Control of Foreign Relations in Modern Nations

Contributors

QUINCY WRIGHT

MARTIN B. TRAVIS, JR.

LUIS QUINTANILLA

PHILIP W. BUCK

J. D. B. MILLER

ARTHUR C. TURNER

GRAHAM H. STUART

MANFRED C. VERNON

DAVID T. CATTELL

JAMES T. WATKINS IV

KAZUO KAWAI

Control of Foreign Relations in Modern Nations

Editors

PHILIP W. BUCK
STANFORD UNIVERSITY

and

MARTIN B. TRAVIS, JR.
STANFORD UNIVERSITY

W · W · NORTON & COMPANY · INC · New York

CONTENTS

V

The United Kingdom
PHILIP W. BUCK
Department of Political Science
Stanford University

The Four Original Dominions in the Commonwealth of Nations
J. D. B. MILLER
Department of Government
University College, Leicester

The Asian Members of the Commonwealth of Nations
ARTHUR C. TURNER
Division of Social Sciences
University of California, Riverside

France
GRAHAM H. STUART
Emeritus Professor of Political Science
Stanford University

The Netherlands
MANFRED C. VERNON
Department of Political Science
University of Alabama

The Union of Soviet Socialist Republics
DAVID T. CATTELL
Department of Political Science
University of California, Los Angeles

Japan

JAMES T. WATKINS IV   and   KAZUO KAWAI
Department of Political   Department of Political
    Science   Science
Stanford University   Ohio State University

QUINCY WRIGHT
Department of Political Science
University of Chicago

MAPS AND CHARTS

FOREWORD

This book analyzes the forces and institutions of the contemporary international scene by studying the foreign policies of selected modern states, since it is impossible to include all the states of the world. The United States, the United Kingdom, and the Union of Soviet Socialist Republics are discussed in three chapters each because the influence they exert in world affairs requires analysis of their past tradition, contemporary situation, and present methods of formulating foreign policy. France and Japan, also influential members of the community of nations, are discussed in two chapters each. The members of the British Commonwealth and the Latin American nations are considered as groups which frequently act in concert, being politically or geographically associated. The Netherlands is included as representative of many small states which have an important share in the affairs of the world. The discussions have been arranged in an order which proceeds from the most familiar countries to the least familiar. Accordingly, the reader is first introduced to the Western Hemisphere, while the Soviet Union and Japan, whose cultural and institutional determinants of foreign policy are widely divergent from western patterns, are reserved for final consideration.

There is no intention in this book to imply any nationalist thesis —it is designed to give a picture of the relations among nations in the world of today by studying the situation of a number of national states and by setting forth the methods their governments use in formulating and administering foreign policy. Stated simply, the intention of authors and editors has been to give a succinct and straightforward account of how each state conducts its dealings with the other states of the world. The restraints imposed upon the policy makers have been described: the capabilities of the states they represent, the national attitudes and social structure of their people, and their traditional foreign policies. The importance of international organization and of associated action by many states appears in the first and last chapters, and in parts of all the chapters in which are described the actions of particular states as they participate in international organizations. The editors and the contributing authors all regard this method of analysis as realistic for a world organized in national states.

Necessarily each state has been treated briefly and generally, but every effort has been made to make each chapter accurate and to include all significant details. Brief lists of books offer suggestions for further study of each country's foreign policy.

The editors and contributors are:

Quincy Wright, emeritus professor of international law, University of Chicago, and Carnegie Visiting Research Scholar, the Carnegie Endowment for International Peace. Educated at Lombard College, the University of Illinois, and the University of Pennsylvania. Author: *The Control of American Foreign Relations; A Study of War; The Study of International Relations;* and numerous other books. Fields: international law, foreign relations, international politics.

Martin B. Travis, Jr., associate professor of political science, Stanford University. Educated at Amherst College, the Fletcher School of Law and Diplomacy, the University of Chicago, and the University of Heidelberg. Duke University travel grant for study of foreign-policy formulation in selected South American countries, 1952. Fields: international relations, Latin American politics and relations, United States foreign relations, international law.

Luis Quintanilla, Mexican Ambassador to the Organization of American States (OAS). Educated at the Sorbonne and Johns Hopkins University. Author: *A Latin American Speaks; Pan Ameri-*

canism and Democracy; and other books in Spanish. In the diplomatic service of Mexico since 1923, in Europe, North and South America. Ambassador to Colombia, the USSR; Delegate to United Nations Assemblies. Chairman of the OAS Council, the Inter-American Peace Commission, and Special OAS Investigating Committees.

Philip W. Buck, professor of political science, Stanford University. Educated at the University of Idaho, Oxford University, and the University of California. Author: *The Politics of Mercantilism*; co-author, *The Governments of Foreign Powers*. Fields: comparative government, political theory, British government and politics.

John Donald Bruce Miller, lecturer in politics, University College, Leicester. M.Ec., University of Sydney. Author: *Australian Government and Politics*; *Richard Jebb and the Problem of Empire*.

Arthur C. Turner, associate professor of political science and chairman of the Division of Social Sciences, University of California, Riverside. Educated at Oxford University and the University of California. Author: *Bulwark of the West*; *Towards European Integration*; and other books. Fields: international relations, comparative government in the British Commonwealth, and area study of eastern Europe.

Graham H. Stuart, emeritus professor of political science, Stanford University, and member of the Advisory Committee of the Foreign Service Institute, United States Department of State. Educated at Western Reserve University, the University of Wisconsin, the Alliance Française, and the École Libre des Sciences Politiques. Author: *French Foreign Policy from Fashoda to Serajevo*; *The International City of Tangier*; *The Department of State*; and other books. Fields: international law, foreign relations.

Manfred C. Vernon, associate professor of political science, University of Alabama. Educated at the University of Cologne, the University of Berlin, and Stanford University. Co-author: *Source Book in European Government*; contributor and collaborator in other books. Fields: comparative government, international politics, foreign policy and diplomacy.

David T. Cattell, assistant professor of political science, University of California, Los Angeles. Educated at Amherst College and Columbia University. Author: *Communism and the Spanish Civil War* and *Soviet Diplomacy and the Spanish Civil War.* Fields: area study of eastern Europe and the Soviet Union, international law, comparative government in Europe.

James T. Watkins IV, chairman of the Department of Political Science, Stanford University. Educated at Stanford University, the Institut Universitaire de Hautes Études Internationales (Geneva), and Columbia University. Author: *General International Organization* (with J. William Robertson); and other books. Fields: international relations, international organization, area study of North East Asia.

Kazuo Kawai, associate professor of political science, Ohio State University. Educated at Stanford University. Editor-in-chief, *Nippon Times,* Tokyo, 1941-1949. Fields: area study of North East Asia, international politics, comparative government in Asia.

The editors join in expressing their deep appreciation of the helpful co-operation of the contributing authors in the preparation of the book. They are particularly indebted to Professor Quincy Wright, who read most of the manuscript and contributed many valuable suggestions. They also wish to express their gratitude for the efforts of the publishers in the arduous task of bringing together the work of a group of contributors.

PHILIP W. BUCK
MARTIN B. TRAVIS, JR.

Control of Foreign Relations in Modern Nations

1. Introduction: Problems in the Conduct of Foreign Relations

CHAPTER 1

INTRODUCTION: PROBLEMS IN THE CONDUCT OF FOREIGN RELATIONS

QUINCY WRIGHT

Department of Political Science, University of Chicago

One approach to the subject of international relations begins at the point where national law and policy meet international law and policy. The society of nations is an extremely loose and decentralized society, yet it has law and organization—law in a body of general principles established by custom or convention and an organization capable of acting for it in certain situations. This organization includes the diplomatic missions sent by each state to most of the others, functioning within privileges, immunities, and powers established by international law and maintained by the diplomatic corps at each capital. The organization also includes the United Nations, the dozen Specialized Agencies, and a number of regional agencies, with headquarters in various cities of the world and with competencies and procedures defined by constituent treaties binding the members. The law of the society of nations, both customary and conventional, and the policies which emerge from its organs—bilateral, regional, and general—in the exercise of their functions, impose limitations upon the nations in the conduct of foreign policy.

3

The nations themselves are much more tightly organized than is the society of nations. Each has legislative, executive, and judicial authorities capable of making decisions to secure the national integrity, to forward the national interests, and to discharge international responsibilities. These decisions are relevant to international relations, insofar as they implement or conflict with the law and policy of the society of nations, or affect the security or interests of other nations. It is impossible to draw a sharp line between such decisions and decisions of purely domestic import. A decision by a local magistrate may affect international relations, if it involves a resident diplomat, consul, or national of another state. So in certain circumstances may national legislation concerning agricultural subsidies, education, military appropriations, currency, taxation, narcotic drugs, or most other subjects of legislation. Executive decisions recognizing foreign governments, instructing diplomats, ordering naval movements, or declaring policies, have a more direct effect on international relations. In sum, a very wide range of activities by almost any governmental agency, local or national, may affect international relations. They may induce representations, protests, preparations, or acts by another government. They may become the subject of discussions, recommendations, or decisions by an organ of the United Nations or of some other international organization.

Legally the line between decisions in the realm of foreign policy and of domestic policy depends on the presence or absence of an international obligation. A sovereign state can regard any decision as legally within its domestic jurisdiction, and therefore as exempting it from protest by another government or from intervention by the United Nations, unless the state is under an obligation of general international law or of treaty limiting its discretion in respect to the substance, or the manner of making or of executing the decision. In other words, a decision is not a domestic question if any other state may validly protest against it on grounds of international law. Otherwise it is.

This definition, however, while suitable for qualifying the legal competence of agencies of the United Nations to "intervene" in matters "essentially within the domestic jurisdiction" of a state, is not suitable for qualifying the political, economic, or social interests of the states or of the United Nations. States may make informal representations or initiate discussions in United Nations organs concerning many decisions made by other governments which, however legal, adversely affect their interests. Furthermore, a government is always free to initiate negotiations with the object of concluding a treaty; and it may always seek co-operation with other states, bilaterally or multilaterally, in regard to any matter which it believes a subject of common interest. To an increasing extent states discuss with other states new matters which they cannot deal with adequately through the exercise of their domestic jurisdictions. Consequently, they frequently accept reciprocal treaty obligations of novel type. Through such "international legislation," states continually diminish their "domestic jurisdiction" in the legal sense.

Thus the area of foreign relations grows and changes. The speed and magnitude of this change is reflected by the development of international communications, trade and travel; by the vulnerabilities of all states to military, economic and propaganda attack; as well as by the increase during this century in the number and scope of bilateral treaties, general treaties, and international organizations. The causes are to be found in the tremendous developments of technology, population, education, and living standards during this period, making it possible for acts or utterances within one state to have important effects in the most distant states. The probability that decisions of national agencies will have international repercussions has, therefore, increased at an accelerating rate. Familiarity with recent history provides ample evidence of this acceleration.

Along with this development of a shrinking and interdependent world, the nation-states have become more closely integrated, more extensively socialized, and more effectively governmentalized. National governments have insisted on more independence to plan the national economy and to formulate and execute the national policy. Peoples have insisted on "self-determination," meaning that they shall become independent and that decisions of the government shall be based only upon national opinion and legislation and shall be implemented without outside interference.

These opposing movements toward more comprehensive and pressing international relations on the one hand, and toward more intensely organized, dynamic, and self-determining national governments on the other, have made the problem of conducting international relations more difficult.

The Dynamics

It is clear that the problem can best be approached from the side of the national governments. The society of nations is so loosely organized and so lacking in capacity to make decisions and to carry them out that the dynamics of the situation comes, not from it, but from the national governments. The discipline of international organization exists, it is true, and the trends toward more effective decision-making by its organs will doubtless in time give increased importance to the approach from the side of international organization. Even today this approach throws valuable light on the course of international relations. Yet the agencies of the United Nations and other international organizations function largely through the making and publication of information and studies, through facilitating discussion, and through recommendation and advice to the nations. They seldom command or order the nations, much less individuals. Their task is less to formulate and carry out international policies than to assist governments in co-ordinating their activities in order to achieve common ends or to avoid conflict, or to assist governments in solving conflicts when they arise. Accordingly, the sources of change, of tension, and of conflict in international relations are the decisions of national governments, especially of the governments of great powers.

These governments, however, face a continuing dilemma. In international relations the state is in theory the unit of action, but the state is an abstraction giving legal form to the nation and practical unity to the people which compose it. Only the government can act, but in conducting international relations it can act only through an individual who directly represents the government, and indirectly represents the state, the nation, and the people. As Walter Lippmann once said, "Two masses of people have no way of dealing directly with each other . . . the very qualities which are needed for negotiation—quickness of mind, direct contact, adaptiveness, invention, the right proportion of give and take—are the very qualities which masses of people do not possess."[1]

The individual, however, can be said to act for the state only if he exercises powers which the state has conferred upon him by its constitution or laws. But in the sudden and unforeseeable contingencies of international negotiation, co-operation, or defense, it may prove impossible for him—if the Constitution and laws impose limitations upon his powers—to meet his national responsibility to advance and protect the national interests, and simultaneously to discharge his international responsibility to observe and enforce the obligations of the state under international law. The two facts, that his powers flow from the constitution and his responsibilities from the international situation and from international law, face him with a dilemma. If he observes the constitutional and legal restrictions upon his power which, in the modern, democratic constitution may be considerable, he may be unable to meet sudden attacks or to discharge international responsibilities. If on the other hand he acts freely in the international field, as could the absolute monarchs of the sixteenth and seventeenth centuries, he may be impeached for violating the constitution or defeated in the next election by adverse public opinion. In constitutional democracies, and especially in the United States, the situation has resulted in continual conflict between the demand of the executive for almost unlimited discretion in the conduct of foreign policy and the demand of nationalistic public opinion, often reflected in legislative bodies, for greater restrictions of law upon executive discretion.[2]

The actual nature of the decisions made by the representative authority of the state, usually the chief executive, depends upon many factors, which may be classified as: (1) his personality; (2)

[1] Walter Lippmann, *The Stakes of Diplomacy*, New York, 1915, pp. 26, 29.
[2] Quincy Wright, *The Control of American Foreign Relations* (New York: Macmillan, 1922), pp. 3ff.

the procedures required by the constitution, laws, or practice to limit his discretion, to assure the concurrence of other organs, or to bring relevant information and opinion to his attention before he makes a decision; (3) the goals, standards, and rules established by the constitution, laws, or practice, to guide the participants in this procedure; and (4) the actual conditions of the situation affecting the practical applicability of these goals, standards, and rules. The relative importance of these four classes of factors influencing the decision-making process differs greatly from state to state, and varies from time to time in the same state.

The Personality

In a dictatorship, the personality of a Hitler, a Mussolini or a Stalin may be the influence of commanding importance, as was the personality of the monarch in the days of absolutism.[3] Even in these cases, institutional arrangements usually impose some restrictions. Even the most powerful leader, in his role of decision-maker for the state, is influenced by considerations different from those affecting his behavior in family, business, or social relations. The importance of the personal influence of the individual in conducting foreign relations also varies during the history of a particular state. In the United States, the personality of Jefferson, Jackson, Lincoln, Theodore Roosevelt, Wilson, and Franklin D. Roosevelt had far more influence in international decision-making than did the personality of the average president. Periods of war and tension probably accentuate the importance of the key personality, but powerful personalities may by their own energy emerge above the shackling influence of procedure, law, and tradition. Studies of types of political personality and of the biographies of particular persons can therefore throw important light upon the probable course of international decision-making, especially under circumstances of permanent or temporary dictatorship. An understanding of the personality of individuals who are influential in international decision-making is in no circumstances unimportant.[4] That is to say, decisions in international politics cannot

[3] Frederick Adams Woods, *The Influence of Monarchs*, New York, 1913.
[4] Harold D. Lasswell, *Politics: Who Gets What, When, How?* (New York: McGraw-Hill, 1936), pp. 181ff.

be thoroughly institutionalized at the national level. Such institutionalization would be more nearly possible at the international level, through effective international law and international organization; but so long as that form of institutionalization is primitive, the national states, if they are to survive, must give wide discretion to the persons who make decisions for them in international politics.[5]

The Procedures

In a constitutional government, the influence of procedures upon foreign-policy decision-making is of importance and may be of major importance in normal times. Such governments tend to be of law not of men, although in the field of foreign affairs this situation is less possible to maintain than in domestic government, particularly in times of tension. John Locke, an apostle of constitutionalism, said of the power to conduct foreign affairs, which he called the "federative power":

Though the well or ill-management of it be of great moment to the commonwealth, yet it is much less capable to be directed by antecedent, standing, positive laws, than the executive (that is, the power to conduct domestic administration) . . . for the laws that concern subjects, one amongst another, being to direct their actions, may well enough precede them. But what is to be done in reference to foreigners, depending much upon their actions, and the variation of designs, and interests, must be left in great part to the prudence of those who have this power committed to them, to be managed by the best of their skill, for the advantage of the commonwealth.[6]

Nevertheless, with the growth of constitutional democracy, procedures limiting the discretion of the individual conducting foreign relations have increasingly been prescribed. It is the recent development of such procedures, together with the blurring of the line between domestic and foreign affairs (which has in itself in-

[5] Wright, The Control of American Foreign Relations, pp. 36off. See also Quincy Wright, Problems of Stability and Progress in International Relations (University of California Press, 1954), pp. 273ff.; The Study of International Relations (New York: Appleton-Century-Crofts, 1955), pp. 168ff.

[6] John Locke, Treatise on Civil Government, Sections 144-148, quoted Wright, Control of American Foreign Relations, p. 142.

creased the demand for such procedures) that has given the subject under consideration its importance. The absolute monarchs who governed most European states when the modern state system came into being in the sixteenth and seventeenth centuries could make domestic law, establish courts and administrative organs to enforce the law, instruct diplomats, ratify treaties, and declare war at discretion. They did not need to distinguish between domestic and international affairs except in regard to the kind of advice and information most useful and the methods most efficient; neither did they need to distinguish between constitutional powers and international responsibilities. They had the legal power necessary to meet the responsibilities of the state. Their problem was merely that of relating national interests and foreign demands to practical calculations of the international power situation.

In England, although in principle the powers to recognize foreign governments, formulate policies, instruct diplomats, make treaties, and declare war were within the royal prerogative, the power of Parliament over appropriations and legislation, and the independence of the courts, often made it necessary for the crown to assure itself of the consent of Parliament in the exercise of these powers. After the constitutional struggle with the Stuarts in the seventeenth century, it became clear that treaties affecting the rights of Englishmen could not be enforced within the realm without implementing parliamentary legislation. It also became clear that war could not be carried on and military discipline could not be maintained without annual appropriations and annual re-enactment of the Mutiny Act. Furthermore, legislation was necessary for recruiting troops and preventing espionage and sabotage by the enemy within the state. Even so, two tendencies— the tradition established by the vigorous Tudor monarchs of reserving foreign affairs to the discretion of the Crown and the workings of responsible government which developed in the eighteenth century—secured the Crown a relatively free hand in conducting foreign affairs until the rise of the Labor Party in the twentieth century. It is true that the inherent complexity of decision-making in this field required a distribution of the Crown's functions among a number of cabinet officers each heading a ministry—the Foreign Office, the Admiralty, the War Office, the Board of Trade, the Treasury, and others—but the principle of Cabinet unity prevented serious jurisdictional controversies. The increasing complexity of the problem and the growing number of officials in the various offices concerned with foreign affairs have made new demands upon the organization of the executive offices to assure that the personnel will be adequate, that the right studies will be made in time, and that relevant information will be before the decision-maker at the critical moment. This, however, is a problem of public administration, faced by all branches of government as government has become more complex and pervasive.

In the United States the above problem was more serious. The Constitution limited all governmental powers by the Bill of Rights, distributed powers between the states and the federal government, and in the latter distributed powers among independent legislative, executive, and judicial branches. In general, power adequate to conduct foreign relations was given to the federal government and within it to the president. But in detail, the impossibility of precise definition of "foreign affairs," its inevitable overlap with "domestic affairs," the sentiment of "states' rights," and the jealousy of executive power (flowing from colonial experience and manifested in the Articles of Confederation) made it inevitable that the participation of other organs in foreign-policy decision-making should be explicitly required by the Constitution in some cases. These conditions likewise made it inevitable that the President's exercise of powers in this field should often be challenged on constitutional grounds even when there were no explicit limitations. The struggle, between the President insisting upon an interpretation of the Constitution enlarging his discretion and the Congress insisting on an interpretation reducing that discretion, has been continuous since the time of Washington. The most recent and also the most comprehensive assault on the President's independence in the field, an independence which has generally been supported by the courts,[7] was the Bricker-amendment movement, which sought to curb presidential treaty-making

[7] *Missouri v. Holland*, 1920, 252 U.S. 416; *U.S. v. Curtiss-Wright Export Corporation*, 1936, 299 U.S. 304.

and judicial enforcement of treaties, in the interest of domestic
jurisdiction, states rights, congressional powers, and senatorial
prerogatives. If adopted in its original form, the Bricker proposal
would have gone far to put the government back to its situation
under the Articles of Confederation which made effective conduct of foreign relations impossible, and which was a major factor
in leading to the acceptance of the constitution in 1787.[8]

The Constitution provides for the collaboration of the Senate
in treaty-making and in diplomatic appointments, and gives Congress power to regulate foreign commerce, to define piracies and
offenses against the law of nations, to make appropriations, and to
declare war. While the President has been able to do much independently by making "executive agreements," appointing "presidential agents," and utilizing his powers as "commander-in-chief"
to employ armed force for national defense, for treaty enforcement,
and for the protection of citizens abroad, he has not been able
to escape the need for senatorial or congressional approval of many
decisions, especially as foreign policy has increasingly taken the
form of economic aid to allies, technical aid to underdeveloped
countries, and the maintenance of a vast military establishment
requiring large appropriations over which Congress has complete
control. As in England, the problem of organizing the executive
agencies for effective co-operation has grown as the personnel
of these agencies has become greater, and as all of the executive
departments have become interested in certain aspects of foreign
policy. In the United States the problem is more difficult than
in England and other countries, because of the greater propensity
of Congress to insist on organizing executive departments in detail
and on supervising them through investigations. The effort to
increase the efficiency of the foreign service, to integrate the
foreign and domestic services of the Department of State, to co-
ordinate the executive departments through interdepartmental
agencies such as the National Security Council, has proceeded
with presidential and congressional collaboration. The difficulties
of the problem of organization, administration, and co-ordination

[8] Quincy Wright, "Congress and the Treaty Making Power," *Proc. Am.
Soc. Int. Law*, 1952, pp. 43ff.

are suggested by personnel statistics. Before World War I the United States conducted its foreign affairs with less than 1000 civilians, nearly all employed by the Department of State, of which two-thirds were abroad in the foreign service. In 1956, the Department of State employed over 15,000 persons, of which three-fourths were overseas. In addition, in 1956, an equal number of civilians were employed overseas by departments other than the Department of State, and each of these other Departments had large numbers of civilian employees engaged in international affairs in Washington. Thus, apart from the military, it appears that more than 50,000 persons were engaged in the conduct of United States foreign relations, more than fifty times as many as before World War I. It is not surprising that the State Department has undergone numerous reorganizations. The conditions of the foreign and domestic services have been frequently changed by legislation and executive order, and devices have been set up to co-ordinate policy both in Washington and in the various foreign capitals.[9]

While the foreign relations problem in the United States has been peculiarly difficult because of the constitutional separation of powers and the tremendous growth of responsibility and personnel during the past generation, the underlying problem has been the same in all constitutional democracies: namely, the reconciliation of the democratic thesis with the efficiency thesis, the one demanding that governmental powers shall be exercised only with the consent of the people, the other that representative authority, in touch with actual conditions of the world, must have wide discretion in the making of decisions. According to the first thesis, the exercise of arbitrary power is not permissible and the representative authority must gain the consent of other organs in making major decisions in order to assure that they shall accord with the Constitution, the law, and public opinion. The efficiency thesis, on the other hand, asserts that the people cannot be expected to understand the situation in foreign countries, that only executive authority with access to dispatches from the foreign service can have the essential information, and that its decisions

[9] Henry M. Wriston, ed., *The Representation of the United States Abroad*, The American Assembly, Columbia University, 1956.

must be made rapidly and authoritatively if disaster is to be avoided. The distinction made by John Locke is emphasized. In domestic affairs what the public wants can, in large measure, be realized by legislation and administration, so the problem of democratic government is to ascertain public opinion, and, when a demand is clear, to implement it. But in foreign affairs, what can be obtained depends upon the policies of foreign governments and upon the power situation. Public opinion can guide only the broad goals of foreign policy. Short-run policies and their detailed applications must be left to the discretion of the executive.

While the cogency of the efficiency argument is recognized by most students of international politics, the progress of constitutional democracy has given increasing force to the democratic thesis. The result has been that in the United States the president has had to work more closely with Congress and the parties, gaining support for major policies through publicity, popular education, and continuous consultation with Congressional and party leaders. While he may act with more independence in times of emergency, it does not appear that future presidents can act in foreign policy with the freedom enjoyed by presidents during the French Revolutionary and Napoleonic periods, or by Lincoln during the Civil War. The solution must be found in effective constitutional co-operation through understanding rather than in rivalry among the organs of government.[10]

This problem has been raised in all constitutional democracies during the nineteenth and twentieth centuries. Parliamentary participation in war-making and treaty-making, elaborate executive organization, a trained foreign service, and education of the public in foreign affairs has in varying degrees been accepted by all such governments. All have abandoned the effort to make sharp distinctions between foreign and domestic affairs and to leave the former exclusively to their foreign offices. Rather, they have recognized the interest of all the executive departments in phases of foreign affairs and the frequent need of co-operation from the legislatures and the courts. Increasingly, the competence of courts to apply international law and treaties as the law of the land has been

[10] Wright, *The Control of American Foreign Relations*, pp. 7, ff., 339ff.

acknowledged in the countries of Western Europe. In some countries, notably the Netherlands, decisions of international agencies
established by treaty have been given a status superior to that of
national legislation; international obligations have thus been given
a priority over domestic law and policy. In the larger countries and
in the totalitarian states the trend has been in the opposite direction, toward the preservation of domestic autonomy, by requiring
express legislation to incorporate international obligations in national law. The United States was a pioneer in giving immediate
legal effect to treaties. The Constitution provides that treaties shall
override conflicting state legislation and be on a parity with Congressional legislation, and judicial practice has always given legal
weight to customary international law. The proposed Bricker
amendment, however, would subordinate all international obligations to Congressional legislation.

The Goals, Standards, and Rules

With respect to the goals, standards, and rules influencing foreign policy-making, governments differ. The executives of great
states have tended to give power position first priority and to seek
flexibility in international decision-making without too great concern for international law and the recommendations of international organizations. They have, as has been noted, sought to
emancipate themselves even from national law, national traditions,
and national public opinion. They have sought guidance not from
these quarters but rather from the latest and best information concerning the capabilities of rivals and allies and the changing attitudes of foreign governments. They have tended to consider diplomatic negotiation and war or threats of war as primary means for
achieving foreign-policy goals, although they have given considerable importance to the use of economic inducements and pressures and to the influencing of foreign opinion by information,
education, and propaganda, in the Soviet Union more than the
west. The legislature has often differed from the executive in respect to preferred goals, standards, and measures, because it is influenced more by traditional formulations and current public opinion, while the executive is influenced more by expert military and

legal advice and by current information concerning foreign attitudes, policies, and capabilities. Even in regard to long-run goals,
there may be differences. The legislature and public opinion tend
to look upon foreign policy and power position as instruments for
domestic prosperity and welfare, while the executive may look
upon domestic prosperity and industrial progress as aspects of
power and instruments of successful foreign policy. The determination of what is the national interest is in its nature a political
question about which the public, parties, and governmental agencies will differ, both generally and in particular situations. Times
of emergency threatening the continued existence of the state tend
to still these controversies and to emphasize the national interest
in security of territory from invasion.

Smaller states depend for existence on the power equilibrium of
the great, which they cannot markedly affect by policies of their
own. They appreciate that the rule of law in international affairs
would diminish their dependence upon the great states and increase their general security. Consequently they tend to govern
their own conduct, and seek to govern the conduct of others, by
the standards and rules of international law, international organization, and treaties to which they are parties. They gain so much
from the rule of law that they are usually willing to qualify sovereignty provided others do likewise, to strengthen the society of
nations, and to enhance the reliability of international standards.
The United States during the nineteenth century, insulated from
international politics and protected by the oceans and the British
navy, gave extraordinary attention to international law and to such
national traditions as Washington's farewell address and the Monroe Doctrine. Public opinion became a factor of increasing importance in the twentieth century, and as the position of the United
States in power politics has become increasingly significant during
World War II and since, international law has occupied a lesser
role, ancient traditions have often been found inapplicable, and
public opinion has frequently been found uninformed and public
wishes impracticable. The result has been efforts of the executive
to base policies on correct information concerning actual conditions, to reinterpret international law and national traditions in

order to justify policies suggested by the needs of security under
these conditions, and to attempt to educate public opinion and
Congress to give support. At the same time, lip service has been
given to the United Nations and other international organizations
with the hope that eventually they may bring about conditions in
which it will be possible to rely on collective security and international law.

While these differences in emphasis exist, every government
must today pay attention not only to its own public opinion and
to its own history and traditions but also to international law and
to the changing conditions of power, technology, trade, and policy
in the external world. In a shrinking, changing, and anarchic world,
all governments must think strategically in the sense of formulating
their goals in terms of their capacities to achieve them, and of
adapting policies to conditions which cannot be altered. Under
such conditions, a government which thinks ideologically, attempting to deduce policy decisions from general principles or historic
traditions, is unlikely to survive. Goals, standards, and rules must
therefore be treated as flexible guides, to be interpreted in the light
of current circumstances.

The Pertinent Conditions

States differ greatly in respect to area, resources, trade, industrialization, wealth, access to the sea, vulnerability to attack, population, cultural homogeneity, education, religion, political stability,
and morale. Similarly, general conditions of the world at large
change in respect to transnational communication, travel, and transportation; to military technology; to political ideology and social
tensions; and to international and regional organization. Such
changes have never been more rapid than in the twentieth century.
For every state, the goals of policy and the means to attain them
are affected by these conditions—not directly, but indirectly as
decision-makers interpret the significance of changing conditions
upon the definition of national interests and the means for forwarding them.

The distinction between the goals and the conditions of foreign
policy is not absolute. While—in general—conditions of the kind

mentioned cannot be changed abruptly, goals of policy can often be changed more rapidly, although not always. National goals and definitions of national interest may become so crystallized and may acquire such a hold upon public opinion that governments cannot easily alter them. A goal then has the character of a condition to which policy must accommodate itself. Furthermore, nearly any condition may be changed in some measure by national effort, and particularly by co-operative effort of many states. Thus it ceases to be a condition, and its change becomes a goal of policy. One problem which foreign-policy decision-makers face is whether to adapt desirable goals and policies to existing conditions—as small states must usually do—or to attempt to modify conditions, perhaps seeking international co-operation to that end, in order that desirable national goals and interests can better be achieved. Large states are obviously in a better position to change conditions than are small states; but even large states can hardly effect significant changes of the conditions of the world without extensive international co-operation through permanent agencies.

The discussions in the succeeding chapters of this book illustrate the relation between the underlying conditions and the national policies of a number of states both large and small, and the procedures by which the governments of these states make decisions designed to serve current interpretations of the national interest. The problem of gearing policy-making at the national level into policy-making at the international level through agencies of the United Nations, the Specialized Agencies, and other international organizations, is not extensively dealt with. It will probably increase in importance as the world becomes smaller, as the destructiveness of war becomes greater, and as closer contacts and vulnerabilities of people become reflected in the increased activity and authority of international organizations designed to preserve the peace and to promote international co-operation. This problem is briefly dealt with in the final chapter.

The United States of America

MARTIN B. TRAVIS, JR.

Department of Political Science
Stanford University

The United States of America

CHAPTER 2

COMPONENTS OF
UNITED STATES FOREIGN POLICY

The destiny of the United States hangs, as never before, upon the wisdom of the foreign policies adopted by its statesmen. A Secretary of State is confronted with a more difficult task than are the other Cabinet secretaries entrusted with domestic policies. He must consider the foreign policies of many other sovereign states, and he must determine what international issues have present or potential importance for the objectives of United States foreign policy. The determination is not easy.

If the Secretary is not alert to key issues, the problem may reach crisis proportions before action is taken. Witness Secretary of State Cordell Hull, who is said to have been more preoccupied with his reciprocal-trade program than with the developing problems of war. The reputed British method of "muddling through," which suggests a certain lethargy in defining situations and a reluctance to grapple with immediate problems, may have been successful when the balance of power was stable and when international contacts were less frequent. There is little doubt that "muddling through" is less effective when a crisis may evoke a catastrophic modern war.

On the other hand, an overanxious Secretary may misinterpret circumstances surrounding an issue. Secretary of State Frank

Kellogg (known as "nervous Nelly" by his State Department colleagues) viewed Nicaraguan instability in 1927 as the work of
"Bolsheviks" who were endangering the security of the Panama
Canal. Historians have not supported his assessment nor his decision to return the United States Marines to Nicaragua. A statesman must be careful about precipitating an issue prematurely or
unnecessarily. He must be alert without being precipitous, cautious
but not lethargic in selecting situations ripe for consideration and
decision.

Once a situation has been identified, the statesman must correlate it with national objectives and must elaborate alternative
courses of action. He must know the relative power position of
his country in a situation identified as a threat to national security
if his diplomats are to bargain from a position of strength. However, a democratic statesman is not always free to apply that
policy which might be best suited to a particular international
situation. In order to keep the confidence of the people who elect
him, he must take their desires into consideration and must convince them that a particular policy will secure these desires or that
these desires should give way to other objectives. A statesman will
also rely on traditional foreign policies, knowing that the policy
has been successful in the past, that foreign governments will
expect him to support these policies, and that the public at home
has endorsed them. Finally, a statesman will not only correlate
past precedents with immediate demands of power and public
opinion, but will also give attention to the future through his concern for international law and justice. To develop a world which
maintains international order and promotes peaceful change requires wise decisions which most successfully balance all these
considerations.

The Relative Power Position of the United States

In a world dominated by power politics, where the average life
of a sovereign state is relatively short, particular attention must be
given to national security as a foreign-policy objective. Statesmen
need to use care in balancing foreign commitments with national

capabilities so that the power of their countries will be most efficiently employed to attain national goals. Both the means and ends of United States foreign policy, therefore, are heavily dependent upon the relative power situation; and United States decision-makers should be kept alerted by the various intelligence organizations.

Even the best intelligence organizations will not pretend to measure power with mathematical exactitude. Power is a relative matter, and sources of information from Iron Curtain countries are uncertain. National power is also continually changing, and the rate of this change is not easy to assess. Figures on the size of the army or armament production might suggest the possibility of precise measurement, but it is more difficult to ascertain psychological factors like morale or reputation abroad. And even the material aspects of power are not entirely free from subjective judgment, since quality as well as quantity must be appraised.

Immediate Material Power

One of the most important results of the development of the thermonuclear weapons and methods for their delivery has been the increasing effectiveness of offensive warfare. The United States will no longer have two or more years to mobilize and arm as it did after 1914 and 1939. Geographical distance has been shortened, and the privileged sanctuary of the North American continent is now exposed. The importance of military preparedness has also been suggested by the reorientation of the world power situation. When the United States was first recognized as a world power in 1898, power was well distributed among a number of European countries and a balance was maintained by Great Britain from an island fortress. Two world wars subsequently destroyed the fulcrum of world power within Europe and left only the Soviet Union and the United States confronting each other. Thus neither a balance of power secured by Britain nor vast ocean distances and arctic wastes now safeguard the United States from possible aggression. Accordingly a premium has been placed upon having power immediately available for American needs. Time and distance no longer afford the protection they once did.

Its geographical position and military strength are among the major elements of material power immediately available to the United States. Its geographic position must be related to that of its major antagonist, the USSR. From this standpoint the entire world may be viewed as a series of defense rings extending from what geopoliticians have called the "heartland"—the great land mass of Eurasia which has in the past protected Russia well. The "interior position" of this heartland in relation to Europe and Asia has given the USSR the theoretical advantage of shorter and less exposed communications. This land advantage, however, disappears when the USSR's poorly developed lines of communication are recognized. The fringing rimlands of Eurasia and the bordering islands and continents thus assume greater importance for United States naval and air power. United States air bases surround the USSR: 42 in Europe, 7 on islands in the Atlantic, 18 in the Orient, 6 in North Africa and 1 in the Near East. Hundreds of additional facilities are provided by allies in Europe, in the Western Hemisphere, and in the Pacific. Lacking similar facilities, on the other hand, the USSR must cross great distances of sea and air to reach the United States continental base. Today, military considerations require that these areas be preserved from local Communist action.

In defending itself against a possible attack from the USSR, the United States has ringed Canada with three chains of radar stations. A "Pinetree" chain is located near the United States border, a "Mid-Canada" ring follows the latitude of southern Hudson Bay, and a third defense line across the Arctic known as Distant Early Warning (DEW) was to be completed in 1958. The latter would give three hours' warning to such cities as Chicago, Detroit, or Cleveland if the USSR were to attack with jet bombers flying at 600 miles per hour. A seaward extension of the radar network has been operated by naval picket vessels, transport planes, and so-called Texas towers in the shoal waters off the northeast coast. The limited effectiveness of this elaborate defense apparatus was revealed in the June 1955 country-wide test by a mock thermonuclear attack. The attack was assumed to have destroyed 58 cities, killed 8.2 million people, and injured an additional 6.5 million. Approximately 20 per cent to 30 per cent of the enemy's imaginary piloted

THE WORLD AROUND THE NORTH POLE

The Arctic Ocean is not a barrier against aerial attack.

bombers had pierced United States defenses. Prevention through the enemy's expectation of retaliation would seem clearly superior to defense under these circumstances.

The offensive power of the United States was second to none during World War II, and since the Korean aggression the United States and its allies have restored their power position. An indication of the rapidity of this rearmament may be seen by comparing the 1948 federal budget of $33.1 billion with that of 1953, which totaled $74.3 billion. It is probable that the appropriations for the fiscal year 1956, amounting to $62.4 billion, would be typical of the cold-war period. An estimated 64 per cent of these budgets was earmarked for major national-security programs.

The lead in atomic development gave the United States an undisputed advantage over the USSR. But the Soviet Union produced its first atomic bomb in 1949 and tested its first thermonuclear bomb in August, 1953, fully seven months before the United States. It was clear thereafter that United States superiority in atomic development was fast waning. According to Mr. Churchill's statement of March 2, 1955, there is no reason why the USSR should not develop "within the next four, three, or even two years" more advanced weapons and full means to deliver them on American targets. Thus the United States lost much of its advantage in strategic nuclear weapons, but in May 1955 it accomplished the successful adaptation of atomic energy to tactical or small weapons. Both the North Atlantic treaty forces in Europe and the American continental troops were being furnished and trained to use these tactical nuclear weapons which could be dropped by plane, fired from guns, and carried by rockets against enemy troops, airfields, and other battlefield targets.

The "awful arithmetic of nuclear weapons" (President Eisenhower's words in a speech to the United Nations General Assembly in 1954) is being applied to the improvement of guided missiles. General H. H. Arnold declared that World War II was the last conflict in which airplane pilots would participate. The USSR has been alert to possibilities in this field and is reported in certain types of missiles to have superiority over the United States. The ultimate weapon in this field is the intercontinental ballistic missile (ICBM), capable of flying accurately across oceans at high speeds and carrying atomic and hydrogen warheads. The United States had three of these under development in 1956: the Snark, the Navaho, and the Atlas. It is probable that the ICBM will be operational before the mid-1960's, both in the United States and the USSR. Already in service in 1956 were surface-to-air missiles like the Nike to guard the cities of the United States against enemy aircraft, and surface-to-surface missiles like the 500-mile-range Regulus and Matador. The air-to-air Falcon has a "brain" of its own which (at least in theory) steers it to anticipate and strike the enemy bomber, no matter how the bomber maneuvers. Weapons like the Nike, however, would have no usefulness against a rocket plunging from the stratosphere at a speed of thousands of miles an hour with a warhead of sufficient power to compensate for errors of aim.

The revolution in warfare resulting from these weapons creates the paradox for policy-makers that they can neither risk doing without them nor afford to fight with them. They must find or devise a transitional policy which can employ both the infantryman with his bayonet and grenade and the jet plane with the hydrogen bomb. The transition policy as elaborated by the Eisenhower administration has assumed that full-scale war is unlikely in the immediate future, and that economic strength of the United States must not be exhausted by the costs of prolonged preparedness. Hence greater reliance is placed on air power and atomic arms as a deterrent to general aggression, while costly overseas-army strength is reduced in favor of local indigenous forces. For the necessary flexibility, a strategic reserve of land forces in the continental United States can be moved rapidly to needed areas when a crisis develops. United States land forces are being kept in Europe, however, where the prize is tempting for a Soviet aggression.

The United States Air Force has been the chief beneficiary of the new weapons which have revolutionized warfare. Between 1949 and 1954 its budget increased nine times and its appropriations for the fiscal year of 1956 were twice those of the Army and 60 per cent greater than those of the Navy. To its Strategic Air Command has been assigned the role of chief deterrent against Soviet aggression. Quantitatively, United States air strength barely equaled the USSR's in 1956, with the Russians having the advantage in such defensive aircraft as fighters, and interceptors. Qualitatively, however, the United States may have possessed an over-all superiority. Battlefield experience in Korea suggested that the Americans were better equipped and had greater pilot and maintenance skills. Furthermore, United States superiority in bombsights, electronics, nuclear weapons, oil, aluminum, and industrial capabilities should not be overlooked.

The United States is overwhelmingly strong at sea; the United States Navy reached a parity with the British after World War I and succeeded to first position after World War II. The Navy's successful adaptation to nuclear and air power and the surface link it provides with the nation's allies have been recognized as important for strategic planning. Its continuing contribution to traditional warfare was noted in the Korean conflict. Five 60,000-ton aircraft carriers have supplanted battleships as the backbone of the fleet. Described by some as sitting ducks at sea which could be destroyed in the first hours of atomic warfare, by others they are considered movable air bases possessing the advantage of unpredictable location.

On land the United States has been relatively weak. However, new tactics and strategy resulting from the utilization of nuclear weapons give a few men great killing power. Great mobility is provided through the use of large air carriers that can transport weapons and troops rapidly to distant areas of the world. Compared to the USSR, the United States Army has emphasized quality as against quantity, highly mobile as against less mobile troops, a flexible and decentralized command as against a highly centralized organization, relatively small numbers of highly trained personnel as against masses wherein the individual soldier has few skills.[1]

Potential Power of the United States

President Eisenhower has remarked that it is as dangerous for a

---

[1] For a recent assessment of the United States' power position compared with that of the Soviet Union, see Henry L. Roberts, *Russia and America: Danger and Prospects* (Harper and Bros., 1956).

nation to arm too early as for it to arm too late. He referred to the fact that present-day armaments become obsolete rapidly, and that the unnecessary accumulation of immediate power wastes a country's potential strength. The consequent policy of the "long haul" emphasizes the importance of potential strength which provides the foundation for military and economic end-items so useful for bribing, coercing, threatening, or otherwise influencing the policies of other nations. Labor, land, and capital constitute the potential economic strength of a country, and these basic factors of production enter into statistics as population, natural resources, and industrial capacity respectively.

Ever since the United States entered world politics as a great power in 1898 it has ranked as the most populous among the western nations, larger than Britain and France combined. By 1955 its population of 165 million and the USSR's 200 million people were exceeded only by China and India. The birth rates of the two forecast 190 million people in 1970 for the United States as compared to 244 million for the USSR. However, the Soviet orbit in 1970 (excluding China and East Germany) may total 320 million persons. Since the turn of the century, also, the United States has had 60 to 65 per cent of its population in the employable age group from 15 to 64 years. The employable age group in the USSR is growing rapidly, and will be half again as large as that of the United States in 1970.[2]

There is little doubt, however, that the population of the United States is better educated, enjoys a higher standard of living, and has greater technical skills. The United States is educating twice as many college and university students as the Soviet Union, but significantly enough the latter is graduating almost twice as many engineers as the United States.

The economic potential of the United States is high because of the abundance of its natural resources—both food and raw materials. Its continental land area of 3 million square miles makes it one of the five largest states of the world, and the equal in size of four

[2] Legislative Reference Service of the Library of Congress, *Trends in Economic Growth: A Comparison of the Western Powers and the Soviet Bloc* (Government Printing Office, 1955), p. 22 and *passim*.

of them. The Soviet Union's 8.6 million square miles, however, represents one-sixth of the world. The arable land in the United States totals 437 million acres; that in the USSR totals 556 million acres; Europe outside the USSR has only a little more than 300 million acres. Colin Clark has estimated, however, that the Soviet Union has only about 70 per cent as much standard farm land as the United States.

Less than one-sixth of the United States population is engaged in agriculture, while one-half the population of the USSR is so employed. The difference is explained by the effective mechanization of the farms in the United States. Between 1940 and 1953 the growth in this respect has been astounding. Tractors increased 300 per cent, motor trucks 250 per cent, grain combines 500 per cent, field corn pickers 600 per cent, farms with milking machines 700 per cent. The 4½ million tractors and 940,000 grain combines in the United States were respectively 4½ and 3½ times the number available in the USSR during 1953.

A recent survey of United States resources concluded: "No material obstacle appears to stand in the way of our producing enough food and fiber in 1960 for both domestic and foreign markets, for civilian consumption, for our armed forces here and abroad and for regular and foreign aid exports."[3]

Both the United States and the Soviet Union are well endowed with raw materials. However, the United States consumes more than the Soviet Union or any other country, and for this reason the depletion rate has been more rapid. Until 1940 the United States was generally self-sufficient in raw materials as a whole, although tin, chromite, manganese, nickel, tungsten, and rubber have been imported for many decades. Since 1940, the United States has imported more raw materials than it has exported, and the deficit has tended to grow, even after 1945 when war requirements were no longer pressing. By 1950 the United States was consuming $900 million more industrial raw materials than it was producing. New materials were added to the list of imports; these included the entire supply of asbestos, graphite, antimony, beryl,

[3] James F. Dewhurst and Associates, *America's Needs and Resources* (Twentieth Century Fund, 1955), p. 810.

cobalt, diamonds, and quartz. Varying amounts of bauxite, lead, mercury, magnesium, tungsten, copper, and zinc also came from abroad. The most important and critical scarcity items were petroleum, copper, lead, zinc, and such ferroalloy metals as nickel, cobalt, and tungsten.

Since the United States must depend upon foreign countries for raw materials, it is fortunate that many can be supplied by western allies and that some can be stockpiled for an emergency. In addition, improved methods of discovering mineral deposits are being developed, more thorough extraction processes are being introduced, products formerly discarded are now being used, and potentially abundant new metals like titanium have been brought into the technology. In short, human ingenuity has increasingly overcome geographical niggardliness. But if it were denied free access to world raw materials, the United States would be confronted with mounting industrial costs, a larger proportion of human and material effort would be required, and more than the present 4.5 per cent of its total manpower would be necessary to exploit the abundant low-grade reserves or to produce substitutes.

With hardly 6 per cent of the world's population, the United States produces about 40 per cent of the world's output; western Europe produces 30 per cent and the Soviet area 20 per cent. In 1955 the gross national product of the United States reached almost $400 billion, more than that of all free Europe and an estimated three times that of the USSR. World War II and the Korean War were two important periods of industrial expansion in recent United States history. The experience gained from these wars indicates that the United States has reached a stage of economic development and technical competence where inadequate industrial and commercial capacity can be quickly overcome. The annual rates of growth for the United States economy and for that of the Soviet Union are approximately equal, so the present gap between their annual productions will probably stand.[4]

[4] *Trends in Economic Growth*, op. cit., p. 219. Roberts (op. cit.), claims this is too optimistic, but economists Colin Clark, and Dudley F. Pegrum together with George F. Kennan, among others would argue in its support. However, Roberts does note that even with the USSR's favorable annual rate of growth, the absolute difference between United States and Soviet levels of

Steel is a pace setter for modern industrial economies and provides the foundation upon which they rest. In 1953, the United States produced 101 million tons of steel, twice as much as the Soviet bloc. Its iron-ore production was similarly twice as great, while in coal production it did not quite equal the Soviet colossus. In general, the United States has maintained a 40-year lead over the USSR in steel production, and estimates for 1960 suggest little change in this ratio.

Power resources of the United States were greater than those of the Soviet Union and western Europe combined in 1950. In 1953 the electric power utilized by the Atomic Energy Commission alone was equivalent to one-fourth of all the electric power available to the Soviet Union during that year.

The United States possesses a substantial part of the world's transportation facilities and equipment. It owns 30 per cent of the world's rail mileage, one-third of the highways, and nearly four-fifths of the motor vehicles. Its air-transport systems and pipe lines exceed those of any other nation. An effective network of communications reinforces these transportation facilities. Important both for rapid military mobilization and for an efficiently developed economy, this network forms another great strength of the United States.

Morale

The capabilities of a country in its foreign relations depend upon the extent of public support for its foreign policies as well as upon the comparative abundance of its resources, population, and technology. A highly motivated people will make sacrifices willingly by working more intensely and longer, and will thereby increase the economic and military efficiency of the country. Thus morale in foreign relations is a function of the degree of determination with which a nation supports its foreign policies. In the United States this determination is conditioned by the material well-being and the national character of the people.

During 1948 a public-opinion survey was made in nine countries

---

production is increasing because of the larger level of production in the United States today.

to determine among other things, the citizens' personal security, their attitude towards the regime in power, and their satisfaction with life in the country. The results were identified as a "national security index," but they might have been called an index of national morale. The United States rated second only to Australia and equal to Norway in this security index.[5]

The policy-makers of the United States have a number of advantages in securing the continuing support of the people for foreign policies. A network of communications and transportation in a highly literate country gives them a large audience quickly. The people themselves have developed a surprising consensus on many issues, the more surprising in view of their dissimilar cultural backgrounds; perhaps the democratic system minimizes any frustration of cultural minority groups by guaranteeing basic individual liberties for all. The existence of a large middle class may also have contributed to this consensus. Indeed, Americans are overwhelmingly agreed on their own national values—the bipartisan foreign policy of the Democratic and Republican parties reflects the extent of this agreement.

On the other hand, the policy makers have disadvantages peculiar to the United States. Our complex industrialized society fosters conflict in the interests of various trades, businesses, and professions. The government's policy-makers are also handicapped in soliciting public approval because they have no clear monopoly over the minds of citizens. Long and extended public debate may improve the general level of understanding, and even modify a policy in the public's interest, but it is not calculated to heighten the determination with which the people support foreign policies.

While United States policy-makers, in comparison to those in authoritarian countries, are handicapped as to methods for securing the support of the people for a given foreign policy, certain appeals have proved successful for this purpose. A patriotic fervor throughout the country may be galvanized by an appeal to the fears of

[5] William Buchanan and Hadley Cantril, *How Nations See Each Other*, a *Study in Public Opinion* (a UNESCO study published by University of Illinois Press, 1953), pp. 24-37. The United States, Australia, Great Britain, Norway, Mexico, France, Italy, Netherlands, and West Germany were surveyed.

foreign aggression and of threats to national security. Both the Berlin blockade in 1948 and the Korean aggression were successfully presented to the public in this light by United States leaders. Economic self-interest may be used for this purpose; the State Department encouraged support for the Marshall Plan by appealing to the profit motive of United States businessmen. But an appeal to principle is sometimes more successful than an appeal to the pocketbook. Henry L. Stimson, as Secretary of War, declared in 1941:

At the same time that we leave no stone unturned for the protection and welfare of our soldiers, we must not forget that it is not the American ideal to bribe our young men into the patriotic service of their country by thoughts of comfort and amusement. Moving pictures and soda water have their places, but endurance of hardship, sacrifice, competition, and the knowledge that he is strong and able to inflict blows and overcome obstacles are the factors that in the last analysis give the soldier his morale. And such is the growing morale of our present Army.[6]

The Allies of the United States

While high morale is necessary if the material aspects of power are to be effectively produced and utilized, a good reputation is equally important if the United States desires allies in time of need. Indeed, when high morale is artificially created by xenophobic appeals, it is purchased at the expense of the nation's reputation abroad. The frenzied witch-hunting of Senator McCarthy did promote loyalty oaths and chauvinistic patriotism throughout the United States; the discriminatory immigration policy of Senator McCarran professed to protect American cultural values; and the proposed Bricker Amendment suggested the desire to preserve American political values. But the harm that these have done to the reputation of the United States may be greater than any contribution they may have made to national morale.

The importance of allies has grown as the world has become smaller. The effective containment of the Soviet power has required the United States to locate dozens of its air bases in foreign

[6] Henry L. Stimson and McGeorge Bundy, *On Active Service in Peace and War* (Harper and Bros., 1948), p. 379.

countries. Allied troops are protecting their respective countries from a potential aggressor whose success would threaten the security of the United States. Collective security not only makes aggression less attractive but also allows the United States to share defense costs with its allies. The United States is now a member of eight collective defense arrangements embracing 43 different countries. Strategically, the defense of these countries against internal revolutions and foreign aggression is important if the "rimland" is to be kept free from Soviet domination. Economically, the allies of the United States provide a source for critical raw materials. Politically, the United States welcomes the voting support of its allies in the United Nations and diplomatic conferences.

Money is not the best catalyst for cementing alliances and promoting co-operation among allies. The United States dispensed $41 billion in the form of lend-lease and relief to its allies during World War II. Soviet aggression and the developing cold war prompted a large part of the $51 billion which the United States transferred abroad in the decade following the end of the war. The United Nations Relief and Rehabilitation Agency, the Marshall Plan, and the technical-assistance program channeled much United States money into the economic development and material improvement of foreign countries. Those Americans who were disappointed with the apparent lack of gratitude on the part of the recipient countries were alerted to the fact that allies cannot be purchased. Nor did the European countries increase their respect for the United States because it was a Great Power; Professor William Rappard has said "Zeus has no friends!"

By mid-1956 the United States leadership in the western world was weakening; a relaxation of the cold war had reduced the general fear of Soviet aggression, while the restoration of economic and political stability had relieved European dependence upon United States assistance. The bipolar international situation was rapidly developing into a more widely distributed power system. German sovereignty and the neutral Asiatic states made it increasingly impossible for the United States and the USSR, even if they wished, to arrange the world between them. For the United States, persuasive abilities had therefore taken on a new importance and the conditions which established the country's reputation abroad needed to be re-examined. These conditions are not easy to assess; they differ from country to country and they are continually changing. In addition, the reputation of the United States rests not only on its foreign policy but also on its domestic policy and on the characteristics that foreigners attributed to its people. If, as its allies charged, the United States placed too heavy reliance upon military solutions, was unwilling to accept for itself the foreign economic policies it was urging upon its allies, lagged in applying both abroad and at home the finally accepted principles of human rights and self-determination of peoples, or practiced an inflexible and inexperienced policy of moralizing in lieu of any concrete practical plan, then only a revamped foreign policy would maintain the leadership of the United States in the western world.

That leadership was under severe stress at the end of 1956. The United States found itself separated from Great Britain and France in the Suez crisis, with the Soviet Union employing the situation as an opportunity to champion Egypt and the Arab states in their opposition to western influence and power in the Near East.

However overwhelming the material resources, both immediate and potential, at the disposal of the United States, its relative power position is less dependent on these than upon its morale and its allies. The responsible foreign policies required of a Great Power must have the steady determination of the people behind them and must secure the support and sympathy of allies abroad. The determination of the people and the co-operation of allies was not difficult to secure as long as the USSR was dramatizing its aggressive intentions during the first postwar decade. Future United States policy will have to balance the nationalistic appeals which help build morale with the international appeals which win allies. The statesman's task would be helped by educating the people of the United States for their long-run responsibilities and by developing in foreign countries a greater sympathy for and understanding of American character and institutions.

Public Opinion in the United States

It would be quite enough to consult the power situation alone if a foreign policy could be formulated as a rational response to changing conditions abroad and if the objective of national security could be promoted by weighing a nation's commitments against its capabilities. But policy-makers must consider the various objectives, values, and expectations of the public as well. Public opinion influences foreign-policy decisions. To say this is not to suggest that the influence of public opinion is or should be as great for foreign policy as it is for domestic policy. Whatever wishful objectives the public may have in the international field, a nation's ability to carry out these objectives is more restricted than it is in domestic politics. A degree of public restraint is both desirable and necessary if foreign policy is to maximize the national interests.

Public opinion in the United States has been viewed both favorably and unfavorably. Alexander Hamilton is reported to have remarked, "Your people, sir, is a great beast!" and recently, Walter Lippmann has warned:

The unhappy truth is that the prevailing public opinion has been destructively wrong at the critical junctures. The people have impressed a veto upon the judgments of informed and responsible officials. They have compelled the governments, which usually know what would have been wiser, or was necessary, or was more expedient, to be too late with too little, or too long with too much, too pacifist in peace and too bellicose in war, too neutralist or appeasing in negotiation or too intransigent. Mass opinion has acquired mounting power in this country. It has shown itself to be a dangerous master of decisions when the stakes are life and death.[7]

Professor Thomas A. Bailey has adapted from Emerson the motto, "The man in the street cannot see the stars in the sky" to support the same point of view. On the other hand, idealists like Sir Norman Angell feel that the common man should always be the final court of appeal, and Woodrow Wilson anticipated a peaceful world

[7] Walter Lippmann, *The Public Philosophy* (Little, Brown and Co., 1955), p. 20.

when the public everywhere exercised full determination of foreign policies.

Decision Making and the General Public

Whether its effect on foreign policy has been good or bad, public opinion plays an important role in the determination of United States foreign policy. A policy-maker must have some degree of success in selling his foreign policy if he is to remain in office. The United States public as a consumer is free to buy the most attractive offer in a competitive market. Policy-makers, therefore, who are confronted with a situation which calls for the containment of Communism, must suggest policies which are palatable to the people as well as effective in promoting national security. While it is true that the United States public may buy an interventionist policy when a fear of aggression exists, the cold-war situation has also produced conditions which result occasionally in erratic behavior. The fear of a catastrophic atomic war, the psychological fatigue which results from continued great tension, the drain of natural resources which has accompanied continued great economic sacrifice, the hostility engendered against the USSR, and withal the complexity of the foreign situation, have all been confusing and perplexing for the general public. The result has been ambivalence: support of withdrawal policies on the one hand, capricious activism on the other.

The people of the United States have been characterized as lacking tolerance for cultural differences. This intolerance has been explained in terms of their overwhelming agreement on capitalist, middle-class, democratic, liberal values; it has also been called the result of a puritan heritage. Whatever the explanation, cultural intolerance affects foreign policy.

A tendency towards mood simplification has also been noted in the United States. The popularity of "unconditional surrender" and "nonfraternization with the Germans" during World War II has been followed by "agonizing reappraisal" and "massive retaliation" more recently. Mood simplification is also reflected in UNESCO studies which indicate that Americans, like others, have acquired certain inaccurate stereotypes of various foreign peoples.

Americans are also described as being idealistic, but happiest when they can cloak good business with morals.

Whatever may be said about the validity of these generalizations (Alexis de Tocqueville, James Bryce, and Margaret Mead, among others, would give at least partial support to them), there is less doubt about how various social groups respond to foreign policy. Gallup polls have indicated that persons under thirty are more optimistic, internationalistic, and better informed than older people. Differences between the sexes are not significant for foreign affairs. The middle class is more optimistic and possesses a greater sense of involvement in the world than does the working class. Regional distinctions between an isolationist Middle West, a free-trade South, and an interventionist East have become less important with the development of communications and travel and with the industrialization of the South. Rural groups are inclined to be more traditionalist, less attentive to foreign affairs, and more pessimistic than urban dwellers. In total, a foreign policy of idealism, optimism, and internationalism is likely to be supported by the youthful elements, by city dwellers, upper income brackets, and by women. A foreign policy of cynicism, pessimism, isolationism, on the other hand, is likely to commend itself to older groups, rural residents, and lower income brackets. Since all these groups overlap, a synthesis of the opposing tendencies has been characteristic of the climate of United States public opinion.

The policy-maker should be interested in the general public if only to learn the changing mass mood. At least 80 per cent of the people of the United States population are uninformed and uninterested in foreign affairs.[8] Yet they participate indirectly and passively in the public opinion, by indicating pleasant or unpleasant attitudes towards the foreign policies which have affected them. Mass indifference to international problems was most recently indicated in a survey conducted under the chairmanship of Professor Samuel A. Stouffer. He discovered that personal problems were listed twelve times more frequently than international problems as reasons for worrying. Such unconcern explains the ignorance of

[8] Gabriel A. Almond, *The American People and Foreign Policy* (Harcourt, Brace and Co., 1950), *passim*.

international issues. Martin Kriesberg wrote in 1949 that 30 per cent of the electorate was unaware of almost any mentioned event in United States foreign affairs, that 45 per cent was barely aware of important events but could not be considered informed, while only 25 per cent of the electorate consistently showed knowledge of foreign problems.[9]

The Attentive Public

Only one-fifth of the total United States population, therefore, has any familiarity with foreign policy. This group has been called the interested or attentive public. It includes the college-educated who are more international, optimistic, and better informed on international problems than groups with less formal education. The attentive public provides an audience for opinion- and policy-makers and holds them to responsibility for their policy declarations. The United States differs from most other countries in the relatively large size of its attentive public; in other countries even less than 20 per cent of the public is attentive.

Opinion and Policy Leaders

The opinion and policy leaders represent 1 per cent of the total population of the United States. They are divided into administrative, special-interest, and communications elites. The administrative elites are the civil-service career officers whose interest and familiarity with various aspects of foreign affairs makes their specialized contribution valuable in the formulation of foreign policy. They will be discussed in the next chapter. The communications elites are those which control the press, radio, and movies. They also include teachers, clergymen, and writers. Finally, there are special-interest elites—those who represent economic, foreign-origin, ideological, or religious groups that have a direct interest in various aspects of foreign affairs.

An elite which controls opinion and formulates foreign policy need not be incompatible with democracy. The elites in the United States are different from the Soviet ruling groups. They are sepa-

[9] Lester Markel and others, *Public Opinion and Foreign Policy* (Harper and Bros., 1949).

rated from each other—even in the government, which provides
for judicial, legislative, and executive independence. In the Soviet
Union, on the other hand, not even the interest groups and communications elites are free from governmental authority. Leaders
in the United States must compete for the support of the public,
while Soviet elites may employ coercion and command. The elites
in the United States have no ideological discipline like Communism to which they must conform; any common policy which
arises from these heterogeneous groups must develop naturally as
a consensus. While the conditions in the United States permit a
broader participation in the formulation of policy, the formulation
is obviously slower and less flexible.

The communications elite in the United States is perhaps more
influential in the field of foreign relations than it is in domestic
affairs. The public is dependent almost exclusively upon mass communications for its foreign news, and perhaps feels less competent
to make its own evaluations in an area so complex and confusing.
The several large publishers each tend to present a special point of
view. The Hearst publications suggest a strong ideological orientation in their opposition to Communism and support for General
Franco in Spain, and the Chicago Tribune of the McCormick-
Patterson chain is noted for its extreme and conservative nationalism. Henry Luce's Time-Life-Fortune periodical syndicate has
dubbed this the "American century." On the other hand, the international responsibilities of the United States are emphasized by
the New York Times which has been called an "elite" press because
its readers belong to the attentive public and to the elite groups.
Newspaper and radio analysts play an equally important role as a
communications elite. Walter Winchell's Anglophobia, Gabriel
Heatter's humanitarian isolationism, and Drew Pearson's crusade
for international democracy all have mass audiences. James Reston
of the New York Times and Walter Lippmann provide penetrating, balanced analysis of world events for a relatively restricted
public.

Among special-interest elites, in 1950, Gabriel Almond found a
broad consensus in the field of foreign policy. The great majority
of the groups agreed that Communist aggression should be resisted

by economic, diplomatic, psychological, and military means. They were interested, furthermore, in reconciling individual freedom with mass welfare. A similar consensus was found to exist in 1954 when the Council on Foreign Relations conducted a nation-wide survey. Nine out of ten civic leaders supported the United States policy toward the USSR. This consensus was weakest in respect to a liberal trade policy and a strong national-security program. Foreign-origin groups viewed the developing aspects of the containment policy from the special outlook of their country of origin.

Changing conditions make it necessary for policy-makers to keep interest elites informed and committed to evolving foreign policies. It is a rare week that fails to bring two or three of these groups to the Department of State, and for a number of years the Department has held a national conference on United States foreign policy for the leaders of some 200 of the chief private organizations in the country. Here the Department reports on its conduct of foreign policy, and Department officials hear the views of representatives of many areas of American life. It will be increasingly difficult for these interest elites to give their continuing support for the realistic and economically burdensome policies that may be necessary as United States policy necessarily changes.

A mention of some of the important interest elites will be sufficient to suggest the nature of the problem. The American Federation of Labor and Congress of Industrial Organizations (AFL-CIO) has supported the general containment policy against the USSR, although before the two organizations merged in 1955 the CIO had been slower to adopt this position and was not notably militant or nationalistic in supporting it. President Meany of the American Federation of Labor declared in 1955: "The policy of massive retaliation, which was put forward in the early spring as the policy of the Eisenhower administration, has vanished into thin air. Let us hope that it will not be replaced by a policy of massive appeasement on a world scale that would make Munich of [1939] pale into insignificance." The Federation also qualified its approval of the Reciprocal Trade Program, fearing the competition of cheap foreign labor.

Among business organizations, the United States Chamber of

Commerce has been less idealistic than the Junior Chamber of Commerce in its crusading demands for spreading the gospel of free enterprise, but both support the economic policies of lower tariffs, rearmament, and foreign aid. The National Association of Manufacturers has gone along with its fellow business organizations except for its antagonism toward tariff reductions and economic aid.

Three major agricultural organizations have agreed on over-all United States policy. The American Farm Bureau Federation, the largest, has taken a central position. The Grange has combined a moderate pacifist internationalism with an economic nationalism. The Farmer's Union has adopted an unqualified pacifistic internationalism.

It is to be expected that the major veterans' organizations, as well as the business groups, will support universal military training as necessary for the United States defense posture. Except for the liberal and internationalist American Veterans Committee, veterans organizations like the American Legion and the Veterans of Foreign Wars are more nationalistic, patriotic, and distrustful of foreigners than other organizations which support the United States foreign policy. In September, 1954, for example, the American Legion recognized the need for stepped-up defense and for giving serious consideration to cutting off diplomatic relations with Soviet Russia.

The foreign policies of the women's organizations have been among the more idealistic and internationally biased. The nonprofessional, middle- and upper-class housewives in the General Federation of Women's Clubs are least critical of United States foreign policy. The National Federation of Business and Professional Women's Clubs is influenced by its close ties to the business organizations, while the League of Women Voters does not allow its concern for defense to overcome its long-run international goals.

Religious groups, both Protestant and Catholic, have given broad support to United States foreign policy. Ethnic groups have been particularly active in opposing Soviet aggression against the countries of their sympathies. It has been possible to channel such feeling into affirmative influence in foreign countries; a massive letter-writing campaign was stimulated among Italian-Americans on one occasion when an election in Italy threatened to go for the Communists and against the United States. Polish and Hungarian sympathies were particularly engaged in the last months of 1956 when the satellite regimes in those countries were struggling with Moscow. Zionist groups have been notably active in support of the interests of Israel, and thus have at times been in opposition to United States policy in the Middle East.

The broad consensus found in 1950 by Almond and in 1954 by the Council on Foreign Relations thus embraces numerous departures from central tendency. In general, labor, agriculture, religious, and international groups oppose universal military training, while business, patriotic, and veterans' organizations are more inclined to support it. Lowering of trade barriers finds least support from certain business and farm organizations. Labor, religious, and internationalist organizations alone took a clear stand against the proposed Bricker Amendment. Deviant groups which have not supported this general consensus include the radicals, like the Communists and extremely conservative nationalists like the Daughters of the American Revolution. Pacifists include the Friends Society and the Socialists, while extreme internationalists are represented by the United World Federalists.

In summary, public opinion makes a two-fold contribution to the formulation of foreign policy. In the first place, the mass mood establishes the limits and general nature of policy objectives. The public's susceptibility to oversimplification with its resulting support for extremist measures should caution policy-makers to limit their generalized public appeals to periods when rapid change of policy is required. For the implementation and refinement of a general policy, decision-makers must appeal to leaders of opinion and to special-interest groups for support and guidance. But because these groups are neither so well informed nor so generally concerned with the national interest as they are with their own interest, and because foreign-policy decisions cannot always wait for a consensus to form among these groups, the elites must exercise self-restraint in demanding participation in the decision-making process.

Traditional United States Foreign Policies

Traditional principles of United States foreign policy are closely related to public opinion, since they have been endorsed by the public over a long period of time. In one sense, they reflect crystallized public opinion, and policy-makers would be correct in assuming substantial public support for them. Statesmen find it helpful, therefore, to interpret or apply these policies to new situations. Foreign governments as well as the people of the United States are relatively unlikely to question a policy which over the years they have come to regard as characteristic. The application of traditional policy, in short, assures policy-makers some degree of public support.

But the United States, like other great powers, is confronted by a world in which foreign policies are rapidly changing. The past cannot be an effective guide to the future when conditions characteristic of former situations have been radically altered. This truism is not stated to suggest that new conditions necessarily demand new policies. They may well implement the traditional policies; nuclear weapons, for example, may induce general acceptance of the historic United States reliance on international law and peaceful negotiations.

History has presented three different periods which have defined the limits and content of United States foreign policy. The formative period extended from 1776 to the end of John Quincy Adams' administration in 1828. This was the classical age of United States diplomacy described by Gerald Stourzh as a period of realism and dedication to the national interest of survival, while tempered by the democratic ideal. The United States was occupied primarily with the task of securing its independence from Britain, first in the Revolutionary War and then in the War of 1812.

A new national spirit was apparent after the inauguration of Andrew Jackson in 1829. The cold realism of the classical period was no longer imperative, nor possible in the former degree after the masses had been enfranchised. The United States could now afford the luxury of indulging in continental expansionism and economic growth as long as the ocean provided an effective barrier, as long as Europe's power remained balanced, and as long as the balancer, Great Britain, was generally sympathetic to United States policy. Whereas conditions abroad and the relative power situation were responsible in the main for the choice of policy alternatives during the classical period, domestic conditions and attitudes, except for the Civil War, were more significant for this second phase.

The third period of United States foreign policy may be said to have begun near the opening of the twentieth century when the United States entered the world scene as a Great Power. This third period is one in which the international responsibilities of the United States were recognized by the President and State Department, which nevertheless found it necessary to disguise for an isolationist Congress and public opinion the real significance and necessity of what was being done in foreign relations. Accordingly, as Quincy Wright has written, United States participation in international organization and in world politics was "half-hearted, belated, and ineffective."[9a] The popular moods of isolationism and imperialism during this period were more strongly reflected in United States policy than was a tempered recognition for the need to adjust to foreign conditions. Compared to the first and second periods, it may have been that this more recent phase reflected the ascendancy of the traditional principles of foreign policy in the decision-making process. Facts of the international situation were interpreted to fit the principles of United States diplomacy even more than these principles were adjusted to the changing conditions abroad.

Some would argue that this third period ended with World War II, when it was clearly apparent that the European balance of power no longer existed, and when technological inventions were revolutionizing political institutions.

Isolationism

One of the most persistent principles of United States foreign policy until 1940 was its determination to isolate itself from

[9a] Quincy Wright, *Problems of Stability and Progress in International Relations* (Univ. of California Press, 1954), p. 48.

European affairs. Born of colonial experience, and reflected in the Declaration of Independence, the policy was reinforced during the first period of United States diplomacy by the feeling that the republican system of government had little in common with the European monarchies and by the awareness that America's anti-colonial attitude was antipathetic to European empires. The need for detachment from Europe and its overwhelming strength was implicit in Washington's farewell address. Keeping clear of Europe's power systems, moreover, had patent economic advantages. Withal, this splendid state of isolation was reinforced by geographical facts; the American continents were effectively separated from the European power center by a broad expanse of water.

Particular policies which reflected this principle of isolation may be briefly mentioned. There was the policy of no permanent alliances with the European states, and the 1778 treaty with France proved to be no exception because it was honored only in the breach. There was the policy of an automatic declaration of neutrality upon the outbreak of European wars, and there was also a policy of recognizing de facto regimes reflected in the prompt inauguration of relations with the Latin American states. The United States thereby refrained from pronouncing any moral judgment upon an aggressor in the event of war (thus permitting itself freedom of trade with all belligerents), or upon the constitutionality of a new state. It also preferred to make bilateral rather than multilateral peace treaties, thereby restricting foreign commitments.

There were few changes in the principle of isolation during the period 1828-1898. During the Jackson administration public attention shifted from Europe-oriented New England to westward expansion. The Mexican War of 1846 did not involve Europe. The Civil War did, what with French and British assistance to the Confederate States during the hostilities. In 1875 the United States began the practice of attending international conferences dealing with such technical matters as weights and measures, submarine cables, and the African slave trade. In 1884 it even attended a Berlin Conference dealing with the Congo, and the first Hague

Conference in 1899 inaugurated a system of co-operation with Europe for the promotion of peace and the limitation of wars.

Isolationist policy was subject to necessary modification after the United States had become a Great Power. President Theodore Roosevelt promoted the settlement of the Russo-Japanese War at Portsmouth, N.H., in 1905. The United States was represented at the Algeciras Conference the following year. But the entry of the United States into World War I in 1917 was considered by many as rather less a violation of the isolation principle than as an enforcement of the neutrality laws which were being violated. The disavowal of the League of Nations and the Versailles Treaty, the refusal to guarantee the territorial integrity of France, and the successive neutrality laws of 1935, 1937, and 1939 indicate that the isolationist principle was not yet dead. Indeed, Langer and Gleason have concluded that President Franklin Roosevelt and Cordell Hull pursued an unnecessarily isolationist policy before Pearl Harbor. But it was clear that the maintenance of national isolation was increasingly difficult. All the original bases for isolation had disappeared; much of Europe was now democratic, the United States was no longer an inferior power, neutrality was neither possible nor profitable, and technological development had shortened the distance between the two continents. The fact that the policy continued at all after World War I was a reflection of the importance which traditional principles and party politics may have had in the formulation of foreign policy during this period.

The Monroe Doctrine and Pan Americanism

The United States policy of isolation was directed principally towards Europe; the policy of the Open Door was cut to fit the Chinese problem. The twin policies of the Monroe Doctrine and Pan Americanism expressed America's regional intentions in Latin America. As finally declared, the Monroe Doctrine was a two-sphere doctrine, in which the United States asserted the isolation of the American continents from the European sphere. In a restrictive sense, the Monroe Doctrine of 1823 was a warning to Europe to keep its hands off this hemisphere; noncolonization, nonextension of European systems of government to the Americas, and prohibition of European intervention in American continental affairs were its chief tenets. Older than the doctrine itself was the United States policy of opposing the transfer of colonies in the western hemisphere from one European country to another.

The Monroe Doctrine was associated from the very beginning with Pan Americanism. Secretary of State John Quincy Adams hoped to rid the American continents of British influence, and for this reason favored United States participation in the first Pan American Congress at Panama in 1826. Henry Clay strongly endorsed the project in Congress as a means for expanding America's commercial interests in the area. The two "doctrines of the two spheres," therefore, reconciled the principles of isolationism from European affairs and expansionism in the western hemisphere.

Between 1828 and 1898 the Monroe Doctrine assumed the coloration of the period. At first the United States was so preoccupied with its own development that the Doctrine was ignored. Then in 1845 President Polk dusted it off as a warning against British interference with the westward expansion of the United States into Texas and California. The era after the Civil War found the United States with greatly increased material and military power. As a result of Secretary Seward's opposition to the establishment of the Maximilian empire in Mexico, the conviction grew that henceforth force would be used to prevent political interference by Europe in the Americas. By 1889 the United States industrial production had reached a level that made foreign markets desirable. Pan Americanism was conceived by Secretary of State James G. Blaine as a co-operative procedure whereby the Latin American area could be stabilized and a market for United States goods could be developed. The Pan American Conference in Washington, D. C., in 1889 permitted the United States to cast itself in the role of tutor for its southern neighbors. Both the Monroe Doctrine and Pan Americanism were unilateral policies of the United States. The first would shield the Latin American republics from Europe; the second would develop the area economically for United States markets. Even the Bureau of American

Republics was little more than an office within the Department of State in 1890.

The United States established itself as a Great Power in the area reserved for the Monroe Doctrine. British influence in the Caribbean had begun to recede by 1856 and had diminished still further after the turn of the century. German and French influence had been only sporadic at best. The threat of European intervention was not great, except perhaps in the forceful collection of unpaid debts. As the irresponsibility of the turbulent Latin American republics was forced on the attention of United States policy-makers, there seemed but one way to justify the continued insistence on a "hands off" policy. The Roosevelt Corollary of 1904 called upon the United States to exercise an international police power over impotent and wrongdoing Latin American regimes. The Monroe Doctrine, which had interposed a shield against Europe, thereby acquired a lance pointing southward. Thereafter Cuba, the Dominican Republic, Haiti, Nicaragua, and Panama became de facto United States protectorates at one time or another, and interventions were frequent. The Pan American conferences and the Pan American Union in Washington stood in the shadow of the Washington Monument. Nevertheless, the shielding function remained; German threats to the American continents in World War I and World War II suggested that the Doctrine could still be useful against ambitious aggressors and that it therefore had not lost its significance for United States security.

Not until the Buenos Aires Conference of 1936 were Pan Americanism and the Monroe Doctrine really shared with the Latin American countries. The legal and economic discussions heretofore characteristic of the inter-American conferences had produced disappointingly sterile results. However, in 1933 the United States began to be less demanding about the constitutionality of the regimes it recognized, and it took an oath of nonintervention in Latin American affairs. By 1936, therefore, the American countries were prepared to consult together in the event of any emergency, and with the advent of World War II it was clear that what was once the unilateral determination of the

United States to ward off a European threat had, with few exceptions, become a multilateral effort within the hemisphere.

Freedom of Trade and Freedom of the Seas

A third principle of United States foreign policy concerns free trade and freedom of the seas. The trading interests of the United States were strong during its early period, and the vigorous support of international law was reinforced by policies designed to extend and liberalize the traditional rules of navigation. Indeed, the American Revolution had been motivated in part by a general resentment against British trade restrictions during the colonial period. New England, with its tradition of seamanship, its shipbuilding industries, and its extensive overseas commerce, was an interested supporter of this principle. Likewise the South was anxious to exchange its tobacco and agricultural products for imported manufactured items. Withal, the geographical situation recommended hearty endorsement of this principle; the usefulness of Atlantic Coast harbors and of the St. Lawrence and Mississippi Rivers, whose mouths were controlled by England and Spain respectively, depended upon liberalizing shipping and trading opportunities.

During the early period of its diplomacy the United States restricted its territorial waters to three miles, pursued an active policy of clearing the Mediterranean waters of the Barbary pirates, and on the high seas granted the right of visit and search only during war. Its early commerce treaties provided for the conditional most-favored-nation clauses. The St. Lawrence and Mississippi were opened to shippers in the United States.

As long as its exports were primarily agricultural, the United States interest in low tariffs continued. Indeed, the Marcy-Elgin Treaty of 1854 with Canada was a model of liberality. After the Civil War, however, increasing demands for tariff protection arose from the rapidly industrialized sections of the country. The most-favored-nation clause disappeared from commerce treaties and other measures were taken to protect the domestic market from foreign competition. As the power and interests of the United States had grown, so had its claims over the high seas; the nation was now asserting its sovereignty over the Bering Sea and Chesapeake Bay. After 1898 tariffs were raised progressively until, in the Smoot-Hawley Tariff Act of 1930, they reached an all-time high. If reciprocal trade agreements were negotiated, they were either left unratified by Congress or terminated by a subsequent tariff act. Further inroads were made on the doctrine of free seas. The Anglo-American Liquor Treaty of 1924 accorded to the United States protective jurisdiction over a zone extending one hour's sailing distance from its shores. Previously, the conservation of fur seals on the Pribilof Islands had led to a treaty in 1911 which restricted the use of the high seas for pelagic sealing.

The reversal of the higher-tariff trend awaited Secretary of State Cordell Hull, who combined the traditional low-tariff beliefs of a Southern Democrat with the conviction that international trade is a cornerstone of international peace. The United States reciprocal trade agreements made under the program inaugurated in 1934 had incorporated in them the unconditional most-favored-nation clause. The United States, after seventy years, had again recognized that trade is a two-way street.

The Open Door Doctrine

Another traditional United States policy has been called the open-door doctrine. It refers to the equal opportunity for all nations to trade with China, and for this reason it has been closely associated with the principle of free trade. The open door emerged as an international issue in 1899, although its foundations were laid in the most-favored-nation provisions of the 1842 treaties between China and the foreign powers. Equal commercial rights of the United States were threatened in the area by the European powers who were establishing leaseholds and spheres of influence. Secretary of State John Hay accordingly asked the powers in 1899 to declare formally that the equality of commercial treatment would prevail for all countries alike, no special preferences being given by the respective countries to their own nationals within their respective spheres of influence. A year later the principle of equal and impartial trade with all parts of the Chinese Empire was joined by its logical corollary, the preservation of Chinese territorial and administrative entity.

Subsequently, the United States waged a losing battle in demanding respect for the open door. Russia in 1902 assumed a pre-emptive position in Manchuria, but was arrested by Japan in the Russo-Japanese War. The Root-Takahira exchange of notes in 1908 pledged Japanese support for the open door, but in 1917 the Lansing-Ishii notes recognized Japan's "special interests" in China. The Nine Power Treaty in 1922 conventionalized the policy, but a decade later Japan had forcefully acquired Manchuria and thence much of northern and western China. It was Japan, indeed, which shut the open door. But the United States refused to withdraw from the orient or to forsake its principles.

Territorial Expansionism

A fifth principle may be called territorial expansionism. At first it was motivated by the land hunger of the pioneers and the desire to control the Indians. It was also supported by those who feared the proximity of an imperial power to the United States and looked upon expansionism as a form of preventive defense. Finally, it reflected a desire for power—the United States should board the bandwagon of destiny. The vague and undefined area of Louisiana was purchased from Napoleon in 1803. This acquisition was followed sixteen years later by the Florida treaty with Spain. The opinion the United States had a "manifest destiny" to occupy the continent was thus well launched in the first period of its diplomacy. John Quincy Adams told the British minister, in 1821, "Keep what is yours, but leave the rest of this continent to us."

After 1828, the United States continued plucking territory where it was easy to pluck. The acquisition of Texas in 1845 was followed in 1846 by the successful assertion of title to Oregon. The war with Mexico in 1846-1848 not only secured the Rio Grande boundary and Upper California but the vast intermediate area as well. In three years the area of the United States had grown by 66 per cent or 1.2 million square miles. The decades before and after the Civil War were periods of growing United States interest in areas outside the continent, but except for the occupation of the Midway Islands in 1867 and the purchase of Alaska from Russia in the same year, little territory was actually added.

A feeling for a new manifest destiny was already apparent in 1894 even though in that year President Cleveland rejected the Hawaiian Annexation treaty. Hawaii was eventually annexed in 1898. Public support for overseas ventures came from the popularization and interpretation of Charles Darwin's concepts of the "survival of the fittest" and the "struggle for existence." It was not difficult to believe in the superior quality of Anglo-Saxon institutions and the superior power of the "Anglo-Saxon race" as discussed by popular writers and public men like Alfred T. Mahan. The Spanish-American War ushered in the new era of oceanic empire. Cuba, Puerto Rico, the Philippines, the Panama Canal Zone, together with a miscellaneous assortment of Pacific islands, all came under the American flag. Even under the anti-imperialist administration of Woodrow Wilson the Virgin Islands were purchased from Denmark in 1917. The Philippine independence act of 1934 may not have been the first step, but undoubtedly it was the most dramatic, in reversing this traditional United States policy of expansionism. American humanitarian objectives would thenceforth be accomplished by economic and technical co-operation, while its strategic objectives would be served by leased territory and by trusteeships.

Peace and Disarmament

In addition to its traditional policies which have been related to geographical regions or economic interests, the United States has pursued policies with universal application. These policies are more closely related to ideals than they are to interests, and some have argued that United States foreign policy has been unique in supporting them. The first such policy which could be mentioned is one favorable to peace and disarmament. Benjamin Franklin was famous for his dictum that "there has never been, nor ever will be, any such thing as a good War or a bad Peace." In spite of Washington's advice, the United States never established an effective standing army. Inexperienced volunteers furnished the manpower for its wars in the nineteenth century, supplemented by conscripts in the armies on both sides of the Civil War. William Jennings Bryan, Secretary of State, in 1914 opposed the development of a trained army, asserting that a million Americans would spring to arms overnight to defend the country from attackers. The United States had no strong professional navy until the Spanish-American War, however famous some ships and some officers. The Jeffersonian Republicans were not enthusiastic about navy expenditures; Jefferson felt that a few score gunboats for harbor defense were all that the country needed. He had hoped—in vain—that embargoes and nonintercourse acts would coerce Europe into peaceful relations. Not until 1883, when the United States realized that the Chilean Navy included armored cruisers which outclassed any ship possessed by this country, was there any effort to construct a modern navy.

Since before the United States had become a Great Power, the peace movement has had forceful advocates. Organized after the War of 1812, it had become an effective pressure group favoring arbitration treaties instead of large military appropriations. The Hague Conventions of 1899 and 1907 favored this movement. Woodrow Wilson declared that World War I was a war to end all wars and made disarmament the fourth of his Fourteen Points. In 1921-1922 the Washington Conference halted a costly and dangerous competition in armaments between the world's three leading naval powers. The Kellogg-Briand Pact in 1928 condemned recourse to war for the solution of international controversies and renounced it as an instrument of national policy. However unrealistic these peace policies may have appeared to some, they had become, nevertheless, an important factor in United States policy.

It is pertinent to mention that since 1871 the United States and Canada have had unguarded common boundaries.

Democracy and National Self-Determination

United States policies have also favored democratic governments and encouraged the self-determination of peoples. It was natural that a successful popular government should encourage the development of democracy elsewhere to gratify its own people, to reduce the danger of ambitious aggressors, and to promote the cause of human dignity. A de facto recognition policy strengthened and encouraged the emerging democracies of Greece, France, and

Latin America. The monarchic systems of Europe were proscribed in the new world by the Monroe Doctrine, and in 1848 the liberal revolutions in Europe had the sympathy though not the material aid of the United States. The escaped leader of the abortive Hungarian revolution, Louis Kossuth, was even feted in the White House, while liberties were taken with international law to secure the release of still other revolutionary leaders.

President Woodrow Wilson, more than any other, is credited with articulating democracy as an important tenet of his foreign policy. He is associated with the "constitutional" recognition policy inaugurated to discountenance the seizing of power by military leaders in Latin America. Self-determination was a conspicuous component in more than half of his Fourteen Points.

These principles have proved useful guides for policy formation in the past. Together with the traditional reliance on international law, they have affected the decisions and the behavior of the United States before the world. But each of these policies has been adapted to the developing public moods within the United States, and more slowly to changing conditions abroad. Nationalism, nuclear weapons and aircraft, and the disappearance of the European balance of power have revolutionized contemporary world conditions. If the historical principles of democracy and self-determination are to be adapted successfully, they must be interpreted broadly without losing their essential purposes. Emphasis must be placed on co-operative rather than unilateral action to avoid antagonizing nationalistic sensitivities. Regional policies must be universalized to adjust them to the air and nuclear age. Accordingly, the United States has had to modify its general policy of isolation from Europe to a policy of refraining from intervention in the domestic affairs of all foreign states. If such adjustments are made effectively, United States foreign policy can keep the stability and predictability that accompany the use of traditional policies, and yet maintain the flexibility requisite for necessary accommodation to events abroad. In short, principles must be pursued and facts must also be accepted in order to formulate effective policies. Withal, public support for traditional policies is more quickly and easily secured than for new policies which must stand the test of debate.

International Law

Just as the United States in its foreign policies has traditionally favored democracy, peace, and disarmament, so has it been predisposed towards international law. Like the other traditional principles, international law is a conservative force, and while a foreign policy which relies heavily on international law will gain in predictability, it will also be less flexible and adaptable. The legal approach to foreign relations is a deductive one; policies logically flow from a general premise. Long-run objectives are thereby emphasized. Both the opinion and power approaches are inductive; policies are developed from the facts of what the people want or from the changing power situations. Both international law and historic principles contribute a perspective to the short-run considerations of power politics or the fickle demands of the public. The employment of the legal approach reduces the danger of adopting expedient policies which may prove disastrous in the long run.

For a small nation, law is obviously preferable to force; for large nations, law-abiding small nations are convenient colleagues in international society. The American founding fathers were enthusiastic in their use of international law, and their strong advocacy of it encouraged the European powers to recognize the United States. The early American statesmen were well versed in Blackstone and Vattel and were undoubtedly better informed on international law than were their European counterparts. Indeed, Vattel's *Law of Nations* was the first book withdrawn from the New York Public Library, and the borrower was George Washington. One reason for Vattel's popularity was his liberal treatment of river navigation, which the United States could cite to support its claims for shipping rights in the foreign-controlled mouths of the Mississippi and St. Lawrence Rivers. The constitutional ideal that force was subordinate to law also encouraged the new republic to value international law more highly than the European monarchies did. Rules which were particularly useful for the United States policy of this period included those relating to the equality of states, neutral rights, impressment of seamen, enemy property in war, and arbitration.

After the formative period, from about 1829, international law guided the foreign policy of American statesmen while their chief attention was directed toward domestic affairs. Congress continued to give effect to international law by passing laws which enforced the obligations of treaties or maintained United States neutrality. The Supreme Court left a wide field for international law by interpreting legislation so it would not conflict with treaties. Presidents Hayes and Arthur vetoed Chinese Exclusion Acts because they violated treaties with China. There were occasions, however, when Congress and public opinion refused to accept the responsibilities of the United States under international law. Congress passed the Chinese Exclusion Act of 1882 in spite of treaty obligations, and the Senate frequently refused to accept general treaties for international arbitration. The President at one point interpreted an act of Congress so that he could extend United States sovereignty over the entire Bering Sea, but the United States did submit the matter to international arbitration for settlement. On the whole, as Quincy Wright has written, the tendency of the Department of State until the twentieth century was to treat most issues as cases in international law.[10] There were instances— such as the Mexican War, Spanish American War, and expansions in pursuit of "manifest destiny"—when the United States acted in the national interest without much reference to the law, although even then the United States tried to justify its actions on the basis of international law.

After the United States was recognized as a Great Power, its support for international law dwindled. In spite of the fact that most of the Secretaries of State were lawyers (and some like Elihu Root, Robert Lansing, and Charles Evans Hughes were outstanding in their profession), international law was honored neither by the courts nor by Congress as often as before. Supreme Court allusions to international law were much less frequent after

[10] Quincy Wright, "American Foreign Policy and the Concept of International Law," Chapter 1 in Alfred H. Kelly (ed.), *American Foreign Policy and American Democracy* (Wayne University Press, 1954).

1917 than they had been during the time of Marshall and Story, and the Court has been inclined to hold that international issues are political questions. If presidential policies gave more weight to power politics than they did to international law, the country's new power position may have explained why. President Wilson could and did justify United States entrance into World War I on the basis of enforcing national rights on the high seas against German submarines violating them; but the postwar world, he felt, required that a law violator be punished by an international authority rather than by the offended nation. An international organization was also needed to make international policy, since democracies lose out in the game of power politics. Democracies successful at power politics were likely to become garrison states where individual liberties were sacrificed for national security, secret diplomacy, and rapid decisions. The failure of the United States to join the League of Nations, however, prevented international law from acquiring a new and active role in foreign policy. To make matters more confused, neither did the United States formulate its policies on the basis of power politics. Instead, it reverted to an isolationist policy which revered the nineteenth-century positive international law. After 1924 career foreign service officers had to demonstrate their knowledge of international law before being admitted to the service; but it was a static law, narrowly construed. Critics of this period of United States foreign policy have called it unrealistic and legalistic, but their real objection could have been to the particular brand of international law that was applied. Neither responsible policy officials nor influential leaders in the American Society of International Law had adjusted their thinking to the conditions of the twentieth century.

Since World War II, the United States acceptance of the United Nations Charter has committed it to certain new principles in international law. Quincy Wright has called these the "new international law."[11] The nineteenth-century principles of international law have had to be modified for the present century. War and neutrality have given way to collective security. State sovereignty

[11] Quincy Wright, *Contemporary International Law: A Balance Sheet* (Short Studies in Political Science, Doubleday and Co., 1955).

has been broadened increasingly to allow individuals to participate as subjects in international law. The prophylactic use of unilateral force to settle disputes has been succeeded by therapeutic co-operation for economic and humanitarian purposes. Hostilities are illegal unless they are necessary for self-defense or for international policing by the United Nations. States must submit their disputes to some form of pacific settlement if diplomacy fails. Individuals are not only objects but subjects of the law. They are responsible for international crimes and are entitled to fundamental human rights. Finally, the United States and other members must co-operate in raising standards of living and preparing colonies for independence.

These new principles of international law are better suited to the air age than are the old horse-and-buggy rules of the nineteenth century. But they cannot be made effective until the United States can forget its primary concern with national security, and this it cannot afford to forget as long as a polarized situation exists in the world. To some extent power has been redistributed in recent years, however. Europe's growing strength and independent position, together with the increasingly autonomous policies of Japan, China, and India, all tend to recreate a little of the stability which characterized the nineteenth century. The general availability of atomic weapons for all countries will also contribute to this redistribution of power. It is not impossible that the United States may soon find itself in a position to formulate its foreign policy within the framework of international law.

Conclusion

Walter Lippmann is undoubtedly right when he notes the influence that mass opinion has had over United States foreign policy. It may well be the greatest single factor today. Neither international law nor historic principles, perhaps not even the power situation, have been so influential in the determination of contemporary policy. Certainly recent changes in strategic thinking were quite as much determined by economy-minded businessmen as they were by conditions abroad.

Concededly, many fortunate decisions have been made in the face of the need to keep the relative power situation in equilibrium. They would be especially fortunate if they were made out of the realization that we are living in a revolutionary age in which principles must be adapted before they can meet contemporary needs, in which rapidly changing conditions place a premium on flexible policy in contrast to long-run legalist and traditionalist policies. If, however, they were temporizing decisions born from the facts of opinion and power, they may not have been truly fortunate.

To maximize democratic procedures in foreign-policy formulation may be insuperably difficult in a world of power politics. For such a world all but demands highly flexible national leadership and initiative, complemented by generally vigorous support from a self-restrained public. Thus United States foreign policy for the present would be improved if an enlightened leadership were to assume major responsibility for the elaboration of policies which effectively respond to changing conditions abroad—particularly in terms of promoting the power and strengthening the attachment of allies. The posture of the United States in foreign affairs would be more confident if the communications and interest elites that articulate its public opinion were to exercise self-restraint in the foreign field, holding the leadership responsible for success in large objectives rather than hampering it by insistent minor stipulations. These two demands are not likely to be entirely fulfilled, and if fulfilled they might be criticized as imperfectly democratic.

Only under some such conditions, however, can the United States have a foreign policy capable of achieving long-run objectives, solutions of the long-run problems that confront the world and the United States in the mid-twentieth century.

BIBLIOGRAPHY

The plethora of literature on both substantive and procedural aspects of United States foreign policy makes the problem of selection a particularly difficult one. Among periodicals, an international point of view is reflected in the articles and reviews which appear in *World Politics*, and in the *American Journal of International Law*. The weekly *Department of State Bulletin*, and the quarterly *Foreign Affairs* include articles by American statesmen in defense of their policies. Similarly, the indispensable *New York Times* generally supports administration policies. The objective and independent analyses of James Reston, its Washington Bureau Chief, and of its military correspondent, Hanson Baldwin, should be noted. So should the syndicated columns of Walter Lippmann.

For an assessment of United States foreign policy in terms of its power position, Hans J. Morgenthau, *In Defense of the National Interest* (University of Chicago, 1951), and George Kennan, *American Diplomacy, 1900-1950* (University of Chicago, 1951), are best known. More recently Louis J. Halle, *Civilization and Foreign Policy* (Harper and Bros., 1955); George F. Kennan, *Realities of American Foreign Policy* (Princeton University Press, 1954); Charles Burton Marshall, *The Limits of American Foreign Policy* (Henry Holt and Co., 1954), all writing from practical experience in the Department of State, not only castigate the American public's immaturity in foreign affairs but argue that the United States should pursue a policy of power politics with limited and attainable objectives, being careful to balance objectives with capabilities. A thoughtful review of United States power vis-à-vis Russia which carefully avoids overstating Russia's position can be found in Henry L. Roberts, *Russia and America* (Council on Foreign Relations, 1956). Legislative Reference Service of the Library of Congress, *Trends in Economic Growth: A Comparison of the Western Powers and the Soviet Bloc* (GPO 1955) takes an even more optimistic stand on the United States power position, and is generally supported by James F. Dewhurst et al., *America's Needs and Resources* (Twentieth Century Fund, 1955). The argument over military strategy in an age of atomic stalemate has extended beyond the Department of Defense. One of the most recent studies, William W. Kaufmann (ed.), *Military Policy and National Security* (Princeton University Press, 1956), argues strongly for an upgrading of traditional warfare and potential power and cautions against exclusive reliance on the Strategic Air

Command. The psychological problem relating to the United States reputation abroad is considered *inter alia* by Otto Klineberg, *Tensions Affecting International Understanding: A Survey of Research* (Social Science Research Council, 1950), and by William Buchanan and Hadley Cantril, *How Nations See Each Other, A Study in Public Opinion* (UNESCO, 1953).

The effect of United States public opinion on foreign policy has been systematically and analytically surveyed by Gabriel A. Almond, *The American People and Foreign Policy* (Harcourt, Brace and Co., 1950). The descriptive works on American character of Alexis de Tocqueville and James Bryce, and the sociological studies of Margaret Mead, Geoffrey Gorer, and Clyde and Florence Kluckhohn are used by Almond. Thomas A. Bailey, *The Man in the Street* (Macmillan, 1948), negatively relates public objectives and desirable foreign policy—a conclusion which is strongly endorsed by Walter Lippmann, *The Public Philosophy* (Little, Brown and Co., 1955). A predictive approach, suggesting that the United States foreign policy will embark again upon an introvert phase in the 1960's is convincingly developed by Frank L. Klingberg, "The Historical Alternation of Moods in American Foreign Policy," *World Politics* IV, 2 (Jan., 1952), pp. 239-273.

Traditional foreign policies have been developed by Thomas A. Bailey, *A Diplomatic History of the American People* (5th ed., Appleton-Century-Crofts, Inc., 1955), and by Samuel F. Bemis, *A Diplomatic History of the United States* (4th ed., Henry Holt & Co., 1955). The latter applies principles of traditional international law and foreign policy as a criterion for effective policy as compared to Bailey's use of public opinion. Julius W. Pratt, in his *A History of the U. S. Foreign Policy* (Prentice Hall, Inc., 1955), has associated himself with viewpoints (e.g. that on the United States entry into World War II) which have not been widely accepted by recent scholarship. Hollis W. Barber, *Foreign Policies of the United States* (Dryden Press, 1953), lacks the detail of the previous works, but is useful for general purposes.

The varying impact of international law throughout the history of United States foreign policy has been briefly described by Quincy Wright, "American Foreign Policy and the Concept of

International Law," chapter 1 in Alfred H. Kelly (ed.), *American Foreign Policy and American Democracy* (Wayne University Press, 1954). The American Society of International Law is embarking upon an extensive survey of this subject, and Quincy Wright, *Contemporary International Law: A Balance Sheet* (Short Studies in Political Science, Doubleday and Co., 1955), has referred to the "new international law" as a developing source for foreign policy. Edwin D. Dickinson is more optimistic about the continuing impact of international law on the domestic United States legal system in "Law of Nations as National Law: Political Questions," *University of Pennsylvania Law Review*, vol. 104, No. 4 (Jan., 1956), pp. 451ff.

CHAPTER 3

THE CONTROL OF UNITED STATES FOREIGN POLICY

The Constitutional Structure

The problems confronting statesmen in the formulation of United States foreign policies are procedural as well as substantive. In a world of power politics where conditions are rapidly changing, foreign policy must be determined and executed quickly to be effective. A country which does not respond readily to these changing conditions may well endanger its national security or fail in its other national objectives. But rapid formulation of policy necessarily entails the concentration of authority in the executive power and this concentration tends to jeopardize the democratic process. This is the dilemma confronting the United States today. National security and international order must be promoted through rapid and flexible processes; yet individual liberties, guaranteed by the democratic process, must be safeguarded.

The constitutional system of the United States does not provide a clear and orderly guide for the formulation of foreign policy. The Constitution itself is vague, there have been inconsistent interpretations at different periods of history, and the courts have tended to regard questions involving foreign relations as political matters not subject to their jurisdiction. But Quincy Wright has noted that the underlying reason for this confusion lies not with the nature of the Constitution itself but rather with the dual position in which United States policy-makers find themselves.[1] In representing the United States abroad, policy-makers are expected to meet international responsibilities in a manner which on occasion is denied them by the United States Constitution. For example, the President of the United States may conclude a treaty which the Senate may refuse to accept or Congress may refuse to enforce by neglecting to appropriate money or even by passing contradictory legislation.

The United States has dealt with this conflict in a typically pragmatic manner. It has used political understandings, both domestic and international, to reconcile any legal conflicts between its international responsibilities and the Constitutional powers of its agencies. It has expected foreign countries, for example, to tolerate Congress's reluctance to ratify a signed treaty, and it has expected the executive branch to act in a way that other organs will approve. Thus Presidents have not forced a reluctant Congress to accept and execute all treaties which other countries might like to negotiate, but once a treaty has been approved, Congress has not been permitted the arbitrary power to determine whether it was expedient or not to make it effective.

The Federal System

The increasing scope of foreign affairs has meant that matters formerly reserved for domestic consideration have now become international in nature. While the United States Constitution specifically restricts the role of the several states in the formulation of foreign policy, the influence of the states over foreign policies has increased as these policies have come to deal with local matters. The paradox exists, therefore, that the states are accorded a very minor control of policy through the legal machinery but have been asserting a larger voice through the political machinery since World War II. As states have become more influential in policy making, the control over policy has necessarily been dispersed, and flexibility has been sacrificed. However, the areas in which the sev-

[1] Quincy Wright, *The Control of American Foreign Relations* (The Macmillan Co., 1922).

eral states are influential are not those primarily concerned with
national security but rather those concerned with individual rights
and local police powers.

The Constitution was motivated in part by the desire to eliminate the impotence of the United States in foreign relations under
the Articles of Confederation. In the Constitution, the national
government was assumed to possess an undivided sovereignty in
foreign affairs, to be a subject of international law, and to have a
power in this field which was more than a collection of all the
powers bestowed somewhere in the Constitution. Article 1 Section 10 of the Constitution specifically restricts the states from
making treaties (although Congress may, it never has given its
consent for the making of foreign agreements by states), imposing
tariffs, or engaging in war. Article VI Section 2, known as the
supremacy clause, states that all treaties made under the authority
of the United States shall be the supreme law of the land. This
important power of making international agreements is thus reserved for the national government, and the responsibility for
enforcing these agreements is largely given to Congress in Article 1
Section 8 of the Constitution.

Genuine states rights are incorporated into the Constitution in
Article IV Paragraphs 3 and 4. Here the states are guaranteed territorial integrity, republican form of government, and immunity of
their government organs from national taxation. It is clear, however, that with the possible exception of the first of these guaranteed states rights, none of them limit the treaty-making power of
the national government. The consent of Massachusetts was obtained before the Webster-Ashburton treaty of 1842 adjusted the
Maine boundary. A state's consent, however, would hardly be
insisted upon in practice if territory had to be ceded in order to
conclude an unfortunate war. It is likewise possible that a treaty
might under necessity make a protectorate of a state or otherwise
subvert its government. Indeed, the courts approved the military
government of Texas after the Civil War and have declared that
what constitutes a republican form of government is a political,
not a legal question.

The so-called reserved rights of the states are another and more

disputed limitation of the powers of the federal government in
international affairs. They are derived from the Tenth Amendment
which declares that powers not delegated to the United States by
the Constitution, nor prohibited by it to the states, are reserved to
the states respectively, or to the people. These reserved powers
include the regulation of state land and resources, the control of
state public services, and police control in behalf of public safety,
health, morals, and economic welfare. However, none of these
powers may interfere legally with the national enforcement of a
treaty. The Supreme Court held in the Missouri v. Holland (1920)
case that the power of the federal government to make treaties,
the power of Congress to pass laws to enforce them, and the supremacy clause making treaties the supreme law of the land are
not affected by the general terms of the Tenth Amendment. Congress has passed varied legislation (prohibiting white slavery and
protecting migratory birds and dealing with other matters normally
within the reserved power of the states) which would have been
considered unconstitutional had it not been enacted to carry out
the terms of a treaty. Even without a treaty, federal legislation
which bears upon foreign affairs has taken precedence over a state
law although it interferes with a state's police power. The Alien
Registration Law of 1940 was thus allowed to invalidate a Pennsylvania law which regulated the activities of enemy aliens.

If the Tenth Amendment does not prevent the national government from fulfilling its treaty and other international responsibilities, neither does it legally affect the power to make treaties. In no
case involving a clear treaty obligation to permit an alien to own
land and exploit natural resources, to use public schools or to work
on public projects, and freely to immigrate, to labor, and to conduct business, has the treaty failed to supersede a conflicting state
law. Since the Civil War, treaties have encroached upon the states'
rights to regulate and tax property and inheritance as well.

But the states' political role in the control of foreign policy
has been increasing since World War II. The Senate, necessarily,
has been jealous of states rights, even though the Seventeenth
Amendment has provided for the popular election of senators since
1913. The Senate has agreed with the dicta of courts and the opin-

ions of statesmen that the treaty power should seldom interfere with state control of land, natural resources, and public services, and that it should not interfere unnecessarily with the state's police control in behalf of public safety, health, morals, and economic welfare. But this is precisely the area with which many treaties since World War II have been concerned. The Genocide Treaty, which outlaws the planned extinction of whole national, racial, or religious groups, is not likely to be approved by the Senate for this reason. Even if it were, the treaty requires all signatories to supply needed legislation to make it effective. Indeed, all treaties that are not self-executing, like the Genocide Convention, give the Senate an opportunity to consider the effect of each new treaty on states rights. The State Department makes a practice of inserting in those treaties which affect states' interests a federal-state clause. This clause is intended to postpone the applicability of such a treaty within a state until the state has passed the necessary legislation. State and local governments have also become more involved in making foreign policy as civilian defense has assumed importance in the atomic age. The Eisenhower administration has consulted with state governors, for example, in the field of foreign affairs and defense. The assertion of claims by Texas and Florida to submerged oil lands beyond the three-mile limit suggests the difficulties of extending the role of the states in the formulation of foreign policy.

Separation of Powers

Whatever may be said of the states' powers in the control of foreign policy, it must be admitted that they do not compare with those possessed by the national government. As was noted in the Curtiss-Wright case in 1936, the Constitution gives the President a discretion and freedom over foreign policy not admissible in domestic policy. Legally the national government is unrestrained in the realm of foreign policy if Congress and the President are agreed upon a course of action. While treaties cannot authorize what the Constitution forbids, no treaty has ever been declared unconstitutional by the Supreme Court. Indeed, the courts have respected the pronounced will of the legislature and executive over foreign policy. Withal, the control over foreign policy in the United States system has been the product of political development to a greater degree than constitutional development.

On the national level, as Edward S. Corwin has stated, the Constitution is an invitation to struggle·for the privilege of directing United States foreign policy.[2] History has shown that the President is in a position to propose, Congress to dispose; the divided power has required co-operation between the two organs of government for all important decisions. The President is in a relatively advantageous position, however, and strong Presidents like Lincoln, Wilson, and the two Roosevelts have monopolized the control over foreign policy during critical periods in history. Nevertheless, the need to collaborate with Congress is apparent when the important powers of appropriations, appointments, war-making and treaty-making are to be exercised. It is clear that the President could make few important decisions without at least the tacit consent of Congress. Under these circumstances, a bipartisan support for foreign policy is always advantageous; and during periods when Congress is controlled by a party which is not the President's, a bipartisan policy is a necessity.

The President has vague and vast executive powers as head of the state. The Constitution has granted him explicit and implied powers, while statutes and custom have further implemented his position. The President's Constitutional power of nominating diplomatic representatives has been the basis for his legal monopoly over information in external affairs, since he is the sole organ of official communications with other governments. That this information need not be shared with Congress is evidenced from the fact that the Department of State—alone among the executive departments—is *requested*, not *directed*, to report to Congress. Since the Logan Act of 1799, statutory law has prohibited all but the President and his representatives from speaking for the nation in foreign affairs, and the President's position in this respect has made his influence especially effective in shaping the public mind. The power to appoint special diplomatic agents, like the power to make

[2] Edward S. Corwin, *The President: Offices and Powers* (3rd ed., N.Y. University Press, 1948), chaps. 5, 6.

executive agreements, has actually limited the Constitutional role of the Senate in the areas of treaty-making and appointments. Special statutes have conferred extensive emergency powers upon the President, and during wartime his position as Commander in Chief gives him complete control over troops and allows him to take such defense measures as the relocation of the West Coast Japanese during World War II.

Congress shares with the President those additional powers which arise by virtue of the fact that the United States is a sovereign nation. These powers include acquiring territory, and waging war. Congress also has been granted special Constitutional powers in the foreign field, although they are not as extensive as those accorded the President. The approval of the Senate, for example, is required of treaties and diplomatic appointments. Other powers of Congress can be and are used to achieve influence in foreign policy. Since 1940 the appropriations power of Congress has become an increasingly important factor in the conduct of foreign policy, and the practice of incorporating foreign-policy "riders" on appropriations acts may force the President to accept the will of Congress in some particular regard rather than veto an entire bill. Congress also regulates foreign commerce, although it has delegated this right in part to the President in the Reciprocal Trade Agreements Act. From its power to establish uniform rules for naturalization Congress has established its right to regulate the admission of persons to the United States. Concurrent resolutions may express the sense of Congress on various aspects of foreign policy, and members of Congress frequently serve on diplomatic missions. The power of investigation associated with the Congressional privilege of immunity has given the legislative branch a tremendous influence in making foreign as well as domestic policy. The Congressional power to impeach the President might be used to influence foreign policy, but has not been thus exercised.

It is clear from the foregoing that the President has a position of initiative and leadership in the formulation of foreign policy but that Congressional co-operation must be secured if the policies are to be made effective. The necessity for this close co-operation can be seen if the Constitutional provisions relating to the use of force, to the making of treaties, and to the conclusion of executive agreements are explored.

The president, as Commander in Chief in peacetime as in war, may deploy United States troops anywhere in the world. More than 150 times the United States Navy has been ordered out to protect American lives and property; troops have been sent into Texas in 1845, into Mexico in 1917, and into Iceland in 1941 to defend the national interest. As Commander in Chief, the President also is empowered to execute treaties. The President has exercised these rights in the occupation of defeated enemy states. President Truman's decision to send troops to Korea, therefore, could be seen as an exercise of his Constitutional powers in defense of United States strategic interests, for safeguarding United States forces in Japan, in implementation of the United Nations Charter, or to protect United States properties and lives.

The President, however, would be unwise to ignore the Congressional stake in defense. Congress, after all, must provide for raising and supporting the defense establishment, and its appropriations power allows it to exercise a negative control over military policy. This was evident in 1955 when Congress refused to authorize the funds requested for military assistance to foreign countries. However, President Eisenhower could not be compelled to restore a personnel reduction of the Marine Corps when Congress appropriated a larger sum for the Corps than he had requested. The power of appropriations nevertheless permits Congress to limit the over-all size of the military establishment and to impose its views on the relative strength of the Army, Navy, and Air Force. Legislative action also reflects public opinion and to this extent legislative support strengthens presidential policies. For this reason, President Franklin Roosevelt was gratified by Congressional authorization for his occupation of Iceland and for the exchange of United States destroyers for British air bases, although in neither case was it legally necessary.

The Constitution authorizes Congress, not the President, to declare war. This power is more nominal than real, however, since every war in which the United States has participated except for that of 1812 was brought about by executive action.

The treaty-making power is another which is jointly shared. The President again has the major responsibility in this field. Under his authority treaties are negotiated and signed. He is free to accept or reject alterations recommended by the Senate, and once the treaty is ratified, the President has the power of interpretation, implementation, and termination. The latter powers, however, are shared with other organs of government. Congressional authority in this field is centered in the Senate, which has considered more than six treaties per year during the first half of the present century. During its history the Senate has amended or added reservations to about a sixth of the treaties submitted to it, and it has turned down only 14 treaties. However, such important instruments as the Versailles Treaty and conventions for obligatory arbitration were rejected, while apprehension of such action has discouraged the executive from negotiating treaties which it feared one-third of the Senate would disapprove.

Political treaties are interpreted by Congress as well as by the executive, while self-executing treaties which create private rights are enforced by the courts. A treaty which calls for appropriations or implementing legislation requires action on the part of both houses of Congress. While the House of Representatives has insisted it is not obligated to take such action, it has habitually done so. Finally, Congress may direct the President to terminate a treaty or may pass contradictory legislation which then becomes the law of the land. The United Nations Participation Act of December 20, 1945, illustrates the Congressional role in the execution of treaties. The act declares that any implementation of the Charter is based on the national legislative power, not on the presidential prerogative. The right of Congress to be informed on United States participation in the United Nations is established, and all special agreements regarding the number and type of armed forces designated for United Nations purposes under Article 43 of the United Nations Charter must be submitted to Congress. While such military agreements have never been concluded, it seems clear that the Act lays the basis for a division of responsibility between Congress and the President; in regard to obligations to use military force, the former will give general approval to over-all size and strength of forces while the latter will maintain the initiative in committing the forces to any particular action.

Executive agreements often require close co-operation with Congress in spite of the fact they do not need Senate approval. The President concludes many of them in pursuance of the express will of Congress which has delegated him this authority in such areas as trade agreements, trade marks, postal affairs, or foreign aid. Other executive agreements, like the Lend Lease agreements, require Congressional appropriations or other legislation to make them effective. Altogether it has been estimated that 85 per cent of the executive agreements which have been concluded required the participation of Congress. The rest are self-executing and are made by the President under his authority as Commander in Chief or under his diplomatic powers as chief of state. Typical of these were the Japanese surrender on the battleship *Missouri* on September 2, 1945, the Rush-Bagot agreement to demilitarize the Great Lakes in 1817, and the Litvinov Agreements of 1933 which led to the recognition of the USSR. Treaties like the Charter of the United Nations often contemplate the conclusion of executive agreements to implement them. Like the military agreements already noted, these may require Congressional endorsement.

The Presidential Prerogative—The Bricker Amendment

The Constitutional system of the United States has accorded the President more authority in control over foreign policy than in control over internal affairs. Moreover, the enlarged scope of foreign policy has expanded the President's foreign-policy role into an area formerly reserved for domestic questions. The concern of the United States for promoting individual welfare and liberty throughout the world has raised the possibility that the President could commit this country by means of self-executing agreements to a policy which would further human rights and social reform and in so doing affect adversely the current rights of United States residents and of the individual states. Accordingly, Senator John W. Bricker has led a Congressional movement to amend the Constitution in a way which would restrict the President's powers over foreign affairs. The pertinent provision of his proposed amendment, in the version that was approved by the Senate Judiciary Committee in a 11-2 vote on March 5, 1956, reads thus:

A provision of a treaty or other international agreement which conflicts with any provision of this Constitution shall not be of any force or effect.[3]

There was doubt by many, including President Eisenhower and his staff, as to the meaning of this latest revision. Senator Thomas C. Hennings of Missouri, who led the opposition in defeating a similar proposal in 1954, along with Senator Estes Kefauver, declared it either meant too much or too little. It was clear, however, from the majority report of the Judicial Committee that an expansive interpretation was intended. The "three little words" of the proposal—"with any provision"—were intended to override Justice Holmes' decision in the Missouri v. Holland case and, by applying the Tenth Amendment broadly, to limit treaties to subjects that did not fall within the reserved powers of the states or the Bill of Rights.

The Supreme Court has frequently declared that a treaty cannot violate the Constitution. For example, the Constitution does not permit the federal government to encroach upon the guaranteed individual liberties contained in the first ten amendments. A treaty, which the Constitution declares is the supreme law of the land and which the Supreme Court (in the Missouri v. Holland decision) determined could override the "invisible radiations" of the Tenth Amendment, would under this proposal be subordinated to the vague and unspecified residual powers given the states. The President's foreign policy powers could thus be seriously jeopardized. The amendment would render illegal a treaty which protects the United States citizen abroad and which necessarily must offer reciprocal rights to aliens in the United States. The national government, in short, would have no more authority over foreign relations than it does over domestic questions.

[3] *Constitutional Amendments Relative to Treaties and Executive Agreements*, Report of Judiciary Committee, 84th Congress, 2nd Session Part 1 and 2 (GPO, Senate Report No. 7193 and 7194, March 27, and April 11, 1956).

Basically the proposed amendment would downgrade the President from spearhead to figurehead in foreign affairs. Executive agreements not authorized by Congress would be ineffective until Congress had ratified them. Foreign states would never be sure that the United States would execute treaties which the national government had concluded. As was the experience under the Articles of Confederation, the United States would claim to be one state when making treaties and 48 when expected to enforce them. The rights of the several states would thus be safeguarded not only by the two-thirds vote of the Senate, but also by the provision that valid treaties cannot conflict with any vague reservation of powers to the states or to the people as stated in the Tenth Amendment.

The authors of the Bricker Amendment have contended that the United States has been moving too rapidly into the international arena, particularly in the field of social reform and human rights. They feel that the limitation of the treaty power would slow up this process and would give the people of the various states, with their different customs and habits, time to accommodate themselves to new conditions. But recent Supreme Court decisions on the desegregation of schools have highlighted the fact that the important invasion of traditionally held states rights has come not from the international but from the domestic field. The Supreme Court has recognized the growing scope of domestic legislation on the national level by its liberal interpretations of the Fourteenth Amendment, and of the commerce, taxing, and general-welfare clauses. The Bricker Amendment is concerned with the danger of unwelcome social innovations through the back door of treaties and executive agreements, when the front door of domestic reform has been left wide open. The Bricker proposal thus locks the back door unnecessarily, and it sacrifices in the process what little flexibility exists in the control of United States foreign policy.

It is true that the Constitutional system today gives the President of the United States a broad and necessary prerogative to meet emergencies as he defines them. His authority furthermore has been increased by extensive delegations of power by Congress. The Supreme Court has not yet exercised its right to declare a treaty or executive agreement unconstitutional. It has been left to the President, therefore, to recognize the enlarged scope of Congress over implementing legislation in foreign policy. The states have made no legal intrusion into the function of making foreign policy. Nevertheless the President's control is not absolute. The Senate has been given a voice in the appointive and treaty powers, while Congress possesses the initiative in appropriation measures. The legal necessity for the President to co-operate with Congress is reinforced by political factors which will be discussed later. Indeed, it is this co-operation which provides the Constitutional key whereby the flexibility necessary for safeguarding the national security is balanced by the broader participation in the control of foreign policy required of democracies.

The Executive and Foreign Policy

President Woodrow Wilson once wrote: "The office [of the Presidency] is so much greater than any man could honestly imagine himself to be that the most he can do is to look grave enough and self-possessed enough to seem to fill it." What was true in Wilson's day is all the more true now. The President holds a pre-eminent position in foreign affairs not only as the result of the generous allotment of Constitutional power but also by the nature of the office. As a single individual, the President is capable of more rapid and effective decisions than is a bicameral Congress. He can function as promptly as his temperament permits when a foreign crisis occurs and demands immediate action; he is the one national figure who is elected by all the people, and his statements are given immediate and complete circulation by the press, radio, or television. Through press conferences and press releases he can educate, persuade, and mobilize the public. His Constitutional position gives him a monopoly of information on foreign affairs; this information is analyzed by a permanent staff of experts and is privileged in that it may be kept secret. Furthermore, rapid transportation and instantaneous communication have enabled the President to deal directly with foreign chiefs of state.

The role of the President in foreign affairs is affected by his personality and by the world situation he confronts.[4] In the present century, the two Roosevelts and Woodrow Wilson chose to view their role expansively. President Eisenhower, following Harry Truman's example, on the other hand, made it a policy to encourage Congressional participation in making foreign policy. President Franklin Roosevelt has been characterized as imaginative, sophisticated, and subtle, preferring to exercise his own judgment and negotiating ability. President Truman was more inclined to appeal to common sense and to depend upon his advisers. President Eisenhower is said to think in broad generalizations and to be a man of heartfelt, earthbound sincerity; not being studious or reflective, he depends all the more upon the oral advice of his associates, particularly that of the Secretary of State and the National Security Council.

But while President Eisenhower has desired to forbear in executive control of foreign policy, world events and the demands of the public have forced him to take initiative. Such initiative is demanded in any period when aggression threatens the national security. It is also demanded in a world situation characterized by an unstable balance of power, by rapidly changing conditions of power or opinion, or by authoritarian regimes. The mounting importance of foreign relations will never again allow a President to assert the restricted view of the executive so characteristic of the 1920's, and of most of the period between 1826 and 1900.

This expanded role of the executive does indeed permit foreign policy to adjust more rapidly to changing conditions abroad. But it raises a question regarding the President's responsibility to Congress and to public opinion. The Constitution, of course, provides a system of checks and balances, but in foreign policy all too often the checks can be exercised only after an action has been taken. Congressional investigations have been most effective in this regard. The press has exerted an informal and continuing restraint on Presidential power, but in the last analysis, decisions which require secrecy and dispatch and may be described as self-executing

[4] Richard C. Snyder and Edgar S. Furniss, Jr., *American Foreign Policy* (Rinehart and Co., 1954), chapter 5.

are the sole responsibility of the executive. Nevertheless, Presidents rarely flout public or Congressional opinion. Even a President as dynamic as Franklin D. Roosevelt, according to Professors Langer and Gleason, never moved more rapidly than public opinion during the critical pre-war years, and occasionally fell behind.

Presidential Co-ordination of Foreign Policy: the White House Staff

Effective co-ordination at the executive level not only speeds up the decision-making process but also assures the maximum use of all pertinent information. It is likewise important if the United States is to speak with one voice at more than 400 international conferences each year, or in the United Nations where 25 government agencies have connections. Co-ordination of these executive agencies creates particular difficulties in the United States: first, because many of them are equal in authority; and second, because their functions are often unclear and overlapping. The problem could be mitigated if major responsibility were to be given to one agency like the Department of State, or if the functions of each interested organization were carefully delineated. Short of this plan, participants in the co-ordinating process can only be self-restrained and stand prepared to make concessions in terms of the "big picture."

The President may perform this co-ordination function directly or delegate it to assigned officers on the White House staff. In either case the effectiveness depends directly upon Presidential power. At a lower level, "line co-ordination" is accomplished through interdepartmental committees like the National Security Council, or through the most interested single agency, which may be the Department of State for general policy or the Department of Defense or the Central Intelligence Agency for their special interests.

The need for effective staff services to supervise and unify both the formulation and execution of executive policy was first recognized by President Roosevelt in 1939 (one week after Germany invaded Poland), when he established the executive office of the President. Two innovations which President Eisenhower has brought to the functioning of the White House staff are (1) a much clearer line of authority channeled through a chief of staff, and (2) the introduction of a corps of special assistants to the President.

The White House staff has thus been reorganized into a cohesive group of intimate personal assistants reporting to Sherman Adams as chief of staff.[5] The staff is divided into seven service chiefs who handle problems relating to the press, appointments, legislation, speeches, economic affairs, and liaison with Congress. In addition there are Presidential assistants who have been placed in charge of specialized fields; these presently include atomic energy, national-security affairs, foreign economic problems, cultural and psychological aspects of foreign relations, and disarmament.

All of the special assistants attend the National Security Council and are intrusted with certain co-ordinating responsibilities in their respective fields. The foreign economic adviser chairs the Cabinet-level Council on Foreign Economic Policy. He is responsible for producing a unified governmental policy in the secret weekly meetings of the Council. In this way such disagreements as existed between the former director of the Foreign Operations Administration and the economy-minded Secretary of the Treasury over the size of the Asiatic developmental program can be kept within the administrative family. The special assistant on disarmament performs a clearing-house service for proposals on world peace and is the chief United States negotiator on these matters in the United Nations and at general conferences on disarmament. Presumbly, these co-ordinating assistants will change as new problems demand the special attention of the President.

The White House staff thus systematizes and co-ordinates the flow of information to the President in problem areas of foreign policy. The President has been provided with a $1.5 million budget for this staff of 250 persons which keeps him briefed through oral presentations or one-page summaries of significant problems. The procedure reduces the probability of erratic and ill-considered policies occasionally attributed to President Roosevelt, but it makes the President unusually dependent upon his staff's thinking. President Eisenhower's too-hasty dismissal of Chou En-lai's peace feelers from Bandung in May 1955, indicate that the procedure is no cure-all. Furthermore, it does suggest the need for top men who are not only loyal, technically efficient, and industrious, but who possess an unusual intellectual aptitude as well. However, much clutter has been removed from the President's desk, and if this new-found freedom is devoted to the consideration of "big" problems, much has been gained.

Presidential Co-ordination of Foreign Policy: the National Security Council

While the White House staff provides a systematic flow of information to the President, the co-ordinating functions of the National Security Council (NSC) assist him in the actual formulation of important foreign policies. The Council brings together, at the Cabinet level, the chief points of view in foreign policy. Under the Eisenhower administration it has become the most powerful agency of the government under the President, and the most important arm of the Presidency.

The National Security Council was established by statute in 1947 along with the Department of Defense, the Central Intelligence Agency, and the Office of Defense Mobilization (ODM). It was modeled after a similar organization in Great Britain, which was established during World War I. Compared to the President's Cabinet, the Council was smaller, and for this reason could reach decisions more quickly. It also had the advantage of keeping departmental disputes on foreign policy from being aired among all Cabinet members. In times of emergency it provided for the close co-operation between the Departments of Defense and State, but from the beginning Secretary of State Dean Acheson felt that it endangered the political determination of policy by institutionalizing the policy-making role of the military. There was no doubt but that the Council restricted the key position of the Department of State in the formulation of foreign policy.

The President, accompanied by his staff co-ordinators, presides

over the secret weekly meetings of the Council. The military is
represented by the Secretary of Defense and the Chairman of the
Joint Chiefs of Staff, while foreign-policy costs are the concern of
the Secretary of the Treasury and the Director of the Budget.
Facts concerning conditions abroad are the responsibility of the
director of the Central Intelligence Agency, while the director of
the Office of Defense Mobilization safeguards United States military potential. A broad political and diplomatic viewpoint is
reflected by the Secretary of State. The presence of the Vice
President gives the country an informed possible successor to the
Presidency. The Council contributed to 1,277 Presidential decisions between 1947 when it was organized and 1955. Recently it
has been responsible for more than 200 decisions a year. The
"new look" in the military establishment, the defense ring around
the southern boundaries of the USSR, and the partition of Indo-
china have all been considered by the National Security Council.

The President's special assistant for national-security affairs has
been assigned chief responsibility for the Council's secret weekly
meetings.[6] He chairs three weekly meetings of the Council's
Planning Board (representing at the Assistant Secretary level the
same organizations that are in the Council and assisted by a 28-man
permanent staff), wherein an agenda is discussed, the drafting of
working papers is assigned to relevant agencies, and preliminary
discussion of the problems takes place. Top priority is given the
preparation of the working paper, which is composed of five parts:
a statement of the basic elements which underlie the issue, a
statement of the objectives in view of the problem, a recommended
course of action, its cost, and finally the documentation (which is
its thickest section). Before the three-hour session of the Council,
the special assistant carefully briefs the President and at the
meeting itself he reads the agenda, calls on members to speak in
turn, and steers the conversation. Subsequently he writes a "record
of action" which may cover two to six major problems and which

    [6] Robert Cutler, "The Development of the National Security Council,"
Foreign Affairs (April, 1956), pp. 441-459. Also see Dillon Anderson, "The
President and National Security," *The Atlantic* (Jan., 1956), pp. 42-46.

becomes official policy after it has been initialed by the President as soon as possible after the meeting.

To oversee the execution of the policies recommended by the National Security Council, the Eisenhower administration established the Operations Co-ordinating Board (OCB) in 1953.[7] In 1956 the Board was chaired by the Under Secretary of State and was composed of the Presidential assistants for defense and psychological warfare, the Under Secretary of Defense, and directors of the Central Intelligence Agency (CIA), the International Co-operation Administration (ICA), and the United States Information Agency (USIA). The OCB has been characterized as an anticonfusion device to see that a big government which is getting bigger does not have one department carrying out overseas policy in one way and several other departments carrying it out some other way. The OCB has established an elaborate procedure for implementing the NSC policies which have been assigned to it. Committees (some forty in 1956) representing the participating agencies agree upon an operating program for the new policy, and subsequently submit semiannual progress reports to the NSC. Occasionally, as they did with the Department of Defense project for propagandizing the world with the ten basic tenets of "militant democracy," they declare a policy too obscure for implementation. Some have criticized the OCB as a wholesale time-killer; its progress reports are given little attention and it has no overseas staff to supervise continuing operations in the field. Nevertheless, by general consent, the OCB is a useful new device of the President that is developing authority in unifying United States actions abroad.

While the National Security Council is too new for any final assessment, none would doubt that it is a necessary extension of Presidential intelligence and decision-making. It cannot supplant the power of the President, nor can it provide the authoritative direction which the President must give its work. But the Council does provide for a systematic and institutionalized co-ordination

[7] Dale O. Smith, "What is OCB?" *Foreign Service Journal* (Nov., 1955), pp. 26ff.

of the several departments which are especially concerned with national security. The effective functioning of the NSC depends upon efficient staff and informational services which are provided by the Planning Board, the permanent staff, and the CIA; these contribute to the collaborative recommendations by Cabinet members and other "line" officers who are concerned with the day-to-day operations of national security. The quality and wisdom of the Presidential decisions which result from this process, and their effective implementation of these decisions through the Operations Co-ordinating Board (OCB), in the last analysis, measure the success or failure of the National Security Council.[8]

Several criticisms and suggestions have been offered regarding the NSC. The Hoover Commission recommended that Council membership be extended to all members of the Cabinet (since domestic affairs no longer can be separated from foreign affairs); but such increased membership might present obstacles to rapid and effective orientation toward the rapidly changing conditions abroad. The jurisdictional friction between the participating members would be increased. Another criticism has been that the predominance of military influence is creating an "industrial Sparta." But since 1949 the only regular military participants in the Council have been the Secretary of Defense and the Chairman of the Joint Chiefs of Staff. Moreover, a reorganization of the Department of Defense in 1953 was designed to implement civilian direction and improve the co-ordinating power of the Department over the respective military services.

Co-ordination of Intelligence Agencies

The specific responsibility of keeping the President and the members of the NSC abreast of the changing world picture belongs to the Central Intelligence Agency (CIA). This Agency is accountable to the NSC, and its director (currently Allen Dulles) opens the weekly NSC meetings with a fifteen-minute assessment of the latest international developments. The agency also gives

[8] Arthur W. Macmahon, *Administration in Foreign Affairs* (Univ. of Alabama Press, 1953), suggests the need for one department of foreign affairs to secure the necessary co-ordination.

top priority to securing information related to the problems which the Planning Board has selected for the Council's agenda.

The CIA, which is believed to have between 10,000 and 15,000 employees, operates on a secret budget, estimated to be as much as $500 million. Its basic function is to secure effective national intelligence estimates, and this it does by co-ordinating data gathered by itself and other national agencies and by co-ordinating the activities of these agencies. However, it has no direct power over the other agencies except the right to inspect their files. Its director chairs the Washington Intelligence Advisory Group, in which the directors of the FBI, the Atomic Energy Commission, State Department Intelligence, Army Intelligence (G-2), Air Force Intelligence (A-2), Office of Naval Intelligence, and the Defense Department's supersecret National Security Agency agree upon a co-ordinated intelligence policy.

As the successor of the war-born Office of Strategic Services, the CIA was, at the time of its organization in 1947, primarily interested in the collection of covert information. For this purpose it has agents in each of the United States embassies abroad and inside the country maintains 25 branch offices which act as regional headquarters for the collection of foreign intelligence. The Hoover Commission, in 1955, was the third investigating committee to draw attention to the inadequacy of the data, particularly on the USSR, which the CIA was collecting. However, the organization has shifted its chief emphasis from the collection of covert intelligence (which at best represents one-tenth of the necessary information) to the general evaluation of all intelligence. The United States intelligence objective (as compared to the British) is said to emphasize the capabilities of foreign states rather than their intentions. Both, of course, must be considered in policy-making, since a country's policies and actions are not necessarily related to its relative power situation. Effective interpretation of intentions demands able area specialists who have a cultural and sociological appreciation of the respective countries, and these have been in short supply during the postwar years.

Large intelligence organizations, necessary as they are to policy formulation, contain inherent threats to democratic governments.

They cannot be subjected to publicity and public opinion—their security must be safeguarded; yet overcautious policies which have not distinguished between unnecessary secrecy and desirable security often lead to inefficient and costly operations.[9] More important in the long run, policy-makers may find themselves in a position of formulating policy on information which cannot be shared with the general public. A serious danger to democratic institutions is that the intelligence agencies may not distinguish between evaluating information and making policy. The intelligence agencies can so interpret information as to suggest only one course of action, leaving no alternatives for policy-makers. They also reflect a vested interest in preserving the secrecy of intelligence—an interest which was reflected during the spring of 1956 when they actively discouraged policies which would broaden exchange of personnel between the United States and the USSR. Alerted to these dangers, the Hoover Commission in 1955 suggested the creation of a joint Congressional watchdog commission which would give the legislative body a more formal liaison with the CIA. To serve this purpose, and yet to safeguard vital information from potentially indiscreet use by Congressmen, a Presidential commission was appointed early in 1956.

The Defense Establishment

The important role of the military in "peacetime" has been an important aspect of the revolution in United States foreign policy. Conditions abroad and at home during the postwar decade have contributed to the growing military influence. Public opinion has demanded a larger defense establishment as international tensions have increased. The deterioration of United States-Soviet relations, which culminated in the Korean War, reflected the importance of implementing collective and regional military arrangements. The prestige and experience of military leaders like General George C. Marshall have made them natural candidiates for policy-making positions.

Recent foreign policy has been greatly influenced by this new

[9] Roger Hilsman, Jr., "Intelligence and Policy-making in Foreign Affairs," *World Politics* (October, 1952), pp. 1-46.

military imperative. Co-operation with the dictatorial Franco government, for example, grew out of the need of the United States for air bases in Spain; the establishment of special trusteeships over the captured Japanese mandates in 1946 was deemed necessary for security reasons; and the sympathetic concern for the Arab countries in part reflects a military appreciation of their valuable oil resources and strategic location. The United States Occupation policies toward Germany and Japan were in large part determined by Generals Lucius Clay and Douglas MacArthur, respectively. Indeed, in 1948, President Truman was assisted by Admiral Leahy as his Chief of Staff, by General George C. Marshall as Secretary of State, by General Bedell Smith as Ambassador to the USSR, and by the NSC, in which until the following year the military had a four-to-one majority.

A curtailment of military participation in policy-making was effected in 1949 when the Secretary of Defense and the Chairman of the Joint Chiefs of Staff were made the military establishment's only statutory participants in the NSC. In 1951 President Truman reasserted civilian supremacy when he dramatically removed General MacArthur from his command in Korea for refusing to execute orders of the Commander in Chief. Subsequently, President Eisenhower further reorganized the Department of Defense with this objective in mind. The authority of the Secretary of Defense, of the Chairman of the Joint Chiefs of Staff (JCS), and of civilian leaders in the establishment has been enhanced by the provisions which unify and centralize the defense leadership under an Undersecretary and 10 Assistant Secretaries of Defense, and thereby give the Secretary of Defense a concentration of authority in a department which operated on a budget of $35 billion in 1956 (eight times that of General Motors Corporation).

As the agency second only to the Department of State in the conduct of foreign relations, the Defense Department not only advises the NSC and the President on military implications of foreign policy but also provides strategic plans for the support of national objectives and executes these plans when military operations are required. In addition to the Joint Chiefs of Staff, whose special proficiencies in the policy-making role are self-evident, the Assistant Secretary for International Security Affairs should be mentioned. This official is responsible for developing Defense Department views with respect to the Mutual Security Program, NATO, the United Nations, the NSC, psychological warfare, international conferences, and military-political affairs in general. Other Assistant Secretaries of Defense are responsible for research and development, supply and logistics, public affairs, manpower, and atomic energy. In spite of the new authority given the Department of Defense and in spite of joint strategic planning at the JCS level, however, it is clear that unification of the Army, Navy, and Air Force is limited by fundamental disagreements on strategy and by rivalry for funds.

In perspective, it would appear that exaggerated fears of a "garrison state" controlled by the "military mind" have been unfounded.[10] In truth, wise and cautious counsel was frequently provided by the trained and experienced military advisers while adventurous policies were proposed by civilian politicians. Nevertheless, Theodore Roosevelt's admonition that experts should be kept on tap and not on top applies with particular force to the military. The flexibility and adaptability required of those handling political problems are not the essential qualities of a soldier whose strategic objectives can be more narrowly construed and whose tactical procedures can be more precisely analyzed than can political problems. As Quincy Wright has written in The Study of International Relations, "Professionals in the art of war, intent on immediate requirements, are doubtful guides to foreign policy."[11]

Co-ordination of the Foreign Economic Program

The United States is now confronting a world situation in which it must increasingly employ economic and psychological instruments of foreign policy. In December, 1954, President Eisenhower

[10] Burton M. Sapin and Richard C. Snyder, The Role of the Military in American Foreign Policy (Doubleday Short Studies in Political Science, No. 7, Doubleday and Co., 1954), passim.

[11] Quincy Wright, The Study of International Relations (Appleton-Century-Crofts, 1955), p. 156.

announced, "We must now concentrate on developing economic weapons in the cold war because we are going to hear less gunfire and see less blood flow." It is unfortunate, therefore, that the agencies for the co-ordination of these policies have been neglected. Not until December 11, 1954, was the Council on Foreign Economic Policy (CFEP) created in the Presidential Office with Joseph M. Dodge serving both as chairman and as special assistant to the President. The Council provides line co-ordination for foreign economic policy. Its purpose is to assure the orderly development of economic programs and to co-ordinate economic policies of various departments. For example, it ascertains whether farm-surplus disposals conflict with the aims of economic aid in particular circumstances, and it examines United States tariff policies. Its members include the Secretaries of State, Treasury, Commerce, and Agriculture, the Director of the International Co-operation Administration, and the special assistant to the President for national-security affairs. Co-ordination of the work of the NSC and CFEP is provided by overlapping membership of the two organizations, as well as by regular contact of the respective staffs.

In addition to the CFEP, the National Advisory Council on International Monetary and Financial Problems was established in 1945 to co-ordinate United States policies with those of the World Bank and other agencies which participate in making foreign loans. The National Advisory Council is chaired by the Secretary of the Treasury, and includes the Secretaries of State and Commerce, the Chairman of the Federal Reserve Board, the President of the Export-Import Bank, the Director of the International Co-operation Administration, and the Chairman of the CFEP. During the Eisenhower administration the guiding figure in both the Council and the CFEP has been the Secretary of the Treasury, George M. Humphrey, who also participates in the NSC meetings. It has been reported that while both Defense Secretary Wilson and Secretary of State Dulles took their cues from President Eisenhower, the President took his cues on economic policy from Mr. Humphrey. The result has been a conservative policy in which both military- and foreign-aid expenditures have been rigorously examined in the light of the United States economy.

The economic development program (Point 4) is the responsibility of the International Co-operation Administration (ICA). Established in June, 1955, it succeeded the Foreign Operations Administration and before that the Economic Co-operation Administration. As presently organized, the Director formulates his policies in close co-operation with the Under Secretary of State, who chairs the Operations Co-ordinating Board of the NSC, in which both participate.

These three organizations (CFEP, ICA, and National Advisory Council) are responsible for developing and co-ordinating administration policies relating to international trade, finance, and development. Overlapping membership of these organizations with the NSC would suggest that the points of view of the Cabinet members who are not participants in the NSC meetings are nonetheless represented there. However, it cannot be claimed that an effective co-ordination of foreign economic policy has yet materialized.[12] It may develop out of the records and procedures of the CFEP which have been established by the pioneering efforts of its first chairman.

Co-ordination of Cultural and Psychological Policies

The importance of influencing the peoples as well as governments of foreign countries has enhanced the role of propaganda and cultural exchange. Institutions for the implementation of this phase of foreign policy were slow in developing; Congressmen were suspicious that a government-sponsored organization for propaganda abroad would not reflect the national interests, and might even be used in the home country to enhance the political fortunes of the administration. Nevertheless, the Division of Cultural Relations in the Department of State was established in 1938, and during World War II the Office of War Information, the Co-ordinator of Inter-American Affairs, and the War Department

[12] *The Political Economy of American Foreign Policy*, Report of a Study Group for the Woodrow Wilson Foundation and the National Planning Association (Henry Holt and Co., 1955), ch. 10.

were all engaged in propaganda activities. During the Truman administration, foreign information programs were sponsored by the Mutual Security Agency and the Technical Co-operation Agency, while the International Information Administration (within the Department of State) operated the Voice of America. President Truman also established the Psychological Strategy Board, which under the Eisenhower administration has become the Operations Co-ordinating Board.

During the Presidential campaign in 1952, Eisenhower declared that effective psychological warfare involved the selection of principal targets within broad national objectives. He noted that the maximum psychological impact could only be made by an effectively co-ordinated operation in which well-directed and properly timed action was taken against the chosen targets. He therefore established a special assistant to the President for cultural and psychological aspects of foreign relations, separated the International Information Agency and the United States Information Agency from the Department of State, renamed them the United States Information Administration (USIA), and provided for these agencies to be co-ordinated by the OCB. The Department of State continued its responsibility for the exchange-of-students program.

While the OCB has failed to keep administrative officials from making countless contradictory statements, it has been effective in developing cultural programs and trade fairs which have been administered by the USIA. Nevertheless, the inherent difficulties of operating a peacetime propaganda program within the framework of a democracy are enormous. When Senator McCarthy sponsored the purging of United States libraries abroad by Messrs. Cohn and Schine, it became clear that Congressional pressures can upset the entire program. The lack of effective co-ordination between the Secretary of State and the other agencies responsible for this program has also weakened its effectiveness. It may be that a long-run program through which foreign peoples will come to understand the positive as well as the negative aspects of the American way of life is all that can be expected. It may also be that an international agency like UNESCO, free from the taint of prejudice, offers the best avenue for this activity.

The administrative superstructure, described above, has been largely a postwar response to the more active role of the United States in world affairs and to the political, ideological, and technological developments in the international situation. The National Security Council and the White House staff have attempted to channel and order the information and points of view of the 40 executive organizations which the Commission on Organization of Executive Branch of Government (Hoover Commission) found to be directly concerned with aspects of foreign policy. It is clear, however, that the effort has been more successful for political-military policy than it has for the economic and psychological areas. This difference in part may be explained by the fact that conflicting domestic interests are more closely involved in the latter areas, making ready compromise more difficult.

The Department of State and the Foreign Service

Whatever may be said of the developing position of the National Security Council and the other interdepartmental co-ordinating agencies, the Department of State continues to be the principal staff and operating arm of the President in foreign affairs. Indeed, the NSC may be viewed as the Department's instrument for securing the effective support in political matters of the other interested agencies. The Secretary of State is the principal adviser to the President on foreign affairs. The Secretary also voices important political considerations which his colleagues on the foreign economic committees must heed. The Undersecretary of State, furthermore, chairs the OCB, suggesting thereby the leading role which the Department assumes in the conduct as well as in the formulation of foreign policy. The policy supervision which the Department gives to both the USIA and to the ICA further indicates its controlling importance.

The growth of the Department of State's budget, personnel, and functions since 1930 gives some indication of the revolution which has transformed United States activity in foreign relations.[13] In 1930 its Departmental and Foreign Service staff totaled 4,726 with a budget of $15.4 million. These had grown to 12,592 employees and a budget of $129.7 million in 1955. Approximately half of the 1955 appropriations were for purposes which had not been recognized in 1930: participation in international organizations, international information programs, and contributions to the governments in occupied areas. In addition, the increasing responsibilities of the Department itself can be noted in the growth of its home staff from 703 to 3,686 and of its budget from $1.4 million to $20.2 million. Likewise the costs of regular Foreign Service activities have increased more than eight times.[14]

High-Level Officers in the Department of State

The ideal Secretary of State should possess the qualities of an astute and flexible negotiator, a wise policy-maker and adviser to the President, an able administrator of his Department, and an effective advocate of his policies before Congress and the public at large. No Secretary can be equally effective in all these areas, not only because his time and capabilities may be limited, but also because of the competing nature of these various responsibilities. An appeal to Congress, for example, may be most successful if oversimplified in terms of limited national interests; an appeal in such terms by the Secretary of State may well jeopardize his negotiations with foreign governments.

The negotiating responsibilities of the Secretary have so increased that Secretary Dulles was traveling 100,000 miles a year. A heavy responsibility has thus been thrust upon the Under Secretary, who is Acting Secretary during these absences.

The chief policy co-ordinator for the Secretary and Under Secretary is the Deputy Under Secretary. He is concerned primarily with integrating the views of the regional bureaus and the Bureau of International Organization Affairs. He also meets fort-

[13] Graham Stuart, *American Diplomatic and Consular Practice* (2nd ed., Appleton-Century-Crofts, Inc., 1952); and Graham Stuart, *The Department of State* (Macmillan, 1949).

[14] *The Department of State, 1930-1955*, Department of State Pub., 5852 (GPO, August, 1955).

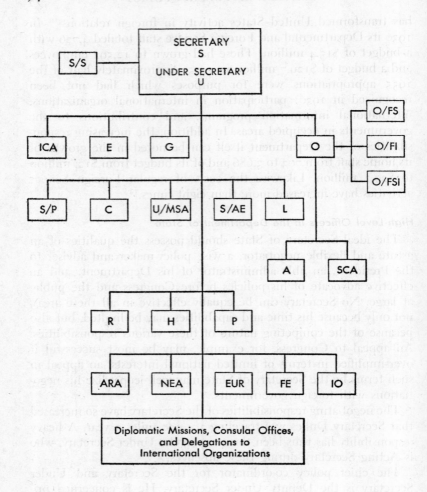

ORGANIZATION OF THE DEPARTMENT OF STATE, JUNE 1, 1956

The significance of the boxes identified by initials in the above diagram is shown on the facing page, together with a list of subordinate personnel and organizations under each functionary.

The organization shown is not permanent. The Department publishes new charts of this type about twice yearly, showing organization at the time of report.

A   **Assistant Secretary-Controller**
Office of Personnel—PER
  Management & Services Div.—MSD
  Employment Division—EMD
  Personnel Operations Div.—POD
  Allowances Div.—ALD
  Classification & Wage Admin. Div.—CWD
Office of General Services—OGS
  Div. of Supply Management—SD
  Div. of Operating Facilities—FD
  Div. of Records Management—RM
  Despatch Agency—DA
Office of Special Services—OSS
  Div. of Communications—DC
  Div. of Visual Services—VS
  Div. of Publishing Services—PB
  Div. of Language Services—LS
Cryptography Staff—CY
Foreign Reporting Staff—REP
Arts and Monuments Adviser—AM
Clemency and Parole Board—CPB
Safety Director—DS
Office of Budget—OB
  Div. of Program Review—DPR
  Div. of Financial Management—DFM
Office of Finance—OF
  Div. of Accounts—ACD
  Div. of Audit—AUD
Office of Foreign Buildings—FBO
Regulations & Procedures Staff—A/RP

ARA   **Assistant Secretary, Inter-American Affairs**
Office of Middle American Affairs—MID
Office of South American Affairs—OSA
Office of Inter-American Regional Political Affairs—RPA
Office of Inter-American Regional Economic Affairs—REA

C   **Counselor**

E   **Deputy Under Secretary for Economic Affairs**
Office of International Financial & Development Affairs—OFD
  Lend-Lease and Surplus Property Division—LL
  International Finance Division—FN
  Economic Development Division—ED
Office of Transport and Communications—TRC
  Aviation Division—AV
  Shipping Division—SH
  Telecommunications Division—TD
Office of International Trade and Resources—ITR
  Economic Defense Division—ECD
  Fuels Division—FSD
  International Business Practices Division—BP
  Trade Agreements and Treaties Division—TAD
  International Resources Division—IRD

EUR   **Assistant Secretary, European Affairs**
Office of British Commonwealth and Northern European Affairs—BNA
Office of Eastern European Affairs—EE
Office of German Affairs—GER
Office of Western European Affairs—WE
Office of European Regional Affairs—RA

FE   **Assistant Secretary, Far Eastern Affairs**
Office of Chinese Affairs—CA
Office of Northeast Asian Affairs—NA
Office of Southeast Asian Affairs—SEA
Office of Southwest Pacific Affairs—SPA

G   **Deputy Under Secretary for Political Affairs**

H   **Assistant Secretary, Congressional Relations**

ICA   **Director, International Cooperation Administration**

IO   **Assistant Secretary, International Organization Affairs**
Office of Dependent Area Affairs—ODA
Office of UN Political & Security Affairs—UNP
Office of International Economic & Social Affairs—OES
Office of International Conferences—OIC
Office of International Administration—OIA

L   **Legal Adviser**

NEA   **Assistant Secretary, Near Eastern, South Asian, and African Affairs**
Office of Greek, Turkish and Iranian Affairs—GTI
Office of South Asian Affairs—SOA
Office of Near Eastern Affairs—NE
Office of African Affairs—AF

O   **Deputy Under Secretary for Administration**

P   **Assistant Secretary, Public Affairs**
International Educational Exchange Service—IES
UNESCO Relations Staff—URS
News Division—ND
Public Studies Division—PS
Public Services Division—SEV
Historical Division—HD

R   **Special Assistant, Intelligence**
Office of Intelligence Research—OIR
  Div. of Functional Intelligence—DFI
  Div. of Research for American Republics—DRA
  Div. of Research for Western Europe—DRW
  Div. of Research for USSR and Eastern Europe—DRS
  Div. of Research for Far East—DRF
  Div. of Research for Near East, S. Asia, & Africa—DRN
Office of Libraries and Intelligence-Acquisition—OLI
  Div. of Acquisition and Distribution—LAD
  Library Division—LR
  Div. of Biographic Information—BI

S/AE   **Special Assistant, Atomic Energy Affairs**

SCA   **Administrator, Bureau of Security and Consular Affairs**
Office of Refugee and Migration Affairs—ORM
Passport Office—PPT
Visa Office—VO
Office of Special Consular Services—SCS
Office of Security—SY
  Div. of Physical Security—SY/P
  Div. of Evaluations—SY/E
  Div. of Investigations—SY/I
Office of Munitions Control—MC

S/P   **Assistant Secretary for Policy Planning**

S/S   **Director, Executive Secretariat**

U/MSA   **Special Assistant, Mutual Security Affairs**

nightly with the Joint Chiefs of Staff and co-ordinates matters involving labor's interest in foreign policy, for which he has a labor adviser. In 1947 a Policy Planning Staff was established to formulate long-term plans and to anticipate problems. The director of the staff frequently acts as a principal adviser to the Secretary in international negotiations, and is the Department's representative on the NSC's Planning Board. The regular adviser to the Secretary and Under Secretary, however, is the Counselor of the Department. A top-level secretariat has been provided these officers since 1944; this Executive Secretariat includes a director who facilitates the decision work of the Secretary and Under Secretary, a Protocol Staff, and a staff which assists the top Secretaries in international conferences, prepares daily summaries of important developments, and follows up action assignments within the Department.

Functional Offices

As with foreign offices of other Great Powers, the Department has distributed its various responsibilities among geographical and functional bureaus, each headed by an Assistant Secretary. The latter serves as an operating executive and makes the decisions for his area except those which require the approval of a higher-level officer. Following a suggestion of the Hoover Commission, the geographic bureaus now have specialists in economics, intelligence, administration, and public affairs in order to co-ordinate all relevant considerations with respect to each region. Each of the geographic bureaus, together with the Bureau of International Organization Affairs, maintains close alliance with the Foreign Service officers stationed at the respective missions overseas.

The Department has five functional divisions. These pertain to economic affairs, relations with Congress, public affairs, legal matters, and intelligence. Each of the first three is headed by an Assistant Secretary; the legal adviser is considered of equivalent rank.

Departmental responsibilities for foreign economic policy include economic-assistance programs which are administered by the ICA, trade policies which are co-ordinated with CFEP, financial policies, and international communications policy.

As foreign relations have become increasingly dependent upon large legislative appropriations, the Department has needed closer liaison with Congress. Since 1949 an Assistant Secretary has been regularly in charge of answering Congressional inquiries (some 6,126 in 1954), and arranging frequent consultations.

The need for ascertaining public opinion on proposed foreign policies and the even greater need to gain public support for the policies is recognized in the Division of Public Affairs. Its international operations include relations with UNESCO, the educational exchange service, and policy co-ordination for the USIA. Domestically, it analyzes public opinion and utilizes mass media for information programs.

The Office of Legal Adviser passes upon questions of domestic, foreign, and international law. The unprecedented volume of legal problems in recent years has been in part a legacy of the war, and also has resulted from the subversive activities of the USSR, from technological developments, from new treaty commitments, and from military and economic programs. To handle these complex questions, the legal office is organized along departmental lines, having the respective geographical and functional areas.

The Special Assistant for Intelligence is responsible for the interpretation and evaluation of overt information in political, cultural, and sociological fields. The Foreign Service is a primary source of information on foreign countries, and the analyses made by this division are subsequently co-ordinated by the Central Intelligence Agency.

Geographical Offices

There are four geographical bureaus: Inter-American Affairs; Near Eastern, South Asian, and African Affairs; European Affairs; and Far Eastern Affairs.

The task of countering the Communist threat through economic reconstruction and military alliances was most formidable in Europe. The Bureau of European Affairs has been delegated these tasks. It has five offices dealing with British, German, USSR, West European, and NATO affairs, and its "desk" officers for each of the countries. The Bureau of Near Eastern, South Asian, and

African Affairs presently exceeds the Far Eastern Affairs Bureau in total personnel, due in part to the rapid growth of independent states and in part to United States assumption of British security responsibilities here. The nonrecognition of Communist China has limited diplomatic activity in the Far East, but the postwar problems of neutralism, nationalism, military occupation, the Korean aggression, and military pacts have fully occupied the departmental personnel assigned to this region.

Historically, the Monroe Doctrine has drawn the United States closer to Latin America than to any other area; since the war, the collectivization of the Doctrine through the Rio de Janeiro defense pact and the Charter of the Organization of American States has continued to justify the maintenance of the second largest staff of all the areas.

The Foreign Service of the United States

Since the United States Foreign Service was given career status in 1924 with the Rogers Act, it has met with imposing difficulties in the development of the necessarily highly talented and trained personnel. A career officer and former Ambassador to the USSR, George Kennan, wrote in 1955:

. . . our Foreign Service was weakened beyond real hope of recovery. The present administration inherited not a going professional service but an administrative ruin, packed with people who had never undergone the normal entrance requirements, hemmed in and suffocated by competing services, demoralized by anonymous security agents in whose judgment and disinterestedness its members had little confidence, a helpless object of disparagement and defamation at the hands of outside critics. This was the tragic ending of an experiment launched with high hopes and with none but the most innocent and worthy intent, three decades earlier. As of the year 1953, it was no exaggeration to say that the experiment of professional diplomacy, as undertaken by the United States in 1925, had failed.[15]

In March, 1954, the Foreign Service reached its lowest strength in

[15] George F. Kennan, "The Future of our Professional Diplomacy," *Foreign Affairs* (July, 1955), p. 568. For an analysis of the personal characteristics of the Foreign Service personnel in 1952 see James L. McCamy and Alessandro Corradini, "The People of the State Department and Foreign Service," *The American Political Science Review* (Dec., 1954), pp. 1067-1083.

five years; no new appointments had been made for two years and 142 members had resigned or retired during the first fifteen months of the Eisenhower administration.

Secretary of State Dulles therefore appointed an independent committee, headed by Dr. Henry M. Wriston of Brown University, to investigate the problem. The committee's findings covered a wide range of subjects, and provided the basis for a major reorganization of the Foreign Service. One of the most important changes was the expansion of the 1,300-man foreign service by the addition of 1,440 State Department officials and 1,200 members of the "staff corps" (the administrative specialists in the foreign service who had not taken the regular examinations for admission) within two years. Like those in other foreign offices, career officers of the Department would now be eligible for experience in the field, while Foreign Service personnel would be brought back to Washington at regular intervals. New applicants were encouraged by limiting the written entrance examinations to one day (it was formerly three days), and by increasing the number of those admitted. By August, 1957, 1,200 posts in Washington and 2,400 posts abroad were to be filled by members of the newly integrated service. In addition, new life was given to the Foreign Service Institute so that in-service training at the junior, middle, and senior level would be available.

Today there are roughly 300 American Foreign Service offices and 180 consulates general or consulates in the capitals and major cities abroad. Large embassies like those in London, Paris, or Mexico City have as many as 500 persons, and are run on the order of a miniature Department of State. The functional subdivisions include consular, administrative, economic, cultural and information, and political areas. The Reorganization Act of 1939 transformed overseas representatives of the Commerce and Agricultural Departments into commercial and agricultural attachés who were to function under the direction of the Ambassador. In addition, each Embassy may have a number of attachés from the military services, the Central Intelligence Agency, and other organizations.

It has not been easy for United States ambassadors of these large embassies to give unity and purpose to the conduct of foreign policy. The increasing size of the establishments has imposed real difficulties. More directly, the arrival of frequent Presidential emissaries or of special negotiating teams, often headed by the Secretary of State himself, have interrupted the normal course of operations. Lacking the intimate familiarity with the local scene, and enjoying a greater latitude in interpreting United States policy, these missions from Washington tend to hamper the successful attainment of the Embassy's objectives and to weaken its continuing prestige. Another factor which handicaps diplomatic efficiency has been the autonomous representation abroad of many independent United States agencies. In 1950 there were 43 government departments, agencies, or units which employed 74,879 civilians abroad.[16] In recent years, however, the Ambassador's immediate authority over these agencies has been increased, and any continuing differences are ironed out at the Washington level.

International Conferences and the United States Mission to the United Nations

Direct diplomatic intercourse between the United States and each of the independent states of the world has been the primary responsibility of our foreign missions. The Foreign Service has represented United States interests, negotiated treaties and agreements, and kept the United States government informed of the changing political, economic, social, and military conditions of other countries. While the informational tasks of foreign missions have been increasing, changing world conditions have created difficulties for their negotiating functions. The democratization of Foreign Services everywhere has, by introducing personnel of narrow background, enhanced the parochial at the expense of the cosmopolitan point of view, and to this extent has limited understanding and agreement. More important has been the pressing demand for rapid negotiations; international communications have expanded and resulting disputes are more widely known. As a result, crises are more frequent and must be settled more quickly than ever before. Furthermore, most crises now affect the interests

[16] The Brookings Institution, *The Administration of Foreign Affairs and Overseas Operations* (GPO, 1951), p. 244.

of more than two nations, and they can no longer be localized in the European area as they were in the nineteenth century. Bilateral negotiations are no longer sufficient; new diplomatic institutions have had to be developed.

"Conference diplomacy" has been used to expedite and coordinate the conduct of United States foreign policy. In a quarter of a century, the frequency of United States participation in international conferences has grown fourfold, to about 300 conferences annually. The United States mission to the United Nations participates in more than 1,000 additional international meetings each year. Continuing multilateral consultation is characteristic of the Organization of American States, of NATO, and of the specialized agencies to which the United States belongs. The United Nations and the regional organizations, indeed, have permanently institutionalized the new diplomacy in which the processes of continuous interaction with representatives of other states modify or implement United States foreign policy.

Accordingly, the United States Mission to the United Nations has assumed an important role in the postwar diplomatic machinery.[17] Like the embassies in foreign capitals, it is a miniature Department of State, but the multilateral nature of its negotiations demands a greater degree of flexibility. Henry Cabot Lodge, the permanent United States representative to the United Nations and Chief of Mission, attends meetings of the National Security Council and is an intimate adviser to the President. The permanent staff of the Mission numbers 167, which rises to 280 when the United Nations General Assembly is in session. A Secretary General of the Mission handles diplomatic and social problems, conference services, reporting and documenting facilities (there are three telephone tie lines in addition to teletype service connecting the Mission with the Department of State), and public information. Permanent substantive experts are responsible for security affairs, economic and social affairs, political and legal affairs, trusteeships, the Economic and Social Council, and International Organization affairs. A Counselor engages in behind-the-scenes negotiations, ex-

17 Daniel S. Cheever, "The Role of the United Nations in the Conduct of United States Foreign Policy," *World Politics* (April, 1950), pp. 389-404.

ploiting intimate political contacts among the delegates. These substantive experts are headed by a chief of staff and have regular meetings with the Chief of Mission. They also advise the United States delegation to the United Nations General Assembly, which is appointed annually and except for the period 1947-1949 has had bipartisan representation from Congress.

Thus, the United States Mission to the United Nations is much more than an information-gathering agency. It organizes support for the United States position, it provides liaison with more than 50 permanent missions and with the United Nations Secretariat of 3,500, and it co-ordinates United States and United Nations activities in such areas as economic development. Through Congressional participation in the delegations, the Mission assists the co-operation of the legislative and executive branches of government, and it broadens the perspective of the geographically or functionally oriented Foreign Service officers who are assigned to it.[18] On occasion the Mission has even been responsible for initiating policy; in January 1956, both the President and the Secretary of State endorsed the statement of the United States delegation to the United Nations General Assembly. The statement was viewed by the press as the adoption of a new foreign policy. It read in part:

The present period in history may one day be recognized as a major turning point in the struggle between Communism and freedom. It appears to be clearly a shift in the cold war, in which economic and social problems have moved to the forefront . . . We are in a contest in the field of economic development of underdeveloped countries which is bitterly competitive. Defeat in this contest could be as disastrous as defeat in an armaments race.

Congress and Foreign Policy

We have seen that the President has greater Constitutional authority in foreign relations than he has in domestic affairs. Since the war, however, Congress has been devoting more energy to foreign-policy matters through hearings, debates, and investigations than ever before. Indeed, half the bills introduced in the first ses-

[18] Channing B. Richardson, "The United States Mission to the United Nations," *International Organization* (February, 1953), pp. 483-9.

sion of the Eighty-first Congress dealt with foreign policy. It could be argued that although the Constitution clearly provides for limited participation of Congress in the formulation of foreign policy, the political role of the legislative body has far exceeded Constitutional expectations. Furthermore, the United States Senate has lost its clear ascendancy in the foreign field to the extent that the House of Representatives has asserted its control via the appropriations power. The responsibilities for supervising and checking the vast new foreign expenditures likewise promote Congressional participation in this area. It has been truly said that the House watches the purse while the Senate watches the President.

Congressional Sources of Information on Foreign Policy

The behavior of Congress is greatly influenced by the inadequacy of its information, by the personal motivations of its key members, and by the nature of its committee and party organizations.[19] It is remembered that Senator William E. Borah suggested to Secretary of State Cordell Hull, shortly before the outbreak of World War II, that his information differed from the Secretary's and that there would be no war in the near future. Some information on foreign policy cannot, by its very nature, be made available to Congress, while much information which is available cannot be adequately assessed by the Congressmen themselves or by limited Congressional corps of staff experts. In addition, the work-load of Congress has increased tremendously since World War II, and has diverted attention from substantive problems. It has been estimated that from 50 per cent to 80 per cent of a Congressman's working day is devoted to his constituents (compared to 25 per cent in Great Britain), while much of the remaining time is taken up with roll calls, committee meetings, and periodic visits home.

Most Congressmen rely heavily on the mass media for their information—newspapers, columnists, weekly news magazines, or radio commentators. The Congressional committee staffs, the Legislative Reference Service of the Library of Congress, and the few

[19] Robert Dahl, *Congress and Foreign Policy* (Harcourt, Brace and Co., 1950).

knowledgeable Congressional leaders cannot compete with the talent available to the executive branch. For these reasons Congress is likely to have a less accurate understanding of the international situation than the executive, and a less precise appreciation of the policy alternatives which are available. The President's State of the Union Address and Congressional hearings provide Congress with that information which will induce them to support a proposed policy.

Congressional deliberation is restricted by the fact that foreign-policy proposals are frequently made at the eleventh hour—when indeed there is no alternative but to accept the suggestion of the executive.

Personal Influences on Congressional Decisions

The tendency of Congress to assert itself in foreign policy is enhanced by the freedom accorded its individual members. While it is true that the United States Congress is more restrained than the French parliament, it has none of the disciplined characteristics of the British House of Commons. The difference is explained in part by the loose character of the party system in the United States and in part by the political advantage which accrues to those who gain the spotlight. The "prima donna" characteristics of the Senate, furthermore, are encouraged by the custom of extended debate, about which Representative William M. Colmer of Mississippi declared in February 1955 that "the sky is the limit and the Lord's Prayer could be offered as an Amendment."

Congressional action on foreign policy, therefore, is less guided by a rational understanding of the foreign situation than it is influenced by personal considerations involving re-election, sectional orientations, and private convictions. Members of the House, who stand for re-election every two years, are somewhat more exposed to the pressures of their constituents and of the special-interest lobbyists than are Senators, who enjoy a six-year term (although half of the 435 members of the House in 1955-1956 had ten years or more of experience as compared to a third of the Senate). Congressional leaders, however, who have gained their position through long service, are less subject to constituent pressures since their re-election is assured by the party regularity of their districts or states. Sectional interests are more likely to be influential in their case. The Midwest traditionally re-elects Republican congressmen, and Southern Democratic Congressmen have likewise established tenure records. Congressional leadership, selected from these senior members, tends to be Midwestern in a Republican Congress and Southern in a Democratic one. For example, the Republican Eighty-third Congress was dominated by the Midwest, which controlled 13 of the 19 key chairmanships in the House and 9 of the 15 in the Senate. The Democratic Eighty-fourth Congress (1955-1956) gave Southerners the same proportion of chairmanships in both houses.

Midwestern influence has been characterized as isolationist, pro-Asia and anti-Europe, budget-conscious, and disinclined to tolerate foreign influences like the United Nations in the decision-making process.[20] The South has been internationally predisposed; it has been oriented towards Europe, has supported low trade barriers, and has encouraged military-defense policies. As the South has become industrialized, however, and as foreign affairs have encompassed social policies, this area has forsaken its stand on free trade, has resisted economic aid for underdeveloped countries, and has opposed the international development of human rights. Easterners of both parties tend to be the most enthusiastic internationalists in an economic and social as well as in a political sense.

Congressmen are also influenced by their own backgrounds and personalities. Their comparative maturity (in the Eighty-fourth Congress, the average age of a Senator was 57 as compared to 51 years for a Representative) and their legal background (two-thirds of the Senators and more than half of the Congressmen in the Eighty-fourth Congress) would predispose them to a conservative outlook. William F. Knowland of California established the reputation for allowing his own personal convictions to determine his position on foreign policy, even when he was the Senate Republi-

[20] George L. Grassmuck, in his *Sectional Biases in Congress on Foreign Policy* (Johns Hopkins University Press, 1952), studied the problem from 1935 to 1941; and H. Bradford Westerfield, in his *Foreign Policy and Party Politics: Pearl Harbor to Korea* (Oxford Univ. Press, 1955), carries the analysis to 1950.

can leader. He supported the Bricker Amendment against the wishes of his own administration, he attacked the Republican Secretary of State for agreeing to discuss Indochina at the Geneva conference, and he threatened to resign as majority leader of the Senate if Communist China were brought into the United Nations.

Congressional Committees

Except for the full-dress debates on critical issues, Congress has delegated the major legislative role to its committees. There are fifteen standing committees in the Senate and nineteen in the House. The Senate Committees on Foreign Relations, Armed Services, and Appropriations, and the House Committees on Foreign Affairs, Ways and Means (for tariffs), Armed Services, and Appropriations are among the most important for foreign policy. Duplication of committee functions and resulting rivalries occasionally handicap efficient operations, and a special effort must be made to co-ordinate the policy viewpoints of the various committees. In 1946 the number of standing committees was reduced, so an additional burden was thrust upon the surviving committees. Subcommittees have been entrusted, therefore, with the primary task of formulating the committee reports, although experienced Congressmen are not always available for these smaller groups. The committee chairmen have great power over legislation; they decide committee procedures, appoint subcommittees, control hearings, and can hold back a bill from the floor. Chairmen are appointed as the result of long service, so they do not have to exercise their committee powers with any special regard for party loyalty or for their expertness in a particular subject. Committee hearings, therefore, may take the form of uncritical attacks which confirm the chairman's prejudice, instead of being used as a source of information.

The Senate Foreign Relations Committee is one of the most important in the upper house. Its chairmen have included some of the most distinguished names in the history of the Senate—the first Henry Cabot Lodge, William E. Borah, Key Pittman (1934-1940), Tom Connally (1940-1946; 1948-1952), Arthur Vandenberg (1946-1948), and Walter F. George (1955-1956). Some of them, like Senator Borah, claimed to run a separate department of government, equal in status with the President. Others like Pittman, Connally, and George have been administration leaders, and George during his chairmanship was considered the third most important man in the field of foreign policy—ranked only by the President and the Secretary of State. There are fifteen members of the Foreign Relations Committee and as many as nineteen subcommittees with jurisdiction corresponding to the respective bureaus in the Department of State. Each committee member serves on two subcommittees; the latter have three members, two of which represent the majority party. Overlapping membership with the Committee on Appropriations subcommittees, together with occasional meetings with members of the House Committee on Foreign Affairs, has facilitated legislative co-ordination. Many of the Committee's sessions are secret, and its procedures are often time-consuming—working up a favorable report on NATO took six months. The Committee is responsible for the consideration of treaties, nominations for diplomatic posts, and the organization of the Department of State. A small permanent staff, formerly headed by the able Francis Wilcox, has given the Foreign Relations Committee the benefit of its systematic and expert advice.

Parties and Bipartisanship

While the two-party system in the United States has played an invaluable role in providing a choice of candidates for election and in organizing the legislative and administrative branches of government, it does not have similar values for making foreign policy. The President's position as leader of his party is reinforced by his control of patronage and the attention he receives in the press; these assets, however, are counterbalanced by the importance of local issues in off-year elections and the independence of Congressional leaders whose positions are attained by seniority rather than by party loyalty. The real disagreements over foreign policy have been regional, economic, or ideological, rather than partisan. The Republican Party is divided between the New England liberals and the Midwestern conservatives, and the Democratic Party is split between North and South. Accordingly, political parties in the United States have been defined as loose confederations of warring tribes who get together during an election. There is less danger than is commonly supposed that foreign policy might become a political party football with consequent jeopardy to national security, or interruption in the continuity of policy when administrations change.

Indeed, bipartisan foreign policy has excluded certain issues from Presidential campaigns, has encouraged support from both parties in Congress for an administration bill, and, most important, has secured effective co-operation between the legislative and executive branches of government. The purpose of bipartisanship has been to secure harmony and consistency through agreement on fundamental objectives. Co-operation between the parties and between the administration and Congress have been the means for attaining these ends. Confronted by a Democratic Congress for 1955-1956, President Eisenhower issued an executive order on December 15, 1954, ordering cabinet officers to confer with Congressional leaders *before* they formulated policies relating to foreign affairs, defense, or mutual-security aid. To use the language of Harold E. Stassen, this plan would allow the Democrats to be co-pilots in the foreign policy take-offs as well as in the crash landings.

The growth of bipartisan policy-making paralleled the developing United States involvement in world affairs. President Franklin Roosevelt appointed two Republicans as his War and Navy Secretaries three years before Secretary of State Cordell Hull met with John Foster Dulles in 1944 to agree that peace would be a nonpartisan topic in the forthcoming Presidential campaign. While bipartisanship broke down in 1949, there was a broad area of agreement during the 1952 Presidential campaign on NATO and on the necessity for containing Communism. During the 1954 election campaign Secretary Dulles canceled a number of scheduled speeches because they fell just before election day. In 1955-1956, the Democratic Congress responded more readily in many instances to the foreign-policy leadership of the Republican administration than had its Republican predecessor. Close and sympathetic bipartisan co-operation was in part responsible for this response.

The Need for Leadership

Under the United States system of government, the executive is in a position to make an accurate appraisal of changing international conditions and to maximize the achievement of foreign-policy objectives through rationally defined policies. While the President represents the whole nation and stresses over-all national objectives, Congress is sensitized to the diversities in American society and reflects these parochial interests with varying intensity. Congressional thinking, as compared with executive thinking, is also more closely associated with domestic matters and these are necessarily weighed more heavily in forming Congressional foreign-policy attitudes. The concurrence of Congress is needed, nevertheless, if United States policies are to be systematically and effectively executed. Legislative support provides the strength and determination required for maintaining order and for promising peaceful development in a shrinking world.

The responsibility for alerting Congress to the international position of the United States rests with the executive. Secretary of State Dulles has followed the precedent set by Elihu Root and Cordell Hull in meeting regularly with Congressional leaders. The foreign-relations committees have been organized so there are almost daily communications with the Department of State, and participation in diplomatic assignments has given Congressmen of both parties a lively awareness of the international position of the United States. But institutionalizing the regular flow of information from the administration to Congress is not enough, as President Eisenhower discovered within six months of taking office. Congress cannot respond with sufficient speed and skill to maintain a co-ordinate position with the President in the formulation of foreign policy. A dynamic leader, with vitality, courage, sensitivity, and intelligence is needed to present the actual world situation effectively to Congress and to secure its support for those policies best calculated to promote the national interest.

BIBLIOGRAPHY

Quincy Wright's classic, *The Control of American Foreign Relations* (The Macmillan Co., 1922), provides a legal interpretation which gives perspective to the Constitutional distribution of powers in the United States with reference to international responsibilities. Another classic is Edward S. Corwin's *The President's Control of Foreign Relations* (Princeton University Press, 1917) which discusses the role of the President in the formulation of foreign policy and the conduct of foreign relations as seen by the constitutional lawyer. *The President: Offices and Powers* (3d ed., New York University Press, 1948) chapters 5 and 6, and *Total War and the Constitution* (Alfred A. Knopf, 1947) chapter 1, are Corwin's more recent analyses of the developing role of the President vis-à-vis the states and Congress. The Constitutional powers of the President as Commander in Chief have been treated by Francis O. Wilcox in "The President's Authority to Send Armed Forces Abroad," *Proceedings of the American Society of International Law* (Washington, 1951). Elmer Plischke's text, *Conduct of American Diplomacy* (D. Van Nostrand Company, 1950), clarifies the treaty-making process and provides an excellent background for the many recent articles on the Bricker Amendment. These include Quincy Wright, "Congress and the Treaty Making Power," *Proceedings of the American Society of International Law,* pp. 43-58, and P. Perlman, "On Amending the Treaty Power," *Columbia Law Review* (November, 1952). The Reports and Hearings of the Senate Judiciary Committee on the Bricker Amendment, for the years 1952-1956, assemble rational and visceral responses to the problem.

In considering executive control of foreign policy, Richard C. Snyder and Edgar S. Furniss, Jr., *American Foreign Policy* (Rinehart and Co., 1954), develop the decision-making process from the multidimensional approach of motivation and personality, coordination of information, and role of the decision-maker. This is the most comprehensive and recent text on the control of foreign policy. *United States Foreign Policy, Its Organization and Control,* Report of a Study Group for the Woodrow Wilson Foundation (Columbia University Press, 1952), raises important Constitutional and administrative problems and suggests certain reforms. Its tolerance of Presidential co-ordinating agencies like the National Security Council contrasts with the conclusion of Arthur W. Macmahon in his brilliant series of essays entitled *Administration in Foreign Affairs* (University of Alabama Press, 1953) which supports the need for grouping all foreign-affairs functions within one executive department. Important for its discussion of the many-faceted impact of foreign affairs on the executive branch of government and for its behavioral analysis of the Foreign Service is J. L. McCamy, *The Administration of American Foreign Affairs,* chapters 4 and 8 of which were updated in his article in collaboration with Alessandro Corradini, "The People of the State Department and Foreign Service," *The American Political Science Review* (December, 1954), pp. 1067-1083.

Recent authoritative articles on the operation of the National Security Council are written by special assistants to the President; Robert Cutler, "The Development of the National Security Council," *Foreign Affairs* (April, 1956), pp. 441-459, and Dillon Anderson, "The President and National Security," *The Atlantic* (Jan., 1956), pp. 42-46, both describe the development and functioning of the Council from their experience in the Eisenhower administration. Roger Hilsman, "Intelligence and Policy-making in Foreign Affairs," *World Politics* (October, 1952), pp. 1-46, implements the excellent consideration of these problems by Sherman Kent, *Strategic Intelligence for American World Policy* (Princeton University Press, 1949). Burton M. Sapin and Richard C. Snyder, *The Role of the Military in American Foreign Policy,* Doubleday Short Studies in Political Science, No. 7 (Doubleday and Co., 1954), is unexcelled and provides a useful bibliographical note of additional works in this field. Jerome Gregory Kerwin, in *Civil-Military Relationships in American Life* (Walgreen Foundation Lectures, University of Chicago Press, 1948), ably discusses the role of the military in a society that traditionally has insisted upon the subordination of the military to civilian control.

The co-ordination of economic foreign policy has been all too briefly considered both in and out of government; chapter 10 of *The Political Economy of American Foreign Policy*, Report of a Study Group for the Woodrow Wilson Foundation and the National Planning Association (Henry Holt and Co., 1955), concludes that the National Security Council and the President together must provide the needed policy integration and action in the foreign economic field. *The Hidden Weapon*, by Royden James Dangerfield and David Livingston Gordon with a foreword by Thomas K. Finletter (New York: Harper, 1947), is a factual account of economic warfare. Edward W. Barrett, *Truth Is Our Weapon* (Funk and Wagnalls Co., 1953), discusses the operation of information agencies prior to the Eisenhower administration. Dale O. Smith, "What is OCB," *Foreign Service Journal* (Nov., 1955), pp. 26ff, is an authoritative and sympathetic treatment of the agency which replaced the Board of Psychological Warfare.

Graham Stuart has long been the academic specialist on the Department of State. His *The Department of State* (Macmillan, 1949) and *American Diplomatic and Consular Practice* (3d ed., Appleton-Century-Crofts, Inc., 1952) provide a historical perspective to the developing problems of the Department which is most concerned with the control and conduct of foreign affairs. *The Department of State, 1930-1955*, Department of State Pub., 5852 (GPO, Aug., 1955) in 66 pages briefly summarizes the present organization and functions. *The Foreign Service Journal* is the professional periodical of the Service, and has followed the changes resulting from the Wriston Report with lively interest. George F. Kennan, one of the most able and articulate critics, who writes with the authority of a former career officer, has few words of praise for these reforms in "The Future of Our Professional Diplomacy," *Foreign Affairs* (July, 1955), pp. 566-587. An excellent discussion of the Foreign Service is contained in Henry Wriston (ed.), *The Representation of the United States Abroad*, Report of the Arden House Discussion in June, 1956 (Columbia University Press, 1956). The present and potential role of the United Nations in the formulation of United States foreign policy is discussed by Daniel S. Cheever, "The Role of the United Nations in the Conduct of United States Foreign Policy," *World Politics* (April, 1950), pp. 389-404, and in the perceptive analysis by Channing B. Richardson, "The United States Mission to the United Nations," *International Organization* (Feb., 1953), pp. 483-489.

The role of Congress in making foreign policy has been developed historically by Daniel S. Cheever and H. F. Haviland, Jr., *American Foreign Policy and the Separation of Powers* (Harvard University Press, 1952). These authors illustrate the pattern of executive-legislative relations with a wealth of cases. Robert Dahl, *Congress and Foreign Policy* (Harcourt, Brace and Co., 1950), provides a sympathetic analysis from a behavioral point of view. In suggesting that the position of Congress could and should be implemented, he reflects a greater awareness of the domestic as distinguished from the international implications of making foreign policy.

CHAPTER 4

THE FOREIGN POLICIES OF THE UNITED STATES AFTER WORLD WAR II

Since the outbreak of World War II the basic mood of the people of the United States has been internationalist. Their statesmen have had wider latitude than before in committing the country to an active role in foreign affairs. Frank L. Klingberg predicts that this mood will continue at least until the 1960's, and others claim that a shrinking world will never again permit the United States to return to isolationism. The postwar decade, accordingly, has witnessed expanding United States influence in international affairs, and there is strong indication that the next decade will continue in the pattern of the past.

The various forms assumed by these activist policies have been largely determined by the changing world situation. Since 1945, three successive broad situations have required three different sets of policies. The first extended from 1945 to 1947 and was characterized by the economic, political, and social devastation following the war. In 1947, the United States was generally alert to the aggressive and nonco-operative policy of the Soviet Union. The Communist coup d'état in Czechoslovakia in February, 1948, followed in June by the Berlin blockade, demonstrated to the public at large a change in the international situation. After the Geneva Conferences in July and October 1955, fully two years after Stalin's death, the American people began to perceive a recession in the Soviet military threat and noticed that Japan, Germany, India, and the British Commonwealth were beginning to share the world stage with the United States and Russia. Nationalistic ideologies, along with Communism, were recognized in this period as important factors in world dynamics.

Postwar Reconstruction: 1945–1947

The immediate postwar years held no apparent threat to the power position of the United States, which alone possessed the secret of the atomic bomb and was producing this weapon in ever greater numbers. As the "arsenal of democracy," the United States not only had raised and equipped an army of several million but had supplied its Allies as well—the USSR having received aid estimated to equal 10 per cent of that country's own military production. The United States, spared from wartime bombing, had a national production in 1945 equal to twice that of 1929. Europe, in contrast, was devastated and the USSR's productive areas had been victimized by the Nazi occupation. The western powers controlled the industrial heart of Germany and General Mac-Arthur directed the destiny of Japan.

There was general confidence in the peaceful intentions of the victors. While it was clear at the Yalta Conference in February, 1945, that Soviet hegemony would be maintained in Eastern Europe, this area was nevertheless promised control over its own domestic affairs. The war seemed to have given rise to a new kind of Soviet Union: nationalistic appeals had supplanted Communist symbols, the Comintern had been abolished, and churches had been given some freedom. Indeed, Soviet objectives in both Asia and Europe appeared legitimate and easily satisfied; at home, agricultural and industrial reconstruction might well absorb the time and energies of the Soviet leaders.

The United States thus considered itself freed from compulsion toward the kind of expedient decisions which had been necessary to win the war or which would be required if the international situation suggested the need for an immediate preoccupation with its own security. It would not have to occupy Germany for long— Roosevelt had told Stalin that United States troops would be kept there for only a short time, perhaps two years. The industrial capacities of Great Britain and France would be restored quickly, and these countries could protect themselves against a weakened Germany. Accordingly, the United States would devote its attention to the long-run problems of promoting law and order through the United Nations.

The United States and the United Nations

The United Nations came into existence largely through the efforts of President Franklin Roosevelt. In August 1941, the politically sensitive President avoided a clear-cut statement of the need for international security arrangements, but the changing public mood after the attack on Pearl Harbor emboldened Roosevelt to establish a special staff within the Department of State to develop plans for the new organization. Secretary Cordell Hull secured Soviet approval for the project in 1943, and at the Teheran and Yalta Conferences the Great Powers again pledged their support. A preliminary planning conference was held in 1944 by the United States, the USSR, Great Britain, and China at Dumbarton Oaks, an estate near Washington. The League of Nations system was strengthened in the plans made here by substituting a two-thirds vote for the unanimity rule in the General Assembly, and by introducing an international military force. At Yalta, the USSR was induced to forgo its veto privilege on procedural matters and on questions relating to the pacific settlement of disputes. Specialized organizations to deal with labor, agriculture, postwar relief, finance, and aviation were established at conferences in Philadelphia, Hot Springs, Atlantic City, Bretton Woods, and Chicago between 1943 and 1945 and were related to the United Nations system.

The new international organization was formally brought into being at San Francisco in 1945, and seemed eminently workable. There was reason to hope that the Great Power co-operation, born of wartime alliance, would continue. Even if it deteriorated, the force of world opinion would help dissuade a Great Power aggressor, while nonmembers and small powers without a veto would be subjected to the collective decisions of the Security Council. As an instrument for economic and social development, the United Nations Educational, Scientific, and Cultural Organization (UNESCO) would lay the groundwork for effective international co-operation, while the other agencies would aid in the reconstruction of the war-torn countries, raise the standard of living, foster international trade, and promote human rights and self-government in the dependent areas and trusteeships. The United Nations, with its specialized agencies, thus multilateralized and institutionalized the traditional objectives of the United States. Backed fully by Congress and the public, the Truman administration undertook to support the United Nations at all points, to ensure full debate in the United Nations of all issues, and to approach as many problems as possible within the United Nations framework. The selection of New York as the headquarters for the new organization symbolized the continuing support of the United States for international procedures.

With the successful handling of its first dispute, the Security Council seemed to justify the trust which the United States had placed in it. The case involved the refusal of the Soviet government to withdraw its troops from Azerbaijan, the northern province of Iran, as it had agreed to do six months after the cessation of hostilities. After the Iranian government (supported but not prompted by the United States and Great Britain), submitted the dispute to the Security Council, the USSR was persuaded to change its policy and it withdrew its troops in May, 1946. Another instance of the successes of a policy of international co-operation and full discussion came with the protests of Syria and Lebanon on February 4, 1946, that the presence of British and French troops in their respective territories infringed upon their sovereignty. Although the USSR vetoed the resolution proposed in this situation because it did not demand immediate withdrawal, a formula was found that was acceptable to the parties directly concerned. Likewise, a common policy toward Spain was formulated. None of the Allied governments looked with favor on the Franco regime, which had come to power through the help of Hitler and Mussolini and which had favored the Axis cause during the war. Refusing to accept the Soviet demand for severing diplomatic relations with Spain, the General Assembly nevertheless recommended the recall of ambassadors and ministers from Madrid and resolved to bar Spain from membership in all international agencies.

Even in the field of disarmament, the United States could be guardedly optimistic although there was almost no specific achievement. The General Assembly had established an Atomic Energy Commission on January 24, 1946, and the United States had volunteered the following June to surrender its leadership in atomic weapons to international control pursuant to the Baruch Plan. Progress was blocked by the USSR's demands that atomic weapons should be destroyed as a preliminary step and that control and inspection should be subject to the veto. The negotiations for the creation of an international military force likewise broke down, primarily on the issue of whether contributions should be proportional to national strength or should be the same from all nations regardless of size. Nevertheless, the USSR accepted a resolution sponsored by the United States in the General Assembly on December 14, 1946, which outlined the general principles of disarmament. This resolution separated the control of atomic weapons from the control of conventional weapons, stressed the importance of international inspection, and considered disarmament as part of the process of regulating force. Leading as it did to the establishment of the Commission for Conventional Armaments in February, 1947, this resolution held out some hope for the future.

Economic Policy

On the economic front, international activity got off to a slow start. The United Nations Relief and Rehabilitation Administration (UNRRA) had been established in 1943 by 46 nations and the United States had contributed two-thirds of its total $3.7 billion expenditures. However, the United States was becoming dissatisfied with the inefficiency of UNRRA and as the largest contributor did not welcome its anonymous status. "We want to give

aid as the United States," Under Secretary of State Acheson announced on November 13, 1946, "and not as a member of an
international organization." Nevertheless, the World Food Board
was formed to continue the relief work, and the International
Refugee Organization assumed the repatriation responsibilities of
UNRRA. After the overwhelming approval by Congress of the
International Bank for Reconstruction and Development, and of
the International Monetary Fund (which began functioning in
spring, 1947), access to United States capital resources was re-
opened for those European governments which had defaulted on
their World War I debts to the United States and had therefore
been debarred by the Johnson Act from further United States
loans. The United States also co-operated with other governments
in establishing the Preparatory Committee on the International
Conference on Trade and Employment early in 1946. This committee arranged for a conference in Geneva between April and
October 1947, in which twenty-three nations subscribed to the
reciprocal-trade principles that were written into the General
Agreements on Tariffs and Trade. Congress, however, traditionally
jealous of its tariff-making powers, refused to approve the International Trade Organization which the Geneva Conference had
drafted in treaty form.

The United States also assumed a responsibility independent of
the United Nations for granting relief, fostering economic recovery, and restoring world trade. In July, 1946, Congress approved
a $3.75 billion loan to Great Britain, a country which already had
received two-thirds of the United States Lend-Lease aid before it
had been abruptly terminated on September 2, 1945. The Export-
Import Bank's lending power was quintupled (to $3.5 billion) in
the summer of 1945. The Reciprocal Trade Agreement act was
extended for three years, and the War Department, through the
Armed Forces Civilian Supply Program, administered relief programs in occupied Germany and Japan.

Peace Settlements with the Defeated Powers

Article 107 of the United Nations Charter permitted the Allied
states to conclude peace treaties on their own with the defeated
powers. The Big Four meeting of foreign ministers (United States,

USSR, Great Britain, and France) met unexpected difficulties in Soviet demands at London (September 1945) and at Moscow (December 1945), but found itself in general agreement after two meetings at Paris (April-July; July-October, 1946). As finally formulated in New York in December, 1946, the peace treaties with Hungary, Bulgaria, Rumania, and Italy recognized the continuing control of the USSR over the eastern European states (through the device of securing reparations), and gave Trieste neither to Yugoslavia as the Soviets had demanded nor to Italy as the western powers had wished; but to the United Nations as an internationalized port.

The peace treaties with Germany and Austria could not be agreed on. The USSR's excessive demands for reparations in these areas were reinforced by its control of the easternmost of the four administrative zones into which Germany and Austria had been divided. Neither France (which had been overrun three times by Germany) nor the Soviet Union viewed the problem with the detachment of the United States and Great Britain. The United States had already forsaken Secretary of the Treasury Henry Morgenthau's plan for a Carthaginian peace and had adopted a policy of rehabilitating Germany within a democratic framework. To allay the fears of the USSR and France, Secretary of State Byrnes proposed a long-term treaty which would guarantee the continued demilitarization of Germany, but Soviet recalcitrance prevented a four-power agreement. Formal peace for Germany did not come until 1952, and not until 1955 with respect to the USSR. The Austrian peace treaty was concluded in 1955.

Far Eastern Policy

Among the great powers which were assigned a permanent seat and a veto in the Security Council, China symbolized the growing voice of Asia, just as France reflected the fading prestige of a dying age in Europe. Postwar China was in economic chaos and politically divided between the Kuomintang Nationalists in the south and the Communists in the north. During 1945-1946, the USSR supported Chiang Kai-shek's Nationalists as the strongest and most co-operative faction in China, while United States efforts were aimed at unifying, stabilizing, and democratizing the country. A succession of United States efforts by various generals failed to bring the Communists and Nationalists together—the nearly successful year-long negotiations of General George C. Marshall during 1946 collapsed when extremists of both factions refused to co-operate. United States monetary and military aid to the corrupted Nationalist regime did not strengthen Chiang's position and it antagonized the Communists.

Elsewhere in northeast Asia, the United States strengthened the forces of democracy where it could. Unhampered by divided control in Japan, General Douglas MacArthur decentralized the large industrial monopolies, imposed a new Constitution in 1947, reformed the educational system, gave women the right to vote, and demilitarized the country. Political and military war lords, including Tojo, were tried and executed. The Philippines assumed full independence on July 4, 1946, and in return for a United States payment of $620 million and for United States trade preferences, they accorded equal rights with Filipinos to United States investors. United States military services were established in twenty-three bases with ninety-nine-year leaseholds. The United States strategic position in the Far East was further consolidated when a reluctant Security Council approved its trusteeship over 1,400 islands formerly Japanese mandates—the Marshalls, Carolines, and Marianas.

The Period of the Containment Policy: 1947–1950

In 1947 the world situation did not conform to the 1945 expectations of the policy-makers. The Soviet Union had proved itself most unco-operative, and neither the British nor French economy had been revived. The USSR's abuse of the veto in the Security Council dramatized both its aggressive intentions and the incapacity of the United Nations to act when the Great Powers were divided. During 1946 the USSR had ten times thwarted decisions of the Security Council with its veto. On one of these occasions the USSR had indicated that it could prevent action even on procedural matters through the use of the so-called "double veto." The demobilization of Soviet armed forces had not kept pace with that of the western powers, the Soviet Union had failed to honor its Yalta commitments with regard to free elections in eastern Europe, it had supported its Balkan satellites when they aided Communist guerrillas in Greece, and it had pursued obstructive tactics in the German peace settlement.

Not only had Soviet postwar intentions been falsely assessed, but in view of the failure of the economic recovery in Britain and France, its relative capabilities were greater than had been estimated. The winter of 1946-1947 was one of unparalleled severity in Europe and served to direct attention toward the insolvent position of the British. The French economic crisis was compounded by political chaos. Inflation was rampant everywhere in western Europe, currency restrictions and trade barriers hampered trade, and the shortage of dollars prevented importation of needed goods from the only country which could easily supply them. Great Britain simply could not afford the costs of maintaining its position of power in the subcontinent of India, in Palestine, or in Greece; the dismemberment of the British Empire had become a matter of necessity. British weakness created a power vacuum in strategic areas abroad; French instability provided an internal problem upon which the Communist Party could capitalize. The multipower European situation had thus failed to materialize; the United States alone would have to confront the USSR.[1]

From the beginning, President Truman had been somewhat more skeptical about Soviet behavior than his predecessor, who had assumed that Stalin would respond to a generously co-operative policy. Under Truman, as military aid Harry Vaughan put it in 1945, the White House forsook its diet of caviar and returned to good old-fashioned ham and eggs. The President spoke sharply to Molotov about the Soviet policy in Poland on the occasion of their first meeting in the White House before the San Francisco Conference. Truman's increasing irritation with his Secretary of State, James Byrnes, reflected in part his desire for a sterner policy with the Russians.

[1] Richard C. Snyder and Edgar S. Furniss, Jr., American Foreign Policy (Rinehart and Company, 1954), pp. 668-674.

One of the most percipient foreign-policy advisers in the Truman administration was George F. Kennan, a career diplomat and chief of the policy-planning staff of the Department of State. As early as February 1946, he had sent a long warning from Moscow on the aggressive nature of the Soviet foreign policy and had suggested the response that should be made to it. He publicly restated this assessment in an anonymous article entitled "The Sources of Soviet Conduct," which was published in the July 1947 issue of *Foreign Affairs*. Kennan recommended that, since the Soviet Union was weaker than the unified western world and since its leaders were sensitive to the logic of power, the United States should pursue a long-range containment effort. The Soviets should be confronted with "unalterable counter-force at every point when they show signs of encroaching upon the interests of a peaceful and stable world." The United States effort, therefore, must be global, and it must be applied "at a series of constantly shifting geographical and political points, corresponding to the shifts and maneuvers of Soviet policy." While a trained diplomat like Kennan was the first to recognize that this policy alone would not bring a fundamental change in the Communist regime, it would at least, he felt, impress the Soviet leaders to the degree that they might consider alternative policies within ten or fifteen years.

By 1947 the people of the United States were as alert to the new situation as were the leaders. Public-opinion polls reported that 70 per cent of the public felt that the United States would be involved in another war within a generation; only 40 per cent and 60 per cent had felt so in 1945 and 1946 respectively. The opinion polls also showed that 77 per cent of them thought that Soviet aims were aggressive in 1948 as compared to 58 per cent with this opinion in 1946. Likewise, 72 per cent of the public felt in 1948 that the United States should adopt a firmer attitude toward the USSR— an increase of 12 per cent in two years.

The containment of the USSR to safeguard the national security of the United States thus became the dominant foreign-policy objective. The development of law and order through the United Nations had been handicapped by the lack of Great Power agreement and by the fact that decisions could not be made rapidly and effectively to maintain peace in specific emergencies. Regional agencies and unilateral policies which permitted quick and flexible action were not only preferable but necessary in a system of power politics. The United Nations had lost its utility as a bridge between East and West and was reduced to a secondary role as an instrument of United States diplomacy—providing at best the moral support and the international banners under which the United States could fight the cold war.

Containment, by its very nature, was a negative policy in which the long-run objectives of promoting democracy, self-government, and human dignity gave way to the expedient practice of supporting authoritarian regimes whose internal stability often depended as much upon the use of coercion as upon persuasion. Walter Lippmann, in a series of articles, pointed out other serious objections to the containment policy, but he offered no feasible alternative. He noted, for example, that the United States system was not geared to the needs of power politics—Congress was notoriously slow in acting. He felt that the overwhelming costs of a prolonged program which would contain the entire perimeter of the Soviet sphere of influence, as Kennan had recommended, would regiment our free economy. Constructing coalitions in the Near and Far East would embroil the United States in war when these coalitions broke down. Effective containment would require the revival of German strength, and with it the more effective articulation of demands for German unification. Since the Soviet-held East Germany was the key to reunification, the bargaining power of the USSR would increase, not decrease. These, indeed, were the risks of the new policy.

But under the circumstances, containment was both necessary and preferable to alternative policies. Preventive war would be catastrophic, and would destroy with it all democratic values; cooperation with an intractable Communist regime had proved unfeasible. Containment, therefore, became the key objective of United States foreign policy, while other objectives were either correlated with it—as, for example, the economic reconstruction of Europe was justified in terms of withstanding Soviet aggression—

or were given low priority in policy considerations and budgetary appropriations.

Economic Aid to Europe

The United States opened a frontal attack on the USSR by throwing its economic resources into the reconstruction of Europe. Great Britain had been prompted by its waning strength to terminate full-scale economic aid to the Greek government in February 1947. The unstable rightist government in Greece, which had been plagued by Communist-supported guerrillas, could easily fall victim to the same fate that had overtaken the other Balkan regimes. President Truman therefore asked Congress, on March 12, 1947, to appropriate $400 million for economic and military aid to Greece and Turkey. He declared that one of the primary United States objectives was to create conditions in which all nations could work out a way of life, free from coercion. Both United States security and international peace were jeopardized by the direct and indirect aggression of totalitarian regimes. Accordingly, the United States must pursue a policy of supporting free peoples who were resisting attempted subjugation by armed minorities or by outside pressures. The Soviet Union did not have to be mentioned by name; the implication was clear.

As Great Britain's defense of an authoritarian Polish government inaugurated World War II, so did United States support for rightist Greece, in the form of the Truman Doctrine, initiate the cold war. Ideologies were cast aside when the stakes were national security. Traditional policies were again molded to fit new conditions. President Monroe had forsworn intervention in Greece, but as Thomas A. Bailey noted, the United States defense line in 1823 was the Gulf of Mexico whereas in 1947 it was the Gulf of Corinth. The Truman Doctrine also reflected a certain unilateral truculence on the part of the United States. Greek and Turkish aid was not intended to be channeled through the United Nations and perhaps entangled in international red tape, although a Congressional amendment provided that the United Nations was free to assume the burden at any time it chose. There was little danger that the significance of the Truman Doctrine had been lost on the USSR.

The Doctrine was announced just as Secretary of State George C. Marshall was reportedly rejecting the Russian demand for a large United States loan.

A far more ambitious proposal for economic aid to Europe was made by Secretary Marshall in a commencement address at Harvard University in June 1947. He suggested that if the European governments would collaborate in an economic-development program involving self-help and mutual assistance, the United States would support them with financial help. Sixteen western European nations (Molotov walked out on the planning conference and subsequently prevented the satellite nations from participating) joined in forming the Organization for European Economic Co-operation (OEEC) to co-ordinate their plans.

Congressional approval for such an elaborate program—President Truman asked for $17 billion to be spent over four and a quarter years—might well have been denied, had it not been for the vigorous and heavy-handed response of the USSR to the Marshall Plan program. They not only refused to participate in the European Recovery Program, but also took counter measures to consolidate their own sphere. They instituted an economic-integration plan of their own and in September 1947 they established the Cominform, which began disseminating propaganda about United States imperialism. The cleavage between east and west was again dramatized in February 1948, when a Communist coup d'état overthrew the Benes-Masaryk regime. The Czechoslovakian Foreign Minister, Jan Masaryk, had previously courted Soviet disfavor by indicating his willingness to co-operate with the Marshall Plan. In March, the USSR withdrew from the Allied Control Council in Germany and in June it imposed such drastic restrictions on traffic between the Western Zone and Berlin that they amounted to a blockade of the city. Congress resented this Soviet behavior and approved the appropriations act for the European Recovery Program so clearly directed against the USSR. Nationalist China was also given $463 million, and there was strong pressure to include Franco's Spain because of its demonstrated opposition to Communism. While Congress refused to bind itself to a long-term appropriation, it was understood that the funds for the

Marshall Plan would be renewed during the following three years.[2]

Paul G. Hoffman was placed in charge of the Economic Co-operation Administration (ECA) to supervise the expenditure of Marshall Plan funds. The European recipients matched the dollar grants with equal deposits of local currencies, called counterpart funds. From April 3, 1948, when the program was finally approved by the President, until June 30, 1950, when the Korean aggression initiated a new phase in foreign relations, a total of $10.28 billion was made available for European recovery. Altogether, the United States gave $15.6 billion in foreign aid between June 1947 and June 1950; of this Europe received 80 per cent, Asia 15 per cent, and Latin America 1.3 per cent. While the Marshall Plan was not successful in integrating the European economy, it did help defeat the Communists in Italy during the 1948 elections and it raised over-all production in the countries that received funds.

Beginnings of Military Containment

As tension between the USSR and the United States mounted, it was clear that a policy limited to economic recovery would not be enough. The crucial area of conflict was Germany. The United States and its Allies reached the conclusion at the London Council of Foreign Ministers in December 1947, that the Soviet Union was not willing to proceed with a German treaty except on its own terms. They decided, therefore, to rebuild West Germany, since it was a vital element in the development of Western Europe and in the checking of Soviet expansion. The British and United States zones had already been consolidated in May 1947, and closer ties with the French zone were now established.

The West was not deterred by the Soviet responses to these moves, that followed in rapid succession during the winter and spring of 1948: the Czech coup, the plans for the creation of an East German state, and most striking of all, the Berlin blockade. The blockade, which continued for almost a year, actually boomeranged in favor of the West; instead of capitulating, the Americans and British instituted a successful air lift to supply the city.

[2] Thomas A. Bailey, *A Diplomatic History of the American People* (5th ed., Appleton-Century-Crofts, Inc., 1955), p. 880.

The blockade convinced the reluctant French that West Germany must be unified. In April 1949, a three-power agreement providing for German economic rehabilitation and for the creation of a German Federal Republic was reached. Germany thereupon became a full-fledged participant in the United States European aid program, and the restrictions on its economic production were progressively removed.

Even with West Germany unified and released from strict economic controls, the European powers needed to be safeguarded against the USSR by more than economic strength. Indeed, they would never have agreed to the policy on Germany at all were it not for the threatening Soviet actions. The fifty-year pact between Britain, France, and the Benelux countries, known as the Brussels Treaty, probably would not have been hastened to completion in March 1948 had it not been for the impetus given by the Czech coup. The Brussels Treaty not only strengthened the economic co-operation already reflected in the OEEC, but it also created a military alliance directed against the renewal of German aggression. The signing of it precipitated the Soviet withdrawal from the Allied Control Council in Berlin. United States support for the Brussels Treaty was forthcoming from President Truman, and in June, 1948, the Vandenberg Resolution gave Congressional endorsement for the security arrangements that had been made. Congress, furthermore, passed an unprecedented peacetime conscription law and approved an unprecedented peacetime military budget. With the course thus charted, Secretary Marshall began negotiations for the North Atlantic Treaty in the fall of 1948. The pact was signed in Washington on April 4, 1949, by twelve nations: United States, Canada, Britain, France, Italy, the Benelux countries, Norway, Denmark, Ireland, and Portugal. It was a twenty-year military alliance which promised collective action, including armed force, if any one of them, or their islands, or French Algeria, were attacked by an aggressor. Full implementation of the treaty awaited another outburst of Communist aggression in Korea, although President Truman secured $1.31 billion from Congress to arm the western allies.

The North Atlantic Treaty had been attached to the United

Nations Charter through Article 51. But Article 51 itself had been an afterthought, added at the last minute in San Francisco, and it reflected the percipient forebodings of those who were never confident that the system of collective security in the United Nations would work. In a very real sense it was a calculated loophole, an escape clause whereby threatened nations could band together for collective defense, free from the veto of a potential aggressor. Thus Article 51 legalized military alliances, and NATO was essentially a military alliance. The strengthening of NATO indicated the return to power politics, which was necessary and effective in the short run to contain a threatening aggressor, but which in the long run would be destructive of international law, peaceful change, and democratic processes. The North Atlantic Treaty was an expedient, not a finality.

The United Nations

The cold war restricted but did not eliminate the role of the United Nations. President Truman summed up the United States position in his inaugural address in January, 1949: (1) unfaltering support of the United Nations and renewed efforts to strengthen its authority and increase its effectiveness, (2) continuation of United States programs for world economic recovery, (3) strengthening the freedom-loving nations against the dangers of aggression by means of regional agreements, (4) the undertaking of a "bold new program" for making the benefits of United States technological advances available for underdeveloped areas. We have seen how the economic recovery programs (Point 2) and the development of regional agreements (Point 3) were addressed primarily to Europe. Truman's Point Four program was put into operation during the next period and will be discussed later.

The cold-war problems that were brought to the attention of the United Nations were considered in an atmosphere of hostility which seemed less like that of a deliberative meeting of the world than a gladiatorial combat. The United States forced Soviet vetoes into the record in order to dramatize Soviet truculence. Communist initiatives were chiefly taken in the General Assembly, which succeeded the veto-bound Security Council as the chief organ for security matters late in 1947. In proposing their disarmament plans and demanding the reduction of world tensions, members of the Soviet bloc pointed accusing fingers at the United States as the leader of the warmongering capitalist powers. But the western powers were invariably successful in defeating these proposals or shaping them to suit their own purposes. Thus the General Assembly, in spite of Soviet opposition, approved a plan in November 1948, whereby the United Nations Atomic Energy Commission would be empowered to inspect atomic power plants. The Assembly also ignored Soviet protests when it declared that the disarmament of conventional weapons would have to accompany the establishment of an international police force, the control of atomic energy, and the conclusion of peace treaties with Japan and Germany. In 1949 the Assembly was used for the purpose of publicly condemning infringements of human rights by the Balkan satellites in violation of their peace treaties. Finally, the Special Committee on the Balkans kept watch over the outside Communist pressures on Greece.

The United States found the United Nations a useful forum for demonstrating leadership in meeting problems which were not intimately involved in the cold war. These problems concerned the emerging national governments in the Near and Far East. The United States, for example, worked actively within the United Nations to promote the independence of Indonesia. As a participant on the Security Council's Committee of Good Offices, it assisted in bringing about a military truce between the Dutch and Indonesian forces in January 1948. When Holland repudiated the truce in December and commenced military operations, the United States delegate to the United Nations, Philip Jessup, requested a cease-fire order and censored the Dutch action. Simultaneously, the United States withheld from the Netherlands the Marshall Plan aid that was destined for use in Indonesia. Holland was finally persuaded to participate in a round-table conference at the Hague, and in December 1949 a United States formula for the recognition of the Republic of Indonesia was approved.[3]

[3] Leland M. Goodrich and Anne P. Simons, *The United Nations and the Maintenance of International Peace and Security* (The Brookings Institution, 1955), pp. 50-52.

The evolution of Palestine from a British mandate to an independent state was another such problem. The British, overwhelmed by their economic difficulties and embarrassed by the Zionist and United States pressures to allow increased Jewish immigration into Palestine, placed the question of the future of their mandate before the United Nations in the spring of 1947. The General Assembly's recommendation that Palestine be divided satisfied neither the Jews nor the Arabs. The day before Britain's mandate over the area terminated on May 15, 1948, the Jewish authorities proclaimed the State of Israel. President Truman recognized the new state with precipitate haste. Fighting with the Arabs ensued, but the Israelis were successful in expanding their territory by one-third and forced 900,000 Arabs out into exile. An armistice was arranged in 1949 by the United Nations mediator, Ralph Bunche, and Israel was admitted to the United Nations in May 1949. The United States, drawn inexorably into the midst of Middle East politics, had to balance its concern for Arab oil and strategic position with its sympathy for the new Israeli state. These conflicting considerations would have to be reflected in the policies of the United States regarding the refugee problem, the internationalization of Palestine, and the demarcation of permanent boundaries. Temporarily it sought to stabilize the area by joining with the British and French on May 25, 1950, to guarantee the status quo.

Other instances of United Nations palliative capacity were its handling of the Kashmir dispute between India and Pakistan in 1948 and 1949, and the 1949 decision to give Libya full independence from Italy.

Latin American Policy

Since the beginning of World War II, United States relations with Latin America have suffered from our preoccupation with problems and areas which were more insistently concerned with international security. President Roosevelt reflected this lowered concern when he scribbled on one of the policy papers for Latin America: "Give them the crumbs and keep them happy." Once the United States had relinquished continentalism for internationalism, the strategic importance of Latin America was lessened. A two-ocean Navy and an air force reduced the relative value of the

Panama Canal; it was at once more vulnerable and less necessary for strategic purposes. Latin governments were neither as turbulent as the emerging nationalists in the Near and Far East, nor as powerful and strategic as those in Europe and in the countries on the Soviet periphery; their long-run problems could be by-passed to deal with short-run concerns elsewhere. The area, however, was not devoid of importance. It possessed twenty votes in the General Assembly, it produced critical raw materials like oil and copper which were increasingly scarce in the United States, and above all it held a high priority as an area of traditional United States interest.

The cold war had a twofold effect on the United States policy for Latin America; it encouraged closer relations with the dictatorial Peron administration in Argentina (just as it had with Franco's Spain), and it fostered the development of a regional security system. The unfortunate and ineffective opposition of United States Ambassador Braden to Peron's Presidential ambitions and the Department of State's publication in 1946 of the Blue-Book which exposed Nazi influence in Argentina had to be overlooked. By 1949, the Export-Import Bank had loaned Peron $125 million in return for Argentine concessions to United States business interests and for Argentine ratification of the Inter-American Treaty of Reciprocal Assistance.

This Rio Defense Treaty, as it was called, originated with the Act of Chapultepec in 1945, but its significance in 1947 was not alone the institutionalization of sanctions to keep the hemispheric peace. More importantly, it was a warning to the USSR to keep its hands off the western hemisphere. In treaty form, it multilateralized the Monroe Doctrine; future threats, whether they originated from without or from within, or whether they took the form of armed attacks or subversion, would give rise to consultation by the Council of the Organization of American States (OAS) or by a meeting of the foreign ministers.[4]

The Ninth Inter-American Conference which convened in 1949 in Bogota, Colombia, contributed to the further development of

[4] Martin B. Travis, Jr., "Inter-American Affairs," Americana Annual, 1949, 1950, 1951.

the regional security system. An uprising of unusual proportions in Bogota during the meeting was blamed on Communist influences and alerted the delegates to the necessity of adopting a resolution, sponsored by the United States, which committed their countries "to take all necessary measures to impede and uproot Communist activities." The Latin American representatives were told quite frankly that the United States' first line of economic and military defense was Europe and loans to Latin America would be given secondary consideration.

The Conference also approved a Charter of the Organization of American States which put the fifty-nine-year-old inter-American system in treaty form as a regional arrangement within the United Nations. The system had operated with real success in settling western-hemisphere disputes, for several important reasons: tensions involved in inter-American disputes were not so great as those elsewhere, the Latin countries were not powerful, inter-American settlement procedures were well developed and effectively manned, and the overwhelming economic, political, and military power of the United States was available for enforcement action. When Costa Rica complained, just a week after the Rio Treaty had come into effect in December, 1948, that it had been attacked by Nicaragua, prompt and effective action by the OAS forestalled further military engagements and culminated in an amity pact a year later. Again in January 1950, when Haiti charged the Dominican Republic with aiding an exiled Haitian conspirator, a Special Committee of the OAS made a careful investigation and pinned full responsibility on the Dominican government.

In other ways the inter-American organization was performing its regional tasks as provided by Chapter VIII of the United Nations charter. The Pan American Sanitary Bureau served as the regional branch of the World Health Organization, the Inter-American Economic and Social Council was closely identified with its United Nations counterpart in New York, and the exchange of information with the United Nations secretariat working smoothly. The Latin American countries were "in the club" and United States power was being channeled through the OAS to enforce their collective decisions.

The Korean War and Its Aftermath: 1950–1955

The Far East Front

The aggression of North Korea on June 25, 1950, inaugurated a new phase of the cold war which emphasized military rather than economic tools of foreign policy and which transferred the main theater of operations from Europe to Asia. There were more obstacles to the creation of an Asian defense alliance than there had been in Europe. Many of the thirty independent or nearly independent nations in non-Communist Asia had a feeling of relative security, separated as they were from the Communist countries by jungles, deserts, seas, or mountains. There existed, in addition, interstate frictions stemming from religious and dynastic differences or—in the case of Japan—from past aggressive behavior. Their prevalent attitude was anticolonialism, which contributed to neutralism toward the Korean venture. These countries associated the United States policies quite understandably with those of the Dutch, French, and British, the experience of the Philippines notwithstanding.

The fate of the 500 million Chinese, who occupied an area larger than the United States and Alaska combined, further complicated the situation. The Communists' success in forcing the Nationalists to evacuate the mainland for the island of Formosa in 1949, reinforced dramatically their ideological appeal, and the United States could do little about it.[5] Soviet support for the Communists had been no greater than United States support for the Nationalists, but the Communists' program, which promised the peasants title to their land, was more attractive to the majority than that of the landlord-dominated Nationalists. The Republican Party blamed the Truman administration and the allegedly disloyal career Foreign Service for this unhappy state of affairs; but Senator Vandenberg, at least, confessed that it was good practical

[5] Henry Wei, *China and Soviet Russia* (D. Van Nostrand Co., 1956), p. 228, suggests that the United States limited its support for the Nationalists after 1947, but he describes how the USSR was expanding its interests by negotiating with both the Nationalists and Communists in China before that time.

politics to criticize the Democratic administration in an area where there could have been no satisfactory solution in any case. Under the circumstances, a foreign policy which was guided by the rules of power politics would have recognized the Communist control of China; but the United States held aloof while the USSR concluded a military alliance with Mao Tse-tung in 1950, and Great Britain accorded him de facto recognition early in the same year. Vocal elements in Congress and the public imposed this policy on the United States. Secretary of State Acheson, nevertheless, indicated in a speech to the National Press Club that this country would leave the defense of Formosa and South Korea to the United Nations, and would itself concentrate on a defense perimeter which included Japan and the Philippine Islands. The United States was not, in short, going to make any unilateral commitments to defend the Nationalists in Formosa.

United States policy quickly changed when on June 25, 1950, the North Koreans, trained by a 3,500-man Soviet advisory group and equipped with Soviet and Japanese materiel, fell upon the South Koreans. The United States took the situation to the United Nations Security Council, which promptly declared North Korea to be an aggressor, urged a cease-fire, and requested United Nations members to render every assistance in restoring peace. By coincidence the USSR at the time was boycotting the Security Council for the reason that Communist China had not been permitted to replace the refugee Chiang government in the United Nations, and hence could not cast a veto.

United States forces entered the fighting immediately. The United States was designated by the United Nations to direct the military effort, and General Douglas MacArthur was named to command. By the end of October his troops had cleared the invaders out of South Korea and had advanced to the border between North Korea and China. In these circumstances the opportunity for forcefully unifying Korea under the anti-Communist government of Syngman Rhee, president of South Korea, appeared highly attractive to the United Nations General Assembly and to United States public opinion. In November, however, the Chinese Communist forces, nominally "volunteers," entered the fighting as they had threatened to do.

The turn of events re-established the popularity of the limited containment objective, although General MacArthur continued to believe there was no substitute for victory and argued for bombing the "privileged sanctuary" of Manchuria. MacArthur's truculence resulted in his dismissal by President Truman in April, and by spring the belligerents were once again stabilized approximately at the 38-degree parallel. Truce negotiations through United Nations channels commenced in July 1951, and continued for two years, with interruptions for heavy sporadic fighting. The disposition of prisoners became the crucial issue. After the death of Stalin in the spring of 1953, the Communist leaders decided to call a halt to the impasse of their own creation and to agree that a neutral custodial commission, headed by Indian officials, would take charge of the disputed prisoners. The respective commands would be allowed to reindoctrinate their own nationals, and then—and this was a victory for the United States and its Allies—the prisoners would be permitted a free choice as to whether they would reassume their former allegiance. The Communists were successful in persuading 138 of their 21,000 to return, while 3,901 of the 4,000 United Nations troops chose repatriation (77 of the 99 who stayed with the Communists were South Koreans).

The Korean situation prompted a new United States foreign policy elsewhere in the Far East. The United States dropped its hands-off attitude toward the Chinese civil war. President Truman in June 1950 instructed the Seventh Fleet to neutralize the Formosa Strait, separating the Chiang Nationalists from the Communist mainland. Generous allocations of United States funds helped rehabilitate Formosa and strengthen Chiang's army. By the time President Eisenhower came to office, defense of the island by the United States fleet no longer seemed necessary. The neutralization order was countermanded and it was announced that Chiang's troops had been "unleashed." While the Formosa government was quietly told not to engage in adventurous activities, it was clear that the United States considered it an established regime and would defend it.

A mutual-security treaty gave formal recognition to this relationship between Formosa and the United States in February 1955. Similarly, the United States guaranteed the integrity of South Korea (culminating with a treaty in January, 1954) as an inducement to President Rhee to accept the United Nations truce terms. Japan also was brought within the security network. John Foster Dulles, who was entrusted with these negotiations, in 1951 found the other Asiatic states more amenable to a revived Japan than the European Allies had been to a reconstructed Germany. A Japanese peace treaty was signed in San Francisco in September 1951, without the USSR. An accompanying security treaty provided a legal basis for the continued presence of United States troops in Japan, and pointed the way for eventual Japanese participation in the containment front. These treaties thrust the main burden for defensive action upon the United States. They also raised the question as to whether other nations, whose integrity was guaranteed only by the United Nations Charter, would also be promptly supported in the event of aggression.

In Indochina, the United States found itself torn between its new containment policy and its traditional support for self-government. The eight-year (1946-1954) Indochinese struggle for independence was a complex mess involving the French, their supporters and adversaries among the Indochinese, and Communists and anti-Communists among the adversaries. The diplomatic problem for the United States was complicated by the fact that France had become, both strategically and politically, the keystone of European defense. Also, the Chinese Communists, freed from their involvement in Korea, in 1953 began sending troops in ever-increasing numbers to the aid of the Viet Minh faction. While France welcomed United States financial support for the war (toward the end, $800 million a year), it was reluctant to submit to United States political or military interference which might weaken its hold on this area. Nevertheless, during the critical winter of 1953-1954, Secretary of State Dulles threatened the Chinese Communists with "massive retaliation," and reportedly would have engaged the United States in an all-out effort to support the French in defending Dienbienphu, had he not been overridden by the

President.[6] The British, in any event, refused to be associated with such a policy. The French lost Dienbienphu, and Mr. Dulles endorsed the peace settlement between France and the Communists in June 1954. Militarily, the containment policy had suffered a severe blow; the three Indochinese states were prevented by the treaty from joining a military alliance, Vietnam was divided into a northern Communist and southern free sector, and Laos was virtually surrounded by Communist territory. But politically, the peace treaty marked a welcome termination of French colonialism in this area under an arrangement that had not jeopardized United States relations with France.

The United States now found it necessary to extend the containment front to South East Asia. Secretary Dulles, together with British Foreign Minister Sir Anthony Eden, called a conference of the states in this area. Four of them—India, Burma, Ceylon, and Indonesia—refused to attend, but Pakistan, Thailand, the Philippines, Australia, and New Zealand met with France, Great Britain and the United States in Manila on September 8, 1954. The resulting South East Asia Treaty Organization (SEATO) followed the pattern of the other security pacts, and established a council with a Secretariat at Bangkok. Both Great Britain and the United States preferred to retain their freedom of action in this sphere, so no joint military command was established. Nevertheless, Communist China was placed on notice that the United States and its Allies would act should the territory of Indochina or that of the member states be subjected to aggression.

The United States containment policy in the Far East was thus well established by 1955. Military-security pacts, together with economic and military assistance, reinforced our position in the area. But the limitations of a security policy were more apparent in the undeveloped countries of Asia than they had been in Europe; unstable governments needed more than military pacts to win the allegiance of their people, and without this loyalty both their policies and their institutions were subject to revolutionary change. It was not a happy augury that many of the governments which

6 New York Times, January 13, 1956, p. 2.

had allied themselves most closely to the United States were least inclined to improve the lot of their own people.

The European Theater

The West was more favorably situated in Europe during 1950-1955 than it had been in Asia. Yugoslavia had defected from Soviet control in 1948 and the Allies had successfully countered the Berlin blockade with the air lift. Nevertheless, Soviet military forces were well entrenched on the western European border, and posed an ever present threat. Negotiations with the USSR had so far deteriorated that Secretary Acheson in February 1950 described further talks as fruitless until western strength should equal that of the Soviet powers. But it took the North Korean aggression to convince Congress that greater military funds should be appropriated. General Eisenhower was persuaded to leave his position as president of Columbia University in December 1950 and to throw the full weight of his prestige behind the effort to translate NATO's paper obligations into actual military strength. The United States secured additional pledges amounting to $15.4 billion from the NATO countries. NATO itself was enlarged and reorganized; a permanent council with a secretariat was established in Paris, and Greece and Turkey were accepted as members of the alliance.

As the strongest and largest single contributor to European defense, the United States played an important decision-making role in the Atlantic alliance. The supreme military authority of the organization, representing the chiefs of staff of the United States, Britain, and France, was located in Washington. The most important command post in Europe, with headquarters near Versailles (Supreme Commander Allied Forces Europe or SACEUR) was awarded to an American; Generals Eisenhower, Ridgway, Gruenther, and Norstad successively occupied the post. SACEUR had the responsibility for defending Europe from Norway to the Black Sea. The United States Sixth Fleet, which dominated the Mediterranean, was kept under United States control by creating the Mediterranean Command in 1953, and an admiral of the United States Navy was placed in charge of the Atlantic Command with headquarters in Norfolk, Virginia.

NATO's military effectiveness depended heavily upon a rearmed Germany. West Germany had the greatest economic potential and largest manpower reserve in Europe, and it was strategically located in an area which invited Soviet aggression. It was necessary, however, to persuade a reluctant and distracted French government that its traditional enemy should be revived not only economically but militarily as well. French Minister of Foreign Affairs Robert Schuman proposed a first step in this direction. As approved in 1952, his plan provided for the establishment of a supranational European Coal and Steel Community, composed of France, West Germany, Italy, and the Benelux countries. The Community was given full power to regulate this important segment of the European economy, and quieted French fears that an independent German steel industry would once again place itself at the disposal of an aggressive government.[7]

Another plan devised by the French in 1952 proposed to merge the armed forces of these same countries into a single European Defense Community (EDC). But the French developed doubts about this proposal when the USSR offered to unify and neutralize Germany in 1952, and when the Korean truce was settled the following year. Because of its preoccupation with colonial and domestic quarrels, the French National Assembly delayed the vote on EDC until August 1954. In spite of Secretary Dulles' threat that the United States would undertake an "agonizing reappraisal" of the entire French position (presumably he would deal directly with Germany) if EDC were defeated, the French Assembly did not approve the treaty. With British initiative, a substitute plan was drafted for incorporating West Germany and Italy into the Brussels Pact. The new defense organization was called Western European Union, and it gave France a reassuring degree of control of German rearmament but did not provide for full integration of the armed forces. Great Britain also promised to keep five divisions on the Continent, and the United States indicated that it would maintain its current strength of six divisions. The treaty

[7] The International Studies Group of the Brookings Institution, *Major Problems of United States Foreign Policy, 1950-1951, 1951-1952, 1952-1953, 1954.*

was finally ratified by all the participating states on April 28, 1955. Germany, after granting special control over its armed forces to NATO, recovered its full sovereignty.

The dissident Communist regime in Yugoslavia also became a nominal partner in the containment effort. The United States hoped that by supporting this heretic, it would encourage other satellites to break away from the USSR. Between 1949 and 1955, Yugoslavia received financial and military aid valued at $502 million from the United States. Since Yugoslavia was no longer supporting the Greek guerrillas, steps were taken to link that country in a common defense front with Greece and Turkey, and indirectly with NATO. The defense treaty was finally concluded in 1954, just as a final settlement with Italy (through the mediation of the British and Americans) was being reached on the disposition of Trieste.

A more favorable orientation towards Fascist Spain was also undertaken by the United States. In 1950, the United States joined with Latin America to rescind the United Nations recommendation on Spain. United States military leaders, who desired air and naval bases behind the natural barrier of the Pyrenees Mountains, strongly endorsed the new policy, and Congress voted economic and military aid for Spain. An agreement on the military bases was finally reached in September 1953, when Spain was permitted to draw upon the $226 million which had already been appropriated.

The United Nations after the Korean Aggression

By taking the Korean dispute to the United Nations, the United States temporarily injected new life into the world organization. It also found the United Nations a convenient agency for mobilizing world opinion behind United States leadership, and it could disassociate itself by this tactic from the incubus of imperialism. If the United Nations no longer bridged the West and the East, it nevertheless aided in synthesizing the moral objectives of the idealists with the practical necessities of power politics. The fortuitous absence of the USSR from the Security Council, and the chance location of a United Nations commission in Korea were important factors in the prompt decisions that were made in the summer of 1950. But these conditions for successful United Nations decision-making could be institutionalized if certain procedural changes were built into the system. Secretary Acheson therefore proposed the "Uniting for Peace" resolution, which was approved overwhelmingly by the General Assembly on November 3, 1950. The resolution provided that any seven members of the Security Council could request the General Assembly to consider a dispute or situation when the veto-bound Security Council was unable to act. In addition, United Nations members were asked to earmark military forces which would be immediately available for general security purposes. A Peace Observation Commission would observe and report on any international situation which might lead to a breach of the peace.

Enthusiasm in the United States for the United Nations was quickly dissipated during the course of fighting and negotiating in Korea. The United States had contributed 90 per cent of the non-Korean troops, had spent a total of $20 billion, and had suffered 136,029 casualties, 24,281 of them deaths. Furthermore, most members ignored the Uniting for Peace Resolution or failed to earmark troops for collective action. Indeed, the general public discouragement with the Korean venture was so pronounced during the 1952 Presidential campaign that the Democratic Party suffered heavily for having been its sponsor. United States enthusiasm was further dampened by the revelations that former American Communists were employed by the United Nations. Some political figures, Senator Bricker being one, took exception to the liberal economic and social objectives of the international organization. The public discussion that followed the military reverses during the first winter in Korea brought forward much opinion that the United Nations was ineffective or objectionable or both, and that the United States should withdraw from Europe, hole up in the American continent, or perhaps concentrate its resources and attention in Asia. This latter-day isolationism did not prevail, but the viewpoint had an indirect and harmful effect on United States participation in the world organization.

Nevertheless, the United Nations was a useful arena for propaganda in the cold war. It was used to unmask the Soviet Union and to dispel Allied fears of what many called the saber-rattling

policies of the United States. For example, the United States
agreed with the USSR that a joint Disarmament Commission be
established, and then proceeded to introduce proposals for atomic
control and disarmament that were not at all what the Soviets
desired. The USSR first tried to ridicule these proposals. Mr.
Vyshinsky, in untimely derision, told the unimpressed delegates:
"I could not get to sleep last night—because I was choking with
laughter." To avoid further embarrassment, the Soviet delegate
turned to the offensive with the charge that the United States was
using bacteriological warfare in the Far East. It was a year before
the United States finally came to grips with that rumor in the
United Nations. None of such unilateral United States efforts as
the Voice of America, or the floating broadcasting station, had the
dramatic appeal of the action-geared proposals in the United Nations. One of the most successful of these was President Eisenhower's "Atoms for Peace" project which Winston Churchill
dubbed the "Republican equivalent to Mr. Truman's Point Four
Plan." The project was presented in December, 1953, and suggested the establishment of an international agency for the peacetime development of atomic energy throughout the world. People
everywhere were thus apprised of United States concern for the
peaceful as well as the military aspects of atomic energy.
UNESCO's decision in 1951 to engage in cold-war propaganda
also proved helpful for United States foreign policy. To discourage
further military aggression, UNESCO forsook its earlier neutrality
and sponsored an information program which capitalized on the
United Nations action in Korea.

The United States had also initiated the United Nations technical-assistance program. President Truman assessed the importance of this program:

"Communist propaganda holds that the free nations are incapable
of providing a decent standard of living for the millions of people in
the underdeveloped areas of the earth. The Point Four Program will
be one of our principal ways of demonstrating the complete falsity of
that charge."

While the United States contributed only a small fraction of its
own technical-aid appropriations to the United Nations (in 1950
it gave $7.5 million, but this was doubled by 1955), the world

organization possessed many advantages in administering the program. Technical specialists from many countries were available to the United Nations, the specialized agencies were already familiar with the needs of the undeveloped countries, and the sensitive recipients of aid were not inclined to suspect the motives and activities of the United Nations agents.

The United States found the United Nations less successful as a moderator of disputes in which the emerging nationalisms were a factor. The United Nations was better equipped to deal with disputes between states than with quasi-revolutionary movements which were sweeping half the world and which respected neither legal boundaries nor legal and administrative forms. Tensions had increased, and the policy-makers of the United States were not inclined to jeopardize their main objective of containment by pressing for the minor one of self-determination. Furthermore, both Great Britain and France were now involved in such disputes, hence neither would support the traditional United States position on nationalist aspirations. Accordingly, the United States found itself caught between the metropolitan powers on the one hand and the Arab and Latin American countries on the other, in disputes involving South African treatment of Indians and French policies in Tunis and Morocco. The United States was sympathetic to the theory of self-government, but it was realistically aware of the unpreparedness of many to govern themselves. By 1952 the nationalistic sentiments in the Near and Far Eastern countries outweighed their concern about the East-West struggle. Voting patterns in the General Assembly had shown that a combination of Asian, African, and Latin American states, together with the five votes of the Soviet bloc, could deprive the United States of a working majority. Since the Latin American countries held the balance of power, the United States turned to the renewal of its traditional friendships in that area.

The Middle East as an Area of Containment

The Korean dispute alerted the United States to the need for embracing the Middle East in its containment plans. The area bordered on the USSR and supplied most of Europe's oil requirements. The United Nations, as we have seen, was not effective in settling Middle Eastern disputes with Great Britain and France, or in overcoming Arabic neutralism when collective-security matters were at stake. Indeed, most of the Arab countries had adopted a neutral or at best indifferent stand on the Korean crisis. United States objectives in the Middle East, therefore, included the defense of the countries on the Soviet border and the development of co-operation with the others.

Technical assistance was extended to these Middle East states in 1951. Syria, however, reflected its strong Arabic nationalism by rejecting the United States aid. Military aid was extended to Turkey, Greece, and Iran, and an air-base site in Dahran was secured from Saudi Arabia. In 1952 Egypt refused to go along with Great Britain, France, and Turkey in establishing a Middle East Command because of its involvement with Israel and the Suez Canal. The United States hoped to reduce nationalistic tensions in Egypt by encouraging the British to withdraw from the Canal. Since this British "life-line to the Orient" had lost much of its strategic value in the presence of the hydrogen bomb, Winston Churchill agreed in 1954 to withdraw the British troops after Egypt had guaranteed the international control of the Canal, leaving its operation to the Suez Canal Company.

The Republican Party was less committed to Israel than the Democrats had been. Under its administration the United States gave less sympathetic consideration to Israel in its border disputes with the Arabs, and in several instances supported United Nations censure of Israel.

Thus the United States generally supported Arab nationalism, but this policy did not hold for Arab nations along the Soviet perimeter. In Iran, President Eisenhower refused to make financial assistance available to Premier Mossadegh as long as the country made no move to settle its dispute with Great Britain over the expropriation of oil properties. The expected fall of the Iranian government materialized, and the army intervened just in time to forestall a Communist effort to seize power. A settlement on the expropriated oil properties was thereupon reached, and the United

States extended $45 million in emergency aid to stabilize the new regime.[8]

In 1954 the United States also determined upon a course of action that would make the "northern tier" countries of Turkey, Iraq, Iran, and Pakistan defense partners in the free world. All of them shared common boundaries with the USSR, and were for that reason sensitive to their security needs. With Pakistan also a member of SEATO and Turkey participating in the counsels of NATO, this final agreement completed the ring of committed states around the Soviet Union. It was not a strong alliance, however. Pakistan was divided geographically and hostile towards India. The young Shah of Iran was oriented towards the West, but he did not have the allegiance of strong nationalistic groups in the country. Pan Arabic sentiments also divided Iraq. Although Britain adhered to the alliance in April 1955, the United States, by not joining, kept a free hand in dealing with the neutral Arab countries.

Latin America and the Containment of Communism

The United States policy on the Korean conflict evoked a more favorable response from Latin America than from any other under-developed area of the world. The Council of the Organization of American States immediately expressed its collective support of the United Nations action and reaffirmed its pledge of continental solidarity. The flood of enthusiastic messages which poured into Washington from the Latin capitals was subsequently supported by token offerings—as for example, a Colombian frigate and infantry battalion. While the limited resources of the Latin American countries prevented their making large military contribution to the defensive effort, they nonetheless exerted a strong voice and moral support in the counsels of the United Nations and the Organization of American States. At a consultative meeting of the Latin American foreign ministers in Washington on March 26, 1951, called to dramatize the seriousness of the world situation, the Latin delegates resolved to tighten their internal controls on

[8] Marshall Knappen, *An Introduction to American Foreign Policy* (Harper and Bros., 1956), pp. 475-485.

Communism, to strengthen their military defense, and to increase the production of strategic raw materials. By the time of the Korean truce, the United States had distributed $140 million in military aid to the Latin American area. Mutual-security agreements were also concluded with eleven Latin countries by 1955, and a reinvigorated inter-American Defense Board elaborated plans for safeguarding sources of strategic materials and for protecting communications channels.

In 1952, however, inter-American co-operation was handicapped by a resurgent nationalism and by the United States preoccupation with the Soviet threat in Europe and Asia. The growth of Peronism seemed to many to be a greater peril in the area than Communism (except in Guatemala), but it received less attention from the Department of State. Nationalistic feeling in the Latin American countries was reflected in the extension of territorial waters from the conventional three miles to 200 miles; Chile, Peru, and Ecuador concluded a treaty to this effect in 1952 to keep United States craft from exploiting their fish resources. Mexico asserted concern for the welfare of its legal (braceros) and illegal (wet backs) emigrant farm hands in the southwest United States, who were often exploited by American but not by Mexican standards. Neither Secretary Acheson's trip to Brazil in 1952, to call attention to the dangers of Russian subversion, nor the 1953 five-week fact-finding junket by the President's brother, Milton Eisenhower, did much to impress the Latin Americans. Since the days of Elihu Root they had become calloused to amenities unaccompanied by deeds.

The Eisenhower administration was at first handicapped in its Latin American policies by its inexperience and by the relaxation of urgency that followed the truce in Korea. At the Tenth Inter-American conference, held in Caracas in 1954, Secretary Dulles attempted to re-energize continental determination with an anti-Communist declaration. It provided that a consultative meeting of foreign ministers would be called when an American state was dominated or controlled by Communists. There was a manifest lack of enthusiasm for the proposal in the more democratic states, as well as direct oppositon by the Communist-dominated Arbenz regime in Guatemala.

But the timeliness of the declaration was apparent two months later, when munitions from the Iron Curtain countries arrived in Guatemala to reinforce its faltering government. Rebellious forces, eventually successful, were aided and abetted by Guatemala's un-neutral neighbor, Honduras, and by United States Ambassador John E. Peurifoy. The Guatemalan situation raised a question regarding the proper participation of the United Nations and the Organization of American States in regional disputes. Guatemala submitted the dispute to the United Nations where it could count on the friendly intervention of the Soviet delegate. The United States delegate to the United Nations, Henry Cabot Lodge, strongly supported by a near-unanimous vote of the Senate, employed resourceful tactics to have the dispute submitted to the Organization of American States. By the time the regional organization was entrusted with the case, the rebellious forces were victorious. However well-intentioned Washington's objectives may have been, the United States was criticized by Latin America and Europe for the procedures it had employed.

Little United States attention was given to the long-run economic problems of Latin America during this period. A much-delayed economic conference was held in Rio de Janeiro during the last months of 1954, but the United States delegates used the occasion to alert the Latin countries to the prior need for internal reform before private capital could be induced to flow from the United States. Secretary Dulles did secure the reversal of a decision by the economy-minded Republican administration to abandon the Export-Import Bank, and was able to announce to his relieved Latin colleagues that governmental loans would still be available.

Peaceful Competition: 1955–1956

The policy-makers and the attentive public in the United States were once again reassessing the international situation in 1955. Soviet deeds as well as words seemed to indicate a new and more

co-operative approach in world affairs. An Austrian peace treaty
was signed on May 15, 1955, which provided for the withdrawal
of Soviet troops and for the neutralization of Austria. A friendly
visit of Bulganin and Khrushchev to Yugoslavia resulted in important concessions by the USSR—including the subsequent dismissal of Foreign Minister Molotov and the disbandment of the
Cominform. The "Summit Conference" at Geneva, which convened July 18, 1955, convinced both the USSR and the United
States that neither of them was bent on an all-out atomic war.
Though the Russian leaders promised arms to the Arab countries,
refused to reunify Germany, and violently attacked United States
policies in the Supreme Soviet, they nevertheless instituted significant internal reforms, institutionalized collective leadership,
and in February 1956 set about destroying the Stalin myth.

People in the United States at first were skeptical about these
changes, but by July, 1956, Secretary Dulles declared:

> It is not a matter for this year or next year, but I believe this second
> postwar decade in which we are, will see these new forces [in the USSR]
> take charge of the situation and that we can really hopefully look for-
> ward to a transformation of the international scene.

Thus the world situation appeared in the summer of 1956.

Earlier in the year President Eisenhower had announced that
international conditions were changing so rapidly that what was a
good policy six months earlier was no longer valid when he spoke.
While others were cautioning that the Soviet Union was changing
its manners but not its long-run objectives, George F. Kennan
noted that objectives were only ends, while methods were means.
"As a nation bred in the Christian tradition, we should understand something of the importance of method," he wrote. "We,
of all people, should know that it is method—not the objective—
which, in the last analysis, determines the outcome."

Soviet capabilities were also being reappraised in the light of
the developing situation. There was increasing agreement that
observers in the United States had overstated these capabilities
during the period of containment, just as they had underestimated
them in 1941. The Soviet announcement in the spring of 1956

that the USSR was reducing its armed forces by 1.2 million men supported this new estimate. Soviet ability to make war was growing nevertheless, and might continue to grow more rapidly than that of the United States. But if the USSR was the second-greatest power in the world, as Khrushchev announced in 1956, it no longer shared the world stage with the United States alone; Communist China, Germany, the British Commonwealth, and perhaps Japan could not be discounted as important world powers. This wider distribution of power and the general fear of atomic war lessened the possibility of immediate conflict and gave a new importance to industrial and economic strength. Rightly or wrongly, policy-makers were confident of United States competitive capacities for the "long haul." And in an age of technological revolution defense needs might well be met by the threat of retaliation from American-based intercontinental ballistic missiles and atomic-powered planes. This strategy would permit underdeveloped countries to advance socially and economically with United States and United Nations assistance.

United States objectives were reviewed in terms of this new situation. Short-run considerations of containment did not now demand exclusive priority. But until an international disarmament plan should find general acceptance, security objectives could not be neglected; the policies of the USSR had proved fickle in the past and the behavior of the emerging powers could not be predicted. Lessening tensions nevertheless permitted the United States to consider policy objectives which had been put aside or subordinated since 1950. Long-run international stability required the advancement of self-government, nonintervention in the domestic affairs of foreign states, greater recognition of human rights, and better standards of living. Progress toward these objectives was also necessary to palliate the confusing and irrational turbulence of the emerging nationalisms. In some of these countries, military pacts made during the containment phase had shored up unpopular regimes. There was also a growing discontent with having United States troops stationed at these foreign bases.

By 1955 the people of the United States were discovering that the world situation was far more complex than they had been accustomed to think. The USSR seemed neither so good as they had thought in 1945 nor so evil as it had appeared in 1950; however sinister and cruel the Stalin regime may have been, it should not have been confused with the Hitler regime and its reckless program. Self-determination created additional international problems, and it required tolerant and understanding policies toward the strident nationalisms. Thus multidimensional objectives were required for a complex international world, and a variety of procedures were needed to implement them. The United States had found in 1946 that it could not rely exclusively upon the United Nations to solve its international problems, and its democratic form of government did not allow it sufficient flexibility to engage successfully for any length of time in power politics. The policy-makers of the United States had discovered that its short-run objectives of defense and the settlement of disputes were often handled most expeditiously within a bilateral or regional framework, while its long-run social and economic objectives could be carried out most effectively through the United Nations.

Foreign Economic Policy

The United States policy of economic assistance was unaffected by the "Spirit of Geneva." While the USSR had expanded its foreign aid tenfold within a year (Soviet aid totaled more than $1 billion between July, 1955, and July, 1956), the United States had not increased its appropriations for this purpose since 1953. In addition, recipients of Soviet aid were not overburdened with military costs, whereas the chief beneficiaries of the $1.7 billion annual United States aid were countries like Korea and Formosa which needed defense support. In all, the United States provided a meager $205 million for economic aid that was not related to military programs and $152 million for technical assistance. Less than 20 per cent of the $3.76 billion foreign-aid appropriation for 1957 was for strictly economic purposes.

The United States was thus pursuing a conservative policy in a revolutionary epoch. Producing 40 per cent of the world's goods, twice the share of the USSR, it was giving economic assistance neither as large nor as effective as that of the USSR. Projects

that the United States sponsored may have been sound economically, but they did not cater to the immediate desires of the
underdeveloped countries. Clearly the United Nations technical-
assistance program promised greater success; United Nations spon-
sorship removed the taint of military side-taking, reduced or
eliminated colonial memories, and helped steer the world's economic and technical revolution away from dictatorial solutions.
Most importantly, the United Nations brought the vigilance of
world opinion and the sanction of world condemnation to bear
upon any Communist attempt to use aid as an instrument of
Soviet imperialist penetration. But only with difficulty was a reluctant Congress persuaded to approve a $15.5-million contribu-
tion to the $28.9-million economic-resistance budget of the United
Nations in 1956. To the United States, the United Nations foreign-
aid program was a stepchild.[9]

The Eisenhower administration has nevertheless encouraged the
development of world trade. The Reciprocal Trade Agreement
Act was extended for three years, and tariff reductions were made
on 900 imported items at the Geneva meetings of GATT. Accordingly, United States imports increased by $1.6 billion between
1955 and 1956, with Europe the chief beneficiary of this "trade
not aid" policy. But foreign merchants could not count on the
continuing accessibility of United States markets as long as trade
policy was subject to the erratic behavior of Congress. In 1955,
the administration initiated a permanent organizational framework
for GATT which was called the Organization for Trade Co-operation (OTC). But Congress, fearing that the administration was
infringing upon its right to regulate foreign commerce, refused to
bring the OTC to a vote in 1956.

Public and private loans from United States sources also contributed to better living standards abroad. The capitalization of
the Export-Import Bank was increased to $5 billion, and the
International Finance Corporation was established in 1956 as an
American-inspired offshoot of the World Bank. With a capitaliza-

9 *The Political Economy of American Foreign Policy*, Report of a Study
Group sponsored by the Woodrow Wilson Foundation and the National
Planning Association (Henry Holt and Co., 1955), pp. 205-218.

tion of $100 million, the IFC encouraged private loans to under-developed areas. The United States also contributed a third of the $9 billion capital to the World Bank. Loans from this agency were concentrated largely on public projects such as power, transport and other utilities. Private investments abroad reached $19.6 billion in 1956, of which $6 billion was invested in Latin America and the same amount in Canada. Indeed, Latin America was one of the most important beneficiaries of all these lending agencies.

The United States also turned to economic policies to prop up faltering regional organizations. NATO was originally designed to meet the threat of Soviet aggression. As East-West tension had lessened, European members were less enthusiastic supporters of the alliance. Military budgets were reduced, France withdrew several divisions to fight in North Africa, Germany was slow to rearm, and Iceland's voters had demanded the withdrawal of United States troops. The military alliance was destined to fall of its own weight unless remedial measures were taken. Secretary Dulles therefore proposed, in May 1956, that NATO should henceforth be concerned with economic and political as well as military matters. A similar development occurred in the Latin American area. At the Panama Conference, in July 1956, President Eisenhower proposed that an Inter-American Committee on Human Problems should be established. The committee would recommend plans for the peaceful use of atomic energy and for raising living standards to the Organization of American States.

Education for International Understanding

Since the early days of the cold war, the United States had been developing an information program to win international support for its foreign policy. More recently, the main effort of this program was directed at exposing Communist aggression and undermining Soviet strength both in the satellites and in the uncommitted areas. The Geneva Conference in 1955, however, inaugurated a new policy of moderation and understanding. Cultural, scientific, and scholarly exchanges were arranged between the USSR and the United States. The Voice of America, however, continued to exploit such opportunities as the publication of

Khrushchev's secret denunciation of Stalin. Although the 1956-1957 budget for the United States Information Agency was set at $113 million and an additional $20 million was approved for the exchange-of-students program, the United States campaign to sell itself was supported by only an insignificant fraction of the national income.

The foreign propaganda and cultural activities of the United States had suffered from lack of experience, failure in co-ordination, interference of untrained and unperceptive politicians (the Mc-Carthy-inspired purge of the information libraries abroad, to mention only one), and unfamiliarity with foreign cultures. Many of these difficulties were inherent in a democracy which speaks with many diverse voices.

But self-advertising is necessarily subject to skepticism. Action alternatives such as the United Nations programs of disarmament, atoms for peace (which the USSR finally accepted), and Eisenhower's open-skies aerial inspection plan were likely to have a wider appeal. There remained the need to broaden international understanding and to develop a world-wide appreciation of the responsibilities for living in one world. The United Nations Educational, Scientific, and Cultural Organization (UNESCO) could best perform this task, unhampered by prejudices that a propagandizing national program might encounter.

German Reunification

While the United Nations promised effective support for the social and psychological policies of the United States, its apparatus lacked the flexibility, speed, and secrecy that were often necessary in negotiating key political questions. The problem concerning the reunification of Germany was best adapted to the procedures of traditional diplomacy. After the Geneva Summit Conference in July 1955, the significance of an armed Germany appeared in a new light. The defense posture of the western allies had already deteriorated as the result of the receding concern over militant Communism and the increasing preoccupation with developing nationalism. In 1956, Egypt's expropriation of the Suez Canal had engaged the attention of Great Britain and Algeria's struggle for independence had diverted French troops to North Africa. The Balkan defense pact had disintegrated as Yugoslavia moved closer to the Soviet Union and as Greece and Turkey became engaged in the dispute over Cyprus.

Important changes were also taking place within Germany. Generous United States aid and prodigious native efforts had increased German productivity to the point where it now challenged every other western European power. Chancellor Adenauer's party and policies were losing popularity; protests against having United States troops garrisoned in Germany, concern over NATO's defense strategies which would make Germany a battleground, and protest against rearmament were all being voiced by the opposition. The people of West Germany were united on the need for reunification with Communist-controlled East Germany. But Adenauer's assumption that the Soviet Union would be compelled to accept reunification after a strong West Germany was firmly linked with NATO seemed no longer to matter, since western strength was disintegrating and Soviet procedures had changed.

Under these circumstances the United States needed to reassess its own policy toward central Europe. West Germany was now independent, and its domestic opinion had replaced United States guidance in the making of its foreign policies. The division and weakness of Germany, which France and the USSR had formerly viewed as an element making for stability in the international situation, were creating frustrations among the Germans that might rather contribute to instability. If neutralization were to be imposed on the Germans as the condition for reunification, and if they should accept this condition, then the "alarm system," as NATO has been called, would be moved back to the French borders. But significantly enough, the reunification and neutralization of Germany might diminish tensions both within Germany and within the Soviet bloc. And if they were so diminished, the attitude of the Soviet leaders toward the satellite states might grow more liberal, as indeed it had seemed to be doing since Stalin's death. The United States stood to gain much from a policy of furthering such liberalization and relief of tension.

Arab Nationalism

In the Middle East, the United States has attempted to balance European imperial interests with the nationalistic demands of the Arabs. After the Korean War, however, the containment policy identified the United States more closely with Europe's interests than with those of the Arab countries. The new situation suggested the desirability of re-establishing a balance between the dynamic objectives of self-determination demanded by the Arabs and orderly international behavior required by the British and French.

During 1955-1956 the Arab bloc, led by Egypt, strengthened its position and increasingly asserted its independence from the West. At the Bandung Conference in April, 1955, all but Turkey, Iran, and Iraq supported neutrality in the cold war. The attempt to include then British-controlled Jordan in the Middle East Treaty Organization in January 1956, provoked national uprisings and resulted in the expulsion of General Glubb, who had been the symbol of British influence. Antagonism toward Israel was a focus, as before, of Arab policy. Both the Arab states and Israel took increasingly tough attitudes; there was a reciprocal policy of reprisal, each violence being revenged with a still more violent act. As these incidents accumulated, Arab antagonism and Arab cohesion increased.

United States policies in the area were designed to salvage the deteriorating western prestige in the Arab world. The United States had refused to sell arms to the Arabs, but it also denied the Israeli request to buy arms after Egypt had made its arms-for-cotton deal with Czechoslovakia. The United States also sponsored Sudan as a new member of the United Nations, joined Great Britain and France in United Nations condemnations of Israeli aggression, and initiated United Nations mediation in the Israeli-Arab disputes. The Egyptian recognition of Communist China in May 1956 was not favorably received in the United States, however, and on July 21, the Egyptians were told that the United States would not help finance the $1.3-billion Aswan High Dam. Secretary Dulles had been irritated by the attitude of the Egyptian ruler, Colonel Nasser, who had presumed to exploit his position as a neutral by turning alternately to the USSR and to the United States. For this decision, Mr. Dulles received enthusiastic Congressional support from the cotton-growing areas, who feared Egyptian competition, and from Israeli sympathizers. Egypt's response was to nationalize the Suez Canal and propose to divert its revenues to the High Dam project. This action was unexpected; it was obvious that the United States had underestimated the fervor of the Egyptians. United States influence was successful in tempering the belligerency of Great Britain and France for several weeks, and Mr. Dulles prevailed upon them to call a series of conferences in London for the purpose of arranging international supervision of the Canal's operations, before discussing the problem in the Security Council of the United Nations.

The Far East

United States foreign policy in the Far East was confronted with three important problem areas: Communist China, Japan, and the neutralist bloc in South East Asia. The Chinese Communists were established more securely than many recognized Latin American governments, and their aggressions had been partially condoned by the Korean truce in 1953; but their truculent and unconciliatory leaders had given little evidence of understanding the western world. The United States not only refused to recognize the Communist government but also actively opposed its admission to the United Nations. With the USSR and its satellites members of the United Nations, Communist China's exclusion puzzled some observers, while others recalled the United States policy of diplomatically ignoring the USSR from 1917 to 1933. The nonrecognition policy, in any case, was morally satisfying to public sentiment in the United States, however unrealistic it may have been in a world where coexistence was the only alternative to nonexistence.

Japan's position in the Orient was not dissimilar to Germany's in Europe. The 1951 peace treaty had looked forward to Japan's being a counterbalance against Communist power, and had provided for the indefinite stationing of United States forces on its territory. Japan's foreign policies would reflect, sooner or later, domestic opposition to the presence of the United States garrisons.

Certain observers argued that it might be preferable under these circumstances to neutralize the Japanese archipelago; neutralization might conceivably reduce tensions between the Communist and free worlds, and eventually Japan might become a bridge between the two great world systems.

The Bandung Conference in April, 1955, had separated the neutralist countries in South East Asia from those committed to the West and to the Communists. The neutralists were led by India, and aided by the United Nations through the Colombo Plan. These countries felt, as Vice President Richard Nixon saw it, that their own internal problems compelled them to abstain from mutual-security pacts. Somewhat reluctantly Secretary Dulles accepted this sympathetic approach to Asiatic neutralism, and the United States has made more spirited efforts to increase economic aid to these countries.

The Evolution of a New International Situation?

United States policy-makers are compelled by rapidly changing world conditions to reassess the world situation in which they are operating. The dramatic events which accompanied the disruption of the Soviet satellite empire and the Egyptian crisis during November, 1956 precipitated the need for a careful reconsideration by the United States President and his advisers. Characteristic of the new developments, both in Eastern Europe and in the Near East, was the use of force as an instrument of foreign policy.

The first sharp test of the new Soviet policy in the satellites came in Poland on October 21, 1956, when a nationalistically oriented Communist, Wladyslaw Gomulka, was reinstated as secretary of the Polish Communist Party. The Soviet leaders gave their reluctant approval of the subsequent changes in the personnel and domestic policies of the Polish government. A similar situation in Hungary, however, was viewed in Moscow as having been the result of effective sabotage by the imperialist camp. Indeed, the Hungarian people, embittered by a decade of Soviet rule, had risen up, first against the USSR, and then against Communism itself. The Soviet response on November 4, 1956, was a brutal military attack on Hungary which broke active resistance within ten days. But the difficulties of the new Soviet-dominated regime were enormous; the country had been devastated, the people were sullen, and a general strike prevented reconstruction. An occupation policy of revenge was evident in the herding of men, women, and children indiscriminately into freight cars and sending them presumably to slave camps in the USSR.

Under the circumstances, President Eisenhower refused to use the Hungarian rising to lead a crusade for the liberation of the satellite countries. He furthermore disassociated the United States from a policy which had encouraged rebellion in these areas. Instead, the United States chose to bring the floodlight of world opinion upon the Soviet ruthlessness, in the forum of the United Nations. While this United States policy recognized the Soviet Union's special relationship with the satellite areas, the action helped publicize to the uncommitted areas of the world the intrinsically evil nature of Soviet policy.

Military force also figured heavily as the new policy component in the Middle East. Seizing advantage of the Soviet preoccupation in the satellite areas, and of United States involvement in presidential elections, Israeli troops attacked Egypt on October 30, 1956, swept through the Sinai peninsula to the Suez Canal and seized the Egyptian-held Gaza Strip on Israel's doorstep. Presumably in concerted action, France and Great Britain thereupon announced that their forces would occupy the Suez Canal Zone to insure continued traffic through the Canal, and bombed Egyptian airfields and barracks as a prelude to forceful entry when Egypt refused to accept the ultimatum. It was clear that all three governments hoped that their actions would so embarrass the Egyptian ruler, Gamal Abdel Nasser, that he would be forced to abdicate.

Initially, there was little reason why the United States should have responded sympathetically to these military acts; France and Great Britain had broken their treaty pledges by not consulting the United States in advance, both countries used military equipment from the United States which was committed exclusively for NATO objectives, the United States policy of reducing tensions in the area had been frustrated, and the way had been opened for greater Soviet involvement in the Middle East. Nevertheless, the United States once again appealed to the United Nations for a solution. The United States found itself aligned with the USSR against its western allies, who vetoed Security Council action in the matter. When the USSR subsequently announced that it would send volunteers to help the Egyptians, however, President Eisenhower took exception—but he declared that he would strongly support counter-action within the United Nations. An eventual cease-fire in the Egyptian conflict was secured under United Nations auspices and immediate steps were taken to develop the first United Nations emergency police force with which to supervise the evacuation of the foreign troops and stabilize the area.

Temporarily, at least, the United States policy was assuming that the brutal suppression of freedom in Hungary would have no sequel, that the USSR would not send its volunteers to support the Arabs, and that the Kremlin would not return to the Stalinist policies which had been disavowed so recently. Whether this appraisal of the situation was correct, only time would tell, but none would deny that the United States objectives in implementing the long-run purposes of the United Nations were nobly inspired. To be sure, the experience of that organization would not encourage optimistic hopes for its success in dealing with questions concerning the cold war and emerging nationalism. It remained to be seen whether the United Nations would be more successful now that it was vigorously supported by the United States.

Conclusion

Since 1945, the makers of foreign policy for the United States have had only limited success in defining the international situation as it has actually existed. At some times they defined it wrongly. George Kennan's remark in 1955, "I do not recognize the world of which Mr. Dulles is speaking," could with modifications have been applied to 1945, 1947, and 1950. The inexperience of President Truman and his Secretary of State, James F. Byrnes, may have been in part responsible for their oversimplified interpretations of the international situations they confronted. Mr. Truman's own forthright personality may have contributed to the stereotypes

into which the areas of the world were categorized. The same predilection for distinguishing right from wrong without noting intermediate positions has been characteristic of Mr. Dulles's statements on foreign policy.

Policy-makers have also been propelled toward oversimplification
by the need for securing the attention of an indifferent public
opinion and of the special interests in Congress. On occasion their
dramatization of the world situation has been too successful, and
the overreaction of a frightened public has resulted in the sacrifice
of desirable objectives. A country with immense capabilities for
promoting international order and progress can afford to have a
greater confidence in the success of its foreign-policy objectives. It
should not ignore the long-run need for international stability by
failing to assist underdeveloped areas, to promote self-government,
to implement human rights, and to institutionalize co-operation
in the United Nations. At the same time it must not overlook the
short-run considerations of national security and the settlement of
political disputes.

Policy-makers should therefore recognize with more accuracy
the complex international situation, while Congress and the public
should support multiple- rather than single-purpose objectives to
meet the situation. Finally, the procedures which are selected to
carry out these objectives should be executed with humility and
understanding. The victories of democracy occur not when men
are destroyed but when they are made wiser and more tolerant. The
citizens of the United States should remember that they are the
agents, not the authors, of the eternal truths in which they believe.
They should not see or claim as their personal power what in
reality is the power of these truths. Moderate and flexible procedures are as necessary as they are desirable for promoting short-
and long-run objectives in a complicated and continually changing
world.

BIBLIOGRAPHY

The problem of selectivity is raised when the substantive aspects
of United States foreign policy are considered. The general text
which best illustrates the dichotomy between the international

responsibilities of the United States in a changing world and the responses of public opinion is Thomas A. Bailey, *A Diplomatic History of the American People* (5th ed., Appleton-Century-Crofts, 1955). Marshall Knappen, *An Introduction to American Foreign Policy* (Harper and Bros., 1956), views the last decade as representing one situation, and is convinced that the flexible application of power politics through military alliances is still the best policy for the United States. The problem-solving approach has been developed for the years 1947-1954 under the guidance of the late Leo Pasvolsky, *Major Problems of United States Foreign Policy* (The Brookings Institution). The entire decade has recently been canvassed in *United States Foreign Policy, 1945-1955* (Brookings Institution, 1956). The series published for the Council on Foreign Relations and written until 1949 by J. C. Cambell *et al.*, and thereafter by R. P. Stebbins *et al.*, *The United States in World Affairs,* *1945-1947; 1948-1949; 1950; 1951; 1952; 1953; 1954; 1955* (Harper and Brothers), presents in a felicitous style the respective foreign and domestic factors involved in developing and executing foreign policies. The bibliographies and chronology of world events at the ends of these volumes are particularly useful, along with the short appraisals by Henry L. Roberts, "Recent Books on International Relations," in the quarterly *Foreign Affairs*. These publications should be compared with the international point of view reflected in the annual *Survey of International Affairs* (Royal Institute of International Affairs), a series developed by Arnold Toynbee for which Peter Calvocoressi is now responsible. The *New York Times* presents the best single contemporary coverage of foreign policy, but its approach in certain areas, as for example the Near East, should be compared with that of the *Christian Science Monitor*, which is more favorable to the Arabs.

Long-run responsibilities of United States foreign policy are necessarily emphasized in Goodrich and Simons, *The United Nations and the Maintenance of International Peace and Security,* (Brookings Institution, 1955), and Daniel S. Cheever and H. F. Haviland, Jr., *Organizing for Peace* (Houghton Mifflin, 1954). The limitations of United Nations procedures in settling ideological and political problems relating to Communism and nationalism are noted here. A study in a series sponsored by the Carnegie Endowment for International Peace, *The United States and the United Nations* (Manhattan Publishing Co.), promises to be the definitive work on this subject.

The inherent difficulties of the United States effort in foreign propaganda are sympathetically noted in Edward W. Barrett, *Truth Is Our Weapon* (Funk and Wagnalls, 1953), and are critically described by the Hungarian, Bela Szunyogh, *Psychological Warfare* (William-Frederick Press, 1955). Paul M. A. Linebarger, *Psychological Warfare* (Infantry Journal Press, 1948), reflects the short-run, military approach which may not be germane in a period of lessening tensions. John Scott, *Political Warfare: A Guide to Competitive Coexistence* (John Day Company, 1955), is a useful volume on techniques in which the author rejects preventive war, isolationism, and purely passive defense. Recent articles by Barbara Ward, George F. Kennan, and others (specifically placed elsewhere in this bibliography) have called attention to the possibilities of UNESCO, ECOSOC, and the specialized agencies as being more effective than national instruments as social and psychological tools of foreign policy. Philip Jessup et al., *International Regulation of Economic and Social Questions* (Carnegie Endowment for International Peace, 1955), surveys the developments in this field. Also emphasizing the international approach is Gunnar Myrdal, *An International Economy* (Harper and Brothers, 1956). The basic facts of the various disarmament proposals can be found in *The Disarmament Question 1945-1954* (British Information Service, 1954), and the use of the disarmament issue as a propaganda device has been described in the series *United States in Foreign Affairs* which has been mentioned.

Within the framework of power politics, Kenneth Ingram, *History of the Cold War* (Philosophical Library, 1955), dramatizes the importance of the interaction between the major contestants in the cold war as the important factor in creating the international situation. He notes that Soviet truculence has been on occasion a response to the western "get tough" policy. Henry L. Roberts, *Russia and America: Dangers and Prospects* (Harper and Brothers, 1956), reflects the conclusions of a two-year study for the Council of Foreign Relations, and suggests that while the United States should keep its powder dry, normal relations between the United States and the USSR can develop to the extent that the desires of the people of the Soviet Union become more important in decision making. George F. Kennan's appraisals of the softening of the Russian line appear in *US News and World Report* (June, 1956) and in *Harper's* (August, 1956). A contrary point of view can be found in Philip E. Mosely, "Soviet Foreign Policy: New Goals or New Manners?", *Foreign Affairs* (July, 1956).

The question of NATO and German reunification has been fully canvassed in recent periodical literature and in William W. Kaufman (ed.), *Military Policy and National Security* (Princeton, 1956). George Kennan and James Warburg represent a minority view in their support for neutralization of Germany, as does Jean-Louis Astier, *La Politique Étrangère des États-Unis vers l'Allemagne* (Librairie Nizet, Paris; 1956). Lord Ismay, *NATO—The First Five Years, 1949-1954* (Bosch, Utrecht; 1955), suggests the problem of maintaining the European defense establishment as tensions have lessened.

Recent books on United States foreign policy in Asia have emphasized the need to implement economic and psychological rather than military approaches. Edwin O. Reischauer, *Wanted: An Asian Policy* (Alfred A. Knopf, 1955) suggests that security pacts are least effective, that economic development is too slow and costly, and that propaganda and education can contribute the most for this area. Lawrence H. Battistini, *The United States and Asia* (F. A. Praeger, 1956), feels that the fight for freedom in Asia should be against its most pernicious scourge—abject and degrading poverty. W. W. Rostow and Richard W. Hatch, *American Policy in Asia* (John Wiley and Sons, 1955) are sympathetic toward a policy of recognizing Communist China, and a legal case for recognition can be found in Quincy Wright, "The Chinese Recognition Problem," *American Journal of International Law* (July, 1955), pp. 320-339.

The problem of nationalism in underdeveloped countries has been extensively considered. Miriam S. Farley, *United States Relations with Southeast Asia* (Institute of Pacific Relations, 1955), and William Henderson, *The New Nations of Southeast Asia* (Foreign Policy Association, 1955), highlight these situations and the responding foreign policies. Halford L. Hoskins, *Middle East* (Macmillan, 1954) is sympathetic to the Arab problem. An authoritative Israeli writer should also be mentioned—Walter Z. Laqueur, *Communism and Nationalism in the Middle East* (F. A. Praeger, 1956).

Latin America

LUIS QUINTANILLA

Ambassador of Mexico
to the
Organization of American States

Latin America

CHAPTER 5

BASIC TENETS OF LATIN AMERICAN INTERNATIONAL POLICY

Latin America is an important factor of international politics. It occupies twice the area of Europe and two and a half times that of continental United States. Its population compares with that of the United States and Canada combined, and is growing at the rate of 2.5 per cent annually, among the highest in the world.

The twenty Latin American republics are not only increasing their population steadily; they are also making great strides in the fields of culture and modern industry. At present only two cities on the American continent,[1] New York and Chicago, are larger than Buenos Aires, Mexico City, or Rio de Janeiro. Among "Latin" capitals only Paris ranks any of these. All of them far surpass in population either Rome or Madrid. Portuguese-speaking Brazil is the most populous "Latin" country on earth, exceeding Italy by about 20 per cent. And, in order to suggest the significance of the Latin American capitals, one could mention that Mexico City is an outstanding international center in modern painting as well as in archeology and architecture.

For the United States, Latin America has special significance.

[1] "Continent" is used, in this and the following chapter, in the singular. Latin Americans never pluralize "continent" when it applies to America as a whole (from Canada to Argentina). They hold that America is essentially one continent. Geography, if nothing else, supports their view.

The North American nation shares the continent with sister republics whose twenty votes have often proved decisive in the making of momentous United Nations decisions, not to mention measures adopted within the Organization of American States, known as the OAS.

The annual trade of the United States with Latin America is about $3.5 billion in each direction. In a report to the President by Dr. Milton S. Eisenhower, as special ambassador, this highly respected scholar wrote in 1953: "As a market for our commercial *exports* Latin America is as important to us as all of Europe and more important than Asia, Africa, and Oceania combined. As a source of United States *imports*, the Latin American republics have even greater relative importance, standing well ahead of Europe or other continents."[2]

In matters of foreign policy, each Latin American country faces many specific problems arising from individual domestic conditions. So, when examining the international position of Latin America, we must limit our analysis to only a few general aspects, more or less generic to all the members of that large community. We shall consider here the following: *national sovereignty, peaceful solution of international controversies, collective security, peaceful coexistence, eagerness for democracy, economic co-operation, and inter-American solidarity.*

National Sovereignty

The countries of Latin America are passionately independent. From the territory of the colonies that revolted against Spain, eighteen nations emerged and not even the extraordinary genius of Simón Bolívar could hold them together. In contrast, the Anglo-Saxon[3] and Portuguese colonies became single countries after winning their freedom. Had the Spanish colonies acted in like man-

[2] "Report to the President, United States-Latin American Relations," by Milton S. Eisenhower, Department of State Publication 5290, Inter-American Series 47, December 1953, pp. 2-3.

[3] This expression, convenient to Latin Americans, dismisses many components in the national cultures of Canada and the United States, as the expression "Latin America" likewise dismisses many components in the national cultures of the states it embraces.

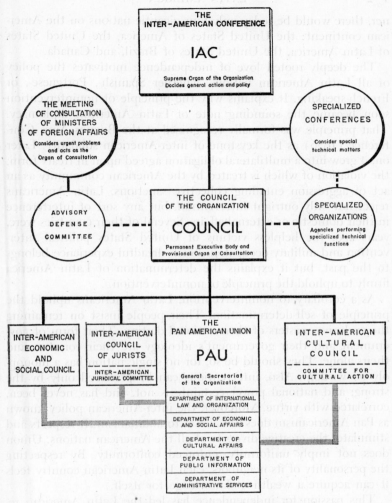

THE
INTER-AMERICAN CONFERENCE

IAC

Supreme Organ of the Organization
Decides general action and policy

THE MEETING
OF CONSULTATION
OF MINISTERS
OF FOREIGN AFFAIRS

Considers urgent problems
and acts as the
Organ of Consultation

SPECIALIZED
CONFERENCES

Consider special
technical matters

THE COUNCIL
OF THE ORGANIZATION

COUNCIL

Permanent Executive Body and
Provisional Organ of Consultation

ADVISORY
DEFENSE
COMMITTEE

SPECIALIZED
ORGANIZATIONS

Agencies performing
specialized technical
functions

INTER-AMERICAN
ECONOMIC
AND
SOCIAL COUNCIL

INTER-AMERICAN
COUNCIL
OF JURISTS

INTER-AMERICAN
JURIDICAL COMMITTEE

THE
PAN AMERICAN UNION

PAU

General Secretariat
of the Organization

DEPARTMENT OF INTERNATIONAL
LAW AND ORGANIZATION

DEPARTMENT OF ECONOMIC
AND SOCIAL AFFAIRS

DEPARTMENT OF
CULTURAL AFFAIRS

DEPARTMENT OF
PUBLIC INFORMATION

DEPARTMENT OF
ADMINISTRATIVE SERVICES

INTER-AMERICAN
CULTURAL
COUNCIL

COMMITTEE FOR
CULTURAL ACTION

THE ORGANIZATION OF AMERICAN STATES

The international organization of the 21 American republics established by
the charter signed at the Ninth International Conference of American States,
Bogota, Colombia, 1948.

The three councils of the Pan American Union have as their Executive Secretaries the Directors of the Corresponding Departments.

ner, there would be today only four gigantic nations on the American continent: the United States of America, the United States of Latin America, the United States of Brazil, and Canada.

The deeply rooted love of independence motivates the policy of all Latin American nations, whether Spanish-, Portuguese-, or French-speaking. It explains why the principle of nonintervention soon became the sounding note 'of Latin American diplomacy. That principle was formally recognized at the Buenos Aires Conference (1936) as the keystone of inter-American solidarity. Later on, it grew into a multilateral obligation agreed upon in treaty form, the violation of which is treated by the American community as an act of aggression entailing collective sanctions. Latin Americans reject not only outright intervention, but any sort of interference in their domestic or external affairs. Several of their countries were, years ago, the helpless victims of United States political intervention and military occupation. Such dreadful experience belongs to the past, but it explains the determination of Latin America firmly to uphold the principle of nonintervention.

As a corollary to nonintervention, Latin Americans uphold the principle of self-determination. Their people insist on remaining the exclusive masters of their national destiny. Their form of government and their government's ideology are their concern, and theirs alone. They should be so, for no single nation has a monopoly on wisdom. Also, interventions can be practiced only by the strong; and national power certainly is not, and has never been, correlated with virtue. Moreover, the inter-American policy known as Pan Americanism does not aim at totalitarianism. It respects and stimulates the creative diversity of all the American nations. Union does not imply uniformity, enforced conformity. By respecting the personality of its neighbors, each Latin American country feels it can acquire a wealth of knowledge for itself.

This passion for independence has led the Latin American republics to clarify the nature and to limit the extent of diplomatic protection. Since they are no longer colonial territories, their governments share the view that no trace of extraterritoriality shall ever be tolerated among them. When a foreign citizen decides to settle and live in a country, Latin Americans assume that he is willing to respect its laws. He must not, therefore, unduly invoke the diplomatic protection of his native land whenever legal dispositions of the country where he has chosen to live become distasteful to him. Otherwise, the double status of such a foreigner would place him in a better position than his countrymen at home, for he could claim at will the advantages of both the laws of his own country and those of the foreign nation of his residence, with the added privilege that "diplomatic protection" would keep him out of whatever juridical situation he might dislike. This policy of Latin America against the abuse of diplomatic protection is similar to that adopted by all other civilized regions of the world. We mention it here because, in the past, this question has been the cause of international trouble.

In fact, the concern for absolute sovereignty led the Latin American governments to proclaim three juridical doctrines which have become a part of Latin American public law: the Calvo Doctrine, the Drago Doctrine and the Estrada Doctrine.

As early as 1868 a celebrated Argentine jurist, Carlos Calvo, stated that it was contrary to fundamental principles of international law to grant foreigners a position of privilege, and that it was an abuse of physical power for a stronger state to exact, on behalf of its nationals, pecuniary indemnity from a weaker state. Local courts, he submitted, had final jurisdiction over the complaints of aliens, and the privilege of diplomatic recourse should be denied to the aliens by their own governments; diplomatic intervention should be ignored as nonvalid by the foreign country in which the aliens were living. This *Calvo Doctrine* has been applied in Latin America to contracts between the government and an alien, and in this sense has been known as the Calvo Clause. It provides that the foreigner "renounces all rights to prefer a diplomatic claim in regard to rights and obligations derived from the contract," or else that "all doubts and disputes" arising under it "shall be submitted to the local courts without the right to claim [the] diplomatic interposition" of the alien's government. In spite of its historical justification and juridical soundness, the Calvo Doctrine was not accepted by the United States and several European countries. But it stands unquestionably as a basic tenet of Latin American policy in favor of the final jurisdiction of local courts.

The *Drago Doctrine* was originated by another distinguished jurist from Argentina, Luis Drago, who was Minister of Foreign Affairs of his country in 1902. In that year Great Britain, Italy, and Germany jointly intervened against Venezuela on the ground that they were seeking to collect unpaid bonds held by their citizens. Drago then submitted a note to the United States Department of State proposing a policy to the effect that "the public debt [of an American State] cannot occasion armed intervention or the occupation of the territory of American nations by a European power." Drago protested against the use of armed force in the collection of public debts. He argued that the purchaser of a foreign bond buys with open eyes and in the price paid takes account of the value of the security, the credit of the debtor government, and all the other factors which enter into the bargain. He added that the emission of the loan and bond is an act of sovereignty; that the creditor knows the payment may be refused or the debt reduced by similar act; that the usual civil remedies are barred and that the state is the sole judge of its ability to pay. He maintained that it is unfair for the people of both countries involved to make this voluntary contract the subject of armed political action involving whole nations, and also make a government the guarantor of its citizens' investments abroad. Professor Borchard points out: "The Drago Doctrine is mainly of interest because it calls attention to the political danger and the undesirability of armed intervention on behalf of private claimants of all kinds, not because the evil which Drago feared was particularly notorious."[4]

There is a third Latin American doctrine also connected with the defense of national sovereignty and political independence: the *Estrada Doctrine*. It was formulated in 1930 by Genaro Estrada, then Minister of Foreign Relations of Mexico. In his statement issued on September 27, 1930, Estrada mentioned the fact that Mexico and various Latin American republics had suffered during

---

[4] "Calvo and Drago Doctrines." Article by Edwin M. Borchard, *Encyclopedia of the Social Sciences*, vol. III, pp. 153-157.

many years the consequences of a policy of recognition of governments "which allows foreign governments to act as the arbiters of the legitimacy or illegitimacy of another government, subjecting to the opinion of foreign powers the legal capacity or the national advent of an administration." Estrada explained that the abuse of the policy of recognition had affected particularly the Latin American countries. Mexico, said he, stands against the practice of "recognition" because it is an insulting practice which hurts the sovereignty of other nations. Therefore—and because Estrada left the consequence unsaid, his doctrine lends itself to some confusion—governments should abandon altogether both the concept and the practice of "recognition" of other governments and limit themselves, as the original Estrada statement did say, to maintaining or withdrawing diplomatic agents without any implication whatsoever as to the legitimacy or illegitimacy of the other governments. In other words, let governments carry their usual diplomatic business according to their national interest, but without thinking in terms of "recognition." It was indeed an original and revolutionary idea. If the Estrada Doctrine had merely stated, "the concept and practice of recognition of governments are things which belong to the past; governments must now forsake them and agree that diplomatic relations do not necessarily imply any endorsement of a foreign government's policy," it would have been perhaps more clearly understood by all. Like the Calvo and the Drago doctrines, it was aimed at preventing intervention and safeguarding the political independence of the American republics.[5]

Peaceful Solution of International Controversies

No sooner had they won their national independence than the Latin American republics began to explore the possibilities of establishing a juridical system for the peaceful solution of all controversies among them. The first step was taken at the historic Congress convened by Simón Bolívar in the city of Panama (1826). At the time, governments were inclined to settle their disputes in traditional terms of military power and political influence. The new emphasis laid by Latin Americans on the supremacy of law

[5] See, however, the paragraph concerning the Tobar Doctrine, p. 185.

for the solution of international differences appeared then rather unrealistic. Yet, as later developments proved, Latin Americans were right. Law is the protection of the weak and also benefits the strong; it assures to both the minimum of stability without which the former would live in constant fear, and the latter in constant peril of abusing his power.

The *"Pact"* of Bogota (not to be confused with the *"Charter"* of Bogota), drafted by the American governments in 1948, is without doubt the most complete and advanced juridical instrument of peaceful solution ever conceived. Nine countries have ratified it up to 1956: Costa Rica, Dominican Republic, El Salvador, Haiti, Honduras, Mexico, Nicaragua, Panama, Uruguay. Their governments are inexorably bound by the terms of this Pact to settle *all* their differences in a peaceful way. The Pact embodies every known procedure of peaceful solution: from good offices to arbitration. It leaves no escape; *all* controversies submitted to the mechanism of this treaty are to be solved peacefully. Latin Americans can be proud of this Pact. If the example were followed by all countries, a decisive step would have been taken in the direction of a permanent international peace.

And there are other notable Latin American contributions in this all-important matter. The *Inter-American Peace Commission* is one of them. Its purpose is not so ambitious as that of the Pact of Bogota. This truly original Commission is staffed by representatives of a small number of American countries periodically selected by all the American governments. It is not a court, nor a tribunal; it never judges, but simply recommends means by which the governments asking the Commission's friendly help could reach a peaceful settlement of their dispute. It only makes recommendations of procedure; it never enters into the merits of any specific case. The interested governments may accept or reject its suggestions. Nevertheless, in spite of the Commission's apparent weakness, it succeeded in promoting the settlement of every inter-American conflict brought to its attention up to 1956. There have been five such conflicts: (1) Dominican Republic v. Cuba (1948); (2) Haiti v. Dominican Republic (1949); (3) the Caribbean "situation" (1949); (4) Cuba v. Dominican Republic (1951);

and (5) Colombia v. Peru (1953), over the Haya de la Torre asylum case, although in this case one of the parties, the Peruvian government, courteously rejected the services of the Inter-American Peace Commission. In the Guatemalan situation (1954)—incredible as it may sound—the Inter-American Peace Commission was expressly excluded because the Guatemalan government then in power bluntly and repeatedly rejected the Commission's assistance when it could have been decisive.

The efficiency of the regional system for maintaining peace in America has been definitely established. The Commission has a truly impressive record. Diplomatic observers, in other parts of the world, would be wise to examine carefully the nature and operation of the Inter-American Peace Commission. Its very existence is a tribute to Latin America's statesmanship, for the creation of this peace-making body came out of a Haitian proposal to the Consultative Meeting of Foreign Ministers held at Havana, Cuba, in the year 1940.

Collective Security

The third original feature of Latin America's international position is its emphasis on collective security, a principle so fundamental that it can be seen as the *raison d'être* of the Organization of American States as well as of the United Nations, the basic philosophy and outstanding function of any conceivable type of international order. In this respect Latin Americans have been, as in other respects, the modest pioneers of a transcendental concept of international law.

In the year 1826, nearly a century before the first League of Nations was created, the plenipotentiaries of the Latin American nations had proclaimed, at the Conference convened by Bolívar in Panama, the determination of the new American family of nations to apply collective security as a policy for insuring permanent international peace. This proposal was sensational since sheer national power had until then been taken as the supreme factor of international politics, and each country was left to assume, alone or in association with a group of allied governments, the defense of its sovereignty, political independence, and territorial integrity. The result of such practice was disastrous: ever larger armies, costly armaments races, a precarious balance of hostile groups, and finally wars and more wars. Unrestricted national power created nothing but international anarchy, a world living in constant fear. Small countries remained at the mercy of big powers and big powers readily succumbed to the temptation of starting bloody wars in order to eliminate their rivals.

"Imperial peace" and "power politics" have seen their day. They are now being replaced by the very policy of "collective security" first advocated by the Latin American governments in 1826, later adopted by the League of Nations in 1920, and still more recently at San Francisco in 1945 by the United Nations. "One for all and all for one": it may take mankind another generation to enforce such policy. But the idea is moving forward and it is to the credit of Latin Americans that their countries led the way. The development shows that quite often what is regarded as idealistic turns out to be most practical, that human ideals may be the anticipation of history.

The Rio Treaty, signed by the American governments in the Brazilian capital in 1947, is a model pact of collective security. The signatories agreed to assist collectively any one of them that might be subjected to aggression or to armed attack. It does not constitute a military alliance. It is exclusively a pact of defensive solidarity. The American republics can apply it only in case of aggression, armed attack, or any other threat affecting the territory, the sovereignty, or the political independence of any of them. It has been applied in four specific occasions: the Costa Rica-Nicaragua conflict (December 1948); the dispute between Haiti and the Dominican Republic (January 1950); also the bitter controversy between the Dominican Republic, Haiti, and Cuba in which Guatemala later became involved (January 1950); and, more recently, the spectacular conflict between Costa Rica and Nicaragua (January 1955). In all these instances, inter-American wars were prevented and the Rio Treaty proved its worth.

There is a side of the Rio Treaty which, however, requires clarification: the Treaty must not be invoked and utilized for collective political intervention. Mexico and Argentina at the

Inter-American Conference of Caracas (1954), and Ecuador and Uruguay in the Council of the OAS (1954), stated concretely their opinion on this point. The issue involved, on this particular occasion, was communist "infiltration" in the republic of Guatemala. The existence of the so-called "cold war" did not encourage examination of the matter with complete objectivity. Nevertheless, Argentina, Ecuador, Mexico, and Uruguay stated in no uncertain terms, at Caracas or later on in the OAS Council, that the Rio Treaty must not be invoked to justify collective action against any American government simply because of the latter's political ideology. The Rio Treaty deals fundamentally with states, not with ideas. It authorizes economic, military, and diplomatic sanctions against aggressor governments, but does not envisage sanctions against a government because its political philosophy happens to be out of step with the political views shared by the other members of the family. The fact that the "charge" against the Guatemalan government was "communism" makes little difference so far as intervention is concerned: a government's ideology is the exclusive responsibility of its people, no matter how unpopular that ideology may seem to others. The fear of intervention remains the best guarantee that "collective security" such as contemplated by the Rio Treaty will never be transformed into an expedient policy available for committing or condoning the very evil it was intended to prevent.

Even so, the American republics, or rather the Latin American republics, would very possibly feel justified in applying the Rio Treaty in order to safeguard the political independence of any of them if a foreign government of whatever ideology, communist or capitalist, were intervening in their domestic affairs through its agents or through acts clearly involving its responsibility. In such a case the Rio Treaty would indeed be applied against the actual intervention of such government, but not against the "intervention" of a "foreign" ideology. Ideologies are made up of ideas, and all ideas are, by their very nature, universal. How could governments, for instance, enforce diplomatic, economic or military sanctions against social theories or philosophical doctrines? Ideas cannot be punished or defeated, except by better and more convincing ideas. Treaty sanctions, under collective security, can be applied only against specific and concrete acts of governments, never against ideologies *per se*. Whether right or wrong or whether right or left, political ideas remain ideas. As such, they are beyond the reach of law. They belong to the intellectual and cultural world and they should, under democratic government, enjoy the constructive privilege of competing freely in the intellectual markets of mankind.

Peaceful Coexistence

The next outstanding trait of Latin America's general policy is the faith that Latin Americans have always placed in peaceful international coexistence. As soon as their independence was established and they had outlined a system of peaceful solution for all their controversies, and also subscribed a pact of collective security tending to warrant permanent international peace, Latin Americans voiced their adherence to the principle of peaceful international coexistence.

In anticipation of the 1826 Inter-American Conference held in Panama, Simón Bolívar wrote in 1815: "May God grant that some day we may have the happiness of installing there an august Congress to discuss and study the high interests of peace and war with the nations of the world." And, in a document dated February 1826, Bolívar predicted: "The New World will be composed of independent nations, all bound together by a common law that will determine their external relations. Perhaps in the march of centuries one nation alone—the Federal Nation—will embrace the universe." Thus, Bolívar envisioned both a regional organization and an eventual world organization. The inter-American system would, for him, serve as an inspiration for the future world organization; in fact, Bolivar had expressed such ideas since 1812. A century later, Woodrow Wilson knowingly or unknowingly followed Bolívar's plan. True, other people in America, as well as in Europe, had thought of maintaining international peace through some kind of world organization, but Bolívar, like Wilson and later Franklin Roosevelt, not only advocated the idea but also implemented it.

In the same document of February 1826, Bolívar summarized further his view on the coming Inter-American Assembly: "This Congress seems destined to form the largest, most extraordinary, and strongest League that has yet appeared on the face of the earth. Mankind will give a thousand blessings to this League. Political society will be given a Code of Public Law to be used as a rule of universal conduct in their relations. The very life of these new states will receive new guarantees. None will be inferior to others and none stronger. A perfect equilibrium will be established in this truly new order of things. The power of all would come to the rescue of any that might suffer from external aggression. Differences of origin and race will lose influence and strength. Social reform will be reached under the holy auspices of liberty and social peace." Here we have, in the year 1826, about a century before the League of Nations, the substance of international order and world organization. Even the name "League" was there.

Practically every important declaration voted upon since then in Pan American meetings brings out the importance of "convivencia." This Spanish word, whose nearest English equivalent is "coexistence," sounds familiar to any Latin American ear. "Convivencia" stems from the Latin "cum vivere," literally "to live with."

The American nations have always been optimistic. The vastness of their continent, their unexplored riches, plus the racial, cultural, and religious diversity of their countries and peoples, helped them to conceive a world in permanent peace. Latin Americans believe in such a world, not because its prospect has now acquired popularity, but because they have always considered it desirable. The apocalyptical possibilities of the atomic age strengthen this belief. No sane person can, in our generation, advocate wars. Nuclear bombs have provided the big powers with a weapon of global extinction which not only can destroy their enemies but can also wipe out civilization and decimate mankind. So there can be no more wars. It is no more a question of choice. Before the atomic age the alternative was peace or war; it has become peace or mutual extermination. And mankind, made up of living creatures, is in no hurry to die. The superbomb, because of its unlimited power of destruction, has in this respect obliged men to establish world peace. The atom has become the effective agent for world peace and may have succeeded where common sense and ethical principles had failed.

Yet Latin Americans are not advocates of peace at any price. A well-known Spanish proverb reads: "Better to die on one's feet than to live on one's knees"; Latin Americans fully agree with it. What they have traditionally claimed is that a peaceful international *convivencia* is both practical and convenient.

The notion of "coexistence" is even less ambitious than the Latin American concept of *convivencia*. Coexistence simply means existence together; *convivencia* means living together. Life ranks higher than existence. Material objects exist, human beings live. Coexistence could imply the mere indifferent toleration of somebody else's existence. *Convivencia*, in contrast, implies finding a way of living as good neighbors. Latin Americans need not be convinced of the wisdom of peaceful coexistence: *convivencia* was in their hearts since the very first moments of Pan Americanism.

Eagerness for Democracy

A somewhat vague but deeply felt eagerness for democracy must now be mentioned as another feature of Latin America's position in world affairs. In international gatherings, as well as in domestic constitutions and laws, Latin Americans always speak for democracy. Not because they contend that their governments have always behaved in the past as models of democracy, or are thus behaving today. Far from it! Their contention is not that all of the Latin American republics have reached democratic maturity, but that a basic democratic aspiration exists in the hearts and minds of their peoples.

Rash statements concerning Latin America's political setbacks are not in order. Where are the perfect democracies? All admit that nations should practice what they preach, but do all conform with such a rule? Furthermore, even sinners can and ought to seek virtue. Democracy is a goal, not an actual possession.

As in the case of the United States, the achievement of independence by the Latin American nations was followed by republican and democratic forms of government, except for short-lived periods of monarchical regimes in three of them. The British revolution of 1688 and the French and American revolutions of the eighteenth century were inspirations to the fathers of Latin America's independence. Their influence can be seen in every Latin American constitution. Popular sovereignty, equality before the law, free elections, division of powers, and a republican form of government: these and other democratic tenets are incorporated in Latin American constitutions. Nevertheless, democracy has not been successfully established throughout the American continent. Americans, North and South, are determined to establish it, and so deeply rooted is their love of democracy that no dictatorship can feel secure on American soil.

Also, it is surprising how vague the word "democracy" can become in the minds of people with different national problems. This magic word embraces so much that those who use it too lightly very often find themselves talking in the end about entirely different values. If such confusion occurs among citizens of one country, the difficulties of understanding the concepts of democracy in foreign countries loom even larger; for the democracy of each nation is likely to possess special characteristics which are the direct result of peculiar domestic conditions.

For one thing, it is agreed that poverty, ignorance, and widespread disease are harmful to democracy. People who are hungry, illiterate, and undermined by endemic diseases can hardly organize themselves anywhere as a militant force for democracy. Unfortunately, a large percentage of Latin America's population is hampered by precisely such material conditions. Until these handicaps are removed, not all the Latin Americans will be able to participate in the active promotion of their national democracy.

The indigenous peoples were exploited during three centuries of colonial rule. Millions of Latin American workers, especially these indigenes, are surviving at present by a miracle of nature. Their diet is so meager that even technical experts, in recent official reports, have reached the sad conclusion that these helpless victims of human greed live in constant danger of physical ex-

tinction.[6] There are, it is true, some international causes at the
bottom of so regrettable a situation, but Latin Americans themselves are directly and mainly responsible for what happens inside
their borders.

Moreover, economic conditions are not the only obstacles in the
path of democracy on the American continent. Democracy cannot
function without due respect for universal suffrage and popular
sovereignty. Free elections are the only assurance that popular
sovereignty will be respected. Democracy always assumes that
political issues can be settled without violence and by majority
rule; that minorities are to abide by such rule; and that majorities,
in turn, will respect minority rights. Furthermore, democracy cannot function without freedom of thought, freedom of assembly,
and freedom of the press. Citizens in a democracy must tolerate
political opposition and dissent, no matter how strongly they feel
against them. Freedom does not mean granting others only the
right to agree, but also the right to disagree; otherwise the difference would be one of mere labels between democracy and
totalitarianism. Democracy welcomes criticism and opposition;
totalitarianism tolerates only obedience and applause.

A further block against the democratic process of Latin America
has been the often abusive interference of the military in political
matters. Citizens properly respect the army, an institution whose
sacred duty is to protect national sovereignty and independence.
Like the national flag, the army is a symbol of nationality. But
militaristic *coups d'état*, wherever they occur, are a blow to democratic institutions. They certainly do not help democracy.

Neither does *caudillismo*, strong-man rule, the evils of which
Latin Americans have traditionally suffered. Democracy has nothing in common with government by force or with arbitrary rule
whether by civilian or military dictators. Democracy can be promoted only under freedom and by democratic means. The only
way to save democracy is to practice it. And not only must it be

[6] "Conditions of Life and Work of Indigenous Populations of Latin American Countries," Report II, Fourth Conference of American States Members
of the International Labour Organization, Montevideo, April 1949; Geneva,
International Labour Office, 1949.

protected from outside threats; it must also be defended from within. What people stand "against" is significant, but what they stand "for" is, to say the least, equally important. Thus, it is not enough for anyone to assert: "I am against communism." He may say it truly, but saying it does not prove that he stands for democracy.

While serving as Foreign Minister of Ecuador, Carlos Tobar stated in 1907 the following: "The most efficient means of putting an end to violent changes of government inspired by ambition, which so often perturb the progress and development of the Latin American nations and cause bloody civil wars, would be for the American governments to deny recognition of accidental regimes born of revolutions until it has been proved that such regimes are backed by the people.[7]

The five Central American republics concluded, in 1907 and 1923, treaties embodying this doctrine, basically incompatible with the noninterventionist doctrine later advocated by Estrada. They bound themselves "not to recognize any government coming into power through a *coup d'état* or through a revolution against duly established authorities, as long as the representatives of the people, freely elected, have not constitutionally reorganized the country."[8] Costa Rica in 1932, and El Salvador in 1933, denounced the treaty of 1923. The well-meaning *Tobar Doctrine* had failed to prosper.

And now it is pleasant to present a favorable aspect of Latin American democracy: its century-old adherence to the theory and practice of political and territorial asylum.

Latin American governments share the view that they must protect, in their embassies or their territories, the lives of political dissenters whose only "crime" has been to oppose actively their own government. This doctrine of asylum is essentially humanitarian. It represents a notable contribution of Latin America to the over-all protection of human rights. Mexico has carried by far

[7] "Curso de Derecho Internacional Público Americano," Carlos Sánchez y Sánchez, Editora Montalvo, Ciudad Trujillo, Dominican Republic, 1943, p. 655.
[8] "Evolución del Panamericanismo," Enrique Gil, Librería y Casa Editora de Jesús Menendez, Buenos Aires, 1933, p. 277.

the heaviest burden in the practice of this doctrine. Its territory and its diplomatic missions abroad have granted protection to a large number of political refugees. In order to survive, the practice of asylum will have to be, however, respected with equal zeal by all Latin American governments, for no single one of them can be expected to assume, unilaterally and by itself, the heavy responsibilities inherent in this humanitarian policy.

Finally, there is an aspect of their social democracy of which Latin Americans can be legitimately proud: racial equality. Latin Americans have no race problems. They stand for complete and absolute racial equality. It must surprise nobody, therefore, that in international conferences Latin American voices always speak strongly against racial discrimination, however masked. As a matter of fact, the great majority of the Latin American countries proclaimed simultaneously their independence and the abolition of slavery.

Of one thing the rest of the world can be sure: Latin America, born under liberty, will remain on the side of democracy.

Economic Co-operation

Economic co-operation between governments is the next feature in this survey of Latin America's international position.

Latin Americans are pictured too often as idealistic and romantic creatures. They do love beauty, and art is for them a vital necessity. Their culture is essentially artistic. But the strong emphasis placed by Latin Americans on the material and economic aspects of Pan Americanism is definite proof that they know how and when to keep their feet on the ground.

Nearly all the theoretical avenues of Pan Americanism have been explored. The philosophy of the inter-American system has reached impressive heights. Latin Americans want now to implement the economic substance of their regional association. Pan Americanism means to them something more tangible than political and juridical commitments. They will insist increasingly on economic measures. They hold that, just as the American governments are helping each other in the field of international politics, they can and must help each other in the field of economics.

In the past, economic *laissez faire* was the national and international policy. Governments were expected to take no economic initiatives and not to interfere with the competitive mechanism of free enterprise. Private initiative was to maintain the entire economy. This viewpoint applied to international policy as well. All that governments had to do was to promote and protect private initiative and private foreign investments. There is nothing evil in such policy. It did help; but it is not enough. Regional and world organizations have introduced a new concept: the direct responsibility of governments to help each other. In this new light, governments have acquired a new obligation which they cannot transfer to private initiative. The complementary action of private initiative and government helps both and harms neither. Private capital and governmental aid support each other; they are not at all incompatible. There are things that private initiative can do, and many others that only governments can accomplish.

Latin Americans know very well the power and possibilities of official help. Within the OAS, which is an association of governments, international co-operation clearly means co-operation *between governments*. And when, for any reason, such co-operation is ignored or relegated to the vague eventualities of private capital, Latin Americans have a right to argue that the OAS Charter is being sidetracked; particularly when Latin America sees that the Washington government follows systematically an official policy of all-out economic co-operation with nations on other continents, and that it does so in government-to-government transactions.

Latin America has never asked for and never received grants or handouts from the United States or any other government. But the Latin American nations are entitled to expect ordinary financial facilities and the adoption of effective inter-American measures likely to promote their economic development. These would not favor Latin America alone; they would benefit the United States as well as Latin America.

In his 1953 report, quoted earlier, Dr. Milton Eisenhower wrote to the President: "Unfortunately, the people of the United States do not seem generally to comprehend the full significance to us of stable economic relations with Latin America. It is difficult to exaggerate the need of South America for capital to promote a sound economic development. The nations of Latin America pay for what they obtain from us. Their purchases from us are governed almost wholly by the volume of our purchases from them." And in a recent publication of the Pan American Union, Dr. Eduardo Zuleta-Angel, then Ambassador of the Republic of Colombia in Washington, commented: "Everything Latin America buys in the United States is paid for with money which Latin Americans earned with the sweat of their brow, while other continents pay for their purchases with money presented to them by the United States."[9]

Investments of private United States capital throughout Latin America amount to $6 billion. They yield a profit of nearly $1 billion annually, which means more than 16 per cent return to the United States investors.

Latin America is willing and ready to increase its business relations with the United States. What it could never do is to freeze its possibilities for progress, should inter-American economic cooperation fail to produce concrete results. In that case Latin America will, of course, notably increase its international trade with other regions of the world, for inter-American solidarity can never be bought by giving up Latin America's prosperity. If financial policies of the United States handicap or prevent Latin America's trade with the North American republic, then Latin America may have to trade with countries of different ideology.

Latin America and the United States

A survey would be incomplete if it failed to mention another feature of Latin America's international policy: the special ties of friendship that bind it to the United States.

The Latin American countries had, in the past, a great deal of trouble with the United States. Happily for inter-American solidarity, the days of "dollar diplomacy," the "big-stick policy," and outright military occupation have given way to the "good-neighbor policy." There is today no basic antagonism between Latin Amer-

[9] "A Program of Inter-American Public Relations," Pan American Union, Washington, D.C., 1955.

ica and the United States. The two have a common denominator: the western hemisphere, or something which could be called "Americanity."

There exists no cleavage between the two Americas and it is absurd to think that Latin Americans dislike their northern neighbor. In spite of past difficulties, and some present misunderstandings, Latin Americans as a whole are sincere friends of the United States. They admire its people, whose technical ability, business genius, and humanitarian spirit have succeeded in creating one of the very great nations of history.

Latin Americans are the best customers of the United States and the United States is the best customer of Latin America, and regardless of economic reasons, Latin Americans are proud of the spectacular success achieved by their Anglo-Saxon neighbor. A tribute rendered to the United States is taken by them as a tribute to the American world. In this respect, Latin Americans have always been ahead of the United States: to them, the word "America" embraces the entire continent. They share an intuitive feeling of Americanity.

Since the early days of independence, Latin American statesmen have kept in mind the totality of the continent. Pan Americanism was conceived as a policy embracing all the members of the American family. It is natural, therefore, that Latin Americans feel so close to the United States, not only geographically but historically and sentimentally as well. And because of it, they expect a reciprocal attitude of friendship from the United States. When the Washington government seems to ignore them, they resent it. And they have been ignored quite often.

Unlike other countries, the Latin American republics have neither asked nor received economic handouts. All they ask, properly so, is to be treated as friends. They have grown up so much that they should not be forgotten. History is on America's side. The "Latin" Republics of the western hemisphere have always co-operated and are still co-operating with the United States in the promotion of international peace and human welfare. And they have always given a good account of themselves whenever the United States has suffered aggression. But the Washington government must never make the mistake of thinking that Latin Americans are unconditional friends. Their proud ancestry, their dynamic present, and their hopeful future entitle them to be treated as equals among equals. Latin Americans believe in friendship, not in servitude. They expect their political ties with the United States to be profitable for *all* concerned. They are not satellites, but *bona fide* partners. They are convinced that the American family of nations still has many battles to win: the consolidation of inter-American prosperity and the gradual strengthening of a world order resting on justice under freedom. They are not skeptical or pessimistic. They share an untiring faith in their continent and in mankind. It would be a political blunder to destroy such faith.

As far as inter-American relations are concerned, the worst is over. The American republics have established forever their international personality. Theirs can easily become the continent of co-operation, mutual respect, and constructive friendship. In other continents there is no similar feeling of solidarity. European, Asiatic, and African statesmen have tried and are still trying to develop it among countries sharing their continents. In the case of the American republics, this feeling of solidarity sprang from the heart of the American populations as soon as they had won their independence: this is, indeed, an original aspect of the American world. The Organization of American States is truly a regional organization, not a political alliance based on fragile motives of military expediency.

It is hard for non-Americans to properly understand this inter-American feeling. But it would be harder for Americans, North, Central, or South, to ignore it or destroy it. We are eager to keep on moving forward, united and respecting each other. A spectacular exhibition of inter-American solidarity was the meeting held at Panama (July, 1956) where nineteen Presidents of the American republics gathered at the invitation of President Ricardo Arias Espinosa to join in the OAS commemoration of Simón Bolívar's historical Congress of 1826 (the first Pan American conference ever held). On that occasion the presidents of the American republics solemnly subscribed the following Declaration:

1. The destiny of America is to create a civilization that will give tangible meaning to the concept of human liberty, the principle that the State is the servant of man and not his master, the faith that man will reach ever greater heights in his spiritual and material development, and the proposition that all nations can live together in peace and dignity.

2. The full realization of the destiny of America is inseparable from the economic and social development of its peoples and, therefore, makes necessary the intensification of national and inter-American co-operative efforts to seek the solution of economic problems and to raise the standards of living of the Continent.

3. The accomplishments of the Organization of American States, an assurance of peace among the Member States and security for the Continent, demonstrate how much can be achieved in the various fields of international endeavor through a loyal co-operation among sovereign nations, and move us to strengthen the inter-American organizations and their activities.

4. In a world in which the dignity of the individual, his fundamental rights and the spiritual values of mankind are seriously threatened by totalitarian forces, alien to the tradition of our peoples and their institutions, America holds steadfastly to its historic mission: to be a bulwark of human liberty and national independence.

5. An America united, strong and benevolent will not only promote the well-being of the Continent but contribute toward achieving for the whole world the benefits of a peace based on justice and freedom, in which all peoples, without distinction as to race or creed, can work with dignity and confidence in the future.

Other official documents and presidential declarations have expressed similar or higher concepts. But never in history had the chief executives of an entire continent convened to manifest freely and jointly some fundamental principles shared in common by their peoples. This most successful meeting is an added proof of Pan American solidarity. And those who refuse to acknowledge the purity of such continental feeling will never understand America.

SELECTED BIBLIOGRAPHY

The material on Latin America is extensive and of excellent quality. An annotated bibliography on Latin American affairs has been published annually since 1940 in the *Handbook of Latin*

American Studies, each volume of which lists some 4,000 items. Little, however, has been published on the control of foreign relations. The writer, therefore, is particularly indebted to his diplomatic colleagues in Washington for supplying him with invaluable, unpublished materials dealing with the respective foreign offices and the foreign services. There are listed below only a few of the most accessible English sources which deal with various aspects of the chapters on Latin America.

Alfaro, R. J., Commentary on Pan American Problems 1938.

Alvarez, Alejandro, The Monroe Doctrine: Its Importance in the International Life of the States of the New World. New York, 1924.

Ball, M. Margaret, The Problem of Inter-American Organization. Stanford, Stanford University Press, 1944.

Bannon, J. F., and Dunne, P. M., Latin America, an Historical Survey. Milwaukee, 1947.

Bartlett, Ruhl J. (ed.), The Record of American Diplomacy. New York, 1948.

Bemis, Samuel Flagg, The Latin American Policy of the United States. New York, 1943.

Bingham, Hiram, The Monroe Doctrine, an Obsolete Shibboleth. 3rd ed., New Haven, Conn., 1915.

Bolton, H. E., History of the Americas: A Syllabus with Maps. New ed., Boston, Ginn, 1935.

Bryce, J., South America: Observations and Impressions. 1914.

Callahan, James M., American Foreign Policy in Mexican Relations. New York, 1932.

Chapman, C. E., Hispanic America: Colonial and Republican. New York, 1942.

Childs, Marquis W., and Stone, William T., Toward a Dynamic America: The Challenge of a Changing World. New York, Foreign Policy Association, Headline Books, 1941.

Clark, J. Reuben, Memorandum on the Monroe Doctrine. Washington, 1930.

Cleven, N. A. N., in A. C. Wilgus, ed., *South American Dictators*. Washington, 1937.

Crawford, W. R., *A Century of Latin American Thought*. Cambridge, Mass., 1944.

Crow, John A., *The Epic of Latin America*. New York, 1946.

Diffie, Bailey W., *Latin American Civilization: Colonial Period*. Harrisburg, Pa., 1945.

Duggan, Stephen, *The Two Americas: An Interpretation*. 1934.

Eder, Phanor J., *A Comparative Survey of Anglo-American and Latin American Law*. New York, 1950.

Fenwick, Charles G., *The Inter-American Regional System*. New York, D. X. McMullen, 1949.

Fitzgibbon, Russell H., ed., *The Constitutions of the Americas*. Chicago, 1948.

Frank, Waldo, *South American Journey*. New York, 1943.

Freyre, Gilberto, *The Masters and the Slaves*, tr. by Samuel Putnam. New York, 1946.

Garcia-Mora, Manuel R., *International Law and Asylum as a Human Right*. Washington, Public Affairs Press, 1956.

Gordon, Wendell, *The Economy of Latin America*. New York, 1950.

Herring, Hubert, *History of Latin America, from the Beginnings to the Present*. New York, 1955.

Houston, John A., *Latin America in the United Nations*. New York, Carnegie Endowment for International Peace, 1956.

Humphrey, John T. P., *The Inter-American System: A Canadian View*. Toronto, Macmillan, 1942.

Humphreys, R. A., *The Evolution of Modern Latin America*. New York, 1946.

Inman, S. G., *Latin America, Its Place in World Life*. Rev. ed., New York, 1942.

Ireland, Gordon, *Boundaries, Possessions, and Conflicts in South America*. Cambridge, Mass., 1938.

Ireland, Gordon, *Boundaries, Possessions, and Conflicts in Central and North America and the Caribbean.* Cambridge, Mass., 1941.

Kelchner, Warren H., *Latin American Relations with the League of Nations.* Boston, World Peace Foundation, 1930.

Lockey, James B., *Pan-Americanism: Its Beginnings.* New York, 1920.

MacQuarrie, Heath Nelson, *Pan American Union and Canadian Foreign Policy.* New Brunswick, 1949.

Manning, William R., *Diplomatic Correspondence of the United States: Inter-American Affairs, 1831-1860.* 12 vols., Washington, 1932-1939.

Massey, V., "Canada and the Inter-American System," *Foreign Affairs* 26:693-700, July 1948.

Padilla, E., "Meaning of Pan-Americanism," *Foreign Affairs* 32: 270-81. January 1954.

Perkins, Dexter, *Hands Off: A History of the Monroe Doctrine.* Boston, Little, Brown & Co., 1941.

Perkins, Dexter, *The United States and the Caribbean.* Cambridge, Mass., 1947.

Quintanilla, Luis, *A Latin American Speaks.* New York, Macmillan, 1943.

Rippy, J. Fred, *Latin America in World Politics.* New York, 1931.

Rippy, J. Fred, "Pan-Americanism and the World Order," pp. 203-219 in *Inter-American Solidarity,* Walter H. C. Laves, ed. Chicago, University of Chicago Press, 1941.

Rippy, J. Fred, *Historical Evolution of Hispanic America.* 3rd ed., New York, 1945.

Rippy, J. Fred, *Latin America and the Industrial Age.* 2nd ed., New York, 1947.

Rippy, J. Fred, in A. C. Wilgus, ed., *South American Dictators During the First Century of Independence.* Washington, 1937.

Stuart, G. H., *Latin America and the United States.* 5th ed., New York, 1954.

Tannenbaum, Frank, *Whither Latin America? An Introduction to Its Economic and Social Problems.* New York, 1934.

Thompson, Wallace, *Greater America: an Interpretation of Latin America in relation to Anglo-Saxon America.* New York, 1932.

CHAPTER 6

CONTROLS AND FOREIGN POLICIES IN LATIN AMERICAN COUNTRIES

It is hard to perceive real and permanent "controls" of foreign relations in states without parliamentary regimes. True, in the western hemisphere as elsewhere, legislatures must approve treaties and declarations of war. But in the Latin American republics, as in their northern neighbor, foreign relations are conducted essentially by the executive, and to most of them "executive" means the president and nobody else.

The western hemisphere is characterized by presidential initiative in foreign relations. Chiefs of state, and they alone, are responsible for making their nations' foreign policy. In those American republics where people can vote freely, the sole control over the executive is the ballot box; and it is a control only when voters take interest in specific international issues. However, once in power, the new president becomes another undisputed master of his nation's foreign policy. He can ignore the opinion of his cabinet and, popular or unpopular, his foreign secretary is accountable only to him. The people must wait until the next presidential election to show their approval or disapproval of an administration's policy. No other legal permanent "controls" are available.

Throughout the American republics sporadic contacts are kept between the executive and the legislative power, concerning measures of international policy: but these contacts cannot be termed "controls." Foreign secretaries may exchange views with special committees of legislatures; they may consult official agencies, or representative groups. Such steps do not tie the hands of the executive. Decisions on foreign policy still remain very much the president's exclusive business.

In other continents, more specifically in countries under a parliamentary system, the making of policy is the task and responsibility of the prime minister and his cabinet. They, in turn, always act under the vigilant control of the electorate, as represented by the members of the parliament. So exacting is parliamentary control that prime ministers and their cabinets are put out of office whenever an important measure they advocate does not meet with the approval of the parliament. For that reason a parliamentary system of government can frequently prove cumbersome and irritating: cabinets may fall in quick succession. But the fluctuating mechanism of a parliamentary system is definitely more responsive if less stable than strictly presidential rule.

Could it be said, now, that presidents of the United States or of Latin American countries are free to do exactly as they please in formulating their countries' policy? Theoretically, yes; in practice, not quite. Even they must through qualifications take into account: *public opinion*, provided there is freedom of expression and press; *representative groups*, in countries where they can function freely; and last but not least, the *opinion of the legislature*, when the latter is not a mere instrument of the executive. These practical limits do not always apply in all the Latin American republics.

On the other hand, there is a moral force which no country can ignore: history. Diplomatic tradition operates in practice as a "control." Presidents interpret history to the best of their ability and in accordance with their own political belief. They may make wise or unwise decisions; but they cannot safely ignore the national traditions of their people. So, since it is difficult to detect in Latin America other equivalents to policy "controls," the present survey takes note of a few historical antecedents.

It must also be said that the diplomatic services of most Latin American countries are improvised and subject to political contingencies. Usually nonprofessionals are chosen as ambassadors or

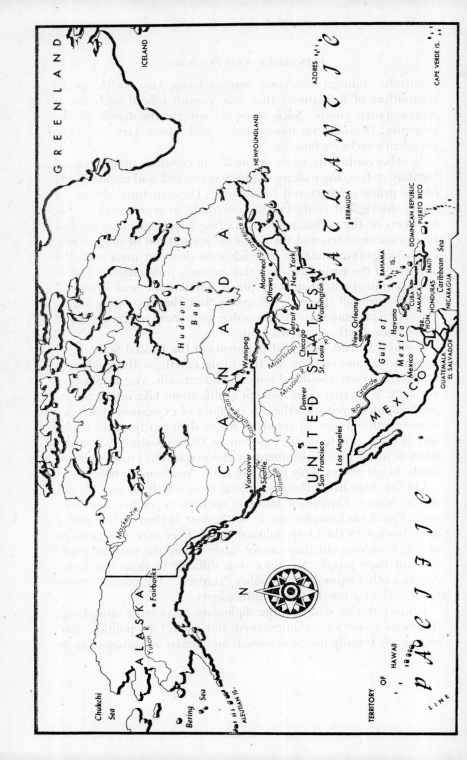

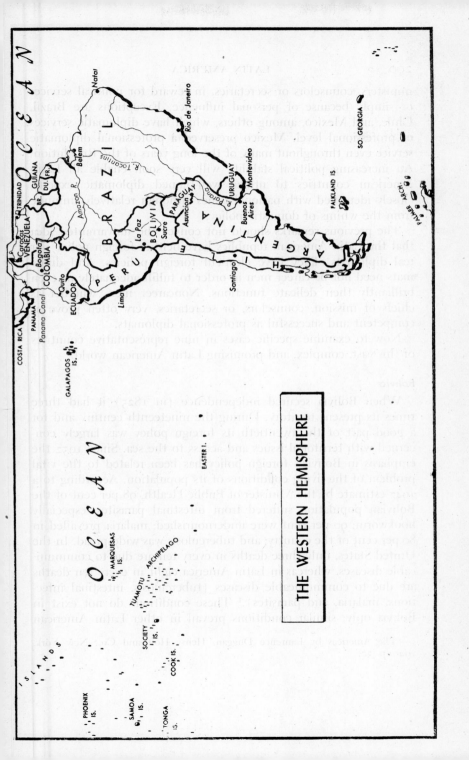

THE WESTERN HEMISPHERE

ministers, counselors or secretaries, in reward for political services or simply because of personal influence. Exceptions are Brazil, Chile, and Mexico, among others, which have diplomatic services of professional level. Mexico preserved a professional diplomatic service even throughout many of the long years of the Revolution. An increasing political stability will very soon enable all Latin American countries to utilize well-trained diplomatic experts, closely identified with national issues although relatively immune from the whims of domestic policy.

The previous remarks should not convey the unwarranted idea that the Latin American republics have neither foreign policy nor real diplomats. They have clear-cut foreign policies. And diplomats need not be career men in order to fulfill adequately or even brilliantly their delicate functions. Noncareer men, whether as chiefs of mission, counselors, or secretaries, very often prove as competent and successful as professional diplomats.

Now to examine specific cases in nine representative countries of this vast, complex, and promising Latin American world.

Bolivia

When Bolivia secured independence (in 1825) it had three times its present territory. During the nineteenth century and for a good part of the twentieth its foreign policy was largely concerned with territorial issues and access to the sea. Since 1952 the emphasis in Bolivia's foreign policy has been related to the vital problem of the living conditions of its population. According to a 1947 estimate by the Minister of Public Health, 98 per cent of the Bolivian population suffered from intestinal parasites, especially hookworm; 90 per cent were undernourished; malaria prevailed in 80 per cent of the country; and tuberculosis was widespread. In the United States, only three deaths in every ten are due to communicable diseases, whereas in Latin America *eight* in every ten deaths are due to communicable diseases (tuberculosis, intestinal infections, malaria, and parasites).[1] These conditions do not exist in Bolivia only; similar conditions prevail in other Latin American

[1] *The Americas* by Laurence Duggan, Henry Holt and Co., New York, 1949, p. 30.

countries where, since the Spanish colonization, indigenous populations have been the victims of merciless exploitation. These conditions seriously impair a country's manpower; yet they can easily be removed. Communicable diseases can be wiped out by social-minded democratic governments. Yet some people cannot (or pretend they cannot) understand why there are revolutions in such countries, where human beings refuse to accept forever the punishment of brutal exploitation and official cruelty!

Bolivia, sometimes called the "American Tibet," must import about 70 per cent of its food. Since independence there have been more than sixty "revolutions," more than a hundred lesser uprisings, and some forty presidents, of whom eight were assassinated. But in April 1952 the "National Revolutionary Movement" launched what was to be the first authentic revolution in Bolivia's history. Under Victor Paz Estenssoro's administration, and following it under the presidency of Hernán Siles Zuazo, the revolution has endeavored to transform Bolivia's economic and social structure and build a modern state with economic justice for its entire population. Paz Estenssoro ordered the seizure of the Bolivian tin industry, heretofore completely owned by a select monopoly of "tin barons" with foreign connections. The ceremony of expropriation took place on October 1, 1952, in Catavi, where Peñaranda's police had in 1942 shot down the striking miners.

Because it shook the very foundations of national economy and was a step in the direction of integral democracy, the Bolivian Revolution shares many goals with the 1910 Mexican Revolution. The two countries' diplomacy has followed similar paths, all tending to protect the country from foreign interference on behalf of native reactionary elements. Labor organization, agrarian reform, nationalization of natural resources, eradication of illiteracy, care of public health, political democracy: these were some of the goals of the Mexican Revolution and are also goals of the Bolivian movement.

Since the Chaco War (1932-1938), Bolivian governments have worked to connect the productive and commercial areas of the region with the territory of neighboring states. Bolivia has signed railroad and highway agreements with Brazil, Argentina, Paraguay,

and Chile. It has opened means of communication between Cocha-
bamba and Santa Cruz, the most important economic zones of the
country. Presently, the Bolivian government is building a pipeline
for the transportation of oil to Argentina and to Chile. It must
consolidate the nation's economy if the Revolution is to survive.

The recent statute of its Foreign Service reflects Bolivia's revolutionary spirit. Adopted in 1954 under Paz Estenssoro, the new
diplomatic regulations exhibit the wholesome transformation of
Bolivia from feudalism to democracy. The diplomatic statute condemns the mining oligarchy that "sold the freedom of the country" and wasted its natural resources. The document aims at·or-
ganizing a solid and well-trained body of career diplomats. An
Institute of International Law, a dependent organ of the Foreign
Department, is created for the purpose of providing theoretical and
practical training to Foreign Service students. The Institute will
also investigate Bolivia's specific international interests and policy,
as well as traditional questions of international and diplomatic law;
its regulations must be approved by the Foreign Department.

Career men cannot be dismissed without previous administrative
hearings to give them fair opportunity to defend themselves. All
members of the service are subject to rotation and transfer, to and
from the Department at home and the various diplomatic missions.
Before assignment abroad, Bolivian diplomats must spend at least
two years in the Department. They are not to be kept more than
four years in Europe or three years abroad in the American continent; thereafter they return to work in the Department.

Among merits that may lead to promotion, the regulations make
reference to "the publication of books and the writing of studies
on international questions of direct interest to Bolivia."

Congress ratifies treaties; only then do they become law. Should
one of the two houses of Congress reject a treaty, they meet jointly
to consider it further. Congress can suggest modifications or offer
proposals to the executive. The latter may set up official technical
committees to examine treaties or economic agreements, and
choose the persons or agencies to serve on them.

Bolivia's diplomacy has so far succeeded in protecting the Revolution from foreign assaults. That achievement in itself is remarkable because rebellions provide rationale for interference by foreign powers. For years to come Bolivia's main diplomatic concern will continue to be the preservation of the many social and economic gains fostered by its Revolution. Its government will accordingly continue to seek the friendly co-operation of all nations, especially the United States and the sister republics that comprise the inter-American regional system.

Brazil

Before the nominal discovery of Brazil by a Portuguese fleet in 1500, its boundaries had already been juridically defined by the papal *Bulla Inter Caetera* (1493) and by the Treaty of Tordesillas (1494) between Portugal and Spain. It became a Portuguese colony and remained so for three centuries, until the Napoleonic wars.

When Napoleon I invaded the Iberian Peninsula, the Portuguese Prince Regent João moved his government to Rio de Janeiro. Brazil thus changed from colonial to metropolitan status. In 1816 the Regent became King as João VI, but remained in Brazil until 1820, when he returned to Lisbon after naming his son Pedro to be Lieutenant Governor of Brazil. Differences with the Portuguese parliament and government led to the peaceful proclamation of Brazilian independence in 1822 and the coronation of Dom Pedro as Emperor. He was officially recognized by the United States in 1824, when James Monroe was President.

Near the end of 1829, various measures taken by Pedro I were denounced as violations of the Constitution and he was forced to abdicate in 1831. Thereafter, and also without struggle, Brazil was governed by its own nationals. Dom Pedro's son, a Brazilian now, took over as Pedro II, under a regency until 1840. His administration was called a "crowned republic." The Empire lasted until 1889, when a republican form of government supplanted the monarchy, again without violence.

The Empire of Pedro II had put an end to the subtle expansionism of João VI and Pedro I. While safeguarding the borders, it adopted arbitration as a peaceful procedure for solving international controversies. Territorial disputes with Argentina on the

Missoes, with France on the Amapa, and with England on British Guiana were settled by arbitration. Disputes with Peru on the common frontier and with Bolivia on the territory of Acre were settled by direct negotiation.

Brazilian diplomacy has shown competence and efficacy in friendly settlement of controversies, largely because of the talent of Rio Branco, Foreign Minister from 1902 to 1912. This celebrated Brazilian statesman well deserves the international reputation won by his brilliant accomplishments. He promoted a respectable tradition: the use of diplomacy instead of military might. Classic lines were applied by him: the juridical equality of states acclaimed by the Hague Conference (1907) when Ruy Barbosa (another famous Brazilian internationalist) represented his country; nonintervention in domestic affairs; peaceful solution of international conflicts, especially through arbitration; constitutional condemnation of the use of force as an instrument of foreign policy; inter-American solidarity; diplomatic flexibility, as shown in disputes with Uruguay and other conflicts over Leticia and the Chaco; a spirit of moderation and practical realism. These principles and rules became the guideposts of Brazil's international policy. Brazil enjoys high prestige in international relations, and one probable reason is its Foreign Department's constructive spirit of harmony and conciliation.

The Brazilian diplomatic service is outstanding in technical training, organization, and quality. "Itamaraty," the familiar name of the Foreign Department (from the building that houses it), has rightly become a synonym for tactful diplomacy. The Foreign Department consults directly with other executive departments such as the Treasury, Agriculture, Communications, and Public Works, as well as with the Central Railways, the Bank of Brazil, the National Council of Economy, the Federation of Industries, the Federation of Business Associations, the Bank for Economic Development, the Central Commissions for Prices, and the Brazilian Institute of Geography and Statistics. These bodies often provide experts needed in diplomatic missions abroad. The General Staff of the Army, the military departments, and the National

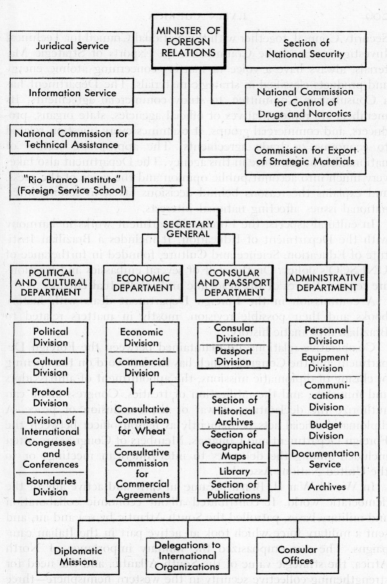

THE BRAZILIAN DEPARTMENT OF FOREIGN RELATIONS ("ITAMARATY")—
GENERAL STRUCTURE

Security Council, together with the National Council for Technical Investigations and the Commission on Exports of Strategic Materials, always have a voice in matters concerning atomic energy and products classified as strategic materials. The Department has a Consultative Committee, to study commercial agreements. Its members are representatives of official agencies, state organs, producers, and commercial groups. It examines every question related to economic or trade agreements. The appropriate sectors of national life have a voice in this agency. The Department also takes very much into account public opinion and the voice of the press, and explains the reasons behind decisions taken in serious international issues affecting national interests.

In cultural aspects, the Foreign Department works in harmony with the Department of Education. It includes a Brazilian Institute of Education, Science and Culture, founded in furtherance of UNESCO's policy. On the staff of several embassies and legations are representatives of the academic and intellectual circles.

A commission in the Foreign Department deals with history books and their possible revision, mostly in matters related to Brazilian diplomatic history.

Co-operative relations are maintained between the Foreign Department and the Congress which has the last word on the opening or closing of diplomatic missions, the appointment of ambassadors and ministers, and the ratification of treaties. Congress alone can authorize the declaration of war or the conclusion of peace. A diplomatic official acts permanently as liaison officer between the Foreign Department and Congress. Members of Congress are often included among the delegates to inter-American meetings or to the United Nations Assembly.

In World War II, Brazil became an early and active ally of the democratic world. It contributed all-out economic collaboration and military bases, patrolled the South Atlantic by sea and air, and sent a military force which took an active part in the Italian campaigns. The war emphasized the military importance of North Africa, the strategic value of the South Atlantic, and the need for strengthening collective security in the western hemisphere—three matters of marked significance for Brazilian foreign policy.

Brazil's European policy after the war was characterized by the promotion of trade relations with England and Germany, of cultural relations with France, and of migratory, economic, and cultural relations with Italy. A special treaty was signed with Portugal in 1952 to create the basis of a Portuguese-Brazilian community of wide scope. In the inter-American field Brazil continues to seek the best possible relations with its sister republics. Particularly significant are its increasing economic relations with the countries of the Plata (Argentina, Uruguay, and Paraguay) and with the United States of America.

In the regional system (OAS), Brazilian diplomacy is guided by the following principles: (a) Inter-American unity and firm opposition to the formation of political blocs within the continent; (b) strengthening of inter-American collective security as set up by the Rio Treaty (1947); (c) nonintervention in the internal affairs of the American republics; (d) peaceful solution of all conflicts and controversies; (e) inter-American economic co-operation on a permanent basis, and not only when a world conflict arises; (f) effective cultural co-operation; (g) opposition to extreme ideologies, and defense of the democratic system; (h) gradual but peaceful emancipation of American territories still controlled by non-American nations; (i) liberal interpretation of the doctrine of diplomatic and territorial asylum; (j) adherence to the Organization of American States and extension of its functions; (k) consideration of inter-American problems in the light of world conditions.

In the world at large, particularly within the United Nations, Brazil has followed this fundamental policy: (a) universality of the United Nations, so as to include all the countries of the world; (b) strengthening of the powers assigned to the United Nations General Assembly; (c) extension of the jurisdiction and competence of the International Court of Justice; (d) preservation and strengthening of the inter-American system; (e) more adequate representation of Latin America in the Security Council; (f) greater autonomy for the United Nations General Secretariat; (g) practical enforcement of the principle of self-determination of peoples, taking into account the corresponding possibilities for

social and political growth; (h) international protection of human
rights, with due respect for nonintervention; (i) development of
international trusteeship; (j) expansion of technical and economic
aid on a permanent basis; (k) peaceful use of atomic energy.

Chile

When Chile embarked on independence (1810), its first *junta*
created only two departments: that of Government and War,
entrusted also with matters of foreign policy, and that of Finance.
A year later, the Chilean Congress was given the delicate task of
directing the foreign policy of the new country, and the General
Secretary of the Congress acted as Foreign Secretary. The first
diplomatic envoy of Chile to the Buenos Aires government was
accredited by the Congress. This fact displays a democratic trend
deeply rooted in the Chilean people and their political institutions:
the high significance of the legislative branch of the government.
But after 1812, the Congress ceased to handle foreign policy and a
foreign minister was appointed. After independence was fully
achieved (1818), an *Oficial Mayor*[2] of the new Foreign Department was designated; later on, an Under Secretary.

From the beginning, emphasis on political democracy and a
deep feeling of inter-American solidarity actuated Chile's diplomacy. Latin America in the early nineteenth century was much
more united than today. In spite of deficiencies in the means of
communication, all the countries shared a feeling of Americanity.
The new nations enjoyed together the novelty of liberty, a common
pride of victory in a common fight. San Martín from Argentina,
O'Higgins from Chile, and Bolívar from greater Colombia, were
indeed brothers-in-arms. Together they had won the total emancipation of South America. National frontiers meant little: a whole
continent was at stake. Morally, South America was but one
gigantic nation.

---

[2] We mention this *oficial mayor* (literally *major official*) because the practice of appointing *oficiales mayores* still prevails in some government agencies
of Latin America, much to the distress of foreign diplomats who have trouble
finding an appropriate translation of the expression. The *Oficial Mayor* is somewhat like a United States Assistant Secretary in charge of administrative and
personnel matters.

The government of Chile did not restrict itself to Chilean nationals in filling official posts of the Chilean state. In 1818, Antonio José de Irizarri, a Guatemalan, became Secretary of the Interior and acted as Chilean Foreign Minister. Francisco Rivas, a Colombian, was appointed *Oficial Mayor*; later he was appointed diplomatic secretary to Irizarri and represented the Republic of Chile in Europe. In 1826, a Spaniard, Juan Francisco Zegers, who had served in the Spanish Foreign Office during the short kingdom of Napoleon's brother Joseph, became *Oficial Mayor* of Chile's Foreign Department. And in 1829, Andres Bello, the outstanding scholar from Venezuela, came to Chile to become *Oficial Mayor* of the Treasury. Bello later held the post of *Oficial Mayor* in the Department of Foreign Relations, where his exceptional mind was instrumental in laying the bases of Chilean diplomacy.

In 1830 Diego Portales outlined, in collaboration with Bello, the fundamental lines of early Chilean foreign policy. They can be summed up as follows: no bilateral entanglements with any specific American nation, in order to avoid conflicts with others; nonintervention in domestic situations of the American sister republics; continental solidarity, preferably without general commitments and taking full advantage of agreements among neighbors.

Chile maintains an excellent Foreign Service. The School of Foreign Service (of the University of Chile) is a notable training center for diplomatic candidates. The President can appoint non-career men as chiefs of mission, but career men are entitled to become under secretaries of foreign relations, ambassadors, or ministers. No diplomatic mission abroad can include more than two honorary attachés.

To enter the Foreign Service, candidates must have completed successfully the requirements of the Foreign Service School. Their grades and merits affect their entry and placement in the service. For the promotion of diplomatic officials, the following are carefully considered: (a) both universal and specialized education; (b) sense of duty and responsibility; (c) spirit of initiative; (d) technical capacity and efficiency; (e) teamwork; (f) personal aptitudes; (g) private conduct. For Foreign Service personnel stationed at the Department, three elements are considered for promotion: (a) efficiency; (b) leadership and methodical work; (c) discipline. When officials are assigned abroad, additional elements are taken into consideration in all cases of promotion: (a) capacity to report; (b) adjustment to foreign environments; and (c) ability to make contacts.

The Chilean Congress ratifies or rejects international treaties. It alone can declare war, and must approve all appointments of chiefs of mission by the President. Article 42 of the Constitution directs the Senate to "give the President of the republic an opinion whenever consulted by him"; the President frequently avails himself of this procedure. The Foreign Secretary, in turn, often appears before Congress or its Committees to explain important aspects of Chile's foreign policy.

The Foreign Minister can obtain advice from two Consultative Commissions composed of technical experts, mostly university professors and former chiefs of mission. The first of these two bodies is dedicated to the codification of international law, as recommended by various inter-American resolutions. The second is concerned entirely with problems of the Antarctic region and the administration of Antarctic territories claimed by Chile.

The Foreign Department keeps in close contact with the Departments of the Treasury, National Economy, and Education, as well as with the University of Chile and the Chilean Commission for Intellectual Co-operation.

Public opinion, through a free press, exerts a notable influence in the formulation of Chile's foreign policy.

The foreign policy of Chile in 1956 embraces the following principal items: (a) peaceful solution of international conflicts and controversies; (b) active collaboration with international agencies; (c) universal, and especially inter-American solidarity; (d) abhorrence of secret diplomacy; (e) rejection of the policy of balance of power, as well as the formation of blocs to implement such balance; (f) constant respect of treaty commitments; (g) juridical equality of states; (h) nonintervention; (i) opposition to the formation of blocs among the American republics; (j) fair treatment to under-

developed countries, with higher prices for raw materials; and
(k) international commitments to maintain stability of prices.

Costa Rica

Costa Rica's independence from Spain dates from 1821, and
its history thereafter for thirty-eight years has much in common
with the history of other countries in Central America—a brief
period of orientation toward Iturbide's Mexican Empire until 1823,
then participation in the Republic of Central America until its disruption in 1839. Thereafter, during the nineteenth century, the
international relations of Costa Rica were colored by boundary
issues with Nicaragua to the north and with Colombia and Panama
to the south. In respect to both, Costa Rica's interests were entangled in the relations between Great Britain and the United
States having to do with the control of shipping in the Caribbean
Sea and the construction and control of the interoceanic canal that
was eventually built in Panama.

Sporadic boundary negotiations with the Colombian government took place in 1825, then in 1865, finally in 1873. In 1873, the
Liberal Party of Colombia held the reins of government and, in a
gesture of revolutionary zeal, handed over to Costa Rica a substantial part of the then province of Panama. One condition was
attached to this unusual deal: Costa Rica was to maintain a
"liberal" policy for the benefit of the population occupying the
transferred territory. The deal was soon canceled by the Congress
of Colombia. The boundary dispute was submitted to arbitration
in 1880. The arbiter, King Alfonso XII of Spain, died before rendering his decision. He was replaced as arbitrator by French President
Emile Loubet in 1897. Colombia accepted Loubet's decision; Costa
Rica did not. In 1903 the former Colombian province of Panama
became independent. New boundary negotiations started between
Costa Rica and the government of Panama. The outcome was the
Guardia-Pacheco Treaty, which did not put an end to the controversy because the Congress of Panama refused to ratify it. In 1940,
still another treaty (Arias-Calderon) settled the issue.

These years of patient diplomacy, required for Costa Rica to
legalize the full ownership of its narrow territory, help to explain

Costa Rica's strong national personality and its faith in the usefulness of diplomatic negotiation.

Members of Costa Rica's foreign service are selected for competence, honesty, good conduct, cultural background, and patriotism. Costa Rica's Foreign Department, as happens in other countries where Church and State are not separated, deals also, although
rather superficially, with religious matters. It is officially called the
Department of Foreign Relations and Cult. The Foreign Secretary
is expected to maintain cordial and good relations with the Roman
Catholic Church and to facilitate whatever the laws and regulations
concede for the exercise of religious services. The Foreign Department's Division of Protocol (not a political division) periodically
informs the diplomatic missions of Costa Rica about pertinent
domestic matters. The Diplomatic Division of the Department is
entrusted with "keeping and investigating the record of nationals
and foreigners whose activities, political creed and origin deserve
to be watched."

The Foreign Secretary may appear before Congress (*Asamblea
Legislativa*). He must submit to the latter a yearly report on the
Department's activities and can recommend projects to the Foreign
Relations Committee of Congress. He must, finally, keep in touch
with other official agencies, to co-ordinate policy affecting inter-
national organizations.

Costa Rica has had, on several occasions, serious diplomatic
incidents with neighboring Nicaragua. The recent ones were settled peacefully, in 1948 and 1955, thanks to the timely and active
intervention of the regional system (the Inter-American Peace
Commission, and the Rio Treaty).

Costa Rica has played in Central America a role somewhat similar to that of Uruguay in South America: both states are relatively
small and both are peaceful and democratic. Both have waged
similar fights for the protection of human rights and the extension
of democratic governments.

Like Uruguay, Costa Rica does not have an "Indian" problem.
Its population is homogeneous, peaceful, literate, and basically
democratic.

The Administration, under President Figueres, has stressed some interesting elements of international policy: firm co-operation with the United Nations and the Organization of American States; political alliance with the United States in the cold war; strengthening of the Central American regional organization (*Organización de Estados Centro Americanos*); continental solidarity; a reserve system to handle surpluses of foods and raw materials.

In his inaugural address (November 8, 1953), President José Figueres criticized in outspoken terms the belief that "private foreign investments represent a desirable means of increasing working capital." He argued that such investments run against the interests of the country that receives them, and ultimately hurt the country that provides them; they take out in dividends, taxes, and salaries the greater part of the wealth they produce; and they tend "to maintain low wages in our [Latin American] countries, thus weakening our purchasing power needed to buy industrial articles." Figueres went so far as to say: "A great investment of foreign capital, even when inspired by legitimate commercial motives, is tantamount in the field of international relations to an economic occupation which in several aspects resembles military occupation." This was a statement not against foreign countries but against economic colonialism. And the President concluded: "The gradual and wise withdrawal of economic occupation would correct one of the gravest mistakes committed in the western hemisphere." The economic emancipation of the United States from British private capital was mentioned to support this view.

Article XXXI of the Costa Rica's constitution reads: "The territory of Costa Rica will be a refuge for all those who are persecuted for political reasons. If their expulsion [from Costa Rica] must be decided because of legal obligations, they must never be sent back to the country where they were persecuted." In this constitutional clause, Costa Rica endorses the popular right of asylum, a notable contribution of Latin America to international law.

Ecuador

The traditional problem of Ecuador's foreign policy since its independence (1830) has been its territorial integrity. In this respect Ecuador's foreign policy has been, up to now, the history of Ecuador's military and diplomatic conflict with its neighbors, particularly Peru, over the possession of Amazonian lands. The fact that at present Ecuador, like Bolivia, covers only one-third of its original area reveals the seriousness of this problem. One must remember, in this respect, that other countries such as Mexico (which lost more than half its territory to the United States) are striking examples of the hardships endured, in Latin America as in other regions of the world, by patriotic peoples determined to preserve their nations' boundaries.

Both the Foreign Secretary of Ecuador and the Under Secretary have "Little Cabinets" of their own. Otherwise, we find here the usual Departments: Foreign Service (including an Economic and a Library section); Diplomatic (with three sections: Diplomatic, Political, and Cultural Relations); International Boundaries; International Organizations (with sections for the United Nations, the Organization of American States, and International Treaties and Conferences); Consular and Trade Matters; Protocol; Documentation and Archives; and last but not least, a Juridical Consultative Group.

There is an organic law for Ecuador's Foreign Service. The pertinent Article states that: "the external sovereignty of the Republic is exercised through the consular and diplomatic representations." And further: "the Foreign Service is a public career and only those admitted in accordance with the regulations [of this organic law] can be appointed to fill the vacancies in the consular and diplomatic service, *as well as in the Department of Foreign Relations*." This article is interesting because it tends to erase the cleavage between diplomatic personnel sent abroad and Foreign Department personnel stationed at home.

To enter the Foreign Service, candidates must meet the following requirements: (a) nationality by birth; (b) a bachelor's degree; (c) registration for military service; (d) well-established morality; (e) intellectual culture; and (f) good health. Candidates who satisfy these requirements are permitted to take a special qualifying examination.

Among the functions and duties of Ecuador's chiefs of mission are the following: to observe the international policy of the continent in which the [diplomatic] mission finds itself; to analyze the international and diplomatic life as well as the political, institutional, and cultural evolution of the foreign country; to inform about these matters in monthly reports sent to the Department, without prejudice of timely communications on other important events when these take place; and to elaborate a general and confidential annual Report, "carefully critical and systematic," in which the chief of mission examines the developments of international policy and the economic and cultural activities of the state to which he is accredited.

The Foreign Department maintains contact with the Congress through the Foreign Relations Committees from the Senate and the House.

The objectives of Ecuador's international policy are explained in detail to representative sectors of the population who appoint delegates to a Consultative Board of Foreign Relations (*Junta Consultiva de Relaciones Exteriores*). Created by the executive department, this Consultative Board includes the Archbishop of Quito, a representative from the armed forces, another from University circles, one from the Senate, one from the Chamber of Representatives, and the President of the Supreme Court, plus ten prominent civilians selected by the President of the Republic. This powerful Board meets at the initiative of the Foreign Secretary, who submits any problem of international policy on which the Board's opinion is deemed necessary. Such an opinion is not always accepted by the executive, but it carries great weight. The Board may also convene at its own chairman's suggestion.

The international policy of Ecuador rests basically on the assumption that the coexistence of states creates between them economic, cultural, and political relations which give shape to a wider international community; and that this international community must be ruled exclusively by international law applied to sovereign states treated as juridical equals. On this premise, the following principles guide Ecuador's international conduct: (a) all conflicts or controversies, whatever their nature, must be solved by peaceful means; (b) Ecuador condemns most emphatically all acts of aggression, and the acquisition by force of the territory of any nation; (c) within the democratic idea, each state has the right to adopt its own ideology and form of government; (d) the existence of an international community imposes the obligation to organize the mutual interdependence of nations within a democratic system of free peoples; (e) the highly developed nations have a duty to help the less developed; (f) Ecuador opposes all forms of colonialism as well as the exploitation of racial minorities or discrimination against them; (g) respect for human rights and for the independence of nations as a basic condition of human solidarity; (h) Ecuador favors the existence and growth of regional systems as long as they remain incorporated into the wider international order, and as long as they are based on sound geographical facts, a common culture, and a common history.

On August 10, 1954, President José María Velasco Ibarra, in his message to Congress, clearly stressed the right of each nation to its own political ideology and form of government. No president in the western hemisphere had been more emphatic on this vital subject. Referring to the Guatemalan situation (June, 1954) Velasco Ibarra declared: "Some people have tried to make it appear as though the [present] intervention in Guatemala were needed, in order to prevent another intervention. Nothing could be more incorrect." And the President continued: "According to international law, the intervention against which juridical declarations have been adopted by the Inter-American System is the direct or indirect interference of a State in the affairs of another State. The ideological influence of a nation, in another country, is not an intervention." Thus, explained Velasco Ibarra, it would be arbitrary to speak of the "intervention" of Spanish Catholicism in the Latin American republics. Taking the same position taken by Mexico in Caracas (1954), Velasco Ibarra stated that communist infiltration in Guatemala was different from an act of intervention by the Soviet Union. "The problem of communism and its repression," he concluded, "must be left to the respective sovereignty of each state and its domestic legislation. Nefarious and dangerous, indeed, would be any theory that would tend to legalize and justify an armed intervention in the territory of a state, because this or that ideology prevails in such state. The adoption of such doctrine would destroy forever the security of all states. Today we would intervene against communism, tomorrow against fascism. Foreign governments would take it upon themselves to qualify the political doctrine of independent peoples. This would mean the end of national sovereignty." Because of its clarity, and the fact that this was a statement coming from a chief executive, the above Declaration will stand in Latin America's diplomatic history as the *Velasco Ibarra Doctrine.*

El Salvador

To appreciate El Salvador's position in the field of foreign policy it is imperative to deal with historical antecedents rather than with a superficial description of any machinery for control of this country's foreign policy. History acts, in this case, as an effective control mechanism.

El Salvador, one of the five provinces under the *Audiencia* of Guatemala (Guatemala, El Salvador, Honduras, Nicaragua, and Costa Rica) was liberated from Spain when Mexico, after a bloody campaign which lasted ten years, finally defeated the last remnants of the Spanish Crown's military power. There was no real warfare against Spanish troops in Central America. In November 1811, Father José Matias Delgado headed a movement for independence in San Salvador, but Matias Delgado's activities were promptly suppressed by Spain. For a while, the new Mexican Empire of Agustín de Iturbide reached far to the south, and included Central America, closely connected with the viceroyalty of New Spain in Mexico. In fact, the captaincy-general of Guatemala (including all Central America, north of Panama) had been an administrative subdivision of the viceroyalty of New Spain. A popular Assembly of the city of Guatemala declared the independence of all Central America. Very soon, however, disjunctive tendencies manifested themselves. Some Central American nations favored joining Guatemala, others preferred to maintain a union with Mexico. The Mexican Emperor Agustín de Iturbide was eager to keep the entire region. In 1822 a majority of votes from the local governments of the towns of Central America favored annexation to Mexico. Thereupon the Creole "Consultative Committee" of Guatemala declared all Central America henceforth a part of Mexico. This decision did not prove popular: Costa Rica, most of El Salvador, and a number of towns in Honduras and Nicaragua refused to approve the union with Mexico. Indeed, in December 1822 a Congress of Delegates in San Salvador voted for annexation to the United States, hoping thus to avoid incorporation into Iturbide's Empire. The proposal met with no response from the then relatively weak Washington government.

Iturbide sent an army into Central America under General Vicente Filisola to put down the opposition. Filisola defeated patriot forces in El Salvador and the issue seemed settled. But early in 1823 Iturbide was deposed and Filisola called a congress of the Central American provinces to meet in Guatemala. The delegates who attended were opposed to a continuance of the union with Mexico. On the first of July of that year, the independence of Central America (from Spain, Mexico, or any other power) was formally declared and a Republic of Central America was constituted. It lasted from 1823 to 1839, finally breaking up into the five countries which, later with Panama, would share the Central American isthmus.

National rivalries had caused the disintegration of the precarious union, but the longing for it has remained. Even today, efforts are being made to restore the Central American nation. The Organization of Central American States (ODECA; *Organización de Estados Centro Americanos*) is a manifestation of such tendency. ODECA, founded in 1951 in San Salvador, is Central America's regional organization. It functions within the wider frame of the Organization of American States. El Salvador preserves its interest in Central American solidarity without prejudice to its adherence to, and support of, the inter-American system as embodied in the OAS.

Article 151 of El Salvador's 1886 Constitution reads: "Since it is a disjoined part of the Republic of Central America, El Salvador remains willing and able to meet with all of them [the present Central American republics] or with any of them, in order to seek the establishment of a single national government, when circumstances will permit it and whenever convenient to its interests." To make clear the full meaning of this constitutional clause, the Article adds: "and this applies to a greater Latin American Confederation." Toward the end of the nineteenth century, this constitutional provision was put into practice. El Salvador, Honduras, and Nicaragua merged into a Major Central American republic (República Mayor de Centro America). This limited experiment lasted only three years. At the dawn of the twentieth century, all of the five Central American countries were again pursuing their individual national lives. In 1921, while celebrating the first century of Central America's independence, another effort in favor of the union took place; again it failed.

The establishment in 1907 of a Central American Court of Justice (in Costa Rica) reflects, in a way, this traditional trend toward Central American confederation. The purpose of this Court was to ensure the peaceful solution of all controversies. Private persons were permitted to bring before it their cases against arbitrary acts committed by any of the contracting governments in violation of treaties, or "other cases of international law"; the only requirement was that the interested parties had previously exhausted the legal procedures of their respective states. The Court lasted until 1917, when the establishing convention was denounced by Nicaragua. The Court can be regarded as a worthy experiment in the direction of an international order.

The Charter of ODECA is called the Charter of San Salvador. The objectives of ODECA are defined as follows in Article I: "Costa Rica, El Salvador, Guatemala, Honduras and Nicaragua have formed the Central American Organization of American States in order to strengthen the ties that unite them, mutually consult on the means to consolidate and preserve the fraternal coexistence of their region of the continent, prevent disagreements and ensure the peaceful solution of conflicts which might occur among them, seek collective answers to their common problems, and promote their economic, social and cultural development, through co-operative and solidary action." As we see, ODECA goes farther than the OAS: it is imbued with a spirit of union entirely absent from the Organization of American States or the United Nations. The organs of ODECA are: (1) the Meetings of Chiefs of State; (2) the Meetings of Foreign Ministers; (3) meetings of other cabinet members (of the Central American republics); (4) a Central American Secretariat (Oficina); and (5) a Central American Economic Council. With ODECA, Central America took a bold step toward internationalism, although on a limited subregional basis.

The OAS Charter, in its Article III, leaves the door open to an eventual Central American union. The Article stipulates: "In the Organization [OAS], any new political body resulting from the merging of several member states, will find place as long as it ratifies this Charter." The text was submitted by the delegation of El Salvador to the Ninth Inter-American Conference (Bogota, 1948) and approved unanimously.

During the Tenth Inter-American Conference held in Caracas (1954), the delegation from El Salvador submitted another project, to set up an Inter-American Court of Justice, an enlargement of the former Central American Court. The Conference asked the OAS Council to examine the matter and decide whether it should be brought to the attention of the next (Eleventh) Inter-American Conference, scheduled to meet in Quito (Ecuador) in 1958.

And as further evidence of El Salvador's determination to reconstruct the Central American union, Article IX of the present Constitution of that country (adopted in 1950) stipulates that: "Because El Salvador is a part of the Central American nation [the union], it is committed to promote the total or partial reconstruction of the Central American Republic." It adds that this can be done through the adoption of a federal, or a central Constitution "as long as republican and democratic principles are respected by the new [Central American] State, and as long as the fundamental rights of persons and groups are fully guaranteed" by all the governments of the five (to be) confederated States.

There is no question concerning El Salvador's international objective: a Central American union. Finally, it is one of the nine Latin American republics which have subscribed the all-important

Inter-American Treaty of Peaceful Solution (1948), known as the Pact of Bogota.

Haiti

Haiti (meaning "place of mountains") was the first Latin American nation to achieve independence. It fought during a dozen years to defeat, in 1804, the forces of French colonialism, when Haitian patriots, mostly former slaves, decisively routed the troops of Napoleon. The Negro nation thus led the way to Latin America's freedom and dealt a significant blow to the absurd current contention that colored races are sentenced by nature to live in perpetual slavery. The entire world followed with keen interest the bloody conflict between slavery and imperialism in the Caribbean island of Hispaniola. The victory of Haiti was taken as a warning to colonial masters and a promise of freedom to Negro people everywhere. Since then, a predominant feature of Haitian diplomacy has been its natural sympathy towards enslaved nations.

Haitian volunteers took part in the North American revolution against Great Britain, even before Haiti won its own freedom. Henri Christophe (the ex-slave who was later to be king from 1808 to 1820) was one of eight hundred Haitians who volunteered for service under Lafayette in the American Revolution and fought at the battle of Savannah. The Negro republic also sent men, money, and guns to help Simón Bolívar in the Latin American fight for emancipation. Toussaint L'Ouverture—former slave, grandson of an African king, and precursor of Haitian independence—tried to promote friendly relations with the United States, even before French colonialism had suffered defeat in his own country. Haiti was treated ungratefully: the Washington government waited more than sixty years before officially recognizing the Republic of Haiti.

Dessalines, another former slave who later became Haiti's first Emperor, supported Francisco de Miranda, the Grand Old Man of Latin American independence, in his scheme for Venezuela's liberation. Alexandre Pétion, first President of Haiti (1808), became the friend and ally of Simón Bolívar, helped him generously, and made it possible for the liberator to return to South America and renew his military campaign against the Spanish Crown. A similar feeling of solidarity was shown by Haiti when President Jean Pierre Boyer (1818) came to the help of the Greek patriotic insurrection. And in our century, Haiti's voice was heard in defense of the Ethiopean nation.

Haiti's foreign policy revolves around two centers: the western hemisphere, and Europe (in this case, France). Haiti's militant anticolonialism does not prevent cordial ties with Europe, especially with France. When the latter recognized the independence of its former colony, Franco-Haitian friendship was promptly restored. The coexistence of Haiti and the Dominican Republic on the same island—two nations with different traditions—has been a source of frequent trouble. One-third of the population lives in two-thirds of the island (the Dominican Republic), whereas two-thirds live in one-third of the island (Haiti).

For economic as well as for political reasons, relations with the Washington government are vitally important to Haiti. As a result of domestic political violence (1908-1915), United States Marines landed in Haiti in 1915 and remained there for nineteen years—until 1934. In the same year Cuba was released from the interventionist Platt Amendment, and Panama from the "protective" iniquities of the Hay-Bunau-Varilla Treaty. These three specific actions witnessed that the Good Neighbor Policy was more than a mere enunciation of theoretical principles.

In the world at large, Haiti endeavors to sell its agricultural products and raw materials in the markets of those countries from which it imports badly needed manufactured goods. The nation is beset with countless economic problems and difficulties. Far forward among them is the fact that its land, mostly mountainous, is being gradually destroyed by implacable erosion. Technical assistance is constantly required in Haiti and can help a great deal, as practical experiments have already proved. The United Nations have co-operated successfully with Haiti in several projects of economic assistance. The government welcomes inter-American co-operation, promotion of international trade, and suppression of tariff walls. Haiti is hopeful that, through national efforts and the understanding of other countries, as well as UN and OAS collaboration, the country can overcome the handicaps of nature and begin a new era of policy and planning to bring its people the material prosperity which they deserve.

International treaties require the approval of both Houses of the Haitian National Assembly. This legislative body also has much to say in establishing new diplomatic missions and fixing quotas for international organizations. The new Haitian Constitution has taken from the National Assembly the right to interpellate the executive. But Congress can request from the foreign minister any information on specific international matters.

The Foreign Service is regulated by an executive decree signed in 1955. Like the French Quai d'Orsay, the Foreign Department has a General Secretary who works closely with the Foreign Minister. A Consultative Council composed of three experts in international matters is appointed by the President of the Republic upon recommendation of the Foreign Secretary. These experts, who receive no salary, give their opinion on any question (political, diplomatic, economic, or even administrative) which the Foreign Secretary brings to their attention.

Haiti, by reason of its special character and history, is almost a unique link in the fabric of international society. Its people being Negro, its culture French, its political and geographic situation American, Haiti may well interpret America to Europe, Europe to America, and both to Africa, the gigantic continent of tomorrow.

Mexico

History has been merciful to some nations: for instance, Brazil established its territory, achieved independence, and changed its political institutions without bloodshed or war. Other states have succeeded in transforming their economic structure from feudalism to democracy without waste of human life. Mexico, on the contrary, has had a violent history. Against foreigners it fought fierce battles: to destroy the armies of the Spanish Crown, to contain the territorial expansion of its northern neighbor, and to defeat the armies of French intervention. In the solution of its domestic problems Mexico had likewise to pay very dearly for the overthrow of dictatorship, for the separation between church and state, for agrarian reform, and for the adoption of a popular form of government. Hundreds of thousands of lives were spent to create and preserve a Mexican way of life.

Hidalgo, Morelos, Allende, Aldama, and Mina, the great leaders for Mexican independence, died facing Spanish firing squads before 1821, when the ten-year war against the Spanish Crown finally came to an end. Thereafter the Mexican people suffered the ravages of two other international wars: one with the United States, which cost Mexico over half its territory (1846-1848), another with France (1861-1867), which ended in the execution of Austrian-born Emperor Maximilian. Benito Juárez, father of Mexican liberalism, hero of the war against French intervention, and champion of nonintervention shines as a striking exception in the long drama of Mexican history: he died peacefully in 1872. But Madero (apostle of the 1910 revolution), Zapata (martyr for agrarian reform), Carranza (statesman of revolutionary Mexico), "Pancho" Villa (the Revolution's guerrillero), Obregón (the military genius of the Revolution)—all met violent death, as though every step in Mexico's social progress required the lives of its great leaders.

Moreover, while the Revolution was at its peak, Mexico was confronted with two serious international incidents: (1) the occupation of Veracruz by the United States Navy in 1914, because Mexico refused to comply with a demand to salute the United States flag after a United States naval officer had been arrested for trespassing on a military reserve in Tampico; and (2) the invasion of Mexican territory by United States troops, after Pancho Villa's men had crossed the border in 1916 and raided the town of Columbus, New Mexico. Not until 1938, when Lázaro Cárdenas nationalized the powerful oil industry, then a property of Anglo-Saxon monopolies, was Mexico able to win an important social victory peaceably.

The nation which would pay so high a price for national existence was from the outset a spokesman for Latin America's freedom. As early as 1814, in the immortal declaration of Apatzingan, Morelos had reaffirmed the sovereignty of Mexico and condemned the use of force as an instrument of international supremacy. And Morelos went further; he stated that any nation trying to subjugate other peoples should be compelled by the international society of nations to respect international law. Morelos spoke not only as a Mexican but as an *American*, for like Bolívar he was conscious of the fundamental brotherhood among the peoples of the new American republics.

So conservative a President as Porfirio Díaz, dictatorial ruler of Mexico for more than thirty years (1877-1910), stood firmly against foreign interventions. In 1896, when United States President Cleveland invoked the Monroe Doctrine against England in connection with a border incident between Venezuela and British Guiana, President Díaz warned Latin Americans of the dangers in the Monroe Doctrine, even though the Cleveland action was popular in Venezuela. "We do not think it sufficient," said he, "that only the United States, in spite of its fabulous wealth, should assume the responsibility of helping the Latin American republics against European aggression." Rather, he proposed, each of them should consider that any aggression from a foreign power against the territory, the independence, or the political institutions of an American republic would be considered as an attack against each of them, and assistance given if the victim of such an attack or aggression should request help.

As early as 1901, thus before the enunciation of the Drago Doctrine, Mexico was proposing agreements among governments looking to the arbitration of claims for damages or losses suffered by their citizens in other countries, looking indeed to the arbitration of all disputes not affecting the sovereignties of nations. During the Revolution, Venustiano Carranza created mixed claims commissions (between Mexico, the United States, and others) to solve peacefully all disputes on foreign claims, until then subject to the abusive mechanism of diplomatic protection. Carranza's view was and is logical: no foreigner can claim for himself a situation other or better than that enjoyed by the nationals of the country where he happens to live. This view directly opposes the interpretation of the Monroe Doctrine which made the United States armed forces bill collectors for foreign creditors of Latin American nations. When Carranza learned that the Versailles Peace Conference was considering the Monroe Doctrine, he declared immediately that Mexico had never accepted it. President Obregón followed Carranza's policy; he flatly refused to subscribe to agreements which were contrary to the Mexican Constitution, such as special guarantees for foreign investments, or against expropriation. When Mexico in 1931 joined the League of Nations, it stipulated that its participation in that League did not imply approval of Article XXI of the League's covenant, where the Monroe Doctrine was specifically mentioned as a "regional agreement."

The anti-intervention principle guided Mexico's policy toward Franco's Spain. When the forces of Falange, helped by Fascist Italy and Nazi Germany, overthrew the legal government of Republican Spain, and placed Francisco Franco at the head of a totalitarian Spain, Mexico held that if a legitimate government became a victim of foreign intervention, the "neutrality" of other countries was tantamount to passive complicity; and that in such case the victim deserved the help of the international community. Thus the voice of Juárez was heard again through President Lázaro Cárdenas. To this day, Mexico has refused to recognize Franco's regime, not because of Mexican objection to totalitarianism, but only because Franco, as was clearly shown by the Mexican Delegation at the San Francisco Conference (1945), had welcomed the open intervention of foreign troops. The ideology of a country, Spain or any other, is a question pertaining exclusively to the sovereignty of that state. On the other hand, foreign intervention is every nation's concern. The Mexican government does not believe that because foreign intervention was successful (in favor of Franco), international law had suffered no blow. Mexico's basic international policy, voiced by Juárez, Carranza, and Cárdenas, persists: to condemn, and never to condone, intervention.

Mexico's opposition to foreign intervention explains also the unflinching position taken by that country at the Tenth Inter-American Conference held at Caracas (1954), which at the initiative of the United States delegation adopted a resolution involving the application of the Rio Treaty against Guatemala, whose government had been denounced as pro-Communist. In Mexico's opinion, the Rio Treaty could and can be applied only in cases of intervention of a state in the affairs of another state; never in cases of "intervention" of an *idea*, Communist or not, in the affairs of any state. Therefore, the Mexican delegation did not subscribe to this Caracas resolution.

Mexico's Congress has some authority in matters of international relations and foreign policy: the Mexican executive cannot declare war without the approval of Congress; the Senate must approve international treaties and agreements signed by the President. Through its committees on foreign relations, Congress keeps in constant touch with the Foreign Department.

Mexico has a Foreign Service, with technical training and administrative stability, although chiefs of mission (ambassadors, ministers, or consuls general) are appointed by the President and can be noncareer men. Chiefs of mission, whether career men or not, must resign when a new administration takes over. The President decides whether to accept the resignations. Other members of the service, from vice consul to counselor of embassy, keep their jobs regardless of political changes at home. The Department supervises periodic examinations to fill vacancies and priority for diplomatic appointment is given to those candidates with the highest marks. Other staff members and minor officials are also appointed by examination. Candidates for the Foreign Service must have completed college and cannot be "members of any religious association, or political sect, contrary to the institutions of the Republic" (Article XII). Personal merit takes precedence over seniority.

On December 1, 1952, President Adolfo Ruiz Cortines summarized as follows the international policy of his administration: "Firm rejection of any form of foreign hegemony; permanent respect for the right of self-determination of peoples; solidarity with the weak and the oppressed; complete rejection of racial prejudice; basic dislike for injustice; unblemished devotion to international peace; adherence to the democratic system; and, above all, an indomitable love of freedom." Mexico, today a good neighbor of the United States, and the only Latin American republic sharing its borders, is viewed by Latin Americans as a faithful and reliable sentry of the extensive Latin American world.

At the meeting of the American Presidents, in Panama (July 1956), Ruiz Cortines stressed the need for all member states of the of the OAS to adopt a parity system so as to maintain the "necessary equity" between prices of primary products (from Latin America) and manufactured articles (from the United States). The President reiterated this recommendation in his Message to Congress (September 1, 1956).

Panama

Panama's brief history as an independent country is inextricably linked with a geographical fact of considerable import: the existence of an interoceanic canal through its territory. In this respect Panama shares with Egypt, and to some extent with Turkey, the dubious privilege of possessing a national territory cut by an international waterway.

Panama has been independent since 1903. Before that time, both under the Spanish Crown and after the successful wars for Latin American independence, it had been a province in Nueva Granada and a part of Colombia. Efforts at secession had been made in 1841, in 1853, and again in 1895.

The question of an interoceanic canal between the Atlantic and the Pacific has always played a prominent role in the affairs of the Isthmus. As early as 1523, Charles V of Spain initiated plans to build a canal. Other projects, plans, and explorations followed, variously in Panama, Nicaragua, and Tehuantepec. The location and control of the canal was an issue between Great Britain and the United States, but in 1876 a French association obtained a concession from the Colombian government to build the canal. In the following year, under the auspices of Ferdinand de Lesseps (father of the Suez Canal), a French Panama Canal company was formed and purchased the concession. From 1880 to 1887, the French did their best to complete the Canal, but money ran short and the company became helpless; yellow fever and tropical diseases complicated matters for the French pioneers who, unlike the United States engineers, did not take the necessary sanitary precautions. The French went bankrupt in 1889.

In 1902 the United States purchased the rights and property

of the French company for $40 million. Under the Hay-Herrán Treaty (January, 1903), Colombia granted canal rights on terms favorable to the United States, but on August 12 the Colombian Senate refused ratification. There were protests in the Colombian "department" of Panama. On November 3 a revolt began; independence was proclaimed at Panama City. Colombian troops, landed at Colon to crush this local insurrection, were stopped by United States Marines. Ten days later, the independence of Panama was officially recognized by the Washington government. Within a week the United States and the new Republic signed a treaty granting to the former the use in perpetuity of a canal zone, along with some extraterritorial rights. (Colombia did not recognize the independence of its former province until 1922.) Within a month after Panama's declaration of independence, the Hay-Bunau-Varilla Treaty granted the United States government the use, occupation, and control of a strip of land ten miles wide, for the purpose of the canal. Work was begun without delay, under the active direction of President Theodore Roosevelt, and the canal was opened in 1914.

The 1903 treaty was first revised in 1936, when the annual rental was raised from $250,000 to $430,000. After extended negotiations, a new instrument was ratified in 1955. It brought Panama several economic advantages, and the annuity paid for the use of the Canal Zone was raised from $430,000 to $1,930,000.

At this writing, there seems to be a serious discrepancy between the views of the Washington government and those of the government of Panama on the touchy question of sovereignty. Secretary of State Dulles, discussing the Suez Canal question, stated the Washington position on United States "sovereignty" in the Canal Zone in words that produced a diplomatic storm (August 29, 1956). After quoting Article III of the Treaty of 1903, he had declared that in the Canal Zone "the United States has all the rights which it would possess if it were the sovereign."[3] And he added: "to the entire exclusion of the exercise by the Republic of Panama of any such sovereign rights, powers, or authority."[4]

[3] The New York Times, August 30, 1956.
[4] The Evening Star, Washington, D.C., August 29, 1956.

Within hours, Panama's Foreign Minister, Alberto Boyd, took issue with Secretary Dulles; he declared that his country had granted to the United States "only certain powers exclusively for the purposes of the canal and nothing else." He also stated that "there is no doubt that the Treaty of 1903 does not grant the United States sovereignty over the Canal Zone. This has been Panama's invariable position since 1904."

It will take tactful diplomacy and inter-American good neighborliness for Panama (youngest and least populated of the twenty-one American republics) and the United States (eldest and most powerful of the American republics) to resolve this issue. However, other important issues have arisen between American governments in the past, and have been solved amicably to the satisfaction of all interested parties.

In the formulation of international policy, the Foreign Minister of Panama consults frequently with members of Congress. He must appear before Congress when a clarification of any international question is needed.

The executive can hardly ignore public opinion in a country like Panama, where the press is free and the citizens are always more than ready to express themselves without inhibition. The international policy of Panama has seldom been imposed from above by the executive. Rather, it is imposed by the people upon the executive.

Conclusions

The relative lack of "controls" over Latin American foreign relations is not the consequence of any particular incapacity of Latin America, but rather of the presidential system prevailing throughout the twenty-one American republics which allows the chiefs of state to act as policy-makers in foreign relations. Should our republics, including the United States,[5] abandon presidential

---

[5] In his excellent study, Edgar Turlington writes: "I suggest for your consideration that, in the absence of vigorous assertion of the powers of control vested in the legislative branch of government, the executive in every one of the

rule in order to experiment with parliamentary systems of government? This is a complex question reaching far beyond the scope of this book.

The Latin American republics *can*, indeed, organize truly professional diplomatic services, immune from political accidents, which can assist them permanently and adequately in the formulation of foreign policy.

Popular "controls" of foreign policy can function only where people can think, vote, and express themselves freely. In other words, only a genuine democracy can tolerate and welcome any kind of popular control.

Continental solidarity benefits *all* the American republics. Pan Americanism has strengthened them all. The OAS protects them both from aggression and from intervention and provides them with an effective procedure for peaceful solution of their conflicts.

Because of their historical tradition of inter-American co-operation, the countries of the western hemisphere are better prepared than those of any other continent to promote the existence of a world order as embodied today in the United Nations. This new internationalism requires a new form of diplomacy and a new type of diplomat. In its present form, diplomacy bears too many marks of an outmoded past. It has been and remains a *de luxe* profession; social manners have too often outweighed technical competence in the choice of diplomatic personnel. It developed in the service of foreign policies devoted almost exclusively to the consideration of national or bilateral interests.

A diplomat of the maturing twentieth century must learn to think and act in terms of world interests, and not of national policy alone. Whereas a diplomat's main mission was once to strengthen the individual power of his country and secure allies

American republics is a potential dictator in this field. This proposition I am prepared to maintain, so far as the United States is concerned, on the basis of the experience which led a competent American scholar to say some years ago that the President of the United States is in many respects a constitutional king." Edgar Turlington, "The Control of Foreign Relations Under the Constitutions of the American Republics," in *Cursos Monográficos*, vol. IV, p. 201, *Academia Interamericana de Derecho Comparado e Internacional*, Havana, Cuba, 1954.

in order to obtain national advantages of strategic character, the new diplomat must become an advocate of mankind as well as a spokesman for his country, and assume the existence of basic interests shared by all states and all peoples. Modern diplomacy must specialize in conciliation rather than in controversy. International organizations such as the United Nations and the Organization of American States are contributing to the advent of this new diplomacy and the training of these new diplomats.

SELECTED BIBLIOGRAPHY

Agan, Joseph, The Diplomatic Relations of the United States and Brazil. Paris, 1926.

Arciniegas, Germán, Caribbean: Sea of the New World, tr. by Harriet de Onís. New York, 1946.

Beals, Carleton, Pan America. Boston, 1940.

Biesanz, J. and M., Costa Rican Life. New York, 1944.

Blanksten, George, Ecuador: Constitutions and Caudillos. Berkeley, Calif., 1951.

Butland, G., Chile, An Outline. London, 1951.

Christensen, Asher N., The Evolution of Latin American Government, A Book of Readings. New York, 1951.

Cline, H. F., The United States and Mexico. Cambridge, Mass., 1953.

Covarrubias, Miguel, The Eagle, the Jaguar, and the Serpent. New York, Alfred A. Knopf, 1954.

Davila, Carlos, We of the Americas. Chicago-New York, 1949.

Duggan, Laurence. The Americas. New York, Holt, 1949.

Early, Lawrence O., The Republic of Panama in World Affairs, 1903-1950. Philadelphia, 1951.

Gordon, Wendell C., The Economy of Latin America. New York, Columbia University Press, 1950.

Gruening, E., *Mexico and Its Heritage.* New York, 1940.

Gunther, J., *Inside Latin America.* New York, Harper, 1941.

Hambloch, Ernest, *His Majesty the President: a Study of Constitutional Brazil.* London, 1935.

Hill, Lawrence, *The United States and Brazil.* Durham, N. C., 1932.

Lockey, Joseph Byrne, *Pan-Americanism: Its Beginnings.* New York, 1920.

Logan, R. W., *The Diplomatic Relations of the United States with Haiti, 1776-1891.* Chapel Hill, N.C., 1941.

McCain, William D., *The United States and the Republic of Panama.* Durham, N.C., 1937.

Mack, Gerstle, *The Land Divided: A History of the Panama Canal and other Isthmian Canal Projects.* New York, 1944.

Mecham, John Lloyd, *Church and State in Latin America: a History of Politico-Ecclesiastical Relations.* Chapel Hill, N.C., 1934.

Mosk, Sanford, *Industrial Revolution in Mexico.* Berkeley, Calif., 1950.

Nerval, Gaston, *Autopsy of the Monroe Doctrine.* New York, Macmillan, 1934.

Quintanilla, Luis, *Democracia y Panamericanismo.* México, D.F., Cuadernos Americanos, 1952.

Shaw, P. V., *The Early Constitutions of Chile.* 1931.

Stanger, F. M., "National Origins in Central America," *Hispanic American Historical Review,* XII, 18-45.

Tannenbaum, Frank, *Mexico: The Struggle for Peace and Bread.* New York, 1950.

Ugarteche, Pedro, *Formación del Diplomático Peruano.* Lima, Villanueva, 1955.

United Nations, *A Study of Trade between Latin America and Europe.* Geneva, 1953.

United Nations, Report 1, *The Population of Central America (Including Mexico), 1950-1980.* New York, 1954.

Whitaker, A. P., *The United States and South America: Northern Republics.* Cambridge, Mass., 1948.

Wilson, C. M., *Empire in Green and Gold: The Story of the American Banana Trade.* New York, 1947.

The United Kingdom

PHILIP W. BUCK

Department of Political Science
Stanford University

The United Kingdom

CHAPTER **7**.

THE CONTEMPORARY SITUATION AND NINETEENTH-CENTURY EXPERIENCE OF THE UNITED KINGDOM

The United Kingdom, which includes England, Wales, Scotland, and Northern Ireland, has an area of 94,207 square miles. Measuring this against the United States and the Soviet Union, it is less than a thirtieth of the size of the former and hardly a hundredth of the size of the latter. Among all the countries of the world the United Kingdom ranks 75th in territory.

In this area live over 50 million people, which fact ranks this community ninth in the world in population. Only three other major countries are more densely populated: Japan, Belgium, and the Netherlands.

The size of neither the country nor the population explains the fact that when the foreign ministers of "The Big Five" or even "The Big Three" assemble for a conference or a consultation on world affairs, the Secretary of State for Foreign Affairs of Her Majesty's Government is one of the group. The British share in the commerce and manufacture of the world, and the widespread territories and peoples of the British Commonwealth lend power and influence to the standing of the government of the United Kingdom in world affairs. In large part, both the commerce of the country and the growth of the Commonwealth are the results of developments during the nineteenth century.

Economic Development and Overseas Expansion in the Nineteenth Century

The Industrial Revolution began in England in the middle of the eighteenth century. In the two centuries preceding, British trade with Europe and with more remote parts of the world had been expanding, chiefly on the basis of a growing commerce in textiles. In the sixteenth and seventeenth centuries English seamen and adventurers began to lay the basis for an expanding colonial empire, in competition with the other nations of Europe. A series of inventions in the textile industries during the course of the eighteenth century greatly expanded productive power and led eventually to the development of the iron and engineering industries.

The significant feature of the whole development is that it led to the creation of factory industry in Great Britain before similar developments occurred in the other commercial states of the world. This gave Britain a long start in the economic expansion of the nineteenth century, so that it is not hyperbole to say that this small community became the workshop of the world. New techniques were created; capital reserves were accumulated; investments were built up abroad. All this activity was accompanied by a rapid growth of population: the population increased fourfold during the course of the nineteenth century—it is worth noting that it increased sevenfold from 1700 to 1955. Old cities grew in size, new cities appeared in the manufacturing areas, and the urban industrial and trading community of England assumed the character it has today.

This brief summary of a long and complicated story must be kept in mind, for the situation of the British community today is the result of the process. Food and raw materials are imported, and manufactured goods and capital must be exported. The balance of trade has become the vital indicator of the welfare of the society.

While economic development was making such progress, the colonial territories which had been acquired during the preceding centuries were slowly consolidated into the Commonwealth. Some areas were lost, notably the North American colonies, but others were acquired in Africa, India, and the Far East during the imperialist competition of the great powers in the last quarter of the nineteenth century. More important than gains or losses of territory, however, was the experiment with new forms of government and association. Canada was the first to achieve what is now called "dominion status." By the end of the century Australia and New Zealand had achieved similar standing, and the same result was achieved for South Africa by 1909, after the Boer War. The new features of self-government for each dominion[1] and consultation among them all on mutual problems were developed in Imperial Conferences, particularly in 1926, and were finally given legal expression by the Statute of Westminster in 1931. This brought into existence what is called by historians "The Second British Empire" and it has been followed by a continued process of extension of dominion status to the Asian communities such as India, Pakistan, and Ceylon. Steps are now being taken to work out similar status for territories and communities in Africa and Malaya and in other dependencies, all of which possess at present some powers of self-government. The Gold Coast, in this program, was scheduled to become independent early in 1957.

In broad outline, then, Great Britain entered World War II as one of the great commercial and industrial communities of the world, importing food and raw materials and exporting manufactures and investment capital to pay for her supplies. She had become the senior partner of an expanding Commonwealth of Nations knit together by a minimum of legal ties, by a willingness to consult on mutual problems, and by a network of economic relationships. The war had far-reaching effects on both the English community and the Commonwealth.

[1] The amenities and the difficulties of terminology for the parts of the Commonwealth and Empire are discussed on pages 301-302, 314, and 400.

The British Situation Today

A short, suggestive phrase is frequently used by British Treasury and Board of Trade officials to characterize the national economy: "a vulnerable economy." The meaning of this phrase is easily guessed from the history which has been summarized: the welfare and the livelihood of the community are heavily dependent on international trade, and Britain's prosperity is closely tied with world economic conditions. For that matter, this situation applies to all nations in the twentieth century—but an American or a Russian can see that his own country is rich in a variety of natural resources and could provide for the employment and living standard of his people in a considerable part or for a considerable time in the face of adverse conditions in the rest of the world.

In 1954 almost a fifth of the total national income of Great Britain (18.2 per cent) was derived from export earnings, and in the same year the proportion of the national expenditure spent on imports was just over a fifth (21.8 per cent).[2]

The British share of the total volume of world trade is significantly large. Britain ranks second among the world's trading nations, taking about a fifth of the world's output of primary products and supplying about a fifth of the total exports of manufactured goods. Its participation in the trade in particular commodities is a further measure of its economic position. It is the world's largest importer of wheat, fodder grains, wool, iron and steel scrap, the largest exporter of ships and textiles, and the second largest exporter of machinery and all kinds of transport equipment. It supplies about half of its own food supplies, and this is a larger proportion than was the case in the years before World War II.

These trading and processing activities were easily sustained in the years before World War I. For more than a hundred years, during the nineteenth century and the early part of the twentieth

---

[2] *Britain, An Official Handbook*, 1956, p. 296. This book, published annually since 1954, is an excellent summary of many aspects of the British scene. Its substance is collected from many official publications of the British Government. It is issued by Her Majesty's Stationery Office (referred to hereafter as HMSO).

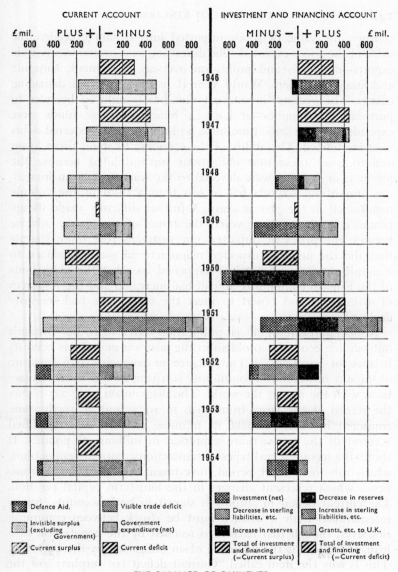

THE BALANCE OF PAYMENTS

From *Britain, An Official Handbook*, 1956 ed., p. 301, by permission of H. M. Stationery Office.

CURRENT ACCOUNT

£ mil. PLUS + | − MINUS
600 400 200 0 200 400 600 800

INVESTMENT AND FINANCING ACCOUNT

MINUS − | + PLUS £ mil.
600 400 200 0 200 400 600

1946
1947
1948
1949
1950
1951
1952
1953
1954

Legend:

- Defence Aid.
- Invisible surplus (excluding Government)
- Current surplus
- Visible trade deficit
- Government expenditure (net)
- Current deficit
- Investment (net)
- Decrease in sterling liabilities, etc.
- Increase in reserves
- Total of investment and financing (= Current surplus)
- Decrease in reserves
- Increase in sterling liabilities, etc.
- Grants, etc. to U.K.
- Total of investment and financing (= Current deficit)

century, the value of goods imported into Britain exceeded the value of the goods exported. The difference was covered by invisible exports—dividends and profits on overseas investment, shipping and financial services. World War II had a number of damaging effects. The overseas investment was greatly reduced by sales to purchase war supplies—at least £1 billion of these funds were expended. At the same time some £3 billion of new external debts were contracted. The ability of the economy to stand these losses and to meet these new obligations was inhibited because the products of industry were devoted to the war effort in an increasing proportion. Exports fell to less than a third of the volume maintained in the prewar years. A further difficulty made its appearance in the postwar years: the terms of trade were adverse because the prices of imported raw materials rose more sharply than did the prices of exported manufactured goods. Reduced to a simple statement, what had happened was that the obligations of the English community abroad had increased and the resources of investment and export to meet the obligations had seriously declined.

A sober and careful official publication stated in 1956: "Britain's outstanding economic problem in the post-war period has been its balance of payments."[3] The balance of payments is a measure of the way in which the community is paying its way in its transactions with the rest of the world. The diagram on page 241 shows the record of the years from 1946 to 1954, and is worth some comment in order to make its meaning clear. It is a simplified account of the transactions, expressed in millions of pounds. It shows the record of two types of transactions: current transactions, which run for a short period; investment and financing transactions, which represent changes in the long-term capital position. The current deficit or surplus is shown in both accounts, for in international trade a balance must be struck between communities, even though that balance is reached by the negotiation of a loan which means the incurring of an obligation by the borrower. This is why the item called "Current deficit (or surplus)" in the

[3] *Britain, An Official Handbook*, 1956, p. 298 (hereafter cited as *Handbook*, 1956).

current account appears as "Total of investment or financing" on either the plus or the minus side of the investment and financing account.

A striking feature of the current account has already been suggested in the discussion of the growth and the present position of the national economy. This is the persistent appearance of the "visible-trade deficit" which expresses the excess of the value of imports over that of exports. This has been a long-standing characteristic of the British trade balance. In the nineteenth century this item was more than covered by the surplus of invisible transactions, which has been reduced in the years since the World Wars by the loss of returns from investment abroad and declines in shipping and financial services.

In summary, this record of the recent balance of payments shows a difficult position for the British national economy, one which requires constant effort to balance accounts with the rest of the world. When it is recalled that nearly a fifth of the national product goes into exports and a fifth of the national expenditure is spent on imports, the importance of this balance is all the more significant.

Two other diagrams, which appear on pages 244 and 245, illuminate the situation further. These express the distribution of foreign trade: one the nature of the commodities imported and exported, the other the geographical distribution of trade. Both diagrams express these relationships in percentages, not in outright units of currency. The bars in the diagrams show how large a proportion of imports are basic materials, foodstuffs, etc., and how large a proportion of exports are engineering products, textiles, etc. Similar proportions are shown in the area-distribution diagram for the sources of goods imported and markets for exports. The "sterling area" includes the Commonwealth countries, the colonial territories, and a few other countries (Burma, Iceland, Iraq, British-protected states in the Persian Gulf, Jordan, Libya, and the Republic of Ireland). The total sterling area contains about a quarter of the world's population and accounts for about a quarter of the world's trade, so it is not surprising that it bulks fairly large in the percentages of geographical distribution.

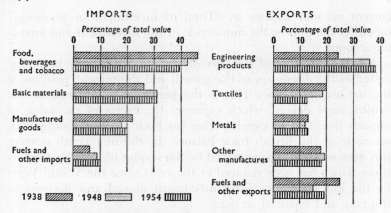

IMPORTS

Percentage of total value

EXPORTS

Percentage of total value

COMPOSITION OF FOREIGN TRADE BY VALUE, 1938-1954

From *Britain, An Official Handbook*, 1956 ed., p. 299, by permission of H. M. Stationery Office.

An interesting feature of the commodity distribution is the increasing percentage shown by the engineering products—machinery, electrical goods, vehicles, and the like. In the nineteenth century the big percentage would have been textiles, but the importance of this industry is now declining as the composition-of-trade diagram shows for the selected years. This reveals the determined effort of the ingenuity of the manufacturing community to find outlets, and so to develop electronic equipment, motorcars, airplanes, and other manufactures which can secure a place in the world market.

The United Kingdom's Productive Power

The foregoing rough and general summary of the balance of payments and the character of foreign trade suggests that the British community has been in a tight spot since the end of World War II and that the future looks difficult, though it need not be regarded as discouraging. It is quite clear that effort and ingenuity will be needed if Britain is to pay her way. The community has been busy in the attempt to solve these problems.

The working population of the United Kingdom at midyear of

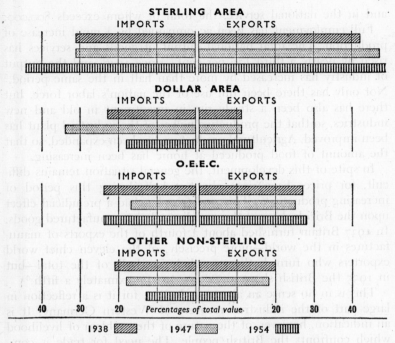

STERLING AREA

IMPORTS   EXPORTS

DOLLAR AREA

IMPORTS   EXPORTS

O.E.E.C.

IMPORTS   EXPORTS

OTHER NON-STERLING

IMPORTS   EXPORTS

40   30   20   Percentages of total value   20   30   40

1938   1947   1954

AREA DISTRIBUTION OF FOREIGN TRADE, 1938-1954

From *Britain, An Official Handbook*, 1956 ed., p. 299, by permission of H. M. Stationery Office.

1955 was just over 24½ million people, nearly half of all the people. All but 5 per cent of the men of 15 to 64 years of age are working or seeking jobs. Of the women, 45 per cent are working, but this difference results from the fact that official manpower statistics do not count housewives who are not doing some sort of part-time work outside the home as employed persons.

Since the war unemployment has never been higher than 3 per cent, and for most of the period has not been higher than 2 per cent.[4] These figures include men and women in the armed forces

[4] Manpower figures from *Handbook*, 1956, p. 252. Unemployment percentages from Command Paper 9725 (hereafter Cmd.), *The Economic Implications of Full Employment*, HMSO, 1956, par. 2.

and in the national service, the total of whom exceeds 800,000.

Full employment has been accompanied by a rapid increase of production. The total national output of goods and services has risen by nearly a third (30 per cent) since 1946; and the output of industry has increased by more than half in the same period.[5] Not only has there been full use of the nation's labor force, but there has also been a steady rise in investment in old and new industries, so that the productive power of the industrial plant has been improved. Agricultural production has been expanded, so that the amount of food produced at home has been increasing.

In spite of this development, the general situation remains difficult, for prices have risen about a half during this period of increasing productivity. This price rise has had a prejudicial effect upon the British share of the world's trade in manufactured goods. In 1937 Britain furnished about a fourth of the exports of manufactures in the world—more precisely, of the eleven chief world exporters who furnish the overwhelming bulk of the total—but in 1955 the British share was down to approximately a fifth.[6]

This is in no sense an alarming decline, for it is a reflection in large part of the industrial recovery of Western Germany. It is an indication, however, of the nature of the problem of livelihood which confronts the British people. The need for trade is compelling, and ideally productivity should rise while prices remain stable if the British are to balance their payments with the rest of the world.

An asset to Great Britain which has already received some comment in the preceding pages is the Commonwealth. It includes eight sovereign and independent states: the United Kingdom, Canada, Australia, New Zealand, South Africa, India, Pakistan, and Ceylon. One state, the Federation of Rhodesia and Nyasaland, has powers of self-government, but is not yet regarded as one of the completely equal and independent partners in the association. Besides these there are all the colonial territories administered by

[5] Cmd. 9725, cited above, par. 3.

[6] Cmd. 9728, *Economic Survey 1956*, HMSO, p. 27. This annual publication is an excellent analysis of Britain's economic situation for each year. It has appeared annually since 1947. For the problem created by rising prices, see Cmd. 9725, referred to in previous footnotes.

the United Kingdom and some of the other member states. The total territory is a little more than 14½ million square miles, and the combined population of all these communities is 631 million. While there are many trade and economic ties among them, and some preferential agreements, all of them trade with many parts of the world outside the association. Nevertheless, Britain's banking, trading, and industrial strength gives her many opportunities within this vast area, which is nearly a fourth of the earth's surface and contains nearly a quarter of the world's population. Many of them are producers of primary products, and this has been an important factor in the balance of trade between the Commonwealth and the rest of the world. A series of Colonial Development and Welfare Acts enacted by the Parliament of the United Kingdom, combined with co-operative efforts like the Colombo Plan, have already contributed to the capital development and the productive power of the Commonwealth and will continue to do so in increasing measure in the future.

The Commonwealth and the colonial territories must be counted as one of the resources which lend strength to Britain's position economically as well as politically, but it must always be remembered that Great Britain in no sense "owns" these territories, in the old sense of empire. Associated action, by agreement and consultation among the communities, can benefit all the members.[7]

Traditional British Foreign Policies

This sketch of Britain's present economic situation, and the development which gave rise to it, suggest that for more than a century there has been a persistent set of conditions which have at least influenced, if not controlled, the course of British foreign policy. Britain's relations with other states of the world have continually to be directed to safeguard the trade of the homeland and

[7] *Economic Development in the Commonwealth*, Reference Pamphlet No. 13, 1956, and *Economic Development in the U.K. Dependencies*, Reference Pamphlet No. 8, 1955, both prepared by the Central Office of Information and issued by HMSO, give a good brief description of the recent economic growth referred to above.

to maintain the connections of the many communities which are now associated in the Commonwealth.

The field of action for policy has been world wide for more than two centuries. The explorations and the establishment of colonies which began in the sixteenth and seventeenth centuries established contacts far beyond the limits of Europe alone, although European affairs were of great concern to British governments. All this is clear enough, but some of the consequences of this wide field of action should be pointed out.

Administrative authorities in many departments of the government as well as in the Foreign Office have a long experience and an accumulation of knowledge to apply to situations in all parts of the world. The published collections of British state papers show a remarkable range of dealings with widely scattered areas and diverse communities. This experience has been gathered by political leaders as well as by expert permanent officials—the substance of debate in the Parliament and in the country is often concerned with foreign affairs, and·has been so concerned for a long period. The official, the political leader, and the general public have become accustomed to giving thought to world affairs. The newspaper-reading public is the largest in the world—611 daily newspapers are sold to every 1,000 persons. Of course, this reflects an interest in football pools as well as in international affairs, but it can be said with confidence that a continued and sustained interest in foreign affairs is natural for a people who are well aware from long experience that their livelihood depends on the conditions of trade between nations.

The wide extent of connections and contacts is accompanied by another condition which has persistently affected foreign policy. The interest of a trading nation lies in the maintenance of peace, order, and stability in international relations. It is perhaps possible to make quick profits out of wartime situations, but over any long period trade flourishes under peaceful and stable conditions. Though Britain was at war several times during the nineteenth century, her economic development was made possible by long periods of peace.

These two conditioning factors—the wide extent of British interests and the interest in peaceful and stable relationships among nations—are reflected in large part in the characteristic policies which have been pursued by the leaders of the community. A few guiding principles of policy which have been quite consistent for a long period can be stated.

Maintenance of command of the seas was clearly imperative, to safeguard the homeland from any threat which might arise across the narrow reaches of the Channel and to protect widely dispersed holdings and trading connections in all parts of the world. For a maritime and trading nation the support of a powerful fleet was a natural and continuous policy. Diplomacy was brought to the aid of the fleet. The neutrality and independence of Belgium and the Netherlands was a constant object of policy, realized in a number of treaties of guarantee.

A continuous interest in the position of Turkey—what diplomatic historians refer to as the "Eastern Question"—accompanied by a concern in the affairs of Greece, Egypt, and the rest of the countries of the eastern Mediterranean, was also a means of protecting the great trade routes and the maritime power of England. British policy in the twentieth century, even after naval parity with the United States had been accepted at the Washington Conference in 1921, is still clearly designed to safeguard the command of the seas.

A second guiding line of foreign policy is expressed in the phrase "the balance of power," which refers chiefly to policy toward the states of Europe. The conception can be stated more accurately if it is put negatively. Britain has tried to prevent the domination of Europe by any one power and has formed alliances, and even engaged in wars, to limit the authority of any one power. The wars against Napoleon are an instance of this purpose, and some of the time between 1800 and 1815 Britain stood alone against the Napoleonic Empire in Europe. It is not straining historical generalization too much to say that the two world wars of the twentieth century follow in the direct line of this policy. So also do many of the peace settlements following the wars: France was not dismembered at the Congress of Vienna, and Germany maintained much of her national position in 1918.

A strategy which has been consistently used by British leaders has been the formation of alliances. This might be regarded as a third guiding principle of foreign policy, which shows a consistency as steady as the two previously described. To a considerable extent it has been enforced by circumstances—while the fleet has always been as powerful as any other, or more powerful, the army has never been as large as the armies maintained by other European powers. From the time of the alliances designed to restrain the power of Napoleon to the alliance which opposed Hitler in World War II, Britain has usually been able to find a basis for concerted action with other powers.

In the world of the twentieth century this policy has been extended beyond limited associations of powers to international organizations. The British record of membership in the League of Nations—and in the United Nations—is an evidence of willingness and ability to act in concert with other powers in order to secure co-operative action for mutual purposes. There are compelling economic and trading reasons for this readiness to seek the basis of general international organization. If stability and order can be established by international action, it is clear that the community of Great Britain can count on an increased security for the future of the "vulnerable economy."

A fourth guiding line of policy should be stated, though it is much more difficult to express. Certainly it can be said that during most of the nineteenth century the foreign policy of Great Britain was accommodated to change in political and social organization in the states of Europe, and of the world. This was the period of the growth of nationalism and of liberal constitutional governments on the continent of Europe. British leaders like Canning, Palmerston, Disraeli, and Gladstone refused to give the aid of their government to any grouping of states which was organized to frustrate or suppress these movements. Public opinion in England was willing to support policies designed to encourage political and social change in France, Germany, and many of the smaller states of the Continent. This is not a consistent and sustained policy; but it is safe to say that British leadership recognized needs for change and development and was ready to accommodate policy to changing conditions in Europe and in the world. This is partly a general practical approach to the problems of international relations and partly a sympathy for the growth of institutions which were like the institutions of parliamentary democracy in England itself. On the whole, both leaders and public are willing to give cognizance to change and to attempt to modify and adjust policy to fit new situations as they appear in the world of states.

Probably it is impossible to characterize adequately the foreign policy of any great state by defining a series of general principles, and the student is warned that the foregoing general statements should not be taken as conclusive or positive. Nevertheless, British foreign policy has been quite consistent for a long period of time—largely because the community's economic situation has progressively led to industrial and trading activity on a world scale. Under these circumstances it was natural that foreign policy would be concerned with command of the seas, order and stability in international relations, and accommodation to change. Restraint of the growth of a single powerful state in Europe, a strategy of alliances, and support for international organizations seem the appropriate methods for securing the conditions which would give a more secure future for the developing commerce of the English people.

Group Influences on Foreign Policy

In the next chapter the constitutional structure and the administrative agencies of British government will be described. The pattern of parliamentary government in Britain has concentrated responsibility for policy in the hands of a Cabinet which is responsible to Parliament and which includes the leaders of the majority party. The most important influences of public opinion on the issues of foreign affairs are without question the two major parties. Both act as agencies for the mobilization of public opinion, and both maintain research organizations which work with party councils and committees to formulate and publicize the program of the party toward international affairs. The action of other groups on important issues is quite likely to work through the organization of the two major parties.

The functioning relationship between party and government has existed for well over a century. This has concentrated the attention of scholars upon this relationship, with the result that there has been little study of the influence of pressure groups or specialized organizations upon foreign policy, or upon government policy in general. Some important groups do exist, however, and though it is not easy to assess their influence it is possible to identify some of the more powerful organizations and to suggest their fields of activity.[8]

The British banking and financial community, concerned with investment in enterprises in all parts of the world, has always exerted influence upon the shaping of foreign policy. There are two convenient channels through which the great banks and investment houses can express their views: the Treasury, with which they constantly deal on questions of regulation of foreign exchange, and the Bank of England, which as the central bank constantly deals with government and with other banks and financial institutions. The weight of opinion in "the City" (referred to by this term because most of the banks, insurance companies, and investment houses have their offices in the City of London) is undoubtedly heeded by political leaders when policies are being framed.

Industry and labor groups also are able to bring their viewpoints to bear on questions of international relations. The Federation of British Industries has a membership which includes about 270 national industrial associations and some 1,600 local and regional associations of employers and managers. The Federation (FBI) is the recognized spokesman for the management side of industry. Since 1939 the need for government controls of the economy has established a regular and formal contact between various government departments, known as "Production Departments," and groups of industries or industrial associations. This provides a formal channel, particularly through the Ministry of Supply, the Board of Trade, the Admiralty, and the Ministry of Transport and Civil Aviation, by which questions of production, trade, and re-

[8] See Beer, Samuel H., "Pressure Groups and Parties in Britain" (in *The American Political Science Review*, March, 1956, vol. L, pp. 1-23), for a shrewd and suggestive discussion of the role of such groups in British politics and government. Professor Beer points out that scholars in England are now exploring this field of investigation.

search and development may be discussed by officials and the leaders of industry.

The most important spokesman for labor is the Trades Union Council (TUC) though many of the big and powerful unions may also exert influence. These groups have a large share of the membership of the Labour Party, and a corresponding degree of influence upon its formulation of policies. In the same ways that industrial and management associations gain access to departments and officials, the trades unions are able to find expression of their viewpoints. The co-ordinating action of the Cabinet brings all these sources of information, influence, and opinion to bear on questions of foreign policy whenever there is relevance to the issues of international relations.

One public service organization should be mentioned: the Royal Institute of International Affairs. It is in no sense a pressure group; it is a research foundation comparable to the Council on Foreign Relations in the United States. Its publications attract wide notice, however, and undoubtedly have influence both on government officials and upon an influential section of public opinion. In the past few years it has organized study groups of distinguished membership to analyze contemporary issues of foreign policy. These reports, by virtue of their quality and through the reputation of their members, undoubtedly have a considerable influence on lines of policy. The Institute itself is restrained by its charter from sponsoring any particular viewpoint and is studiously careful to sponsor objective investigation and study. The Study Groups, however, may and do express opinions and occasionally make recommendations, though their chief care is to make an analysis of the problem under consideration.[9]

There are also public associations which are concerned with foreign policy and international affairs. The United Nations Association is a conspicuous example of this type of organization, and there are others in the history of the years since World War I.

The influence of the press has already been suggested. England has a large number of national newspapers, published in London

[9] A good recent example of one of these reports is: *Britain in Western Europe*, Royal Institute of International Affairs, London and New York, 1956.

254 THE UNITED KINGDOM

and circulated to the whole area of the United Kingdom. There are also a large number of weekly journals of comment and opinion with circulations of tens of thousands. It is impossible to assess the influence of newspapers and journals upon the course of policy because there is constantly the expression of a wide diversity of opinions. The stimulating effect upon public opinion, and the interest in the questions of foreign policy, are undoubted.[10]

It should be repeated that, while all these associations and institutions have influence on the formation of foreign policy, the importance of group influences on policy in Great Britain is being studied with attention and thoroughness. This explains the caution which has been used here in describing them. What has been said should be placed in relation to the discussion of the action of British government which is described in the following chapter. It is safe to say that all the groups which have been mentioned, and many others of more ephemeral character, express the general interest of the British public in foreign policy and certainly have an effect upon decisions taken in the field of international affairs.

The Military Establishment of the United Kingdom

In the imperfect world in which we live it is often not enough merely to negotiate, it seems to be necessary to "negotiate from strength." The risk of war requires Britain, and other nations, to maintain a sufficient force and sufficient reserves to meet whatever conflict may develop. In the vocabulary and the realities of international life since 1945, these forces are defense forces wherever employed—abroad or at home.

Responsibility for defense rests upon a Minister of Defence who is a member of the Cabinet. He speaks there for the three service ministries headed by the First Lord of the Admiralty, the Secretary of State for Air, and the Secretary of State for War. The technical complexity of warfare in an age of nuclear weapons and guided missiles is so great that this co-ordination of the services was

[10] For a compact description of the press, see *Handbook 1956*, Chapt. XIV. For an authoritative analysis of the character of the press, with recommendations for a General Council of the Press which was established in 1953, see Cmd. 7700, *Report of the Royal Commission on the Press*, HMSO, 1949.

established in 1946 and has been maintained since. One of the
results of this organization is to make the *Annual Statement on
Defence*, presented to Parliament in February of each year when
consideration of the budget begins, a good succinct summary of
the status of defense.

Since armaments are now so complex, it is more intelligible to
measure British strength by the figures of the number of people in
the services, and the budget figures of cost, than to attempt a
catalogue of armament. The strength of the total active forces,
which includes people in the national service doing two years of
training, is shown in a table.

	1955 (Actual)	1956 (Est.)	1957 (Est.)
Regular	518,119	465,500	464,600
National Service	284,954	289,100	253,400
Women	20,557	17,400	17,000
Total	823,630	772,000	735,000
Reserves (Volunteers and part-time National Service), men and women	647,382	634,242	

Source for above figures: Cmd. 9691 *Statement on Defence*, 1956, HMSO,
pp. 16, 30. The Statement gives a breakdown of these figures for the various
services.

In view of the relative shortages of manpower in a situation of
full employment, it is worth noting that the total number in the
active forces is a little larger than the labor force engaged in coal
mining and more than a full sixth of the number engaged in the
metal, manufacturing, and vehicle industries which bulk so large
in the export trade of Britain.

The money cost of defense is as impressive as the claim it makes
on available manpower. The budget for the current costs of defense
for 1956-1957 is £1498.7 million, to which £50 million of United
States aid will be added. Since 1952-53 the cost of defense has been
30 per cent or more of the total expenditure of the government,
and since 1955 it takes a full third. Converted into a share of the

total national income or expenditure, it reaches a dimension of just short of a fifth.

The slight decline of manpower which appears in the figures on page 255 is the result of a policy announced by the Prime Minister in October, 1955, and explained in the *Statement on Defence, 1956*. The prospect of war with atomic and nuclear weapons had led to the decision to raise the standard of equipment of all the armed services, to concentrate effort on nuclear research and guided missiles, and therefore to diminish the strength of the forces slightly. However, since this policy will require a higher percentage of men serving longer terms in order to acquire the skills for this type of army, navy, and air force, there have been increases in pay and improvement of conditions in order to attract a larger number of volunteers for longer periods of service. Though the strain on manpower will be relieved a little by this policy, the total costs of defense are quite likely to increase to larger figures in future years.

A great deal of effort and thought is being put into research and development programs for the fleet, the air force, and for the improvement of weapons for the army. The navy has an active building program, ships are being re-equipped and reconditioned, and new vessels are under construction in substantial numbers. An active development of new types of fighter and bomber aircraft also is in progress. Much of this activity is secret, and it is hardly worth while to attempt to characterize it. Official statements are guarded, but they unhesitatingly declare that extensive work is being carried forward.[11]

Summary: Past History and Present Problems

The history of Britain has involved the home and overseas community in steadily widening commitments and obligations. The assets and resources to meet these demands are perhaps not so great now as during the period of expansion. The vulnerable economy of the twentieth century is the result of the commercial suc-

[11] Cmd. 9391, *Statement on Defence 1955*, Cmd. 9691, *Statement on Defence 1956*, and Cmd. 9388, *The Supply of Military Aircraft* (1955), all give some description of arms and equipment. Cmd. 9697, *Explanatory Statement on the Navy Estimates 1956-57*, gives a statement on the deployment of vessels in the fleet, and the nature of the construction program.

cess and industrial development of the nineteenth century. The obligations of the Commonwealth arise from the expansion of trading and colonial connection during the eighteenth and nineteenth centuries.

The problem of balancing payments with the rest of the world requires full employment of the manpower of the community, and under the pressure of maintaining exports there have been surprising shifts from the textile industries to the newer forms of production—electrical equipment, machinery, motor vehicles, and airplanes. Investment outside of Britain has been increasing slowly in the years since 1946, but it is safe to say that the losses of wartime have not yet been made up. Shipping and financial services no longer produce the secure surplus that could be expected during the nineteenth century.

A trading and manufacturing population must seek its employment and livelihood in maintaining an active foreign trade, and that population is four times as large as it was a century ago. To maintain the world conditions which are favorable to trade, the government must undertake a wide range of obligations to international organizations and associations and must sustain an active connection with the countries of the Commonwealth and the developing dependent territories. The British commitment to Europe, expressed in membership in NATO and in association with other European organizations, must be active and determined.

One of the requirements that the state of the world imposes on Great Britain is the maintenance of a large defense establishment. Under conditions of technical change in equipment and weapons, this imposes a heavy burden on the manpower and the income of the community. In this field the government is using research and inventiveness, as well as men and money, to build effective means of defense.

Though material resources may be limited, there are other assets. The history that has been under review created traditions of dealing with the world which are understood by the public and receive support when leaders declare them and put them into effect. The maintenance of a peaceful and orderly world so that trade will be safe is an agreed objective of policy. The need for alliances with other countries in order to achieve this objective is clearly recognized, as is the more extended obligation to participate in international organizations. Even the "balance of power" concept still has its uses—associated action to lessen the possibility of aggressive action by a powerful state is understood as a necessary strategy at times.

In fact, if the traditions can be reduced to a single statement, that statement might well be that British leadership understands the value of action in association with other nations and can count upon the public to support such action. This is a natural response for a people fully accustomed to making their living from the exchange of goods and services in international trade.

While the Commonwealth carries with it obligations, it is also an economic and political asset. The recent record of constitutional and political development among the countries of the Commonwealth shows steady progress toward increasing powers of self-government and the creation of more effective forms of consultation and associated action. "The Third British Empire" is not to be an empire at all in the usual sense of the word, but an association of self-governing communities.

Among these traditional attitudes there is also a tradition of willingness to experiment, to accommodate to the processes of change that go on in the world. This has been evident during the nineteenth century in the formulation of British policy toward Europe, and it is certainly exemplified in the changing patterns of the Commonwealth. This means that leaders of government and opinion have a considerable range of freedom of action in devising policies to meet changing situations in the world.

The formal responsibility for declaring foreign policy rests upon the Secretary of State for Foreign Affairs, though the Prime Minister and the Cabinet as a whole cannot avoid responsibility as well. The means and agencies for the formulation of policies in international affairs will be the subject of the following chapter.

CHAPTER 8

THE FORMULATION AND EXECUTION OF BRITISH FOREIGN POLICY

Her Majesty's Secretary of State for Foreign Affairs is one of the chief members of the government. He is, therefore, a member of the Cabinet, the group of political leaders which carries the power of decision on all matters of policy and which bears the responsibility for proposing legislation to the Parliament. While it is assumed that he will undertake the initiation of foreign policy and will make decisions regarding its administration, he must always be able to win the consent and support of the Prime Minister and his fellow Cabinet ministers. Since these responsibilities are heavy, he has the assistance of two Ministers of State who are not members of the Cabinet but are members of the ministry. Associated with these three are two junior ministers, Parliamentary Under-Secretaries of State, who assist in both the work of devising policy and the practical matters of administration. All these officers are simultaneously members of Parliament, usually of the House of Commons, and all therefore participate in debate and carry the responsibility for defending and explaining foreign policy and responding to questions in the House of Commons on all matters of foreign affairs.

This relationship of ministerial responsibility to the Parliament for all matters of policy and administration is the result of the long history of the growth of parliamentary government in England and is defined more by custom and usage than by legal provisions. The best explanation of it is practical, and the circumstances of the election of May, 1955, are a good illustration of the way in which these institutions work.

The Constitutional Framework of Cabinet Government

Sir Winston Churchill resigned as Prime Minister on April 5, 1955, and Sir Anthony Eden succeeded him on the following day. He made a few changes in the Cabinet, and a week later announced that Parliament would be dissolved and that the election of a new House of Commons would be held on May 26. The election would show whether the Conservative Party still retained the support of the electorate and whether it would, therefore, have a majority in the House of Commons in support of its policies.

The Conservative Party and its allies polled 13.3 million votes and elected 345 members to the House of Commons. The Labour Party polled 12.4 million votes and returned 277 members. Liberals won 6 seats, and 2 Sinn Fein members (subsequently disqualified because they were serving prison terms) were returned from Northern Ireland.

The general effect of the election was more clear and decisive than had been the two preceding elections, in 1950 and 1951. The Conservative Party had a reasonably solid majority of 60 votes, which meant that legislation, and acts of foreign policy, would have the endorsement of this majority. The legal life of a Parliament runs for five years, so the government could count on support until 1960 unless a break occurred in the majority.

Sir Anthony Eden resigned January 9, 1957. After consulting the retiring Prime Minister, and a few other Conservative leaders, the Queen appointed Mr. Harold Macmillan to succeed Sir Anthony. At the time of his appointment Mr. Macmillan declared that there was no need to hold a general election; and if there is no break in Conservative loyalty and discipline, the government will continue in power until 1960. Should the government at some time fail to hold the support of its majority, the Prime Minister would dissolve Parliament before the end of its legal term. A new election would settle the issues by returning a majority supporting the Conservative Party and leadership, or by giving a majority to the Labour Party, now in opposition.

The fundamental principles of parliamentary government and Cabinet responsibility in England are simple and straightforward, as this recent practical illustration demonstrates. Since these arrangements are the product of a long historical development and are dependent on tradition and custom more than on legal and constitutional provisions, they are laced with all sorts of subtleties. Nevertheless, it is not misleading to give them this simple statement. The Secretary of State for Foreign Affairs—or to give him the shorter unofficial designation which the journalists use, the Foreign Secretary—therefore, is involved in three important constitutional relationships, indicated in the diagram on page 262.

First of all, he must be sure that the policies he proposes and the action he takes will receive the support of his colleagues in the Cabinet. He consults with the Prime Minister, and participates in Cabinet meetings, in order to make sure that all his colleagues will join in support of the government's action which he carries out. Sometimes this agreement, if the issue is of great importance, must be worked out among the ministers who are not members of the Cabinet, and in achieving reconciliation of viewpoints at this wider level the Foreign Secretary has the assistance of two Ministers of State for Foreign Affairs. There have been times when he has not been able to agree with his colleagues. Sir Anthony Eden (then Mr. Anthony Eden) was unable to agree with the members of the Chamberlain Cabinet, and resigned as Foreign Secretary in February 1938. In November 1956 Mr. Anthony Nutting, Minister of State for Foreign Affairs, and Sir Edward Boyle, Economic Secretary to the Treasury, both resigned in protest against the action of the Eden government in the Suez crisis. Naturally this situation does not arise often, because any Cabinet member will hesitate to risk his political future by open disagreement with the leadership of his party. Ordinarily differences of opinion can be adjusted by discussion and compromise, and it is the duty of the

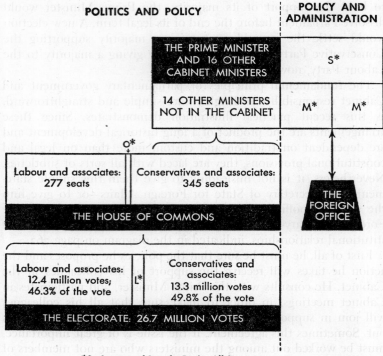

POLITICS AND POLICY   **POLICY AND ADMINISTRATION**

THE PRIME MINISTER AND 16 OTHER CABINET MINISTERS   S*

14 OTHER MINISTERS NOT IN THE CABINET   M*   M*

O*

Labour and associates: 277 seats | Conservatives and associates: 345 seats

THE HOUSE OF COMMONS

THE FOREIGN OFFICE

Labour and associates: 12.4 million votes; 46.3% of the vote | L* | Conservatives and associates: 13.3 million votes 49.8% of the vote

THE ELECTORATE: 26.7 MILLION VOTES

*S = Secretary of State for Foreign Affairs
M = Ministers of State for Foreign Affairs (2)
O = Others: 8 seats
L = Liberal and associates: 1 million votes; 3.9% of the vote

BRITISH POLITICS AND GOVERNMENT

The relation of the Foreign Office and its heads to the Government, Parliament, and the Public in the United Kingdom. The figures are those following the 1955 general election.

Prime Minister to hold his team together so that they speak with a united voice on important issues. Cabinet deliberations are secret, so that conflicts are either told about years afterward in the memoirs of the former ministers or guessed at and gossiped about at the time. It is unlikely that a group of able, determined, and experienced political leaders are invariably in happy unanimity on all matters of policy, but their experience tells ministers that they must reach public agreement if they are not to imperil the authority of the government and the strength of the party majority.

The Foreign Secretary's second constitutional obligation is to defend and explain the government's foreign policy to the House of Commons, and a spokesman for the government must perform a similar duty in the House of Lords. He is assisted in this task by the two Ministers of State, and by two parliamentary secretaries. These are members of the House of Commons or the Lords, and are ministers with less influence and experience than himself.

Debates on foreign policy are fairly frequent in the House of Commons, and the Foreign Secretary must speak for the government against the alert and experienced leaders of the opposition party, some of whom have had experience of his office during their parliamentary careers. He must be able to meet the arguments of his opponents and also to reconcile or silence some disaffected members of his own party who have become dissatisfied with the action of their leaders. The Prime Minister (who may simultaneously be Foreign Secretary) will often take a share of the big debates, because any Prime Minister is deeply involved in foreign policy on account of its importance to Britain. Both men are well equipped to meet the demands of debate, because they have already had a long experience both in opposition and in the government majority during the course of their political careers.

The Foreign Secretary also bears a daily responsibility. He must answer questions put to him during the question hour with which every session begins. A good share of this burden is carried by his immediate associates, particularly the parliamentary secretaries, but on many occasions he must answer for the action of his department or for the general policy of the government. This duty can be very taxing because a question on a difficult point, further elaborated by a skilled and experienced member with a supplementary question or two, may involve him in embarrassing difficulties. Once trapped —and the trap may have been sprung by an injudicious reply by one of the junior ministers—he is at the mercy of the House, and in such circumstances the House can be merciless. What this constitutional obligation means is that the action of the government in all fields, as well as foreign affairs, is constantly subject to the scrutiny and the criticism of the House of Commons.

The Foreign Secretary's third constitutional responsibility is to his own department. He is the head of the Foreign Office and under the conditions of his relationship to Parliament, which have just been described, he must accept responsibility for all the administrative acts and the advice on policy which come from his department. He cannot evade this burden, though in the nature of things the complexity of the work of the Foreign Office may make him responsible for actions of his subordinate officials of which he may have relatively little knowledge. The nature of ministerial responsibility requires him to take these risks, and he is fully aware of all this when he accepts the seals of office.

All Cabinet ministers as well as the Foreign Secretary must sustain a dual character. As members of Parliament, usually of the House of Commons, they are part of a team selected from the majority to develop a program of policy and to carry on the work of government. As heads of government departments, they are administrative officials bearing a heavy executive responsibility. The task of the Foreign Secretary is peculiarly complex and intricate, but he must carry both types of responsibility—the formulation and defense of policy and the tasks of administrative action.

The Foreign Office

The total personnel of the Foreign Office serving in London numbers approximately 4,500 and the number serving abroad in missions and consulates is a little less than 5,000. A German Section, which is being steadily reduced as the status of Germany changes, adds another 3,000 persons to the total. The entire staff at home and abroad is just short of 13,000 people, and this includes many typists, messengers, and others doing simple routine work. The members of what may be called the Foreign Service—officials performing expert and responsible functions—number well under 3,000. The total cost of maintaining the whole establishment, at home and abroad, runs annually to less than £20 million. Considering the vital importance of the task performed by the Foreign Office and the representatives in foreign countries, this is still a modest establishment though it has greatly increased in size during the past fifty years.

The general shape of the home organization is sketched in the diagram on page 266. This sketch is deliberately made rough and general, because the organization changes from time to time and any diagram would go rapidly out of date. This fundamental pattern is quite stable, and does indicate the levels of responsibility and authority and the nature of the various activities carried on.[1] All organization charts are subject to this defect of short life, but one for the Foreign Office is sure to age rapidly.

The responsible political officers who bear the weight of decision and must speak for the organization to the Parliament and the public have already been mentioned. They deal directly with the high officials of the permanent staff, of whom the chief is the Permanent Secretary. The relationship works two ways, as it does in other departments of the British government. The Foreign Secretary, as a member of a Cabinet responsible to a party majority in the House of Commons, undoubtedly says to the Permanent Secretary in his first conference after being appointed to office: "This is the general shape of the party program on which my party won the recent election. We committed ourselves to accomplish the following things, some of which differ from the policies followed by our predecessors. I rely upon you to assist in achieving these objectives, and for your best advice on how, and to what degree, we can realize this program in action."

None of this comes as a shock to the Permanent Secretary. During his years in office he has met this situation more than once. He has been reading the newspapers during the election period, and may well be able to anticipate most of what the new Foreign Secretary tells him. Over his long years of service he has accumulated an expert knowledge of what the office does; and he can rely on the whole staff to bring their resources of experience and knowledge to

---

[1] There are two recent and authoritative accounts of the Foreign Office and the Foreign Service, both written by former high officials. Both give quite precise details of organization as of the time of publication. They are: Ashton-Gwatkin, Frank T., *The British Foreign Service*, Syracuse University Press, 1950; and Lord Strang, and other members of the Foreign Service, *The Foreign Office*, London and New York, 1955.

Political and Parliamentary Leadership	The Secretary of State for Foreign Affairs Two Ministers of State Two Parliamentary Under-Secretaries
Permanent Official dealing with the Secretary of State and political leaders	The Permanent Under-Secretary of State
Permanent officials reporting to the Permanent Secretary for departments in their jurisdiction	Three Deputy Under-Secretaries and Four or five Assistant Under-Secretaries, Director of Communications, Director of Research, Legal Advisers
Permanent officials usually reporting through Deputy Under-Secretaries	Two or three Assistant Under-Secretaries, and heads of various departments
Permanent officials usually reporting through Assistant or Deputy Under-Secretaries	Approximately forty heads of departments, which may be grouped: *Administration*—Personnel, Organization, Finance, Corps of Inspectors, Communications, Archives, Buildings and Establishments. *Political departments*—Africa, American (in two divisions, one for the United States and one for Latin America), Far Eastern, Southern Europe, Northern Europe, and so on. *Departments with special functions*—Treaties and Nationality, Information Departments, Economic Research and Collection of Economic Data, Regional International Organizations (European Economic Co-operation, NATO, Western European Union), United Nations, and UNESCO. [In addition to these, notice above that Archives and Communications, Research, Library and Records, and Legal Advisers usually report direct to the Permanent Secretary.]

Diplomatic posts abroad (subject to changes):
About 50 ambassadors
More than 20 ministers
From 80 to 90 Consulates General

THE BRITISH FOREIGN OFFICE

The organization loosely presented above is very general and approximate because it is subject to frequent changes. (Sources: Ashton-Gwatkin, work cited in text; Lord Strang, work cited in text; *Her Majesty's Ministers and Heads of Public Departments*, No. 50, H. M. Stationery Office, July, 1956.)

bear on the proposals of policy which are put to him by the new leadership. This relationship continues throughout the life of the government, and undoubtedly initiative in decision is shared between the expert officials and political leaders.

The relationship between the Permanent Secretary and the second echelon of permanent officials is not unlike his relationship with the political leaders. Three deputy under-secretaries rank next to him in seniority and authority, each bearing responsibility for some group of activities in the Foreign Office. The various functions are organized in what are called "departments"—a slightly confusing term because the Foreign Office itself is one of the departments of the government. Most of the deputy secretaries "report to" the Permanent Secretary on behalf of a group of departments (the quoted phrase means that they are responsible for, and bring the advice of, a section of the staff engaged in some particular function). One of them bears the responsibility for a group of related administrative functions: the inspectorate, which calls on the offices and missions abroad, the personnel department, establishment and organization, finance, and similar activities. Another ordinarily "reports to" him for the Western Department, which is one of the "political departments" and carries responsibility for study and action for a group of European states including France, Belgium, the Netherlands, the Republic of Ireland, and others. The third has jurisdiction over the departments concerned with international organizations.

Most of the assistant under-secretaries report to one of the deputy secretaries, but some of them report directly to the Permanent Secretary, depending upon the importance of the matters which lie within the jurisdiction of the department or departments for which they are responsible. The director of communications and the director of research and keeper of the papers, like assistant secretaries, report directly to the Permanent Secretary. Reducing all this to a simple practical statement, the important activities and groups of activities are brought to the Permanent Secretary by some responsible official, sometimes called a deputy secretary, sometimes an assistant secretary, sometimes a director of some particular part of the staff.

Naturally all these officials consult with each other and organize interdepartmental committees to assemble data and interpret facts on problems which are wider than the jurisdiction of one department. This technique of using committees to discuss and analyze problems is one of the characteristic methods of British government as a whole. One of its most valuable aspects, quite apart from the necessity of co-ordinating the work of diverse departments when the nature of the problem under consideration requires it, is the experience it gives to junior members of the staff. Ordinarily such a committee includes members of widely varying terms of service, so that a young man who has not been long in the service has the experience of serving with a group of senior officials in the discussion of some problem and in the assembling of the facts and figures required for framing a recommendation.

The range and diversity of the tasks carried on by the Foreign Office is indicated sufficiently by the organization chart given above (page 266). The grouping given there of the functions performed by the forty or more departments is enough to indicate the character of the work done in them. Some words and phrases, however, hardly suggest the extent of the responsibility borne by the department. Economic information and advice covers all sorts of collection of data, analysis of trends, and forecasting of possibilities. The information department is required to do a great deal of work in cultural relations, news contacts, and public relations. Legal advice must be competent throughout the complicated fields of public and private international law and is required in the preparation of drafts of treaties and all sorts of international agreements, which are frequently of a multilateral character that increases their complexity. The corps of inspectors which visit all the diplomatic and consular posts abroad are required to be highly competent in all the latest practices and equipment of administration. A senior official, remembering simpler days, once regretfully remarked that the work of the Foreign Office had become immensely more technical "since economics had crept in." He was, of course, aware that with economics had come the problems of communication, publicity, social and welfare policies, and all the other complications of contemporary society. Since the relations of states run through all these aspects of society, the scope of the Foreign Office must be adjusted to take all these matters into account.

The Foreign Service

What has been said makes it clear that the Foreign Office, and the embassies and consulates abroad, must have a staff of high quality. The recruitment and training of personnel is based upon the "Eden Reforms" of 1943.[2] The essential effect of these reforms was twofold. First, there was a unification of all branches of the service into one organic whole, so that it was possible for any member of the staff to fill a series of diverse assignments in a variety of posts abroad, either consular or diplomatic. Second, there were changes in the method of examination, recruitment, training, pay, and pensions and allowances which opened the foreign service to a much wider range of qualified applicants. In a sense, this meant no more than the application to the foreign service of the principles and methods which had had a long record of success in the rest of the government services. This should not be taken to imply that the service had been staffed before 1943 with a group of young men whose chief qualification was good social standing, because the service had long been of high quality. It did mean, however, that the field of competition was made much wider and that the chances for recruiting high-quality personnel were to be comparable to what they had been made in the rest of the government service by the long record of work of the Civil Service Commission.

There are four branches of the service, and the methods of selection used for them should be briefly described. Branch A corre-corresponds to the administrative class of the general government service. Candidates $20\frac{1}{2}$ to 24 years of age must hold first- or second-class honors degrees from a university, or be able to satisfy an examining board that they can demonstrate equivalent intellectual quality. Competitive examinations, both written tests and extended personal interviews, finally result in the admission of 20 to

[2] Cmd. 6420, *Proposals for the Reform of the Foreign Service*, HMSO, 1943. This statement is an excellent compact description of proposals which have been carried into effect since its presentation, and repays reading.

30 candidates a year to this branch of the service. The standard of
selection is rigorous, and competition is keen enough to result in
the final choice of highly competent candidates.

Branch B is comparable to the executive class of the home civil
service and is open to competition of young people of 16 to 18
years of age for clerical posts. Examinations are used here for selection, but at a lower intellectual level of training than for Branch A.

Branches C and D are all typists, messengers, and comparable
sorts of employees and are also selected by appropriate measurement of qualifications.

Branches A and B are the sources for the future responsible
officials of the foreign service, and it is important to keep in mind
that, after acquiring some experience, members of Branch B have
various pathways open to them for entrance into Branch A. Upon
recommendation by the Foreign Office there is a competition for
Branch B members to enter Branch A between the ages of 25 and
30, and there is the continuous possibility of promotion or transfer
of senior officers of 15 years' experience or more from the one
branch to the other. In all branches there are grades which allow
promotion to more important work and higher pay within the
limits of that part of the service.

Entrants into all branches are given training for some time after
they enter the service. A considerable number choose (and are
sometimes assigned) to language study, with longer time and more
generous allowances for the harder languages such as Chinese,
Hungarian, and others. Language study carries with it study of the
culture, social patterns, and economic characteristics of the area
in which the language is used. The people who go through this
training become area specialists and, while they spend a good share
of their career in the areas appropriate to their studies, they are
also assigned to other areas in the unified service.

All entrants, whatever language and area studies they may pursue, receive a course of training in the general work of the Foreign
Office, so that they have a good working conception of the total
organization of which they are a part. Their first assignments to
posts both at home and abroad take them through various different
kinds of work, so that their knowledge of the whole field of opera-

tions is built up as much as possible. After being in service for some time in some particular part of the service, opportunities are opened to them for either part-time training or periods of leave for training which will enhance their usefulness in the jobs they occupy.

An important aspect of the unified service is the presumption, carried out in practice, that every member may be assigned to serve in any part of the Foreign Office or in any one of the posts abroad, whether it be diplomatic or consular. A graduated scale of pay and allowances which compensate for the fluctuating costs of living either in London or abroad, and for the costs of moving a household from place to place, is designed to make this transfer from post to post, from foreign service to work in the London headquarters, possible for any member of the service without undue hardship. Already this has shown the benefits of variety of experience brought to bear in the differing activities of dealing with the complex subject of international relationships.

Finally, pension and retirement allowances have been made more generous than in the past, so that the person who devotes his career to this service can count upon a satisfactory life after his retirement. A further intention has also been realized, at least in part. With all the care that is exercised in selection and training, some people who enter the service show themselves to be unsuited to it, or not satisfactorily qualified for promotion in it. Increase of retirement benefits makes it possible for people to leave the service without excessive hardship, so that its quality is enhanced by some withdrawals which benefit both the person who withdraws and the service he leaves.

The Eden Reforms have been in effect for little more than a decade, but there is general agreement that the quality of the service has been improved by them. A wider field of selection yields greater diversity of talents, and keenness of competition raises the level of intellectual quality and possibility of growth in competence. The training schemes have imposed upon the old methods of apprenticeship the organized effect of thorough preliminary instruction and the opportunity of further postentry training. The unified service offers better chances for satisfactory careers, and the pension and allowance schemes provide for comfortable transfers from one activity to another and a satisfactory condition of life after retirement. All this has increased the cost of maintaining the service, but the benefits of its enhanced performance are expected to be fully repaid by increasing the effectiveness with which Britain faces difficult problems in the international scene of the twentieth century.

Methods of Operation

In spite of the phrase in one of President Wilson's Fourteen Points—"open covenants openly arrived at"—most of the practical conduct of business among nations is still secret or semisecret. This is not necessarily disgraceful or dangerous—much of the business of the world must be transacted with a moderate degree of secrecy. This imposes a difficulty upon the scholar when he attempts to discuss the methods of any foreign office. Part of the time he must rely on memoirs, which may be true enough for the times and the events described in them, but no longer reflect the methods currently used. Some of the time he is tempted to rely on the gossip collected by journalists who have startled an official into making an unintentional revelation, or have been industriously listening at keyholes. Sometimes he even tries to find a keyhole of his own—though when he does it usually opens into the wrong room.

Though these difficulties exist, it is possible to sketch the methods of operation used in the Foreign Office. Some discussion of the ways in which action begins, and is then carried out, might be put in the terms of hypothetical cases which bear some resemblance to actual events.

One has already been suggested. A new Secretary of State for Foreign Affairs or, for that matter, one who has been in office for some time might well come to the Permanent Under-Secretary saying something like this: "My colleagues in the Cabinet are pledged by their election program to initiate high-level talks with the leaders of the Soviet Union, and other powers, in order to work out a plan for disarmament, or limitation of armaments. Will you explore the possibilities, and suggest methods for implementing such a policy?" The Permanent Secretary then puts the Foreign

Office to work and calls upon the diplomatic posts abroad to report on possibilities. The deputy under-secretaries and the assistant secretaries assemble heads of the appropriate departments: research and records to survey the history, the political departments dealing with interested communities such as the United States, the Western European nations, the countries of Eastern Europe. Interdepartmental committees are formed at the initiative of assistant under-secretaries with suggestions from their superiors.

It soon appears that the Ministry of Defence and the service ministries can hardly be ignored in this discussion—they are the armed forces who might be disarmed. The co-ordinating activities of the Cabinet and the office of the Cabinet Secretariat are now put to work. More committees are organized at the suggestion of the Secretary to the Cabinet and his staff, comprising membership from the staff offices of the Admiralty, the War Office, the Air Ministry, and the Ministry of Defence. The records of the Cabinet Committee on Imperial Defence are brought to bear upon the problems opened up. Data are assembled and past history carefully combed over. The committees which are set up with membership from different ministries usually have officers at the rank of assistant under-secretaries, each of them having been briefed by the committees of his own ministry which have been working on the relevant data. Discussion in such groups is pointed toward the task of framing a recommendation setting forth the possible courses of action.

At the same time that all this activity was begun in the government offices in Whitehall and Downing Street, similar action has been in progress in a number of diplomatic posts. Every diplomatic post, embassy or consulate, bears some resemblance to the Foreign Office. The Ambassador has a first secretary who is often called the Head of Chancery in the mission. There are also legal advisers, information officers, military and naval attachés, and various other specialists. A number of diplomatic missions receive a request from the Permanent Under-Secretary, stating the proposed policy of the Secretary of State for Foreign Affairs and asking for information and advice. All the members of the mission have made contacts in various quarters during their term of service. The Ambassador seeks an interview with the foreign minister of the nation, and other members of the staff assemble all the information they can elicit from their opposite numbers in the foreign government. This is brought together by the Head of Chancery, who organized the initial distribution of work. The amount of overtime put in by all the members of the mission is governed by the urgency of the request that has come to them from London. A report is drafted, sometimes carrying recommendations for action, and is transmitted to the Foreign Office.

Eventually the reports from abroad and the recommendations from the interdepartmental and interministerial committees in London are crystallized by the Permanent Under-Secretary and his aides into a report and recommendation which he lays before the minister. All the complex data have been summarized into intelligible form, and recommendations are made as to possible courses of action: "These are the necessary steps to take for realization of the policy," or "This is not a good time to make the attempt to implement the policy," and many other variants. Briefed by the Permanent Under-Secretary, the Secretary of State goes to a Cabinet meeting, and then perhaps a good share of the work is all to be done over again if the Cabinet decides that none of the recommendations are acceptable in view of its political obligations to the party and the country.

The initial step leading to action of this character may, of course, take other forms. Egypt may decide to nationalize the Suez Canal. Presumably the embassy in Cairo has been reporting developments there carefully and thoroughly to the Foreign Office, and authorities in London are prepared to anticipate action. It must be admitted, however, that the atmosphere of fluster in London in August 1956 created some suspicion that either the embassy had failed a little in its task or that Colonel Nasser had kept his secret so well that no embassy staff could have succeeded in forecasting events.

Regarding this as a hypothetical instance, one may safely say that the process which follows the event is much the same as the one sketched for the preceding example. The resources of the Foreign Office are mobilized at high speed to bring expert information to bear on the problem; the co-ordinating activities of the Cabinet are quickly employed to correlate the action of various ministries. The process is that of making a decision, and the best skill and knowledge are organized to make the decision as effective as possible. Just as in the other instance, the services of several embassies must be enlisted, as the widening circles of the effect of a sudden action involve the interests of a number of nations in the twentieth-century world.

Sometimes the action taken is in anticipation of an important scheduled event, such as a meeting of the Assembly of the United Nations, or its Economic and Social Council, or a special convention or conference of states. In these instances the agenda is known in advance, in fact it has already been the subject of a considerable amount of work in the Foreign Office. The organization sketch already given shows a number of departments concerned with international organizations, and it is upon these that the work of forecasting the probable attitude of member states, working out the possible alternatives of British policy, and briefing delegates to the meeting will chiefly fall. All such conferences and meetings are to discuss subjects with wide ramifications, so that ordinarily all the agencies which have been cited for the instance of disarmament (pages 272-274) will be occupied in searching out data, discussing alternative courses of action, and forecasting possibilities. It should be added that the missions of the United Kingdom to the United Nations and to the Organization for European Economic Co-operation, to mention two examples, are comparable in rank and similar in organization to embassies, but special delegates are often added to their regular staffs.

These instances illustrate questions of high policy, which bring the full resources of the Foreign Office and even the whole operation of Cabinet government to bear on questions of urgency and moment. Many instances might be cited of the routine action which is a regular part of the work of every diplomatic mission: the transmission of routine messages by the Ambassador to the head of the state to which he is accredited, the rescue of a British subject who has unwittingly fallen afoul of regulations, the adjustment of governmental claims. There are also many matters of routine in the Foreign Office in London which never rise higher in the chain of command than a department head or an assistant under-secretary.

While many matters are decided before they reach the desk of the Permanent Under-Secretary, and he in turn does not bring all that reach him to the attention of the Secretary of State, one of the most serious problems of this organization is the number of matters that do come to both of them for decision. Relations between states are now so intricate and involved that many matters that appear at first to be of minor significance turn out eventually to be of serious weight. This is true of all ministerial offices, but it is peculiarly the case in the field of international affairs. Minor issues grow into major crises, and the burden upon the higher officials grows steadily heavier. So long as the traditions of Cabinet government apply, the Secretary of State must be responsible for all the actions of his ministry. The two Ministers of State can take some of the load of work and the permanent officials can analyze the problems and clarify the alternatives, but in the long run the ultimate decision tends to travel up to the Secretary of State and often to his colleagues in the Cabinet.

Some of this load of responsibility might be reduced by some type of planning organization which would devote time and expert resources to the special task of forecasting trends and attempting to meet situations in advance. This kind of activity has been used in other departments of English government for the development of economic policies. It is used in other foreign offices, notably in the State Department of the United States. One of the reasons for the influence exerted by the study groups of the Royal Institute of International Affairs which were referred to in the chapter preceding this one, is that the Foreign Office has been friendly, or at least not unfavorable, to analyses of problems made by groups of distinguished membership. It must be admitted, nevertheless, that reorganization of this kind can go only a short distance toward solving the problem which has been stated. In some ways much is being done in the anticipation of situations and the planning of action, and it has not diminished the load of responsibility which rests on all the higher officials.

It can surely be expected that as time goes by, and the effect of the Eden Reforms becomes more evident, the wider range of backgrounds of the members of the Foreign Service and the level of talent which can be expected from a wider field of competition will materially aid the Foreign Secretary and the Foreign Office in meeting the pressures created by the problems of international affairs.

This chapter and the preceding chapter have begun by describing the situation of Great Britain. That situation has become difficult because the prosperity of the nineteenth century which gave a secure place in the world to a rapidly growing industrial and urban community has been subjected to the strains of two world wars and the troubled period between them. The long start conferred by the early appearance of the Industrial Revolution is now being reduced as other economies adopt new techniques. The population of the United Kingdom is fully employed, and every resource of ingenuity and research is being applied to increasing its economic productivity.

Britain's relationships to other states and the forms of association in the Commonwealth are being adjusted to the new situations. The traditional foreign policies are still useful, but their modification is doubtless necessary.

In the organization of the Foreign Office and in the developing reforms in the foreign service the British government possesses an instrument which can be used to meet these new demands and to repair the losses which have been suffered during the twentieth century. Cabinet government can make especially effective use of the Foreign Office to meet the problems of relationships with other states. Public interest is centered upon these problems, and political leadership can make use of public support if it is able to develop policies and explain and justify the purposes embodied in them.

The next chapter, therefore, will be devoted to an analysis of the recent history of British foreign policy.

CHAPTER 9

RECENT AND CONTEMPORARY
BRITISH FOREIGN POLICY

The nineteenth century really ended for Britain in 1914. The pressures of economic change, arising in part from the growth of other great industrial economies and partly from the changing patterns of British industry and trade, made their full effects felt during and after World War I. After 1918 traditional foreign policies required some modification to deal with the situation that came into existence after the peace settlements at the end of the war. It is therefore proper, even though it may place some strain on the word "recent" in the title of this chapter, to review some of the modifications and adjustments of foreign policy which were the result of the troubled years between the two world wars.

The Years Between the Wars

The two painful and difficult decades that followed the peace settlements at the end of World War I may be divided into three periods. The first ran from 1918 to 1924, and was marked by the efforts of the Allied nations to enforce the peace settlements. The second began in 1924, and the record of the six succeeding years to 1930 is chiefly a story of attempts to modify and adjust the settlements in order to make them workable and to relieve the tensions between the victors, who wished to maintain the new arrangements, and the defeated powers, who sought to revise the treaties. At least one of the victors, Italy, joined in the demands for "revision." The third period is the story of the gathering storm which led to the outbreak of war in 1939. Political dictators who led their countries into aggressive demands appeared in Italy and Germany, and the conflict between them and other powers could not be adjusted.[1]

The problems of these years for British leaders were sharpened by the changes in the position of Great Britain which became manifest at the same time. The changes in the Commonwealth were given full legal recognition in the Statute of Westminster of 1931. Experimentation with the new forms of consultation required by the widening of Dominion status and the increasing freedom of action acquired by each of the Dominions, drew the attention of Cabinets and ministers to the changing patterns of "The Third British Empire." The policies of the home government had to be accommodated to the viewpoints of the Canadians, Australians, South Africans, and New Zealanders. Ireland acquired independent status, first as a Dominion and eventually as an associated republic. Constitutional reforms began in India, with progressive grants of self-government. Great Britain was compelled to give thought to the changing shape of the Commonwealth, and was reluctant to involve herself in heavy commitments to European affairs.

The economic problems which have been described in Chapter 7 for the years since 1945 appeared soon after 1918. Unemployment reached unprecedented dimensions, averaging 14 per cent of the working population in the years from 1921 to 1939, and reaching a peak of 22 per cent in 1932 during the world depression. These effects were produced by the slump in world trade and were immediately reflected in the national economy. These problems led the government into a departure from the traditional free-trade

[1] Three excellent short accounts of this period should be mentioned: Carr, E. H., *International Relations between the Two World Wars 1919-1939*, London and New York, 1947, reprinted 1948, 1950, 1952, 1955; Medlicott, W. N., *British Foreign Policy since Versailles*, London, 1940; and Reynolds, P. A., *British Foreign Policy in the Inter-War Years*, London, 1954.

policies of the nineteenth century, and a protective tariff was adopted by the National government after 1931, and preferential tariff agreements were made with the countries of the Commonwealth at the Ottawa Conference in 1932. The effect of dislocation of world trade was heightened by the persistent problems of reparations and intergovernmental debts.

The foreign policies devised during these difficult years reflected in considerable part the traditional principles which have been described in Chapter 7. The situation demanded modification of the familiar lines of policy, however, and some of the important changes can be stated in brief summary. These changes in strategy and attitudes are all the more important because they reappear in some of their essential aspects in the policies which Britain pursued after 1945.

The Treaty of Versailles included as part of its text the Covenant of the League of Nations. Britain held one of the permanent seats on the Council of the League, and her policies as a League member were to support this new international organization. This was not an entirely new orientation of policy because there was the record of her nineteenth-century association with the Concert of Europe. In the main, the British record in the League is one of affirmative participation in all the activities of the new international organization. Membership raised a few new problems—for one thing the Dominions also were members in equal standing with all other member states. The extent of the League was world wide, and this involved Britain and the Commonwealth nations in heavy commitments. This imposed caution on participation in the worldwide obligations, but British prime ministers and foreign secretaries came to Geneva for the meetings of the Assembly, and the weight of the influence of the United Kingdom was applied to enhance the strength and effectiveness of the general principles of the Covenant. This is not meant to imply that British policy was consistent and unwavering, but it can be said that Britain's part in the League was an important part of her foreign policy throughout the period. It compares well with that of other member states, and reflects the long-standing British interest in maintaining peaceful and stable conditions in the world.

The League suffered from its position as part of the peace settlements, which meant that European problems bulked large in its sphere of action. The persistent problem in Europe throughout the interwar years was the reconciliation of the French demand for security against the possibility of attack by a resurgent Germany with the demands of Germany and other revisionist powers for modification of the peace settlements. The French wanted guarantees, which would imply the enforcement of the treaties to maintain reparations payments and to sustain territorial settlements and the provisions for demilitarization of the Rhineland. The Germans —and the Italians—wanted adjustment of these very same problems to give them a more satisfactory position in Europe and in the world.

The persistence of this problem led British statesmen into a somewhat new relationship to the nations of Europe. The traditional policy of the "balance of power," with its negative implication that it meant no more than an effort to prevent the gaining of a dominant situation by one power on the European continent, changed to a policy of active association with groups of states. At first guarantees were devised in the form of provisions to strengthen the power of the Covenant. This produced the Draft Treaty of Mutual Assistance submitted to the 1923 Assembly by the Temporary Mixed Commission on Disarmament. The following year both Ramsay MacDonald, then British Prime Minister, and Edouard Herriot, Premier of France, appeared at the Assembly, and the intention of the Draft Treaty was formulated in the terms of the Geneva Protocol, which was designed to provide for a compulsory resort to arbitration in the settlement of international disputes. This was too heavy a commitment for a succeeding British government to undertake in the following year, but Austen Chamberlain, as Foreign Secretary for the Conservative government which had been elected in the interval, initiated the discussions which finally led to the Locarno Treaties in 1925. These treaties (for there were a series of agreements) pledged Britain with other powers to a system of mutual guarantees of the Rhine frontier. It is worth noticing that the Dominions refused to act with Britain in accepting these obligations in Europe—this is one of the times when a British government was required to act without the support of the other nations of the Commonwealth because these nations did not wish to participate in the obligations incurred by these policies toward the continent of Europe.

At the same time that these guarantees were offered to the French demand for security, Britain was participating in a series of conferences which were adjusting and modifying the terms of the treaty settlements. The most important of these were the conferences which finally led to scaling down the requirements of reparations. The financial distress of Germany and the eventual effects of the world depression led to the creation of the Dawes Committee in 1924, and the Young Plan in 1929. Though the United States had never accepted the Treaty of Versailles nor membership in the League of Nations, these adjustments of the settlement were made by securing United States co-operation. British leaders were among the first to recognize that the treaty settlements required adjustment if they were to be made workable, and to work with the United States in carrying out the process of modification.

These policies were not pursued with sufficient determination and speed to forestall the growth of dictatorship in Germany and Italy, and the outbreak of war in 1939. It is possible, of course, to condemn British leadership for the eventual failure to maintain peace. Britain's part in the acceptance of German action remilitarizing the Rhineland in 1936 and agreement to the Munich Pact in 1938, which eventually brought all of Czechoslovakia into Hitler's Reich, have been often enough criticized as policies of appeasement which, nevertheless, were insufficient to avert war.[2] This is a criticism which must be applied to other nations as well during that period.

This quick review of the foreign policy of Great Britain during these troubled years is useful here to indicate new orientations of her policy which occurred during that time. The obligations of international organization were new, though comparable commitments had been carried during the nineteenth century. Britain

2 For a careful and temperate assessment and criticism of British policy during these years see P. A. Reynolds, op. cit.

lived up to the terms of the Covenant of the League as fully as did any other great power. Necessities for adjusting the terms of the peace led her into a more active association with the nations of Europe than had been implied in earlier times by the tradition of maintaining the balance of power. This is best exemplified, perhaps, in the terms of the Locarno Treaties and in the discussions of the Geneva Protocol. Finally, the dominant position of the United States in the world was fully recognized; its co-operation in the Dawes and Young plans was welcomed, and British acceptance of naval parity with the United States was combined with participation in the agreements of the Washington Conference concerning the Far East. As has been said already, these changes in policy were reconcilable with nineteenth-century traditions of British action, but it has been useful briefly to review this period because the action of the United Kingdom since 1945 is more readily understood.

The "German Problem" and the Cold War after 1945

It was the intention of the Allied powers to postpone settlements at the close of World War II. Italy had been admitted to the status of a cobelligerent during the concluding months of the war, and an Allied Occupation Administration was established until the new Republic of Italy was finally set up on the first day of 1948. On the basis of the Potsdam Declaration of August 2, 1945, a four-power occupation of Germany was instituted, with Britain, the United States, France, and the Soviet Union each taking responsibility for the administration of a zone of Germany, with a joint authority of the four sharing the administration of Berlin. It was hoped that all the participating Allies could agree to carry out the declared occupation policies in their respective zones.

It proved to be impossible to reconcile the purposes of the Western powers with those of the Soviet Union, and the increasing tensions between them led to the situation which is characterized in the expression "the Cold War." It is unnecessary to tell the story of the increasing difficulties, which finally resulted in the establishment of a Communist-dominated Democratic People's Republic in the Soviet zone in Eastern Germany. Soviet satellite states were established during 1947 in Eastern Europe, and early in 1948 a Communist seizure of power was achieved in Czechoslovakia, followed shortly by similar action in Hungary.

Confronted by this steady growth of Soviet power in Europe and unable to reach agreement with the Russians on joint policies toward Germany, the Western Allies developed concerted action among themselves. Britain co-operated with the United States in setting up a joint administration of their two zones in Germany, and eventually the British, United States, and French governments sponsored the creation of the Federal Republic of Western Germany. The West German constitution was proclaimed in September of 1949. Before that result was accomplished, however, there had been a dramatic contest over the administration of Berlin. The Soviet zone encircled the city, and normal transport into it was cut off by a blockade. The British co-operated with the United States authorities in maintaining an air lift from June, 1948, to May, 1949, during which time all supplies for the western zone of Berlin were brought in by planes.

During this whole period of increasing tension British policy was firmly aligned with that of the Western powers, particularly with that of the United States. At the same time British leadership sought to find means of reconciling the conflict, without yielding on the principles of free elections and the establishment of democratic institutions as the indispensable basis for the unification of Germany.

The problems of economic recovery and reconstruction in Europe as a whole also were urgent during these same years. The need for associated action in both economic and political fields was recognized if Western Europe was to resist Soviet pressure and defend itself against the possibility of military action of the kind which had occurred in Czechoslovakia. Britain and the United States acted with the nations of Western Europe to establish various forms of co-operative action.

The Growth of Western European Union

Several types of association were developed among the states of Western Europe to deal with the problems of the postwar situation. Some of these organized efforts were directly related to the Cold War, some were designed to meet pressing needs quite apart from the tensions between the bloc of Soviet states and the Western European nations.

One of the first to be organized sprang from the speech of the United States Secretary of State George Marshall at the Harvard University Commencement in June of 1947. He declared that the United States was ready to give economic aid to European states which were prepared to assist each other to meet the problems of reconstruction and recovery. Mr. Bevin, Foreign Secretary in the Labour government which was then in power in Britain, immediately took up the invitation made in the Marshall speech. He invited all European nations, including the Soviet Union, to attend a conference in Paris, which met in July, 1947. Mr. Molotov appeared at the conference, but the U.S.S.R. soon withdrew from the discussions, and so also did the other nations of the Eastern European group. The hopes that had first arisen that this economic association might diminish the conflicts of the Cold War were disappointed, but the conference proceeded to develop plans for the economic recovery of all the states which were willing to take associated action and avail themselves of the offer of United States aid.

A report was drafted which made recommendations for the use of United States aid and for economic co-operation among the participating states. On April 16, 1948, seventeen Western European states signed a Convention for European Co-operation in Paris. This was the basis for the Organization for European Economic Co-operation, usually referred to by its initials as the OEEC. A central headquarters was established in Paris, and a considerable organization was built up which collected statistical data, drafted reports and recommendations, and thus made effective use of the economic aid which came from the United States under the Economic Co-operation Act and the Economic Co-operation Administration. The work of the OEEC did not end with the termination of United States aid. It still continued to function as a central clearinghouse of economic information, and it was under the auspices of this organization that a European Payments Union was set up in 1950 to facilitate settlements of trade balances between the European members of the association. These activities of economic co-operation continue to be of great value to the economic health of the Western European states.

United States influence during the period of the Economic Co-operation Administration was exerted in the direction of encouraging economic integration of the national economies of Europe, citing the benefits of the large free-trade area of the United States. It became clear that "integrating" the economies of Europe was too far-reaching a project to achieve ready acceptance, however desirable it might seem in theory. In May 1950, the French government under the leadership of Foreign Minister Robert Schuman proposed the pooling of the iron, steel, and coal industries of the European countries. This proposal eventually developed into the European Coal and Steel Community, called the Schuman Plan in the press reports. Its distinctive feature was the creation of a supranational authority possessing quite extensive powers over production and marketing of coal and steel in all of the six countries (France, Germany, Italy, the Netherlands, Belgium, and Luxembourg). The treaty establishing the High Authority, a Council of Ministers, and an Assembly to carry out the practical work of the plan was signed April 18, 1951, and was ratified by all the six countries by the following June.

Two British governments were in power during the period of the negotiations for the establishment of the Coal and Steel Community—the Labour government, which had barely won the election of February 1950, and the Conservative government, which came into power in October 1951. Both expressed the same attitude toward the creation of this new association of European states. Because Britain had Commonwealth commitments—and exported about eight times as much steel to the Commonwealth countries as to Europe—the government could not become a member of the Coal and Steel Community, but declared approval of the plan and promised as close co-operation with it as possible. This in fact became a consistent policy toward European associations which exhibited supranational and federal features. British participation and willingness to assist were limited by overseas economic and

political connections, but this attitude carried with it a readiness
to work with such associations to achieve the desired objectives.

Besides these economic organizations, a number of political associations and alliances were brought into existence in Europe
during these years. The initiative for one of these came from preliminary discussions of the possibilities of a North Atlantic Treaty,
which will be discussed later in this chapter. In March 1948, the
Brussels Treaty was signed by Britain, France, Belgium, the Netherlands, and Luxembourg. The chief purpose expressed in the agreement was the creation of a defense organization and a Western
European army, but cultural and economic action was promised
as well. A chain of events followed this initial step in creating
what was even then referred to as "Western Union." The creation
of the North Atlantic Treaty Organization (NATO) a year later
led to the discussion of the rearmament of Western Germany to
strengthen the military force at the disposal of the organization.
This in turn was followed by a long period of negotiation and
consultation concerning the establishment of a European Defense
Community (EDC). The prospect of German rearmament roused
the fears of France, and even after an agreement had been framed
at the close of a conference in Paris in May 1952, the French Assembly failed to ratify the treaty in August 1954.

At this point Mr. Eden, then Foreign Secretary in the British
government, made a round of visits to all the participating governments, and at a conference in London a substitute for EDC was
worked out, which was drafted and signed in Paris in October
1954. This was ratified by all the parties by April 1955, and the
Canadian Parliament and the United States Senate both gave approval to the treaties.

British policy throughout the development of these arrangements, which go by the name of "Western European Union
(WEU)," has been quite clear. Part of the time Mr. Eden, representing the government, undertook the initiative in working out
the plans. All the time Britain was ready to accept commitments
to guarantees and pledges of joint action in Europe which would
hardly have been acceptable to either leaders or people in the

years before 1939. The experience of the years between the wars had been a lesson, and the need for association with the nations of Europe was clear enough after the failures of that period.

One other association of European states was brought into existence in considerable part by the initiative of Mr. Churchill, at the time of his greatest reputation in world affairs. A speech of his at Zurich University in September 1946, called for the recreation of the European family of nations. This suggestion led eventually to a conference of political leaders at The Hague in May 1949, and the establishment of a Statute for the Council of Europe to which ten powers agreed. Two bodies were created by the statute: a Council of Ministers and a Consultative Assembly. A secretariat and a headquarters were set up at Strasbourg, and there have been frequent meetings of the organization. At the time of its foundation the organization was regarded by many people as a nucleus for a possible European federation, but the most urgent requirements in Europe have been met by the other agencies which have been described previously. It would be premature, however, to suggest that the Council of Europe may not have an important share in the future organization of Europe. It might even play a part in drawing together the various forms of associated action which had been built up during the years since 1945.

British policy in Europe since 1945 has been quite consistent, and it is worth noting that both Labour and Conservative governments have been in power in Britain during these years. The United Kingdom has accepted commitments and pledged itself to guarantees under the terms of the Brussels Pact and under its later form in the Paris agreements of 1954-1955, which may be given the name of Western European Union. At the same time, while it has been ready to associate itself and co-operate with supranational organization, as in the case of the European Coal and Steel Community, it has avoided the obligations of full membership in such schemes on the basis that Commonwealth connection limits its action in these forms. One of the chief aims of British policy is to move at the same rate and to the same extent that the United States is willing to act in European affairs, so that the organization of the Atlantic community is a guide to the action which leaders are willing to take, feeling sure of public support.

The North Atlantic Treaty Organization

The story of the growth of NATO parallels much of the history of the other organizations which have been established to give effective shape to military and economic co-operation among the countries of Western Europe. In fact, the signing of the Brussels Treaty in March 1948, was followed three months later by the passage of the Vandenberg Resolution by the United States Senate. The resolution declared that the United States was ready to act with other powers under the terms of Article 51 of the Charter of the United Nations, which recognizes the right of states to act individually or collectively for defense. Consultations among the ambassadors of ten states in Washington followed quickly afterward, and the agreement of the Brussels Council to the principle of a North Atlantic defensive pact. The treaty was drafted and signed by twelve states by April 1949, and was ratified by all of them before the end of July of the same year. In 1951 Greece and Turkey were admitted to the organization, so that the total number of associated states stands at fourteen.

NATO has been so widely discussed that it is only necessary to say that it is an association of these states for mutual aid and self-defense. A central headquarters had been established in Europe (SHAPE) and three European commands have been set up. A Council of Ministers deliberates on matters of general policy, and a series of committees and boards having continuous existence work on problems of defense production, develop military plans, and correlate the action of the various member governments.

While the action of NATO has so far been concerned with the creation of effective defense forces in Europe, it is worth emphasis that the treaty provides for economic and political action in association by all the members, and that the long-term goal of the treaty is really the creation of an Atlantic Community. Contributions by the member states to the forces under the command of the Supreme Commander and the commanders of the various regional commands have required careful study of the economic resources of each of them. For this the accumulated experience under OEEC and under the Brussels Pact have been extremely valuable.

In the series of meetings held by the Council since its first meeting in Washington in September 1949, there has been a steady development of the machinery of associated action. In all this Britain has had an active part, and in the Paris Conference of September 1954, which has been referred to above, the initiative of Mr. Eden contributed decisively to the correlation of NATO with the agencies of Western European Union.

Britain therefore stands at present as a member of both the North Atlantic Treaty Organization and the series of overlapping agreements of Western European Union. These memberships entail heavy commitments, which have been assumed in the hope of maintaining the peace and the economic well-being of Europe. At the same time, as has been explained earlier in these chapters, the requirements of the Commonwealth have been increasing. Combined with these obligations are also the demands of the world organization of the United Nations.

Britain's Part in the United Nations

Perhaps it is a token of the way the world has been going since 1945 that discussion of British action in the United Nations has been postponed until after her share in various regional organizations has been described. It is hardly necessary to recall that Britain was a party to the Atlantic Charter during the war and that an able and active delegation from the United Kingdom took part in the Charter Conference in San Francisco in 1945. Earlier experience in the League of Nations had prepared the way for another attempt to work out a plan for a world-wide international organization.

It has been pointed out in the preceding chapter that the Foreign Office has now a special department for United Nations affairs and that the mission to the United Nations has the status of an embassy. This is a reflection of the fact that the government attaches great importance to this activity, and that the quality of British representation to the Council and the Assembly, and to the specialized agencies such as the Economic and Social Council, has been comparable to that of other member states and equal to any other diplomatic mission maintained anywhere in the world. British delegates have continually stressed the desire of their government to make the United Nations effective. A few instances from the record can serve to demonstrate this attitude.

Early in the history of the organization the projected Trusteeship Council was organized to assume responsibility for dependent territories. When the Council was ready to begin work, the British government placed three territories in Africa under the jurisdiction of the Council: Tanganyika, the Cameroons, and Togoland. Britain had been administering these territories under the Mandates system of the League of Nations, and voluntarily accepted the continuance of the authority of the comparable organ of the United Nations. While this was not an act of great importance, it was an earnest of the British intention to accept the authority of the international organization which had been set up under the Charter.

The persistent problem of the United Nations has been a reflection of the Cold War. Disagreement between the Soviet Union, supported by its satellite states in Eastern Europe, and the Western powers has continually blocked the organization of effective action. Attempts have been made to devise procedures to meet this conflict, and the British delegation has supported these efforts. Two of these are worth mention.

The regulation of the use of atomic weapons and the international control of the use of atomic fuels and atomic energy led very early in the life of the United Nations to the establishment of an Atomic Energy Commission. The Baruch plan, proposed by the United States, envisaged the creation of an international authority with powers of controlling research and development combined with authority to inspect developments in all nations. The long and tangled story of the conflict between the USSR and the Western states over this proposal need not be told here. British delegations steadily supported the proposal and the British government committed itself to the development of a scheme for international regulation of the use of atomic energy.

This project, as well as many others, was blocked by the intransigence of the Soviet group of states. In 1947 an effort was made to bypass the use of the veto in the Security Council by organizing an interim committee of the Assembly. The rules of procedure for the Assembly made many decisions possible by majority votes of the members, and if a committee could use these procedures the chances for organizing action would be correspondingly improved. "The Little Assembly," as it was called, was strongly supported by the British delegation.

The most important action taken by the United Nations was the decision to use armed force to resist the invasion of South Korea in June 1950. The British representative on the Security Council fully supported the decision to organize military action. British troops formed a part of the United Nations forces which took part in this action. This crucial decision is the most unmistakable demonstration of the British intention to support the authority of the United Nations, even though most of the forces which took part in the Korean War were from the United States.

The British record in the United Nations shows willingness to accept the jurisdiction of the organization and its constituent agencies, support of efforts to make its action more effective, and prompt participation in the decision to resist the aggressive use of force and require the use of means of peaceful settlement of disputes. This record was established during eleven years, and is the record even if the Suez actions in November 1956 were departures from it.

The action of the British government with regard to the Suez Canal should be briefly summarized, though it is too soon to make a careful analysis of all the factors involved. Behind the whole story lies a long record of difficulty in the administration of the British mandate over Palestine established after World War I, complicated by the conflicts between the Arab states of the Middle East. The independent state of Israel was finally established in 1948. Great-power interests are deeply involved because this whole area is one of the world's greatest sources of oil.

In 1952 a military coup d'état in Egypt ended the reign of King Farouk; and shortly thereafter the British government agreed to withdraw troops from the Suez Canal zone by gradual stages. In June 1956 the last British troops left the zone, and on July 28, 1956, Colonel Nasser, recently elected President of Egypt, nationalized the canal. His action followed weeks of negotiations with the United States and Britain over questions of economic aid to Egypt and of the adjustment of Arab-Israel relations. The British and French governments called a conference on the question of the canal, and at the same time made military and naval preparations. The conference was held in London in the first fortnight of August; but it was impossible to negotiate with the Egyptian government, either on the basis of the London Conference proposals, or later proposals for a canal-users' association. On October 29, 1956, Israeli troops moved into Egypt and occupied the Gaza strip; and two days thereafter the British and French governments sent in bombing planes, and landed parachute troops in the canal zone. The Egyptian government retaliated by wrecking bridges over the canal and by sinking block ships in the channel. After United Nations Assembly resolutions had called for a cease-fire, Britain and France accepted the proposal on November 7, 1956. Soon thereafter a small UN police force was landed to maintain these arrangements. By December of 1956 withdrawals of British and French troops had begun, but the underlying problems remained unsolved. This is a bare recital of the sequence of events. It is worth repeating what has been said above—the British record in the United Nations from 1945 to 1956 stands as described. It will be possible at some future time to analyze this complicated story and assess the action of all the parties concerned.

The Political Parties and Foreign Policy

In the decade following World War II, responsibility for foreign policy was almost equally shared by the two major parties. The Labour government, headed by Mr. Attlee, was in office from July, 1945, to October, 1951. A Conservative government then assumed power, and won a substantial parliamentary majority in the election of 1955. The record of these years, which has been reviewed in the preceding pages, shows a considerable degree of consistency in foreign policy, though each party was in power for part of the time and in opposition for another part.

Consistency in foreign policy is not the result of any formal bipartisan arrangement. It is rather the product of recognition of the needs of Great Britain in the postwar world and the recognition of the importance of the lines of action required to meet them. In parliamentary debates on foreign policy a considerable area of agreement is revealed in the attitudes of both major parties.

Naturally enough, agreement on some of the most important foreign policies was revealed in the manifestoes of the two parties in which they declared their programs in the 1955 general election. Both declarations promised support for disarmament, continued support of the association of the Western states, and active participation in the United Nations. Both pledged themselves to attempt to arrange high-level consultations with the Soviet Union and its associates in the effort to relax world tension. Each placed some stress on particular aspects of these policies, as might be expected, but the agreement between the two parties was much more striking than the points of difference.[3]

Most of the area of agreement shared by the two major parties springs from a quite realistic and frank appraisal of Britain's international position. English party programs tend to be more straightforward than party platforms in the United States, as is revealed in these two declarations. Both parties, however, have acquired a tradition on these matters. Labour has a Socialist foundation and has always expressed the usual Socialist support for international organization. The party looks back to the record of the MacDonald ministries in the interwar period as a demonstration of its consistency in support of international organization. Similarly, the Conservative Party points to the Locarno Treaties of the same period. Both parties have borne the responsibility of directing foreign policy during the twentieth century and both have been committed during this period to the lines of policy described earlier in this chapter. And behind both of them stretches the history of the nineteenth century and the record of a trading nation concerned with stability and order in international relationships.

Neither party is entirely unanimous in its attitude on these important issues. The Labour Party has always had to deal with a

[3] Each party headquarters published its manifesto in a pamphlet. An easily accessible source for the text of both is *The Times Guide to the House of Commons 1955*, London, 1955, pp. 255-264.

group that is more deeply concerned with Socialist principle than is the rank and file of the party. This attitude has been expressed in recent years by Aneurin Bevan, but there have always been members of the party who have favored a more active program of socialism than has been expressed by the official leadership at any time. The Conservative Party also shows occasional groupings within its membership, sometimes the influence of Tory diehards who want a return to the traditions of earlier times and sometimes a group of reformists who strive to change the traditional attitudes. The character of the party system is such, however, that ordinarily the program represents a consensus of most of its membership. This consensus is enforced by the character of the Cabinet system, for once a party has won an election it must assume responsibility for carrying the bulk of its pledges into action.

The function of the parties has already been explained, but it is worth repeating that they are powerful agencies for organizing, and even educating, public opinion. Not only does a general election produce a great deal of discussion of public issues, including the issues of foreign policy, but in addition the constant effect of parliamentary debate between government and opposition leads to a flow of declarations of policy from the councils and headquarters of the two parties. This debate has the effect of keeping public opinion on the alert, and of course influences reporting in the press. What the British citizen reads and hears has a very close relationship to the substance of policy, and is powerfully influenced by the actions of party leadership. The relationship is reciprocal—leadership is made constantly aware of the shifts in public opinion.

The fact that both parties have been for some years committed to a number of foreign policies which either of them is ready to support and to carry into action means that the probability of consistency in the attitudes of British government is high and that public opinion has been ready to accept and support whichever leadership carries responsibility for Britain's part in world affairs.

Britain's Stake in World Affairs

A short review of Great Britain's position can serve to summarize the substance of these chapters. At the beginning of the twentieth century the effect of early industrialization, which had made her one of the great trading states of the world, began to lose its force. Other communities, particularly Germany and the United States, began to match British industrial and commercial importance. The growth of trade during the nineteenth century had been accompanied by a rapid growth of population in the United Kingdom, and at the same time the widespread commitments of the Empire and the Commonwealth had come into existence. At the close of World War II Great Britain's needs and obligations in the world of states were even greater than they had been in the preceding century, but her economic power and political influence had declined. This is a brief and brutal way of stating the matter, but it is a short way of characterizing her present situation.

The method of meeting this situation was already prepared for in some of the traditional lines of foreign policy. Since the Napoleonic Wars British governments have been ready to ally themselves with the other states of Europe in an effort to preserve orderly and stable international relationships. Since the Versailles Treaty there has been an equal willingness to accept the obligations of world-wide international organization. Since 1945 Britain has acted in association with other powers and has supported the action of the United Nations in efforts to preserve peace and maintain international economic and trading activity. There is hardly any other viable policy for a community which is now heavily dependent on international trade and which must watch its trade balance as a barometer of its economic welfare.

The Cabinet system and the disciplined organization of the two major parties makes it possible to recruit experienced leadership and mobilize public support. The resources of the Foreign Office provide the means for carrying out policies, once public support for them is assured.

If international peace and security can be maintained, the changing patterns of British industry can yield the means of economic welfare for the community.

SELECTED BIBLIOGRAPHY

Two standard authoritative works on the history of British foreign policy which must be mentioned:

Ward, Sir A. W. and G. P. Gooch, eds., *Cambridge History of Foreign Policy.* 3 vols. Cambridge University Press, 1922-1923.

Seton-Watson, R. W., *Britain in Europe 1789-1914.* Cambridge University Press, 1955.

For the period 1919 to 1939 three books give a good compact account, with some critical comment:

Carr, E. H., *International Relations between the Two World Wars 1919-1939.* London, 1955.

Medlicott, W. N., *British Foreign Policy since Versailles.* London, 1942.

Reynolds, P. A., *British Foreign Policy in the Inter-War Years.* London, 1954.

For the period since 1945 a penetrating survey of events and an interpretation aimed at suggesting lines of policy are given in the reports of three study groups under the auspices of the Royal Institute of International Affairs, and published by them in London and New York:

Defence in the Cold War. 1950.

Atlantic Alliance: NATO's Role in the Free World. 1952.

Britain in Western Europe: WEU and the Atlantic Alliance. 1956.

A monthly publication of the Royal Institute of International affairs is valuable for current affairs:

The World Today.

There is a steady flow of documentary materials from H. M. Stationery Office, some of which have been cited in the first of the preceding chapters. All these publications are given in:

Government Publications Monthly List, HMSO. This is cumulated each year into a list for the year.

The Four Original Dominions in the Commonwealth of Nations

J. D. B. MILLER

Department of Government
University College, Leicester

The Four Original Dominions in the Commonwealth of Nations

CHAPTER 10

BACKGROUNDS OF FOREIGN
POLICY IN CANADA, AUSTRALIA,
NEW ZEALAND, AND SOUTH AFRICA

It should be emphasized at the beginning that treating the four "original dominions" under one heading is a matter of convenience, and is not intended to suggest that they form a unit in international society. Each is a sovereign state with full control of its foreign policy. Each decides that policy in terms of its national interest, as it conceives that interest; and since the four countries differ considerably in geographical situation, economic development, and social composition, the policies differ in aim and emphasis. It will be the purpose of this and the following chapter to show how national interest is conceived in the four countries, and what policies they have pursued as sovereign states.

But having made this point about the independence of the four countries one from another, it is also important to indicate why they are grouped together, not only here but also in the minds of many writers and speakers, especially in Britain and the United States. They are so grouped because they are member nations of the Commonwealth, and because for many years they were referred to collectively as "the British dominions." Each has Queen Elizabeth as its sovereign; each has made its way slowly from the position of a British colony to that of a sovereign state, without losing its connection with the others or with Britain. But the connection has changed. Whereas in the beginning it was between a sovereign Britain and subject communities overseas, it has become in the course of time an informal connection between countries which recognize one another's independent status but prefer to share a common monarch, in the sense that the Crowns of Britain, Canada, Australia, South Africa, and New Zealand are united in a single person. Something of how the change has taken place, and of the nature of the situation now, is explained below.

Common Development

It is not only a common evolution of international status that encourages the grouping together of these four countries. They have other things in common. Foremost among these is the fact that in the nineteenth and twentieth centuries they have been, like the United States, Brazil, and Argentina, receivers of millions of migrants from an overcrowded Europe. Their populations have been largely immigrant populations, concerned to make a better living in new, "empty" lands. In fact none of the lands was completely empty. Each had a native population which the incoming white men had either to make peace with or subdue. That native population was negligible in Canada and Australia, formidable but potentially co-operative in New Zealand, and massive in potential strength in South Africa. But in each case the incoming white men became the dominant group, and have continued as such. Nearly all the significant political pressures and conflicts have been within the white group—certainly so far as foreign policy is concerned.

The second point of similarity between the four countries is closely allied with their common role as receivers of immigrants. It is that each developed primarily as an agricultural, mining, and pastoral community, exporting food, minerals, and fibers to the growing markets of Europe and especially to Britain. As the nineteenth century drew to a close this was their dominant role: in return for men and capital from Britain, they sent primary products. In the twentieth century each has qualified this position by developing its own manufacturing industry, usually under tariff protection; but each has remained heavily dependent upon exports of primary products.

The third point of similarity is that each is a parliamentary democracy, operating on the pattern of responsible government as practiced in Britain and as recommended for Canada in the Durham Report of 1838. In South Africa the system is more parliamentary than democratic, in that only the white minority has the vote in parliamentary elections; but in each of the other dominions, and in South Africa so far as the white minority is concerned, the parliamentary system is identical with that practiced at Westminster. This gives the four dominions an almost instinctive understanding of one another's political systems, and gives them, moreover, in the field of foreign policy, an executive which is by definition tolerably certain of parliamentary support in its dealings with other states.

The four countries are, then, roughly similar in their demographic origins, their economic development, and their political systems. Each has derived its place in the society of states from its growth out of colonial status to nationhood. Each is a member of the Commonwealth, and each has as its formal Head of State the same person. Now it is time to look at the geographical and social circumstances which differentiate the dominions from one another.

Canada

Canada is a North American country. Ever since the American Revolution, its development and its emerging national interests have been based upon a triangular relationship between the United States, Britain, and itself. From Britain have come people and a political system. From the United States have come manufactured goods, the raw materials of a common North American culture, the challenge of a different type of political system, and all the impact of a dynamic economy; in the twentieth century, capital has also come in large quantities. Throughout Canada's history, there have been prophets who insisted that it was only a matter of time before Canada became incorporated into the United States.

British influence, they have said, would never be strong enough to withstand the pressure of the vigorous United States.

Yet in Canada itself the problem has not taken on quite this aspect. In so far as there has been a continuous argument in Canada, it has been between those who wished to stress the British connection and those who wished to stress the innate Canadian character of the developing country. Historically the reason has lain in the fact that Canada was a French colony from 1608 to 1759, and that the tenacious French-Canadian temperament, developed then, has never allowed itself either to be substantially diluted by British stock or to succumb to cultural pressure from the United States. The French Canadians are one of the world's most remarkable examples of a people which has accepted the economic and political relationships of the country in which it is placed, but has refused to accept with these the religion, language, and law which seemed inevitably to go with them. When Lord Durham came to Canada as governor-general in 1838 he found, in his own words, "two nations warring in the bosom of a single state": the French Canadians would not accept the consequences of their incorporation into the British Empire, if those consequences entailed accepting the social customs of their fellow Canadians of British descent.

Durham's solution was to grant responsible government in the hope that the vigorous majority culture, of British origin, would assert itself over that of the unprogressive French minority. But in fact this did not occur. What responsible government did was to enable the two groups to agree to differ. The French remained solidly set in the province of Quebec (where today more than 80 per cent of the four million inhabitants are of French origin), preserving their own religion, law, and social system. They were cut off from France itself by the French Revolution's denial of religion and seigneurial right; the increasing secularism and cynicism of France in the nineteenth century meant that France drifted even further away from the French-speaking Canadians. All they had left was their own position in Canada, which they proceeded to make impregnable in constitutional terms and which served as the basis of an emergent Canadian national sentiment under such leaders of French extraction as Cartier, Laurier, and St. Laurent.

Yet it would be quite misleading to think of Canada's politics as divided between French, on the one hand, and English, on the other, and of Canadian nationalism as essentially a French-Canadian product. Throughout Canada's history since its federation in 1867, national sentiment has been developed through the skillful co-operation of leaders of both groups and through the vision of a united Canada in which national-origin differences mattered less than the prospect of a great destiny. In the nineteenth century John A. Macdonald, and in the twentieth W. L. Mackenzie King, headed what were in effect intercultural coalitions aiming at the unity of Canada. The force of their appeal was augmented by the prospects of Canadian development (as the prairie provinces came into being and Canada's immense natural resources were progressively revealed) and by the fact that much of the new ground was being broken by settlers who were neither French nor British in origin, but came from farther east in Europe. Scandinavians, Poles, and Russians could not be expected to show enthusiasm for either Britain or prerevolutionary France; only Canada itself could engage their loyalty. During the twentieth century each Canadian government has made the unity of Canada its prime objective. As we shall see, foreign policy has been largely guided by the desire to preserve and enhance that unity. Canadian nationalism has been a product both of reaction against excessive identification with Britain or the United States and of deliberate policy by governments. At any rate, nationalism has proved a unifying factor.

Union of South Africa

In South Africa it has been otherwise. There the attempt to create a distinctive nationalism has been pursued by only one nationality group, whose efforts have led to more division than unity. South Africa was settled first by Dutchmen, Frenchmen, and other Europeans, who merged into a composite group called first Boers and then Afrikaners, speaking a distinctive tongue called Afrikaans, which is descended from Dutch but has become a language in its own right. Later, as in Canada, there came British conquest and British settlers. But the differences from the Canadian situation were profound. In Canada there had been a direct transition from French Empire to British Empire; the French population was cohesive and closely settled; although there was conflict between British and French, it never became thoroughly bitter, and by 1867 the French minority had been guaranteed its own language and the other rights which it wished to preserve within the boundaries of a single Canadian federation. In South Africa the Boers had founded for themselves two independent republics—in the Transvaal and the Orange Free State—and had rapidly established a national tradition, molded by their circumstances as farmers settling on great tracts of land and leading patriarchal lives. Their connection with Holland was small. In the end they had to be conquered before they would submit to full British control—and their final submission did not come until 1902, the end of the Boer War. By this time their sense of national existence was complete; the bitterness and violence of the war gave it extra strength which French-Canadian "nationalism" never possessed.

When the Union of South Africa was established in 1909 it looked like much the same settlement the Canadians had achieved in 1867. The Boers were guaranteed the inviolability of their language and their Roman-Dutch law, and it was plain that in the provinces in which they were a majority of the white population (the Transvaal and Orange Free State) they would have much the same dominance as the French had in Quebec. But they were a larger proportion of the population than the French in Canada; they were to be found in the Cape as well as in the provinces which had been Boer Republics; their religion and their sense of national identity convinced many of them that theirs was the only legitimate South African nationalism and that the British element in South Africa must, in the end, submit to distinctively Boer traditions—since these British had no corresponding African traditions of their own, only their sense of loyalty to Britain, a faraway country.

Statesmen of Boer descent (Botha, Smuts, Hertzog) did their

best to draw the two groups together as Macdonald, Laurier, and Mackenzie King had done in Canada. It was at first thought that the same result had been achieved. But by the 1940's it was clear that Afrikaner nationalism, sharpened by disapproval of British colonial policy and by its own sense of destiny, was firmly in the ascendant. The "British" South Africans—a numerical minority— had no corresponding sense of destiny to sustain them, and were being insensibly drawn into the sphere of influence of Afrikaner viewpoint.

In this process it is essential to remember that the strength of the Afrikaner case lay in its character as an *African* case. Militant Afrikaners insisted that white South Africans had to live in Africa forever, had no other home; they must therefore adopt an attitude toward African problems different from that of European colonial powers or American idealists, who either had no direct connection with Africa or could get out of it whenever they wished. For South Africans the only possible policy must be one of survival; this, as they saw it, meant supremacy over the numerical majority in the country, the non-Europeans (Bantu, Colored, Indian); the tradition to follow was that of the Boer Republics, the original white men's states in Africa. Just as Canadians' sense of national interest had to be developed in the context of the North American continent, so South Africans' same sense must be primarily African, based on their permanent position in the southern part of the continent.

Commonwealth of Australia

Australia has had none of the intercultural difficulties that have perplexed Canada and South Africa, although Australians of Irish descent and Roman Catholic religion have sometimes seemed to form a group of special distinctiveness. Until substantial migration from continental Europe began in the late 1940's, Australia had recruited her population almost entirely from the British Isles. Her people all spoke the same language and professed much the same cultural tradition. Their internal conflicts were those not of race against race, but of class against class, town against countryside, district against district for the economic gains that wages,

profits, and investment might bring.[1] Australia's attachment to the
British connection has been a combination of sentiment (derived
from the heritage of culture, family connection, educational and
religious tradition and the other ties which come from transplant-
ing British people overseas) and economic advantage. Britain trades
more with Australia than with any other single country, Australia
more with Britain. External investment in Australia has been
largely British. Yet such a close connection has led to negative
feelings as well as positive ones. The fact that Britain was so
obviously the source of development capital in Australia has often
led Australian radicals to attack the British investor as a skinflint
or a moneybags. The facts that social status in Australia derived
(and still to some extent derives) from the precedence accorded
by British governors, and may express itself through such essentially British symbols as a knighthood or an education at Oxford
or Cambridge, have also drawn the fire of radicals. Australian
nationalism has therefore been associated more with the Australian
Labour Party than with its more "respectable" rivals, who until
recently were inclined to impute disloyalty to anyone who spoke
of Australian interests as not necessarily being identical with
British. There was a considerable support among Irish Australians
for Australian nationalism in the formative years between 1890
and 1920; here again the opposition was to British domination of
free Australian development.

Australian nationalism has been economic, in so far as it has
arisen out of demands for better markets and more investment, and
out of a vision of how great might be a nation which had at its
disposal the resources of a continent. The economic element has
been mixed with another, the fear of external domination. Here

[1] I am not suggesting that these particular conflicts did not occur in Canada
and South Africa. They did, and still do, and they have been the stuff of
political argument over the years there, as much as in Australia. But in looking
for the background to the formation of foreign policy one looks for those particular elements in national life which go to make the special self-assertiveness
of the nation in question; and there can be no doubt that in Canada and South
Africa these have come from the struggle for national unity, while in Australia
and New Zealand they have come from economic needs and the fear of external
conquest through either excessive immigration or military invasion.

Australia's geographical position is of prime importance. Australians are a European people on an Asian limb. By way of New Guinea, Indonesia, and Malaya, their country is in easy communication with Asia; they cannot move it away, any more than South Africans can move their country away from the rest of Africa. But they are firmly convinced that it should remain a white man's country, neither affected from within by a flood of Asian immigrants nor conquered from without by an Asian power. This is the explanation of the White Australia Policy (a policy dating from the early years of this century, though agitated for long before that, whereby colored people are not allowed to become permanent residents of Australia). It is also the explanation of Australia's anxiety over New Guinea, her long-felt apprehensions about Japan, and her active search for security pacts in the Pacific.

Dominion of New Zealand

Much the same is true of New Zealand, though in a modified way. New Zealand is less clearly linked with Asia than Australia; she is twelve hundred miles from Australia on the side farthest from the Asian mainland. New Zealand is ringed round with ocean, part of no continental mass. Large-scale Asian immigration has never been the same possibility for her as for Australia. Yet her situation in the Pacific, as far as can possibly be removed from Britain, has meant considerable anxiety among New Zealanders about possible invasion—first from some hostile European power and then, following the experience of Japan's southward push in 1942, from a hostile power in Asia.

New Zealand sentiment toward Britain has been stronger than similar sentiment in Australia. New Zealanders have an even smaller admixture from continental Europe than Australians; they have a smaller proportion of Irish Catholics among them; their radicals have been more inclined to embrace British influence than resist it. In any case, there is less room for grandiose national sentiment in New Zealand than in Australia, Canada, or even South Africa. New Zealand is the smallest country of the four, with the smallest population and the least prospect of substantial industrial growth. It has no vast undeveloped areas with which the

mind can play, as it can in Canada and Australia. Racial and
religious conflicts have hardly been known, and class conflict,
while liable to burst forth in small vicious spurts from time to
time, has had nothing like the permanent political place allotted
to it in Australia.[2] The New Zealand role in world affairs was
obviously to be a modest one. New Zealanders have tended to see
it as such, and to ask for a less positive independence from Britain
than any other of the four dominions. Their sense of attachment
to Britain has been strengthened by the fact that the New Zealand
economy has been almost entirely built upon the supply of meat
and dairy products to Britain, and Britain remains by far New
Zealand's principal supplier of imported goods.

Common Factors in Foreign Policy

Having discussed the special twists which social composition and
geographical facts have given to each of the four dominions, it is
possible to show in broad outline where their national interests
and spheres of interest lie. All have been insatiable absorbers of
capital from outside, much of it from Britain. They are still in
this position, though Canada and (in lesser degree) Australia are
now sources of investment capital themselves and though the
United States now has a greater part than formerly in supplying
their capital needs. Canada trades overwhelmingly with the United
States, while the other three conduct most of their trade with
Britain. In other words, all four have strong economic interests
which encourage them to be on the best terms possible with the
United States and Britain; the fact that Canada, Australia, and
South Africa are all intent on large-scale industrialization is no
contradiction of this other fact, but does mean that relations with
Britain and the United States are more complicated than if those

[2] In overt signs of social class, Australia and New Zealand are much the same
sort of "classless" society and are easily confused in the minds of observers of
their peoples' behavior. But in Australia trade-unionism has developed more
strongly on a basis of class conflict than in New Zealand, and the mythology of
the Australian Labour Party is more heavily class ridden than that of the New
Zealand Labour Party. In this sense a "permanent political place" has been
allotted to class conflict in the minds of Australians.

two countries simply supplied manufactured goods and the dominions primary products. It is also worthy of note that the four dominions are competitors in regard to a number of products—meat, wool, dairy products, wheat, metals—and therefore their common interest in good relations with Britain and the United States is liable to be obscured by competition for markets at times when markets are limited and will not absorb all that the dominions wish to export. Similarly, they are competitors for capital: the British or United States investor may well be faced with the conflicting opportunities of a mine or a factory in Australia and one in South Africa.

Each of the four countries is compelled by geography to maintain interest in a particular regional situation. For South Africa this is the African continent, where her obvious relations are with colonial powers such as Britain, Portugal, Belgium, and France, and with emerging nation-states such as Nigeria and the Sudan. For Canada it is the North Atlantic community, embracing herself, Britain, continental Europe, and the United States; at the same time Canada has a Pacific coastline and must take account of events on the mainland of Asia. For Australia the region to be concerned with is the Pacific on its Asian side. Developments in the Asian areas that lead to shifts of power there (for example, the retreat of the Dutch from Indonesia and the change of regime in China) are of first importance to her, as is the interest which the United States shows in Asia. For New Zealand the region is roughly the same as for Australia, with perhaps more concentration upon the islands of the Pacific.

None of the four countries can hope to be dominant in the region in which its prime interest lies: 2½ million white South Africans, 15 million Canadians, 9 million Australians and 2 million New Zealanders are not enough in any of the four cases to play the dominant role, in spite of the very high standard of living which each country enjoys. For each, therefore, foreign policy involves doing the best it can with the material at its disposal—making the firmest and most productive alliances, choosing the strategic moments at conferences, using to the best advantage the connections it has with other Commonwealth members, with Britain, and with the United States, and being as good a neighbor as it can to the countries around it which seem to be important for its future.

But this is a sophisticated, up-to-date view of foreign policy for each of the four dominions. It is relatively new—in the form in which I have put it, it is applicable only to the period since World War II. In the next chapter the policy of each of the four countries since then will be examined in some detail. In the meantime, however, it is necessary to show how the four countries got to the position where it was possible (both legally and actually) for them to take such a view of foreign policy. Doing this means showing how the British Empire of the 1900's, with Britain as its formulator of foreign policy, was changed to the Commonwealth of the 1950's, with each member nation responsible for its own foreign policy and for no other member's; and it means seeing something of the arguments and changes that took place in each of the four countries up to World War II.

Dependence in Foreign Policy

At the beginning of the twentieth century the term "dominions" was not used. The countries with which we are here concerned were called "the self-governing colonies," a part of the British Empire. They were distinguished from nonself-governing colonies in that they were in full charge of their domestic affairs. The British government had the power to exercise a final veto over their legislation by instructing the Governor-General to refuse the royal assent to bills on domestic matters; but this kind of veto did not occur. These autonomous colonies were in full control of their internal affairs. Externally, however, they had no initiative. They were not recognized as sovereign states; indeed, they did not seek such recognition. They had no independent treaty-making powers and no diplomatic representatives. The accepted constitutional doctrine was that the Crown was indivisible, that the Crown in its international negotiations consisted of the monarch, and that the monarch in such circumstances could be advised only by his British ministers, who, in this manner, were responsible for the foreign policy of the Empire as a whole. It was assumed that there was and should be a unitary foreign policy.

In certain ways, however, the self-governing colonies were associated with foreign policy. The most obvious way was in the making of treaties on matters which concerned some colonies but not others—in the main, commercial treaties. The four countries had fiscal systems different from Britain's: Canada and Australia, in particular, were protectionist countries while Britain was still free-trade. So far as Britain was concerned, the difficulty was got over by providing, from the 1870's onward, that the colonies should not be bound by treaties between Britain and a foreign country unless they specifically acceded to these by their own subsequent act. In cases where a particular colony was clearly implicated in any arrangements that might be made between Britain and a foreign country, the custom was to associate the colony directly with the negotiation by allowing it representatives in the British team of negotiators. Here the most obvious examples were treaties and agreements between Britain and the United States, where Canadian interests were involved; and in this way Canada became the first British colony to participate regularly in diplomatic negotiations. This participation by Canada followed naturally from the fact that it was the only major colony situated alongside a major foreign power. At the same time the widespread feeling that Canadian interests were sometimes subordinated to British in such negotiations was an important element in furthering Canadian nationalist demands for a free hand. The Washington Treaty of 1871 was an example of this kind. Later, however, Canadian representatives predominated in the British teams; in 1909 the Toronto correspondent of The Times could claim that "through the orderly course of Imperial development Canada has become the sovereign British power on the American continent, responsible alike to Great Britain and to the Canadian people."[3] The fact remained still that Canada had no power of independent negotiation; Canadian nationalism remained unappeased.

The Imperial Conference

The other main way in which colonial governments were associated with the making of foreign policy was by means of the

[3] The Times (London), May 24, 1909.

Imperial Conference. At Queen Victoria's first Jubilee in 1887 there had been a conference in London of all the colonies, whether self-governing or not. At her second Jubilee, in 1897, the conference was restricted to the self-governing colonies; and this Colonial Conference was transformed in 1907 into an Imperial Conference. The intention was that the conference should meet every four years, that it should be confined to self-governing colonies, that it should be concerned with "matters of common interest . . . as between His Majesty's Government and his Governments of the self-governing Dominions beyond the seas,"[4] that the Prime Minister of Britain would preside, and that the nations represented would have one vote each, without distinction on grounds of size or importance. The conference continued to be held, roughly every four years, until 1937. In the period before World War I there was no question of its being in charge of imperial foreign policy. What happened was that the British Prime Minister or Foreign Secretary gave it a picture of foreign affairs, described the government's policy, invited comments, but was under no obligation to take account of what he heard.

The British government's attitude was that the determination of peace or war was something it could not share. The dominions agreed with this attitude, since it was obvious that the power to decide peace or war must go along with the power to make war; this power resided exclusively in Britain herself, since it was she who financed and ran the Royal Navy, which each dominion considered to be its first line of defense. In fact, there was some controversy before World War I over whether there should be "dominion navies," and Australia did go to the length of establishing her own Royal Australian Navy; but it was understood that

[4] The Report of the Conference, Cd. 3523. This was the first time the self-governing colonies had been distinguished as "dominions." Thereafter they were all called "dominions," until the Style and Title assumed by Queen Elizabeth in 1953 distinguished them as "realms." The new term has not caught on; they are still widely called "dominions," though "Commonwealth countries" (a term which can also include the Republics of India and Pakistan) also is used. Nomenclature is further confused by the fact that the Commonwealth includes the Dominion of New Zealand, the Commonwealth of Australia, the Union of South Africa, and Canada (formerly the Dominion of Canada).

in time of war this would be under the control of the Admiralty. Its instigation was due to a determination on the part of the Australian government that there should be some protection for Australia in the event of a surprise attack in the Pacific. It did not mean that Australia wished to conduct an independent foreign policy. A similar proposal for Canada was rejected by the Borden government in 1913 in favor of an "emergency contribution" to the Royal Navy; New Zealand showed its loyalty during the same period by a similar contribution.

Theories of Imperial Unity

Before World War I the increasing strength and national sentiment of the dominions encouraged much theorizing about their futures and about how the Empire might be organized so as to accommodate them without destroying the principle of imperial unity. On the one hand, the dominions were growing; they had no wish to separate themselves from Britain; they wished to be at least consulted about foreign policy and defense policy. On the other hand, Britain was in control, and wished to remain in control, of foreign policy. It was impossible to envisage the subtle development of British policy in Europe being held up while discussions took place with politicians in New Zealand, who knew little or nothing of the situation. Furthermore, the dominions displayed only an occasional desire to contribute toward the cost of imperial defense. Most of the time they were content to leave this financing to the British taxpayer. They were responsible for their own land defense, and the nationalists among them wanted their own navies as sources of national pride. The situation could hardly be met by occasional consultation; yet frequent consultation was impossible, and the British electorate was not likely to approve of a veto over British foreign policy being given to people thousands of miles away.

In fact the difficulty was not solved until well on into the 1920's. Doubts about it remained until 1939. The way in which it was eventually dealt with is discussed below. Before World War I, however, much effort was put into schemes for imperial federation and for the strengthening of the Imperial Conference. Imperial federation had first been proposed in the 1880's but had languished; it received an injection of spirit in the 1900's through the activities of Lionel Curtis and his "Round Table" groups in Britain and the dominions. But their influence was negligible, except here and there with a dominion minister who explained that the idea was splendid but that his people would not accept it. In the dominions themselves the idea was received with apathy or suspicion, "loyalists" giving it only qualified support and nationalists usually attacking it on the ground that it meant the subordination of national development to British control. Apart from the British government's reluctance to share control of foreign policy with anyone, the scheme met insuperable difficulties in Britain through its association with schemes for tariff preference for goods from the dominions, all of which entailed some interference with the traditional British policy of free trade.

Schemes for strengthening the Imperial Conference were put forward by some of the dominion prime ministers and by such theorists as the Englishman Richard Jebb. They too met with apathy or suspicion. Any permanent secretariat for the Imperial Conference would have to be somehow reconciled with the British system of responsible government a difficult task in any case; and the idea of continuous consultation with dominion prime ministers was made difficult by the fact that a single visit to London by one from Australia or New Zealand meant a three-month absence from his own country, where political attention was in any case overwhelmingly devoted to domestic matters. In the upshot, no principle of imperial control of foreign policy was worked out.

World War I

In August, 1914, the dominions announced their enthusiastic support for Britain's cause; it was assumed that they were at war because she was at war, and there discussion ended. The events of the war itself, however, had a considerable effect upon the development of national feeling in the four dominions, and upon their international status. The fact that each of them sent many thousands of volunteer troops to fight in France and the Middle East gave a fillip to national pride. Each dominion had its own special actions to remember; it is still sometimes said, for example, that "Australia became a nation on the heights of Gallipoli." The organization of troops, consultation over their use with the British government, and the semi-independent management of the war in areas near to the dominions themselves, all gave to the dominion governments a sense of greater maturity. This was accentuated by the fact that their prime ministers were incorporated in a sort of temporary imperial executive, the Imperial War Cabinet. They became figures in the British political world, and there was talk of the Imperial War Cabinet being continued into the peace as a solution to the problem of imperial foreign policy.

But in the dominions themselves events were taking courses which were to run counter to the idea of a single Empire policy, and to encourage the more defiant dominion nationalism of prewar days. In South Africa, Botha and Smuts put down a Boer rebellion, thereby earning for themselves the enmity of Boer extremists who had previously been prepared to follow them in their policy of "live and let live" with British South Africans. In Australia the proposal of the Hughes government that there should be conscription to reinforce the Australian troops in France was the cause of a permanent split in the Labour Party and in due course was turned down by two successive referendums of the people. The Easter Rebellion of 1917 in Dublin had its effect, too, in temporarily widening the gap between many Irish Australians and their more imperially minded fellows. In Canada, Borden's conscription proposals split the Liberal Party and led to an explosion of French-Canadian nationalism and opposition to conscription, the echoes of which were to be heard again in World War II—as were the echoes of the Australian struggle. Only in New Zealand was conscription smoothly undertaken, though there it was opposed by the stripling Labour Party: Peter Fraser, who was to be the Labour Prime Minister in World War II, was sent to jail for sedition on account of his opposition to conscription.

The effect of the war in each of the dominions was to intensify the cleavage between those who wished the country to follow Britain in its international relations and those who wished it somehow to acquire the power to act in its own right. This was not necessarily a cleavage between imperialists and nationalists; it was more a cleavage between respectful nationalists and disrespectful ones. The respectful nationalists were those who loved their country but saw its destiny as inextricably linked with Britain's; they were attracted to the British connection by pride of blood or respect for Britain's power, or both. The disrespectful nationalists were those who dwelt on the horrors of the war, the futility of its results, and, often, the wickedness of financiers and armament manufacturers. Their solution was that their country should not concern itself further with the affairs of Europe but should attend to its own affairs. Disrespectful nationalism in this respect had much in common with isolationism in the United States: much the same arguments, much the same disrespect for crowned heads, diplomatic maneuvers, and Europe generally.

The immediate outcome of the war was that in each dominion the respectful nationalists, those who had been closely associated with the British government in the prosecution of the war, represented their country at the peace negotiations. The peace settlement was signed for "the British Empire" by representatives of Britain and of each of the dominions, which also became foundation members of the League of Nations. At the peace conference itself the main preoccupation of three of them was the retention of ex-German colonies near to their own territory, which they had seized by force of arms. For New Zealand it was Western Samoa, for Australia German New Guinea, and for South Africa the German territory in South-West Africa. It was largely in order to ensure the occupation of these by the dominions, and their treatment as integral parts of the territories of the dominions while still subject to conditions of trusteeship, that the "C class" mandate was constructed. The dominions, led by Hughes of Australia, also were anxious to avoid the inclusion in the peace treaty, by Japan, of a clause declaring racial equality. They feared that this might allow international attack on the exclusionist migration policies pursued by Canada and New Zealand as well as by Australia. In form, the signature of the treaty by the dominion representatives on behalf of "the British Empire" preserved the notion of a single imperial policy. But the fact that each dominion was designated by its own name, coupled with the vigorous appearances which various dominion representatives had made publicly in the deliberations of the conference, made it clear that they would be heard from again in international diplomacy.

Dominion Status and Foreign Policy

The international status of the dominions still remained undefined, however. Were they sovereign states? They had some of the trappings of sovereign states, certainly so far as their internal affairs were concerned. But it was plain that they could not declare war and negotiate independently with foreign countries, since they shared a common sovereign who could not be divided and who (while in symbolic form the king) was in fact the British Parliament and through it the British government. In 1920 it was proposed that the first dominion diplomatic representative should be appointed, a minister plenipotentiary at the British Embassy at Washington in charge of relations between the United States and Canada. He was to be appointed on the advice of the Canadian government; but he was to be stationed at the *British* Embassy and, when the scheme had been agreed on, the British and Canadian governments were quick to point out that it meant no "departure . . . from the principle of the diplomatic unity of the British Empire."[5] It could be argued that this was simply a development from the practice of associating Canadians with British in negotiations with the United States, and that Canada's own status had not advanced at all. No one was ever appointed to the post.

During the next twenty years the status of the dominions was clarified, and they began to enter international life on their own account. To conclude this chapter I propose to discuss, first, the way in which their joint status was defined, together with the reasons for the definition, and, second, the foreign policies which each began to develop before World War II. It is necessary to discuss the joint status first, since until this was achieved the dominions were hardly in a position to embark upon policies of

[5] Announcement in Canadian House of Commons, May 10, 1920.

their own. At the same time it is necessary to distinguish between the path which each of them took, since they were not all of the same mind about the desirability of independent policies.

The problem of what "dominion status" involved became prominent in 1921, when the British government offered Ireland "the same constitutional status in the Community of Nations known as the British Empire as the Dominion of Canada, the Commonwealth of Australia, the Dominion of New Zealand, and the Union of South Africa."[6] When the British Prime Minister, Mr. Lloyd George, commended the Irish Treaty to the House of Commons, he said it would be "difficult and dangerous" to give a definition of dominion status; but he did say that "the Dominions since the War have been given equal rights with Great Britain in the control of the foreign policy of the Empire." Unless there was an elected "Council of Empire," the machinery for carrying out the Empire's policy must remain in London, in the British Foreign Office; the dominions accepted this, but they claimed "a voice in determining the lines of our future policy." The Imperial Conference was now arriving at decisions on policy "with the common consent of the whole Empire." The dominions had earned this opportunity of control through their efforts in the war. But there were advantages for Britain too in the arrangement: "joint control means joint responsibility, and when the burden of Empire has become so vast it is well that we should have the shoulders of these young giants under the burden to help us along. It introduces a broader and a calmer view into foreign policy. It restrains rash Ministers and it will stimulate timorous ones."[7] Ireland was to participate fully in this activity of making foreign policy.

What Lloyd George was saying (and what many people believed) was that the prewar difficulties had been smoothed away by the fact that the dominions had shown themselves willing to support Britain in a great war and that from now on there would

[6] From Article 1 of *Articles of Agreement for a Treaty between Great Britain and Ireland, December 6, 1921,* reprinted in A. B. Keith (ed.), *Speeches and Documents on the British Dominions, 1918-1931* (London, 1932), p. 77.

[7] Speech in the House of Commons, Dec. 14, 1921, reprinted in A. B. Keith, *ibid.,* pp. 83-97.

be no difficulty about their sharing in foreign policy through telegraphic consultation and the Imperial Conference. At the Washington Conference of 1921 this assumption was acted on: "the British Empire" was once again represented by dominion as well as British delegates. But within a year of Lloyd George's confident statement it had become clear that there was in fact no joint control of foreign policy.

In September, 1922, Turkish Nationalists under Kemal Pasha were advancing against fleeing Greek troops at Chanak, by the Dardanelles in Asia Minor. British troops, alone among the former Allied nations, remained to defend the Straits. Lloyd George cabled the dominion governments asking them to send contingents if fighting took place with the Turks. The dominion governments had not been consulted about the beginnings of the situation; nevertheless, New Zealand cabled an emphatic promise of support and Australia a rather less enthusiastic one. But Canada and South Africa both stated that the matter would have to be put before their respective Parliaments and made it plain that they did not consider themselves bound in policies which had not been the subject of consultation. In the following month the British government invited the dominions to take cognizance of the fact that it was sending plenipotentiaries to Lausanne for the conference which would finally end the war with Turkey, and asked them to approve this action. It was pointed out by Canada, however, that the whole procedure was different from that which had been adopted to end the war with Germany: there was no joint "British Empire" delegation, but simply one from Britain, and the dominions could hardly be expected to regard themselves as morally bound by any obligations which the treaty arising from the Lausanne Conference might impose upon former belligerents.

The change from the rosy expectations of 1921 was formally recognized by the Imperial Conference of 1923, and found its expression first in the Locarno Treaty of 1925. The conference decided that each part of the Empire was free to negotiate treaties which concerned only itself and another foreign state, but should make sure that other dominions which might be interested were consulted and, if necessary, associated with the negotiations. If the

whole of the Empire was to be associated with a particular international treaty (for example, one arrived at by way of a general
international conference), each dominion should be represented,
as it had been at Paris and Washington, and should sign the document. This arrangement did two things. It gave approval to the
negotiation of treaties by individual dominions, without the interposition of the British government (earlier in the year Canada had
already followed this procedure in signing the Halibut Treaty with
the United States), and it recognized the fact that British foreign
policy must proceed in certain directions without the participation
of the dominions in the necessary negotiations, and without their
being committed by the policy decided on. This plan was a long
way from the "joint control" envisaged by Lloyd George; but it
was a recognition of the facts: a joint policy was impossible. The
Locarno Treaty of 1925 was negotiated by Britain on this understanding. No dominion representatives were present, and the treaty
contained the provision that it should "impose no obligation upon
any of the British Dominions, or upon India, unless the Government of such Dominion, or of India, signifies its acceptance
thereof."[8] The true nature of the situation was made clear by the
British Foreign Secretary, Sir Austen Chamberlain, in the House
of Commons:

. . . the affairs of the world do not stand still . . . I could not go, as the
representative of His Majesty's government, to meeting after meeting
of the League of Nations, to conference after conference with the representatives of foreign countries, and say, "Great Britain is without a
policy. We have not been able to meet all the governments of the
Empire, and we can do nothing." That might be possible for an
Empire wholly removed from Europe, which existed in a different
hemisphere. It is not possible for an Empire the heart of which lies in
Europe . . . and where every peril to the peace of Europe jeopardizes
the peace of this country.[9]

Yet there remained a dilemma in British foreign policy, in
Europe particularly, for the rest of the interwar period. On the one

[8] Article 9. Quoted in Nicholas Mansergh, *Survey of British Commonwealth
Affairs, Problems of External Policy 1931-1939* (London, 1952), p. 65. In the
event, none of the Dominions signified its acceptance of the Locarno pact.
[9] House of Commons, Nov. 18, 1925. Quoted in Nicholas Mansergh, *op. cit.*

hand, it was impossible to associate the dominions with all the details of British policy, or indeed the specifically European aspects of policy, where British interests were continually at stake. On the other hand, it was clearly undesirable to have the dominions quarreling with British policy and either refusing to follow it or actively opposing it in the League of Nations and elsewhere. As things turned out (see below), none of the dominions wished to pursue an active foreign policy at variance with Britain's, with the partial exception of New Zealand in 1936-1937. This tendency to agreement made the task of British policy-making easier. But the dominions remained as a possible drag or veto on British policy, once that had been formulated: their lack of co-operation, their refusal to take part enthusiastically in the carrying out of policy, might weaken British prestige, create divisions within and between the various parts of the Empire, and put obstacles in the way of a British naval policy that envisaged the active co-operation of the dominions in the deployment, docking, refueling, and other operations of the Royal Navy. Every British foreign secretary had to keep in mind the desirability of a united "Empire front" in any positive policy he put forward. The dominions were thus placed in a position of power without responsibility, no less real for the fact that the outside world had little comprehension of the role they might play in modifying British policy.

By the mid-1920's, then, the dominions had gained treaty-making powers, had been released from any formal "joint control" of British foreign policy, and were in a position to exercise considerable negative influence on that policy if they vigorously made their wishes known to Downing Street. But their status was still undefined. The need for some clear statement of their position was met by the 1926 Imperial Conference, to which came three dominion delegations committed to obtaining some clarification of dominion status. The Irish Free State[10] wished to have the greatest possible independence, since its government was continually under fire from an opposition which wished the ties with

[10] The Irish Free State attended Imperial Conferences as a dominion between 1923 and 1932. It continued to be regarded by the British government as a dominion until 1948, but certainly did not regard itself as one in anything like the same full sense as the four countries with which I am concerned here.

Britain to be cut completely. In South Africa, General Hertzog had been elected to power on a policy which demanded either equality of status with Britain or secession from the Empire. In Canada, Mr. Mackenzie King's government had just emerged from a disagreement with the Governor-General in which the government had challenged that official's right to operate on any advice other than that of his Canadian ministers. Unless the status of dominions could be settled in such a way as to guarantee these three countries full equality with Britain, the Empire might have to do without them. Their attitude contrasted sharply with that of Australia and New Zealand, whose governments wished neither for any change in their relations with Britain nor for any clear definition of their status.

The Statute of Westminster

The 1926 conference appointed an Inter-Imperial Relations Committee, which submitted a report in which the hand of Lord Balfour, the British representative, was clearly seen. It has become known as the Balfour Report and sometimes, less accurately, as the Balfour Declaration. It began by stating that nothing would be gained from trying to lay down a constitution for the British Empire, since it defied classification in its character as a collection of parts at different stages of evolution. But the "group of self-governing communities composed of Great Britain and the Dominions" had now "reached its full development," and their "position and mutual relation" could be readily defined. They were

. . . autonomous communities within the British Empire, equal in status, in no way subordinate one to another in any aspect of their domestic or external affairs, though united by a common allegiance to the Crown, and freely associated as members of the British Commonwealth of Nations.

The Report went on to say that "though every Dominion is now, and must always remain, the sole judge of the nature and extent of its co-operation, no common cause will, in our opinion, be thereby imperilled"; and it concluded with various practical suggestions about how the remnants of formal British control over dominion legislation might be disposed of. It was adopted by the conference, added to by the next conference, in 1930, and given legal effect when the Statute of Westminster was passed in 1931 by the British Parliament. The Statute referred to the "common allegiance" and "free association" of the members of the British Commonwealth of Nations, and proceeded to state that in future any alteration of the Succession to the throne or of the Style and Titles of the monarch would require dominion consent; that no law would be made by the British Parliament, extending to any of the dominions, without the request and consent of the dominion concerned; and that in future each dominion would have full power to make laws having extraterritorial operation. The Statute was, in effect, a self-denying ordinance on the part of the British Parliament, which had been the sovereign power within the British Empire. It was declaring its intention not to use whatever legal sovereignty it might still possess over the dominions, unless they specifically asked it to do so; and it was equipping them with such powers of self-government as they had not previously received.[11]

By 1931, therefore, the dominions were in a position to operate fully as sovereign states. While the Balfour Report and the Statute of Westminster did not refer specifically to diplomacy and foreign policy, they provided the essential characteristic of *status* without which no dominion could pursue a foreign policy. What policies did the dominions pursue in the 1930's?

Beginnings of Independent Policy

In fact, the record shows that, having got their status, the dominions were in no hurry to use it to the full. At the outbreak of war in 1939 neither New Zealand nor Australia was represented abroad by anyone other than their high commissioners in London. Canada appointed a minister to Washington in 1927, with its own legation, and set up legations in Paris and Tokyo in 1928. South

[11] The Balfour Report, the conclusions of the Imperial Conferences of 1926 and 1930, the debates on the Statute in the various dominion parliaments, and the Statute of Westminster itself, are all to be found in A. B. Keith (ed.), *op. cit.*

Africa set up legations in Washington, The Hague, and Rome in 1929, and in Paris, Berlin, Stockholm, Brussels, and Lisbon in 1934; in the last three centers, however, the legations were under the control of ministers at the larger European capitals. In each dominion the department of external affairs was small and inexperienced. Information about world affairs came to New Zealand and Australia entirely, and to Canada and South Africa to a considerable extent, from the British Foreign Office. Each dominion had in London a senior representative (its high commissioner) who was in constant touch with the Dominions Office and could present the views of his government to the British government in this way. There was also considerable telegraphic communication between the centers of dominion government and London. By these means a dominion might influence British policy. But it had little opportunity of working out a policy of its own and then applying it. Only at the League of Nations had it a means to express its independence, if it wished to do so. Generally, it did not wish to do so. Reference to the policies pursued by the individual dominions will show that for each of them the principal desire was a quiet life.

Canadian Policy

Canada was dominated in foreign policy throughout the interwar period by Mackenzie King. His aims were, first, to secure full status for Canada and then, once status had been secured, to ensure that no issue from outside Canada would be allowed to create the sort of national split that had taken place over conscription in 1917. "I believe that Canada's first duty to the League and to the British Empire," he said in 1936, "with respect to all the great issues that come up, is, if possible, to keep this country united."[12] Any adventurous excursions in foreign policy might break the national unity. In any case, before the bombing plane was brought to the pitch of perfection that it attained in World War II, it was customary for Canadians to feel that they could safely isolate themselves from events outside the American hemisphere. In 1924 Senator Raoul Dandurand achieved an assured

[12] Quoted in Nicholas Mansergh, *op. cit.*, p. 111.

mention in all future accounts of the evolution of Canadian foreign policy by telling the League Assembly that Canadians lived "in a fireproof house, far from inflammable materials."[13] Their relations with the United States were obviously of the first importance. Throughout Mackenzie King's prime ministership (which lasted from 1922 to 1930, and from 1935 to beyond the end of World War II), he stressed the North American situation of his country, by trying to prevent the Imperial Conference from adopting policies which ran contrary to United States interests, by opposing schemes for closer integration of the Empire, which might create difficulties in the relations between Canada and the United States, and by cultivating friendly relations with the United States in the defense field—leading to the secret defense talks of 1937 and the Ogdensburg Agreement of 1940 for the creation of a Permanent Joint Board on Defense between the two countries. He had no desire to make Canada subordinate to the United States, but he looked on its links with the United States as necessary (in economics as in politics—so he was opposed to plans for joint preference within the Empire, from which the United States would be excluded) and as bringing the prospect of common North American insulation from European conflicts. In doing this he had to work quietly and constructively. He knew that an election had been won in Canada in 1911 on the slogan, "No truck nor trade with the Yankees." And he never proposed—nor has the Canadian government proposed since—that Canada should join the Pan American Union or Organization of American States. To King, the link with the United States was a combination of necessity and insurance.

In the European crises of the 1930's Canada was concerned to relieve tension and deprecate policies which might lead to war. A Canadian delegate to the League of Nations who showed a desire to strengthen League sanctions against Italy at the end of 1935 was publicly disowned by his government at home. While in this instance the government's action had special relevance to the fact that Catholic French Canadians were strongly opposed to any

[13] League of Nations, Plenary Meetings, 5th Assembly, Oct. 2, 1924.

action against Catholic Italy, its general attitude was essentially one of noninvolvement in European affairs. Canada was, of all the dominions, probably least anxious to participate in a policy of collective security under the League; and when the Munich crisis was in progress, the Chamberlain policy of appeasement had no more fervent supporter than Mackenzie King. His telegram to Chamberlain when the Munich agreement was signed has gained some notoriety:

> The heart of Canada is rejoicing tonight at the success which crowned your unremitting efforts for peace. . . . On the very brink of chaos, with passions flaming and armies marching, the voice of reason has found a way out of the conflict which no people in their heart desired but none seemed able to avert. A turning-point in the world's history will be reached if, as we hope, tonight's agreement means a halt to the mad race in arms and a new start in building a partnership of all peoples. May you have health and strength to carry your great work to its completion.[14]

Yet it must also be made clear that the King government went ahead with Canadian rearmament in 1938 and that the Prime Minister, visiting Hitler in Germany in 1937, had made it clear to him that if there was a war of aggression in Europe, nothing would keep the Canadian people from being at the side of Britain. This conversation was a secret one, which King did not reveal in public until 1944: it was characteristic of his methods that both his discussion with Hitler and his defense talks with the United States should have been held in the same year and should both have been secret. His policy was of no obvious involvement in external affairs.

This policy suited Canadian opinion in the 1930's. To some extent it was a balancing policy: on the right, King's opponents urged him to show more forthright support for Britain in all her policies, while on the left, from extreme opinion in the prairie provinces and in Quebec, he was urged to declare a studied policy of neutrality. His party depended for its majority on the fact that it was acceptable to Quebec. If he adhered to either of the strong policies recommended to him, he would alienate support and, in a

[14] Quoted in Nicholas Mansergh, op. cit., p. 132n.

crisis, split the country. In the end, when he invited the Canadian Parliament to declare war on Germany in September, 1939—an action which it took a week after the British declaration of war, thereby demonstrating Canadian independence in the most momentous of foreign-policy decisions—he carried majority opinion with him. But it is widely considered that so definite a step could not have been successfully taken at any earlier date. Up to that point Mackenzie King's policy had been one of influence and suggestion, not of public declamation.

Australian Policy

The position in Australia was not dissimilar, though from rather different causes. Between 1917 and 1941 Australian governments were recruited from the non-Labour side in politics, with the exception of the brief period 1929-1931 when a Labour government was in office. Thus, although Australia pressed hard for a clarification of status at the 1930 Imperial Conference, at no other time did she have a government which wished to hasten the development of dominion status or, once that status was achieved, to practice an independent policy. In Canada, King pursued a policy of independence quietly, more by suggestion than by open revolt against British influence; in Australia, S. M. Bruce and J. A. Lyons took the line of acquiescence in British policy, or of private disagreement through consultation wherever they did not find that policy suitable to them. In public, "Follow Britain" was their watchword. In private they strove to perfect the system of consultation and to instigate means whereby a common "Empire policy" could be made a reality. Australian governments accepted the view that in a world war Australia might fall a prey to aggressive attack unless she was closely associated with a great power, that power being Britain. The idea of neutrality or nonbelligerency in a war in which Britain was involved was an impossibility to them. In any case, they constantly strove for preferential markets in Britain for Australian products; and this orientation gave them an extra inducement to pursue policies which would draw tighter the formal bonds of Empire. At the same time they were anxious that Australian interests should not be subordinated to British interests and that Australian ministers should be informed about British policy in time for them to state their views on it. Characteristically, Australia's method of exerting international influence in the interwar period was not to create her own diplomatic posts even in countries of prime importance to Australian interests; it was to station an Australian civil servant in the Foreign Office in London, where he could see British policy in the making and inform the Australian government, either direct or through the High Commissioner in London. The combination of such an officer and of a high commissioner of the political stature of S. M. Bruce (the former Australian Prime Minister who represented his country in London throughout the 1930's) meant that Australia probably had the most *direct* influence on British policy of all the four dominions. But there was nothing spectacular about such influence; it went largely unregarded by Australian radical nationalists, except when they accused it of subordinating Australian development and interests to the British government.

In the Italo-Abyssinian crisis the Australian government was as little enthusiastic about sanctions as the Canadian—and for much the same reasons. It had a large Roman Catholic minority to deal with and it had to meet the complaints of those who said "sanctions mean war." Once the Abyssinian affair was settled, Australia was particularly active in attempting to bring Britain and Italy into closer relations: this is perhaps the one instance in British foreign policy in the 1930's in which it can be said that the pressure of a dominion upon Britain was able to exercise any strong positive influence. In the Munich crisis, Neville Chamberlain received as strong support from Canberra as from Ottawa.

Australia's most direct concern with foreign affairs, however, was in the Pacific, especially in relation to Japan. Australians in general felt doubts about Japanese intentions, fearing that population pressure would lead Japan to demand entry into Australia's "wide open spaces"—which were in fact mostly desert, a point which Australians themselves, in their pride of ownership and desire for development, came only reluctantly to admit. In the 1930's there was little disposition in Australia to question Japan's activities on the Asian mainland: so long as Japan was occupied in China she would hardly turn south. It was also realized by the government that League of Nations action against Japan was impossible in the absence of support from the United States. The government therefore adopted a policy of attempting to establish cordial relations with Japan, for trade reasons and on general political grounds. It was a complicated position because, while Japan was a profitable market for Australian wool, imports from Japan tended to displace British imports and even incommode protected Australian industries. A quiet life with Japan was difficult to achieve, apart altogether from Japan's own intentions. To meet a possible Japanese threat, the government relied upon British naval power and welcomed the construction of the Singapore naval base. In any plans for rearmament, however, it had to meet strong opposition from the Labour Party, either on grounds of "warmongering" or in terms of aerial defense being preferable to naval. The Australian government had in this opposition a problem of "national unity," but on nothing like the same scale as Mackenzie King's in Canada. It was widely believed that if Britain were ever in danger Australia would spring to her support.

South African Policy

In South Africa the position was quite different. Here, throughout the interwar period, the argument over status continued. Apart from economic problems and the relations with the Negroes, South African politics revolved around questions of national anthems, national flags, bilingualism, and the sanctification of the Afrikaner past. The structure of political parties demanded that all questions of external relations should be tested in terms of the possibility of Britain "domineering" over South Africa, and of the exact constitutional relationship in which the two countries stood. This argument took place largely within the Afrikaans-speaking community. The English-speaking community was in a numerical minority (40 per cent) and was closely attached to the symbols of Empire and a close tie between South Africa and Britain. In the province of Natal, where there was an actual English-speaking majority, extreme imperialist views flourished; but elsewhere English-speaking South Africans were anxious for co-operation with moderate Afrikaners, and prepared to support a political party (first the South Africa Party and then the United Party) with an Afrikaner at its head. J. C. Smuts was, throughout the period, the symbol of the attempt to merge the two nationality groups in a common pride in South Africa and a common loyalty to the British Commonwealth of Nations. To Smuts, the British Commonwealth was something of a *deus ex machina*, sent to solve the special problems of South African national unity. It offered an opportunity for nations such as South Africa to develop in perfect freedom in their domestic affairs, displaying whatever linguistic and cultural diversity was natural to them, and yet to form part of a world-wide group of states in which no single member was dominant but all contributed to a more enlightened understanding of common problems. Smuts constantly reiterated this viewpoint: South Africa was free, but the British Commonwealth gave her an enlargement of freedom.

Against this Commonwealth outlook the Nationalist Party stood for the view that the only true development for South Africa was development in the traditions of the Boer Republics. The South African people could be united only behind these traditions: unless English-speaking South Africans accepted them, they could not properly qualify as part of the South African nation. So long as they looked to Britain as their homeland they were strangers and sojourners in South Africa. To the Nationalists, those Afrikaners like Smuts—who tried to link the two peoples and not give precedence to the Afrikaner traditions and way of life—were traitors.

General J. B. M. Hertzog was at first the leader of Nationalist opinion; after his fusion with Smuts in the United Party in 1933, this role was taken up by Dr. D. F. Malan, whose Purified Nationalist group was at first only a small section of the South African Assembly but grew steadily to the stature of a majority party after World War II.

From 1924 to 1939, Hertzog's efforts as prime minister were first devoted to the achievement of status, then to its practical expression in the cutting of formal ties with Britain, and finally to a policy in foreign affairs which would safeguard South Africa's interests in the African continent and preserve her from the dangerous effects of European quarrels. Hertzog's basic attitude—shared by most other Afrikaners, and to some extent by Smuts—was that the Treaty of Versailles had been an unjust treaty, that it had given Germany many legitimate grievances, that the League of Nations was a source of hope in Europe so long as Germany's grievances were righted, but that South Africa's own special gain from the treaty—her possession of South-West Africa—must be retained at all costs. In African affairs, this attitude led to a curious dualism in South Africa's approach to the question of ex-German colonies. South Africa made it quite clear that it would not give up South-West Africa, and Hertzog firmly put down attempts at Nazi indoctrination and control among the German-speaking inhabitants there. But at the same time South Africa was the most active among the dominions in initiating discussions with Germany about the restoration of *other* ex-German colonies, or, alternatively, the provision of African colonies for Germany at the expense of smaller European colonial powers such as Belgium and Portugal. This dog-in-the-manger approach was not taken seriously by Nazi Germany, but was welcomed in so far as it supported, in a qualified manner, the Nazi claim for the return of all prewar colonies.

Another strand in the specifically African aspect of the Hertzog policy was its concern lest there should be a new "struggle for Africa" among European powers, leading to outrages against native peoples, the arming of native troops, and the eventual blotting out of white influence in Africa. Afrikaner theory drew a distinction between such Europeans as the Afrikaners, who came to Africa to settle permanently, and those European powers who claimed great tracts of Africa either for imperial glory or to use African resources for their own ends. The Afrikaners disapproved of the latter. When Italy invaded Abyssinia in 1935, the South African government's view was that a testing time had come: if the League of Nations could not stop this new onslaught on Africa, then no part of Africa would be safe in the future. South Africa therefore showed herself far more determined to apply League action to Italy than did Canada and Australia. Her reaction against the Hoare-Laval pact was correspondingly greater, and her bitterness against the great powers for refusing to move against Italy was correspondingly more outspoken. After this event, Hertzog's inclination was to withdraw from external commitments and put "South Africa first." South Africa had to allow Britain the use of the Simonstown naval base in time of war, as agreed during the Churchill-Smuts conversations of 1921; but she had no other commitments, and Hertzog reasoned that she should accept none. Letting Britain use Simonstown would not, in his view, involve South Africa in war.

With the successive German moves in Europe in the late 1930's Hertzog showed little concern. His own view that it was right to rally and cherish the distinctive "South African people" (the Afrikaners), on a basis of language, made him sympathetic toward German claims for the ingathering of German-speaking peoples. When the Czech crisis of 1938 was in progress, he and Smuts and their Cabinet agreed that South Africa would be nonbelligerent "in the event of war in Europe with England as one of the belligerents."

The existing relations between the Union of South Africa and the various belligerent parties shall, so far as the Union is concerned, remain unchanged and continue as if no war were being waged, with the understanding, however, that the existing relationships and obligations between the Union and Great Britain and any other of the members of the British Commonwealth of Nations in so far as those relationships and obligations are the result of contractual obligations concerning the naval base at Simonstown; or of its membership of the League of Nations; or in so far as the relationships, etc., must be regarded *impliciter* as flowing from the free association of the Union with the other members of the Commonwealth, shall remain unaltered and shall be maintained by the Union; and that nobody shall be permitted to make use of Union territory for any purpose calculated to infringe the said relationships and obligations.[15]

The satisfaction of the South African government with the Munich agreement was considerable. It has been widely suggested that

[15] The Cabinet agreement, as drafted by Hertzog; quoted in Nicholas Mansergh, *op. cit.*, p. 257.

the knowledge of South Africa's intended nonbelligerency, together with doubt about whether the Canadian Parliament would
go to war on such an issue as the Sudeten one, and the promptings
of the Australian government, was a material influence in deciding
the British government against any resistance to Hitler at this
point.

Smuts, who could go along with Hertzog in sympathizing with
German claims for the Sudeten lands, was not prepared to endorse
Hitler's actions early in 1939; and when South Africa's attitude
had to be settled in September 1939, the South African Parlia-
ment decided by a majority of only 13 in a House of 147 to follow
Smuts and endorse the British declaration of war against Germany.
Hertzog resigned, still demanding nonbelligerency.

New Zealand and the League

In New Zealand the course of events was quite different. New
Zealand had made no quest for status, and up to the election of
her first Labour government late in 1935 had made little effort
to formulate a foreign policy: at one stage she had even asked
for her formal communications as a member of the League of
Nations to be routed through London, so that she would have
no direct contact with Geneva. Up to 1935 she was governed by
coalitions of farmers and businessmen who were proud of being
British and saw no reason to change the existing state of affairs.
At Imperial Conferences they looked with dismay on the way the
Irish, South Africans, and Canadians went to work to weaken the
bonds of Empire. By 1935 this attitude was beginning to change.
New Zealand governments had been impressed by the growth of
dictatorial power in Europe, and the Italian invasion of Abyssinia was recognized as a test of League solidarity. The Nationalist
government introduced sanctions legislation against Italy, and
had the support of the Labour opposition in carrying it through—
a contrast with Australia, where the Labour opposition, with the
exception of one member, opposed the Lyons government's proposals for sanctions in accordance with the call of the League.

When, shortly afterwards, the Labour government took office,
it showed itself to be firmly attached to the League and to notions

of collective security. Among its ministers were a number who had decided views on foreign affairs: these were roughly the same as those of the left wing in British politics, except that the New Zealanders did not shrink from arming the League with extra powers or from the implication that this might mean an armed clash with one of the dictator countries. When the League showed itself powerless in 1936 to stop Italy, New Zealand expressed herself as forcefully as South Africa in condemnation of the great powers—including, by implication, Britain. But the New Zealand government did not read the lesson of the League's failure in the same way as did the South African government: instead of turning away from the League and concentrating on its own affairs, it advocated changes to make the League structure stronger, and in due course proved the only one out of Britain and the dominions to refuse official recognition to Mussolini's conquest of Abyssinia. It also clashed with Britain over nonintervention in the Spanish Civil War, considering that the Spanish republican government had a case against Germany and Italy on the ground of their interference in Spanish affairs.

There was a notable contrast between the ambition of New Zealand's schemes for collective security against the dictators and her own capacity to contribute to the striking force needed to oppose Germany, Italy, and Japan. This disparity was felt by the New Zealand government itself. It considered, however, that collective security was a correct policy, and that New Zealand's strength or weakness was not a material factor in deciding what should be a correct policy for League members to pursue. Nevertheless, the New Zealand government showed considerable concern for rearmament. At the same time it was reluctant to continue with public criticism of British policy, which by 1937 had largely bypassed the League. The Labour government was no exception to other New Zealand governments in its attachment to Britain and its determination to side with Britain in a war. So, from the beginning of 1938 onward, New Zealand took a less prominent place in international discussion. At the Imperial Conference of 1937 (see below) New Zealand support for appeasement was rather less strong than that of the other dominions, and at the time of the Munich agreements New Zealand's congratulations for Chamberlain were rather primmer than those of Canada, Australia, and South Africa.

The extent of support in New Zealand for the government's attachment to collective security will never be known. It was not made an issue at a general election. Some critics have said that it was mainly the New Zealand Labour Party's inexperience in foreign affairs that provoked such an apparently doctrinaire attitude. Others have said that support for the policy went beyond the Labour Party's supporters, and embraced a good many people who habitually voted Nationalist. Certainly the issue was not one to be settled by the ordinary economic considerations of New Zealand politics; and since the British connection was never repudiated by the government, it is likely that the policy proved for many New Zealanders an exciting new experience in national self-assertion and an opportunity to defend international morality.

The Coming of World War II

By now it should be clear that when war approached in 1939 each dominion had its own problem to solve in formulating its attitude toward the conflict. New Zealand's was the simplest: she had labored for collective security and therefore had a clear conscience, her people were united in their support for Britain, and she had a Labour government which was in no mood to argue constitutional niceties. If Britain was at war, New Zealand was at war—and this in spite of the fact that during the previous year there had been considerable coolness between the governments of the two countries, over a flight of British capital from New Zealand and difficulties in renewing a New Zealand loan.

In Australia the government headed by R. G. Menzies was a resolutely imperialist one, which accepted the view that Australia was at war automatically when the King went to war. This view was challenged by the Labour Opposition, which tended to take the Hertzog-Mackenzie King view that the Statute of Westminster had given each dominion the right to declare war or stay neutral. But the Labour Party did not deny that Australia should be at war with Germany: it simply wanted the process to be a different one, in order to show Australia's independence.

In Canada it had been the custom of Mackenzie King to say that the Canadian Parliament should decide such matters as peace and war. Up to the time of the Statute of Westminster, his view had been that Canada was at war when Britain was, but that the extent of her participation in the war was a matter for her to decide. This doctrine he had inherited from Sir Wilfrid Laurier. In the 1930's he took the view that Canada had full power to decide the act of war for herself. At any rate, Canada enjoyed a week of symbolic neutrality after Britain's declaration of war on Germany, this neutrality being recognized by both Germany and the United States. Then the Parliament met, and declared war with only negligible opposition. Mackenzie King had kept the situation fluid for so long, refusing to commit himself, that when it came to a decision he was able to carry the whole country with him, except for even less extremist opposition in Quebec than had been expected.

In South Africa the decision was closest, and the consequences most fateful. Smuts took office from Hertzog when the nonbelligerency which Hertzog recommended was turned down by the House of Assembly, and won the next election handsomely on a "win the war" program. But for many Afrikaners this meant the end of Smuts as a possible standard-bearer of Afrikaner interests and traditions; in postwar elections his party was to reap the consequences of its action, in the loss of much Afrikaner support to the Nationalists under Malan.

The outbreak of war marked a decisive stage in the evolution of dominion foreign policy, in two ways. In the first place, it showed conclusively that the Crown was divisible and that "common allegiance to the Crown" did not mean common automatic support for the Crown's policies in Britain: Canada's week of neutrality and Ireland's continued neutrality did not prevent them from being regarded as dominions. In this sense the final ambiguity of the dominions' relation with Britain was resolved. They were left free to pursue their own way in foreign affairs, each with its own Crown incorporated separately in the person of the King.

In the second place, the outbreak of war represented the failure of the first common policy which the several dominions (with the partial exception of New Zealand) had separately arrived at—the policy of appeasement. At the 1937 Imperial Conference they had gone on record as follows:

Finally the members of the Conference, while themselves firmly attached to the principles of democracy and to parliamentary forms of government, decided to register their view that differences of political creed should be no obstacle to friendly relations between governments and countries, and that nothing would be more damaging to the hopes of international appeasement than the division, real or apparent, of the world into opposing groups.[16]

The policy of appeasement, sincerely embarked on because it seemed to offer a quiet life in the world of states, had shown itself bankrupt: the world was divided into opposing groups, and each dominion wished, in its own interests, to be part of the group which emerged victorious from the war. This failure of appeasement was to have profound influence upon the policies of each dominion, as these developed and ramified during the war and afterward.

SELECTED BIBLIOGRAPHY

A study in depth of the growth and character of the dominions is W. K. Hancock, *Survey of British Commonwealth Affairs* (London, 1937, 1940, 1942). North Americans who wish to study the history of the dominions outside that continent will find it well summarized in R. M. Crawford, *Australia* (London, 1952); H. Miller, *New Zealand* (London, 1950); and A. Keppel-Jones, *South Africa* (London, 2nd ed., 1953). The relations of Canada with Britain and the U.S.A. should be studied in J. B. Brebner, *North Atlantic Triangle* (New Haven, 1945). A valuable comparative study of the four countries considered here is A. Brady, *Democracy in the Dominions* (Toronto, 1947). There are good studies

[16] Report of the Conference: Cmd. 5482, p. 16.

of the growth of foreign relations of two dominions: G. P. de T. Glazebrook, *A History of Canadian External Relations* (Toronto, 1950), and F. L. W. Wood, *New Zealand in the World* (Wellington, 1940).

For dominion status and policy between the wars, see Sir Cecil Hurst and others, *Great Britain and the Dominions* (Chicago, 1928); A. Toynbee, *The Conduct of British Empire Foreign Relations since the Peace Settlement* (London, 1928); A. B. Keith (ed.), *Speeches and Documents on the British Dominions 1918-1931* (London, 1932); A. G. Dewey, *The Dominions and Diplomacy: The Canadian Contribution* (London, 1929); C. A. W. Manning, *The Policies of the British Dominions in the League of Nations* (London and Geneva, 1932); G. M. Carter, *The British Commonwealth and International Security* (Toronto, 1947). N. Mansergh, *Survey of British Commonwealth Affairs: Problems of External Policy 1931-1939* (London, 1952), is a work to which this chapter is heavily indebted.

CHAPTER 11

FOREIGN POLICY IN CANADA, AUSTRALIA, NEW ZEALAND, AND SOUTH AFRICA: ITS FORMULATION AND RECENT CHARACTER

Since 1939 the four original dominions have functioned as fully sovereign states in international society, each going its own way to secure its national interests as it has conceived them. But they have also continued to be associated in certain aspects of their foreign policy, first as partners in World War II and then as members of the expanded Commonwealth of Nations after the war. This chapter discusses, first, how policy is framed in each of the four countries; second, what part is played in their lives and policies by their membership of the Commonwealth; and third, the directions taken by their individual policies under the pressure of events in the wartime and postwar worlds.

Before I discuss the formulation of policy in each country, it is necessary to sound a warning for readers in the United States: In none of these countries is foreign policy made in the same atmosphere as in the United States. The reasons are partly historical, partly constitutional; they are worth rehearsing in order to put the dominions into a broad perspective of difference from the United States.

Formulation of Policy

Differences from the United States

In the first place, the making of foreign policy is a comparatively recent affair for each of the four dominions. As was indicated in the previous chapter, Canada has the longest continuous experience of international dealings, New Zealand the shortest; but in each case the country's capacity to act as an independent force in international affairs is a fairly recent development when compared with the fact that the United States has been acting in this way since the very beginning of the republic. In the politics of each dominion the idea of foreign policy as a live issue is still new. Its principal period of operation has been the decade since World War II, when there has been less opportunity for difference of opinion about foreign policy than in most previous decades of the twentieth century. It is true that in each case the question of relations with *Britain* has been a live issue in politics for many years. But this was largely a question of each country's status, of its constitutional position in association with Britain; since the settlement of this question by the Statute of Westminster and the events of 1939, it has become of less importance in its own right and has merged into general considerations of foreign policy. For foreign affairs, then, there is not the same "public" as in the United States, since foreign affairs are matters on which political strife and agitation have not been concentrated. In each of the four dominions, interest in them is largely confined to specialists, although each political party feels an obligation to declare itself on broad issues of foreign policy.

This state of things is accentuated by the fact that none of the dominions has in its population anything like the same collection of powerful ethnic, religious, and national groups which in the United States have been the main source of pressure upon politicians for particular action in foreign policy. The Zionist, Polish, and Italian groups in the United States have no counterparts of anything like the same influence in any of the dominions. In Canada and Australia there are now substantial immigrant groups from Eastern Europe, but they have had little impact on foreign policy. Nowhere has a dominion government found itself subjected to the same steady, powerful, persistent pressure, backed by votes, that has become a commonplace in United States politics. Similarly, none of the dominions has developed the same phenomenon of organized pressure upon a government to take some particular action in foreign affairs, as epitomized by ad hoc Committees for Some Proposal or Activity, sending telegrams, petitions, and postcards to congressmen on the eve of some significant vote at Washington. This technique has not been adopted in domestic matters either. The explanation lies largely in the differences between the presidential-congressional system of the United States and the parliamentary system which each of the dominions has taken over from Britain.

The Parliamentary System

In the parliamentary system, responsibility for foreign policy lies squarely with the government of the day, which can avail itself, if it wishes, of the prerogative of the Crown in making treaties or in either going to war or making peace. In fact, governments in the dominions have tended to reinforce the power of the prerogative by asking parliamentary assent to treaties and to declarations of peace and war. But the existence of the prerogative gives the government (that is, the Prime Minister and Cabinet) the initiative in foreign policy. Since the government is responsible to Parliament, and stands or falls as it retains or loses the confidence of the lower house, any significant challenge to its foreign policy becomes a matter of confidence in the government itself, and will be treated as such: the government has behind it, in practice, a well-disciplined party or coalition majority which will support it on a matter of major importance. In financial matters the same applies: criticism of the money which the government intends to lay out on particular aspects of its foreign policy (for example, on its activities in NATO or the Colombo Plan) must be criticism of the government's whole financial policy as expressed in its budget, and so becomes again a matter of confidence in the government as such.

The effect is that only the more important questions of foreign policy are likely to be debated independently in Parliament, and that the government will be in danger only if it has committed some error or enormity which alienates its customary majority of members. The defeat of General Hertzog's nonbelligerency proposals in September 1939, mentioned in the preceding chapter, is an example of how important a foreign-policy issue must be before it seriously embarrasses a government in one of the dominions. Of course, the government is accustomed to continual criticism of its day-to-day actions by the opposition, and may even have to meet a motion of censure on some aspect of its diplomacy; but unless a truly vital question is involved, it will be in no danger of defeat. This customary support strengthens its hand, and makes potentially less effective than in the congressional system the activities of groups which wish either a special policy or a particular decision to be accepted by the government. It also means that such groups, if they exist, may find that they need to concentrate upon one of the parties rather than upon members of Parliament at large, if they wish to see significant parliamentary force put behind their proposals. This kind of activity is rare in the dominions, as it is in Britain. There is no reason why it should not develop if there exist groups sufficiently cohesive and determined to carry it through, and if they can promise votes in the right numbers in areas which are important for political strategy. So far, however, these conditions have not applied on any large scale in any of the dominions. In their absence, the power of the government, the lack of general interest in foreign affairs, and the fact that the parties conduct their disputes on other issues than those of foreign policy, have combined to give foreign-policy formulation rather more aloofness than in the United States, whose great debates on foreign policy of the postwar decades have not been paralleled in any of the dominions.

Canada

The Canadian Department of External Affairs was established in 1909. Its title indicated that it was not thought of as a specifically "foreign" affairs agency; in fact, one of the main reasons for establishing it was to canalize Canada's dealings with the United Kingdom. In common with similar departments or sections of departments in the other dominions during the same time, this was its principal occupation. It was given a minister and a permanent head, and has continued to function as a unit ever since. From 1912 to 1946 it did not have a separate minister, but was the responsibility of the Prime Minister. Thus Borden and Mackenzie King were their own foreign ministers, Mackenzie King for the whole of his long prime ministership. Since 1946 there has been a separate minister. For most of this time the office has been filled by Lester B. Pearson, who resigned from the permanent career staff of the department and entered Parliament so as to become Secretary of State for External Affairs when Louis St. Laurent succeeded Mackenzie King as prime minister. Canadian foreign policy has been subject to continuity of management of an exceptional character.

The growth of the department has gone along with the growth of Canadian representation and responsibilities abroad. The establishment of legations at Washington, Paris, and Tokyo in the late 1920's was followed by a ten-year lull on account of the depression of the 1930's; when World War II came Canada had just begun to move again, with a new legation in Brussels. The outbreak of war called for closer relations with the other dominions, and high commissioners were sent to Australia, New Zealand, South Africa, and Ireland. During the war legations were established in China and the U.S.S.R., and a single minister was accredited to the refugee Allied governments in London. For the first time, too, Canada embarked on a policy of closer association with Latin America, sending representatives to Chile, Mexico, Peru, Cuba, Brazil, and Argentina. In 1943 a number of legations were converted into embassies; Canada thus embarked upon diplomatic representation at its highest level.

Since the war the list of countries to which Canada sends diplomatic missions has been widened again. The European list has been filled up by the addition of World War II neutrals and former enemy countries; Colombia, the Dominican Republic, Uruguay, Venezuela, and Haiti have been added among American states; representation has been extended into the Middle East, with missions in Egypt, Israel, and Lebanon. Perhaps the most important development has been the new links with Asian countries (Ceylon, India, Pakistan, and Indonesia) to which Canada gives special emphasis. Apart from these formal diplomatic ties, Canada has developed a consular service, and has had to staff a number of missions and commissions. There are permanent missions to the United Nations at New York and Geneva, permanent delegations to NATO and OEEC in Paris, and a military mission in Berlin.

To meet its various commitments in the international field, Canada has developed a more elaborate organization than any of the other dominions. Below its permanent head are four Assistant Under-Secretaries and a department organized in eighteen divisions, plus a section for political co-ordination and a press office. The eighteen divisions are partly geographical, serving the principal world regions and the United Nations, and partly functional, dealing with such matters as international economic policy, protocol, legal affairs, defense liaison, consular matters, personnel, information, finance and properties, establishment, historical research, and communications.

Like the other dominions, Canada has tackled the problem of recruiting diplomatic personnel by special entry of university graduates. Candidates must have a university degree and must pass a competitive examination; they must be Canadians of at least ten years' standing. The standard is high. In 1954, 19 officers were recruited from an examination for which there were 170 candidates. Official bilingualism in Canada has been an advantage, since English and French are basic languages for the practicing diplomat. In appointing its ambassadors and ministers Canada has chosen to appoint career officers rather than former politicians and service officers, although some of the higher posts have gone to men outside government service.

The need for co-ordination of the policy of different departments toward foreign countries is met in Canada (as in the other dominions) primarily by the Cabinet system. The Cabinet is the final decider of policy, and disputes between departments about the policy to be adopted will finally be resolved by ministers there. But at the departmental level an effort is made to co-ordinate policies before they reach the Cabinet level. The methods can be illustrated from two of the most important policy fields, economics and defense. In economics it is the responsibility of the Economic Division of the Department of External Affairs to co-operate with the Departments of Finance, Trade and Commerce, National Revenue, Agriculture, and Transport, and with the Bank of Canada. Discussions will embrace such matters as commercial treaties, assistance to foreign countries, loans, civil aviation, telecommunications, exchange questions, and the balance of payments. If no joint policy emerges from consultation with other departments, the Cabinet will have to decide from the submissions made by the various ministers. In defense the organization is more complicated, because of Canada's membership of NATO and her special arrangements with the United States. Here the Department of External Affairs, through its Defense Liaison Divisions, maintains a link with the Department of National Defense and the other departments which abut on defense. NATO questions and those relating to the Permanent Joint Board on Defense (a member of which is a senior officer from the Canadian External Affairs Department) are discussed in interdepartmental committees; the department's permanent head attends meetings of the Chiefs of Staff Committee; the department provides the chairman of the Joint Intelligence Committee. There are various other bodies at the departmental level which bring together the service and supply departments and External Affairs; and at Cabinet level there is a Cabinet Defense Committee of which the Secretary of State for External Affairs is a member. The aim is that of bringing together civil servants from all the departments involved, together with senior military officers, to co-ordinate policy in terms of what the Cabinet has already agreed to, and to suggest new policies for Cabinet discussion and approval. In the process, departmental rivalries of the kind familiar in the United States are exhibited; personalities make their impact in committee and in memoranda; and there is likely to be a clash between service and civilian opinion, and between departments within the civilian field.

But the differences from similar procedures in the United States must be stressed. In Canada (and the same applies to the other three dominions considered in these chapters) the Cabinet is a more powerful body than in the United States, and the heads of departments have more permanency. The fact that the Canadian Cabinet is a body with power, which is collectively responsible to Parliament and not simply the chosen instrument of an elected chief executive, means that a stubborn minister has, by and large, a better chance of getting his way than in the United States. He may lose his Cabinet post if he becomes utterly recalcitrant or fails to back up his colleagues; but his loss of office may precipitate a Cabinet and party crisis, which the Prime Minister and the rest of the Cabinet will go a long way to avoid. Within the Cabinet, then, power is more evenly shared than in the United States Cabinet; and if it were proposed to set up in Canada or one of the other dominions a special body such as the United States National Security Council it would have to be either a committee of Cabinet or under obligation to report to it. In form, at any rate, a prime minister could not set up such a body on his own account, unless he were completely dominant over his Cabinet and could get automatic acceptance of whatever he proposed. Most Cabinets are not like this.

The fact that in Canada (and in all the other dominions) the heads and subheads of departments are permanent officials, creates another important difference from the United States. In so far as there is conflict and jockeying for position between these heads, it is usually carried on in silence. The public does not hear of it, unless there is some leak which all concerned will be anxious to stop. When the heads of departments are permanent officers absolved from personal responsibility (all of which is taken by the minister in charge of the department, himself a politician), there is less room for an appeal to the public or to Parliament than in a country where it is customary to fill the major posts in key departments with presidential nominees. The homeric battles between heads of agencies and departments in the era of Franklin D. Roosevelt would not be likely to occur in any of the dominions.

In Canada there is no direct parliamentary supervision of either foreign service or foreign policy, but the House of Commons has a Standing Committee on External Affairs. Its main function is to study the Estimates of expenditure submitted by the department. It is empowered also to examine and inquire into any matters submitted to it by the House. In considering the estimates and other matters, it may call as witnesses officers of the Department of External Affairs, officers from other departments, and persons from outside government service. It confines itself to questions of fact and particularly to the economy or otherwise of particular expenditures; any challenge to policy is met on the floor of the House by the Minister. The committee usually takes a month or two months to complete its work, before the departmental Estimates are presented to Parliament for approval.

The party situation in Canada tends toward stability and continuity of policy. The Liberal Party has been in office since 1935, first under Mackenzie King and then under St. Laurent. It is the only party which operates in all the provinces, although its main strength still lies in Quebec. Canadian parties are sometimes difficult to distinguish in terms of policy, but the Liberals can be said to be traditionally a party stressing the north-south axis of trade and culture, as against the emphasis of their principal opponents, the Conservatives, upon the east-west axis within Canada and between Canada and Britain. The Liberals' strength in Quebec has meant that they have supported provincial rights in theory, although the exigencies of government have made this support sometimes tenuous in practice. In economic policy the Liberals have stood on the free-trade side of the line which separates free trade from protection, while the Conservatives have stood on the protectionist side with its associations of imperial preference; but here again the distinction has been tempered by the demands of day-to-day politics. In terms of foreign affairs, substantial party differences now lie in the past. The background of the Liberals is one of emphasis upon Canada's independent status, and reluctance to interfere in the affairs of Europe; here the French-Canadian element, with its emotional rejection of British symbols and European conflicts, has been a powerful influence. But this state of mind is now largely out of date, and is frankly admitted to be so by the leaders of the Liberal Party. Once isolationist, it is now clearly interventionist, in the sense of favoring participation in international alliances and associations, and an active foreign policy. The most important thing about the Liberal Party, however, is that it is the government: it cannot afford doctrinal extravagance and cannot ignore significant international developments, since it has the continued responsibility of protecting Canadian interests. As indicated below, it has found those interests in recent years to center in the North Atlantic community; and it is committed to this view of them.

The Liberals' main rivals, the Progressive Conservatives (who were last in office under R. B. Bennett from 1930 to 1935), have their main strength in Ontario, where something of a British-Protestant orthodoxy has sustained itself over the years by contrast with the French-Catholic orthodoxy of Quebec. It is only in emphasis that the Progressive Conservatives differ from the Liberals; they are the party in Canada most likely to cherish the symbols of Empire and to be watchful in case British interests are completely neglected in the policy of the government. But they have so far shown little likelihood of presenting an alternative foreign policy.

Two other parties are significant in the Canadian House of Commons, each a radical party with a special twist. They are the Co-operative Commonwealth Federation (CCF), a farmer-labor party with its main strength in the prairie province of Saskatchewan; and the Social Credit Party, which provides the provincial governments of Alberta and British Columbia, but has so far not done so well in federal politics. The CCF presents the principal alternative to the government's foreign policy, adopting a line rather similar to that of the British Labour Party but modified in terms of traditional Canadian prairie radicalism. The Social Credit Party is mainly noted in foreign affairs for its enmity toward the Soviet Union and its fear of international finance. Neither party is likely to secure sufficient support in populous eastern Canada to give it office.

Until some considerable change occurs in the basis of Canadian politics, the Liberal Party has the prospect of being a perpetual government. Like other such parties in democratic states, it can perform this role only by providing within itself something of a coalition of the main social forces at work in the country. So far it has done so without alienating its basic support in Quebec (although Quebec votes for an extremist French-Canadian party, the Union Nationale, in provincial elections, and rejects the Liberal Party in that context). In foreign policy it has met no significant opposition since World War II from its political opponents (the CCF, in spite of its interest in more radical policies, fully recognizes the need for Canada's North Atlantic alignment), and this state of things is likely to continue. At the same time, the Liberal government has not been subject to strong pressure from outside the organized parties; and this has made its formulation of foreign policy very much a matter of the estimation of chances by the government itself. It must step cautiously on matters which affect the consciences of Roman Catholics (for example, on the question of recognition of Communist China), but there is almost complete public unanimity on a policy of opposition to Russian aggression and of alliance with the United States, France, and Britain. Such a policy is hand-made for national unity, since it brings into a harmonious coalition of interests all the divergent elements of opinion in the community.

Australia

The Australian Department of External Affairs was set up in 1901, when the Australian federal government was brought into being; it was the first department in any of the dominions to bear that name. Like that of Canada, it was largely concerned with relations with Britain, but was also responsible for the administration of Papua, the Australian possession in the southeast part of New Guinea. (This responsibility was later transferred to a separate department, now called the Department of Territories.) But it was a weakling growth, and in 1916 was abolished; its work of contact with other governments was taken over by the Prime Minister's Department. In 1921 it was re-established as an offshoot of the Prime Minister's Department, and in 1924 was reorganized. It had no permanent head of its own, and only five officers. The desire of the Bruce government to influence British policy from within led in 1924 to the appointment of an Australian liaison officer in the Foreign Office in London; in 1937, in spite of the fact that the department had been given an independent life two years before, this same procedure was adopted in attempting to get some knowledge of United States policy at its source. An Australian officer was appointed Australian counselor at the British Embassy in Washington. Australia thus refrained from following the example of Canada and South Africa, and setting up her own diplomatic service; it was considered that a separate Australian foreign policy was neither necessary nor practicable and that Australian influence would best be felt from within the circle of British diplomacy.

The outbreak of war rendered this attitude out of date. In 1940 the first Australian legation was established at Washington. It was followed by another at Tokyo. But the department and its responsibilities continued to be small until 1942, when a combination of the Pacific war, a Labour government, and a pushful minister led to an enlargement of its staff and a quickening of its activity which have continued ever since. A legation was set up in the USSR, high commissions in New Zealand and India, and in 1945 a legation in Paris. A consular service was also developed on a substantial scale. There are now embassies in West Germany, Indonesia, Ireland, Holland, France, Japan, Burma, Thailand, the Philippines, and the United States; legations in Cambodia, Brazil, Italy, Viet Nam, and Israel; high commissions in all the Commonwealth capitals, and a commission at Singapore; and missions at Berlin and to the United Nations at New York and Geneva. Like Canada, Australia is a member of the various specialized agencies of the United Nations.

The expansion of diplomatic staff had to be extremely rapid to meet the demands of such widespread representation. In 1943 the department began recruiting staff by a special competitive examination and later by restricting entry to university graduates, who were then given special training to fit them for their work. This selection process continues, and is generally considered to have produced the results that were hoped for. At first the high appointments, of ministers and ambassadors, were filled by prominent persons from outside the department, but it is now customary to appoint career diplomats.

The department itself is organized on somewhat similar lines to its counterpart in Canada. Below the permanent head are four divisions. Under Division 1 come the Pacific and the Americas, South and South East Asia, the European, African, and Middle East, the Defence Liaison, and the Information Branches. Under Division 2 come the Economic Relations, United Nations, Commonwealth Relations, and Economic and Technical Assistance Branches. Division 3 deals with administration in general, including Consular and Protocol affairs. Division 4 deals with Legal and Treaty matters. As with other dominions, there is continual change of personnel between the central office in Canberra and the establishments abroad.

Co-ordination of policy between departments in Australia presents much the same features as the Canadian example, described above. In each case there is an effort to secure agreement of policy at the civil service level before matters come before Cabinet; in each the final work of reconciliation is done by Cabinet or by one of its committees.

There is even less direct parliamentary control of foreign policy in Australia than in Canada. Instead of the Canadian Standing Committee of the House of Commons, primarily concerned with departmental Estimates, there is a Joint Committee of both houses of the Australian Parliament, which discusses matters referred to it by the Minister for External Affairs. As a representative body it is vitiated by the fact that the opposition, the Labour Party, refuses to nominate members to it on the ground that the committee has no independent life, cannot initiate subjects for discussion and can see officials and records only with the concurrence of the Minister. Its function was conceived as that of providing in Parliament a group of members with special knowledge of foreign affairs, and so giving more life and realism to debates on the periodical statements by the Minister for External Affairs. Opinion differs about whether this has occurred; but certainly the committee is in no position to carry out an independent inspection of the government's foreign policy.

From this example the reader will gather that party conflict over foreign affairs is rather more serious in Australia than in Canada. There are two roughly equal sides in Australian politics, each of which has shown a distinctive approach to foreign affairs since World War II. The Labour Party was in office from 1941 to 1949; its opponents, the Liberal and Country parties, have been in office in a coalition government since then, under the prime ministership of R. G. Menzies. This Liberal-Country Party government is a direct descendant of the Bruce and Lyons governments of the 1920's and 1930's. Its principal links are with business and farming, and it is officially an anti-Socialist government. In foreign affairs its basic tenets are imperial, but it has recognized the logic of Australia's wartime isolation in the Pacific and of the grouping of forces after the war; it is a strong upholder of the alliance with the United States which it has helped to cement in the ANZUS treaty and the South East Asia Collective Defense Treaty (SEACDT). The government is doubtful of the efficacy of the United Nations, though prepared to go along with it, provided that Australia's security is buttressed in other ways, particularly by alliance with the United States. It views with sympathy the efforts of the new Asian countries to establish viable states and values the link with India, Ceylon, and Pakistan which the Commonwealth provides. But it is emotionally attached to the symbols of Empire (also to the prospect of favored markets in Britain for Australian primary produce) and is still likely to speak of "the Empire" rather than "the Commonwealth."

The Labour Party is a trade-union party, officially Socialist in policy. It was isolationist in the 1930's, remembering with bitterness the conscription struggle of World War I, which split the party and helped to keep it out of office for most of the interwar period. But when it did attain office in 1941 it was faced with the need to manage a war effort which soon became an all-out one with the coming of war in the Pacific. The party's postwar attitude to foreign affairs has been a mixture of its former feelings and of the lessons which it learned during the war. Its approach has been personified by H. V. Evatt, who was Minister for External Affairs throughout its term of office from 1941 to 1949 and has since been its leader. The party has remained an opponent of capitalism and imperialism, but its opposition to these forces has been expressed in different ways from those which it chose before the war, when it preferred isolationism to any positive action. The Evatt policy was one of welcome and recognition for the new countries which appeared out of the ruins of the European empires in Asia at the end of the war, and of international action to administer dependent territories and to prevent the anarchic tendencies of prewar international economics. For security the Labour Party looked to the United Nations, but also to the tie with Britain and, if possible, to an association with the United States which would continue the co-operation between the two countries during the Pacific war. The policy was a mixture of Australian nationalism and internationalism: not a doctrinaire policy, since it had to take account of the actual circumstances in which Australia found herself during the Labour government's time in office, but a policy which envisaged international bodies working in ways which would suit Australia's interests.

Since 1949 the Labour Party has been in a state of confusion over its attitude to communism at home and abroad. The Irish-Catholic elements in the labor movement have been agitated over the growth of Communist power in Europe and in Asia, and the more militant among them have challenged the Evatt leadership on the grounds of its "softness to communism." In reply, the dominant section, led by Evatt, has tended to take a rather more radical view of international affairs (in the sense of one more favorable to Soviet and Chinese claims) than it might have done if opinion in the party had not been polarized by internal warfare, or if the party had been in office.

There is thus room for difference of emphasis between the two sides of Australian politics. In fact, however, it is difficult to imagine an Australian government which revoked the ANZUS or SEACDT pacts and so antagonized the United States. The parties are basically at one in their desire to preserve Australian living standards, to use the Commonwealth of Nations to the full as an instrument of policy, and to retain United States support for Australian security. The only alternative policy ever presented (aside from the Communist policy, which does not differ between one country and another) is that of dropping all alliances and siding with India in its "nonalignment" policy. But this is very much a minority opinion and carries little weight.

Pressure groups in foreign policy are rarely found in Australia. The most persistent have been those trade-unions which, under Communist control, have attempted to force Communist policies upon Labour and non-Labour governments alike. The Waterside Workers' Federation, for example, staged a dock strike in protest against Dutch ships taking arms to Indonesia during the Indonesian struggle for independence. But there is no evidence that this kind of pressure has proved effective, outside the narrow limits of specifically industrial demands. Although Australians are extremely adept in organizing themselves into industrial and vocational syndicates of one kind and another, they do not adopt this kind of procedure in foreign policy; the few organizations which exist have difficulty in keeping alive. As in Canada, foreign policy is made within the government. But in Australia, by reason of the more evenly balanced party situation, opposition criticism is more voluble than in Canada. Foreign affairs are still, however, very much a minority interest in politics.

It is worth noting that, unlike Canada, Australia is a colonial power. This provides a further point of formulation for foreign policy. Australia controls the whole eastern half of New Guinea (the southern part by right of ownership, the northern part as a trust territory from the United Nations), and Nauru, a phosphate island in the Pacific (as the administering authority on behalf of Britain, New Zealand, and herself, who are the joint trustees). Both of these territories were invaded by the Japanese in World War II. New Guinea is regarded by all Australians as vital to Australia's security: a possible threat to New Guinea is one of the few issues of foreign policy which can excite public opinion, in particular the opinion of the well-organized veterans' associations, which are ordinarily concerned only with pensions, hospital facilities, and jobs. In consequence, each party is called upon to state its policy whenever the status or security of New Guinea is called into question, and each has shown its determination to retain Australian control. A by-product of this issue is the fact that

Australia habitually finds herself among the "colonialist" minority in the United Nations Trusteeship Council, where she is a target for Russian attack, Arab-Asian criticism, and United States ambivalence. New Guinea affords one of the few examples of a set point in Australian policy: whatever fields that policy is free to move in, it must remain fixed on retention of New Guinea.

South Africa

South Africa has the oldest tradition of diplomatic activity of all four dominions: the tradition of the negotiations with foreign powers carried on by the Boer Republics in the latter part of the nineteenth century. The South African Republic of the Transvaal made treaties with Portugal, Belgium, Holland, and Germany; had an Under-Secretary for Foreign Affairs; organized a consular service; and had a Minister at The Hague who was accredited to various European countries. The memory of this independent diplomacy remained with many Boers after the republics were defeated and merged with the British colonies to form the Union of South Africa. The desire to be represented again in the councils of the nations, and especially to negotiate on equal terms with the other European powers in southern Africa, was one of the strongest desires of the National Party; and soon after the declaration of the Imperial Conference of 1926 had made it clear that South Africa could do this, General Hertzog began the business of independent diplomacy.

His first move, in 1927, was to establish a Department of External Affairs, on much the same lines as the departments in Canada and Australia. (Previously, external relations had been the responsibility of the Prime Minister's Department.) The establishment of diplomatic relations with a number of European countries has already been described in the preceding chapter. At the outbreak of war in 1939, South Africa had the most widespread diplomatic representation of the four dominions. She did not expand her representation during the war so substantially as Canada and Australia did, but has extended it since the war to all areas where it is considered that South African interests demand representation. The prewar legations in Belgium, France, West Germany,

Italy, Holland, Portugal, and the United States have become Embassies. There are high commissions in Britain, Canada, Australia, and the Central African Federation of Rhodesia and Nyasaland. New legations have been established in Greece, Egypt, Switzerland, Spain, Argentina, and Brazil. Special importance is attached to relations with colonial areas in Africa. Since these are not sovereign states, ambassadors and ministers cannot be accredited to them; but the Union has a commission in Kenya, and representatives in the Belgian Congo, Angola, Portuguese Mozambique, and French Madagascar. South Africa does not exchange high commissioners with the Asian Commonwealth countries (India, Pakistan, and Ceylon) because of a long-standing dispute about the treatment of Indians in South Africa.

The Department of External Affairs formerly was closely linked with the Prime Minister's Department, but has now achieved the independent status of the departments in Canada and Australia. Administratively, the department is divided into three divisions: Political and Protocol; Africa and International Organizations (two sections); and Economic and International Trade (four sections). On matters in which more than one department is concerned, such as external trade, there are interdepartmental committees of the same character as those discussed for Canada and Australia. It should be remembered, however, that governmental organization is on a smaller scale in South Africa than in those two dominions, and that the co-ordination of policy is made correspondingly easier through the close personal relations of a few departmental heads.

One of the distinctive characteristics of the South African Department of External Affairs is its application of the official bilingualism of the Union. Correspondence written in the department itself is written in English and Afrikaans in alternate months. Financial returns to the Treasury and to the Controller and Auditor-General are submitted in English and Afrikaans in alternate years. A reference to the South African diplomatic list shows that senior officers' names are roughly half Afrikaner and half English, although in the civil service of the Union generally Afrikaners preponderate. Recruitment to the department is on much the same lines as in Canada and Australia: candidates must have a university degree, preferably in law or economics, must be bilingual, and must pass a departmental examination during their three years' probation.

The effect of the South African party system upon the making of foreign policy is complicated by the fact that South Africa is the only dominion where questions of status are still prominent political issues. The debate which went on in the 1920's and 1930's is still in progress, although it has ceased in the other three dominions. This is not in itself surprising. The debate was always more bitter in South Africa, and the objectives of South African nationalists were always further distant than those of Canadian nationalists. It is the republican ideal that now divides South Africans when the question of status is raised. There is no dispute that South Africa is a sovereign state, and that Britain can no longer decide policy for South Africa. But extreme Afrikaner nationalists still maintain that South Africa will not have reached her destiny until she organizes her government in the form traditional in Afrikaner history—that of the Boer Republics. English-speaking South Africans retain their firm attachment to the monarchical ideal and would strongly oppose any attempt to make South Africa a republic. But they recognize that the ground has, to some extent, been cut from beneath their feet by the acceptance, by the Commonwealth Prime Ministers, of India and Pakistan as republics within the Commonwealth. Previously they took their stand on the view that it was impossible for a nation to be in the Commonwealth unless it owed allegiance to the Crown and that to make South Africa a republic would be automatically to cut it off from the Commonwealth. Plainly, this interpretation will no longer stand; and the South African Nationalist government was glad to give its ready acceptance to the formulation of Commonwealth relations made by the Prime Ministers in 1949.

The National Party is the dominant party in South Africa, having come to power in 1948 and repeated its electoral success with an increased majority in 1953. It was led at first by D. F. Malan, who headed the revolt against Hertzog when Hertzog fused the National Party with Smuts' followers in 1934; Malan's Purified Nationalist group grew into the National Party of today.

The leader is now J. G. Strijdom. Its Cabinet is entirely Afrikaner in composition, and it embodies the full myth of the Afrikaners as the European people sent by Providence to govern South Africa. However, the party has not wished to discriminate against English-speaking South Africans, but to persuade them that adherence to that myth (involving electoral support for the National Party, and full support for its republican objective and its racial policy) will give them a better future than the forlorn attempt to retain a sentimental connection with Britain. Central to this government's policies since it took office has been its determination to apply a policy of *apartheid*, or separate development, for the various races in South Africa. The Nationalists believe in white supremacy (i.e., that the determination of South Africa's affairs, at home and abroad, should be solely in the hands of Europeans) but also in the right of each race—European, Coloured (mixed-blood), Asian and Bantu—to develop its own characteristic life in separate surroundings. The *apartheid* policy involves not only the denial of all rights in national politics to non-Europeans, but also the provision for each racial group of separate facilities for development, areas within which the races will be free to make their own domestic arrangements for themselves. It is a complex policy, which differs from traditional South African practice only in the singlemindedness with which it is enunciated and pursued. South Africa has traditionally denied political opportunities to non-Europeans and reserved favorable economic opportunities for Europeans, but this has been usually put forward as a policy of expediency rather than of deep principle, as the Nationalists have made it. In so far as the policy seems to advance the interests of Europeans, and restrict the power of the increasingly prosperous Bantu and Asian communities, it is a popular one with European voters; other things being equal, the Nationalists can expect increasing white support.

In foreign policy the distinctive Nationalist policy has been isolationism, along something like the same lines as the French Canadians of Quebec. But this has greatly lessened in the postwar world. It shows itself, in an attenuated form, in the resentment Afrikaners feel toward the criticisms of South African racial policy that are voiced at the United Nations and in the newspapers of

Britain and the United States: the tendency is for the Nationalists to turn their backs on such criticism and refuse to argue. But in the relations of states the Nationalists have deserted their isolationism because of their fear of the USSR. It is a widespread belief among white South Africans (not confined to Nationalists) that the USSR pursues an unrelenting policy of inciting non-white peoples to rise against their white masters. It follows that a world in which the USSR was dominant would be one in which there was no place for the Afrikaners, who are firmly convinced that white supremacy must continue. The Nationalist government is prepared to join in any movement which is opposed to the interests of the USSR, and particularly any movement which unites colonial powers in defense of their African possessions. With certain reservations, this is a continuing policy which contrasts sharply with the Nationalists' prewar determination to keep out of other people's affairs.

The Nationalists retain a good deal of their prewar suspicion of Britain. They consider that Britain still attempts to control South African economic life through the large concentration of British capital in the gold mines and other industries; but, even more, they dislike British colonial policy, the objective of which is the creation of independent African states. The Nationalists were strongly opposed to the policy of giving independence to the Gold Coast and Nigeria, but have now accepted this as a *fait accompli*. They would view with disfavor any attempt to make black men supreme in the Rhodesias or the British dependencies in East Africa. Above all, they resent Britain's policy of retaining control of the three "High Commission territories" (Bechuanaland, Basutoland, and Swaziland) although she gave an implied promise earlier in this century that these areas would be handed over to the Union. Thus, in spite of the advances made in the field of status for South Africa, the Nationalists still have plenty to blame Britain for.

The United Party, the principal opposition party, has shown increasing uncertainty and confusion since the death of Smuts in 1950. It has no positive alternative to the Nationalists' racial policy, and retains its still substantial vote mainly because of many townspeople's dislike of the Nationalists and especially of the past policy of the Nationalists in opposing South African participation in World War II. The United Party stands for the maintenance of bilingualism against a possible Nationalist move to make Afrikaans the dominant language, and for a monarchical system and continued membership of the Commonwealth. It has a predominantly English-speaking following, although it also secures a substantial Afrikaner vote. In the 1948 and 1953 elections it actually secured a greater number of votes throughout the country than the National Party, but failed to secure a majority of seats because in South Africa there is an electoral "weightage" in favor of the rural areas, where Nationalist opinion predominates. It is thus still possible that the United Party might become the government.

Apart from the question of status, there is not much controversy over foreign affairs in South Africa, in Parliament or in the press. There is no parliamentary committee on foreign affairs. In so far as South Africa pursues a foreign policy, it is bipartisan: both parties agree that South Africa should hold on to South-West Africa, that she should not endure what her white citizens regard as perpetual insults from the United Nations on racial policy, that she should work for peace in Africa in order to further her trade and prevent the arming of black peoples, and that she should clearly state her position as an anti-Communist country. South Africa has a white population smaller than the population of Chicago; this "political nation" is bound together so closely by its antipathy toward the prevailing racial ideas in other countries that it is unlikely to develop substantial differences of opinion on foreign policy.

New Zealand

In New Zealand the "political nation" is even smaller than in South Africa (just over two million) but is not divided on racial or cultural grounds—the Maori people are accepted as full citizens—and has no legacy of quarrels over status or of ambivalence toward Britain. Nor has opinion on foreign policy shown the same difference of emphasis in recent years as in Australia. Since World War II, New Zealand has had a more or less uniform foreign policy and has preserved the most modest diplomatic establishment of the four dominions.

The New Zealand Department of External Affairs was established in World War II. Its permanent head is also permanent head of the Prime Minister's Department, and there is a considerable degree of interchangeability with that Department. The Minister for External Affairs is, however, a separate Minister. Within the Prime Minister's Department is a Cabinet Secretariat with three officers, one of whom is styled Secretary of the Cabinet. These three officers are usually drawn either from External Affairs or Treasury. The Secretary of the Cabinet has normally a permanent appointment, while his subordinates are usually appointed for two years.

The External Affairs Department has two Political Sections covering Europe, Asia, and the Americas; a Trusteeship and South Pacific Section; and Economic, Legal, United Nations, Specialized Agency, Colombo Plan, Information, Consular and Protocol Sections.

New Zealand has embassies in Siam and the United States. She has high commissions in Britain, Australia, and Canada, and a commissioner at Singapore, who has a roving commission to cover South East Asia generally. She has legations in France and Japan. There used to be a legation in the USSR, but this was closed for economy reasons when the Nationalist government took office. Career officers are rarely appointed to the highest posts, the usual appointments being those of politicians. Since the diplomatic service is so small, recruitment does not require the fairly elaborate procedures of Canada and Australia: a high academic standard is required from university graduates who apply, but there is no special examination. Half a dozen at the most might be appointed in a year, sometimes none.

New Zealand has the most elaborate arrangement of all four dominions for parliamentary consultation on foreign policy. There is an External Affairs Committee of Parliament (the New Zealand legislature is unicameral) consisting of the Minister and of members of Parliament drawn from both sides of the House. The department provides a secretary for the committee, and also provides it with material. The committee meets regularly, about once a month. It has no special functions in regard to expenditure, and there has been no difficulty in getting both sides in Parliament to co-operate in it. It is principally a source of information for members, and is intended (as was the case with the Australian Committee) to improve the standard of foreign affairs debates. The New Zealand Parliament devotes considerable time to discussion of foreign affairs. But there is little division between the parties.

The Nationalist Party has been in power since 1949, when it took office following fourteen years of government by the Labour Party. The term "nationalist" is misleading: it does not mean the assertion of an independent nationalism, as in South Africa, but the declaration of national unity as opposed to class conflict. The New Zealand Nationalists are roughly equivalent to the Liberal-Country Party coalition in Australia, allowing for the fact that New Zealand is much less heavily industrialized than Australia and is, to a considerable extent, a "farmers' republic." The party is against socialism and in favor of free enterprise. In external relations its traditional line is "follow Britain." On coming back into office after a long absence, it was inclined to deprecate the expansion of diplomatic activity that had taken place under the Labour government, and to suggest that the task of representing New Zealand's interests abroad could be adequately performed by Britain, as in the 1930's. But it quickly discovered that the principal problem for New Zealand was that of making herself indispensable to the United States. For this purpose independent representation in Washington was essential. It discovered too that, as New Zealand's responsibilities increased because of her commitments to ANZUS and SEACDT, fresh representation—such as that of a commissioner at Singapore—became necessary. The Nationalist government is, therefore, unlikely to reduce the extent of New Zealand diplomacy. But it is certain to retain the strongest ties with Britain and to be the most outspoken of all Commonwealth countries in its commendation of things British.

The Labour Party, in opposition, does not quarrel with the
foreign policy which the government pursues, although it is likely
to give a more radical emphasis to some of the policies which it
advocates. Labour is proud of having provided the government that
made New Zealand an object of world-wide interest for its social
services in the 1930's, and for the collective security stand which
its representatives took at Geneva. It is proud of having directed
the New Zealand war effort in World War II, of having provided
all the troops and supplies demanded of it and of having reintro-
duced conscription after the war (New Zealand is the only dominion to have done so) when Communist aggression seemed
to threaten the same kind of attack as Hitler had made ten years
before. It has, therefore, few of the remaining inhibitions in foreign policy from which the Australian Labour Party has not yet
shaken itself free. It supports internationalism in security matters
and in economic questions, but is anxious that New Zealand's
security should be guaranteed by alliance with Britain and the
United States. In foreign affairs it has had no dynamic single
personality comparable with Dr. Evatt in Australia, and so there
has not been the opportunity to personify its policy in the same
way as Dr. Evatt has embodied the Australian Labour Party's.

Within the New Zealand community discussion of foreign
policy is largely confined to intellectuals, among whom it has often
been warm and vigorous. The churches have shown themselves
rather more interested in foreign issues than those of Australia;
the newspapers are more serious-minded than their counterparts
in Australia and carry more foreign news. To outside observers,
New Zealand liberal intellectuals sometimes seem to have carried
over, in their isolation, the assumptions of the "pink decade" of
the 1930's more fully than similar intellectuals in the other
dominions, in Britain, or in the United States. The reason may
simply be that in New Zealand the tradition of Protestant rectitude is less alloyed than in most other countries where it became
established. Foreign affairs are discussed with seriousness and moral
fervor in New Zealand. But there is no far-reaching disagreement
within the community, and New Zealand policy in the future is
predictable, whichever party should happen to be in office.

Formulation of Policy: Some Comparisons

It will be seen that there are numerous similarities between the formulation of foreign policy in one dominion and its formulation in another. The system of responsible government produces a basic pattern which has been adhered to in all four dominions, and which has not been affected by the existence of Foreign Affairs Committees in three of the parliaments. Foreign policy is the responsibility of a minister, who shares his responsibility with a Cabinet; criticism of foreign policy must be severe indeed if it is to shake the Cabinet's resolve, once that has been formed. In each country pressure groups are weak or do not exist in matters of foreign policy. Protest against the government's policy must be made through the party machinery if it is to prove effective. In each country there is still a sense of newness about the carrying on of an independent foreign policy. One of the new aspects is that each dominion now possesses a staff of career diplomats and experts in foreign affairs, who remain in their posts in spite of changes of government, and exert considerable influence upon the foreign policies which governments follow.

The fact that in each dominion the External Affairs Department is either connected with the Prime Minister's Department or has been separated from it within fairly recent times is an indication of the direction which external relations took until recently. From the beginning of the century onward, the Prime Minister in each of these countries was responsible for its contacts overseas, so far as those related to high policy; and those contacts were, to a great extent, contacts with Britain. It was the Prime Minister who went to the Imperial Conference, and it was the Imperial Conference which provided the main part of high-level external relations. Until the 1930's, this was true of Canada and South Africa as it was of Australia and New Zealand; and it continued to be true of Australia and New Zealand until World War II. It is necessary to recognize that connection with Britain, through dominion high commissioners in London and through other means explained below, is still an important part of each dominion's external relations and is still not thought of as "foreign affairs" by any except possibly South Africa.

The main reason for this is that the matters which the dominions have been accustomed to discuss with the British government have been those of trade, immigration, and investment rather than those which are usually associated with the work of foreign offices. For many years the dominion governments endeavored to persuade the British government to give preference in British markets to dominion primary products, by levying a duty on foreign goods of a competitive character. This campaign achieved a qualified success in 1932, when an Empire Economic Conference at Ottawa inaugurated a system of agreements between various dominions and Britain, whereby certain specified goods were given a privileged place in the British market in return for a favored position for British goods in the dominions. This was the system of "imperial preference," which has frequently come under fire in the United States. It is perhaps worth pointing out that the dominions did not get anything like the concessions they wanted from Britain, either in the variety of goods covered by the agreements or in the rates of preference allowed. Since Ottawa the effect of new agreements and changes in the nature of trade has been to minimize the importance of these agreements in both the British economy and the economies of the dominions.

Preference in trade aside, Britain remains an important factor in the economies of the four dominions. She is the country with which each dominion except Canada has done most of its trade, and from which most of its imported capital and its immigrants have come. Australia, New Zealand, South Africa (and Canada to a lesser extent) have had a basic interest in good working relations with Britain. This need was not altered by the quest for status in the 1920's and 1930's, though it may have been overshadowed in some cases. Similarly, in the 1940's and 1950's, it has not been obscured by the quest for American support in the field of security. It is, therefore, worth while considering this relationship in its formal setting, that of the Commonwealth of Nations. Britain and the four dominions are all member nations of the Commonwealth. What does this imply in terms of formal connection, how has it arisen out of the situation at the time of the Statute of Westminster, and what part does the Commonwealth relationship play in formulating the foreign policy of each dominion?

The Commonwealth, and Its Influence on Foreign Policy

When World War II ended it was plain that "dominion status" included more independence than some people had thought before the war. In particular it meant the right of neutrality. Wartime experience had also shown that the prewar search for "an Empire policy" in foreign relations was a failure; each dominion would in future be closely associated with other countries, notably the United States, and a concerted policy was not possible. In its place the Australian government, through Dr. Evatt, put forward the idea of Commonwealth regionalism, of each dominion assuming general Commonwealth responsibilities in the area where its own interests clearly lay. Such a policy was actually pursued in the treatment of Japan, Australia providing a British Commonwealth member of the War Crimes Tribunal, and a British Commonwealth member of the Allied Council in Japan. To strengthen the "regional" notion of Commonwealth association, Australia and New Zealand had signed a pact of mutual association in the South Pacific in 1944. But such an interpretation of the relationship between the dominions, while it might suit the particular situation of Australia and New Zealand, could not settle the incipient conflict between South African and British native policies in Southern Africa, and met with no favor from the Liberal government in Canada. It lost even its relevance in the Pacific area when new dominions were created in India, Pakistan, and Ceylon and when, two years later, the Asian situation was transformed by the Communist revolution in China.

It was the granting of dominion status to India, Pakistan, and Ceylon in 1947, and the acceptance of India as a republican member of the Commonwealth in 1949, that finally changed the Commonwealth from its still ambiguous prewar situation to the position which it now enjoys—a position in which, although the members are less closely bound than they were in prewar days, their constitutional status is clear and the limitations of their association are evident.

The eight states which in 1956 comprised the Commonwealth—the United Kingdom, Canada, Australia, South Africa, New Zealand, India, Pakistan, Ceylon—are recognized by each other as sovereign, in no way subordinate one to another in any aspect of their domestic or foreign relations. Their sole constitutional link is that they recognize Queen Elizabeth as "Head of the Commonwealth." But this is only a symbolic position, and gives the Queen no functions of a practical character. Such functions as she does perform are confined to the six "realms": Britain, the four original dominions, and Ceylon. India and Pakistan are republics. The Queen is the monarch of each of the realms, but in all except Britain she is represented by a governor-general who is appointed on the advice of the ministers of the government concerned (not of the British government) and must accept their advice in the performance of his duties. In each of her realms the Queen has a different "Style and Title," indicating that for each one she is a separate ruler. Such a system can work only on the assumption that in each realm the Queen is a completely constitutional monarch and acts only on the advice of her relevant ministers. This assumption is fully observed, and it is not unusual for the Queen, in formal terms, to take contradictory actions in more than one of her realms. As Queen of Britain, for example, she recognizes the Communist government of China; as Queen of Canada, Australia, and New Zealand she recognizes the government of Chiang Kai-shek as the Chinese government. The Crown has become completely divisible, with no loss of prestige and no special difficulty in arranging the machinery.

The fact that the eight nations are members of the Commonwealth is signified by their periodic attendance at meetings of the Commonwealth Prime Ministers. These meetings are the lineal descendant of the Imperial Conference, but that name has fallen into disuse. The Commonwealth Prime Ministers do not meet regularly, do not arrive at decisions, have no permanent secretariat, and agree to raise no matters which would involve dispute among themselves. They meet for discussion only, and do not expect to agree on a concerted policy. The assumption behind the Imperial Conference, that the dominion prime ministers were under an obligation to agree, is no longer tenable; it is assumed at meetings of Commonwealth Prime Ministers that agreement is unlikely, but that if it does occur it is to be welcomed. The term "British Commonwealth" has been tacitly dropped, and replaced in official reports simply by "Commonwealth."

The Prime Ministers' meetings are a means of "consultation," an ambiguous word which has a long history in Commonwealth relations. It has always been the practice for the Commonwealth Relations Office in London (formerly the Dominions Office, and before that a section of the Colonial Office) to send to dominion governments a great deal of cabled information about British international policies. The dominions, on their part, have always had the ready ear of the British government for any comments they might make upon British policy. Between the wars it was widely assumed that this telegraphic communication was intended to form British policy, since British policy, as indicated in the previous chapter, was considered by many to be imperial policy. This assumption was certainly made in Australia and New Zealand, and under Smuts in South Africa. Today, however, it is clearly recognized by all Commonwealth governments that the consultation which takes place by cable is intended only to inform, not only British policy (which is not regarded as any longer representative of the dominions) but also the policies of the several Commonwealth members. There is, for example, a heavy traffic in cables between Delhi and Canberra, and between Canberra and Wellington, apart from the bilateral communication which each overseas country maintains with Britain. The cables from one member to another are meant to inform, to clarify, and to influence. They are not public documents, and they are less formal than the ordinary communications between countries in the usual diplomatic relations with one another. The informality which characterizes this world-wide traffic in information about one another's policies is regarded by the various Commonwealth governments as extremely valuable. But none of the consultation which takes place in this way commits any of the senders or receivers.

In a similar way, it is usual for the Commonwealth representatives at the United Nations meetings to have informal discussions about the coming agenda, not in order to reach a common policy but merely to inform each other of what their policies will be. In London the high commissioners of the various Commonwealth countries meet regularly to discuss the movement of world events and to enlighten each other about policy. Each high commissioner has direct access to the British government in London, either through the Commonwealth Relations Office or by direct negotiation with the departments in Whitehall with which he wishes to make contact. Again, this sort of consultation does not commit the governments taking part in it. It is for information only, though naturally if governments wish to make special arrangements or understandings with one another they may do so.

It may be asked what value the member nations derive from this consultation, and from this relationship with one another which carries with it no decisions and no commitments. The answer is that each country finds that its interest is served by an arrangement which brings it into close contact with so many other powers (especially with a great power, Britain, and the foremost non-Communist power in Asia, India) without any formal obligations. Throughout the crises of recent years, especially those of Asia and the Middle East, such an assembly of countries has been well worth belonging to, if only because of its great value as a listening post. Since there is no pretense of automatic agreement, it is possible for members to disagree openly about major questions of foreign affairs (such as the Bagdad Pact or the recognition of Communist China) and still preserve their joint membership of the Commonwealth. It is true that if one of the Commonwealth countries became dominated by a Communist party, this arrangement could no longer continue. It is because all the members of the Commonwealth have been either anti-Communist or unaligned that they have been able to agree to differ; they have not had the greatest question of all to differ about, whether to be part or not to be part of the world Communist front.

At the same time they have found that they had a considerable common interest in at least two fields, those of economic policy and of conflict in Asia. All Commonwealth countries except Canada are members of the Sterling Area, which means that their international balances are banked in London with the Bank of England. They share a common gold and dollar reserve to meet their balance of payments deficits (if they have any). The overseas Commonwealth countries find this a congenial arrangement, partly because it fits in with the traditional pattern of their trade, which is still largely with Britain, and partly because banking with Britain means that they have access, for purchases in the dollar area, to the dollar surpluses of British dependencies, arising out of sales to the United States of such things as Malayan tin and rubber, West African cocoa, and Rhodesian copper. This does not mean that the overseas Commonwealth countries are "milking" Britain's colonies: the colonies get goods or credits to the value of the dollar exports which they send away, but the goods which they receive in return are not all dollar goods; they include also goods from sterling and European sources. What the overseas Commonwealth countries get is an opportunity to buy the capital goods which their economies, more up to date than those of the British colonies, require from the United States and Canada. For the time being, at any rate, the Sterling Area has proved a means whereby the overseas countries could achieve greater multilateralism in trade than would otherwise have been available to them, given the difficulty of exporting their primary products to the United States. From the British point of view, the adherence of so many nations to the Sterling Area (which is not confined to the Commonwealth but includes such non-Commonwealth countries as Burma, Iraq, Ireland, and Iceland) is a means of greater multilateralism in trade and an opportunity to extend the area in which British goods can flow freely.

The relevant point about the Sterling Area for our purpose here is that it has no formal constitution and organization. In so far as any statements are ever made on behalf of the Sterling Area as a whole, they are made by the Commonwealth Prime Ministers' Conference—which means that Canada, which is not a sterling but a dollar country, participates fully in discussions of Sterling Area policy. This contradictory situation is explicable only in terms of the informality and mutual confidence which characterize the economic relations of the members of the Commonwealth. Their joint interest lies in exporting more to the United States and in preserving the state of full employment which each of the developed Commonwealth countries has enjoyed since the out-break of World War II. Although they are competitors with one another in a variety of fields, they have found that the nature and direction of their trade make it possible for all except Canada to share a common reserve of gold and dollars. If any one of them found itself trading so heavily with the United States and receiving such an inflow of United States capital as Canada, it would no longer have an interest in remaining within the Sterling Area. But that state of things is not likely to arise, except possibly in South Africa. Leaving the Sterling Area would not mean leaving the Commonwealth, and leaving the Commonwealth would not mean leaving the Sterling Area. But the practical identity of the two bodies makes the Sterling Area something of a buttress to the existing Commonwealth relationship.

Throughout the period since 1949, and especially since the Korean War, the eight member nations of the Commonwealth have had a common desire to avoid a major war in Asia and to restrain the United States from embarking upon a war with Communist China. This temporary unanimity of outlook has prevailed in spite of the fact that most of the members were already allies of the United States in one way or another, and had other means than the Commonwealth of making their views known in Washington. Yet at the 1951, 1953, and 1955 meetings of Prime Ministers it was clear that they thought they could achieve a greater force as a group than separately. This aspect of their common interest is difficult to analyze, since it relates only to the special circumstances of Chinese-American relations, and does not carry over into Asian affairs generally. There is no common attitude on Kashmir, for example, and none on whether Australian and New Zealand forces should be operating in Malaya; India, which participated in the appeals for peace made by the Prime Ministers at the three conferences in question, has also been opposed to the formation of SEACDT. But it is plain that Britain,

Australia, and Canada value the close association with India which the Commonwealth link provides, and that India, Pakistan, and Ceylon, each for different reasons, value a link with the anti-Communist bloc. The unique character of the Commonwealth link means that these Asian countries are not exposed to the taunt that they have been recolonialized; at the same time, while it links them with Britain, it does not saddle them with responsibility for British colonial policy.

These considerations about relations with Asia apply with much less force to South Africa than to Australia, Canada, and New Zealand. Whereas those three countries are all geographically concerned with the Pacific and so with the situation in Asia, South Africa is far removed from Asia by geography and is, in any case, on bad terms with the Asian members of the Commonwealth. But the Commonwealth has other advantages from the government of South Africa's standpoint. Remaining in the Commonwealth is a means of preventing disunity among white men in South Africa, since it assuages the wounded feelings of English-speaking South Africans. The government realizes also that if South Africa did not belong to the Commonwealth she would not belong to anything: she is ill at ease in the United Nations, has no formal alliance with the United States such as all other Commonwealth members except India and Ceylon enjoy, and is neither a Colombo nor a Bandung power. The Commonwealth does at least give South Africa access to a wider company of nations than if she were confined to those with whom her interests as a white man's state in Africa would most obviously associate her—the minor European colonial powers of Belgium and Portugal.

Apart from the advantages which the four dominions derive from the economic strength of the Commonwealth and from the special position in which it puts them in regard to Asia, there is one further advantage which has become apparent to the governments of Canada, Australia, and New Zealand. Each of these knows that the security of its country is ultimately dependent upon the United States. Yet each country is small in population, in spite of its high standard of living and its resources. If it had to treat bilaterally with the United States, it might find itself treated like a "banana republic." This may be a mistaken impression, but it is certainly current among dominion statesmen. The fact that each is a member of the Commonwealth mitigates this danger. It is not that dominion demands upon the United States are made through the Commonwealth; this is true only in the general sense that Commonwealth Prime Ministers, at their conferences, have issued thinly veiled invitations to the United States to be less uncompromising with the Communist bloc and to assist multilateralism in trade by liberalizing its own conditions of trade with other countries. It is rather that a dominion treating with the United States knows that it does so as a country which can expect the informal, benevolent support of at least some other Commonwealth countries, and usually the support of Britain, in its requests. It is not alone. At the same time its association with other Commonwealth countries is so informal as to prevent its being bound to any policies which they may put forward. Such a situation may be confusing and bewildering, and may even seem hypocritical, from the American viewpoint; but it is understandable in terms of the history of the dominions.

The Commonwealth is thus an important factor in the foreign policies of the four countries with which this chapter is concerned. To them it is an association which has advantages and a lack of disadvantages. It gives them enhanced status, enables them to maneuver in their international negotiations, and imposes no obligations upon them. This final point needs stressing, especially in the field of defense. There is absolutely no obligation on the part of a Commonwealth member to come to the defense of any other member, simply because they are both members of the Commonwealth. The Commonwealth is not a military alliance. In fact, there are only two formal military agreements between Commonwealth members that do not involve other nations outside the Commonwealth. These are the agreements between Britain and Ceylon and between Britain and South Africa about the use of bases and facilities for British naval vessels. In neither case is the overseas country compelled to go to war because Britain is at war. So far as other Commonwealth countries are concerned, there is a tacit feeling in Australia and New Zealand that these countries would go to war if Britain were attacked; but this is an understanding rather than an alliance or even an entente. In general, Commonwealth countries would go to war only if their vital interests were affected, and it is probable that they would do so then only in pursuance of the international agreements which they have signed. All are members of the United Nations, and because of this Britain, Canada, Australia, New Zealand, and South Africa sent forces to serve in the Korean War. Britain and Canada are members of NATO, and both have troops stationed in Europe. Australia, New Zealand, and Britain are signatories to SEACDT, and Australia and New Zealand to ANZUS. Pakistan (to take an example outside the range of these chapters) is a member of the Bagdad Pact. In each of these cases, however, it is not only Commonwealth countries that are involved: other nations, notably the United States, are involved too. It is best, then, to look on the Commonwealth not as a defensive alliance but as an association to which belong countries some of which are united in other alliances with each other and with foreign countries, and some of which are members of no alliance at all. Given this state of things, it is still true that there is a good deal of consultation between the Chiefs of Staff of the various Commonwealth countries, not excepting India. There is much standardization of weapons and training, and discussion of tactics and development in armaments. This practical discussion does not add up to an alliance.

Recent Policies

No attempt has been made so far in this chapter to describe directly the policies pursued by the four dominions since the outbreak of war in 1939. But in discussing the attitudes toward policy of their governments and political parties, and the development in Commonwealth relations since the war, their general position has been outlined. In each case they have discovered that the exercise of independence has depended upon the securing of powerful allies and the choice of sides in the cold war. Each has found that independence involves interdependence, less with one another than with Britain and the United States. Each has found that in a particular region it has had to work out policies which would both fit the circumstances of its regional position and keep it secure in terms of the balance of power in the world at large. The threat of Communist aggression, first from the USSR and then from China, has conditioned the whole policy of the dominions in the postwar era. This process can be seen at work in each of the following accounts of individual dominions' foreign policies.

Canada

The war itself proved a turning point in Canadian foreign policy, and in the postwar period Canada has gone even further along the road which she took in 1939. Whereas it has been said that the three dogmas of Canadian prewar policy were "imprecision, no commitments, and a reluctance even to consult with other nations on the major issues which could threaten the peace,"[1] Canada has given increasing precision to an interventionist policy. During the war she became a center of air force training for the whole of the Commonwealth, her troops were prominent in the invasion of Fortress Europe, and she was brought into even closer association with the United States in the defense of the Pacific coast of North America. Canada was the third side of the British-American-Canadian triangle in the development of the atomic bomb. This role of third side of a triangle, or middleman, is a familiar one with Canadian diplomats, and has gained in importance since 1939. In 1941 Mackenzie King played an important part in smoothing the exchange of bases for destroyers between Britain and the United States. Canada finished the war as not a great power, but as the foremost of the "middle powers." It was in this role that she, together with Australia, objected to the great power veto at the San Francisco conference of 1945, which drew up the Charter of the United Nations.

[1] Formulated by Escott Reid in an article in *Canadian Journal of Economics and Political Science*, 1937; quoted by L. B. Pearson in "Some Thoughts on Canadian External Relations" to the Canadian Historical Association, Winnipeg, June 4, 1954.

Two years later Louis St. Laurent, as Canadian Minister for External Affairs, told the General Assembly of the United Nations that more precise obligations for collective security than those proposed by the Charter might be adopted by those countries which were prepared to accept them; and in November 1948, he said, as Prime Minister:[2]

It is no secret to anyone that the leaders of the Soviet Union aspire to world domination. It is equally clear that they count as much on the weaknesses of the free nations as they do on their own armed strength. By demonstrating to the Soviet Union that the free nations of the world are really taking the measures necessary to defend themselves and to ensure respect for the principles of the Charter, the free nations may well convince the Soviets that it would be impossible for them to win a war if they started one. Now no one is likely to start a war with the prospect of losing it . . .

Like many of you, I have paid for fire insurance since I first began to own a home. Happily, there has never been a fire in my house, but I feel no regret for having paid the premiums and I shall continue to pay them as long as I own any property. When I ask you to support a North Atlantic Treaty, I am simply asking you to pay an insurance premium which will be far, far less costly than the losses we would face if a new conflagration devastated the world.

Thus Canadians learned that the days of the fireproof house were over, and that they must join in peacetime military alliance to prevent aggression. This was a complete reversal from the prewar position. Some prewar memories linger: Canada is the only NATO country, for example, which does not impose conscription but must fill its forces by voluntary enlistment. But Canada's national unity has survived the massive change in the nature of her foreign commitments. To a considerable extent, as indicated earlier, the reason is that the enemy is Communist Russia, than whom no other power could be more objectionable to Catholic Quebec. But whatever the responsibility of external pressure for the national unity of today, the Canadian Secretary of State for External Affairs thinks that internal changes have some responsibility too,

[2] Quoted in G. P. de T. Glazebrook, A History of Canadian External Relations (Toronto, 1950), p. 438.

and that now the country approaches foreign policy in a more adult frame of mind than in the past:[3]

. . . Our society of two cultures has by now reached the more mature stage where foreign policy can be formulated as a result primarily of a dispassionate analysis of the foreign situation.

In the '30's we were intensely preoccupied with the effect of our foreign policy on the unity of our country. But in the '50's we are also concerned with the connection between that policy and the unity of the coalition against aggression, in which Canada is playing an active part. Hence the problem of seeking unity has been vastly enlarged in scope and complexity.

It is this latter problem of attaining unity and harmony within the anti-Communist coalition that Canada has tackled in recent years. From the Canadian standpoint it has not been simply a matter of acting as middleman between Britain and the United States. In NATO the problem has hardly arisen. But in Asia it has arisen in forms which have often perplexed the allies in the anti-Communist coalition. On the whole, Canada has thrown her weight on the side of the British, and to some extent the Indian, government in attempting to moderate American policy at times when it seemed possible that the war in Asia might spread. Canada was a member of the United Nations Commission in Korea at the time of the North Korean invasion of South Korea, and so was able to verify the fact of aggression; Canada strongly supported the steps taken against North Korea. Yet it was plain that Canada disapproved of General MacArthur's desire to carry the attack into China, and that she voted with reluctance for the American resolution branding China an aggressor. When firing ceased in Korea, Canada showed herself a supporter of Indian rather than American views in the United Nations, as indeed did the other Commonwealth countries. On Korean prisoners of war and on India's candidacy as a member of the political conference which was to have followed a Korean truce, Canada was on the opposite side to the United States. On the question of recognition of Communist China, no American statesman has gone so far toward

[3] L. B. Pearson, op. cit.

advocating recognition as St. Laurent did during his Asian tour in 1954; and it was hardly with the official blessing of the United States that Canada accepted the thankless task of membership of the International Commissions for Viet Nam, Laos, and Cambodia, established as a result of the Geneva conference on Indochina in July, 1955.

Canadian interest in Asia has not been limited to concern about war. Canada was represented at the Commonwealth Meeting on Foreign Affairs held at Colombo in January, 1950,[4] out of which arose the Colombo Plan, whereby the developed countries of the Commonwealth offered the undeveloped ones technical assistance and a certain amount of actual capital equipment, to assist the local plans of the Asian countries. The plan has since been extended to bring in new donor countries, including Japan and the United States, and new recipient countries in South East Asia. But Canadian help has been largely devoted to India, Pakistan, and Ceylon. A tour of these countries by the Canadian Prime Minister in 1954 attracted considerable attention, as did a tour by L. B. Pearson, the External Affairs Minister, in 1955. Pearson's speeches have frequently stressed the need for the Western countries to understand the different background of India and other "neutralist" nations, to help in their economic advancement, and to take account of their point of view. In this he considers that the Commonwealth link is of great value. In 1956, over the British and French intervention in Egypt, Canada voted against Britain and with India and the United States. She was clearly anxious that the Asian Commonwealth members should not consider that the original dominions sided automatically with Britain. Pearson attached great weight to keeping the Asian countries in the Commonwealth, in the face of Britain's failure to consult with them (or with the original dominions or the United States) over her action in Egypt.

In spite of some differences of opinion with the United States over Asian policy, there has been no slackening of co-operation

4 See its communiqué in Nicholas Mansergh (ed.), *Documents and Speeches on British Commonwealth Affairs, 1931-1952* (London, 1953), p. 1186, and further documents on the Plan, pp. 1053-1073.

between the two North American countries. Canada is largely responsible for the defense of Arctic America, which, through the distant-early-warning radar system, means the defense of the United States against air attack across the North Pole. In economic affairs, the growth of American investment in Canada and the continued buoyancy of the Canadian dollar have contributed to good relations; almost 70 per cent of Canadian exports go to the United States. At the same time, Canadian intellectuals have exhibited a growing concern about the possible blotting out of a distinctive Canadian culture by the flood of printed matter, radio and television broadcasts, books, and films which comes into Canada from the United States. The emergence of distinctive Canadian objectives in foreign policy has been matched by an increasing self-consciousness in the cultural sphere, and a determination to preserve and enlarge what is directly Canadian in the lives of Canada's people. Here, as in foreign policy, the existence of intermediaries between Canada and the United States is seen to be of value. In the 1930's Canada's relations with the United States and with Britain were, in the main, direct. Now, according to Pearson,[5]

... they are to a large extent concerned with them as members of a coalition of which Canada is itself a member. That is one reason why Canada is so strong a supporter of such an organisation as NATO; it is a vehicle of Anglo-American-Canadian co-operation as well as a bulwark of peace. The triangle rests more comfortably in such a system.

Australia

During the war Australia's foreign relations underwent a considerable change, the main aspect of which was the increase in association with the United States. This was a gradual process for the first two years of war, though even then, before the United States became a belligerent, she bulked much larger than before in Australian policy. With the outbreak of the Pacific war, the destruction of British naval and military power in Malaya, and the southward advance of Japanese troops through the Indonesian archipelago, American help became imperative. In a New Year

[5] L. B. Pearson, op. cit.

message to Australians at the beginning of 1942, the Labour Party Prime Minister, John Curtin, said:[6]

> The Australian Government . . . regards the Pacific struggle as primarily one in which the United States and Australia must have the fullest say in the direction of the Democracies' fighting plan.
> Without any inhibitions of any kind, I make it quite clear that Australia looks to America, free of any pangs as to our traditional links or kinship with the United Kingdom.
> We know the problems that the United Kingdom faces. We know the constant danger of invasion. We know the dangers of dispersal of strength. But we know too that Australia can go, and Britain can still hold on.
> We are therefore determined that Australia shall not go, and we shall exert all our energies toward the shaping of a plan, with the United States as its keystone, which will give to our country some confidence of being able to hold out until the tide of battle swings against the enemy.

Following out this policy, the direction of Australian forces was put in the hands of General MacArthur when he escaped from the Philippines, and Australian ministers continually agitated for the creation of a Pacific War Council in Washington. For the rest of the war Australian weight was thrown on the side of argument in the United States that demanded a significant share of manpower and equipment for the war against Japan, rather than all-out concentration upon Europe. The strident character of some of the Australian demands led to occasional coolness with the British government. But in general it could be said that, in an emergency situation, Australia had asserted a legitimate national interest, that of survival.

After the war, as has been indicated, the Evatt policy of internationalization and of encouragement of the new nations in Asia held the stage. At the San Francisco conference in 1945 Australia campaigned for a reduction of the veto power given to the great powers in the Security Council, for a strengthening of the Economic and Social Council, for more international power in the field of trusteeship, for a clarification of the Charter's reference

[6] Nicholas Mansergh (ed.), *Documents, op. cit.*, p. 549.

to domestic jurisdiction (so as to prevent the White Australia Policy's becoming an object of attack by the UN), and generally for greater weight to be given to the middle and small powers. These remained principles of Australian policy, and still remain so to a considerable extent. But in 1949 the Chinese revolution occurred and the Australian Labour government went out of office. Since then events have taken a different turn, and policy has turned with them—assisted by the fact that another party was in control of it.

At first the Liberal-Country Party government under R. G. Menzies seemed to show little awareness of the changes that had taken place in the Commonwealth. In 1950 the Prime Minister himself was still advocating[7]

. . . a Committee on Imperial Foreign Policy, to sit in London and to be attended by the Foreign Secretary representing the United Kingdom Government and by the High Commissioners or visiting Ministers representing each Dominion. It should sit regularly, and its work should be regarded as of major importance.

But in the following year the Menzies government took a bigger step in independent foreign policy than any Australian government had taken before. This was the signing, with the United States and New Zealand, of the Pacific Security Agreement known as the ANZUS Pact, in which each of the three countries promised to regard an attack on one as an attack on all and to "act to meet the common danger in accordance with its constitutional processes." Furthermore, the treaty set up a council, consisting of the three foreign ministers or their deputies, "to consider matters concerning the implementation of the treaty."[8] Although the Australian government hastened to point out that Britain had been kept informed of the negotiations (which had been closely associated with those on the Japanese Peace Treaty; Australia and

[7] R. G. Menzies, *The British Commonwealth of Nations in International Affairs* (Roy Milne Memorial Lecture, Adelaide, 1950).

[8] The Treaty, together with comments on it by the Ministers for External Affairs of Australia and New Zealand, is reprinted in Nicholas Mansergh (ed.), *Documents, op. cit.*, pp. 1171-1177.

New Zealand were generally considered to have been given the Pacific guarantee by the United States as a *quid pro quo* for their adherence to the peace treaty), it became known that Britain had unsuccessfully sought admission to ANZUS, not being included because of American objections. In June, 1953, the British Prime Minister, Winston Churchill, announced in the House of Commons, "I do not like the ANZUS Pact at all." Thus, in a comparatively brief period, an Australian government intent upon greater imperial co-operation found itself out of step with a British government to whose party complexion it was sympathetic. It was recognized widely in Australia, however, that such was the inexorable logic of the postwar world. As Chinese Communist power grew, so did the realization that a link with the United States might prove as necessary as in 1942, even though it meant a lack of close identity with Britain in the particular matters with which the ANZUS Pact was concerned. In fact, Britain, Australia, and New Zealand were already co-operating in military planning in regard to British operations in Malaya. In September 1954, the balance was set right by the signature of SEACDT, which included Britain as well as Australia, New Zealand, and the United States; Britain was once again admitted into major military planning in the Pacific.

In regard to the possible spread of war in Asia, as it revealed itself in the various stages of the Korean War, Australia played a less distinctive part than Canada, although she too tended to support the British and Indian rather than the United States proposals at critical times. In general, Australian policy displayed more concern for American feelings than did Canadian. At the same time it is worth noting that Australia was the prime mover behind the Colombo Plan from the beginning, and has contributed much more to it, in terms of her population, than has Canada; the Australian contribution has been shared out fairly evenly among the various recipient countries and not confined largely to those which are members of the Commonwealth. The Menzies government's Minister for External Affairs, R. G. Casey, a former governor of Bengal, is firmly convinced of the importance to Australia of Asian goodwill and has been responsible for considerable Australian effort, both diplomatic and economic, in this direction. In particular, Australia has welcomed large numbers of Asian students under the Colombo Plan; this has been a quite new experience for a country previously suspicious of Asian intentions.

The Australian position in regard to Asia is a more difficult one than that of Canada, because of Australia's proximity to Asia and her policy of excluding colored immigrants. (Canada has, since the war, organized a quota system for the permanent entry of a small number of migrants from Asian Commonwealth countries; Australia has not.) In particular, Australia has found herself sharply at odds with Indonesia over the future of West New Guinea. This part of the former Dutch empire in the East Indies was left with an undecided future when Indonesia became a sovereign state. Since then the Indonesian government has maintained that West New Guinea is properly part of Indonesia; the Dutch have continued to hold it and have undertaken development plans there. The Australian government—supported by the Opposition—has indicated that it considers Indonesia has no claim to the area and that it would oppose any Indonesian attempts to take it by force. Furthermore, it entered into an agreement with the Dutch in July, 1953, for co-operation in certain fields, as between Australian East New Guinea and Dutch West New Guinea. In consequence, Australia faces the charge of being colonialist and of abetting other colonialists. To this the government answer has been that its deeds under the Colombo Plan have shown that it wishes well toward Asian nationalism. But the issue is likely to cause further trouble.

Just as Canada hopes to mediate between Britain and the United States in cases where the two great powers' policies seem to diverge, so does Australia. In a speech in 1955, Menzies said:[9]

. . . We work incessantly for the closest collaboration between the British Commonwealth and the United States of America . . .

It is very easy to provoke an argument between Britain and America. It is, alas, all too easy for that argument to be exaggerated into a matter of deep and bitter dispute. The Communists, who are masters of

[9] Statement in the House of Representatives, Canberra, April 20, 1955; reprinted in Current Notes (Canberra), Vol. 26, No. 4, April 1955.

propaganda and who are adept at getting their own sentiments repeated by those who think themselves most opposed to Communism, seize on every point of difference. As I said on my return to Australia, their policy is clearly the oldest one in history—to divide and conquer. Most of the British-American arguments so-called which I have heard or read during the last three months have not arisen half so much from genuine differences of policy between the administrations, as from mutual misinterpretations of the views of partisans. . . .

I have myself met men, some of them occupying responsible positions, who have come to regard any praise for the United States as being anti-British and any work for closer British-American co-operation as being subversive of the British Commonwealth relationship. It would be a tragedy if such sorry nonsense became at all widespread.

In this spirit, Australian foreign policy is directed toward a reconciliation of British and American views when these are in dispute. Menzies' work as chairman of the Suez Canal Committee in September, 1956, can be viewed as activity of this kind, as can the abortive efforts of Casey to reconcile British and United States policies after Britain had intervened in the conflict between Egypt and Israel. The fact that the Menzies government supported the British rather than the United States policy is an index of its party complexion; a Labour government would probably have supported the United States, as did the Canadian government.

South Africa

South African foreign policy since 1939 has been less ambitious than that of either Canada or Australia, and has concentrated upon fewer issues. South Africa was not so heavily involved in the war: her territory was not in danger, and her active fighting was confined to sending troops to assist the British effort in North Africa and the Mediterranean. To a greater extent than the other dominions, South Africa had a problem of subversion and disloyalty at home, which occupied much of the government's time. South Africa was less prominent at San Francisco than Canada and Australia, and had less to do in the next few years in the formation of either defensive alliances or bonds with new nations. Her principal preoccupation in external affairs became her position at the United Nations. Since the United Nations began to operate,

South Africa has found herself under heavy fire for her racial policy. This fire has taken three forms: attack upon South Africa for not making South-West Africa a Trust Territory in the same way as Britain, Australia, and New Zealand had made their League of Nations mandates into Trust Territories; complaints about the treatment of persons of Indian and Pakistani extraction; and complaints against South Africa on grounds of her alleged violation of human rights through the *apartheid* policy. In each case South Africa has replied that the matters in question were domestic matters in terms of Article 2 (7) of the Charter and has refused to admit the right of her opponents (notably of India) to question her domestic policy. South-West Africa remains the one mandated territory still dependent upon the Treaty of Versailles; it has now, to all intents and purposes, been absorbed into the Union of South Africa, and members elected by its white population sit in the Union Parliament.

As indicated earlier, South Africa's racial policy has made her a lonely nation outside Africa. Within Africa her attention has been concentrated upon gaining as close co-operation as possible with European powers with interests in Africa. In 1949, largely through her efforts, the Commission for Technical Co-operation South of the Sahara was established; it is usually known as CCTA. This body promotes co-operation in such fields as human and animal health, soil conservation, transport, labor productivity, housing, nutrition, and education. It has 16 permanent technical bureaus and 6 regional committees. By 1956 it had sponsored some 65 international and regional conferences. This kind of international co-operation represents, from the South African standpoint, practical assistance between nations with common problems, and is often contrasted with what are considered to be the barren debates of the United Nations.

The Nationalist government which has been in office since 1948 has distinctive views on the future of Africa. These views were expressed with clarity by Dr. Malan in 1953.[10] They include the need for international control of the Suez Canal, and a British base somewhere in the Middle East: "it is in our interest that

[10] Reply to external affairs debate, Aug. 11, 1953.

there shall be a base to safeguard the gateway to Africa, which will safeguard Africa and us." South Africa must maintain "good neighborship" with the Central African Federation to her north and resist attempts by India to interfere in African affairs—not only those of South Africa, but also those of the British dependencies in East Africa, where there are numbers of Indian traders and settlers. The most notable aspect of Nationalist policy, however, is its demand for an "African Charter," to be agreed upon by South Africa, Britain, France, Portugal, and Belgium. The aim of this would be

To protect the indigenous peoples of Africa against penetration by the peoples of Asia . . . Africa should be safeguarded for the European who has settled here, but the rest of Africa should be there for the benefit of the natives.

The purpose of this Charter, in addition to protecting Africa from Asian infiltration, would be to protect it as far as possible from Communist activity and to prevent its being militarized. This latter point is a fixed one in South African policy: no natives are enlisted in the South African forces, none is trained to arms, and South Africa deprecates the practice of European colonial powers of enlisting black troops. It is this, more than anything else, which makes it difficult for her to co-operate with her neighbors in military matters. Frequent staff conversations are held with the European colonial powers, but they are not likely to issue in firm alliances because of the essential differences between South African forces and those of her potential allies.

In Africa, then, the South African government has been seeking ways of co-operating with her European neighbors. A problem about which South African policy has only recently been clarified is that of the development of British colonies into independent African states. The South African attitude toward the development of Nigeria and the Gold Coast was at first one of hostility; Britain, it was felt, was digging a pit for her own feet, since the new states would prove ungrateful to her, and she was also digging a pit for South Africa, whose own natives would take their cue from those of the emerging African states. In 1955, however, the

Strijdom government issued a number of statements to the effect that South Africa would not discriminate between one state in Africa and another. Strijdom told his Party Congress:[11]

There should be that type of common approach—also in so far as our relationship with non-White states is concerned—which will ensure that we do not regard one another as opponents but as different states and races and communities, each entitled to its own territory and to its own existence in this great continent.

Thus South Africa has accepted the inevitable, and is not likely to attempt to block the entry of new African states into the meetings of Commonwealth Prime Ministers, as once seemed possible. It still remains to be seen what the actual diplomatic relations of these states with South Africa will be. In the meantime, there remains the dispute with Britain over the High Commission Territories (see above) which are either on the borders of the Union or totally enclosed within it. The South African government is determined that these shall become not independent black states, but part of the Union.

Alone of the four dominions considered here, South Africa is not in alliance with the United States. It is unlikely that such an alliance could be forged, if only because Negro service men of the United States would be subject to rigid segregation if they set foot in South Africa. But in any case the two countries have few interests in common, apart from gold (of which the United States is the principal buyer and South Africa the principal supplier) and a common antipathy to communism. South Africa is far away from possible scenes of conflict in a war between the Communist and anti-Communist powers. Nor is it certain that South Africa would favor close association with a country which is officially opposed to the racial discrimination that is official policy in South Africa. In future it seems likely that South African interests will continue to diverge from those of the other Commonwealth countries, and that South Africa will retain the

[11] Statement to National Party Congress, Pretoria, September, 1955; quoted in Co-operative Co-existence in Africa (South Africa House, London, 1956).

Commonwealth connection only so long as her government considers that its interests, at home and abroad, are served by doing so.

New Zealand

New Zealand foreign affairs have been simple since 1939. As suggested earlier, New Zealand is not a big enough state to carry much weight in international affairs. In the war her role was confined to providing troops for service in North Africa, the Mediterranean, and Italy, and serving as a naval and supply base for the United States Navy and her own forces in the Pacific. Nevertheless, her Labour government was extremely active in support of the demands of the Labour government in Australia for a greater allocation of supplies and men for the Pacific. Its attitude at San Francisco was similar to that of Australia. The close relations between the two governments were illustrated by the abortive Canberra, or ANZAC, Pact of 1944, in which Australia and New Zealand bound themselves to continued joint action in the South Pacific. This pact was abortive in the sense that it promised more in the way of co-operation than did in fact occur; this is largely because it was superseded by later pacts. In one regard, however, it has proved fruitful: the South Pacific Commission, of which Australia, New Zealand, and the various colonial powers of the Pacific are members, was foreshadowed in the pact and duly took shape in 1947.[12] It carries out, for the Pacific islands, functions similar to those performed in Africa by CCTA. New Zealand's special interest lies in her possession of certain islands and her trusteeship of Western Samoa.

Since the war the principal features of New Zealand foreign policy have been associated with ANZUS, SEACDT, and the problem of peace in Asia. The Holland Nationalist government which took office on the morrow of the Chinese revolution, and not long before the signing of the Japanese Peace Treaty, was faced with the same problems as the politically similar Menzies government in Australia. In neither country was Japan at all popular, and in both there were many people who thought a

[12] See Nicholas Mansergh (ed.), Documents, op. cit., pp. 1050-1052, for the main articles of the agreement establishing the Commission.

harsher peace should be imposed upon her. At the same time it was recognized that Japan could not be kept under control forever (especially since the control was being exercised exclusively by the United States) and that Australia and New Zealand could hardly make a peace treaty on their own. The ANZUS Pact was something of a bitter pill for loyal New Zealanders to swallow, but again the realities of wartime experience had made it plain that the United States was essential to New Zealand's security. The pact gained fresh significance when it seemed possible that the United States might be drawn into war with China over Formosa; was this the sort of conflict that would involve New Zealand automatically in war? But this issue did not come to the test.

Once American support was ensured to the extent that it was possible to secure American help, New Zealand found herself in the 1950's again in association with Britain, helping with token forces in Malaya and the Mediterranean. Like Australia, she was closely concerned in the negotiations over the Suez Canal in 1956. But by this time her basic foreign affairs position was clear, and was not likely to be changed by disturbances in the Middle East.

Conclusions

The four dominions considered in this and the preceding chapter have now arrived at political maturity. Each is in full command of its foreign policy, so far as formal control is concerned. But each has found that the nature of the postwar world is such that the isolated independence which most nationalists dreamed of in the 1930's has become a delusion, and that small nations can survive only if they are lucky enough to find that their interests are in fact interdependent with those of great powers. Each has discovered that the United Nations is not sufficient for its security. Three have found their interests directly bound up with those of the United States; the fourth, South Africa, has had no formal links with the United States but has enrolled itself by implication in the United States camp, by reason of its strong antipathy toward the USSR. Apart from the problem of relations with the United States, the central problem of policy for each of the four dominions has been that of coming to terms with emergent nationalism in Asia and Africa. Again, this has been a different problem for South Africa, for whom it has been mainly a matter of the impact of expanding nationalism elsewhere in Africa upon the native peoples of the Union itself. For the other three dominions, the problem has been one of creating cordial relations with the new countries of Asia. In this way they have found the Commonwealth and the Colombo Plan useful devices.

Whether in the future these few countries will continue to be classified together is largely a matter of whether they remain within the Commonwealth and of what sort of body the Commonwealth becomes in future. As indicated at the beginning of the preceding chapter, there will always be a superficial resemblance between the positions of the four countries, because of similar demographic and economic development. But that is no reason why the four countries should share a common political future. If the analysis made in this chapter is correct, South Africa is likely to diverge from the other three because of her different racial composition and her concentration upon African affairs. The position of the other three in the Pacific, and their common dependence upon the United States, are likely to draw them closer together. It is also likely that they will continue to regard the Commonwealth as a means of furthering their foreign policies. But it is important to emphasize that it is in this manner, through the furtherance of individual countries' interests, that the Commonwealth will prosper, and not through any separate virtue of its own. This point has been made with force in another context by Max Beloff:[13]

The British Commonwealth, the most enduring example of international co-operation, has functioned only through the process of continuous consultation and has made no headway with the creation of objectives separate from and external to its independent nations.

If the Commonwealth is viewed as a means of satisfying the interests of its members, and not as an organism with a life and

[13] Max Beloff, *Foreign Policy and the Democratic Process* (Baltimore, 1955), p. 104.

interests of its own, its continued survival is more easily explained and the likelihood of changes in its form more easily accepted. Prevailing sentiment in Australia and New Zealand, and among part of the population in Canada and South Africa, is against this way of looking at the Commonwealth. But the changes which have taken place in the institution since World War II have strengthened its utility to each of those countries, and enabled them to co-operate more selectively and more successfully than if a more organic connection between the parts of the Commonwealth had been attempted. National interests will be the operative forces in the Commonwealth of the future. The Commonwealth itself will survive so long as really fundamental disagreement does not arise between its members; and even then, with some of its members gone, it could still survive in a more modest form.

Finally, it may be asked what sort of categorization can be made of the formulation of foreign policy in the four countries: is it sufficiently alike in each case for them to be classified together as examples of foreign policy in the making? The answer must be an affirmative one. There is no significant difference between the way foreign policy is made in one of these countries and in another. The considerations which must be taken into account differ from one to another, but in each the process is basically the same. It approximates more to the British process of making foreign policy than to the American. This is because the four dominions maintain Cabinet government of the British pattern, and have altered it only in small ways, such as the election in some cases of Cabinets by the party in power (instead of their selection by the Prime Minister) and in others the weakening of collective responsibility within the Cabinet, as that is understood in Britain. None of these divergences is significant in the making of foreign policy, which remains firmly in the hands of the Cabinet. The Cabinet is dependent for advice upon career officers of its External Affairs and other departments, but is plainly in final control. In each of the four dominions it is now rare for foreign policy to become a matter of major public discussion; elections are not won and lost on such questions. The "newness" of foreign policy as an election question may bear some responsibility for this state of affairs. But it seems unlikely that in any of the countries foreign affairs will become a matter of far-reaching dispute or that pressure groups of a formidable character will develop to press for particular measures. The first of these prognostications is dependent upon world affairs continuing to be polarized between Communist and non-Communist powers, and the second upon the political habits of the four countries remaining much as they are. Whether both these assumptions can be accepted or not, it is a point of similarity between the four dominions that their foreign policies are governed more by external than by internal factors. Externally, they are subject to the pressures which small, rich, white, non-Communist countries cannot avoid. Internally, they are all more closely united than before World War II. This does not necessarily mean that in all of them, in the words already quoted from L. B. Pearson, "foreign policy can be formulated as a result primarily of a dispassionate analysis of the foreign situation." No country is ever likely to be in quite this position. But it does mean that each of the four dominions is likely to be faced, throughout the foreseeable future, by massive external forces which can neither be exorcised nor controlled by the dominion acting alone; and that this situation will tend to force bipartisanship in foreign policy upon the major contesting parties in domestic policies.

SELECTED BIBLIOGRAPHY

The political systems of the four dominions are compared in A. Brady, *Democracy in the Dominions* (Toronto, 1947). See also S. D. Bailey (ed.), *Parliamentary Government in the Commonwealth* (New York, 1952). The individual systems of the dominions may be studied in H. McD. Clokie, *Canadian Government and Politics* (Toronto, 1950); J. D. B. Miller, *Australian Government and Politics* (London, 1954); L. Marquard, *The Peoples and Policies of South Africa* (London, 1952); L. Lipson, *The Politics of Equality* (Chicago, 1948) (for New Zealand). See also J. C. Beaglehole (ed.), *New Zealand and the Statute of Westminster* (Wellington, 1944), W. Levi, *American-Australian Relations* (Minneapolis, 1947), and A. R. Conan, *The Sterling Area* (London, 1952).

Various aspects of Commonwealth association are listed and explained in H. J. Harvey, *Consultation and Co-operation in the Commonwealth* (London, 1952). But for the "recent policies" with which this chapter is concerned the student cannot do without N. Mansergh (ed.), *Documents and Speeches on British Commonwealth Affairs 1931-1952* (London, 1953).

The Asian Members
of the
Commonwealth of Nations

ARTHUR C. TURNER

Division of Social Sciences
University of California, Riverside

The Asian Members of the Commonwealth of Nations

CHAPTER 12

BACKGROUNDS OF FOREIGN POLICY IN INDIA, PAKISTAN, AND CEYLON

The Commonwealth in Asia

·That the remarkable institution known as the Commonwealth of Nations now possesses three member nations in Asia is one of the most curious, one of the most important, and possibly one of the most auspicious of the facts of contemporary politics. It is not common for nations which have recently and for a long time been subject to foreign rule to be willing, when they have attained control of their own destinies, to continue in any sort of political association, however tenuous and free of compulsions, with the power that was formerly dominant over them. Even within the Commonwealth itself, both Burma and the Republic of Ireland have made another choice, and determined entirely to sever their connection with the United Kingdom—the former at the earliest moment when the opportunity presented itself, in 1947; the latter, after a quarter of a century of steps each of which fell just short of that end, in 1949.

Yet India, Pakistan, and Ceylon, when they attained to sovereignty and independence, chose to remain voluntarily as members of the Commonwealth, and thus to become its first self-governing members in Asia. India remained a member even after becoming a republic in 1949.[1] It is true that, for many reasons stemming from history, Commonwealth membership means to the Asian members something different, and something less, than it does to Canada, Australia, and New Zealand; their membership, really though not formally, is on a different footing from that of those others whom one might, perhaps, call the "charter members." Not only did the Asian members arrive at membership by a different route, but it is noteworthy that their public statements on the Commonwealth underline strongly that full sovereignty is essential for the member nations. While this is sound doctrine, its enunciation with emphasis is somewhat *passé* in the older Dominions, which have realized for a generation or so that the principle is not in dispute. The emphasis on the limitation of the functions of the Commonwealth to providing opportunities for discussion and co-operation, the complete denial of its possession of any central authority, are a natural reflection of the recent emergence from dependent status and are largely dictated by internal political considerations. The same sensitivity, as has been noted in the preceding chapter, is for somewhat similar reasons to be observed among the dominant Afrikaners in South Africa.

[1] See discussion of this point below, pp. 479 ff.
It seems impossible to deal with the Commonwealth without some mention of terminology; which, unhappily, is not always used consistently, even in official contexts. The term "British Commonwealth" is no longer used by India, Pakistan, and Ceylon, which avoid the adjective, though it is still employed by the other members, and especially by Australia and New Zealand. A distinction is sometimes made between "Commonwealth" and "Empire," the former term being used to refer only to the fully self-governing units, the latter to dependent territories. Since this involves an invidious distinction, the preferred usage is now that "Commonwealth" is all-embracing. The useful term "Dominion" was dropping into desuetude even before it became clearly inapplicable to India. Now resort must be had to some such phrase as "member nations" or "sovereign members." A further difficulty is that no other modern language has any real equivalent for "Dominion" or "Commonwealth." French-Canadians are forced to speak inelegantly of "le Commonwealth" and "le Dominion." The scholars who devised the Latin version of the United Kingdom royal title in 1953, however, came up brilliantly with *Consortionis Populorum Princeps* for Head of the Commonwealth. On these and other like questions, which have a certain practical political importance, see S. A. de Smith's pamphlet *The Vocabulary of Commonwealth Relations* (London, 1954).

It is true, also, that Commonwealth membership for the Asian members is neither the determining element in foreign policy formation nor even a very important element, save perhaps for Ceylon. Yet in the case of all three countries the former British connection, continuing into the present most obviously but not solely in the form of Commonwealth membership, is a historic fact of primary importance. It continues in manifold ways to affect them, in some respects as a benefit, in others as a trauma. Into the alien soil of South Asia there were transplanted by Britain many habits, attitudes of mind, and political usages, ranging from an enthusiasm for drinking tea in the afternoon to the tradition of an incorruptible judiciary. How durable such plants will prove in their new soil cannot yet be determined; it is sufficient for our purpose here that they still survive, and in many cases flourish, though British rule in the subcontinent has ceased for almost a decade. Recent achievement of independence may lead to a heavy emphasis on the fact that British rule has been ended, and on the desirability of a similar release for all colonial peoples; it would be amazing if such views were not uttered. But what is interesting and significant is the degree of friendliness displayed (in the presence of criticism, of course) by the holders of power in India, Pakistan, and Ceylon toward their former rulers and the respect accorded to many elements of the British tradition. The carrying-over of so many elements characteristic of British politics into the political structures of these new nations is of great significance to the particular subject under discussion in this volume because, as we shall see, the constitutional processes of foreign policy formation in the Asian members of the Commonwealth do not differ substantially from those found in the United Kingdom, though they certainly operate in a vastly different social and political context.

The presence of Asian member nations in the Commonwealth is welcome and hopeful for many reasons which have little to do with British prestige or British influence. The function of the Commonwealth as a bridge is perhaps its most important characteristic at the present time. It is a bridge between European nations, or nations which had their origin in Europe, and nations

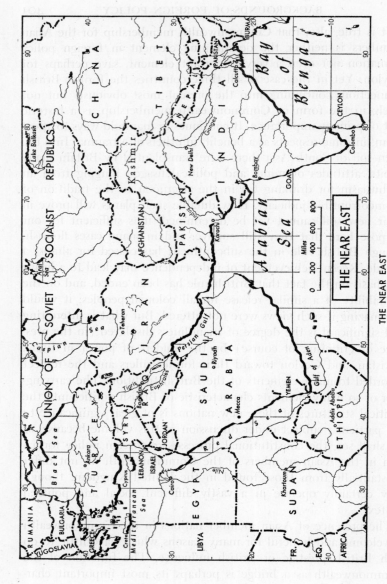

THE NEAR EAST

An area of emerging nationalisms and of difficult problems in international relations.

of the Orient; between white races and nonwhite; between European civilization, with its advanced technology and its concern for political democracy, and the ancient civilizations of the East, with their very different preoccupations.

The relationship between these two parts of the world has not so far been a very happy one. The role of Asia, as of Africa, has in recent centuries been mainly passive. It has been subject to the impact of European colonizing and mercantile activity; large areas, especially of South and Southeast Asia, have been held for long periods under European rule, with all that this implied in the way of social and economic discrimination. Only in recent decades have many peoples of Asia been able largely to free themselves from European domination and attempt to set up house for themselves.

In politics all Asian nations at the present time inevitably focus their attention on certain common themes. These are a lingering resentment—greater in some places than in others, but nowhere nonexistent—at the recent fact of colonial dependence; and a determination to end such conditions wherever they still exist. In economic policy attention is inevitably, and properly, centered on the undeveloped state of the economy. In such countries there is characteristically a large population subsisting almost entirely on a primitive agriculture. The crying need is obviously for more modern methods of agriculture and for industrialization; neither of which can be achieved without large capital expenditure.

The contrast with Europe and with countries settled by emigrants from Europe is glaring, and constitutes perhaps the most explosive fact in the world today. There is a natural tendency for the differences in historical experience and in economic development to be paralleled in political groupings. The Bandung Conference of Asian and African nations in April, 1955, was a sign of this. Such a situation lies open to Communist exploitation, and even without it would be potentially dangerous to the future of the world.

In so far as the Commonwealth tends to prevent the forming of a clear division between the ex-colonial Orient and the West, in so far as it blurs the edges or forms a liaison between the two

THE ASIAN MEMBERS

groups, it is of immense value in world politics. No other organization can attempt such a role except the United Nations, and the UN, unhappily, is all too often merely an arena where contending blocs augment their differences by voicing them. The Commonwealth, therefore, has a unique and helpful line of conduct to pursue as a reconciler and harmonizer between different parts of the world. It can pursue it actively through such schemes as the Colombo Plan, the Commonwealth-sponsored plan for economic development; it can also pursue it merely by existing, by providing a multitude of official and unofficial contacts, of occasions for friendly and confidential discussion in an atmosphere of trust, a family atmosphere.

Yet, while the Commonwealth can do something to mute or to smooth over differences of attitude between its European and its Asian parts, it would serve little purpose to deny that such differences exist. Professor Nicholas Mansergh, in his fascinating account of the Fifth Unofficial Commonwealth Relations Conference, held at Lahore, Pakistan, in March, 1954 (the first conference in the series to be held on Asian soil, itself a fact of import), has drawn attention to the significant differences which showed themselves in the discussions there. "In the last two decades the older European and the newer Asian members had been beset by different cares, preoccupied with different problems, oppressed by the thought of different dangers and seeking different ends, and one result was that the lessons they had learned from recent history were not the same." Here, then, is a fundamental factor in foreign policy formulation which sets apart the Asian members of the Commonwealth from the others.

For the European members, the experience now strongly present in their minds was the struggle against Nazi Germany and the lesson drawn was the necessity to unite in time to resist aggression, from whatever quarter it might threaten. In Asian minds, however,

what remained uppermost was the struggle to overthrow imperialism in the nineteen-thirties, its largely successful outcome in the nineteen-forties, and uncomfortable reminders from South East Asia that it was not yet ended. . . . They regarded the post-war struggle between the Communist and non-Communist world not indeed with any indifference but somewhat remotely. Perhaps as a consequence, they both hoped for, and were more inclined to seek, complete solutions to difficult questions and to analyse them in a perhaps more fundamental, but also less immediately realistic context.[2]

To speak of the struggle between Democracy and Communism in terms of right or wrong appeared to Asian participants in the conference "a presumptuous over-simplification." Such views as these here described were more strongly held by Indians than by Pakistanis or Ceylonese; a distinction which, as we shall see, is reflected in the divergencies between the foreign policies of the three countries.

The Power Position of India, Pakistan, and Ceylon

For India, Pakistan, and Ceylon, as for other countries, foreign policy is arrived at not by a completely free choice among an infinite number of possibilities; it is, rather, the resultant of a large number of forces of different kinds. Of these the most fundamental, the most unyielding, and the slowest to change are such factors as the geographical situation of the state; its population; and its economic situation and resources, developed and undeveloped. Together the factors of this kind act as fundamental determinants, creating a frame within which choices may be exercised, defining the power of the state or the lack of it, setting the limits of the possible.

Geography

Manifestly, the geographical factors are the most fundamental of all. They are subject to change to some minimal extent through such activities as the damming of rivers for irrigation purposes or the reclaiming of land from the sea, but at best these can affect the geographical situation of a country in only a small degree. The only other way in which a country's geography can be altered is through the large-scale gain or loss of territory. This can be impor-

[2] Nicholas Mansergh, *The Multi-Racial Commonwealth: Proceedings of the Fifth Unofficial Commonwealth Relations Conference* (London, 1955), pp. 137-138.

tant. It is improbable, for instance, that an independent but undivided India, occupying the same territory as the former Government of India in British hands, would have followed quite the same foreign policy as does the present Republic of India, which has Pakistan as a neighbor and in consequence does not have as neighbors Afghanistan or the tribes of the North-West Frontier. We shall have occasion to return to such considerations.

India, Pakistan, and Ceylon occupy an area which has a certain clearly defined geographical unity, with India and Pakistan constituting the mainland areas and Ceylon being, in a broad sense, an offshore island. The area occupied by India and Pakistan is generally called either the Indian Subcontinent or (to avoid offending Pakistan) the Indo-Pakistan Subcontinent. The question of nomenclature has its difficulties, since prior to 1947 the whole area could be described as "India," but after the creation of Pakistan "India" necessarily had a different and narrower meaning. There would appear to be something to be said for the adoption of the ancient Sanskrit term "Bharat" to refer to the whole area of India plus Pakistan, but it is as yet too little known to be generally useful.[3] Meanwhile the phrase "the subcontinent" is useful, and serves to draw attention to certain geographical features of the area. It is additionally helpful that no other area of the world of less than continental size seems to have a geographical unity sufficiently marked to earn the use of the phrase. Though a generic term, "subcontinent" is in practice specific. There is no other subcontinent, certainly none whose identity is so clearly established.

The subcontinent is roughly triangular in shape, with its apex pointing due south. The base of the triangle, however, is not a straight line, but is formed by the vast curve of a mountain wall, approaching the sea at the east and west ends of its course, and curving far to the north between. To the northeast the mountain wall is formed by the 1,500-mile long range of the Himalayas, the highest in the world. The mountains to the northwest are not so

[3] The government of India has further confused the issue by the assumption that "Bharat" is an alternative name for its territory. This is a very close analogy to the use for itself by the former Irish Free State of the name "Eire" or "Ireland," which turns a blind eye to the existence of Northern Ireland.

high, though still formidable. It might be argued that to seek the true geographical boundaries of the area at this point one would have to go farther north, to where the Hindu Kush range runs east and west and bisects Afghanistan.

Neither at the east nor at the west end of the northern barrier do the mountains quite come down to the sea; there is, however, a sufficiently clear natural boundary to the west in the deserts of Baluchistan. To the east the boundary is less distinct. Beyond the immense delta of the Ganges and Brahmaputra lie ranges of hills running north to south, and beyond them the valley of the Irrawaddy, the great river of Burma—which until 1937 was administered as part of India. To the south, of course, the limits of the subcontinent are framed by salt water. Thus, contained almost completely between very high mountains and the sea, the Indo-Pakistan area is indeed one clearly and strikingly defined. So difficult to traverse are the geographical limits that no railway line passes out of the subcontinent to any other area; and the old trade routes which lead through the mountains to the northeast climb over the highest passes in the world, open for only a month or two in midsummer.

These mountain barriers which set the northern limits of the subcontinent have never proved an absolutely effective safeguard against invasion. Indeed, all conquerors of India, with the exception of the European nations who arrived by sea from the sixteenth century onward, have come through the mountains, generally from the northwest. It is to the disadvantage of the inhabitants of the subcontinent that the mountains do not form a single chain, presenting equally difficult faces to north and south. They form rather the southern edge of a tangled plateau of immense size. Hence, it is easier to descend from the plateau to the fertile and attractive plains below than it is to proceed in the opposite direction. In order to lessen this condition of vulnerability any strong government that controls the north Indian plains has always sought to extend its power into the nearer parts of the mountain areas with the object of keeping them friendly, or at least of ensuring that they do not fall under the control of any other strong government. This was the typical British policy toward Afghanistan and Tibet:

the former under the domination of Russia, or the latter under the domination of China, would always be a potential threat to the security of the plains. The same considerations applied in regard to British relations with the lesser hill states—Nepal, Bhutan, Sikkim, and the others. Nor have these considerations ceased to be relevant for India and Pakistan. It is noteworthy, and ominous, that independent India, in the face of a strong China, has not been able to continue with success the British policy toward Tibet, which is now entirely under Chinese control.

The subcontinent falls into two great natural divisions. In the north lies a broad plain, roughly following the shape of the mountains and therefore forming an enormous arc. This is the area of the great river systems, the Indus in the west and the Ganges and Brahmaputra in the center and the east. They water a large alluvial plain which supports a high concentration of population. Population density reaches its highest at the eastern end, in East Bengal. South of the plain lies the plateau and mountain area known as the Deccan, which fills in the whole of the peninsula except for the fertile strips of the Malabar Coast, on the west, and the Coromandel Coast, on the east.

The internal geographical barriers within the subcontinent are not, however, important and have not, generally speaking, corresponded to any significant degree with political frontiers. In this India differs strikingly from Europe, to which it might otherwise well be compared, since the area of the subcontinent is approximately the same as that of Europe without Russia. Europe has a strongly articulated geography dividing it into a large number of separate regions which in a majority of cases have had separate national histories. The lack of important internal barriers in India has made the unification of the subcontinent under one government a natural objective for any rising power. The size of the area involved, however, is so great that a position of hegemony over the whole subcontinent has in fact been achieved only four times in history—by the Mauryas in the third century B.C., by the Guptas in the fourth century A.D., by the Moghuls in the sixteenth century, and by the British in the nineteenth. The factor of size probably had the result that British rule was the only one of the four that was actually effective in administering the whole from one center—and even the British never attempted to administer in detail the princely states.

Many factors other than size make even more difficult the achievement of the political unification that is suggested by geography. There is the immense racial diversity of the peoples of the subcontinent, speaking many languages. Sixteen languages are mentioned by name in the 1950 constitution of India, and there are innumerable dialects.[4] The peoples differ widely in social and cultural level. More serious still are the religious differences. These are more important politically than are religious differences in Europe. Europe is in any case all nominally Christian, of one branch or another. Religious differences in the subcontinent approximate the degree of bitterness and political significance which these things possessed in the Europe of the seventeenth century. It was religious differences which brought to an end the unification that British rule had achieved, and enforced the establishment of two independent states, India and Pakistan, instead of one.

The position which the three countries—India, Pakistan, and Ceylon—occupy in South Asia is central and strategic in every sense. If one looks at the globe with the Jovian eye of a Mackinder, one sees that just as Europe projects three peninsulas (the Iberian, the Italian, and the Graeco-Balkan) southward into the Mediterranean, so on a much larger scale does Asia project southward into the Indian Ocean the Arabian, the Indian and the Malayan peninsulas. The position of the Indian peninsula is such that its rulers are bound to look both east and west. On the left-hand side of the map lie the countries of the Middle East (or, as the Indian government has lately begun to call it, West Asia), stretching from the Mediterranean coasts of Egypt and Turkey to West Pakistan. To the east are the countries of Indo-China.

[4] However, twelve languages constitute the mother tongues of more than 95 per cent of the population. Hindi is easily first in the number of those who speak it, 140 million; the other major languages, in order of numbers of speakers, are: Telegu, Marathi, Tamil, Bengali, Gujerati, Kanarese, Malayalam, Oriya, Rajasthani, Punjabi, and Assamese.

Both of these regions on the flanks of the subcontinent are tempting areas for expansion from the north, and both (apart from the new Turkey) lack intrinsic strength. The Middle East, particularly Iran, is a target for Russian probing. On the other flank penetration and conquest by the Chinese Communists have proceeded far in the past decade, and constitute one of the most menacing situations in the world today. The threats to these areas from Russian and Chinese imperialism long antedated communism, however, being inherent in the geopolitical situation, and may well survive it. There were Russian aspirations for a foothold on the Persian Gulf under the Czars; and the Chinese Empire, in its times of greatest expansion, has always included Indo-China within its area of suzerainty.

Certain grave and essential differences, however, mark the situation today. In the nineteenth and the early twentieth century, China was weak, being involved in the last phases of the decay of the Manchu dynasty and later in revolution and civil war. Her power over Indo-China, as over Tibet, was only a matter of historical reminiscence. Russia, too, was not possessed of the power she now has. But more important was the fact that the weakness and vulnerability of the Middle East and Indo-China were countered by the existence of a center of strength in British-held India. There the resources of a world power were employed, economically but coolly and consistently, to maintain the security of the subcontinent and its contiguous areas.

The problem has changed for the worse, and it is to be feared also that the resources to meet it are in sum greatly less and for a variety of reasons are not fully available or fully employed. Even a united but independent India would certainly have had much less power at its disposal than the Indian Empire of the British. In fact, however, the Indian Empire had not one, but two successor states. A politically divided subcontinent is bound to be much weaker than a united one; and the resources of India and Pakistan, far from being jointly employed to deal with the problem of their common security, have been largely employed in keeping watch over each other. Moreover, Pakistan lacks a unified national territory; she exists in two blocks sundered by a thousand miles of

India—a situation so anomalous that it is difficult to think of any parallel in history.[5]

India, by far the larger and stronger of the two states, is much the less inclined to recognize that any threat to the security of the subcontinent exists. This attitude is partly ideological, partly religious in its basis; it is reinforced, as Professor Mansergh pointed out in the passage quoted earlier, by certain ingrained ways of looking at the world which are a result of the recent history of the country.

The adoption of the Indian attitude is also, no doubt, made easier by the fact that the two wings of Pakistan, situated at the western and eastern edges of the subcontinent, are in some sense a buffer between the Republic of India and the regions to west and east. Any threat from the direction of the Middle East is necessarily a threat in the first place to Pakistan, and only secondarily to India, since West Pakistan lies between India on the one side and Iran and Afghanistan on the other. On the eastern side of the subcontinent, though it is true that Assam belongs to India and that therefore both East Pakistan and India have frontiers which march with Burma's, nevertheless Assam is a somewhat remote state, connected to the main territory of India only by a narrow neck of land round the north of East Pakistan; its importance to India cannot be compared with the vital importance to Pakistan of its eastern portion, which contains more than half the country's population and is also of crucial importance economically.

Conversely, for Pakistan geography operates to enforce on her a positive policy to which in any case she would probably tend for other basic reasons. Her position forces her to be, willy-nilly, the bulwark of the subcontinent to both east and west and to assume

[5] In Europe territorial enclaves have, of course, at various times been common, particularly in Germany. But in these cases the distances involved were so small that there is only a weak analogy to the situation of a state whose two halves are at the closest points as remote from one another as London is from Budapest, or Miami from New York. Also, Pakistan enjoys no transit facilities like the special road, rail, and telephone privileges which Poland afforded Germany for communication across Polish territory with East Prussia in the period 1919-1939. India is not interested in making the situation easy for Pakistan or in assisting Pakistan to demonstrate its viability; rather the reverse.

responsibilities for which her resources are, in fact, much less adequate than those of India. She has pursued a more positive policy than has India in the sense that, instead of espousing "nonalignment," she has actually joined in regional alliances and thus forms a part of the free world's security system. Her peculiar geography is reflected in the fact that her alliances comprise both groupings looking to the security of the Middle East and membership in the South East Asia Treaty Organization, which concerns itself with the safeguarding of Indo-China and the region of the western Pacific.

India, Pakistan, and Ceylon occupy an important strategic position, not only from the point of view of possible military threats or Communist infiltration on land but also from the point of view of air and sea communications. The great route from Western Europe by way of the Mediterranean, Suez, Ceylon, and Singapore to China and Japan or Australia has customarily been thought of as a route of importance to the British Empire, but in fact it has a much broader significance. It is one of the main traveled roads of the world. It must always remain the principal sea route from Europe to the Far East, quite independent of whether or not the bases on the route are in British hands. Its importance remains constant in the air age, because even if the political conditions were favorable, which they are not, no airline is ever likely to choose a route which bypasses the great population centers of the south coast of Asia in favor of the Tibetan plateau—the "Roof of the World"—and the wastes of the Gobi Desert.

Thus these three countries sit astride one of the world's greatest routes, and it is of crucial importance to the rest of the world whether or not they are willing to afford facilities for air and sea transportation, not to mention the even more vital matter of military bases. One or two instances may illustrate the significance of their situation. During the Second World War, when Allied forces were driven out of Singapore and Indo-China, it was in Ceylon that combined headquarters for the whole of Southeastern Asia were set up. During the troubles in the Netherlands East Indies, the Indian government showed an awareness of the strategic importance of its territory by denying landing facilities to Dutch aircraft on their way to Indonesia. Also it is of some consequence to the free world as a whole that Britain, by special agreement with an independent Ceylon, has so far been able to maintain air and sea bases in the island, and thus continue at least in some measure to play her historic role of preserving the peace and security of the Indian Ocean.

It was said above that the Middle East and Indo-China had been exposed at earlier times to Russian and Chinese imperialism respectively. This is the case; yet it is in the context of the world struggle against the Communist menace to free societies that the strategic situation of India, Pakistan, and Ceylon takes on its present quality of urgency. In recent years world attention has focused to an increasing degree on this area, and it is easy to see that there are good and sufficient reasons why this should be so. Relative to Europe, Asia is rising in the scale of world importance, and no part of Asia has a future role so important, and at the same time so uncertain, as these three countries. With the strengthening of defenses in Europe through NATO and other means, the crucial region in the world struggle between communism and Western democratic society appears more and more to be Asia, and it is here that communism has scored its greatest successes—indeed, its only successes. China has a Communist government, and a large part of Indo-China has fallen to the Communists. If communism should meet with further success in that area, it is obvious that the next objective would be the neighboring region of the Indian subcontinent. On the other hand, to take the more optimistic view, if the spread of communism in Asia is to be halted, it is most likely to be through the example of the successful working of democratic institutions in strong and free Asian nations. If India, Pakistan, and Ceylon can give such an example, they are so centrally placed that beneficial results will flow throughout the rest of Asia, with advantage to the whole of the free world.

The question which naturally follows is that of the capacity of these countries to deal with the situation in which geography and history have placed them. In other words, what is their power? Geographical location, which we have been discussing, is in itself one element in power—the example of Britain clearly demonstrates the point. In a given geographical setting, however, other elements may cause weakness or strength, and it is axiomatic that, to be successful, a foreign policy must be a function of the strength of the country concerned. Commitments and policies beyond one's strength are a sure road to disaster. Less common—though seen in the history of the United States—is the failure to frame a policy sufficiently positive to match the national power. This leaves the game in the hands of others and is likely to exact greater exertions later. The assessment of national power is an intricate matter, in which it is possible to consider a multiplicity of aspects; some, however, such as size, population, and economic strength, are obviously primary.

Population

Even with Pakistan subtracted, India is the second most important state in Asia (presuming that Asiatic Russia is excluded), coming next after China. The area of China is certainly considerably greater, and the population probably so.[6] Nevertheless, the population of India is very large: it was 357 million at the census of 1951, and, since it increases at a rate of between 4 and 5 million a year, probably approximates 380 million in 1956. In combination with other factors, this makes India easily the most important non-Communist country in Asia, and a real rival to China for leadership of the continent. China and India stand as symbols of alternative and rival approaches to the basic problem of achieving economic development. The dilemmas being tackled in the one by a Communist government and in the other by a parliamentary democracy are similar. This implicit competition is being watched by Asian opinion.

Population provides India with the basic necessity of an ample labor supply, indeed somewhat of an embarrassment of riches in that respect; but many of the workmen are highly skilled artisans

[6] Mr. Colin Clark, the eminent economist, has thrown severe doubt on the over 500 million population claimed by the present Communist government of China. It is unlikely that China possesses the means to take an accurate census, and highly improbable that, if they took it, they would communicate the results accurately to the world. The Indian figures, on the other hand, are reasonably accurate.

and, given a degree of help through the introduction of machinery, the labor force might become a producer of wealth on a large scale.

In the two parts of Pakistan population and area are not consistently distributed. West Pakistan, with 307,000 square miles as against East Pakistan's 54,000, is easily the larger in area, but in population the case is reversed: according to the 1951 census, West Pakistan's population was 34 million, and East Pakistan's 42 million. The total of approximately 76 million, though only about one-fifth that of India, still makes Pakistan one of the world's more populous states. Her population is a little less than one-half that of the United States, but almost exactly one-and-one-half times that of the United Kingdom. It places Pakistan first in point of population among those countries that are predominantly Muslim.[7]

Beside such figures the area and population of Ceylon are small. Its area of 25,332 square miles is about the same as that of West Virginia or the Republic of Ireland, and slightly less than that of Portugal. Its population of 8 million at the 1953 census is almost the same as that of Australia; among the component members of the Commonwealth only New Zealand has a smaller population.

In considering population figures, it is important to bear in mind not only present figures but the rate of growth, since this factor has an obvious bearing on the probable trend in the standard of living. The annual percentage increase in population in India and Pakistan appears to be somewhat under 1.5, which is distinctly lower than the current high figure in the United States, 1.7; nevertheless, in the very different economic situation of the subcontinent, population increase poses grave problems. The rate of increase in Ceylon is a high one, 2.51 per cent.

Economy

The economies of India, Pakistan, and Ceylon, like the economies of almost all countries in Asia and Africa, are undeveloped relative to the industrialized economies typical of Europe and North America. The standard of living is therefore in general low, and conditions of extreme poverty are the rule rather than the

[7] Indonesia is a rival claimant to this title.

exception. None of the three countries in question is actually among the very poorest in the world in terms of standard of living, but they are fairly far down the list. The average real income per head in India is slightly higher than that in Pakistan. Ceylon is in a distinctly better position. It may be bracketed with Japan, Malaya, the Philippines, and Hong Kong as among the most prosperous of Asian communities.

Extreme dependence on agriculture is characteristic of the economies of these countries, and in the cases of India and Pakistan the agriculture is generally of a very primitive kind, wasteful of resources and unproductive. The situation in India is aggravated by the Hindu religious attitude toward the cow, which cannot be slaughtered and thus, though it exists in immense numbers, contributes little to the food supply. In all three countries rural life is the norm, over four-fifths of the population living outside of cities, in innumerable villages. The proportion of literacy in India and Pakistan is low;[8] the governments are taking strenuous measures to raise it.

Among these countries India is easily first in regard to the possession of heavy industries, and therefore comes nearest to possessing the essential industrial basis for being an important power. She cannot compare, however, in point of industrialization with Japan, whose recent history is unique in Asia. There are two considerable industrial concentrations in India, one in and around Calcutta on the east coast and the other on the west centering on Bombay and Ahmadabad. The Tata works, at Jamshedpur, 150 miles from Calcutta, the greatest Indian iron and steel concern, are responsible for more than two-thirds of the Indian output of steel ingots and castings, which in recent years has been pushed up to about 1½ million tons a year—probably more than is produced by China, certainly more than is produced by any other Asian country except Japan, but less than one-fiftieth of the output of the United States. The basis for a vast iron and steel industry is certainly present. The estimated reserves of iron ore in India are twice as great as

[8] Around 10 to 15 per cent in India and Pakistan; in Ceylon 53 per cent in the local languages, 6 per cent in English.

those of either the United States or Canada and are exceeded only by those of Brazil.

The other great pillar of industrial strength is coal. Here, too, India is quite well off. Her annual production is around 30 million tons—about one-sixth that of the United Kingdom, but still a large figure, about two-thirds that of France—and there are large reserves.

The chief industry in the Calcutta area is the spinning and weaving of jute; in the Bombay area, the spinning and weaving of cotton. In both areas, however, there is a tremendous variety of factories and mills of all sorts carrying on a wide range of light industries.

The future development of Indian industry poses many questions, not the least of them being the effect of government policy toward it. The Indian government is strongly influenced by leveling ideas, and on the whole seems likely to become more and more unfriendly toward private capital and especially toward the great concentrations of wealth in a few hands which have hitherto been typical of Indian society. The wealthy are already being subject to heavy progressive income taxes. Government intervention in the economic field also takes place over a wide range. Such conditions are not those most likely to create the developing economic activity and the rapid increase in the production of wealth which India needs if the standard of living is even to remain stable in face of the population increase, let alone be raised. The same discouraging features are seen in the Indian government's attitude toward foreign capital. Recognitions of the need for foreign capital to finance development are strangely mingled with general denunciations and vague threats of confiscation. It is not surprising that the foreign investor has in general shrugged his shoulders and looked elsewhere for a return on his money. The foreign capital which has been made available to India in recent years has almost all come from official sources.

Pakistan has much less industry than India, heavy or light. The territories allocated to the new nation in 1947 were, in fact, precisely the least developed industrially of the subcontinent. Had

Pakistan been awarded the whole of an unpartitioned Bengal, as the late M. A. Jinnah, Pakistan's creator, at first hoped it would be, there would be a different tale to tell. Pakistan would then have had the Calcutta industrial complex (though not the Tata works, which are in Bihar), including the Asansol coal field. As it is, Pakistan possesses an economy almost entirely dependent on primary products: the cotton, wheat, rice, and sugar cane of West Pakistan and the jute, tobacco, and tea of East Pakistan. The partition of Bengal in 1947 between India and Pakistan had one important economic consequence in that the jute supply was in a different country from the jute mills of Calcutta; and for several years political considerations led India to dam the obvious course of trade.

By far the most important elements in Pakistan's economy are the two chief export crops, cotton and jute, which between them constitute almost three-quarters of the value of her total exports. Despite this unsatisfactory dependence on two fiber crops, Pakistan has been on the whole more prosperous than it was thought by many in 1947 that she could possibly be. It is in her favor that she has a world monopoly of high-quality jute production. In September, 1949, when sterling was devalued, Pakistan felt able to refrain from following the other members of the sterling area, and in consequence the Pakistani rupee was at a premium relative to the Indian rupee (to India's annoyance) until August, 1955, when Pakistan fell into line. The Korean War, by stimulating greatly the demand for raw materials, gave Pakistan two and a half years of somewhat illusory prosperity. The artificial demand had begun to disappear by the beginning of 1953, and the government of Pakistan was forced to take vigorous economy measures.[9] The next few years saw Pakistan's economy again on a more even keel, though undoubtedly her dependence on two export crops was extreme and made her economically vulnerable. It is also a weakness that she possesses only two harbors, Karachi and Chittagong,

[9] Including, it is interesting to note here, a somewhat unusual one in the replacement of the ambassadors in Madrid, Peking, Rio de Janeiro and Tokyo, and of the high commissioner in Colombo, by mere chargés d'affaires (who were cheaper). *New York Times*, May 16, 1953.

and only the former is first-class. Pakistan's known and accessible mineral resources are poor, though she may prove to have undeveloped wealth of that kind. She produces a bare half million tons of coal a year, and there does not seem much possibility of any important increase. Only in the development of hydroelectric power and of the recently discovered deposits of natural gas is there any likelihood of finding from native resources the power requirements of modern industry. Nevertheless, despite all handicaps, industrialization is being vigorously pushed forward to provide the country with a better balanced economy. Textiles are now being manufactured on a considerable scale. Krupps is building in Pakistan a steel mill capable of dealing with the low-grade ore available.

Ceylon's economy, like that of Pakistan, depends overwhelmingly on a few basic products, of which the most important, of course, is her tea. Tea accounts for almost half of Ceylon's total exports. Rubber accounts for another 30 per cent. As with all primary products, tea and rubber are subject to rather violent world price fluctuations; nevertheless, on the whole, the island is prosperous. Unlike India and Pakistan, it is at all times heavily dependent on food imports; food, drink, and tobacco amount to almost one-half of all imports, rice alone being almost one-quarter of the total. There are no important manufactures or mineral resources.

In summing up the economic basis of the strength of India, Pakistan, and Ceylon as states, that is, as units in international politics, it must be said that there is a tremendous work of development still to be done. To realize their potential they need to find, somewhere, both a great deal of capital for development and an immense increment both of skilled labor and of professional knowledge. Knowledge of the techniques which could increase their wealth is as yet not nearly widely enough dispersed throughout their populations. Unfortunately, this kind of knowledge— knowledge of engineering, of mining, of medicine—is the kind which the populations of the subcontinent have so far shown themselves least anxious to acquire. Literary education enjoys a higher prestige than even the most advanced education of a practical cast, and it has been the misfortune of these countries in recent decades, a misfortune both political and economic, to have an oversupply of university graduates with a predominantly literary or legal training, for whom there were all too often no professional opportunities, and at the same time a scarcity of entrants into professions whose services their countries badly needed. Such a situation is common to many countries emerging, or recently emerged, from colonial status.

On the credit side of the ledger, India, Pakistan, and Ceylon have certain advantages worth noting. As a result of British rule they acquired much of the material equipment of modern states. Among the many public works built under the British regime two kinds were particularly important, the railways and the canals. The irrigation schemes, mostly in the Punjab, are the greatest in the world. Today they serve both India and Pakistan—and are one of the subjects of dispute between them.[10] The railroads, unequaled in Asia, brought to the subcontinent an effective unity that it never had before. After partition, the territory of India included 34,000 miles of track,[11] that of Pakistan 6,682 miles (5,062 in West Pakistan, 1,620 in East Pakistan). Ceylon has 913 miles. It is also of advantage economically as well as politically that they inherited administrative systems whose efficiency and integrity place them far above the Asian average. In India and Ceylon administration carried on without any break at the transfer of power; in Pakistan, of course, a new structure had to be improvised, but there was a considerable carry-over in personnel from the former regime, and the beneficial influence of the administrative tradition on the new state is an important reality.

Religious Influences on Foreign Policy

In a survey of the foundations of foreign policy in the three Commonwealth members in Asia, at any rate in India and Pakistan, one must certainly consider religion among the fundamentals. Geography and economics determine the limits of the possible,

[10] See page 483.
[11] It is of some interest that the figure for the whole USSR is no more than 57,487 miles.

but religion has a bearing on the general spirit of policy and also shapes attitudes toward certain specific questions. It is a significant element; but also one whose precise significance is difficult to define.

Before going on to discuss the significance of religion in policy, it may be well to describe the distribution of the different religions. The large majority of the population of the subcontinent are Hindus, but there are substantial minorities. In the pre-partition India of 1941, the census reported approximately 255 million Hindus to 94 million Muslims, and some 40 million following other faiths. When an independent India and an independent Pakistan were set up in 1947, the ruling principle was to include in each state the contiguous areas which had, respectively, Hindu or Muslim majorities. But, though religion was the basis of the division, the new states are far from being homogeneous in a religious sense, and each contains a large minority of the other major religion. In the Republic of India, according to the 1951 census, there are 303 million Hindus and 35 million Muslims, as well as over 8 million Christians, over 6 million Sikhs,[12] and almost 2 million Jains. In Pakistan, out of a total population in 1951 of almost 76 million, 12.9 per cent, or approximately 10 million, were Hindus, and 0.7 per cent, or about half a million, were Christians. In Ceylon the predominant creed is the tolerant religion of Buddha, now quite unimportant numerically in India, the land of its birth. The Buddhists in the island number over 5 million. There are also roughly 1½ million Hindus, half a million Muslims, and three-quarters of a million Christians.

There is something of a paradox in the relationship of India and Pakistan to the question of religion. On the one hand, both profess to provide complete freedom of religion. The Congress Party, which after 1947 became the ruling party in an independent India, never regarded itself as being representative only of Hindu

[12] Sikhism might be described summarily as a kind of Hindu Protestantism; and, like Protestantism, founded in the sixteenth century. It is a monotheistic and martial religion whose tenets in some ways resemble Islam. Sikhs are found mostly in the Punjab. In the undivided, pre-1947 Punjab they were politically important. Since then, lacking skilled leadership, they have been much less so. At partition the Sikhs of the West Punjab mostly fled east, to India.

India, but claimed to be the spokesman for all the peoples and religions of the subcontinent. To underline this claim Muslim members of Congress were frequently elected to high offices in it, including the presidency. In this, however, there was something of the wish being father to the thought, something of façade; the hope was always to deny the right of the Muslim League to anything like equal status with Congress as representative of a large community, to claim that there was no need for the Muslim League (or, later, for Pakistan) to exist at all.

The Congress leaders were consistent in that when they came to frame a constitution for an independent India they made it the constitution of a secular state, without a state rĕligion and without privileges for any one religion. Articles 25 and 26 of the constitution adopted in 1950 are devoted to provisions intended to secure that "all persons are equally entitled to freedom of conscience and the right freely to profess, practise and propagate religion," with certain provisos which in principle are not objectionable, such as that "Nothing in this article shall . . . prevent the State from making any law (a) regulating or restricting any economic, financial, political or other secular activity which may be associated with religious practice . . ."

Without in any way questioning the sincerity of these legal provisions, it may be pointed out that for our purpose it remains important that India is a country primarily, though not exclusively, inhabited by Hindus; that, for instance, whatever the wishes of the Indian government, the forces of communalism remain so strong that it is rather unlikely that any Muslim in India will henceforward emerge into political eminence, except perhaps locally as a leader of Muslims. Muslims are already less prominent in both the police and the army. To create a secular state in a part of the world whose modes of thought have not hitherto been secular will not be easy. Indian nationalism, after all, though it involved the participation of some Muslims, was mostly a Hindu phenomenon. Its political form and its tone were both shaped by the Hindu middle classes, and its technique was based on the tenets of Hindu religion. The present government of India is the Congress Party writ large; the things that were true of it before independence are, despite necessary changes, for the most part still true of it. Its distinctive attitude toward questions of foreign policy, for instance, is, even if not invariably adopted, basically an attitude arising out of the Hindu religion.

Pakistan was intended, by its founder at least, to be a state which would not accord any special privileges to Muslims. Mr. Jinnah was not an orthodox Muslim, and in the earlier part of his life he was regarded as an opponent of Muslim political aspirations. Through- out his life he resembled an English gentleman a good deal more than he did an orthodox member of the Faithful. His emphasis always was on the difference of Islam from Hinduism as a total way of life—affecting questions of law, speech, dress, and food, and therefore justifying the claim that the Muslim community in India was a separate nation—rather than on religion in a strict sense. His ideals for the state he had founded were enunciated clearly in his address to the Constituent Assembly of Pakistan on August 11, 1947:

You are free: you are free to go to your temples, you are free to go to your mosques or to any other place of worship in this State of Pakistan. You may belong to any religion or caste or creed—that has nothing to do with the fundamental principle that we are all citizens and equal citizens of one State. . . .[13]

Since the death of Mr. Jinnah, in 1948, there has appeared more of a tendency in the politics of Pakistan to emphasize the Muslim character of the state. Pakistanis reject the implication that the state is heading toward being a theocracy, chiefly on the technical ground that this implies the rule of a priesthood, while Islam has no formal priesthood; in the broader sense, however, there is some reason to suggest that the danger is there.[14] On the whole, the discrimination against Hindus in Pakistan, particularly in East Bengal, since 1947, has been more marked than the converse discrimination against the Muslims in India.

To a certain extent the emphasis on Islam in Pakistan is under- standable, and it was only to be expected that Pakistan would be

[13] Hector Bolitho, *Jinnah: Creator of Pakistan* (London, 1954), p. 197.
[14] On the constitution of Pakistan, see pages 456 ff.

more self-conscious and self-assertive on this point than India. In
a sense it follows inevitably from the fact that Pakistan is the
smaller and less secure country of the two and cannot afford to
accept its own existence so unself-consciously as India can hers.
Pakistan came into existence only because her people (or rather
the politically articulate part of them) strenuously asserted their
separateness and their right to national existence. Separate sovereignty was achieved, but not easily; nor has its maintenance been
easy. Of that separate national existence Islam is the justification,
the badge, and the cement. It is small wonder if it continues to be
emphasized, sometimes at the expense of that completely fair
treatment of members of the other religion for which Mohammed
Ali Jinnah pleaded.

The two great religions of the subcontinent certainly differ
profoundly in almost every imaginable aspect. To the western
mind, Hinduism seems so complex and difficult of definition that
it presents the aspect less of one religion than of a congeries of
religions. It is customary to distinguish between religions, or sects
of the same religion, under the three categories of dogma, methods
of church government, and ritual. What is one to say of a religion
which offers a great variety of supernatural beings for worship
according to the preference of the believer, which has no general
ecclesiastical organization nor any set pattern of ritual? The Hindu
gods are all regarded as aspects of one fundamental reality,
Brahman, which is represented on the highest level in the hierarchy of deities by the trinity of Brahma, the Creator; Vishnu,
the Preserver; and Shiva, the Destroyer. All these have wives, and
Vishnu and Shiva have many incarnations; one of the most popular deities is the attractive Krishna, the eighth avatar, or reincarnation, of Vishnu. Below all these there is an immense proliferation
of lesser gods and supernatural beings. Hinduism thus is capable of
being approached at any intellectual level and may be appre-
hended in any manner, from the austere intellectual belief in an
absolute monism to the propitiation of his local river-god by the
simple peasant. It multiplies the mystery of the Christian trinity
by finding room for a whole pantheon of deities who are yet, in
advanced thought, in some sense one. Hinduism is the most an-

cient, as well as the most amorphous, of all religions. It has no
known beginning, and its complexity and facility in reconciling
opposites appear to be due to the present survival side by side of
all stages of its development. It follows that it is, in the main, a
religion of tolerance, which regards diversity as inevitable and does
not hold up uniformity even as an ideal. This remains true as a
generalization despite the existence of extremist cults, including
some which believe in violence, and of some sporadic attempts at
proselytizing.

Two characteristic parts of Hinduism must be mentioned in
even the briefest account. One is the belief in reincarnation. At
death every creature, human or otherwise, is immediately reborn
in a higher or lower form. His status in the new life depends on
karma, that is, on the balance of his good and evil actions in all
previous existences. By good actions one can gradually win one's
way upward to an eventual release from the cycle of birth and
death in nirvana. Even the best lives, however, have only an asymp-
totic relation to nirvana: in practice the object is to secure for
oneself a more tolerable level in the next life.

The second point is the caste system. Hinduism is a philosophy
and a social system as well as a religion, and the caste system is the
social corollary of the belief in the transmigration of souls. Human
beings are not equal, but are differentiated even at the moment of
birth by different qualities of spirit and mind deriving from all
their past experiences. The caste system recognizes these differences by dividing humanity into different groups with different
functions. Originally there were four castes, of whom the highest,
the Brahmins, are the priestly caste; below them come the war-
riors, merchants, and laborers; at the bottom, and outside of the
original system, are the outcastes or untouchables. The original
scheme has been subdivided into innumerable gradations, and the
original association of a particular caste with a particular social
function is largely ignored.

Over against the easygoing ambiguities of Hinduism stand the
hard, clear certainties of Islam. It was founded at a known time in
a certain place: by the prophet Mohammed at Mecca in Arabia in
the seventh century A.D. Mohammed is not a deity but, to Muslims,

the last and greatest of the prophets. Islam preaches an unqualified monotheism and is dogmatic and aggressive, recognizing a duty to spread what it regards as the only truth. Unlike Hinduism, it regards all forms of image-making and statuary with abhorrence. It is also, unlike Hinduism, essentially a democratic creed, preaching equality among all human beings and the brotherhood of man.

Along with the religious tenets there has grown up a body of Islamic law, common to many Middle Eastern countries, which regulates the affairs of life in some detail. Thus, like Hinduism, Islam is a social system as well as a religion, though one of a markedly different kind.

Both systems of thought and belief are so all-pervasive in their effect on life that it is certainly more relevant to consider their role in the shaping of foreign policy in India and Pakistan than it would be, say, to consider the role of Christianity in shaping the foreign policy of a contemporary European nation. In the latter case, it would presumably be so small as to be hardly discoverable—and not only in Nazi Germany. We have a potent illustration of the political influence of religion in the subcontinent, though it dates from before Partition, in the extraordinary career of Mohandas K. Gandhi (1869-1948), for which it is impossible to imagine any analogue in the secular atmosphere of contemporary Europe. Essentially his achievement was that he made saintliness effective in politics, and through his tremendous personal prestige and influence imposed on the Congress the method of nonviolent resistance to authority which was in conformity with the profoundest Hindu beliefs. Jawaharlal Nehru regarded himself as a disciple of Gandhi, and indeed the Mahatma's authority over the Indian masses, which he used always to inculcate brotherly love and minimize passion and violence, was so great that it was not confined to the Hindu community, but was felt also among the Muslims.

The influence of the Hindu religion on the foreign policy of India, and of the Moslem religion on the foreign policy of Pakistan, must be discussed in two contexts. Of these the first, the more important arena for this kind of influence, is that of international relations *within the subcontinent*. When we think of the foreign

policy of this or that country we are all too likely to think of it in
relation to the world-wide power struggle between communism
and democracy, or to membership of the Commonwealth, or some
such world-wide question. This is not necessarily how countries
themselves see their own foreign policy. Probably for India, and
certainly for Pakistan, the questions in foreign relations that at the
moment really cause anxiety, really exercise thought in Delhi and
Karachi, are the questions arising out of relationship with the other
country, the neighbor in the subcontinent. This is not a happy
state of affairs; but it would be idle to deny that it is the condition
which actually exists.

In this mutual relationship of the two parts of formerly undivided India there is a hostility, or at the best a latent or potential
hostility, in which religious differences are a big factor. The
Hindu-Muslim antagonism which every now and then in the days
of British India, and immediately after Partition, flared into riots
and bloodshed has now a formalized structure in the relationship
of two states. When the holders of power in Delhi think of
Pakistan, their attitude is not a purely *political* resentment against
those who prevented the coming into being of an India united as
well as independent. This attitude is inevitably mixed up with
thoughts and prejudices stemming from the religious difference.
Similarly, when the holders of power in Karachi think of their
neighbors, they think of those who tried to deny nationhood to
the Islamic element in the Indian population. Time may ameliorate this smoldering enmity, but, since there are three or four
unresolved quarrels still on the carpet, its healing influence can
hardly be said to have begun to work.

When we turn to the relations of India and Pakistan with areas
outside the subcontinent, we cannot trace the influence of religion
with quite such certainty, but still it is not entirely absent. It would
not appear to be merely a coincidence that, just as Islam is a
religion clearer and more comprehensible to the West than Hinduism, so also is the foreign policy of Pakistan in Western eyes simpler and more straightforward. The Hindu habit of mind is invo-
luted, subtle, given to the reconcilement of opposites. Would it
be too unkind to say that to many critics in Europe and North

America the same characteristics are to be seen in the foreign policy of India? Or that the foreign policy of Pakistan seems to be a matter of facing choices straightforwardly and stripping things down to essentials in the manner of Islam? The generalizations are, at the least, tempting.

There is also, it would seem, a contrast which at bottom stems from the different character of the two religions in their attitude toward power and its problems. Hinduism holds suspect the taking of a positive part, involving action, for to that religion all temporal phenomena are essentially illusory and transitory. The taking of action is more likely to lead to harm than not. Violence, in particular, as Gandhi taught, is an evil, even if used for a good cause. Now, while it would not do to push the connection of this doctrine with Indian foreign policy very far—India, after all, has not noticeably shrunk from using military force inside the subcontinent—the Hindu attitude toward the use of force is consistent with India's deploring of "power politics" and repudiation of alliance systems, consistent also with her attempts to effect a reconciliation between the Communist countries and the democracies. By way of contrast, Pakistan foreign policy, like the religion of Mohammed, has had a positive character. Pakistan has in the end not shrunk from committing herself, and has chosen to cast in her lot with the democracies. There is here a profound contrast in the policy toward the external world of the two governments; and, though the contrast is at least in part explicable on other grounds than religion, it would seem undeniable that basic religious differences of attitude have played their part in creating the contrast.

One may note also in passing that religion has played a part in the framing of Pakistan's policy in the further sense that she has been conscious of her position as the largest of Islamic nations. She has supported the Arabs against Israel, and the Moroccan nationalists against France, in the United Nations. There seems little doubt that she would like to be recognized as in some sense the leader of the Islamic states. Pan-Islam, however, is a political concept which, though much written about, has hardly had much more contact with reality than Pan-Christianity. Pakistan has not

so far succeeded in winning from her Islamic neighbors any recognition, however vague, of precedence. With the nearest of them,
indeed—with Afghanistan—she is on the worst of terms. Her
friendliest relations in this area are with Turkey, which for a
quarter of a century has been the most deliberately secular of
states, though the population is Islamic. It may well be, however,
that when Pakistan has settled her constitutional questions and
demonstrated her stability she will find it easier to assert that
predominance within Islam to which she feels her size entitles her.

The Historical Background of the Present Situation

There is much in the history of India, even in remote periods,
that is still potent in shaping attitudes and determining policies.
It is not irrelevant to the rivalries of today that from the eighth to
the eighteenth century Muslims dominated Hindu populations
over much of the subcontinent. We cannot discount as unimportant, even today, the whole extraordinary process whereby a trading
company, the East India Company, with its base in a relatively
small island many thousands of miles away, became the dominating power over all India. Later, the bitterness caused on both
sides by the event known in British history as the Indian Mutiny,
1857, was a legacy whose effect has not yet expired. It was also
significant for future social and political developments that in the
British view Muslims bore the greater responsibility for the mutiny.
Consequently, there was for the next two decades a discrimination
against them and in favor of the Hindus which was one of the
reasons why, when new opportunities for advancement opened up
for Indians in commerce, in education, and in the public service,
they were utilized primarily by Hindus.

For practical purposes, however, we must forgo consideration of
the remoter antecedents of the current situation and render account only of those events from the later nineteenth century
onward which pointed toward the eventual achievement of Indian
independence. Such a culmination of British rule in India had,
however, been anticipated by many of the ablest administrators
even as early as the first quarter of the nineteenth century—that

is, from the very time when British control of the subcontinent was becoming substantially complete and long before there was any nationalist resistance to foreign rule in India. It is fairly well known that Macaulay, speaking in Parliament in 1833, had contemplated "some future age" when India would have attained self-government on the European model. "Whether such a day will ever come I know not, but never will I attempt to avert or to retard it. Whenever it comes, it will be the proudest day in English history." Less well known, perhaps, is Munro's remark of 1824: "If we pursue steadily the proper measures, we shall in time so far improve the character of our Indian subjects as to enable them to govern and protect themselves."[15]

Little was heard of such aspirations for the next half century. British administrators were caught up in the fascinating work of spreading the rule of law over the subcontinent, of creating a just and efficient administration where before their coming there had been either anarchy or oppression. This was the heyday of the Indian Civil Service, perhaps the greatest corps of administrators the world has ever seen.

And little was done to prepare Indians for self-government. The abolition of the East India Company in 1858 and the assumption of direct responsibility by the British government was accompanied by the enunciation of the principle that there should be no discrimination on grounds of race or creed in admission to the public service; but the statement of principle had few immediate practical results.

From 1861 onward some Indians were appointed to the Indian Civil Service; but what in the last decades of British rule became a tide of Indianization of the public services had at first been no more than a trickle. In 1861 also, by the Indian Councils Act, provision was made for a few "unofficial" members to sit on the Governor-General's Council and on the Provincial Councils in order to give the administration some information on Indian opinion. A second Indian Councils Act in 1892 went a little further in providing that some of these unofficial members should

15 Quoted in Sir Reginald Coupland, *Britain and India* (London, rev. ed., 1946), p. 58.

be selected by certain local bodies and corporations (city councils, universities, and so forth). These, however, were modest steps.

The emergence of nationalist sentiment was certainly in part a British creation, and this not merely in the obvious sense that it was a reaction to foreign rule. Indian unity was emphasized, if not created, by railroads, telegraphs, and roads. In the realm of ideas, the spread of education along English lines in India meant that Indians absorbed the concepts of liberty, nationalism, and parliamentary democracy from the English classics. Ironically enough, the very political organization through which Indian independence was to be achieved was founded with British encouragement and support. The Indian National Congress assembled for the first time at Bombay in 1885. There was at first no thought of opposing British rule. The mood of the period was expressed by Mr. Bonerji at the second meeting, in 1886:

> I ask whether in the most glorious days of Hindu rule you could imagine the possibility of a meeting of this kind . . . It is under the civilizing rule of the Queen and the people of England that we meet here together, hindered by none, freely allowed to speak our minds without the least fear or hesitation. Such a thing is possible under British rule, and under British rule only.[16]

This attitude ceased to be dominant in the opening years of the twentieth century. The defeat of Russia by Japan in 1904-1905 stimulated the self-consciousness of Asian peoples and demonstrated that European power was not invincible. In India the partition of Bengal by Lord Curzon in 1905, decided upon for reasons of administrative convenience, provoked the suspicion that the most politically articulate of Indian provinces was being divided into a Hindu-dominated and a Muslim-dominated part in order to make it easier to keep under control. Assassination as a political weapon, associated with the worship of the goddess Kali, was urged by the Congress leader B. G. Tilak, and led to several murders of officials and others.

From this time onward Congress was a body with definite political objectives. This period saw also the founding of another

[16] Sir V. Chirol, *India* (London, 1926), pp. 89-90.

political organization destined to be of great importance. Sir Ayed
Ahmad (1817-1899), an eminent Muslim, did much to rouse his
coreligionists in India out of their state of torpor. This process of
reawakening was symbolized by the creation of the All-India Muslim League in 1906. The stage was set for the communal rivalry
between the two religious communities which was the basic element in the Indian problem during all the last years of British
rule, and which is continued in the relations of India and Pakistan.
The communal rivalry is often blamed on the British, but they
neither created it nor could they have suppressed it. The essential
difference, the essential rivalry, was already there in the subcontinent, and it was inevitable that increasing participation by Indians
in every aspect of public life should bring it to the surface. When
a third Indian Councils Act in 1909 (the "Morley-Minto Reforms") extended the elective principle and admitted an Indian
to each of the provincial Executive Councils and to that at the
center, recognition was given to the fact of communalism by providing for separate electoral representation of Muslims.[17] The
necessity for such a step was regrettable and has led to regrettable
consequences, but the necessity was probably there. The western
democratic method of election by territorial electoral districts assumes the existence of a national community, assumes that people
will vote along the lines of differences of opinion about national
issues. But suppose they think in terms rather of other differences,
such as that between Hindu and Muslim? Suppose they regard
themselves rather as (say) Hindus or Muslims than as citizens
of the country? In that case the effect may simply be to condemn
the religious, or other, minority to perpetual subjection to the
majority, unless some constitutional provision is made to prevent it.

At the great coronation Durbar at Delhi in 1911, when King
George V was crowned Emperor of India—the occasion is a convenient symbol for the high-water mark of British power in India—
it was announced that the partition of Bengal would be revoked
and that the capital of India was to be moved from Calcutta to
Delhi, the ancient seat of the Moghuls. The first announcement

[17] A deputation of Indian Muslims headed by the Aga Khan had sought this
from the Viceroy, Lord Minto.

appeased Hindu sentiment to some extent, and at the same time was looked upon by the Muslims as an act of bad faith; the second was regarded as a further blow to Bengal and was resented by Hindu, and particularly Bengali, opinion for that reason.

The First World War stirred nationalist opinion in India, as it did everywhere; nevertheless, Indian help for Britain was freely given during the war in a manner that was to have no parallel during the second struggle. Both Congress and the Muslim League supported the war. Generous financial aid was forthcoming, and a million Indian troops participated on Britain's side. At the same time, agitation for self-government continued. Congress and the Muslim League came together temporarily in 1916 in the "Lucknow Pact," in which Congress recognized the need for safeguards of Muslim rights. There was a change of attitude on the part of the British government also. In 1917, for the first time, the objective of policy was officially recognized to be "the progressive realization of responsible government in India as an integral part of the British Empire," which implied that India was to follow the path of constitutional development already trod by Canada and other Dominions. Effect was given to the new direction of policy by the "Montagu-Chelmsford Reforms," otherwise the Government of India Act, 1919.

This measure marked a substantial advance toward self-government. It set up a federal structure, and in order to train Indians in the difficult arts of governing it transferred certain among those subjects allocated to provincial governments to Indian ministers responsible to elected majorities. This system was known as "Dyarchy." At the center, the Governor-General's Council was transformed into a full-scale bicameral legislature. British control at the center, which dealt with foreign relations and the other subjects reserved for the federal government, was largely retained.

Indian opinion was resentful at the cautious, step-by-step advance to self-government. Even in favorable circumstances the new scheme might not have worked well, and in fact the circumstances were unfavorable. General Dyer's ill-advised attempt at Amritsar in 1919 to restore order in an unruly crowd was remembered with obloquy as the "Amritsar Massacre," and gave the new system the worst possible send-off. Nevertheless, the increased participation in legislative debate, and even in executive government in the provinces, did create a generation of Indian politicians with some training in the tasks that awaited them at independence.

The chief development of the nineteen-twenties was that the movement for Indian independence for the first time became a mass movement, and not merely an affair of the middle class and the intelligentsia. This was the achievement of Gandhi, who, returned from South Africa in 1914, now emerged into prominence. Gandhi's pleas for nonviolent resistance were frequently ignored by his followers. His economic proposals for a return to a village economy could never have been taken seriously (and are not taken seriously) by India. He was not free from inconsistency in his views. Despite all this, what matters is that he roused the masses of the subcontinent to a desire for independence, and thus must be reckoned the greatest single contributor to its achievement.

From the time of the Government of India Act of 1919, with its acceptance of the goal of Dominion Status for India, the British government's aim was not, as impatient Indians thought it was, to delay as long as possible the coming of independence. The aim—and the problem—was rather to find a competent legatee for imperial power. The search went on for a quarter of a century, and in one sense finally failed, in that no one competent legatee could be found. It was a quarter century of increasing bitterness in British-Indian relations. The British view, that ability for self-government had to be learned in stages and demonstrated in practice, was inevitably galling, and was always met by resentment and impatience. The British determination to maintain law and order so long as the responsibility for the governance of India was theirs led to charges of harshness and brutality. There was no repetition of Amritsar, indeed, but it had become a symbol which poisoned relations. A wider historical view, and the vastly increased experience of tyranny which the world has had in recent decades, might well provoke the reflection that the imperial regime in which one incident of that kind could achieve such eminence must have been tolerant indeed. It is not too much to assert that certain peculiarities (as they are regarded in the West) of the present Indian attitude toward world affairs originate in India's extremely limited experience of what a determined modern tyranny can do. The Gandhian technique of nonviolent resistance to authority met with fair success, and this leads Indian statesmen to overestimate its efficacy as a method for general adoption. But it was, after all, tried out against the British: not against the Germans, the Russians, or the Japanese. Had the Japanese ever succeeded in reaching Delhi, it is conceivable that present Indian attitudes might be different.

The Hindu-Muslim rapprochement achieved in the Lucknow Pact of 1916 broke down early in the 1920's, due, first, to the unwillingness of Congress to adhere to its earlier promises in regard to special Muslim electorates and, second, to the outbreak of violence by the Mopla Muslims of South India against Hindus. The breakdown was complete by 1927, in which year the British government announced the appointment of a new parliamentary commission to consider the working of Indian government. This, the "Simon Commission," roused Indian objections because of its all-British composition. It made its report in 1930, recommending complete responsible government in the provinces. The demands of Congress had already outrun this. The three sessions of the Round Table Conference, held in London 1930-1933, were largely boycotted by Congress, which meanwhile began the second "civil disobedience" campaign. Left to produce its own solution of the Indian problem, the British government after long deliberation enacted the Government of India Act, 1935.

This great measure, the supreme attempt by Britain to create a constitutional structure for the whole of India, never went fully into operation as planned. It deserves more than a passing mention, however, for two principal reasons. First, it envisaged the creation of a federation embracing not only British India but also the Indian princely states. These states, 562 in number, which included one-quarter of the population of India and formed on the map a patchwork with the British-ruled provinces, were ruled by their princes as autocrats. By treaties they had surrendered control of foreign relations and recognized the British government as the

Paramount Power, but Britain interfered in their domestic affairs only in cases of extreme misrule.[18] No previous constitutional plan had attempted to integrate them with British India.

The second reason for regarding the 1935 act as of historic importance is that, so far as applicable, it provided the constitutions of both India and Pakistan when they become independent. It continued to be the constitution of India from 1947 until 1950; and it was not replaced as the constitution of Pakistan until 1956.

The provisions for embodying the princely states in the federal government depended on the accession of the princes to the scheme; as they hung back, this part of the act could not come into force, and government at the center necessarily continued along the lines of the act of 1919. In the provinces, ministries dealing with all subjects were to be responsible to elected legislatures, subject only to certain emergency safeguards in the hands of the governors. Congress, however, did not welcome the new act and, though Congress ministries were elected to power in 1937 in eight provinces, they would not accept office before receiving undertakings that the governors' emergency powers would not, in fact, be wielded. With this assurance, Congress ministries took office in the eight provinces and ruled them with fair success from July, 1937, to October, 1939.

The new regime in the provinces, however, strengthened rather than diminished communal differences. The Muslim League had supported Congress in the elections, but the subsequent offers of places to League members in the provincial governments were conditional on their joining the Congress, which, as it would have made them subordinates rather than partners, they refused. In the provinces in which Congress ruled for the next two years Muslims complained of many acts of discrimination against them.

The Congress decision of 1937 has been described by an author-

[18] The position of Viceroy of India combined the functions of Governor-General in relation to the eleven provinces (after 1935) of British India, and Crown Representative to the princely states. The duties of the latter office were exercised through the Government of India's Political Department, which maintained advisers in the states. From the Political Department were recruited after independence some of the personnel of the Ministry of External Affairs. See page 476.

ity as "a grave tactical blunder."[19] It was, indeed, more. It can be seen now that it marked the refusal by Congress of its last chance of achieving the goal of a united, independent India. Congress had been offered the Sibylline Books for the last time and, unlike the Roman king in the legend, had refused finally to buy them. The refusal was, no doubt, due both to a reluctance to admit the justice of the Muslim League's case and to a grave underestimation of the political importance of the League and its president, M. A. Jinnah. Jinnah had, throughout most of his life as a successful barrister, been an apostle of Hindu-Muslim unity. He had pleaded repeatedly that the Hindus should recognize the Muslim claim to reasonable safeguards against oppression, and that, these claims granted, the two communities should work in co-operation for independence.[20] In 1928 he had reached failure in his attempt to persuade Congress to accept certain proposed constitutional guarantees for Muslims.[21] From 1930 to 1934 he lived the life of an eminent barrister at the Privy Council bar in London, being recalled to India only by the pleadings of Liaquat Ali Khan, later to be first Prime Minister of Pakistan, and of Diwan Chaman Lall.

Jinnah it is impossible not to respect. A lonely, cold, and upright man, he had about him an essential fastidiousness and rectitude, a quality of honorableness, a scrupulous fidelity to his pledged word, a passion for legality, a clarity of mind which loathed equivocation. The struggle he was to wage in the next decade for the rights of his people was to prove again the truth of Marvell's words:

> So much one man can do
> That does both act and know.[22]

It was, indeed, only in 1940, when he was already sixty-four years of age, that Jinnah finally gave up the ideal of compromise and

[19] Sir Percival Griffiths, The British Impact on India (London, 1952), p. 340.

[20] "All through the critical period of the thirties they [the Congress leaders] had, in Jinnah, if only they had realized it, a unique instrument for holding India together." The Economist (London), Jan. 1, 1955.

[21] See Bolitho, Jinnah, pp. 93-95.

[22] Andrew Marvell, An Horatian Ode upon Cromwell's Return from Ireland. Jinnah certainly also was to ". . . cast the Kingdoms old/Into another mould."

decided that a separate Muslim state was essential. From then on he worked with single-minded devotion for that objective. He achieved it in seven years: an astounding accomplishment. On the outbreak of war in 1939, the Congress ministries resigned in protest against the fact that they had not been consulted on the question of India's participation. In March, 1940, meeting at Lahore, the Muslim League formally resolved that in any constitutional plan, if it was to be workable, "the areas in which the Muslims are numerically in a majority, as in the northwestern and eastern zones of India, should be grouped to constitute 'independent States' in which the constituent units shall be autonomous and sovereign."[23] In a crucially important speech moving the resolution, Mr. Jinnah said:

> The misconception that there is one Indian nation has gone far beyond the limits. . . . Hindus and Muslims have two different religious philosophies, social customs, literatures. They never intermarry, nor even interdine. . . . Muslims are a nation according to any definition of the term, and they must have their homelands, their territory and their state . . . We wish to develop to the fullest extent our spiritual, cultural, economic, social and political life in a way that we think best and in consonance with our own ideals and according to the genius of our people.[24]

The ideal of Pakistan, adopted at Lahore, though not by name, had first been enunciated by the great Muslim poet Sir Mohammed Iqbal (1876-1938). The name was coined by a group of Indian Muslim ṣtudents at Cambridge University in 1933: in Persian and Urdu it signified "the land of the pure."[25] The demand for Pakistan was at first looked upon by many as no more than a bargaining counter. Those who did so underestimated the deci-

---

[23] Nicholas Mansergh, *Documents and Speeches on British Commonwealth Affairs 1931-1952* (London, 1953), p. 609.

[24] Mansergh, *Documents*, pp. 611-612.

[25] Conveniently, the name could also be derived, more or less, as an acrostic from the name of the Muslim areas: P for Punjab; A for the Afghans of the North-West Frontier; K for Kashmir; S for Sind; and -tan from Baluchistan. It will be noted that this derivation takes no account of Bengal, whose eastern half is now East Pakistan, but whose inclusion in Pakistan as at first conceived was uncertain.

sive quality of Jinnah's mind, his unshakable resolution once his mind had been made up. Nevertheless, there were so many knotty points raised by the project that there was some excuse for the doubters. The initial reaction of most British administrators in India to the idea of Pakistan resembled that of Thomas Hobbes when first confronted with the theorem of Pythagoras.[26] What were the boundaries of the new state to be? What about the mixed provinces? Was Bengal to be included? If so, how was it to communicate with the main block of territory? Would the state have an economy that could survive? Most of these questions, indeed, were not answered until weeks or even days before Pakistan came into existence. It might be maintained that some of the most difficult of them have not been solved yet—witness the Kashmir question. Throughout the seven years of struggle Jinnah refused either to define the proposed boundaries of the state or to become involved in any minor disputes about practicability. He concentrated relentlessly on the main issue.

The behavior of Congress in the war years played into his hands. Opponents of the war effort unless cast-iron guarantees of immediate independence on the morrow of victory were given, the Congress leaders called for another civil disobedience campaign, and as a result spent the war years intermittently in jail.[27] Even when, in the Cripps Offer of 1942, the British government made the proposal of Dominion Status after the war (which implied the right to secede from the Commonwealth) for a federation of all provinces and states that wished to join (thus recognizing the right of the Muslim provinces to stand out), in return for Congress support of the war, Congress turned the proposal down—though it was what they had demanded earlier. Gandhi, in an unjust phrase that was not to his credit, described the offer as "a postdated check drawn on a bank that is about to crash." Only C. Rajagopalachari (Governor-General of India 1948-1950), with rare independence of mind, argued for acceptance.

[26] "By God, this is impossible."
[27] It is characteristic of Jinnah's punctilious adherence to legality that he was never imprisoned. The nearest he ever came to it was as a student, on Boat Race night in London. Bolitho, *Jinnah*, p. 13.

Throughout the war years the Muslim League gained in strength. In the provincial elections held in the winter of 1945-46 the League demonstrated clearly for the first time that it had the overwhelming support of the Muslim community. Over the tangled and essentially barren discussions and negotiations of the period from the end of the war to the beginning of 1947 we need not linger. The chief British initiative was the "Cabinet Mission Plan," submitted to the Indian parties in the spring of 1946 by a delegation of the British Cabinet. A desperate effort to satisfy both parties and yet preserve the unity of India, this has been justly called "the most complicated federal scheme ever invented."[28] It envisaged a three-tier federation: the Hindu provinces were to be federated in one group, the Muslim provinces in another group, and the two federations were to be joined in a superfederation of all India. The plan failed of acceptance. An interim government, to act as a Cabinet for India until power should be transferred, having six Hindu members, five Muslims, and two others, did come nominally into existence in October, 1946, with Jawaharlal Nehru as chairman—but it seldom met, and such business as it did was transacted by correspondence.

Britain still had responsibility in India, but was rapidly ceasing to have power. A new and more vigorous approach was obviously needed if deadlock was not to continue indefinitely. It came early in 1947, which was to prove the year of decision.

[28] Sir Ivor Jennings, "Communal Groups and National Franchise," in *The Listener* (London), July 28, 1955, p. 137.

CHAPTER 13

THE FORMULATION OF FOREIGN POLICY AND RECENT FOREIGN POLICY IN INDIA, PAKISTAN, AND CEYLON

The Transfer of Power

By the beginning of 1947 the Labour government, which was in power in Britain, had come to feel that it was a matter of urgency, in view of the crumbling of civil order in the subcontinent, to carry out in some manner or other, but at all costs to carry out, the long-proclaimed intention of transferring power to Indian hands. On February 20, 1947, the Prime Minister, Mr. Attlee, announced that Lord Wavell, Viceroy since 1943, was to be replaced by Lord Mountbatten; that power was in any event to be transferred by June, 1948, "whether as a whole to some form of central Government for British India, or in some areas to the existing Provincial Governments, or in such other way as may seem most reasonable and in the best interests of the Indian people." The fixing of an early deadline was intended to shock the Indian parties into a sense of responsibility, and Lord Mountbatten was given a wide discretion: he was to achieve an agreed plan for a united India if possible, and if not to accept partition.

Working with extraordinary speed and energy, the new Viceroy launched a series of discussions with the Indian leaders, as a result of which he came to two conclusions. One was that partition was inevitable; the other was that the situation was deteriorating so rapidly that the date for the transfer of power must be brought still closer. As a result there emerged the "3rd June Plan," which provided for a transfer of power to two new Dominions of India and Pakistan. Steps were to be taken to ascertain opinion in the mixed provinces as to whether they should be partitioned. The 3rd June Plan meant that Mountbatten had obtained from the two great communal organizations, Congress and the League, the minimum concessions without which no peaceful transfer of power would have been possible. These concessions were the admission on the part of Congress that they would not coerce provinces, or major parts of provinces, into becoming part of a Congress-ruled India to which they did not want to belong; on the part of the League, the willingness to accept the partition of the Punjab and Bengal, the two great provinces which Jinnah had hoped to obtain intact for Pakistan. The western part only of the Punjab was a Muslim majority area, the eastern part only of Bengal, though each province as a whole had a Muslim majority.[1] Pakistan would then, it could be foreseen from the 3rd June Plan, consist of the solid Muslim provinces of Sind, Baluchistan, and the North-West Frontier Province, plus the western Punjab and eastern Bengal (and the Sylhet district of Assam, in which the Muslims were in a majority).[2] This meant accepting a good deal less than Jinnah's widest requests—which for a few days at the end of May had included a corridor of territory linking West and East Pakistan.[3] The loss of the East Punjab and of West Bengal meant making do with what Jinnah had some months earlier called

[1] There was historical irony in the Congress attitude to the partition of Bengal. They had been infuriated by it in 1905; they insisted on it in 1947.

[2] Referenda were held in the North-West Frontier Province and in the Sylhet district of Assam; both resulted in decisions to join Pakistan.

[3] Alan Campbell-Johnson, *Mission with Mountbatten* (New York, 1953), pp. 94-98.

"a moth-eaten Pakistan."[4] No other settlement, however, had a chance of being accepted by both Congress and League. Any other would have meant civil war.

It was also announced at the beginning of June that power was to be transferred on August 15, 1947—a dramatic decision, leaving little more than two months to effect the preliminaries and bringing home to all parties that Britain was really determined to "quit India," in the words of one of Congress's slogans. Immediate steps were taken to give statutory effect to this intention. On July 18 the Indian Independence Act, 1947, became law, having passed rapidly through all stages in both houses of Parliament and received the royal assent. It provided that, on the appointed day, "two independent Dominions shall be set up in India, to be known respectively as India and Pakistan," and that consequently, from that day

His Majesty's Government in the United Kingdom have no responsibility as respects the government of any of the territories which, immediately before that day, were included in British India.[5]

In the remaining weeks the complex administrative and other implications of the dual change—independence and partition—had to be dealt with at breakneck speed. Partition meant that every administrative organization built up over a century for the service of the whole of British India had to be split into two, with its personnel choosing their future paths. The assets of government also were to be divided, Pakistan to get 17.5 per cent. (It was later claimed that payment in full was never made.) The problem of the future national boundaries running across the provinces of the Punjab and Bengal was put in the hands of two mixed commissions chaired by a British lawyer, Sir Cyril (later Lord) Radcliffe. Both sides gave unconditional assurances in advance that they would accept the Radcliffe commissions' decisions. As it happened, the mixed commissions could not arrive at agreed decisions; Radcliffe had to take the responsibility for drawing the boundaries himself. His decisions, diplomatically not announced until August

[4] To Ismay, on April 9, 1947. Campbell-Johnson, p. 59.
[5] Complete text in Mansergh, Documents, pp. 669-685.

16, were unpopular with both sides, though perhaps more so with Pakistan. The award in the Punjab, in particular, was obviously destined to raise difficult questions in regard to the water supply of Pakistan, and has indeed done so.[6]

Even more overwhelming, perhaps, at the time was the problem posed by the dividing of the fine Indian Army trained under British leadership. Good judges had declared in advance that partition of the army was impossible, but it had to be done. Units were divided according to the religion of the troops, and began to wend their way to their new cantonments. The army inherited by India was weakened, but not destroyed as an effective force; Pakistan's army had to be organized almost from scratch. This disparity in actual military effectiveness explains a good deal in regard to the outcome of the crises between the two new states in the first months of independence. To ease the transition, provision was made in two cases for temporary joint commands in British hands. A Punjab Boundary Force was created in July to supervise the transition in the Punjab. Hopelessly inadequate for the tasks which in practice it had to attempt, it was abolished on September 1. At the highest level, the commanders in chief of the two armies were at first British; above them was Field Marshal Auchinleck as Supreme Commander, with duties limited to supervising the division of the army. The absence of goodwill between the two new Dominions soon made his position untenable, and the Supreme Command was dissolved on November 30; by then, however, most of its intricate task had been discharged.

In this fashion the Indian Empire of Britain died on August 15, 1947, and two new independent states were born. They had constitutions, for the Independence Act had provided that "each of the new Dominions and all Provinces and other parts thereof shall be governed as nearly as may be in accordance with the Government of India Act, 1935." There also was no doubt as to who was to hold power in the immediate future in each of them: Congress in India and the League in Pakistan. India paid Mountbatten the

[6] Jinnah said that even if the boundary award was "unjust, incomprehensible and even perverse," the pledge to abide by it had to be kept. Campbell-Johnson, p. 178.

high compliment of asking him to remain as Governor-General, which office he held until June, 1948. In Pakistan, Jinnah chose to become Governor-General himself. For a time in June he had advocated native Governors-General in the two states, with Mountbatten remaining in the transition period as unifying head over both, but this had been regarded as an impracticable idea. In India, Nehru of course became Prime Minister, the post which in substance he held already, though nominally he had been vice-chairman of the Viceroy's Executive Council. In Pakistan, Jinnah's brilliant lieutenant Liaquat Ali Khan, an administrator trained in the great school of the Indian Civil Service, became his Prime Minister. For legislatures the two states had their respective portions of the Constituent Assembly which had been elected indirectly in 1946 by the members of the provincial legislatures and which had convened on December 9, 1946, but had been boycotted by the Muslim League.

This tremendous historical event, the transfer of power in India to the peoples of the subcontinent, had aspects both praiseworthy and regrettable. It was, in the first place, singular in that it was made voluntarily, or at any rate voluntarily in the sense that the time and manner of the transfer had been chosen by the former ruling power. Again, the transfer, though accompanied by disorder, was effected peaceably so far as relations between the yielding and the successor authorities were concerned. The disorder was intercommunal, not between the old and the new masters of the subcontinent. It was noticed by all observers that, as soon as the British had made clear their intention of going, both Hindus and Muslims became much more friendly toward British people than they were toward each other. Evidence of the smoothness and friendly nature of the transition was to be found in the fact that large numbers of British administrators were asked to remain in various posts, from governorships of provinces down, until the new regimes felt able to replace them. This happened in both countries, but for obvious reasons more so in Pakistan, where the administrative machine had to be formed from virtually nothing. Jinnah asked Sir Archibald Rowlands to be financial adviser to the new government, and Sir George Cunningham to be governor of the North-West Frontier Province. Owing to the shortage of Indians or Pakistanis with military training adequate to the rank of a general officer, India continued to have a British commander in chief until January, 1949; Pakistan until January, 1951. Gradually, of course, all such carry-overs from the old regime were replaced, but the fact that they had been asked to remain at all was a remarkable testimony to their integrity and the trust reposed in them.

Britain, in other words, transferred power peaceably, and to constitutional régimes with a high probability of survival. But, on the other side of the medal, the transfer of power had its profoundly unsatisfactory aspects, nearly all of which resulted from the speed with which, at the last, British power had been withdrawn. In the first place, there simply was not time to make adequate preparation for the foundation of Pakistan. The new country inherited a considerable number of able civil servants from undivided India—but when they came to the new capital, Karachi, the whole structure of government had to be improvised. Administrative cadres were lacking; and so also were, at first, such elementary prerequisites of government as office space, files, and other equipment. Of course, taking the longer view, the necessity for heroic improvisation in the service of their new state evoked a spirit of adventure among the builders of Pakistan which was exhilarating and actually enabled them to accomplish much. At first, however, the problems presented were, in the existing circumstances, beyond human capacity to deal with.

The greatest of these problems was that posed by the appalling outbreaks of disorder which accompanied partition. They had, indeed, begun before it; but the intercommunal violence over wide areas of the subcontinent which flared up toward the end of August outran all expectation. In Bengal a personal intervention by Gandhi prevented grave trouble, but in the Punjab disaster was unrestrained. Sikhs, enraged by the partition of their province, set on Muslims; Muslims slaughtered Hindus where they had the chance; Hindus murdered Muslims. Refugee trains were frequently stopped in unfriendly areas and their passengers exterminated. Horror raged in Central India as it had not done for two centuries. Those who escaped from the areas of anarchy camped pitifully on the outskirts of the towns they had reached—hundreds of thousands of Hindus around Delhi, and of Muslims around Lahore. Not until the end of September was order in any measure restored. No accurate count has ever been made, or ever can be made, of the loss of life. Adding up deaths from violence and those from starvation and disease, the total was probably about half a million. The total refugee movement, which has not yet entirely ceased, involved perhaps a dozen million persons. Nearly seven million Muslims fled from India to Pakistan. Nearly five million Hindus made the opposite journey. It cannot be doubted that the intense bitterness generated by the slaughter and by the refugee movement—and by subsequent quarrels about the property of refugees—continues to be an exacerbating factor in the relations of the two countries.

Possibly even more serious, and manifestly still present in the situation, were the consequences of the British failure to deal adequately with the problem of the princely states. The failure to anticipate the scale of intercommunal violence was, perhaps, understandable. The problem of the princely states, in all its complexity, was, however, there for all to see. It can hardly be said that Mountbatten, or Attlee's government, solved it; rather, they simply shuffled it off to the successor states. Possibly there was no time to do more. But the results have been grave.

The Indian Independence Act contained merely clauses to the effect that "the suzerainty of His Majesty over the Indian States lapses" and with it all treaties on the subject; and stating that there was no bar to the princely states' acceding to either of the new Dominions. In practice, since they had never had the wisdom to act jointly in politics, nor had they the strength to stand individually as sovereign units, this was the only conceivable future for them. Mountbatten urged the princes to sign acts of accession to India or to Pakistan. The choice in each state was a matter for the ruler, since the rulers were autocrats; the Viceroy, however, recognized that regard should be had also to the geographical situation of the state and to the composition of its population— a plebiscite being held if necessary to ascertain their wishes. No order of preference was ever stated among these different, and conceivably conflicting, principles.

Up to a point the accession policy went well. Before the transfer of power all but three of the princely states had acceded to one or other Dominion. Three unresolved cases remained—those of Kashmir, Hyderabad, and Junagadh. The Kashmir case is so crucial—it forms the greatest single point at issue between India and Pakistan—that it must be treated more fully later. Kashmir is the largest of the states, and strategically very important. It has common frontiers with India, Pakistan, Tibet, and China proper. The ruler was Hindu, but three-quarters of his subjects were Muslim. His eventual accession to India led to India's gaining the most important part of the territory, though much of it is in Pakistani hands. Hyderabad is the second largest, and the wealthiest, of the states. The ruler was Muslim, the majority of his subjects Hindu. The Nizam, the most important of Indian princes, had long tried (unsuccessfully) to maintain that he was on an equal footing with the Paramount Power, Britain. When the transfer of power in India drew near he began to pursue dreams of independence. His state was totally surrounded by Indian territory. He therefore showed signs of attempting to accede to Pakistan, as the most likely means to maintain substantial independence. In the winter of 1947-48, the Nizam, a man of enormous wealth, made a loan of approximately $62 million to Pakistan. Negotiations pursued a tortuous course; several times the Nizam seemed on the point of concluding a special agreement with India, but always at the last moment he backed away or repudiated his negotiators. India began to apply pressure. An economic blockade of the state began—unofficial but effective—which precluded the passage even of medical supplies. Finally, in September, 1948, Indian troops entered the state and took it over. The Nizam retained his title and wealth, but his personal power was gone. Junagadh, the third of these states, was less important than the other two: a small seaboard state on the west coast with a population of half a million, mostly Hindus, ruled by a Muslim, it had land frontiers only with India, but, as it had a small port, sea communications with Karachi, not far distant, would have been possible. The ruler signed an instrument of accession to Pakistan on September 15, 1947. Here, too, India settled the issue by force, sending in troops which took over the state on November 9, 1947.

Pakistan now has no claims in regard to Hyderabad. However, she strenuously maintains what she regards as her rights not only in regard to Kashmir, but also in the apparently closed case of Junagadh, which was still shown as a part of the territories of Pakistan on the official map issued by the Surveyor-General of Pakistan in 1954.

These three cases cause immense bitterness on the part of Pakistan. India had the best of it in practice in all three: actual possession of Hyderabad, Junagadh, and the Vale of Kashmir. Yet the variables in the three cases are such that no consistent application of principles could possibly have awarded all three to India (or, of course, for that matter to Pakistan). In two of the three (Hyderabad and Junagadh) a Muslim ruled over a majority of Hindu subjects. In Junagadh the ruler acceded to Pakistan. In Hyderabad the ruler signed no instrument of accession until his state had forcibly been taken over. In Kashmir a Hindu ruled over a majority of Muslim subjects. He acceded to India. It is clear that only by resting on one principle here and another there can India justify possession of all three states. But, of course, India did not obtain them by argument. She obtained them by force, exerted at a time when Pakistan was in no position to respond in kind. The basic justification in the minds of Indian statesmen appears always to have been that, essentially, India is the successor authority to British India.[7]

The intervening years since 1947 have seen a steady process of integrating the former princely states which acceded to India within its political structure and the introduction into them of democratic institutions. Many of the states being very small, all of them except Hyderabad, Kashmir and Mysore have been com-

[7] Note Nehru's revealing remark in a foreign affairs debate in the Indian Parliament on March 29, 1956 (italics added): "Even if Kashmir had not acceded to India, he claimed, it would still have been their duty to defend it; for, *India being a continuing entity*, whatever did not opt out remained Indian until it was decided otherwise." Report in *The Times* (London), March 31, 1956.

bined with others, or with former Governors' Provinces, to form larger units. In the states or unions of states until 1956, the office of governor was called *Rajpramukh* and was held by one of the former rulers. The princes have been compensated for the disappearance of their powers by the guarantee of adequate civil list pensions and personal estates appropriate to their rank. Such guarantees, of course, are obviously dependent on the goodwill of the present government, and on its continued tenure of office. The princes' remaining privileges would almost certainly disappear if Congress were ever succeeded by any of the opposition parties. In Pakistan the smaller number of states which were within its sphere were treated in similar fashion. Four small states were merged in 1952 to form the Baluchistan States Union. The abolition of the personal power of the princes has not, however, especially in the regions of the mountain frontier, gone so far as it has in India.

Political Structures

The Constitution of India

The constitution under which India is at present governed is the work of the Constituent Assembly which convened, less its Muslim League members, on December 9, 1946. Work on the new constitution began even before the transfer of power. On January 22, 1947, a resolution was adopted that India should become "an Independent Sovereign Republic." The main task of shaping the new constitution was performed by the drafting committee appointed on August 29, 1947, under the chairmanship of Dr. Ambedkhar, President of the Scheduled Castes (i.e., Untouchables) Federation. He had been a distinguished member for many years of the Viceroy's Executive Council and was Law Minister in 1947-1951. The basis of work was a draft previously prepared by Sir Benegal N. Rau. With admirable wisdom, a survey was made of other constitutions which might provide concepts worthy of adoption.

The committee deliberated for six months, and presented its report in February, 1948. The draft constitution and proposed amendments were discussed clause by clause in the Assembly, and the constitution was finally passed on November 26, 1949. It came into force on January 26, 1950.

The whole process of drafting, amendment, and adoption was remarkably expeditious in view of the magnitude of the task. The constitution which emerged is the longest in the world. It comprises 395 articles and 9 schedules. The official printed text occupies 254 pages. The constitution is federal in form. In conformity with the resolution of January, 1947, it is a republican constitution. Having been drafted after a wide search had been made for the best models, the constitution has a kinship at certain points with those of Australia, the United States, and the Republic of Ireland. It shows, however, the strongest signs of the influence of the long British connection. Sir Ivor Jennings shrewdly comments:

> Though India has become a "sovereign democratic republic" and will have an elected President, he will in fact be a constitutional monarch. The constitution has been framed by lawyers accustomed to the legal concept of "the Crown." and the conventional system of Cabinet government. Though neither the Crown nor Cabinet government appears in the Constitution as such, they are in fact there. The drafting would have been simpler and the Constitution would have worked in almost precisely the same way if there had been a Governor-General appointed by the King and Governors appointed by the Governor-General.[8]

In some cases the borrowing from the British constitution is quite explicit. Article 105(3) states that, until parliamentary privilege shall have been further defined, "the powers, privileges and immunities of each House of Parliament . . . shall be those of the House of Commons of the Parliament of the United Kingdom . . ." The definition of the relations of the two houses, which turns on their respective powers in regard to financial matters, is based on the provisions of the Parliament Act, 1911, limiting the powers of the House of Lords in regard to a Money Bill— the term which is actually used in the Indian constitution.

British usage is, however, deserted in favor of the example of the United States and other countries in some parts of the consti-

[8] Jennings, *The Commonwealth in Asia* (London, 1951), p. 92.

tution which, though interesting in themselves, are not especially relevant to our present purpose. Part III of the constitution (Articles 12 to 35) constitutes a comprehensive attempt to define "Fundamental Rights." Part IV (Articles 36 to 51) spells out "Directive Principles of State Policy," which partake of the character of a preamble, in that, though they are declared "fundamental in the governance of the country" and it is the duty of the state to apply them, they shall "not be enforceable by any court." Nothing in events since the adoption of the constitution has disproved the contention, which might be urged against these provisions, that what matters more than the formal enactment of great principles is the will on the part of the national community to uphold them.[9]

Under the constitution the states which compose the union were divided into three groups. The first, Part A States, are substantially the former Governors' Provinces of British India, less territories lost to Pakistan.[10] Part B States are former princely states or unions of such states.[11] Part C States consist of areas which are not yet competent for self-government, and comprise three former Chief Commissioners' Provinces and a number of minor princely states or unions of states.[12] Part D lists the Andaman and Nicobar Islands.

The powers of government in the Part C States are exercised at the discretion of the central executive and legislature. It is

[9] For example: the abolition of Untouchability (Article 17) and of all forms of discrimination (Article 15) is no more than an aspiration until some considerable passage of time has led to the growth of new social conventions. Again, despite the guarantee of freedom of speech and expression (Article 19) the Government of India has in fact proceeded rather far in restricting this right by a constitutional amendment in 1951 and a statute in 1952, and has frequently threatened to proceed even further.

[10] I.e., Assam, Bihar, Bombay, Madhya Pradesh (the former Central Provinces plus Berar), Madras, Orissa, Punjab, Uttar Pradesh (the former United Provinces), and West Bengal. A new state of Andhra was created in 1953. See also page 455 concerning the States Reorganization Act of 1956.

[11] I.e., Hyderabad, Jammu and Kashmir, Madhya Bharat, Mysore, Patiala and East Punjab States Union, Rajasthan, Saurashtra, and Travancore-Cochin. See also page 455 concerning the States Reorganization Act of 1956.

[12] I.e., Ajmer, Coorg and Delhi; and Bhopal, Bilaspur, Himachal Pradesh, Kutch, Manipur, Tripura, and Vindhya Pradesh. See also page 455 concerning the States Reorganization Act of 1956.

only, therefore, in regard to the Part A and B States that the constitution may be considered a federal one. The powers of the federal government and of the governments of Part A and Part B States are extensively defined in long lists—the Union List, the State List, and the Concurrent List. On the Union List are found, as is normal in a federation, "War and Peace," "Foreign Affairs; all matters which bring the Union into relation with any foreign country," and various other items connected with the same subject. The distribution of powers as between the general government and the states is not exceptional. It is, however, worthy of note that the tendency of the constitution is to favor the federal government at the expense of the states. Not only are all residuary powers not specifically allocated left in the hands of the federal government; it also possesses extensive powers of altering state boundaries and of superseding the state governments, as for instance on a Proclamation of Emergency; or in the case of the breakdown of the constitution in a state; or in case of disobedience of central executive directions by a state; or in case of a financial emergency. It is clear that the states are less clearly autonomous entities than the states of the United States; though much, of course, will depend on how the constitution is developed in practice.

The head of the central executive is the President, who is elected for a term of five years by an electoral college containing the elected members of both the central and state legislatures. There is also a Vice-President elected by members of the central legislature. The President is substantially in the position of a constitutional monarch or the Governor-General of a Dominion. He has wide powers of intervention in an emergency to enable the constitution to continue to function. Many of the powers which are vested in him will presumably normally be exercised on the advice of his Prime Minister. The Prime Minister is selected by the President, and the Prime Minister selects the colleagues who with him will form the Council of Ministers—the Cabinet under another name. Article 75(3) lays it down that the Council of Ministers is collectively responsible to the lower house.

India has had (to this writing) only one President, Dr. Rajendra

Prasad (the sole candidate for the post, and formerly President of Congress), and only one Prime Minister, Pandit Jawaharlal Nehru.

The central legislature is called Parliament. Its lower house is named *Lok Sabha*, the House of the People, and its upper house *Rajya Sabha*, the Council of States. The House of the People consists of 500 members, and is elected on a basis of manhood suffrage. Its normal term is five years, but it may be dissolved earlier by the President. The Council of States consists of 250 members, of whom 12 are nominated by the President on grounds of personal distinction in "literature, science, art and social service." Unlike the United States Senate, the Council of States does not give equal representation to the states. Representation is roughly in proportion to population. Members are elected by members of the state legislatures by the method of proportional representation with the single transferable vote. Like the United States Senate, the Council of States is a continuing body, one-third of its membership retiring each two years.

One of the most difficult problems faced in framing the constitution of India was the language question, which is a problem also for Pakistan and Ceylon. The dilemma is that, while English is the language of the former rulers and there is a natural desire to abandon it, it is in fact the only common language within each of these countries. It is the only language in which the generation of politicians who achieved independence communicate with one another; it is also the language in which the constitutions of India, Pakistan, and Ceylon are written. The impulse to abandon English is a nationalist one; but the use of any other language or languages will be antinationalist in effect, because it will focus attention on local separatisms, diminish the effective unity of each of these countries, and perhaps lead to other steps such as the creation, forced on the Indian government in 1953, of a Telugu-speaking state of Andhra carved out of Madras. Hence the numerous realistic qualifications which hedge about the statement in Article 343(1) of the Indian constitution that "The official language of the Union shall be Hindi in Devanagari script." For fifteen years English shall continue to be used for the official purpose of the Union, and Parliament may extend its use beyond that time. The proceedings of the Supreme Court and of the High Courts are to continue to be in English until Parliament otherwise provides.

Intimately linked with the language question is that of the reorganization of the Indian states. The provincial divisions of British India were arbitrary, resting on historical accident or the convenience of the imperial power. During British rule the Congress Party had advocated as part of its platform the redivision of provinces on a linguistic basis. Once it was itself installed in the places of power, it found that to reconstruct the divisions of the country on a basis of reason opened wide the door to internal jealousies, rivalries, and undesirable local patriotisms. The Dar Commission (1948) gave warning of this; but the redrawing of boundaries remained official policy. The pressure for it increased. The creation of Andhra set a precedent, and led to the appointment in December, 1953, of a special commission to consider the whole question of the reorganization of the states.[13] Their report was submitted in October, 1955. It showed an awareness of the dangers to national unity of the whole proposal, yet it did recommend that the political map of India be redrawn on linguistic lines in such a way that sixteen states would replace the existing twenty-seven. Despite the inflammatory effect on local passions which the proposals had, shown particularly in the riots in Bombay, the government pushed ahead with a modified version of the plan, which became law as the States Reorganization Act. As a result of the act, since November 1, 1956, India consists of 14 states.[14] In addition, there are six centrally administered territories, of which the capital, Delhi, is one.[15]

[13] It consisted of three members: Mr. Justice Fazl Ali (Chairman), Dr. H. N. Kunzru, and Sardar K. M. Panikkar.
[14] Andhra Pradesh, Assam, Bihar, Bombay, Jammu and Kashmir, Kerala, Madhya Pradesh, Madras, Mysore, Orissa, Punjab, Rajasthan, Uttar Pradesh, and West Bengal.
[15] The others are: Andaman and Nicobar Islands; Himachal Pradesh; Laccadive, Amindive, and Minicoy Islands; Manipur; and Tripura.

Pakistan in Quest of a Constitution

The experience of Pakistan in the vital field of constitution making has proved much less satisfactory than India's. The problem has proved to be one of immense difficulty. It remained unsolved from 1947 to the spring of 1956. Until the latter date the government was still functioning on the constitutional basis of the Government of India Act, 1935—an extraordinary situation. The course of developments from 1947 to 1956 was, from both the legal standpoint and the standpoint of internal politics, extremely complicated. These difficulties and controversies have now, presumably, been happily resolved; yet, since they were indicative of strains within the country which have not ceased to exist, they are worthy of a brief backward glance.

Three of these basic, permanent factors which caused the confusions of the interim period are of particular importance. One is the tension between East and West Pakistan, which are not only distant from each other but differ ethnographically and in many other ways. A second factor is the question of how far the Muslim religion should be a dominating consideration in the law and life of the state. Khwaja Nazimuddin, Governor-General 1948-1951 and Prime Minister 1951-1953, tended to exalt the influence of Islam. Most of the Western-educated leaders of Pakistan, however, including Jinnah, Mohammed Ali (Prime Minister 1953-1955), and emphatically including the present President, Iskander Mirza, have favored a secular state; in this they are probably far in advance of most of the people they rule, for Pakistan lacks an educated middle class.[16] Third, a real threat to constitutional stability in Pakistan is the lack of national spirit in many of her politicians, especially provincial politicians, too many of whom are guilty of a petty provincial spirit and also of venality. The strongest and soundest elements in Pakistan are the army and the Civil Service, but they are, unhappily, not integrated in the population as a whole.

[16] "The Government wants a secular constitution, but the people thought the reason for partition was religion, and they want an Islamic Constitution." Taya Zinkin, "Pakistan in Transition: Moslem and Secular," in Manchester Guardian Weekly, Jan. 20, 1955.

The Constituent Assembly of Pakistan, being Pakistan's part of the all-India body elected in 1946, functioned as a legislature as well as a Constituent Assembly. In the early years so many pressing problems needed its attention in its former capacity that only in 1949 did it begin to give its attention seriously to constitution making. Already the new state had suffered a severe blow in the death of its creator and first Governor-General, Mr. Jinnah, in September, 1948. It was to suffer another when the very able first Prime Minister, Liaquat Ali Khan, was assassinated in October, 1951. Had they survived, their personal eminence would have facilitated the solution of problems that have plagued their successors. The Governor-General from 1951 to 1955, Ghulam Mohammed, a man whose iron will was housed in a fragile body, was a tower of strength in succeeding crises. (He died August 29, 1956, at 61.)

In 1949 the Assembly proceeded as far as the adoption of an "Aims and Objectives" resolution which included a preamble to the constitution invoking the name of Allah. The next step was the presentation in December, 1952, of the report of the Basic Principles Committee. The committee envisaged the creation of a federal system of five "units" (four being in West Pakistan) with a bicameral central legislature. East and West Pakistan would have equal representation in *both* the lower house, the House of the People, and the House of the Units. The special status of East Pakistan would also be recognized by other complicated constitutional provisions. The Head of the State would appoint the Prime Minister, and the Cabinet would be collectively responsible to the federal legislature. Great difficulties were raised by the proposal that any law contrary to "the Holy Quran and the Sunnah" would be void. It was also laid down that the Head of the State must be a Muslim. The principle of communal representation, given up in India, was retained.

Discussion of the proposals proceeded throughout 1953. In April of that year, the Governor-General replaced Khwaja Nazimuddin as Prime Minister by Mohammed Ali, at that time ambassador in Washington. The committee's proposals underwent various modifications. One was that each unit should have equal representation in the House of Units (i.e., East Pakistan would

not have half the seats). The influence of the new Prime Minister
was also exercised in the direction of secularization. Nevertheless,
in November, 1953, it was resolved that Pakistan should become
an Islamic Republic.

At the end of 1953 further consideration of the constitutional
draft was deferred to await the outcome of the provincial elections
in East Pakistan in March, 1954. These resulted in a disastrous
defeat for the Muslim League and the beginning of a chronic
constitutional crisis. The victorious party was the United Front,
an amalgam of parties of leftward inclination, including Communists. The Muslim League had obviously lost its original zeal,
and also was reaping the result of its failure to deal with the poverty
of East Pakistan.

Iskander Mirza, Secretary of Defence from 1947, was appointed
Governor of East Bengal (i.e., East Pakistan), and the province
was taken under Governor's Rule on May 30. In the next crisis,
in the fall, parliamentary government failed at the center. The discussion of the draft constitution was proceeding; although it could
hardly be called smoothly, completion of the process was hoped
for by the end of the year. On October 16, 1954, the Prime Minister arrived in Washington to complete negotiations for military
and economic aid. Disturbed by dissensions, the Governor-General
summoned him home on October 21 and appears to have given
him the choice of co-operating in drastic measures or resigning.
The Prime Minister remained, but there was a Cabinet reshuffle.
On October 24 the Governor-General proclaimed a state of emergency throughout the country, dissolved the Constituent Assembly on the ground that it had ceased to be representative (which
was true) and promised new elections as soon as possible. On
November 22 the merger of West Pakistan into one unit by the
abolition of the various provinces was announced. In a broadcast
the Prime Minister explained the step as being intended to combat
provincialism. He said that, while "the best form of government
is naturally the unitary type," geography forbade that. "As it is
not possible to unify the whole of Pakistan we should at least
unify the whole of West Pakistan."

The action of the Governor-General in dissolving the Constituent Assembly was challenged in the courts. The Sind Court

decided against him, but was overruled by the Federal Court on May 10, 1955. Elections for a new Constituent Assembly were held in June, from which the Muslim League emerged as the largest party, gaining 25 of 72 elective seats, but with no majority. In August the offices of both Governor-General and Prime Minister had new incumbents. Ghulam Mohammed, who had been very ill for several months, went on indefinite leave, and Iskander Mirza became Governor-General, "acting" at first, until the former's resignation on October 6. Mohammed Ali, whose prestige had been much eroded by the events of the previous fall, lost his position as president of the Muslim League, and was succeeded in both that and the premiership by the former Finance Minister, Chaudri Mohammed Ali.

The new coalition government formed by the Muslim League and the United Front pushed rapidly ahead with work on the constitution. There was a feeling in the air that an agreed solution of this issue was essential for the future of the country, and that failure would be absolute and final. The draft constitution was finally presented to the Constituent Assembly on January 8, 1956; and, having been approved without extensive modification, passed the final stage in debate on February 29, and received the Governor-General's assent on March 2. The new constitution came into force on March 23, on which day the Islamic Republic of Pakistan was proclaimed. Governor-General Iskander Mirza became the first President of Pakistan.

As in India, the President is the formal head of state. He is to exercise his functions normally on the advice of his Cabinet, headed by a Prime Minister, chosen by the President on the basis of being the "most likely to command the confidence of the majority of the members of the National Assembly" (Articles 37[3] and [7]). The constitution is a federal one, but strikingly unusual in that the federation consists of two provinces only, East and West Pakistan. One of the most significant features of the constitution is the scrupulous attempt to make the two provinces equal in all respects in their constitutional powers and functions. Even in the matter of the seat of government, though it is physically necessary for it to be in one or the other province, and in fact it remains at Karachi, to conciliate East Pakistan opinion there are provisions that "at least one session of the National Assembly in each year shall be held at Dacca," the capital of East Pakistan (Article 50), and that the Supreme Court shall sit in Dacca at least twice each year (Article 155).

The legislature at the center is a one-chamber body of three hundred members, half from each province, to be known as the National Assembly, though the National Assembly plus the President is called "the Parliament of Pakistan." The National Assembly has a normal term of five years. During the first ten years, there are to be ten women's seats, to be filled by voting in special constituencies created for that purpose. All citizens of Pakistan of the age of twenty-one or over are eligible to vote in either national or provincial elections.

The structure of government in each province closely parallels that at the center. Each province has a Governor, appointed by the President, a Cabinet of Ministers with a Chief Minister at its head, and a one-chamber Provincial Legislature, consisting of three hundred members plus, initially, ten women members. Powers of government are allocated between the general government and the provinces by a Federal List, a Provincial List, and a Concurrent List. The Federal List, of course, includes all aspects of defense and foreign affairs.

The constitution of Pakistan again resembles that of India in including a lengthy section (Part II) on "Fundamental Rights." Unlike the Indian constitution, however, it is not a purely secular document. Apart from specifically naming the state the Islamic Republic of Pakistan, the religious origins of the country are recognized in the Preamble, "In the name of Allah, the Beneficent, the Merciful . . ."; in the requirement that the President must be a Muslim; and in the "Islamic Provisions" (Articles 197 and 198). These articles provide for the creation of an organization "for Islamic research and instruction in advanced studies"; and, further, that "No law shall be enacted which is repugnant to the Injunctions of Islam as laid down in the Holy Quran and Sunnah . . . and existing law shall be brought into conformity with such injunctions." To give effect to these requirements the President is, within one year of the promulgation of the constitution, to appoint a commission to report within five years. This is not quite postponement *sine die*, yet it obviously represents a compromise in which extreme Islamic views have yielded a good deal of ground to the claims of practical necessity.

The approach to the question of superseding the use of English is, as might be expected, even more cautious than that adopted in India. Article 214 provides that "The State languages of Pakistan shall be Urdu [for West Pakistan] and Bengali [for East Pakistan]"; but the use of English is to continue for twenty years, and may be prolonged beyond that time by Parliament. The President is to appoint a commission to make recommendations for the replacement of English.

Pakistan thus, at length, possesses a constitution of its own, but until national and provincial elections have been successfully held the constitution can hardly be said to be a going concern. Prime ministers and cabinets succeed one another on a basis of personal considerations and of the balance of power between groups rather than on a basis of possessing or losing the confidence of the legislature. There was another such change of this kind in September, 1956. On September 8 Chaudri Mohammed Ali resigned from both the premiership and the Muslim League, and on September 12 Mr. H. S. Suhrawardy, leader of the Awami League, an able man who was Chief Minister of undivided Bengal at the time of Partition, and Law Minister of Pakistan 1954-1955, became prime minister. The new government is a coalition of the Muslim League and the Awami League.

There is reason to hope that the formation of governments will soon rest on the more regular basis of support in a directly and recently elected legislature. In July, 1956, the government set in motion the somewhat lengthy procedures which must necessarily come before elections, by appointing an Election Commission, and a Delimitation Commission to map electoral districts. It is also planned to pass a Representation of the People Act to frame the details of electorates. No doubt there is a sincere intention to push through these stages as fast as possible. Nevertheless, it seems likely for a number of reasons that for some time to come Pakistan will be a qualified rather than a complete democracy. The constitution leaves large reserves of discretionary power in the hands of the national government, and particularly in the hands of the President. This is a direct continuation of the tradition of the years 1947-1956, that the office of Governor-General was more important in Pakistan than in any other member of the Commonwealth. Mr. Jinnah set the precedent for this. Pakistan's rulers, almost to a man trained by British administrators and previous participants in government under the British *Raj*, have no love for despotism. Law is important to them. But so is order, and they will not let blind obedience to democracy, in a country still so backward in many respects, imperil the maintenance of order and sound administration. President Iskander Mirza's model is understood to be the late Kemal Ataturk of Turkey, whom in some respects he resembles. Like him, he believes in a secular state. Some true, but tactless, sayings are attributed to the President that give an insight into his views, views that are bound to be unpopular with many in Pakistan: "Religion and politics have nothing to do with each other"; and again, "There can be no democracy with 13 per cent literacy."

The Constitution of Ceylon

Ceylon, the legendary Serendip or Taprobane of the ancients, is still in many respects a fortunate island. Its standard of living is higher than those of India and Pakistan. It has, admittedly, a diversity of peoples and religions. Besides the 5½ million Sinhalese, there are nearly a million Ceylon Tamils, and another million fairly recent immigrants from India, in addition to almost half a million Moors and a few score thousand Dutch Burghers, Eurasians, and Europeans. The Sinhalese are Buddhist and speak Sinhalese; the Tamils and Indians are Hindus and speak Tamil. There are almost a million Christians (mostly Roman Catholic) and half a million Muslims. English is more widely spoken by the middle class than in either India or Pakistan. Despite all this diversity, intercommunal problems have never been as serious as they are on the Indian mainland. Nor was the path to independence a thorny one, and for that reason it has not been necessary to trace it here. Independence came rapidly, fairly smoothly, and in the main by agreement.

Ceylon was taken over by Britain, during the French Revolutionary Wars, from the Netherlands to protect sea routes, and was retained at the general peace in 1815. Recent constitutional developments began in 1910, but it was in 1924 that more than half the seats in the Legislative Council became elective. In 1931 communal electorates were abolished, the franchise was extended to all adults, and a considerable but by no means complete measure of self-government was established. Most of the present statesmen of Ceylon learned their trade as ministers under the constitution of 1931. It was a clumsy constitution and unsatisfactory in many ways, but principally in that it divorced power from responsibility. In 1943, when the Cripps Offer had just been made to India, an offer of internal self-government, but not Dominion Status, after the war, was made to Ceylon. A constitutional scheme was worked out by the Ceylon ministers, led by Mr. D. S. Senanayake, in 1944. A British commission visited the island in 1944-45 and recommended minor changes in the scheme. Mr. Senanayake continued to press for Dominion Status, and the British government agreed in 1947, when it removed the remaining restrictions on self-government from the constitution conferred on the island by Ceylon (Constitution) Order in Council, 1946, itself largely a product of the Ceylon ministers' scheme of 1944. Thus, when Ceylon became independent on February 4, 1948, it had an already functioning constitution of its own making. The constitution may be amended by the vote of two-thirds of the membership of the lower house. At the same time as the granting of independence, there were signed the Defence and External Affairs Agreements between Ceylon and the United Kingdom, which are of importance in that they contribute to Commonwealth co-operation in the foreign policy field.

The constitution of Ceylon is unitary.[17] The bicameral Parliament has a House of Representatives and a weak Senate. The Crown is represented by a Governor-General. The House of Representatives has 101 members. The representation of the various

[17] It is a short constitution of some twenty pages. The drafting was the work of the eminent constitutional lawyer, Sir Ivor Jennings, then Vice-Chancellor of the University of Ceylon. In 1954 he was commissioned to advise the Government of Pakistan on the drafting of a constitution. He drafted the order unifying West Pakistan in November, 1954.

districts of the island is weighted by an ingenious device which slightly overrepresents the more sparsely populated areas where the non-Sinhalese mostly live. In this way, without the necessity of communal representation, the rights of the minority communities are adequately protected. The Senate has 30 members; 15 elected by the lower house, the other half nominated by the Governor-General—since 1948, on the advice of the Prime Minister. A somewhat unusual feature is that certain matters that are only conventions of government in the United Kingdom receive specific enactment in Ceylon. Section 4(2) provides that the Governor-General shall exercise his power "in accordance with the constitutional conventions" applicable to the actions of the monarch in the United Kingdom. Section 46 defines the Cabinet, the office of Prime Minister, and Cabinet responsibility to Parliament.

Since independence, government in Ceylon has worked well. The United National Party held a monopoly of power, and there was indeed no effective opposition, until the abrupt reversal of the general election of April, 1956. Don Stephen Senanayake remained Prime Minister until his death in a riding accident in March, 1952, when he was succeeded by his son Dudley, who voluntarily resigned office in the next year, and Sir John Kotelawala took office. During his premiership, in July, 1954, the first Ceylonese Governor-General, Sir Oliver Goonetilleke, was installed. The 1956 general election resulted in a catastrophic defeat for the United National Party and brought to power a coalition government whose parties are leftward in inclination and place great emphasis on the independence of the island. The new Prime Minister was S. W. R. D. Bandaranaike.

The Predominance of the Executive

The constitutions and political systems of India, Pakistan, and Ceylon have certain common features which are of paramount importance from the point of view of foreign policy determination. States, including democratic states, differ widely in regard to the concentration or dispersion of the foreign policy-making function. In the United States the function is dispersed very widely (some would say almost to the point of anarchy) and policy is eventually arrived at by a process of pulling and hauling, a sort of "higgling of the market" of opinion and power within the government—all parts of which are very mindful of an important and vocal public opinion.

This kind of dispersion of the policy-framing function is much less likely to occur in countries which possess a parliamentary executive rather than a presidential executive; which have, to put it another way, the British rather than the United States type of democratic government. India, Pakistan and Ceylon, like the older members of the Commonwealth, have all adhered closely to the British model in this respect. In the constitutions of all three countries the Cabinet is a committee of the legislature, and is usually composed of the leading members of the majority party. The formal head of the state normally acts on the advice of his ministers and is not the active leader of the executive. The ministers must be members of, and must be supported by a majority in, Parliament. In such a system power is entrusted to the Cabinet, and effective decision on all questions is in their hands to a far greater extent than it ever is in the hands of the President or his Cabinet in the United States system. It is quite true that the grant of power to Prime Minister and Cabinet is revocable if the legislature feels sufficiently dissatisfied with them, but this happens comparatively rarely. It is of great assistance in evoking steady support from the legislature that the head of state possesses the power to dissolve the legislature (or at any rate the lower house, as in India and Ceylon) before its normal term has expired, and in the British system will normally exercise this right when asked by his Prime Minister to do so—thus holding over the heads of recalcitrant members the threat of the expense and uncertainty of an election. This strongly reinforces party discipline and prevents frivolous votes against the government.

The power of formulating foreign policy is perhaps even more concentrated than this outline of the constitutional position would suggest. Foreign policy has always, with good reason, been looked upon as the highest and innermost function of government, the *arcana imperii.* And nowhere in the democratic states of the mod-

ern world has "the tradition handed down from the age of absolute
monarchy that the conduct of foreign relations is largely executive," in Quincy Wright's words,[18] been maintained to a greater
degree than in the British political system. That system is, after
all, at bottom a modification by evolution of what was originally
a royal executive, and still is that in form.

The general assumption of the British system is that there is a
responsibility in the hands of Prime Minister and Cabinet for the
conduct of foreign policy. It is their business to see that the realm
takes no harm. Their responsibility is a conditional trust, and
they must answer for their conduct of it to Parliament and,
eventually, to the electorate. They would be obviously foolish
to do anything widely out of line with the general trend of thinking in Parliament or in the country. Nevertheless, granting these
limitations, the shaping of policy is conceived as their function.
Their initiatives will be supported, the game will be (within
limits) left in their hands. They will not be subject from day to
day to a microscopic examination and criticism of their actions
by public opinion and other bodies in the government, rivals or
coadjutors in the framing of policy.

This is the British system; the essence of it is present also in the
cases of India, Pakistan, and Ceylon. If one looks at the monu-
mental *Commentary on the Constitution of India* of D. D. Basu,
or Gledhill's work on the same subject, or Jennings and Tambiah
on the constitution of Ceylon,[19] one will find little or nothing
about the machinery for the making of foreign policy. This evidence, though negative, is most revealing. What it implies is the
unquestioned, and perfectly sound, assumption that British procedure is invariably followed in practice. Of formal constitutional
factors operating on foreign policy there are practically none be-

[18] Quincy Wright, *The Study of International Relations* (New York, 1955),
p. 175.
[19] Durga Das Basu, *Commentary on the Constitution of India* (Calcutta,
2nd ed., 1952), 1032 pp. Alan Gledhill, *The Republic of India: The Development of its Laws and Constitution* (London, 1951). Sir Ivor Jennings and
H. W. Tambiah, *The Dominion of Ceylon: The Development of its Laws
and Constitution* (London, 1952).

yond the responsibility of the Cabinet and the ultimate control of the legislature based on the power of the purse. There is no equivalent in any of these countries to the Senate's Foreign Relations Committee or the House's Foreign Affairs Committee in the United States. Mr. Nehru was asked in Parliament on June 12, 1952, whether he proposed to have a parliamentary committee on foreign policy, but he did not look with favor on the suggestion.[20] Nor, in these countries, is there any multiplicity of agencies dealing with foreign relations. In each of them one foreign office, under whatever name, handles everything in that category. Centralization of the direction of foreign policy goes further. In India, in the whole time since independence, Mr. Nehru has been both Prime Minister and Minister for External Affairs. There is no constitutional necessity for this, but Nehru has obviously chosen the dual role because of his great interest in foreign policy. In Pakistan the same situation prevailed from October, 1954, when Sir Zafrullah Khan, Foreign Minister up to that time, became a judge of the International Court of Justice, until the appointment in September, 1955, of Mr. Hamidul Haq Choudhury. In Ceylon the identity of prime minister and foreign minister is laid down in the constitution.[21]

The cardinal fact, then, in regard to foreign policy formation in India, Pakistan, and Ceylon is the predominance of the executive. Since this is so, and since these countries have in fact had very short histories as independent entities, the influence of a few personalities over their foreign policy has been overwhelming. In India it would not be quite true, but it would be very nearly true, to say that foreign policy has been Nehru's policy. There

[20] Nehru said: It has been asked "whether the Standing Committee of the Ministry of External Affairs was going to be constituted. Well, Standing Committees were constituted in the old British days in a peculiar way and for a special purpose. They serve no useful purpose now." *Jawaharlal Nehru's Speeches 1949-1953* (Delhi, 1954), p. 222.

[21] "The Prime Minister shall be in charge of the Ministry of Defence and External Affairs and shall administer the matters relating to that Ministry in addition to such other matters as he may determine to retain in his charge." Mansergh, *Documents*, p. 739.

the Prime Minister is fundamentally in harmony with his countrymen. He represents and voices their consensus. His brilliance and fluency as a speaker is such that he has always been able to overwhelm the few questioning voices that are raised in Parliament from time to time. While the Indian Prime Minister makes up his own mind, it is noteworthy that he relies to a considerable extent on the advice tendered by a small inner circle of intimates. Among these may be mentioned his sister, Mrs. Pandit (prominent as an Indian ambassador abroad); the late Sir Benegal Rau, for several years India's chief representative at the United Nations; the late Sir Girja Shankar Bajpai; Sir Sarvepalli Radhakrishnan; K. M. Panikkar; and V. K. Krishna Menon. Bajpai (like the great majority of the most prominent men in India, Pakistan, and Ceylon at the present time) had an English education, being a scholar of Merton College, Oxford. The foreign office of India is in a large degree his creation. He was one of the first Indian representatives abroad, as Agent-General in Washington 1941-1947. He then became Secretary-General (i.e., permanent head) of the Ministry of External Affairs, holding that central post in the formative period from independence until he became Governor of Bombay in 1952. Radhakrishnan, of the same generation as Bajpai, went into diplomacy after an academic career that included an Oxford chair. From 1949 to 1952 he was Indian ambassador in Moscow; since then he has been Vice-President of India. Panikkar and Krishna Menon are both younger men whose influence with the Prime Minister seems to have been growing in recent years. Panikkar, an extremely able and prolific author of scholarly works in history and politics, has had a varied career which has included a period as Dewan (Prime Minister) to the Maharaja of Bikaner, and ambassador to Nationalist, and afterwards to Communist, China. His later writings stress the themes of former European exploitation and contemporary Asian renascence that are popular with the "neutralist" intelligentsia to whom he addresses himself. Krishna Menon leans over backwards in the effort to be fair to the Communist world. He spent the nineteen-thirties as a left-wing intellectual in London and was for several years a member of the borough council of St. Pancras. He returned to London as High Commissioner for India in 1947, remaining until 1952. In recent years he has fulfilled important functions as Indian representative to the United Nations and as roving ambassador. His magnetic personality and fluency of speech make him an effective representative. In what direction his influence is wielded is difficult to determine. Many of his utterances are unfriendly to the West, yet some have seen in him a restraining influence on Nehru. He has not expressed himself as being against the Commonwealth connection.

In Pakistan there is only one name that need be mentioned in addition to those of the Prime Ministers and Governors-General— that of Chaudri Sir Muhammad Zafrullah Khan, who was Minister of Foreign Affairs and Commonwealth Relations from December, 1947, until October, 1954. He was of the first importance in shaping Pakistan's policy during all the early years of independence. Educated in London, at King's College and Lincoln's Inn, Zafrullah Khan was leader of the Indian delegation to the League of Nations in 1939. He became India's Agent-General in China in 1942, and was leader of the Pakistan delegation to the United Nations from 1947 to 1951, pleading her cause brilliantly in the crucial debates on Kashmir. He made an excellent foreign minister, vigorous yet temperate in his views; his elevation to the International Court of Justice in 1954, while an honor to his country, was also a loss. In Ceylon, foreign policy has so far interested few statesmen. Policy from 1953 to 1956 was dominated by the Prime Minister, Sir John Kotelawala—English educated, of a sincerity bordering on tactlessness; a "bonny fighter." He had a strong personal antipathy to communism, not on economic grounds but because it is unpatriotic—a threat of foreign domination. His successor, Solomon West Ridgeway Dras Bandaranaike, is difficult so far to evaluate. Western educated—he was up at Christ Church, Oxford, at the same time as Sir Anthony Eden—he achieved the premiership as the leader of an anti-Western coalition. His views are not fixed and adamantine, as is shown clearly enough by his secession from the United National Party in 1952. There is some reason to suppose that he is much less extreme than many of his followers.

The Parliaments and the Parties

The experience of Western democratic states suggests that the chances of stability are greatest when there is a two-party system. Even more important is the fundamental agreement of the different parties on maintaining the constitution and other national institutions. This alone makes possible a smooth change of government after an electoral reverse. None of these conditions so far obtains completely in India, Pakistan, or Ceylon. In all of them the party situation continues to be exceptional. Until recently politics in each of these three countries was dominated by one party. This is still the case in India. In Pakistan power is in the hands of a coalition of two parties, each of which finds its strength in one of the two parts of the country, an uneasy situation. Ceylon, perhaps, is nearest to having achieved conditions allowing for a peaceful alternation of parties in office, yet perhaps even in Ceylon there is a lack of agreement on fundamentals.

Neither Congress nor the Muslim League is now—that is, in conditions of independence—fulfilling its original function. Before 1947, the justification of the Congress Party was to oppose the British; of the Muslim League, to oppose the Congress Party. In the gentler atmosphere of Ceylon the same situation existed, though less harsh: the United National Party had considerable experience of governing before in 1948 it took over in independence. Since all these parties focused within themselves the aspirations which led to the achievement of independence, it would naturally take many years before there could exist rival parties of any importance or, consequently, any prospect of smooth alternation of governments of different parties.

In India there is a large number of parties, but only a few are worthy of mention. In the only election so far, held in the winter of 1951-52, Congress obtained an overwhelming majority, with 363 of 489 elective seats. The Communists and allied parties were next, with 27 seats, though they were not next in voting strength. That place was held by the Socialist Party, which split off from Congress in 1948. The Socialist Party secured almost ten million votes—about double the poll of the Communists—but only 12 seats. The Kisan Mazdur Praja (Peasants', Workers', and People's) Party secured 10 seats, and has since merged with the Socialists to form the Praja-Socialist Party. The Hindu Mahasabha, the fanatic religious group, obtained 4 seats.

The most formidable threat to Congress is from the Communists. Their strength is greatest in the south of India. In the central legislature they create, as always, a disturbance disproportionate to their small numbers. They have no loyalty to the constitution or to the democratic process, and should they ever succeed Congress in power it would, of course, mean a new form of government, not a mere change of parties. In domestic politics they have been active in support of the rearrangement of state boundaries according to linguistic divisions, because this would tend to destroy national unity. It is scarcely necessary to say that their advent in power would also imply a revolution in foreign policy; but, indeed, this is hardly less true of the other parties mentioned. The Praja-Socialist Party and the Hindu Mahasabha alike would repudiate the Commonwealth connection. The former would pursue a policy much less friendly to the West and much more so to Russia. The latter would probably embark on war with Pakistan.

These, however, are remote contingencies. In practice, discussions on alternative foreign policies are discussions not between parties but *within* the dominant party. The Congress Party is so broad that there are bound to be conflicting opinions within it. Occasionally these differences come to the surface, as for instance in 1950, when one of the things distinguishing rival candidates for the post of President of Congress was their different attitudes toward Pakistan.

It is not only since 1947 that Congress has had a foreign policy. Since the party was the heir apparent of British power in India, it had long looked abroad and proclaimed opinions on the world scene—though certainly such matters were not its primary interest. Congress established a "Foreign Department" in 1925 as a research and policy-recommending body, and this was reorganized in 1936 with a view to maintaining contacts with other bodies abroad having similar purposes. At Congress meetings resolutions on foreign affairs were passed on such themes as the following: congratulations to other colonial countries on approach to, or achievement of, independence; friendship with China; sympathy for, and admiration of, the Communist experiment in Russia; opposition to imperialism and "imperialist war." One could trace a long series of such resolutions which would show a high degree of consistency with present Indian foreign policy. The meeting of Congress at Jaipur in 1948, just after independence, proclaimed an intention which has, in fact, been followed when it resolved that "The foreign policy of India must necessarily be based on the principles that have guided the Congress in past years."

In Pakistan the dominance of the Muslim League was complete until the East Pakistan elections of 1954 showed that it had completely lost its hold there. In the new Constituent Assembly elected in June, 1955, in the first general election since 1946, the League gained 33 out of 80 seats.[22] The United Front gained 25 and the Awami (People's) League 12; other parties were of no significance. The Muslim League thus had only a plurality, not a clear majority. Moreover, only one of its seats was in East Pakistan, though in West Pakistan it gained 24 out of 32 elective seats, and the two rival parties gained none. The lack of a clear majority combined with the necessity of conciliating opinion in East Pakistan meant the end of the Muslim League's monopoly of power, though it remained the leading party. The two governments which have subsequently held office have been combinations of the Muslim League, the dominant party in West Pakistan, with one or other of the two leading parties of East Pakistan—the United Front, led by Mr. A. K. Fazlul Huq, and the Awami (People's) League, led by Mr. H. S. Suhrawardy. Chaudri Mohammed Ali's government of August 1955 to September 1956 was a case of the former of the two alternatives; the successor government, Mr. Suhrawardy's, is of course the alternative variation. The changes in the party complexion of the government have made little or no differ-

---

[22] The election, like the original election of 1946, was an *indirect* one, the electors being the members of the state legislatures, whose own mandate in West Pakistan was by this time nine years old.

ence in Pakistan's foreign policy, which seems to be determined basically by the country's feeling of need for external support. The United Front is a combination of leftish parties. The Awami League, formerly known as the Jinnah Awami League, is a splinter party that was formed of seceders from the Muslim League led by Mr. Suhrawardy, and it claimed to interpret more faithfully than the Muslim League the political testament of Mr. Jinnah. It has had some small body of opinion in its favor in West Pakistan, but its main source of support is in the eastern part of the country. One of the first acts of Mr. Suhrawardy as Prime Minister was to make it clear that there would be no major change in foreign policy and that his country would stand by its international commitments. In a broadcast on September 12 he said, "We must abide by our pledged word and agreements. Let it be understood that we mean what we say and that our word is our bond." Continuity of foreign policy was also indicated by the fact that the new Foreign Minister, Malik M. F. K. Noon, is a member of the Muslim League.

In Ceylon, until the spring of 1956, there was only one party worthy of mention—Sir John Kotelawala's United National Party. The party had more than maintained itself in the general election of 1952, gaining 54 of the 95 elective seats and, with the support of independents, controlling three-quarters of the lower house. In 1956 Sir John decided to hold a general election, eighteen months earlier than was necessary, on the issue of replacing English by Sinhalese as the national language. In this he was reversing his earlier attitude that there should be equality of status between Sinhalese and Tamil, the language of the Indian and Indian-descended minority. The light vapors of Sinhalese nationalism which Sir John himself had fanned rose rapidly to gale force and blew him and his party out of office. Nationalist sentiment was exploited by the newly formed and somewhat amorphous coalition of opposition parties, which campaigned under the name of the Mahanjana Eksath Peramuna (People's United Front) and under the leadership of S. W. R. D. Bandaranaike. Bandaranaike had been a member of the United National Party, and indeed a Cabinet member as Minister for Health and Local Government, from 1947 until in 1952 he resigned to lead the opposition.

The People's United Front coalition comprises the Sri Lanka Freedom Party, the Lanka Sama Samaj (Trotskyist) Party, the All-Ceylon Bhasa Peramuna, and a group of independents. In the election it appealed to the nationalist, Buddhist, anti-Christian, anti-Western feeling in the island, in which appeal it was powerfully aided, indeed swept to victory, by the efforts of the Buddhist monks.

Of the elective seats the People's United Front secured 51; the United National Party was left with only 8. The policy of the new government is as yet difficult to define with precision. It had campaigned on promises of expelling the British bases from the island; of avoiding any links with the Western powers and seeking instead a complete neutrality; of nationalizing the great tea plantations. But some elements inside the coalition are much more extreme than others; and, while it is certain that the new government is much more leftish and neutralist than was the United National Party, it is by no means certain that its election program will be carried out in its full rigor.[23]

The Foreign Offices and Foreign Services

In all countries with highly developed administrative systems the influence on foreign policy formation of the civil servants who man the missions abroad and staff the foreign office in the capital tends, on account of their permanence, experience, and their role as information gatherers and interpreters, to be very considerable. This is as much the case in India, Pakistan, and Ceylon as elsewhere.

In creating these services the three countries have had to overcome enormous difficulties, first, in the field of personnel and, second, in finance. The cost of maintaining missions abroad in a large number of capitals is very great. For this reason, none of these three countries has a foreign service on the scale of the major

[23] See also page 481.

Western states. India comes nearest to it. The Indian Prime Minister has all along laid great stress on the creation of an adequate foreign service. Speaking in the Constituent Assembly on March 8, 1949, he said:

I am told, sometimes, that I have some kind of bee in my bonnet; that I forget the trouble in India . . . and that I think only of sending ambassadors from Timbuktu to Peru. . . . If we do not go out and have our foreign establishments, somebody will have to look after our interests. Who is that somebody? Are we going to ask England to look after our foreign interests in other countries as Pakistan has done in many countries? Is that the type of independence that we imagine? What does independence consist of? It consists fundamentally and basically of foreign relations. That is the test of independence. All else is local autonomy.[24]

The foreign service of Pakistan is a considerable way behind that of India in scale of organization, while that of Ceylon really does not attempt to compete with the vast expenses under this head of the larger powers. We may therefore treat India's foreign service as a kind of model to which those of Pakistan and Ceylon approximate. The problems that all three countries faced in building up a foreign service, and the kind of solutions adopted, have had much in common.

India

Some decades before independence India, as by far the largest and most important of British possessions overseas, had come, in a somewhat anomalous way, to have an international existence. India was separately represented at Versailles in 1919 by two Indians, Lord Sinha of Raipur[25] and the Maharaja of Bikaner. She signed the Treaty of Versailles and became a charter member of the League of Nations.[26] She also joined the United Nations at its foundation.

[24] *Independence and After: Speeches of Jawaharlal Nehru (1946-1949)* (Delhi, 1949), p. 237.
[25] Lord Sinha of Raipur was the only Indian ever to be elevated to the House of Lords. At least two Indians, however, Messrs. Dadabhai Naoroji and Saklatvala, have been elected to the British House of Commons.
[26] An anomaly; but less so than the charter membership in the United Nations of Byelorussia and the Ukraine.

From 1919 she had a High Commissioner in London, though his duties were mainly commercial. At Delhi there was an External Affairs Department, functioning directly under the Viceroy and staffed by members of the Indian Political Service, which was responsible for maintaining British diplomatic representation in the countries adjacent to India. The proportion of British personnel in the Political Service was, however, higher than in the purely internal services. With the approach of independence, Britain sanctioned the creation of two quasi-diplomatic posts manned by distinguished Indian civil servants, one of whom was appointed Agent-General for India in Washington in 1941 and the other in Chungking. When independence came, however, there was barely a score of Indians who had any acquaintance with the problems of negotiating with foreign governments.[27] In these circumstances, the building of an adequate foreign service in a few years has been a praiseworthy achievement.

The period of emergency recruitment lasted until 1949; since then a permanent system has been instituted. The new service was to man India's diplomatic and consular posts abroad as well as the Ministry of External Affairs in New Delhi, and a few posts in the Ministry of Commerce. Emergency recruitment was from three main sources: a few members from the Indian Civil Service and rather more from the Indian Political Service; second, young men of ability recently discharged from the armed forces; a third category, the great majority, was drawn from business and the professions. Heavy recruitment from this group was necessary since it was impossible to have a service entirely composed of young men, however able, without experience. Since 1949 recruitment to the Indian Foreign Service has been made by the Union Public Service Commission on the basis of a competitive examination. Women are eligible on the same basis as men, though few have come forward. The examination is open to university graduates aged 21 to 24. Those appointed, who number about half a dozen annually, have a probationary period of three years. They spend a

[27] Indian Year Book of International Affairs, Vol. 1, ed. Charles Alexandrovicz (Madras, 1952), p. 28.

few months at the Administrative Service Training School in Delhi; then a year abroad at a foreign university; thereafter, another year's training at the Ministry in Delhi, ending probably with a time as an attaché with a mission abroad. The final hurdle is a language examination, after which the recruit is a full-fledged member of the Foreign Service. This is the regular pattern of entry; heads of missions, however, are appointed directly by the Minister either from inside the service or from outside it.

At the head of the Ministry of External Affairs in Delhi is the political chief, the Minister, a post at this writing held by the Prime Minister. He is assisted by a Deputy Minister and two Parliamentary Secretaries; these three are all Members of Parliament. On the permanent, civil service, side the head of the organization is the Secretary-General; below him are two Secretaries, called the Foreign Secretary and the Commonwealth Secretary. These are officers of ambassadorial rank. Below them are Joint Secretaries in charge of Divisions, Deputy Secretaries and Under-Secretaries. The total number of career officers in the Ministry is small, approximately fifty. The work of the Ministry is organized in three territorial Divisions. There is also a Conferences Division dealing with the UN and other international bodies, a Historical Division, a Protocol Division, an External Publicity Division and an Administrative Division.[28] Thus the allocation of work within the Ministry follows the normal pattern in being partly territorial and partly functional.

India in 1956 maintains abroad twenty-four embassies, six legations, two special missions, five High Commissions in other Commonwealth capitals as well as eight other offices in Commonwealth or British colonial territories. There are also about thirty consular or commercial posts abroad. These figures are constantly being increased, but even so it is clear that India has not so far the finances, the personnel, or probably indeed the need, to maintain representation in all foreign capitals. In 1952 ten of her heads of mission were accredited to more than one country each, some to as many as three. The total strength of the Indian Foreign Service is less

28 *Indian Year Book of International Affairs*, Vol. 1, pp. 32, 366-368.

than two hundred. This, however, does not include those filling junior and clerical posts in Delhi or abroad. Branch "B" of the Foreign Service, recently instituted, will comprise this group.

Pakistan

In Pakistan all the difficulties experienced by India have been felt, and generally in a more intense form. Emergency recruitment was, of course, necessary to supplement the numbers of the members of the Indian Civil and Political Services who opted for Pakistan and who were suitable for the work of the Ministry of Foreign Affairs and Commonwealth Relations and its missions abroad. Many more of the British personnel of these services had to be invited to remain for the time being. Recruitment to the united Civil Service of Pakistan is made through the Pakistan Public Service Commission. There is still a marked shortage in the middle and upper brackets of the foreign service and other branches; in consequence, promotion for young men of ability has been rapid. Pakistan has not felt able to establish missions in as many foreign countries as India has; nevertheless, she has in being a foreign service that is efficient, zealous, and almost adequate to her needs.

Ceylon

Ceylon has a limited program of foreign representation and consequently a small foreign service. Regular recruitment is conducted by the Ceylon Public Service Commission. Ceylon's application for membership of the United Nations was vetoed by Russia until 1955. She therefore until 1956 did not recognize diplomatically any Communist government. Ceylon maintains diplomatic representation only in London, Washington, New Delhi, Karachi, Rangoon, Canberra, Tokyo, Rome, and Jakarta. The services of United Kingdom embassies and consulates are freely available to her wherever she wishes to make use of them and she has found this arrangement entirely satisfactory. The reports of Ceylon's representatives are supplemented by the information supplied by the United Kingdom Foreign Office and distributed to all Commonwealth governments by the Commonwealth Relations Office.

Policy Areas

Intra-Commonwealth Relations

We have discussed the background of Indian, Pakistani, and Ceylonese policies, and the political and administrative structures by which present policy is framed. It remains to outline briefly some of the typical policies which have been the outcome of these various forces. Relations of India, Pakistan and Ceylon within the Commonwealth may be divided into relations with the center, that is, with the United Kingdom, and relations with Commonwealth members other than the United Kingdom. The former have been very satisfactory. Since these countries gained independence Britain has handled her relations with them skillfully, tactfully, and with understanding. The relations of the three countries with one another and with South Africa (the only other Commonwealth member with which they have important dealings) have been much less satisfactory.

The most important step in relations with the center has been the decision on India's part to continue membership in the Commonwealth even as a republic, and the readiness of the other members to accept this. On April 27, 1949, at the end of a meeting of Commonwealth Prime Ministers, a historic declaration was issued which included the following words:

The Governments of the United Kingdom, Canada, Australia, New Zealand, South Africa, India, Pakistan and Ceylon, whose countries are united as Members of the British Commonwealth of Nations and owe a common allegiance to the Crown, which is also the symbol of their free association, have considered the impending constitutional changes in India.

The Government of India have informed the other Governments of the Commonwealth of the intention of the Indian people that under the new constitution which is about to be adopted India shall become a sovereign independent republic. The Government of India have however declared and affirmed India's desire to continue her full membership of the Commonwealth of Nations and her acceptance of The King as the symbol of the free association of its independent member nations and as such the Head of the Commonwealth.

The Governments of the other countries of the Commonwealth, the basis of whose membership of the Commonwealth is not hereby changed, accept and recognize India's continuing membership in accordance with the terms of this declaration.[29]

There was some resentment in Pakistan that India should have been accorded this new and unique status, and Pakistan was no doubt thereby pushed in the direction of a republicanism that otherwise she might not have regarded as an essential feature of her polity. On February 4, 1955, at the conclusion of another Commonwealth Prime Ministers meeting, an announcement was made, closely parallel in language to that just quoted, the gist of which was that in the near future Pakistan would adopt a republican constitution, but that she desired to continue her full membership of the Commonwealth of Nations and to recognize the Queen as Head of the Commonwealth; and that the other members recognized her continuing membership on this basis. Pakistan's membership of the Commonwealth assumed the same form as India's on March 23, 1956, when her new republican constitution became effective.

Ceylon was therefore left as the only Asian member of the Commonwealth retaining the monarchy; but not, probably, for long. The communiqué issued at the end of the Commonwealth Prime Ministers Meeting of June 27-July 6, 1956, stated that "During the course of the Meeting, the Prime Minister of Ceylon [Mr. Bandaranaike] stated that, in accordance with their declared policy, the Ceylon Government proposed to introduce in due course a republican constitution for Ceylon." But Ceylon wished to remain a member of the Commonwealth; and the other Prime Ministers expressed their agreement to this.

In consequence, in the near future the distinction between those members of the Commonwealth that have a substantial proportion of their population consisting of white people of British descent and those in which this element is negligible in number— the distinction, in other words, between the "old Dominions" of Canada, Australia, New Zealand, South Africa, on the one side,

[29] Mansergh, *Documents*, p. 846.

and the three Asian members of the Commonwealth, on the other—will be paralleled by a distinction between those members of the Commonwealth possessing a monarchical and those possessing a republican form of government. This development may make it more difficult for the Commonwealth to perform its function as a bridge and harmonizer between the Asian-African world and the Europeanized Western world.

The change of government in Ceylon also brought up the question of the future of the British bases in the island, and this, too, was discussed when Mr. Bandaranaike was in London in July, 1956. The official announcement of July 6, 1956, seemed to offer some possibility that, while Ceylon would "take over" the bases, means would be found to allow Britain to continue to make use of them. "The discussions," said the announcement, "have been concerned with:

(a) the declared intention of the Ceylon Government to make available to the United Kingdom Government at their request certain facilities enjoyed at present in Ceylon for communications, movements and storage;

(b) the declared intention of the United Kingdom Government to provide assistance to the Ceylon Government . . . for the expansion, development and training of the Ceylon Armed Forces."

Representatives of the two governments were to meet in London and, later, Colombo, to make the necessary arrangements.

It would not be surprising if even the Bandaranaike government continued to rely for security to some extent on the United Kingdom. Ceylon is a very small country, with no armed forces adequate to defend it. There is no present threat to the island's security, but it is conceivable that some successor to Mr. Nehru might be inclined to pursue the dreams of "manifest destiny" which are sometimes mentioned by South Indian politicians with their eyes on Ceylon and its large Indian minority. From the United Kingdom point of view, it is highly desirable to have bases in the island. These complementary needs were the foundation of the two special agreements which accompanied the grant of independence, the Defence and External Affairs Agreements of November, 1947. The former was an agreement to provide mutual military assistance, this in practice meaning that the United Kingdom would undertake the defense of Ceylon in return for the use of naval and air bases on it. The latter agreement brought Ceylon within the system of exchange of information between Commonwealth governments, and arranged for the United Kingdom diplomatic representatives to act for Ceylon at her request in any country where Ceylon did not have representation. It seems probable that the substance of these agreements will be continued in some form.

The most important breaches in intra-Commonwealth harmony are the issues between India and South Africa and between India and Pakistan. There are also less grievous questions concerning India and Ceylon. The issues between India and Pakistan are the only ones that might possibly lead to war. The points which have arisen between India and Ceylon concern the one million Indians in Ceylon, and their status and future. Indians are attracted to Ceylon because of its better standard of living—indeed, they still contrive to enter it illegally—but they continue to look to India as their home. Ceylon legislation has disfranchised them unless they definitely opt for Ceylon citizenship, which necessitates five years' residence and other tests. The Ceylonese position is that unless so registered they remain citizens of India. The Indian position is that they are citizens of India only if so registered with the Indian authorities. Under a Ceylon-India agreement of January, 1954, facilities for registration were set up, but it has proceeded slowly. The Indians in Ceylon prefer to remain stateless rather than risk deportation to the mainland.

The issues between India and South Africa (which to a lesser extent involve the sympathies of Pakistan and Ceylon) concern the long-standing question of the treatment of Indians in South Africa. Recent legislation by Nationalist governments in South Africa launching the policy of *Apartheid* has exacerbated the question. It touches India to the quick because it turns on the whole matter of discrimination on grounds of color. India ceased to have diplomatic relations with South Africa in 1951, and in the same year tried to bring economic pressure to bear; in which move, however, she was not seconded by Pakistan. India has repeatedly brought up the matter in the United Nations, but with little effect. It is difficult to foresee any lessening of this tension. India is not likely to give up her interest in persons of Indian descent in South Africa, nor to cease to resent discrimination such as the South African government exercises. The South African government, at the same time, is intensifying its policy.

Of the several disputes between India and Pakistan two are especially serious: that about the Punjab rivers and the Kashmir issue. The question of the rivers concerns the Indus and its five tributaries on which the thirsty land of West Pakistan depends for water. Of the tributaries three—the Ravi, the Beas, and the Sutlej—are liable, owing to the frontiers drawn for the West Punjab at partition, to have substantial parts of their waters diverted in Indian territory, and it is the Pakistan claim that this has been happening and will happen to an increasing extent when certain works now in construction by India are completed. A solution is possible, since it would be practicable for Pakistan to obtain all the water she needs from the Indus itself, which is entirely within Pakistan territory. This would, however, require a large expenditure for new canals and other works. The World Bank has been interested in facilitating a solution along these lines and, provided India can avoid giving fresh reasons for alarm in the meantime, it is likely that there will be a slackening of tension on this question.

The Kashmir imbroglio gives no equal promise of an easy resolution. Of this exceedingly complicated question, a running sore in the relations of India and Pakistan for almost a decade, it is impossible to give a full account here. The Maharaja, a Hindu though four-fifths of his four million subjects were Muslim, could not decide in 1947 which Dominion to join. He had a freer choice than most of the princes, since he had frontiers with both, and a definite decision for either before August 15, 1947, would probably have been decisive.[30] On August 15 he made a "Standstill Agreement" with Pakistan. Concurrently the persecution of Muslims in the state led to a rebellion in Poonch, in western Kashmir, and

[30] For a definitive account of the Kashmir question see Josef Korbel, *Danger in Kashmir* (Princeton, 1954).

the setting up there of the Azad (Free) Kashmir government, which has maintained itself to the present. The reports of persecutions of Muslims led to an incursion into the state at the end of October by North-West Frontier tribesmen from that province, and also from Afghanistan. India maintains that this invasion took place with the help of the Pakistan authorities. It is more likely that in the then rudimentary state of the Pakistani Army they would have been quite unable to prevent what the Pathan tribesmen regarded as a jehad, a holy war. The tribesmen nearly reached Srinagar. The Maharaja saved himself only by acceding to India on October 26. Indian troops were flown in and were able to save Srinagar and to regain possession of most of the vale of Kashmir, the only fertile and reasonably horizontal part of the state. In accepting the accession, Mountbatten said that it must be confirmed by a referendum later. Nehru repeated this on November 8. He added, however, that invaders must be cleared from the territory first. To Pakistan this means that the plebiscite will be held under Indian supervision and control. This is one of the irreconcilable differences of attitude that still remain.

In January, 1948, India took the issue before the UN Security Council. Sir Zafrullah Khan's counterattack brought up the issue of Junagadh and alleged that India had not really accepted the existence of Pakistan. In April the UN set up a commission to visit Kashmir and exercise its good offices. In the spring of 1948 Pakistan regular forces began to assist the tribesmen, and a curious and limited war began which was brought to an end on January 1, 1949, when a cease-fire was arranged by the commanders in chief of India and Pakistan—both then still British. Essentially, at this point there began a deadlock which has persisted ever since. Discussion still centers round the principles adopted in the UN resolutions of August 13, 1948, and January 5, 1949: that there should be, first, a "truce" period in which would take place the withdrawal first of the Pakistan troops and then of Indian troops except those necessary for the maintenance of order; second, a "plebiscite" period when the future of the state would be settled "through the democratic method of a free and impartial plebiscite." In theory both sides accept this outline of procedure; in practice there have been enough objections on various points, chiefly from the Indian side, to prevent any progress. In 1949 Admiral Chester Nimitz (U.S.) was appointed to be plebiscite administrator, but neither the mission of Sir Owen Dixon (Australia), in 1950, nor that of Dr. Frank Graham (United States), 1951-1953, has created conditions in which he could fulfill his functions. Meanwhile, Kashmir has been more and more brought effectively into integration with India, and thus India's chances in any eventual plebiscite enhanced year by year.

The issue is a great one for both India and Pakistan. It is not only a matter of possessing that state which Nehru, whose ancestors came thence, once compared to "some supremely beautiful woman,"[31] it also involves the principles on which the two states base their existence. For Pakistan, Kashmir seems essential because it is a Muslim state contiguous with Pakistan. For India, possession of Kashmir with its Muslim population would reinforce the thesis that India is not a communal state. It is difficult to see how the issue can be compromised. The only likely solution is reluctant acceptance by both parties of what has been the situation since 1949. In any case, apart from the Vale of Kashmir, this would be consistent with the religious division of the population in the various parts of the state, which has no intrinsic unity. East Ladakh, with its Buddhists, would go to India. Gilgit, Hunza, and Baltistan would remain with Pakistan, as also would Poonch. Jammu province could be divided. This would mean, of course, that the Vale of Kashmir, the pearl of the whole state, would remain to India; but there seems little hope of prying loose India's hold there without war.

Other Foreign-Policy Areas

The main feature of India's foreign policy in regard to the rest of the world has been, as is well known, "nonalignment," the refusal to become a member of any power blocs. India has deliberately not become a member either of the democratic or of the Communist grouping. "Our general approach has been, as far as possible, one of non-interference in the various conflicts in other

31 Nehru, *The Unity of India* (New York, 1942), p. 223.

parts of the world."[32] At the same time, this policy is not regarded either as one of neutralism or as being purely negative. To admit the charge of "neutralism" would be to concede the existence of the division of the world into two camps, the very condition which India deplores and seeks, so far as possible, to avoid. "I have often ventured to point out, in this House, that the policy we were pursuing was not merely neutral or passive or negative but that it was a policy which flowed from our historical as well as our recent past."[33] Nehru, however, has not welcomed the suggestion that India become the nucleus of a "third bloc." He prefers to put it, rather, that India aims at creating an "area of peace."

The refusal to join any bloc, combined with the dislike of "imperialism" wherever it shows its head, has not, curiously enough, resulted in any animosity to Britain. For India, as for much of Asian opinion, the United States is the new standard-bearer of imperialism, and it is toward her that suspicion is directed. These attitudes, however, have not prevented the acceptance of American economic aid.[34]

The attempt to create goodwill in international relations has been given a practical and visible form in the visits exchanged by Nehru and the Russian, Chinese, and Yugoslav leaders, in 1954-1956, and also by the diplomatic endeavors of his right-hand man, Krishna Menon, to build a bridge between Russia and China, on the one side, and the United States and Britain, on the other. These middleman's efforts may often seem to Western opinion to go rather far in making verbal gestures toward the Communist world—politenesses which are seldom directed toward the United States. This can easily be explained, however, as the outcome of Nehru's realistic appreciation of the situation. Impoliteness toward the Communists may be dangerous. Toward the United States,

---

[32] Nehru on March 17, 1950. *Speeches 1949-1953*, p. 143.

[33] *Loc. cit.*, p. 144.

[34] The total amount of grants and credits to India and Pakistan in the period 1945-1954 is as follows: India, $275 million; Pakistan, $103 million. Aid to Ceylon is banned by the Battle Act on account of her trade with China; but in 1956, before the fall of the Kotelawala government, steps were being taken to circumvent this prohibition. (Figures from Department of State Publication 5801, Near and Middle Eastern Series 18 (May, 1955), p. 35.)

however, it is not. Indeed, despite the play that Nehru and other Indian statesmen make with various ideal concepts, doubtless sincerely held, there is little or nothing in Indian policy that is not explicable in simple terms of an eclectic policy based on the maintenance of the national interest. Where strength and the firm hand are likely to pay off—as toward Pakistan, or Goa, or (earlier) toward Hyderabad, or Junagadh, or the French enclaves in India— Indian policy lacks nothing in toughness. Where the strength of the other party demands that India tread softly, as in her relations with China, she treads softly. She has not the military strength to figure in the quarrels of the great powers, and she wishes these disputes to be muted, played down, as far as possible. Nehru himself has conceded the importance of the national interest:

We may talk about peace and freedom and earnestly mean what we say. But in the ultimate analysis, a government functions for the good of the country it governs and no government dare do anything which in the short or the long run is manifestly to the disadvantage of that country.[35]

In internal politics Nehru realizes clearly the risk of Communist subversion and fights it resolutely. In bordering states where action can be successfully taken against Communist influence it is taken —as in Nepal.

Pakistan has a dispute with her neighbor Afghanistan as well as her neighbor India. The issue with Afghanistan arises out of the latter's attempt to push a hypothetical new state called "Pashtunistan," to be carved out of the Pathan-inhabited lands of the North-West Frontier Province—though not, apparently, out of the equally Pathan-inhabited border regions of Afghanistan.[36] This is not likely to come to pass; meanwhile, however, it has led to attacks on Pakistan's missions in Afghanistan, and to the rupture of diplomatic relations.

In her relations with the broader world, Pakistan since 1954 has

[35] On Dec. 4, 1947. *Independence and After*, p. 205.
[36] Pashtun, Pathan, Pashto (their language), are all forms of the same word. On the many absurdities of this far from spontaneous agitation, see Peter Mayne, *The Narrow Smile* (London, 1955).

adopted a notably positive role. She has chosen her partners, and they are on the democratic side. "I am not a neutral, personally or politically," said Pakistan Prime Minister Mohammed Ali on October 15, 1954. "The neutral has no mind of his own. God gave us a mind and we should use it to come to conclusions."[37] Of this new decisiveness in Pakistan's policy there have been three principal instances. On April 2, 1954, Turkey and Pakistan signed an agreement for friendly co-operation in various fields, including possibly the military sphere. This agreement became absorbed in the Bagdad Pact, which Pakistan joined in September 1955, and which also includes Iraq, Iran, Turkey, and the United Kingdom. On May 19, after several months of negotiations, Pakistan and the United States signed a Mutual Defense Assistance Agreement providing for United States economic assistance to Pakistan for purposes of defense. It did not, as at first reported, provide the United States with bases in Pakistan; nevertheless, it was bitterly resented in India, which made it the excuse for breaking off current bilateral negotiations on Kashmir. Finally, in September 1954, Pakistan joined with the United States, the United Kingdom, Australia, France, New Zealand, and—in Asia—the Philippines and Thailand to create the South-East Asia Treaty Organization, a treaty for collective defense against both armed attack and internal subversion. Pakistan has thus aligned herself with the democratic world by joining one of the regional security arrangements which the United States has built, and another (the Bagdad Pact) which the United States supports, though not as a member.

Ceylon's relationship to the world power struggle is paradoxical. Unlike India and Pakistan, she did not until 1956 recognize the Communist government of China. Unlike them, however, she has a substantial trade with China. Ceylon's need to import rice and China's need of rubber led to the signing of the five-year Rubber-Rice Agreement in 1952, by which China buys rubber from Ceylon at a price higher than the world price and sells her rice at less than the world price. The prices are renegotiated each year. Ceylon has not so far joined any anti-Communist alliance, but under Sir John

[37] *New York Times*, Oct. 16, 1954.

Kotelawala she was veering nearer to Pakistan's attitude than to India's. This trend has been reversed since the rise to leadership of S. W. R. D. Bandaranaike.

Though Ceylon's foreign policy is not of world importance, the island has been prominent of late because of the naming for her capital of both the Commonwealth plan for economic aid to undeveloped countries—the Colombo Plan—and the concept of the "Colombo Powers." The first meeting of the Colombo Powers —that is, of India, Pakistan, Ceylon, Burma, and Indonesia, the five countries of that part of the world which had recently emerged from colonial status—was held at Ceylon's invitation in Colombo, April 28-May 2, 1954. The final communiqué included the courageous statement that "The Premiers discussed Communism in its national and international aspects. They affirmed their faith in democracy, and their determination to resist interference in the affairs of their countries by external Communist, anti-Communist or other agencies."

Another meeting was held at Bogor, Indonesia, in December, 1954. On this occasion emerged the idea of holding a much larger gathering—the portentous Afro-Asian Conference held at Bandung, Indonesia, on April 18-24, 1955. That the conference did not go on record only with the crypto-Communist sentiments expected was largely due to the sturdy common sense of Sir John Kotelawala, who said in a notable speech on April 21 that if the conference was united in its opposition to colonialism it should declare its opposition to Soviet colonialism as much as to western imperialism. "While, properly conceived, co-existence is the only alternative to destruction, the existence of the Cominform, the central agency directing all forms of subversion in Asian countries, makes talk of co-existence a snare and a delusion." Back in Colombo on April 26 and 27 he had to face a parliamentary vote of censure, which was easily defeated. At the same time he was reported to have said, on the question of recognizing China, that it called for "a policy of wait and see," and to have hinted that Ceylon might join a defense pact. In all this he was probably far more pro-Western than the bulk of public opinion in the island, as the 1956 general election suggests.

Conclusion

The foreign policies of India, Pakistan, and Ceylon are the product less of a long national history, as is the case with the countries of Europe, than of a long cultural, social, and religious tradition which has only recently taken, or taken again, the form of independent statehood. The long period of dependent status is one of the very important factors in the formation of present-day policy. It is natural, therefore, that there should be in these countries an ingrained suspicion of the West which it will take long years of patience and restraint to smooth out. This factor is strongest in India, least so in Ceylon, but nowhere is it absent.

Politically, these countries are organized as democracies, and democracies after the British model. Since they have not yet evolved any satisfactory party system, however, the question of their long-term viability cannot be said to have been answered more convincingly than by the cautious Scotch verdict of "not proven." Even so, their present political condition as practicing democracies is a shining example in a region of the world where democracies are few. On their ability to maintain their institutions, and on the foreign policies which emerge through the working of these institutions, much will depend in the future of South Asia and the world.

SELECTED BIBLIOGRAPHY

BIBLIOGRAPHICAL AIDS

Excellent full-scale bibliographical aids are available to the student of India, Pakistan, and Ceylon. The most complete and recent is *Government and Politics of India and Pakistan 1885-1955: A Bibliography of Works in Western Languages* (Berkeley, 1956), compiled by Patrick Wilson. This splendid work, issued by the South Asia Studies section of the University of California's Institute of East Asiatic Studies, may be supplemented by the monthly hand list of *Books on South Asia* added to the Berkeley Library, issued by the same Institute. A current list on a larger scale, cataloguing additions to the Library of Congress, is the quarterly, *Southern Asia Accessions List*, formerly (through January 1956) called *Southern Asia: Publications in Western Languages: A Quarterly Accessions List*. A bibliographical essay of great utility on publications down to 1952 is David G. Mandelbaum, "A Guide to Books on India," *American Political Science Review*, December, 1952. Publications on India, Pakistan, and Ceylon are listed *inter alia* in Henry L. Roberts's comprehensive *Foreign Affairs Bibliography 1942-1952* (New York, 1955).

GENERAL BACKGROUND

The geographical setting is described in masterly fashion in O. H. K. Spate, *India and Pakistan: A General and Regional Geography* (London, 1954), which may be supplemented for historical study by C. Collin Davies, *An Historical Atlas of the Indian Peninsula* (Madras, 1949). An excellent general description combining history, sociology, and politics is to be found in Daniel and Alice Thorner's chapter on India and Pakistan in *Most of the World*, ed. Ralph Linton (New York, 1949). By far the best introduction available in one volume is W. Norman Brown, *The United States and India and Pakistan* (Cambridge, Mass., 1953). Professor Brown has also edited a collection of articles originally written for the *Encyclopedia Americana*. These were published under the title *India, Pakistan, Ceylon* (Ithaca, 1951) and cover briefly almost all aspects of the three countries. A work of graceful and compact lucidity is Percival Spear, *India, Pakistan, and the West* (London, 1952). Lord Birdwood, an extremely well-informed British soldier whose family has a tradition of service in India and who himself knows the subcontinent intimately, deals informatively with the transfer of power, the political conditions in India and Pakistan, and the Kashmir problem in *A Continent Decides* (London, 1953). The climate of Indian political thought from early times to the present is surveyed in D. Mackenzie Brown, *The White Umbrella: Indian Political Thought from Manu to Gandhi* (Berkeley, 1953).

OFFICIAL PUBLICATIONS AND REFERENCE WORKS

All three governments publish annual or (in the case of Pakistan) biennial information volumes which are indispensable sources of political and statistical information. The Indian volume is on the largest scale of the three. The most recent in each series to appear are: *India: A Reference Annual: 1955* (New Delhi, 1955); *Pakistan 1954-1955* (Karachi, 1955); and *Ceylon Year Book 1955* (Colombo, 1955). The official *Parliamentary Debates* of the three countries are, of course, extremely useful records of discussions of foreign policy and other topics; but there are very few libraries in which they are available. The fortnightly *Commonwealth Survey: A Record of United Kingdom and Commonwealth Affairs*, issued by the Central Office of Information, London, lists all policy decisions affecting any part of the Commonwealth and provides texts of communiqué and important speeches. An extremely comprehensive unofficial reference work is *The British Commonwealth 1956* (London, 1956), which is a treasury of information on a wide variety of topics. It also contains admirable interpretive articles by Gerald S. Graham, Nicholas Mansergh, and A. D. Knox.

CONSTITUTIONS

The text of *The Constitution of India* is published by the Government of India Press, New Delhi (1950, with revised editions from time to time to cover the latest amendments). The Ministry of Law, Government of Pakistan, has just published *The Constitution of the Islamic Republic of Pakistan* (Karachi, 1956). The constitution of Ceylon, which is not a single document, is most conveniently found in *Documents and Speeches on British Commonwealth Affairs 1931-1952*, ed. Nicholas Mansergh (2 vols., London, 1953).

COMMENTARIES ON CONSTITUTIONS

The constitutions of India and Ceylon have already attracted a considerable volume of scholarly examination and comment. There has not yet been time for this to be true of the new constitution of Pakistan. On the Indian constitution, the lengthiest commentary is Durga Das Basu, *Commentary on the Constitution of India*

(Calcutta, 1952). The author makes many comparisons with constitutional law and usage in other countries. The series of volumes *The British Commonwealth: The Development of its Laws and Constitutions* (general ed., George W. Keeton) has the excellent *The Republic of India: The Development of its Laws and Constitution* (London, 1951), by Alan Gledhill. There is also a series of lectures by Sir Ivor Jennings, *Some Characteristics of the Indian Constitution* (Madras, 1953). A good treatment in short compass is C. H. Alexandrowicz, "The Indian Constitution," in *The Year Book of World Affairs*, 1953 (London, 1953). See also a critical examination by D. N. Bannerjee, "The Indian Presidency," *The Political Quarterly*, January-March 1955. On Ceylon, see Jennings, *The Constitution of Ceylon* (London, 1948), and, in the Keeton series, Jennings and H. W. Tambiah, *The Dominion of Ceylon* (London, 1952). Jennings is the leading authority on Ceylon, as well as being a considerable authority on Pakistan and India, having been during 1942-1955 variously constitutional adviser to the governments of both Ceylon and Pakistan, and Vice-Chancellor of the University of Ceylon. The volume on Pakistan in the Keeton series has not yet appeared.

COMMONWEALTH RELATIONS

The Mansergh volumes of documents, mentioned above, are indispensable. Of the companion work by Mansergh, *Survey of British Commonwealth Affairs*, one admirable volume has so far appeared: *Problems of External Policy, 1931-1939*. The other promised volume is eagerly awaited by all students of Commonwealth affairs. Meanwhile, there is illuminating commentary to be found in his essays *The Commonwealth and the Nations* (London, 1948), and in his report of the Fifth Unofficial Commonwealth Relations Conference, *The Multi-Racial Commonwealth* (London, 1955). The same themes are dealt with in Jennings, *The Commonwealth in Asia* (Oxford, 1951). Jennings on his return from Ceylon gave an interesting series of broadcasts, reprinted in *The Listener* (London): "A Great Experiment in Government" (Feb. 10, 1955); "Making Self-Government Work" (Feb. 17, 1955), and eight articles on the general theme of "Self-Government in the

Commonwealth," with particular reference to Asian areas; *The Listener*, July 14-Sept. 1, 1955. A more recent article by Jennings, "Crown and Commonwealth in Asia," *International Affairs* (London), April 1956, has expressed apprehension about certain recent developments. A general survey of Commonwealth questions is to be found in H. Duncan Hall, K. C. Wheare, and Alexander Brady, "The British Commonwealth: A Symposium," *American Political Science Review*, December 1953. Some interesting suggestions which point in the direction of strengthening the Commonwealth are to be found in two articles on "The Future of the Commonwealth," by an eminent member of the present Government of India, K. M. Panikkar, in *Manchester Guardian Weekly*, June 21 and 28, 1956.

INDIA UNDER BRITISH RULE

Many general histories of India have been published in English. That on the largest scale is the incomplete co-operative work *The Cambridge History of India* (1922-1937). Among the most useful are J. C. Powell-Price, *A History of India* (London, 1955), and a work in three volumes by three Indian scholars, R. C. Majumdar, N. C. Raychaudhuri, and Kalikinkar Datta, *An Advanced History of India* (London, 1946). The standard work on the history of British administration is E. J. Thompson and G. T. Garratt, *The Rise and Fulfilment of British Rule in India* (London, 1934). The completed story is surveyed in Sir Percival Griffiths, *The British Impact on India* (London, 1952). Some outstanding works of imaginative literature are still irreplaceable guides to the *ethos* of British India. Such are Rudyard Kipling, *Kim* (London, 1901), and E. M. Forster, *A Passage to India* (London, 1924). The voluminous writings of the late Sir Reginald Coupland on the problems of India as they appeared in the last years of British rule still have value. The one-volume edition is *The Indian Problem* (New York, 1944). The transfer of power is narrated from the published documents in E. W. R. Lumby, *The Transfer of Power in India 1945-7* (London, 1954). The last stages of the story with much fascinating personal detail are given in diary form by Alan

Campbell-Johnson, press secretary to the last viceroy, in *Mission with Mountbatten* (New York, 1953).

NEHRU AND GANDHI

An understanding of the two leading figures of the Congress Party is essential to an understanding of modern India. Gandhi's autobiography is published under the confused title *Gandhi's Autobiography: The Story of My Experiments With Truth* (Washington, 1948). Both *Towards Freedom: The Autobiography of Jawaharlal Nehru* (New York, 1941) and the same author's *The Discovery of India* (London, 1952) are in substance autobiographical. The latter also contains many historical and political reflections of value. It is the fruit of the author's enforced leisure in prison during 1944. An excellent biography is Frank Moraes, *Jawaharlal Nehru* (New York, 1956). Nehru's speeches are available in official volumes, of which two have so far appeared: *Independence and After: Speeches of Jawaharlal Nehru, 1946-1949* (New Delhi, 1949) and *Jawaharlal Nehru's Speeches 1949-1953* (New Delhi, 1954). Annual volumes of the Indian Prime Minister's press conferences also are published, and these throw some light on the development of foreign policy.

INDIA: CONTEMPORARY PROBLEMS

There is a wealth of substantial and illuminating articles on all aspects of the current Indian scene to be found in the major periodicals. Among them may be mentioned the following: *Current History* for February 1956, devoted in its entirety to a useful *Report on India* by various hands; on regional particularism and the problem of states reorganization, Selig S. Harrison, "The Challenge to Indian Nationalism," *Foreign Affairs*, July 1956, and Satish Kumar Arora, "The Reorganization of the Indian States," *Far Eastern Survey*, February 1956; on the major challenge to democracy in India, John H. Kautsky, "Indian Communist Party Strategy since 1947," *Pacific Affairs*, June 1955; on economic problems, Jerome B. Cohen, "India's Foreign Economic Policies," *World Politics*, July 1955, and E. P. W. da Costa, "India's New Five-Year Plan," *Foreign Affairs*, July 1956.

INDIA: FOREIGN POLICY

There is a wide variety of articles, some of which always impinge upon or deal directly with Indian foreign policy and its formulation, to be found in *The Indian Year Book of International Affairs*, ed. Charles Alexandrowicz (Madras, annual since 1952). The volume for 1955 is the latest to appear so far. J. C. Kundra, *Indian Foreign Policy 1947-54: A Study of Relations with the Western Bloc* (Groningen, 1955), is a careful and unbiased survey, more valuable for India's relations with the United States than for her Commonwealth relationship. Publications of the Indian Council of World Affairs are, of course, worthy of consultation. Two may be mentioned particularly: *Indian-American Relations* (Bombay, 1950), digest of the discussions at an Indian-American conference, and K. P. Karunakaran, *India in World Affairs* (New York, 1952). A valuable article is Taya Zinkin, "Indian Foreign Policy: An Interpretation of Attitudes," *World Politics*, January, 1955. The historical roots of contemporary Indian views are surveyed in *The Foundations of India's Foreign Policy, Vol., I, 1860-1882*, by Bisheshwar Prasad (Calcutta, 1956). Subsequent volumes covering the more recent periods should be of great interest. The Indian High Commissioner in London, V. L. Pandit, expounds current policy in "India's Foreign Policy," *Foreign Affairs*, April 1956. A sympathetic interpretation by an American observer is Chester Bowles, "A Fresh Look at Free Asia," *Foreign Affairs*, October 1954. A detailed and scathingly unsympathetic analysis of the views of former ambassador K. M. Panikkar is Guy J. Pauker, "Panikkarism, the Highest Stage of Opportunism," *World Politics*, October, 1954. Some indications of Indian public opinion may be gathered from Margaret W. Fisher and Joan V. Bondurant, *Indian Views of Sino-Indian Relations* (Berkeley, 1956), in the Indian Press Digest Monograph Series. Robert A. Scalapino, " 'Neutralism' in Asia," *American Political Science Review*, March, 1954, is one of the best discussions available of its subject. An excellent study of India's place in world affairs, still valuable though now several years old, is Werner Levi, *Free India in Asia* (Minneapolis, 1952). In 1955-1956 a Study Group of the Council on Foreign Relations held discussions on foreign policy in India with a Study Group of the Indian Council of World Affairs. The "Working Papers" prepared before the conference are exceedingly discerning, but are unfortunately not available to the general public; the conference proceedings, however, will probably be published.

PAKISTAN: BACKGROUND

Wilfred Cantwell Smith, *Modern Islam in India* (London, 1946), is indispensable, but needs to be used cautiously on account of its leftward major premises. The *locus classicus* on *The Making of Pakistan* is Richard Symonds's book of that name (London, 1950; 2nd ed., 1951). The best life of the Quaid-i-Azam is Hector Bolitho, *Jinnah: Creator of Pakistan* (London, 1954), written with the approval and co-operation of the Government of Pakistan but without access to Jinnah's papers, since this was refused by Miss Jinnah, his sister; in the circumstances, an excellent book. Three good books on the culture and attitudes of Pakistan: *Crescent and Green*, a miscellany (London, 1955); S. K. Ikram and Percival Spear, eds., *The Cultural Heritage of Pakistan* (London, 1956); and Ishtiaq Husain Qureshi, *The Pakistani Way of Life* (London, 1956). Ian Stephens, *Horned Moon* (Bloomington, 1955), gives a sympathetic account of Pakistan by an Englishman long resident in pre-partition India, and former editor of the *Calcutta Statesman*.

PAKISTAN: INTERNAL POLITICS

There have been many good articles on Pakistan's internal difficulties, and some of these are still worth consulting; among them are: F. M. Innes, "The Political Outlook in Pakistan," *Pacific Affairs*, December 1953; Ardath W. Burks, "Constitution-Making in Pakistan," *Political Science Quarterly*, December 1954; Stanley Maron, "The Problem of East Pakistan," *Pacific Affairs*, June 1955; and Keith Callard, "The Political Stability of Pakistan," *Pacific Affairs*, March 1956. Herbert Feldman, *A Constitution for Pakistan* (Karachi, 1956) is not, despite its title, an analysis of the constitution of Pakistan; it is a round-by-round account of the difficulties encountered in drafting a new constitution, from partition to the eve of the adoption of the constitution in 1956. It is a useful and clearly written survey, and still has relevance, for the forces which made a constitution difficult to frame will continue to interpose difficulties in the working of the constitution.

PAKISTAN: FOREIGN POLICY

Little of value has been written on the foreign policy of Pakistan since it assumed its new orientation and relinquished neutralism. Some basic factors are well stated in the collected speeches of the able first Prime Minister of Pakistan: Liaquat Ali Khan, *Pakistan, Heart of Asia* (Cambridge, Mass., 1950). The diplomatic background of the United States-Pakistan treaty is reviewed, as far as known at present, in James W. Spain, "Military Assistance for Pakistan," *American Political Science Review*, September 1954. The strategic situation of Pakistan is well outlined in William H. Hessler, "Pakistan and the Himalayas," *United States Naval Institute Proceedings*, August, 1954.

CEYLON

The articles by Sir Ivor Jennings cited above under "Commonwealth Relations" have a particular value for Ceylon. See also, by the same authority, "Politics in Ceylon since 1952," *Pacific Affairs*, December 1954. Sir John Kotelawala's autobiography, *An Asian Prime Minister's Story* (London, 1956), has naturally suffered a certain loss of interest since the author ceased to be prime minister almost at the moment of publication. It also is somewhat thin in its account of the Bandung Conference, precisely the topic on which one might have hoped it would be most illuminating. The electoral reversal of 1956 in Ceylon is so recent that its significance has not yet been assessed adequately in print. See, however, a useful note, "The Unorthodox Left and the Ceylon Elections," *The World Today*, May 1956.

QUESTIONS AT ISSUE

On Kashmir: The two best books on the Kashmir dispute, both thorough and unprejudiced, are: Josef Korbel, *Danger in Kashmir* (Princeton, 1954), and Lord Birdwood, *Two Nations and Kashmir*

(London, 1956). Prem Nath Bazaz, himself a Kashmiri and a resolutely independent thinker, has two good books on the subject: *The History of Struggle for Freedom in Kashmir* (New Delhi, 1954) and the slighter *Azad Kashmir (Free Kashmir): A Democratic Socialist Conception* (Lahore, n.d.). Also worth noting are Michael Brecher, "Kashmir: A Case Study in United Nations Mediation," *Pacific Affairs*, September 1953, and Murray Green, "Kashmir, Valley of Indecision," *United States Naval Institute Proceedings*, December 1955.

The Water Dispute: The intricate question of the Radcliffe Award and the subsequent disputes concerning the use of the water in the Indus tributaries is clearly set forth in two articles—Lord Birdwood, "The Quarrel of the Canals," *International Relations* (London), October 1954, and F. J. Fowler, "The Indo-Pakistan Water Dispute," in *The Year Book of World Affairs 1955* (London, 1955).

On "Pakhtunistan": This bone of contention in Pakistan-Afghan relations is dealt with in "The Implications of 'Pakhtunistan,' " *The World Today*, September, 1955, and illuminated by Peter Mayne's travel book, *The Narrow Smile* (London, 1955).

France

GRAHAM H. STUART

Emeritus Professor of
Political Science
Stanford University

France

CHAPTER 14

THE BACKGROUND OF FOREIGN POLICY IN THE FRENCH FOURTH REPUBLIC

A vital factor in any consideration of the foreign policy of France is that Frenchmen never forget that their country is the oldest state in continental Europe and has played an important role as a Great Power, continuously from the Dark Ages up to the Second World War. French kings during feudal times had begun to assert the power of the monarch over the barons, and the story of Joan of Arc became the basis of a national sentiment. The community was disrupted by the religious conflicts of the Protestant Reformation, but after this period Henri de Navarre was able to reform and strengthen the royal power during his reign as Henri IV (1589-1610). Henri's reign ended with his assassination, and his widow conferred the direction of the realm on one of the greatest of the king's ministers in French history, the able and ruthless Cardinal Richelieu. Henri's son, Louis XIII, was only nine years old when he succeeded to the throne, but the power of the monarchy was increased by the industry and skill of Richelieu and of his successor as chief minister, Cardinal Mazarin.

When the Grand Monarch, Louis XIV, came to the throne of

France, royal authority was firmly entrenched and France had practically achieved the position of a well-organized and well-administered national state. Royal absolutism, maintained throughout the whole reign of Louis XIV (1643-1715), established France more firmly than ever as one of the great states of Europe. Louis XIV benefited from the aid of able and skillful ministers, particularly Colbert; but the wars he waged taxed the resources of the kingdom even though the successes of his generals made France the dominant power of the continent. The glittering court he maintained at Versailles also became a burden to his people.

The age of absolute monarchs was waning. It ended suddenly and catastrophically in France with the Great Revolution of 1789. In spite of the violence and disorder of the Revolution, the prestige of France in Europe was enhanced. The revolutionary armies carried the new doctrines of equality and liberty far beyond the old boundaries of the kingdom. Then the force of the Revolution fell into the hands of Napoleon Bonaparte, and the Napoleonic Empire dominated the whole European scene until its military success was finally ended at Waterloo. The Congress of Vienna in 1815 restored some of the boundaries and political institutions of pre-Napoleonic times, and restored the Bourbon monarchy in France itself.

This Bourbon restoration was followed in 1830 by a revolution that resulted in the establishment of a constitutional monarchy under Louis Philippe, and for more than a decade there was peaceful economic development. In 1848, revolutionary movements in Europe found expression in France as well as in other countries, and a republic was established in the revolutionary year; Louis Napoleon, a nephew of Napoleon Bonaparte, was its President. He was able to seize power in 1852 and have himself endorsed by a plebiscite as Emperor. Napoleon III, as he called himself, was able for some time to make himself a diplomatic force in European affairs. His career ended in the crushing defeat of France by Prussia in 1871, and the Second Empire collapsed.

The Third Republic was established in the midst of the uncertainty and confusion which followed this Prussian victory, and the constitutional laws under which it functioned were not finally adopted until 1875. In spite of this inauspicious beginning, the Republic was able to extend the influence of France. A great part of the French overseas empire was built up after 1875. Alliances were made with England and with Russia which enabled France to emerge as one of the victors in World War I. French diplomacy after 1918 was primarily concerned with security against the power of a resurgent Germany, and for many of the years between 1918 and 1939 France made herself one of the most important states in Europe by virtue of the alliances which were made with this purpose in view.

In 1939 France had not fully recovered from the injuries she had suffered in World War I. The French birth rate had been declining since 1900, and the great excess of deaths over births from 1914 to 1918 had created a population deficit which was barely balanced by heavy immigration and the annexation of Alsace and Lorraine. The economic damage and dislocation of these same years had been very slowly remedied, and social policies had been moving slowly also. The equipment of the army was obsolete by modern standards, and was unable to withstand the *Blitzkrieg* which began in 1940. The defeat of France was complete by June 1940, and five dark years of Nazi occupation followed. Finally victory was achieved by the United Nations, assisted by the heroic efforts of the French underground resistance, and the Fourth Republic began its life in 1946.

This brief summary of the history of the French nation is designed to explain some of the attitudes of many Frenchmen today. They look back on a long history—taught to them in their school days—which records the early organization of France as a national state. The history shows long periods in which their country was one of the great states of continental Europe—even when struggling through revolutionary disturbances. The Great Revolution actually contributed to national prestige—it carried the mission of equality and democracy beyond the French frontiers, even when its character changed to that of the Napoleonic dictatorship. Paradoxical though it may seem, Napoleon Bonaparte was regarded as "a son of the Revolution." Though the Third Republic fell in 1940, it is not surprising that many Frenchmen regard their country still as a Great Power: great in its past prestige and strength in Europe, and great also in its "civilizing mission."

The defeat of the Third Republic, and the problems of political and economic reconstruction confronting the Fourth Republic, have diminished the prestige of France both in European and in world affairs. The United States and the Soviet Union have taken over principal roles in Europe under the conditions of the "cold war." French leaders face a new situation. It is no longer possible for them confidently to assume that their country must be regarded as one of the great powers. The foreign policy of the Fourth Republic must be accommodated to this situation, which differs greatly from that of the nineteenth century and the more recent period preceding World War II.

Factors of Weakness

Some elements of weakness, which had to be taken into account while policy was being formulated under the Fourth Republic, need discussion.

An exposed strategic position in Europe has long created anxiety in the minds of those who have made French foreign policy. The frontier which has been their most serious concern lies in the west —the Franco-German frontier across which invasion has come twice during the twentieth century. The construction of the Maginot line in the days of the Third Republic was designed to reduce this risk, but the events of 1940 showed that such fortifications could be turned or by-passed. It is proper to remark that in these days of airplanes and atomic weapons all nations are strategically exposed. Nevertheless, it must be said that since 1870 French leaders have been preoccupied with security as a basic problem of foreign policy.

A greater urgency is imparted to this concern by the fact that the natural resources of France are not abundant as to coal and iron ore, the basic materials for industrial development. Industrialization has been slow. In 1955, barely a third of the working population was engaged in industry, and almost a third was engaged in agriculture and fishing. These proportions contrast, for example, with those in the United States, where less than a tenth of the working force is in agricultural employment, and more than two-fifths in industry. One other measure of industrial development might be mentioned. Nearly three-fourths of the French industrial labor force is employed by firms with fewer than a hundred employees—the corresponding proportion in the United States is one-fourth. Although its industrial potential is increasing, France still remains a country of small-scale manufacture in comparison to the other great powers of the world. Industry is a vitally important factor in defense, and the lack of this component of power has increased the dangers of the French strategic situation. Naturally enough, foreign policy has been directed toward building up alliances and toward developing a system of international guarantees, which would protect frontiers and would compensate for deficiencies in industry and natural resources.

Leaders of the Fourth Republic have also in mind the factors which brought the Third Republic to its inglorious end. One very evident cause was weakness in manpower. In 1936 the deficiency of births which occurred during World War I was sharply revealed. The number of young men inducted annually into the army from then until the outbreak of World War II was less than a fourth of the number in the annual classes before 1914. The army, thus reduced in size, was inadequately equipped. A young instructor at the École de Guerre, Colonel Charles de Gaulle, as early as 1934 urged the utilization of tanks and bombing planes and mechanized equipment, but this advice went unheeded.

A further weakness lay in the demoralization of domestic politics as deep cleavages of opinion appeared. Successive crises revealed more clearly than ever the classic problem of French politics—the problem of finding strong and effective leadership.

The greatest weakness was the wavering conduct of diplomacy. The purpose of French policy was quite consistent—to safeguard the security of the country against the possibility of renewed aggression by Germany. Methods for achieving this purpose varied widely. At the Paris Peace Conference in 1919 Clemenceau had hoped that France would be given a frontier on the Rhine, as a "physical guarantee" of future security. The other Allies refused to grant this claim on the ground that more than five million

Germans lived on the left bank of the Rhine and would be separated from their homeland. The Versailles Treaty finally provided that Allied forces should occupy the Rhineland for fifteen years, and that the territory should be permanently demilitarized. At the same time a promise was made that both the United States and the British Empire would negotiate treaties with France, giving assurances that each power would come to the aid of France in the event of any unprovoked move of aggression against her by Germany. The United States never ratified the Versailles Treaty so this pledge was not carried into effect. The British government offered such a guarantee in 1922, only to have Prime Minister Poincaré refuse it because it was not accompanied by a military convention specifying the assistance to be rendered. French leaders began the interwar period, therefore, with the feeling that their country had given up territorial claims, which might have yielded security, without receiving treaty guarantees in return.

The reparations clauses of the Versailles Treaty were expected to limit German power as well as compensate France for war damage. Clauses provided that voluntary failure by Germany to meet payments would allow the Allied powers to take such measures as their governments deemed necessary to compel Germany to meet reparations obligations. In 1923, accordingly, the French and Belgian governments occupied the Ruhr, although the British representative on the Reparations Commission refused to vote that Germany was in voluntary default. The Germans met this attempt to enforce the clauses by a passive resistance which brought the economic life of the region to a standstill. The action which Poincaré had initiated failed of result, and Franco-British relations were seriously strained.

In 1924 an association of moderate left parties won an election in France, and Aristide Briand began a long tenure of the office of Foreign Minister in 1925, holding it through various changes of ministries until 1932. Under his leadership French policy changed from the earlier efforts at rigorous enforcement of treaty provisions to one of conciliation and adjustment. He strove to strengthen the League of Nations as a means of preserving peace, and he pledged France to the Locarno Pacts which were designed to guarantee the Franco-German frontier. During these same years Édouard Herriot, another moderate leader, supported the Dawes Plan which in 1924 began a realistic adjustment of the scale of reparations payments.

In 1930 Hitler's National Socialist party won more than a hundred seats in the German Reichstag, and at the same time the world depression produced an economic crisis in all the countries of Europe. French foreign policy abruptly changed its orientation. Pierre Laval first came into office in 1931 and then in 1934 returned to the Foreign Ministry after the assassination of Louis Barthou, who had tried to strengthen and consolidate the French system of alliances in Eastern Europe and the Balkans. Laval after 1934 began to make deals with the dictators. He acquiesced in German rearmament and he consented to Mussolini's conquest of Abyssinia and his support of Franco in the Spanish civil war. Édouard Daladier, shortly after he became Prime Minister in 1938, followed Neville Chamberlain's initiative and agreed to the Munich Pact that dismembered Czechoslovakia, although France had clear commitments to Czechoslovakia under a treaty of 1925. Winston Churchill's condemnation of these policies at the time may be recalled: "France and Britain had to choose between war and dishonor. They chose dishonor. They will have war." Even after German troops had crossed into Poland on September 1, 1939, Foreign Minister Georges Bonnet refused to join the British in a warning to Berlin. France entered the war unwilling and unprepared, and her defeat came in 1940.

Daladier was Premier at the time war was declared, but criticism mounted during the successes of Germany in the Scandinavian countries, and Paul Reynaud became Premier in March of 1940. When the German invasion made swift advances into France in May, Marshal Henri Philippe Pétain was brought into the Cabinet. In June Pétain became Premier, and immediately sued for peace. The armistice, published in the last week of June, provided for German occupation of the northern part of France and all of its Atlantic coastline. The remainder was to be under the charge of a French government, subject to some control by the German authorities in the northern zone. Members of Parliament were called to a special session in Vichy, and the 700 who attended voted, with only a few dissenting, to end the Republic and establish a new government headed by Marshal Pétain as Chief of State. This government, which had a brief and inglorious life, is referred to as the Vichy government.

On the day after Pétain decided to sue for peace, General Charles de Gaulle broadcast an appeal from London asking all French men and women who wished to carry on the fight against Germany to get in touch with him. A year later a French National Committee was set up in London, and in 1943 the French Committee of National Liberation was established in North Africa. This Committee, under General de Gaulle's leadership, worked with the underground forces of resistance which were organized in France. When Allied invasion was successful, General de Gaulle arrived in Paris in August 1944, a provisional government was set up, and the task of rebuilding France was begun.

The Creation of the Fourth Republic

The provisional government proceeded promptly—perhaps too promptly, in view of the many problems which confronted it—to create a new constitution. An Assembly was elected on October 21, 1945, and at the same time a referendum asked the French citizen to declare whether this Assembly should have power to draft a constitution, and further asked whether authority should be given to the Assembly and the provisional government to direct the affairs of the community until the constitution should be adopted. The constitution was finally proposed for ratification by a referendum on May 5, 1946, and failed of adoption. A second Assembly was elected on June 2, 1946, and presented a second constitution to the voters on October 13, 1946. This second constitution was adopted by a vote of 9 million to 8 million, in approximate figures, but nearly 8 million voters abstained from voting. At the time this seemed to make the future of the document insecure, but it has remained in force and serves as an adequate basis for the Fourth Republic.

The debate on the two constitutions was exacerbated by the attitude of the Communist party, which had strongly advocated the first. During the year that these debates were occupying the attention of the Assemblies and the citizens, it was necessary to undertake the pressing tasks of economic reconstruction and to adjust the relations of France with the other states of the world.

It is not surprising, therefore, that the Big Three—Great Britain, the USSR, and the United States—did not invite France to attend the conferences at Yalta and Potsdam in spite of the vigorous protests of General de Gaulle. Neither did France play an important role in the conference at San Francisco which drew up the Charter of the United Nations. One French correspondent characterized his country's situation with mournful cynicism: "The fall in our fortunes has left us only a corner seat at the table in the high councils of the United Nations." Nevertheless the United States, over Soviet protests, had insisted that France participate in the occupation of Germany, even though her zone be taken from the United States occupied area. When the Peace Conference met in Paris in July 1946, and France with a permanent seat in the Security Council of the United Nations was recognized as one of the Big Four in European affairs, it seemed that *la Grande Nation* was on the road to regain at least a part of her former prestige.

Insistence on Claims Against Germany, 1946-1948

In the first years of the Fourth Republic the attitudes of 1919-1920 reappeared in foreign policy. A weak and disunited Germany was regarded as desirable, and even necessary, in order to safeguard the security of France. For more than two years, from 1946 to the end of 1948, French leaders opposed every Allied suggestion looking toward the recovery of Germany either politically or economically. In August 1946 the governments of Britain and the United States proposed to reduce occupation costs by combining the three occupation zones for economic purposes, but the French government refused to co-operate with such a scheme.

The French Foreign Office at the Quai d'Orsay continued to insist that the Rhineland and the Ruhr should be detached from Germany. If that separation were not feasible, then the territories should remain under international control, and in any case no German government should be established until a settlement in regard to their future status should be reached. As to the type of German government, the French practically insisted that it should have the form of a federal system so that Prussia should never again have a dominant influence.

Inasmuch as the Saar was wholly within the zone of occupation assigned to France and the need for Saar coal was critical, Foreign Minister Georges Bidault at the Moscow Conference of the Powers in 1947 demanded that the Saar mines become the property of the French state, that the Saar be included in the French economic and monetary system, and that the territory be removed from the jurisdiction of the Allied Control Council. The other powers refused to go that far until the German peace settlement should be decided, but the representatives of both the United States and Great Britain showed some sympathy for the French demands. The problem of the Saar finally was the subject of consultations between French Foreign Minister Robert Schuman and Chancellor Konrad Adenauer of West Germany in 1954, and progress was made toward establishing a European statute for the territory.

This early phase of foreign policy can be understood. It reflects French anxieties of long standing. At the same time it was an effort to recover influence in the councils of the great powers. Co-operation with other states became the guiding line of policy after this initial period of intransigence.

European Co-operation

The Marshall Plan offered an opportunity for European co-operation to which French leadership gave enthusiastic support. The conference which drew up plans for making use of aid offered by the United States met in Paris in July 1947. The headquarters of the Organization for European Economic Co-operation (OEEC) was established in Paris in 1948, and continues to function as an agency for associated action by seventeen western European states. The Brussels Treaty of Alliance, signed by France, Britain, and the Benelux countries on March 17, 1948, created a basis for European political co-operation.

The first concrete proposal toward uniting Europe was taken

by the Consultative Council of the five signatories of the Brussels Treaty in January 1949, when it was agreed that a Council of Europe consisting of a Committee of Ministers with an adjunct advisory representative body should be established. The French view that the members of this European Assembly should be chosen from the various groups in the national parliaments was accepted. Inasmuch as the Foreign Affairs Committee of the French National Assembly had overwhelmingly approved a resolution advocating a constituent European Assembly, the French delegation advanced enthusiastically upon the road to a federation of Europe and a European parliament. The British delegation opposed a federal European system, and warned that Britain would not participate in it. Some convinced French federalists such as MM. Bidault, André Philip, and Reynaud were inclined to go it alone without the British, but the French delegation as a whole refused to take such a drastic step and agreed to proceed by way of functional associations with limited powers.

The Council of Europe, as established by a statute signed in London on May 5, 1949, consisted of three bodies: a Council of the Foreign Ministers of the ten signatory states plus those which subsequently adhered; a Consultative Assembly of 127 representatives, 18 each from the four principal states (Britain, France, Italy, and West Germany) and smaller numbers from the others; and a Secretariat of 200 members. It must be granted that the Council of Europe has not acquired actual powers of authority, but it continues to be a center of discussion for various plans of association and even federation of European countries. It might well become the headquarters of some form of European Union.

Just a month before the setting-up of the Council of Europe there was signed in Washington the defense pact creating the North Atlantic Treaty Organization, which brought the United States and Canada into a treaty alliance with ten western European states (Belgium, Denmark, France, Iceland, Italy, Luxembourg, the Netherlands, Norway, Portugal, Britain), to which Greece and Turkey were added in February 1952. It might well be argued that a large part of the initiative for this result came from an appeal made to the United States on February 25, 1949, by the

French Prime Minister, Henri Queuille, who declared, "The
United States can never permit France and western Europe to be
invaded by Russia as they were by Germany. . . . France, as an
outpost of Europe, cannot hold out alone. Nor can she hold out
only with the aid of the Benelux countries on the one hand and
of Great Britain on the other. That is why western Europe must
be in a position to count on the aid of the United States."

The European Coal and Steel Community, another important
agency for co-operative action, was the result of French initiative.
It was proposed by Foreign Minister Robert Schuman to make
war between France and Germany, according to his statement,
". . . not only unthinkable but in actual fact impossible." It was
designed to integrate the industry of the Ruhr with that of its
less powerful neighbors, and thereby prevent any European nation
from securing an advantageous position in the utilization of these
vital sinews of war. Franco-German co-operation was indispensable
to any plan of European integration. The treaty was announced
on May 9, 1950, and was enthusiastically received by many
Europeans and Americans. Great Britain, though she refused to
join, promised full co-operation with the purposes of the plan.
M. Schuman extended an invitation to those states participating
in the Marshall Plan, declaring that the "French government proposes to place Franco-German production of steel as a whole
under a common higher authority within the framework open to
the participation of the other countries of Europe . . . the first
concrete foundation . . . of European federation."

There was bound to be opposition on both sides of the Rhine—
M. Daladier called it a "Pan-German Europe" and Dr. Kurt
Schumacher, leader of the German Social Democrats, stigmatized
it as a "Pan-French" conception. M. Guy Mollet, as Minister of
European Affairs in the last half of 1950, opposed the plan unless
Britain would join; and the Socialist M. Jules Moch, Defense
Minister, would have no deal of any sort with Germany. Fortunately, M. Jean Monnet, the technical advisor who had formulated
the details of the plan, had a great and deserved reputation based
on his direction of internal development plans in France. The plan
benefited from his skill, and from the prestige of the successful

years of the "Monnet Plan" in France. As ultimately initialed in March 1951, and ratified by the French Assembly on December 13 after a week's strenuous debate, the plan included France, West Germany, Italy, Belgium, the Netherlands and Luxembourg. These countries produce 60 per cent of Europe's steel and 48 per cent of its coal. The Strasbourg Assembly of the Council of Europe endorsed the plan and Chancellor Adenauer vigorously supported it. Aside from the economic advantages which arise from it, it has proved the most successful postwar effort yet made towards a permanent settlement of the relations between France and Germany.

As the relationship between the United States and Soviet Russia became more tense, the need for strengthening NATO by adding the support of West Germany became evident; nevertheless the idea of German rearmament was as distasteful to France as to the Soviet Union. In fact, when General Lucius Clay, in a speech in New York on May 7, 1950, suggested the rearming of Germany, Prime Minister René Pleven violently opposed the proposal in a speech before the Council of the Republic. However, the outbreak of war in Korea in June 1950 produced a situation where it was clear that the United States could not protect Europe and at the same time carry on a major war in the Far East. In July the United States High Commissioner in Germany stated frankly that Germany should have the means to defend itself if attacked. When, towards the end of September 1950, NATO declared that there was a need for Germany to participate actively in the defense of western Europe, France was forced to act.

In October 1950, M. Pleven proposed the establishment of a European army in which no country would predominate and which would be devoted solely to the protection of Europe. To reconcile French citizens who opposed any German rearmament, Foreign Minister Schuman pointed out that the Pleven Plan would be arming Europe to protect Europe, since the inclusion of Germany in a common defense system, organized and controlled by the participants exercising collective authority at all stages, was not arming Germany. Furthermore, it would strengthen the idea of European co-operation. Incidentally, but advantageously, it would reduce the strain on the French military budget. To make the plan more acceptable in France, it was provided that Germany would not make any contribution to European defence until after she had agreed to the Schuman Plan.

Nevertheless opposition was bitter and widespread. French fears of a reappearance of German militarism outweighed the threat of a vast Soviet armament already in existence and being used aggressively. The French Communists were unanimous in their determination not to antagonize the USSR. Those who supported de Gaulle feared that the plan would mean the disappearance of a strong French national army. A considerable group of neutralists wished to play the role of a third force—to stand as mediators between the United States and the Soviet Union. However, no responsible French minister could contemplate antagonizing the United States.

Matters were brought to a head when the Foreign Ministers of the western powers, meeting in Washington in September 1951, agreed to recognize the Federal Republic of [West] Germany as independent and to utilize their occupation troops to help defend West Germany against Soviet aggression, with the definite understanding that there would be German co-operation in these defensive measures. The next step was a Contractual Agreement signed in Bonn by Britain, France, West Germany, and the United States on May 26, 1952. This was supplemented the following day by a treaty signed in Paris setting up the European Defense Community. France, Italy, West Germany, and the Benelux countries were parties. The agreement was to run for fifty years, and was accompanied by a British treaty of guarantee and a protocol which extended the guarantees of NATO to EDC. An annex provided for the establishment of an active army of 40 divisions of which 14 would be French and 12 German. France had tentatively committed herself to recognize Germany's right to rearm and to fight, if necessary, to repel Communist aggression.

Although the representatives of the French government had signed the agreement for EDC, French public opinion was unwilling to accept it, and the Assembly failed to act to ratify it. It was at last debated in the Assembly in August 1954, and after scenes of bitterness and recrimination the Assembly voted to proceed to other business and neither ratified nor refused to ratify the treaty.

Secretary of State Dulles and Foreign Secretary Eden expressed the disappointment of both their governments. A conference was called in London in September 1954, and the series of agreements which collectively are known as Western European Union (WEU) were worked out and signed at a conference in Paris October 1954. These agreements extend the military provisions of the Brussels Treaty of 1948, link this military system to NATO, create a machinery of consultation by which the participating governments can develop co-operation in defense and in other fields, and finally provide for a European Statute for the Saar Territory. They set limits on German armament to allay the fears which French leaders and citizens felt about EDC. The WEU agreements were accepted by the French Assembly and Senate by March 1955. A large part of the purposes of EDC is realized, though the WEU agreements lack much of the supranational character of the earlier treaty. The final effect of French participation in Western European Union will probably be to place her firmly in a system of European co-operation.

The French Union and France Overseas

French leaders and many French citizens knew in 1946 that a new organization of colonial territories was needed if these overseas possessions were to be held in any association with France. The intention to initiate reforms has been expressed in several official declarations. While fighting continued in Europe and while the provisional French government still had its headquarters in North Africa, General de Gaulle called a conference of colonial administrators in Brazzaville. Proposals for representation of the colonial communities in a future constitutional assembly were discussed, although the conference went on record against the granting of independence.

The first of the French constitutions drafted in 1946 declared that the French Union was to be based on the free consent of its members. The second constitution of 1946 established the existing institutions of the French Union, and the preamble to this constitution declares that "France forms with the people of its overseas territories a union based upon equality of rights and duties without distinction of race or religion." It further goes on to declare that "France proposes to guide the people for whom she has assumed responsibility toward freedom to govern themselves and democratically to manage their own affairs." These are pious declarations of intention, however. The actual institutions of the French Union do not go far to realize the intentions in practice.

The President of France is also President of the Union, and the Union's organs of government are a High Council and an Assembly. The High Council, which was established by law in 1949, has representatives from the French government and from the associated states. Its functions are purely advisory and consultative, and are expected to deal chiefly with intercolonial affairs. The Assembly of the French Union, which in 1956 had 204 members, is made up of representatives from the overseas territories (chosen usually by the assemblies which exist in those territories), and 104 members chosen by the National Assembly of metropolitan France. The Assembly of the French Union must be consulted on any law modifying the status of any territory, and may be consulted on other matters of concern to the overseas communities.

It is evident that these constitutional provisions do not go far toward giving any real substance to the declarations which have been quoted above. The shortcomings of these institutions have been dramatized by nationalist revolts in a number of the colonial territories. A long and exhausting war that began in Indochina in 1946 was ended by an armistice in 1954, which left an independent government in the northern part of the country while the southern part, Viet Nam, remains an associated state of the French Union. In the North African territories of Tunisia, Morocco, and Algeria Nationalist movements have arisen, complicated by conflicts over the rights of the French residents of these areas and the rights of the native communities. As 1956 was ending, Tunisia and Morocco had reached independent status and Algeria was in the midst of extremely bitter conflict. The relationship of these territories to France, in fact and in law, is difficult to describe or predict.

The overseas territories are of great importance to France— heavy investment has been put into them over a long time, and markets and raw materials offer possibilities of development. The intention to organize these communities into a real association of states holds promise for the future. Algeria, it should be mentioned, is organized as three departments (districts) of France, and Martinique, Guadeloupe, Guiana, and Reunion also have this status. As departments of France, these communities are represented in the National Assembly. The overseas territories, the trusteeship territories, and the associated states are located in Africa, in the Far East, and in the Pacific Islands. It is still too early to estimate the prospects for organizing these diverse peoples and scattered areas into an effective union, but the attempt is being made and may well prove of great importance to France and to the peoples of the overseas territories.

The French Economy

A little has been said earlier in this chapter concerning the slow rate of industrialization in France. It is still a community of small-scale enterprise, both in industry and agriculture. Traditional methods persist in both, and limit productivity.

French students and public men have been concerned about this situation. Maurice Duverger, writing in *Le Monde*, declared that "the decline of France comes from the determination with which the middle classes insist upon retaining outworn economic methods to the detriment of their own interests." President Vincent Auriol, in the fall of 1952, wrote that "France was living upon the riches of the past, her industry was obsolescent, her labor badly utilized. . . . France can no longer afford to remain a bastion of economic individualism." Granting that two world wars within one generation have devastated considerable areas, have devalued her currency, and have decimated her manpower, France still has the greatest ore reserves and the largest area of fertile agricultural land per capita in western Europe.

The use of these resources has improved since 1948 as a result of three important developments, two of an international character and one entirely domestic. The first was the Marshall Plan, whereby the United States granted over $12 billion to western Europe, of which France received over $2½ billion. The second was the Schuman Plan, which placed Franco-German production of steel under a common high authority and opened to any participant in the Marshall Plan the advantages of a widened market and greater access to materials. The third was the Monnet Plan, which created a planning commission representative of French agriculture, industry, and labor, and developed proposals to modernize equipment and increase wages in a number of key industries and in agriculture. The Marshall Plan supplied a flow of capital which stimulated the other two projects from 1948 to 1951, and very successful results were achieved in many industries. French steel mills were made highly productive, there was a vast increase in the development of hydroelectric power, a practically new oil industry was created, and French railways were among the most efficiently run in western Europe.

In an interview with the press in November 1955, Premier Edgar Faure pointed out that France had recently made creative technical achievements. She had produced the fastest locomotive in the world (205 miles an hour) and the most rapid electronic brain (5800 operations per second). He might also have mentioned that France had recently constructed in the Rhone River the largest dam in western Europe.

Nevertheless, much remains to be done. Inflation continues to be a serious threat to the French economy, housing is far short of meeting needs, and both industry and agriculture still need to increase their productive power by increased capital investment and improvement of organization and methods. Pierre Mendès-France aptly summed up the situation after an investigation by an economic committee: "France will accept neither the discipline of planning nor that of free competition; she prefers a controlled economy based upon the protection of the established status quo."

The Character of French Foreign Policy

The consistent purpose of French foreign policy has been to safeguard the security of France. French leaders have been remarkably faithful to this purpose throughout the life of the Third and Fourth Republics. It has been difficult to achieve because the geographical position of the country is somewhat exposed, and because the rate of development of large-scale industry has been slower in France than in neighboring states.

The central problem for French foreign ministers has been to devise the methods by which security might be won. They have sought alliances and guarantees, and once treaties have been negotiated they have striven for precise fulfillment of obligations. If one looks back upon the record since 1870, this strategy is readily understood.

Insistence upon the letter of agreements is frequently irritating to allies. Accommodation to changed situations has often been belated and grudging.

For part of the interwar period, and during most of the years since 1946, French leaders have embarked on bolder policies of international organization. The abiding concern with security has occasionally obstructed the adjustments and accommodations which international co-operation requires. Nevertheless, some of the most distinguished and inventive advocates of international association have been foreign ministers of the French Republics. It may well be that in the future France may find security in plans that give assurance of security to all nations.

A list of Selected Readings appears on pages 548-551.

CHAPTER 15

FRENCH FOREIGN POLICY: ITS FORMULATION AND ITS RECENT CHARACTER

Parliamentary Control of Foreign Policy

To a citizen of the United States, accustomed to the overwhelming power of his President in the conduct of foreign affairs, the French system under which the Cabinet, the Ministry, and the Assembly play the leading roles seems highly anachronistic. The American remembers that under the Articles of Confederation, when the fear of autocracy was still prevalent, the control of foreign relations was vested in a committee of the Congress with highly unsatisfactory results.

The French had even greater distrust of executive authority and the safeguards in their constitutions have gone even further than the Articles of Confederation in their efforts to preserve popular control. Probably no democratic government in the world has allocated as much power to the legislative body in the field of foreign relations as does the Fourth French Republic.

The constitutional authority of the representative assembly—the Chamber of Deputies under the Third Republic and the National Assembly under the Fourth Republic—is given practical force by the political and party relationship of the Cabinet to the legislature. The position of the President in France is comparable to that of the monarch in England. All of his actions must be countersigned by a minister, and the ministers are responsible individually and collectively to the legislative body. In practice, therefore, any Cabinet of the Fourth Republic must have the support of a majority in the National Assembly, and whenever it loses that majority support it must resign. This relationship of Cabinet to legislative assembly was established in the Third Republic, and continues into the Fourth. It is similar to the relationship of the Cabinet to Parliament in England—in fact, the devices of countersignature of the formal acts of the President and the responsibility of the Cabinet to an elected assembly were modeled upon English constitutional practice.

No French Cabinet, however, can count upon the support of a disciplined majority, because the majority is composed of a number of parties. Sometimes the coalition is quite firm and solid, but often it is an uneasy and unstable association of diverse party groups. An English Cabinet, relying upon the power of leadership and the authority of party organization, is normally confident that its policies can be carried into effect. A French Cabinet may often enjoy equal power; but if its majority is uncertain because its member parties may refuse to act in concert, its power is much diminished.

It is not easy, therefore, to characterize the Assembly-Cabinet relationship under the Fourth Republic, because this relationship changes as the party situation changes. Whenever the Cabinet's majority is unstable, the power of the Assembly is great and it is able to control the policies of the Cabinet and to interfere in matters of high policy. On the other hand, when the supporting majority is firmly knit together—often by virtue of the strength of its leaders in the Cabinet—the power of the Assembly is much less. Under these circumstances the position of the Cabinet is comparable to that of an English Cabinet.

In either situation the Cabinet has one resource which strengthens its position—it can rely on the expert assistance of the permanent officials in the government service. This gives the Cabinet a considerable advantage in dealing with the Assembly, especially in foreign relations, where detailed knowledge and expert analysis are of great importance in the formulation of policy.

One must therefore remember that it is not easy to state simply and clearly where the real power of policy formulation lies at any particular time under the Third and Fourth Republics. A precarious balance of power exists, and authority shifts from Cabinet to Assembly according to the nature of the majority. Throughout the life of both Republics, the legislative assembly has striven to dominate policy because of the tradition of distrust of executive authority. At all times, however, the services of the expert permanent officials help the Cabinet to take the lead in devising and administering policy.

If these general aspects of Cabinet-Assembly relationships are kept in mind, the often contradictory and inconsistent character of the action of the French government can be understood. The observer and student is forced to consider the strength of parties at any given time, as well as the more constant factors of constitutional rules and the work of permanent officials, whenever an interpretation is made on matters of policy.

It must be conceded that in practice throughout the life of the Third Republic the Chamber of Deputies was not so interested in foreign affairs as it was in domestic problems, and as a result the Cabinets had a fairly free hand in charting the international relations of France. Furthermore, in spite of all theories regarding the need for democratic control of foreign policies, it is axiomatic that large deliberative bodies are too cumbersome and slow-moving to formulate and execute policies which require despatch and a considerable degree of secrecy. Even such theorists as Rousseau and de Tocqueville, who were insistent upon control by the people, conceded that an elected representative assembly is not adequately equipped to carry on relations with foreign states. Rousseau frankly stated that "the exercise of power in foreign affairs is not proper to the people" and de Tocqueville declared that "it is particularly in the conduct of foreign affairs that democracy seems to be most inferior to other types of government."

A means of checking Cabinet policy which has existed under both the Third and Fourth Republics is the so-called interpellation of the Cabinet ministers by members of the legislative body. The legislators may also obtain information through the use of written and oral questions. Nevertheless, the secrecy with which foreign affairs are conducted, the technical character of many of the problems, and the lack of interest on the part of the majority of legislators combine to put the Cabinet in a position to control regardless of these intended safeguards. A Cabinet almost never falls on a question of foreign policy; and in the words of Professor Joseph Barthélemy, writing in 1919, "In final effect, the government is the sole maker of major international policies."

Before 1914 the French governments carried on their relations with foreign states with very little consideration of parliamentary or public opinion, whereas after World War I there was greater insistence upon democratic control. Even so, there were very few debates and still fewer interpellations upon questions of foreign policy after the Treaty of Versailles. Although the procedure of posing written questions to the government was introduced in 1909 primarily to permit parliamentary control of foreign policy, the number devoted to this subject was exceedingly small.

Unquestionably the most effective instrumentalities for the parliamentary control of foreign policy have been the committees on foreign affairs. The Foreign Affairs Committee of the Assembly is particularly important. It must prepare reports on any questions of foreign policy submitted by the Assembly and through its *rapporteur d'information* it obtains information from the Ministry of Foreign Affairs and from the various other ministries. Its reports are adequate presentations of all the information essential to enable the Assembly to make a decision upon the policy under consideration. On occasions other committees must be consulted, particularly the Committee of Finance when the expenditure of funds is contemplated, and there have been occasions (for example, in the resumption of relations with the Vatican in 1923) when the views of the Finance Committee prevailed.

Due to the intimate knowledge of foreign affairs gained by the normally lengthy service of its members, the Committee of Foreign Affairs has considerable influence. In fact, it may even bring about the fall of the Cabinet. For example, in 1932 when Édouard

Herriot, Prime Minister and Minister of Foreign Affairs, wished to make a token payment to the United States on the French war debt, his Cabinet was forced to resign because the Committee of Foreign Affairs and the Committee of Finance bitterly opposed the payment.

Before World War I the report to the Chamber of Deputies on the annual budget furnished a means for criticism of foreign policy, inasmuch as a lengthy report on the government's activities was an important section of it. However, between the two wars such reports were very brief and after 1926 there was no general discussion of the Budget of the Ministry of Foreign Affairs. It should be noted, however, that any demands for extraordinary credits for the Ministry of Foreign Affairs require consideration and debate in the National Assembly.

The Committee on Foreign Affairs of the French National Assembly, under the Constitution of 1946, is perhaps the most important of the Assembly's 19 general committees. The other three principal committees are National Defense, Finance, and Overseas Territories, all of which have close relations with the Committee on Foreign Affairs. In the period between the two World Wars several of the presidents of the Committees on Foreign Affairs have served as Foreign Ministers—in fact, this chairmanship is often a stepping stone to a ministerial post that is considered as important as the premiership.

The Council of the Republic also has a Committee on Foreign Affairs but its influence is somewhat limited since the Council is a consultative rather than a legislative body. Nevertheless, on occasions, the Foreign Affairs Committee of the Council of the Republic plays an important role. For example, in the thorny question of setting up a European Statute for the Saar within the western European system it was the Council's Committee that laid down special conditions to be fulfilled before acceptance of the agreement (February 1, 1955). Later, on March 18, 1955, Minister of Foreign Affairs Antoine Pinay submitted to the Council's Foreign Affairs Committee a letter from Chancellor Adenauer regarding political freedom in the territory. Finally, the Council of the Republic approved the Franco-German Agreement on the Saar without amendments on March 26, 1955, by a vote of 217 to 92.

It might be noticed in passing that according to Articles 26 and 28 of the constitution of 1946, treaties duly ratified and published have authority superior to that of French internal legislation. In spite of this clear statement on the subject, in two cases French courts, in interpreting rights of Spanish citizens under the Franco-Spanish Consular Convention of 1862 which permitted nationals of the contracting parties to engage in industry and commerce on a parity with nationals, ruled in one case that a decree-law of 1938 requiring a special card for such activity must be complied with, and in the other that the granting of the card was obligatory. In the third case, decided in 1952, the court held that the decree law of 1938 was not compatible with the Consular Conventions of 1862, and according to the provisions of the constitution of 1946 could not be enforced. Upon appeal the Court of Cassation in 1953 reversed all three court decisions and ruled that in questions of international public order the courts must adopt the official interpretation of the French Government and therefore the Minister of Foreign Affairs had jurisdiction in the case.[1]

The Role of the President in the Conduct of Foreign Policy

We have already seen that the President of the Republic is subject to the control of both the Cabinet and the legislature; nevertheless he may exercise considerable influence in directing the foreign relations of the state. Since it is his prerogative to appoint the Premier (President of the Council of Ministers), subject of course to parliamentary approval, he is often able to secure the choice of a person whose views on foreign policy coincide to some extent with his own. Inasmuch as he is elected for a seven-year term, he has the time and opportunity to familiarize himself with the background of international problems facing the country. This

[1] See the well-documented article on the subject by Louis C. Beal in the American Journal of International Law, vol. 49, No. 3 (July 1955), pp. 347, 355.

tenure contrasts with the ephemeral character of French Cabinets, wherefore the advice of one whose stable position has given him the opportunity to be fully conversant with the ramifications of the problem under consideration is not usually disregarded. The President can advise and he can warn, and if his stand is based upon an objective consideration of facts obtained through his presidential position his influence may prevail.

Article 31 of the 1946 constitution specifically requires the President to be kept informed of the progress of international relations. He therefore has the right to learn from his ministers all developments in the foreign relations of the Republic. He presides at the formal meeting of the Council of Ministers; he retains the minutes and is in a position to influence the direction of foreign policy indirectly through his knowledge of the attitudes and predilections of the members of the Cabinet. Thus his success depends to a considerable extent upon his own personality and the personalities of his ministers.

Various examples might be cited of the President's influence in the determination of foreign policy. Unquestionably President Loubet helped Foreign Minister Delcassé achieve his long-desired Entente Cordiale with Great Britain. President Poincaré, who had already served as Foreign Minister and Prime Minister before his election to the presidency, continued to exert considerable influence in foreign affairs throughout his term of office, particularly in maintaining cordial relations with Russia. Vincent Auriol, the first President of the Fourth Republic, at times intervened actively in parliamentary discussions to the great advantage of the state, although he had himself proposed to reduce to the vanishing point the powers of the President. His successor, René Coty, has made few declarations, yet even he, disturbed by the serious situation in North Africa, declared in June 1955 that he supported Premier Faure's policy for a peaceful interdependence in North Africa and condemned the "abominable violence" by Frenchmen against the Arabs.

Articles 30 and 31 of the 1946 constitution give the President the power to appoint and accredit ambassadors and special envoys to foreign powers and to have ambassadors and special envoys ac-

credited to him. The appointment of ambassadors is actually performed by the Minister of Foreign Affairs in consultation with the
Cabinet; they take into account background, experience, and the
requirements of the permanent diplomatic service. Although technically foreign diplomats are accredited to the President, in actuality they carry on their negotiations with the Minister of Foreign
Affairs or with the officials of the Foreign Ministry at the Quai
d'Orsay.

Although the constitution of 1875 specifically provided that the
President of the Republic should negotiate and ratify treaties, in
practice all treaty negotiations were initiated and carried on by the
Minister of Foreign Affairs or his subordinates, and the Cabinet
assumed the responsibility for the results. In the constitution of
1946 the President of the Republic is not mentioned with reference
to the treaty-making power, yet as the head of the state he must
append his signature to treaties and exchange ratifications according to established practice in international law. Behind the scenes
he may use his influence for or against the ratification of a treaty,
as President Auriol is alleged to have done in warning successive
governments against an overhasty ratification of the European
Defense Community Treaty.

An interesting situation arose in France in September, 1955,
when the question of revising the French Protectorate Treaty of
1912 with Morocco was being considered. President Coty sent the
resident-general of Morocco a letter to be delivered to the French-
imposed Sultan, Moulay ben Arafa, directing him to vacate the
throne and to proceed to Tangier on a French destroyer. When
Foreign Minister Pinay objected to the action on the ground that
he had not been consulted as to the wording of the instruction,
the letter was withdrawn. However, the very next month the Sultan
left his palace in Fez to proceed to Tangier and received a letter
from President Coty praising his act of renunciation.

Although it has often been said that the function of the French
President is to hunt rabbits, nevertheless the so-called "prisoner of
the Elysée" is in a position to exert considerable influence on foreign policy through his advice gained from experience, and from

his inner-sanctum position, where he sees all that is going on with the broader vision of the over-all needs of the state.

The President of the Council of Ministers

The position of Premier or President of the Council of Ministers in the French Republic has never been a happy one nor one of long duration, but only rarely does a French Premier fall on a question of foreign policy. Often the French Premier is also Minister of Foreign Affairs. In fact, during the Third Republic almost half of the Premiers held the two portfolios at the same time and some made outstanding reputations as statesmen through positions they took on foreign policy. A few examples will suffice. Léon Gambetta has been justly designated as the "incarnation of French patriotism"; Jules Ferry, although criticized as a rabid imperialist at the time, was later honored for adding Tunis, Indo-China, and Madagascar to the French colonial empire; Raymond Poincaré prepared France for the German attack in 1914; and Aristide Briand strengthened her in the subsequent peace. In the Fourth Republic Robert Schuman gave his name to the most important contribution to the economic development of Europe in the period since World War II, and Pierre Mendès-France provided the only workable solution for the French situation in North Africa.

In the French Cabinet system the ministers act as a unit and the Prime Minister is in actuality only a sort of chairman of the group. Each minister is expected to carry his own weight and be responsible for his own field to the Cabinet as a whole. Unless he is serving as Foreign Minister himself, the Premier will as a rule expect that the Foreign Minister will be conversant with all current problems of foreign policy, be prepared with a program, and be ready to defend it when it comes before the whole Cabinet for discussion and possible adoption. A Premier indifferent to questions of foreign policy will give the Foreign Minister free rein and support his point of view in meetings of the Cabinet. For example, Premier Charles Dupuy supported wholeheartedly his scholarly Foreign Minister Gabriel Hanotaux even when it was a question of appropriating a very considerable sum to send a large force to Madagascar to seize the capital and occupy the island. Five different Premiers during a full seven years allowed Foreign Minister Théophile Delcassé to work out a Dual Alliance with Russia, an Entente Cordiale with Great Britain, and an imperialist policy in Morocco which brought France to the brink of war with Germany, before any action was taken to control him.

A very strong Premier may upon occasions use the Foreign Minister to carry out such foreign policies as he himself has determined upon. This seemed to be the case during Clemenceau's premierships from 1906 to 1909 and from 1917 to 1920, when Stéphen Pichon was his Minister of Foreign Affairs. When both Premier and Foreign Minister are strong-minded men and of somewhat different points of view, as were Premier Poincaré and Foreign Minister Briand in the period from 1926 to 1929, compromise is necessary. In this instance the nationalistic Poincaré seemed to give way to the internationalist Briand even to the extent of approving the famous Briand-Kellogg Pact for the renunciation of war.

The Fourth Republic had seventeen different Cabinets between 1947 and 1956. Obviously, although it has long been realized that the position of President of the Council of Ministers needs strengthening and although the 1946 constitution endows the office with somewhat more authority than it formerly had, nevertheless the Premier is still merely a political leader and his control over foreign policy leaves much to be desired.

The Minister of Foreign Affairs

The Minister of Foreign Affairs in France, like his counterparts in Great Britain and the United States, is almost always a political appointment. However, since in foreign affairs background and experience are almost a *sine qua non*, the tendency is to reappoint the same Foreign Minister in the different Cabinets which rise and fall so rapidly. For example, in the Third Republic Louis Decazes served continuously from 1873 to 1877—a full four years but under five different Premiers. Aristide Briand was Premier six different times and during three of these occasions he served also as Foreign Minister. He was also Foreign Minister under seven other Premiers, having a total tenure of 114 months, of which 62

were continuous, from July, 1926, to September, 1931. Théophile
Delcassé had the longest continuous tenure as head of the Foreign
Office: 84 months from June 28, 1898, to June 17, 1905, under six
different Premiers. Since World War II, two men have practically
monopolized the office of Foreign Minister: Georges Bidault and
Robert Schuman. Except for the brief one-month's interlude of
Léon Blum, they served through nineteen different cabinets from
1945 to 1954, Bidault on three different occasions for 64 months
and Schuman continuously for 53 months. When Pierre Mendès-
France became Premier in June, 1954, he also took over the Ministry of Foreign Affairs.

Although it has been asserted that the Foreign Minister should
above all be the first diplomatist of his country, very few professional diplomats have held the position of Foreign Minister. In
fact, during the Third Republic only two might be so classified,
Flourens and Hanotaux, and the latter is renowned rather as a
brilliant historian. William Henry Waddington, it is true, became
an ambassador after his service as Foreign Minister and represented
France adequately both in Moscow and in London. However it
should be noted that Pichon, Boncour, Herriot, Barthou, Poincaré,
Briand, and in the Fourth Republic Bidault and Schuman devoted
themselves to a considerable extent to the study of foreign affairs.

We have already indicated that many factors control the influence and power of the Minister of Foreign Affairs. Although he is
directly responsible for the relations with other powers he is ordinarily subject to some control by the Prime Minister, by his colleagues in the Cabinet, by the Foreign Affairs Committees in the
National Assembly and the Council of the Republic, and finally
by public opinion as it may be evidenced by the representatives in
the Assembly. However, since he has under his direction the experts of the Quai d'Orsay and both the diplomatic and consular
services in the field, he is in a position to direct the foreign policy
in normal times with very little interference. He is criticized only
when he has made a serious mistake which may have brought about
a crisis or when the country is aroused on some question of great
public interest. Both Poincaré and Briand practically dictated the
foreign policy of France while they were Foreign Ministers and

no man has had a greater influence than Robert Schuman on the
foreign policy of France since World War II.

In addition to playing an important role in the formulation of
foreign policy, the Minister of Foreign Affairs must spend considerable time with the diplomatic representatives of foreign states. He
is usually present when a new ambassador or minister presents his
credentials to the President of France. He must be available for
individual conferences with the representatives of foreign states
upon all occasions when they request an audience, and must allot
a certain amount of time each week for the reception of foreign
diplomats. He must entertain and be entertained almost constantly; the social factor is not to be overlooked in diplomatic
negotiations.

Both Premier and Foreign Minister are in a position to make
public declarations on foreign policy when the situation requires it.
While Edgar Faure was Premier and Antoine Pinay Foreign Minister in 1955, it was often said that France had two Foreign Ministers
since both men were equally interested in the direction of foreign
policy. And although M. Faure was regarded as opposed to the
rearmament of Germany, and M. Pinay favored the rearming of
Germany within NATO, the two worked together to integrate
Germany into the European defense system without substantially
changing their fundamental positions.

The Foreign Minister has a fairly large office staff and a cabinet
of experts chosen by himself who are largely diplomats of experience. These advise with him and do all the necessary routine
preparatory work in order to lighten the load of work borne by the
Minister. He also heads the elaborately organized Ministry of Foreign Affairs—the Quai d'Orsay as it is usually called, since it is
located at number 37 of the Quai d'Orsay on the left bank of the
Seine.

The Foreign Minister has certain appointive powers both as to
positions in the Quai d'Orsay and also in the diplomatic and con-
sular service overseas. However, the French have a well established
Foreign Service based upon merit, similar to that of the United
States, and career men usually fill the top positions both in the
Foreign Office and in the diplomatic service.

The Quai d'Orsay

The French are often quite sarcastic in their remarks concerning their Foreign Office. It has been designated as the Sanhedrin to be addressed only on one's knees; as the house of the dead; as a dusty museum; as a drawing room of high-society imbeciles. Nevertheless the personnel of the Quai d'Orsay, drawn as it is from the career Foreign Service and from the Civil Service, is an organization of trained experts qualified to perform their functions effectively and discreetly.

A very substantial reorganization of the Foreign Office was made in 1880 by Charles de Freycinet who was serving as both Premier and Foreign Minister. Subsequently the Foreign Office has developed intermittently in accordance with the requirements of the government, usually by executive decrees rather than by legislative action. For example a decree in 1916 reserved the most important positions in the central administration to Foreign Service officers who had already served abroad.

Another important development came after World War I when a decree dated January 20, 1920, established the position of Secretary General, whose duty it was to co-ordinate the manifold activities of the Quai d'Orsay. The Secretary General is the top administrative officer and also the most important policy-making official under the Foreign Minister. In the latter's absence the Secretary General acts in his place. The Secretary General regularly has the rank of ambassador and is one of the most important permanent officials in the French administration. Indeed, a parliamentary investigating committee after World War II declared that French foreign policy was almost exclusively the work of the central administration of the Quai d'Orsay, that is, of the Secretary General and his staff. Twenty years earlier, Professor Albert Guérard had pointed out the importance of the bureaucracy in France: "Parliament might very well shut up shop. President and Cabinet ministers might grow lettuce or translate Horace and France would miss nothing vital."

The careers in office of two Secretaries General are of interest.

The first Secretary General of the Quai d'Orsay, Philippe Berthelot, had been well trained in the administration of foreign affairs. He happened to be in charge of the political-affairs division of the Quai d'Orsay just before the outbreak of World War I in 1914, when President Poincaré and Premier and Foreign Minister Viviani were in Russia on a mission. His astute and effective handling of the situation proved his exceptional ability and by the end of the war he had become director of the division of political and commercial affairs. In the fall of 1919, during the illness of Foreign Minister Pichon, Berthelot functioned as the Minister of Foreign Affairs in fact. At the Conference of Versailles it was said that in remaking Europe, Wilson alone acted generously and Berthelot competently.

With this record, in the autumn of 1920, Berthelot was named Secretary General. For the next twelve years, except for a three-year interval, he directed the Quai d'Orsay. As advisor to Aristide Briand, he helped formulate French foreign policy of the Locarno period. He was the architect of the Briand policies of peaceful co-operation with Germany. Berthelot kept in the background and, although conversant with every document that entered the Foreign Office, he destroyed all his papers and has remained an enigma to the historians.

The second Secretary General, Alexis Saint-Léger, was in many ways just as remarkable as his predecessor. He had a brief assignment in the French Embassy in Peking before he took a position on the Asiatic desk in the Foreign Office. Briand noticed the young diplomat, invited him to join his personal cabinet, and made him chief in 1925. Like Berthelot, he aided in drafting the Pact of Locarno and the Kellogg-Briand Pact. Unfortunately, Briand was dead when Saint-Léger succeeded Berthelot as Secretary General in 1933, and none of the eight Foreign Ministers with whom he served were in the same class with Briand. Saint-Léger valiantly strove to maintain the Locarno edifice which he regarded as the keystone of the arch of European peace; but Foreign Ministers such as Laval, Flandin, and Bonnet had other ideas, and they made their deals with Mussolini and Hitler in spite of Saint-Léger's strong protests. He accompanied Flandin to League Council meetings, but was not invited to participate and was not sympathetic to Flandin's appeasement policy. He assisted Daladier at Munich but did his best to oppose concessions. Although the Quai d'Orsay played an uninspired role in the events which led to the outbreak of World War II, Saint-Léger as Secretary General was a constant curb on the policy of appeasement. His dismissal in 1940 by Reynaud was due largely to machinations of Reynaud's mistress, Comtesse Hélène de Portes, and against the advice of the technical experts of the Quai d'Orsay. Saint-Léger's dismissal was worth more than seventy votes for Reynaud in the Chamber.

The French ambassador to London at this writing, Jean Chauvel, served as Secretary General of the Foreign Office from 1945 to 1949. From 1949 to 1955 Alexandre Parodi, who had represented France as permanent member of the Security Council of the United Nations, held the position of Secretary General of the Quai d'Orsay. Secretary General René Massigli, who was named to this position in 1955, has had a long and distinguished career in the Foreign Service of France. Among other assignments, he was ambassador to Great Britain from 1944 to 1955.

Directly under the Secretary General is the *Secrétariat Particulier* and the *Secrétariat des Conférences*. The latter agency, established since the Liberation, has become particularly important since multilateral diplomacy has largely superseded the former bilateral method. The Conference Secretariat prepares the agenda for international conferences, serves as liaison between the French government and the United Nations and the international agencies, and prepares all necessary documentation and special studies for technical and political programs. At present three of its top officials have the rank of minister.

The largest division of the Quai d'Orsay and perhaps the most important is that of Political and Economic Affairs, and its director-general has the status of a minister plenipotentiary. Its Political Division is divided into geographical areas—Europe, Asia-Oceania, Africa-Levant, and America—and these are subdivided into smaller sections. For example, Europe is divided into Northern Europe, Central Europe, Southern Europe, Eastern Europe, the USSR, and the Council of Europe. The Political Division has a press section which covers all communications to the press and to the public; it also surveys the press at home and abroad; summarizes important information; and prepares all documentation for the press both foreign and domestic. Its director has the status of minister plenipotentiary. The Economic and Financial Affairs Division is geographically divided into a half-dozen sections, covering economic relations with the entire world. Two other large sections are responsible for the economic problems associated with the occupation of Germany and with the European Coal and Steel Community. Another section covers the field of economic cooperation, including the United Nations and its various organizations. Still another is concerned with transportation in all its forms, petroleum, literary property and questions relative to atomic energy. The section entitled Private Properties and Interests is self explanatory and is under the direction of a minister plenipotentiary.

Another large division covers Personnel and General Administration. At the head of the personnel section is the Inspector General of Diplomatic and Consular Posts, who has the rank of a minister plenipotentiary. His organization has charge of the recruitment, promotion, and retirement of all diplomatic and consular officers, the administration of foreign posts, auxiliary services, secretaries, and other employees. A second section has charge of budgetary questions, including expenses of international conferences, technical matters including upkeep of establishments abroad, organization of international conferences, internal services, supplies, social security, and kindred matters; an elaborate accounting organization deals with all expenses of the Foreign Service officers. Under the heading of general administration are the courier and pouch services, telegraph, telephone, and correspondence, and the translation bureau.

A large division of the Quai d'Orsay is devoted to such matters as the diffusion of the French language abroad, exchanges of students, documents, books, periodicals, films, and literary and artistic materials. France has always been interested in cultural activities, particularly in relation to other nations, through its overseas establishments.

A division is responsible for the carrying out of the provisions of various administrative and social conventions concerning immigration matters, circulation of persons, the status of French citizens abroad and foreigners in France, the granting of visas, and the maintenance of consular privileges and immunities.

Although protocol does not play as important a role as formally, the diplomatic service has an elaborate ceremonial code and the Chief of the Service of Protocol must receive ambassadors and ministers, arrange ceremonial banquets and receptions, and take care of all questions of a ceremonial nature. The chief of protocol has the rank of a minister plenipotentiary.

To answer any question of international law or a question pertaining to industrial, commercial, literary, or artistic property rights there is a Juridical Service in the Quai d'Orsay. There is also a counselor for religious affairs and a counselor for historical matters. The archives and library have the necessary officials to maintain them and assist in their utilization. An office of protection of refugees and expatriates is perhaps a temporary agency.

The Quai d'Orsay today, with its personnel numbering more than four hundred, has outgrown the antiquated structure which houses it (begun in 1845 and completed 1855). The visitor has a feeling of confusion and cluttered activity because of the overcrowding and the small and unattractive reception rooms. Nevertheless, its location adjacent to the Palais Bourbon, facing the beautiful left bank of the Seine with the sumptuously ornamented Pont Alexandre III almost in front, and the historic Esplanade des Invalides in the rear, is one of the finest that Paris can provide.

The Diplomatic and Consular Services

Although Venice claimed to be the "school and touchstone of ambassadors," Louis XI of France was one of the first European monarchs to establish permanent missions at the courts of neighboring kings; François I set up a completely organized diplomatic service; and Louis XIV possessed such a remarkable diplomatic organization that French gradually displaced Latin as the diplomatic language of Europe. During the monarchy the nobility largely constituted the personnel of French diplomatic representation abroad and ambassadors and ministers were appointed by royal decree. The advent of the Third Republic brought the beginning of a career service in the lower ranks based upon ability and experience. A decree dated February 1, 1877, provided that secretaries of embassy third class be required to pass a qualifying examination, and three years later these examinations were made competitive and consular posts were included. Beginning in 1907 examinations were held annually and a regular promotion in both consular and diplomatic services was inaugurated. In the diplomatic service it usually took a minimum period of ten years to pass through the three classes of secretaries of embassy or legation to reach the position of counselor of embassy. After three years as counselor, the officer might be promoted to the position of minister, second class; then, after another three years to minister of first class. To become an ambassador required nomination by the Foreign Minister and approval by the Cabinet, with the President signing a decree making the appointment official. Some ambassadors were appointed on a political basis but the majority were men who had already proved their worth in the diplomatic service or the Foreign Office.

The qualities of the French Foreign Service may be suggested by mentioning some of its personalities. Many are so famous that they need only be named: the brothers Paul and Jules Cambon, ambassadors in London and Berlin respectively before World War I; Jules Jusserand, ambassador in Washington from 1902 to 1925; Paul Claudel, his successor to 1933 and a playwright, poet, and member of the Academy; André François-Poncet, sometime ambassador in Berlin, Rome, and Bonn, also a member of the Academy. Jean Chauvel, appointed ambassador to Great Britain in 1955, was Secretary General of the Foreign Office from 1945 to 1949, delegate to the United Nations from 1949 to 1952, and held other posts with distinction at various times. René Massigli, Secretary General of the Foreign Office at this writing, was ambassador in London from 1944 to 1955, with such success that the British government awarded him the Order of Merit. Maurice Couve de Murville, appointed ambassador to the United States in 1955, had been ambassador to Italy and to Egypt, and had served as director-general of political affairs in the Foreign Office. Radio listeners in the United States in November 1956 had the opportunity to hear

Louis de Guiringaud, a career diplomat and once consul at San Francisco, speak for the French delegation to the United Nations.

Under the Fourth Republic new regulations were set up for all important career governmental positions. With the establishment in 1945 of the Ecole Nationale d'Administration all candidates for the foreign service must have met the requirements for entrance into this institution and have spent three years completing its curriculum. The applicants are from two groups. The first group consists of graduates of well-known schools or universities, who as a rule must not be over twenty-six years of age. The former École Libre des Sciences Politiques, taken over by the state in 1945 to become the Institut d'Études Politiques of the University of Paris, is unquestionably the preferred institution for those preparing to enter the Foreign Service. The second group consists of state functionaries with or without diplomas who have served a minimum of four years and are between the ages of twenty-four and thirty. Separate competitive examinations are offered to each group of candidates but all candidates must pass a written examination on a subject pertaining to political, economic, or social developments since the middle of the eighteenth century, and an oral examination of a general character to show the candidate's personal judgment, natural gifts, and aptitudes. If they have satisfactorily met these proofs of admissibility, the candidates are then examined in written and oral examinations within the fields of their proposed specialization. The group coming from the universities must pass a written examination in some modern language other than French, whereas the functionary group is required to make satisfactory summaries of documents presented to them. Those candidates who wish to enter the Foreign Service must also pass examinations in diplomatic history and international law.

After being admitted, the candidate desiring a diplomatic career follows a curriculum similar to that required for Foreign Service officers by the Foreign Service Institute in the United States. The first year is devoted entirely to probatory work in the field of his choice under the direction of officials, the second to advanced study, the third to both study and practice.

The French diplomatic service has increased materially in size since World War II, both because of the larger number of sovereign states and because of the additional duties in the fields of economics, technical matters, cultural subjects, and public relations which are now an important part of an embassy's jurisdiction. France has also followed the new practice of naming ambassadors instead of ministers to all posts of interest to the home government, regardless of their intrinsic size or importance. For example, in 1938 France sent abroad 14 ambassadors and 36 ministers, a total of 50 diplomatic representatives, whereas in 1955 there were 56 ambassadors and 15 ministers, totaling 71, an over-all increase of more than 40 per cent, but an increase in the ratio of ambassadors to ministers of more than 300 per cent.

The consular service of France, like that of the United States, is wholly a career service. It is possible to transfer from the consular to the diplomatic branch but transfers are not so common as in the United States Foreign Service. The duties are also approximately the same: promotion and protection of trade, protection of seamen and other nationals abroad, and some passport and visa work. However, in French consulates the latter is never as heavy as in certain United States consulates where large numbers of nationals wish to emigrate to the United States. Also as in the United States Foreign Service, some consuls have a dual commission and serve both as consul general and minister plenipotentiary. Owing to its extensive utilization of consular agents who carry on their own affairs in addition to their consular work, France has one of the largest consular staffs in the world; of some 700 French consular representatives about 450 are such consular agents.

Although not the most important, San Francisco is regarded as one of the choicest French consular posts. The consulate is housed in an attractive edifice in an excellent location; since it is so far from Washington the consul general has the status of minister plenipotentiary or counselor of foreign affairs and performs a number of diplomatic duties. Above all, this office is often a stepping stone to the position of consul general in New York or to a post on the French delegation to the United Nations.

Recent and Contemporary Policy

The foreign policy of France during the decade when it was directed by Foreign Ministers Bidault and Schuman was unfortunately based upon a fundamentally false assumption, namely that France was still a powerful nation and could carry out its commitments in Europe, Africa, and the Far East. As the period neared its close, failure was evident in all three fields. The European Defense Community, initiated by France and sold by France to her allies, was thrown overboard by France after her allies had been persuaded to accept it. The policy of France in Indo-China was too grandiose for a nation which could not afford the necessary expenditures in either money or troops. In North Africa it appeared that Morocco and Tunisia might go the way of Indo-China unless nationalistic demands were met by statesmanship rather than bayonets. By mid-1954, the Laniel-Bidault Cabinet could no longer carry on a policy of imperialism dependent upon United States help to sustain it after it had repudiated the basic requirement upon which the United States had staked its support. With the rejection of the European Defense Community by the French National Assembly and after the débacle of Dien Bien Phu in Viet Nam, the Laniel Cabinet resigned on June 12, 1954, and President Coty requested Pierre Mendès-France to form a new government.

Mendès-France displayed the courage to face the realities of the situation. He had proved his bravery in the underground and in flying for the Free French. He had proposed a drastic plan of austerity in 1945 for the reconstruction of postwar France, which the time-serving politicians feared to adopt. He had constantly warned of the need of greater production, better housing, inflation control, and a limitation of objectives. He foresaw the development of nationalism in the French overseas empire and urged action to meet its just demands. In his address to the Assembly Mendès-France made no effort to curry favor—in fact he was bluntly frank. He declared the war in Indo-China had become an unbearable burden and a negotiated peace was essential. This matter was so vital that he promised that if he failed to obtain a cease-fire within a month he would resign. He proposed to formulate a "coherent

program of recovery and expansion" internally, he would face the
European Defense Community problem and give the allies a definite constructive answer, and he would re-establish peace and
security in Tunisia and Morocco by keeping French promises to
let these peoples conduct their own affairs. The National Assembly
confirmed his investiture by a vote of 419 to 47.

Mendès-France won his gamble to obtain peace in Indo-China
by facing up to the situation and making concessions which could
no longer be avoided. He flew personally to Tunisia and worked
out a program of autonomy with the Bey which was ultimately
accepted by the Nationalist party. He proposed certain changes in
the EDC treaty and met the foreign ministers of the allies at
Brussels, where he tried valiantly to obtain their acceptance. When
he could not, he supported ratification of the original agreement in
a long address to the Assembly. When the Assembly refused ratification, he got together with British Premier Eden and worked out
a new arrangement for expanding the Brussels Treaty Organization
to include Germany. Again the interested powers' representatives
met—this time in London—and perfected an agreement admitting
Germany and Italy to the Brussels Agreement and accepting Germany into the North Atlantic Treaty Organization. The National
Assembly, chastened by the deluge of criticism showered upon it
for its repudiation of EDC, accepted the London Agreements by
a vote of 350 to 113.

Mendès-France had taken over the portfolio of the Minister of
Foreign Affairs as well as the Presidency of the Council of Ministers. Instead of taking up his residence in the magnificent quarters
of the premiers in the Hotel Matignon he moved into the Quai
d'Orsay. He quickly put new life into the Foreign Office. He began
his day at 8:45 instead of 11 and his assistants were expected to do
likewise. His appointments were numerous but rationed in time;
he often had a sandwich luncheon at his desk, an unheard-of violation of established protocol. He held press conferences and gave
direct answers, and every week he broadcast to the people of
France. In one of these broadcasts made on October 24, 1954, he
was able to announce to the country that he had finally settled the
troublesome question of the Saar which had long poisoned Franco-

German relations, and that the two countries could now work toward political and economic co-operation.

Such drastic methods were bound to produce opposition, particularly since Mendès-France drove ahead ruthlessly. His advocacy of more milk and less wine raised a storm among the vineyardists. His Jewish background made him an object of suspicion to certain groups. He refused Communist support and the far right could not abide him. But the opposition which brought him down stemmed from his North African policy of getting together with the Arab Nationalists. Although his program for Tunisia was a constructive policy to preserve French rights and interests by co-operation, his government fell on February 5, 1955, through the influence exerted by the French colonials upon the Assembly.

President Coty found the task of replacing Mendès-France a most difficult one. His first choice was Antoine Pinay, who as premier in 1952 had been successful in cutting civilian expenditures; Pinay tried to form a government but failed. The efforts of Pierre Pflimlin, a comparative newcomer in politics, were equally unsuccessful. The next choice was Christian Pineau, who had held several previous Cabinet posts, but he too was unable to gain the Assembly's approval. More than two weeks elapsed before Edgar Faure, who had served as Minister of Finance in the Mendès-France government and just before its downfall as Minister of Foreign Affairs, was able to form a government acceptable to the Assembly. He chose Antoine Pinay as his Foreign Minister.

Foreign Minister Pinay found it advisable to follow closely the policy charted by his predecessor. He followed up the Mendès-France arrangements regarding the Saar, and represented France in the North Atlantic Council meeting which welcomed the accession of the West German Federal Republic to NATO. The chief progress made by the Faure-Pinay government in the field of foreign affairs was largely limited to an honest effort to solve the serious crisis existing in the relations with North Africa. With Tunisia, where Mendès-France had laid down an excellent foundation for mutual co-operation with internal autonomy, Prime Minister Faure signed an agreement on June 3, 1955. Although there was some opposition by the extremists, the majority of the Neo-

Destour or Nationalist Party, including its popular and able leader, Habib Bourguiba, accepted the agreement. In the debate in the French National Assembly it was made clear that French interests were well protected and the agreement was adopted July 9, 1955, by a vote of 538 to 44. The Council of the Republic ratified the agreement August 3 by a vote of 254 to 25. The six conventions and annexed protocols gave Tunisia complete internal autonomy, transferring to Tunisian persons and institutions full responsibility for conducting the internal affairs of the country. France agreed to continue financial aid and the two countries were to co-operate in foreign affairs and national defense. The first all-Tunisian government was invested by the Bey on September 17, 1955, and the transfer of the various powers was carried out in accordance with the terms of the conventions. The final step was taken March 20, 1956, when France recognized the independence of Tunisia and abrogated the Treaty of 1881 and those provisions of the 1955 agreement contradictory to the new status.

The situation in Morocco was more serious and difficult to solve. When Premier Faure assumed office in 1955 the throne was held by Moulay Mohammed ben Arafa, installed with the support of the French in 1953 when they brought about the deposition and exile of Sultan Sidi Mohammed ben Youssef. The exiled Sultan's return was demanded by aroused Moroccan Nationalists, against whom stood the stubborn French colonials. It was quickly brought home to the French government that half-way measures were not enough. The people of Morocco wanted ben Youssef back on the throne and would not compromise. When El Glaoui, who in 1953 had helped the French unseat ben Youssef, switched to the Nationalist side and Moulay ben Arafa agreed to abdicate, it only remained for the French to work out an agreement with ben Youssef, with his return as Sultan fundamental.

Early in November, therefore, Mohammed ben Youssef returned in state to Paris, Foreign Minister Pinay flew back from the Conference of Foreign Ministers in Geneva to welcome him, El Glaoui begged forgiveness at the Sultan's feet, and on November 6, 1955, the French government recognized him as the legitimate Sultan of Morocco. It only remained to determine whether full independence was assured and under what conditions. However, before final action was taken the parliamentary elections in France produced a Socialist Government with Guy Mollet as Premier and Christian Pineau as Minister of Foreign Affairs.

Negotiations opened in Paris in the middle of February, and on March 2, 1956, a joint declaration recognizing the independence of Morocco was signed by the delegations of both countries. The Treaty of Fez of 1912, which established the Protectorate, was specifically abrogated. The Sultan of Morocco, styled His Majesty Mohammed V, would have a national army and would direct the foreign relations of the country. New agreements were to be concluded defining the status of interdependence and guaranteeing the rights of French persons in Morocco and Moroccan persons in France. It was later agreed that the Sultan would be Commander in Chief of the "Royal Armed Forces," an army of twenty thousand, and that his son would be general in charge.

Many problems of co-operation remained to be solved. One was the agreement for the United States air bases in Morocco, which was negotiated with the French without consulting the Moroccans. Another was the status of the international city of Tangier. Regardless of details, the basic requirement was expressed by Foreign Minister Pineau, chairman of the French delegation in the negotiations looking towards independence within interdependence: "Interdependence finds its definition in the objective recognition of the common interests of our two peoples. Our negotiations must establish through freely concluded agreements the means whereby this interdependence can be organized and made a living thing."

The problem of Algeria is far different from that of the two former protectorates, Tunisia and Morocco. Algeria is the largest and the most populous of the three areas and since 1848 has been considered by the French an integral part of France. Its northern part is divided into three departments which are administered as departments of France. The Moslem natives have been accorded French citizenship and representation in the French National Assembly. The French have built railroads and highways, developed power, provided water by huge dams, and equipped hospitals and schools. The French Government regards the million French colonials in Algeria as sons of France and entitled to her protection. The Algerian question, in the eyes of the French, is strictly a domestic problem and Foreign Minister Pinay withdrew with the French delegation from the United Nations Assembly in September, 1955, when the subject of Algeria was placed upon the Assembly's agenda.

However, the creation of a modern community in Algeria has strengthened the feeling of nationality. Since 1943 the demand for independence has increased steadily. The movement sparked a reign of terror in 1945 when thousands were killed. Its brutal repression stimulated greater nationalism. Since 1955 there has been constant killing of people, burning of crops, destruction of buildings, a veritable orgy of violence. Premier Mollet personally flew to Algeria to view the situation and was booed and reviled by the French populace. The situation had become so serious by the spring of 1956 that the National Assembly granted French Resident Minister Lacoste special powers and increased contingents of troops to put down what has become a widespread rebellion. Premier Mollet has received almost unanimous support in his determination to retain control of Algeria. Present French policy is clearly stated in his address of February 16, 1956, to the National Assembly: "To both Europeans and Moslems I once again solemnly declare that the union between Metropolitan France and Algeria is indissoluble. . . . There is no future for Algeria without France." But a strong Moslem movement, in Algeria and in the Arab world generally, rejects this view. When a group of five Algerian independence leaders was captured by the French in Algeria in October 1955, after their plane had been drawn off its route, Arab resentment was expressed by violence against French consulates and institutions in such distant cities as Jerusalem and by expressions of deep indignation from Moslem authorities in Tunis and Morocco.

This brief survey of French conduct of foreign policy and its results enables us, in the words of Mendès-France, "to judge the profound error of French foreign policy." She has backed and filled in Europe to such an extent that she has lost the confidence of her western allies. Her anachronistic colonial policy has brought about savage massacres in Madagascar (1947-1948), a disastrous debacle in Indo-China, and bloody revolts in Algeria, Tunisia, and Morocco. The recent increase in representation of the Communists in the Assembly and the success of the Poujadist malcontents, coupled with the continuous instability of governments, has produced a feeling of tragic uncertainty both at home and abroad as to the present dependability of France. André François-Poncet recently called France "the sick man of Europe."

However, the French are an intelligent, logical people. They are critical of their own weaknesses and have recognized the need for reform in governmental procedure. They have accepted independence in Tunisia and Morocco and have promised radical reforms in Algeria. France possesses a strategic position in Europe, great natural wealth, and a homogeneous hard-working people able to exploit it. The nation's potentialities should encourage its people to strive spiritedly for a future commensurate with an illustrious past.

SELECTED READINGS

Paul Alland, Le Quai d'Orsay. Paris, 1938.—One of the very few books which confines its field to the French Foreign Office and the French Foreign Service. It gives a historical sketch of the Quai d'Orsay followed by a description of its organization and work. The author covers the foreign service and the methods of recruitment employed at the time of writing. The book is enlivened by the descriptions of personalities who have played important roles in French diplomacy.

D. W. Brogan, France Under the Republic, 1870-1939. New York, 1940.—Although this study is limited to the Third Republic it is still a valuable contribution. The approach is general with particular emphasis upon political aspects.

P. E. Charvel, *France*. New York, 1955.—This is essentially a study of France under the Fourth Republic. The background and provisions of the Constitution of 1946 are analyzed and the problems of administration, the judiciary, and colonialism discussed in detail. The economic factor is covered quite fully and the author concludes that France can no longer afford to remain a bastion of economic individualism. The author is pessimistic as to the future of the Fourth Republic.

Gordon A. Craig and Felix Gilbert, *The Diplomats, 1919-1939*. Princeton, 1953.—This interesting volume which narrates diplomatic history by graphic accounts of the men who made it is a very valuable contribution. For those interested in French diplomacy the chapter by Richard D. Challener on the French Foreign Office and the chapter by Elizabeth R. Cameron on Alexis Saint-Léger are highly recommended.

Edward M. Earle (ed.), *Modern France*. Princeton, 1951.—A collection of essays on present-day France which includes a number on politics, government, and international affairs that are among the best in the volume.

Paul Farmer, *Vichy: Political Dilemma*. New York, 1955.—An objective study of the Vichy Government which controlled France from 1940 to 1944. An excellent bibliographical essay is included.

C. I. Gavin, *Liberated France*. New York, 1956.—An interesting integrated history of the Fourth Republic colored by a very evident distaste for de Gaulle.

Albert Guérard, *The France of Tomorrow*. Harvard, 1942.— *France: A Short History*. New York, 1946.—Written by an American of French origin, the first of these volumes is a brilliant presentation of certain problems of the French national state, and the second, a brief synthesis of all French history, told in a most fascinating manner. Both are highly recommended.

J. E. Howard, *Parliament and Foreign Policy in France*. London, 1948.—An analysis of the methods of parliamentary control of foreign policy during the Third Republic, particularly from 1919 to 1939. The book proves that parliament can control foreign policy but does not always use its powers.

Herbert Luethy, *France Against Herself*. New York, 1955.—The author is a Swiss journalist who has lived during the past decade in France and who views the French situation objectively but frankly. Its brilliant style and stimulating analysis make it one of the outstanding books on the present French political and economic structure. It should be required reading for everyone interested in France.

Donald C. McKay, *United States and France*. Harvard, 1951.— In addition to covering the international relations of France and the United States, the author gives an excellent interpretation of the French character and political situation. The book is informative and sound.

Ronald Mathews, *Death of the Fourth Republic*. New York, 1954.—A first-hand survey of postwar French politics by an English newspaperman who had become painfully disillusioned by the indicated disintegration of a country which he cherished. Time has already proved that the author was overly pessimistic.

François Goguel-Nyegaard, *France Under the Fourth Republic*. Cornell University, 1953.—A brief interpretation of French political behavior written by a leading French political scientist. Rather overemphasizes electoral reform and the election of 1951.

S. K. Padover, *French Institutions*. Stanford, 1955.—A brief study of French political institutions, social problems and foreign policy. Useful for the understanding of France today.

Dorothy M. Pickles, *The French Political Scene*. London, 1938. —*France Between the Republics*. London, 1946.—*French Politics: The First Years of the Fourth Republic*. London, 1953.—These three volumes by an able, well-informed British woman give an excellent picture of the French political scene as seen by an objective observer from the outside. All three volumes are very factual and if the author had only been willing to interpolate a few pungent remarks from time to time, it would have added to the piquancy of the treatment.

David Thomson, *French Foreign Policy*. London, 1944.—*Democracy in France*. 2nd ed., London, New York, 1952.—Both of these volumes, which are concerned with the Third Republic, were written by an eminent British scholar who knew whereof he wrote. Both are substantial contributions to the subjects covered.

P. M. Williams, *Politics in Post War France*. New York, 1954.— This excellent study is limited to an analysis and evaluation of the parliamentary machinery of the Fourth Republic. The author tells how it works and who controls it. It is a scholarly contribution.

Gordon Wright, *Reshaping of French Democracy*. New York, 1948.—A first-hand picture of the birth of the Fourth Republic by an American professor of history. The style is vivid, the characterizations accurate, and the contribution to the subject highly worthwhile.

The Netherlands

MANFRED C. VERNON

Department of Political Science
University of Alabama

The Netherlands

CHAPTER 16

THE BACKGROUNDS OF
NETHERLANDS FOREIGN POLICY

One of the least known and discussed countries in international affairs—despite all its accomplishments, its prestige and its general contributions to mankind—is the little Kingdom of the Netherlands.[1] A faithful ally of the West, it has perhaps done more toward the progress of humanity than any other nation of its size. It is a hard-working nation, believing in the great principles of the West, with a particular interest in the problems and progress of international law. It has a record of frequent sacrifices of self-interest and generous treatment of the oppressed of other lands. Many of these merits are known only to a few interested observers. Yet they should have the widest of publicity in order to present fairly the country's impressive share in the field of international relations. The story of the little country could very well be a lesson in better and peaceful life for our troubled world.

While most other countries were involved in warfare between 1850 and 1920, the Netherlands during this period preserved nonbelligerency and neutrality. In fact, for more than a century, from the War of 1830, which led to the independence of Belgium,

[1] The Netherlands and Holland are the names to be used interchangeably and without any particular reason throughout these pages. While Holland actually has been the name of only a part of the country (The Netherlands) the word has been increasingly used for the entire country.

until May 1940, when the Germans invaded the kingdom, the Dutch nation was able to avoid involvement in European wars. One probable reason was that such a small country, with its specific geographical situation, could not afford to entertain aggressive designs. There were probably more reasons. Whichever was decisive, the Dutch were able for a long time to enjoy and utilize the habit of peaceful living. The habit became a goal.

The Nation and the Sea

A typical small country, the Kingdom of the Netherlands covers in Europe an area of about 12,850 square miles, which is slightly smaller than the combined size of Massachusetts and Connecticut.[2] The capital of the realm in Europe is Amsterdam; the seat of the government is The Hague. The population, which has grown steadily from 8.6 million before World War II to about 10.7 million in 1955, lives in one of the world's most densely inhabited areas; the ratio is more than 800 persons to the square mile.

The Dutch have been always hard-working people, full of initiative and capable of material as well as cultural accomplishments. Certainly, prior to World War II, agriculture, industry, trade, and shipping had given the country a feeling of great contentment and security. The nation's proximity to the sea had made its people both fighters against the sea and also seafarers. Perhaps as early as the tenth century and certainly by the twelfth, the inhabitants of the Lowlands began their struggle against the sea by building a system of dykes and reclaiming land below sea level. While it was a slow process—and there were also instances of failure—the undertaking continued to great success. A large and fertile part of the country has been reclaimed from the sea—about 40 per cent of the total surface area.[3] But as recently as 1953, parts of the

[2] According to official information the Kingdom of the Netherlands (Koninkrijk der Nederlanden) consists of four parts: (a) The realm in Europe (Rijk in Europa) (Nederland) sometimes called Holland; (b) Surinam, sometimes called Netherlands Guiana; (c) The Netherlands Antilles (de Nederlandse Antillen) consisting of the islands of Aruba, Bonaire, Curaçao, Saba, Saint Eustace and part of Saint Martin; (d) New Guinea (Nieuw Guinea)

[3] About one-fourth of the total area of the country lies below sea level and is protected by some 1,500 miles of dykes.

country were flooded by the sea, with severe damage of about 1 billion guilders. The whole population joined to repair this damage and within two months more than 90 per cent of the flooded area had been reclaimed. Truly, there is much to the saying that God created the world, but the Dutch made Holland.

The Dutch developed into one of the world's foremost seagoing nations and have retained this position, even though the Napoleonic wars brought the loss of important bases overseas to England and ended the era of Dutch world supremacy in commercial shipping. The merchant fleet by 1955 had surpassed its 1940 tonnage.[4] The colonial holdings of the Netherlands before World War II, both in the western hemisphere and in the East Indies, gave the nation special incentive and advantage in ocean shipping, just as the river shipping on the Rhine gave it a significant position for trade.

The colonies, throughout the centuries, provided both a sizable part of the national income and a home for those Dutchmen who went to live in "tropical Holland." The Dutch had a feeling of great love for these colonies, and the territories had become part of the people and their land; regardless of the postwar developments, the former East Indies meant home to many people of Dutch background. Much work and much ingenuity were invested to develop them.

Modern Economic Conditions

The economy of Holland, like the land, is largely made by the Dutch people, carrying on in conditions that have made things look bleak and the future seem well-nigh hopeless. In 1945, they set out to mend the war's damage to their economy, just as in 1953 they set out to mend the flood damage to their country, in both tasks manifesting the same tenacity and persistence that are part of the Dutch character and life.

Formerly prosperous Holland, badly hit by World War II, particularly during its closing period in late 1944 and 1945, found

[4] Whereas on January 1, 1940, the total mercantile marine numbered 1,153 units and had a gross registered tonnage of 2,869,813, the respective amounts as of January 1, 1955, were 1,337 units and 3,375,610 tons.

itself close to complete ruin. German occupation and general destruction had caused great damage and reduced the national wealth by almost 30 per cent. An exhausted population, dangerously short of food and housing, suffering of the loss of machinery to the enemy, and facing greatly reduced agricultural production, encountered an overwhelming problem of reconstruction.

The rebuilding had to be started while inland and overseas traffic was completely paralyzed. About 400 ocean-going vessels had been lost, representing about 50 per cent of the 1940 tonnage of the country. The changes in the world economy had left the country in the midst of an enfeebled and indebted western Europe and made it feel the acute shortage of dollars. To top matters, the heavily suffering East Indies, formerly a source of income for the mother country, were in need of help in order to recover from damage inflicted during the Japanese occupation.

Thus Holland had to face reconstruction, a significant change in economic structure, and, above all, the problem of how to increase its production capacity. Marshall Plan help was largely responsible for getting matters started and developed, and the hard work of the government and of the population showed results far beyond expectation; in January 1953, the Netherlands government, most certainly to its great satisfaction, was able to inform the government of the United States that the economic situation the Netherlands had improved to such a degree that United States economic aid was no longer needed.[5] The result showed the strength and determination of the Dutch. Within less than ten years, against terrific obstacles and without any great publicity, the country had succeeded in working its way again toward the top of the economic ladder, almost doubling its industrial production within this period. Increased productivity was accompanied by a shift of working people to industry; in comparison to prewar days, when 30 per cent of the working population was to be found in industry, the percentage in the postwar years has risen

[5] The story of this successful period has been described in a publication by the Director General for the Economic and Military Aid Program of the Ministry of Foreign Affairs, *Road to Recovery* (The Hague, 1954).

to 45 per cent. In addition, the national income has doubled since prewar days. By August 1, 1955, *Forbes Magazine* could say:

Holland presently is enjoying a prosperity second to none despite a substantial population increase . . . It has more jobs than workers and today Amsterdam is topping London as a source for export capital. Their recovery is referred to pridefully in The Netherlands and wonderously in other lands as "The Dutch Miracle."

Also from 1947 to 1953 total production increased by more than 40 per cent, which enabled the general supply level of the country to be considerably improved despite the growing population. One of the most impressive accomplishments was the growth in value of total Dutch exports from 2.7 billion guilders in 1940 to 8.1 billion in 1953, an increase of 200 percent. Also of special significance was the development of exports to the United States and Canada, which increased from 85 million guilders in 1948 to 700 million in 1953. In 1947 the country suffered a deficit in the balance of payments; it amounted to 1.6 billion guilders. Yet in 1952 it had developed a surplus of 1.9 billion guilders. This success was made feasible through Marshall Plan aid, but it was also accompanied by close co-operation within the Organization for European Economic Co-operation and other international organizations; it largely developed because of a Dutch sense of loyalty toward international co-operation. The epilogue to *Road to Recovery* may give a feeling for the reaction of the Dutch nation to the development:

The Dutch people met the many problems with which they were confronted after five years of war and occupation in a spirit of co-operation. They have been prepared to live a moderate life without slackening their efforts because they were aware that their future was at stake. It was this spirit and Marshall aid support during the years now behind us that enabled the government, management and labor to lay a foundation on which the nation could build its future prosperity without further outside help.

On September 15, 1953, in the Speech from the Throne with which the new session of Parliament was opened, Her Majesty Queen Juliana was able to say:

"The change for the good, which already had made its appearance in foreign payments, was not a passing symptom. Gold and currency received from the United States of America from 1948 to 1953, and which has so considerably contributed to the economic recovery, could be terminated. The preservation of the regained equilibrium and continuation of the normal growth of the economy require constant attention. The rapid increase of our population compels us to continue existing sources of prosperity."

With these words Her Majesty the Queen pointed out to the Netherlands people the results of their labors during the past years and their task for the years to come.

Execution of this task will demand the efforts, energy and perseverance of the Dutch people, not only nationally but also internationally. The economy of no other country is so sensitive to international economic events. Promoting international economic co-operation which within the Benelux has already borne such good fruit will therefore continue to demand the attention and application of the nation. In this field, too, an important stimulant has already been given by the effect of the European Recovery Program.

If, in the coming years, results can be obtained in the international field which, in significance, can be compared with those of the Netherlands recovery over the past years, the Netherlands people can face the future with full confidence.

Since then the record has become an even more impressive one. According to the *Foreign Commerce Weekly* of April 2, 1956, the value of Netherlands foreign trade in 1955 reached a new high of 22.4 billion guilders, which was almost 12 percent above the 1954 level of 20 billion (1 guilder = $0.264). Exports had risen to 10,860 million guilders. Germany had become the Netherlands' most important trading partner, followed by Belgium and Luxembourg. There had been also a steady decrease of government interference and restrictions, particularly in the field of foreign exchange. The rate of employment had remained so high that labor shortages were in fact hampering production of some industries, particularly the metal, construction, and wood industries.

Educational and Cultural Accomplishments

A country with such a hard-working and successful population would be expected to achieve a high educational level. And some of the personalities of the Netherlands have reached intellectual and cultural eminence that places them among the great of all times. The country's recognized great impact in the field of knowledge was made possible in part by an early developed system of education; the world-famous University of Leyden was opened in February 1575 and immediately became an attraction for the leading scholars of the European continent—among many others, the French philosopher René Descartes. The Dutch themselves produced men of intellectual greatness, such as Grotius, international lawyer as well as poet, philosopher, and historian. Among the many Dutch citizens who opened new fields of knowledge in biology were Jan Swammerdam, first to study the metamorphoses of insect life, and Anthony van Leeuwenhoek, exploring infinity in the invisibly small and discovering the microbes in a drop of water. Christiaan Huygens, truly an intellectual giant, constructed the first pendulum clock, invented a micrometer, discovered the rings of Saturn, and developed the wave theory of light. There were the many artists who during the seventeenth century contributed vastly to the fine arts. This century, the "golden age" of the Dutch, saw such men as Rembrandt van Rijn, Jan Vermeer, Frans Hals, Jan Steen, Pieter de Hoogh, and Jacob van Ruysdael, all of whom have gained immortality in their field and made "art the chief glory of the Golden Age of the Netherlands."[6]

Great though these men were, it is perhaps in the field of speculative thinking that Holland has produced some of the greatest minds of this world. While the Reformation found many adherents in the Low Countries, largely as a reaction to the ruthless techniques employed by the Spanish inquisitors and overlords, and while many of the Dutch Protestants found their inspiration in the religious fervor of the Calvinists, there was also a great influence for tolerance, initiated in the late fifteenth and early sixteenth centuries by the famous humanist, Desiderius Erasmus of Rotterdam (1466-1536). Then, and ever since, the Netherlands has been known for tolerance and enlightenment and has been a haven for many that were oppressed and driven out for differences in thought, religion, and general beliefs from their countries. It is

[6] Adriaan Jacob Barnouw, "The Seventeenth Century: The Golden Age" in Bartholomew Landheer, ed., *The Netherlands* (University of California Press, 1943), p. 58.

perhaps symbolic and significant that the descendant of such immigrants, the world-famous philosopher Baruch Spinoza, should develop his thoughts in such a surrounding.

While past centuries thus had many outstanding personalities, Holland has many contemporaries who excel in the fields of science, architecture, art, engineering, shipbuilding and aircraft construction, business, and diplomacy that their names would fill pages—all quite natural since the population of Holland enjoys a high standard of literacy and has the opportunity to attend outstanding schools on the grade-school level and exceptional universities of the caliber of Leyden, Amsterdam, and many others.

Humanitarianism

It is necessary to notice and insist on the innate sense of the Dutch for tolerance and their strong feeling for justice. Throughout the centuries the country has opened its borders to victims of religious and political persecutions: the Jews expelled from Spain and Portugal at the end of the fifteenth century; the English Puritans, who had a temporary haven in Leyden before they returned to England and emigrated to Massachusetts in 1620; the Huguenots, who had to leave France after the revocation of the Edict of Nantes in 1685. Some descendants of these immigrant groups belong now to the most distinguished families of the nation.

The policy of furnishing refuge for the oppressed was continued during the nineteenth and twentieth centuries, despite the fact that the country had become one of the most densely populated in the world. Victims of the 1903 pogroms in Russia were taken in. During World War I, despite the official neutrality, Holland gave refuge to thousands of Belgians from the war zone.[7] In 1920, when a demand came to the Dutch government from the victors in the war to extradite the former Kaiser Wilhelm II, who had taken refuge in Holland, the demand was rejected twice since granting it would have been contrary to what the Dutch deemed right and justice and would not have been reconcilable with the country's national honor.

The Netherlands continued the tradition by taking in refugees

---

[7] Also, despite official neutrality, the Dutch people expressed strong resentment after the German sinking of the *Lusitania*.

from Hitler Germany and from Austria and Czechoslovakia after Hitler's occupation of both countries. On the other side, there had always been a willingness to help the children of Germany or Austria after World War I, to feed them, to have them visit Holland for vacations, and to follow their growth to adulthood.

More recently, great interest has been taken in the problem of the displaced persons and refugees of the period following World War II. The population provided material help and homes, and Queen Juliana pleaded in their behalf, in letters to Presidents Truman and Eisenhower in which she expressed the serious consideration of the Netherlands for the problem.[8] Her second message on this subject accompanied her expression of gratitude to President Eisenhower for the sympathy and help of the people of the United States during the Netherlands flood of 1951. It is interesting to note that as a consequence the Dutch government in 1954 asked the Council of Europe to institute a fund to help all hardship cases. The government has continuously supported the office of the United Nations High Commissioner for Refugees financially,[9] and the Dutch people set up a special Committee for Help to Refugees.

A typical example of the work of the Committee may be seen in a nation-wide voluntary aid campaign that was launched in October 1954. The organizations representing industrial workers, clerks and civil servants announced that their members would give up one hour's wages to help the refugee fund, while the employers (including the government) announced that they would contribute the same amount collected by their employees. The final total exceeded 4 million guilders and was turned over to the fund at the

[8] The letters were sent, and the general actions referred to took place, after the termination of the International Refugee Organization in 1951 and the appointment of the High Commissioner for Refugees, who works with very limited financial means.

[9] The first High Commissioner was a Netherlander, Dr. G. J. van Heuven Goedhart, with a distinguished career in international relations work. He died July 10, 1956 of heart failure, a disappointed man who had intended to resign because of difficulties in raising funds in the United Nations for his refugee program. It was largely his influence and work that contributed to the decision of the Nobel Prize Committee to award its prize for peace in 1955 to the United Nations for aid to refugees.

disposal of the High Commissioner for Refugees in addition to the Dutch government's official contribution.

Another interesting expression of Dutch initiative to help others took place in September 1955. A conference met then in The Hague upon invitation of the Netherlands government in an effort to provide refugee seamen with some legal status by correcting oversights in the 1951 agreement on refugees made at Geneva. An estimated 8,000 seamen were at sea without any country, because they had failed to ask for asylum in the port where they escaped from a ship of their native country. Some of these persons had been mustered on board other ships and since they were lacking any legal papers many of them could not go ashore for years.

The humanitarian attitude of the government and people of the Netherlands is perhaps their greatest contribution to mankind. In a German reference publication, the country is recognized as "the classical haven for all the innocent persecuted and for political exiles the protection of whom is an axiom of honor."[10]

Military Potential

Whatever the questions as to the value of any military contributions that might come from the Dutch, Holland since the end of World War II has clearly indicated its willingness to participate in any war that might be forced upon the West. The Netherlands policy of neutrality in world affairs is outmoded, since the leaders of the country realize that its geographical position and the growing interdependence of the world would automatically involve it in a conflict. The defense potential of the country, taken by itself, can concededly be only of minor significance. Any Dutch effort to be militarily prepared ought therefore to be seen and evaluated only in connection with similar efforts of other powers. Although Holland has not had much experience in modern land warfare, it has capable personnel in its armed forces and it has a small but very efficient navy. But no small country can produce much manpower. Nor has Holland the terrain to provide the West with a formidable barrier against an aggressor. The defense planning of the British and the French during World War II, as to the Dutch, contemplated that the Netherlands could delay, at best for some time,

[10] *Politisches Handwörterbuch* (Leipzig, 1923), vol. 2, p. 189.

a possible German move. The flat country was considered by them to be strategically important as a coastal area for the shipping of troops and equipment, or for an evacuation area. Thus the proximity of the North Sea and of the British Channel contributed, as it still does, to the strategic value of the Netherlands. The country can be easily flooded to delay mechanized armies—unless as in 1940 the enemy by surprise or treachery secures control too soon. But such delaying action is of significance only in terms of traditional warfare, not significant in the presence of nuclear weapons and guided missiles. Yet modern warfare is probably beyond the reach and power potential of any country of western Europe.

It is quite certain that the Netherlands is a loyal and faithful partner in the western European defense system. The Dutch government has always agreed that the joint western defense efforts will have to be maintained and that the country would have to try to strengthen its own defense even further. The nation was to furnish under the originally agreed North Atlantic Treaty defense plans five infantry divisions. This quota eventually appeared to be unfeasible because of the lack of manpower. New consultations led to the decision that by the end of 1954 a complete army corps of three divisions plus the sustaining corps troops would be ready, and the formation of the remaining divisions would be left to successive years. Despite the willingness of the country to pay quite heavily for these preparations, it was also realized that the Netherlands could not fulfill this task all by itself although it was willing to contribute as much as possible.

The Dutch financial contributions to NATO have been increased each year; according to the organization the country has given the following amounts:

1949	680 million guilders
1950	901 million guilders
1951	1060 million guilders
1952	1253 million guilders
1953	1330 million guilders
1954	1583 million guilders
1955*	1800 million guilders

* Forecast by NATO on December 16, 1955.

The Netherlands has become also a part of the co-ordinated air-defense and radar-warning system of NATO. The Dutch have built up a modern air-defense command of their own, equipped with relatively modern planes and backed by an excellent civil telephone and telegraph network. Quite a few of the fighter planes are constructed in the Netherlands by such qualified builders as the Fokker Works at Amsterdam.

International Law

To international law, in its theoretical aspects as well as in its formulation and application, the Netherlands has contributed at least as much as any other nation. The country produced some of the most outstanding thinkers in the field. The interest in the subject may have been the expression of a desire of the Dutch to find better ways to international understanding and to world peace; it certainly responded to the need for a little country to remain at peace with its neighbors. The Dutch, throughout the centuries, have manifested respect for law, and in particular for international law; the world became so much aware of this interest and attitude that the Netherlands was considered as a center of internationalism and of peace organizations and activities. The Hague became a kind of "peace laboratory."[11]

HUGO GROTIUS. Modern international law cannot be discussed without a reference to the great accomplishments of Dutch authors. Among these writers belongs, above all, the "father of modern international law," Huig de Groot (1583-1645), better known through his Latinized name of Hugo Grotius, who has contributed to the greater glory of his homeland. Though he is known mainly for his writings in the field of law, his chief interest was the pursuit of classical and theological studies; he excelled as an eminent historian and was, in addition to being well versed in philosophy, an author on Roman Dutch law. His concern for the rights of nations to liberty of navigation, commerce, and fishing on the high seas led him to write on international law. After having re-

[11] Amry J. Vandenbosch, "Netherlands Foreign Policy" in Bartholomew Landheer, ed., The Netherlands (University of California Press, 1943), p. 140.

ceived his degree of doctor of laws from the University of Leyden, he wrote *Mare Librum* (1609), championing the then unpopular thought of freedom of the seas.[12] His most significant and most famous work, *De jure belli ac pacis* (1625), was written while he was in exile in Paris. Believing in the universal supremacy of justice, without which the community of states cannnot be preserved, he had been concerned with the problem for a long time. It has been discovered by now that *De jure belli ac pacis* was actually an enlargement of a brief or legal opinion which he had prepared in 1604 for the Dutch East India Company.

The great contribution of Grotius to international law was that he gave, for the first time, a "fairly complete system of international law" which was "built up as an independent branch of the science of law" (Oppenheim). Perhaps the most significant part of the work is the one on "the law of peace," which, according to his countryman, the distinguished law expert Professor V. van Vollenhoven, "had no parallel in the work of any predecessor; it was a marvel of inductive juridical composition and formed the foundation of the whole system."[13]

Another contribution of the great Dutch author in a related field, that of diplomacy, has been the subject of a recent description by Harold Nicolson, who points out that Grotius helped develop the general theory of diplomacy and the conduct of international relations. Grotius, a man of reason in an age of severe religious conflict, asserted that there was no sense at all in the religious divisions of the time seeking to impose their specific dogmas on each other and pleaded for tolerance and understanding. Nicolson further describes him as the "first systematic philosopher to propose that some institution should be established whereby the Law of Nature could be administered and enforced. His idea was that the Christian Powers, whether Catholic or Protestant, should create 'some kind of body, in whose assemblies

12 He had written already *De jure praedae*, which, while probably finished during the winter 1604-1605, remained unpublished and, in fact, unknown until 1864. It was finally published in 1868.

13 *Encyclopaedia of the Social Sciences*, IV, p. 177.

the quarrels of each one might be terminated by the judgment of others not interested'."[14]

BYNKERSHOEK. Cornelius van Bynkershoek (1673-1743), an eminent eighteenth-century jurist and President of the High Council for the Provinces of Holland, Zeeland, and West Friesland, a post which he held from 1724 to his death in 1743, had been a student of Roman law and became particularly interested in matters concerning international maritime law. He is now known as one of the most significant scholars in the field of positivist thought in the international legal sphere. Less of a general systematizer than an enunciator of specific doctrines, he developed quite a few principles in the field, such as the original thoughts on the "three-mile limit." In his work De dominio maris (1702) he concluded that a state can take possession of the waters washing its shores and thus hold them under its sovereign control as far as it can extend such control; such possession can be made effective by a cannon fired from the shore. Since in Bynkershoek's time the range was about three miles,[15] the young lawyer proposed that a nation should occupy and exercise ownership over waters within three miles of low-water mark.

Bynkershoek, with great pride, had this to say about his countrymen and their respect for the seas open to all:

I am not the sort of person who will lie for the benefit of my own people. It is some time since the Netherlanders excelled in naval glory, but I do not remember that I read they possess the open sea or that they ever possessed it with intent of ownership. Nay, their modesty is so great that, content in the use and enjoyment of the sea, they neither arrogate to themselves sovereignty, nor do they envy others who are delighted by pride of names alone.[16]

[14] Harold Nicolson, The Evolution of Diplomatic Method (The Macmillan Company, New York, 1954), p. 49f. (For detailed information on Grotius see, among many publications on the person and his writings, W. S. M. Knight, The Life and Works of Hugo Grotius (The Grotius Society Publications, No. 4, London, 1925) and the publications by the Carnegie Endowment for International Peace, The Classics of International Law, edited by James Brown Scott).

[15] James Brown Scott, ed., The Classics of International Law: De Dominio Maris Dissertatio by Cornelius van Bynkershoek (Carnegie Endowment for International Peace, 1923), pp. 15-17, 20f.

[16] Ibid., p. 75.

INTERNATIONAL CONFERENCES, COURTS, AND ORGANIZATIONS. The human contributions of the Netherlands to better international relations, its general interest in the subject, its proximity to the sea, and its consequent very active commerce were probably the main reasons why the nation has often been the host for international conferences pertaining to matters of law. For much the same reasons, it has been the home of many international courts and other institutions. The reasons mentioned led the Abbé de Saint-Pierre to suggest one of the Dutch towns, such as Utrecht or The Hague, as the seat of his envisaged international organization for the maintenance of perpetual peace.

The most famous conferences of their kind, the Hague Conferences of 1899 and 1907, belong to the most significant meetings in the general field that have taken place in the Netherlands. The Hague was then chosen both times at the request of the head of a foreign state: the first conference after the suggestion of Tsar Nicholas II of Russia, the second one after a proposal by President Theodore Roosevelt. From 1893 to 1956, seven diplomatic conferences were held in the same city in connection with the codification of private international law. On July 15, 1955, the Statute of the Hague Conference for Private International Law, drawn up in 1951, providing for a permanent office of the organization to be located in The Hague, went into effect. The Netherlands Government was to retain "the diplomatic protection of the Conference while, under the Statute, the Netherlands State Commission for International Private Law will continue to determine the scientific policy for the Conference."[17]

The Hague has also been the seat of the Permanent Court of Arbitration; the Minister of Foreign Affairs of the Netherlands has been President of the Administrative Council of the Court; the International Bureau of the Court, established since 1900 in the Hague, has been under the control of a Secretary-General of Dutch nationality. In 1913 the Bureau was moved to the Peace Palace, built with money given by Andrew Carnegie, after its dedication on August 28 of that year. While most of the thirty-six

[17] *ANP-ANETA News Bulletin,* July 27, 1955.

men who were members of tribunals of the Court served but once in that capacity, the Netherlander de Savornin Lohman was a member of five tribunals.[18]

The Permanent Court of International Justice, also housed in the Peace Palace, was opened on February 15, 1922; the public inaugural meeting was held in the presence of the Queen of the Netherlands and representatives of the League of Nations and of a large number of states. Dr. B. C. J. Loder, a member of the Court of Cassation of the Netherlands, was elected as the first President of the Permanent Court of International Justice on January 30, 1922. He had participated in the preparatory work to set up the Court, together with a number of distinguished jurists from many countries.[19] This Court, organized under the League of Nations, has been succeeded by the International Court of Justice under the United Nations.

Many other organizations concerned with international law have settled in Holland—among them have been the International Academy of Comparative Law, the International Bureau for the Unification of Criminal Law, the Academy of International Law, and the International Office of Legal Translations.

THE GOVERNMENT AND CONSTITUTION OF THE NETHERLANDS IN RELATION TO INTERNATIONAL LAW. The official concern of the Netherlands government with the problem of international law and a need for its use in the relationship between nations has been expressed many times by official spokesmen of the country. A dynamic plea of this nature was made by Dr. J. M. A. H. Luns in the commemorative session of the United Nations at San Francisco on June 23, 1955, on the occasion of the tenth anniversary of the organization:

[18] The only other person to serve five times was the Frenchman Louis Renault. Manley O. Hudson, *The Permanent Court of International Justice 1920-1942* (New York, 1943), p. 33f. A case that involved the Netherlands and the United States before the Permanent Court of Arbitration was the *Island of Palmas* Case (1928), in which it was decided by the single-member arbitral tribunal, the Swiss Max Huber, that the island in its entirety was Netherlands territory.

[19] The American member was Elihu Root, former Secretary of State and then a member of the Permanent Court of Arbitration at The Hague.

. . . Whenever . . . the United Nations upholds the rule of international law and lets world interest prevail over the special interests of its members, it ushers in a brighter future for international relations.

In this connection I should like to draw attention to one feature of the practice of our Organization which, in the view of the Netherlands Government, is fraught with disturbing implications: the sometimes marked disregard of international law. How often has not political expediency prevailed over legal rights in matters dealt with by the General Assembly? And what have we done to develop international law: Few monuments of international legislation have emerged from our workshop; the drafting of legal documents has not always been done by competent hands. The United Nations has shown a lack of interest in matters of law which, if it should prevail, would do much harm to its authority, since no country will feel obliged to obey the recommendations of an organization which behaves like a political gathering of competing pressure groups rather than reflecting in its deliberations and decisions something of the majesty of the law.[20]

The attitude of the Netherlands toward international law, as expressed by its government, was also clearly indicated in connection with the amendments to the Dutch constitution since World War II. While the war was still in progress, the demand for a revision of the constitution, particularly in the field of foreign relations, had become intensified. As a result of investigation and recommendation by a committee under the chairmanship of an eminent expert, Jonkheer W. J. M. van Eysinga, who had been a member of the Permanent Court of International Justice, the relationship of the country to the principles of international law has been prescribed by Article 58: the King, in charge of the supreme direction of foreign relations, "shall promote the development of the international legal order."

Some of the discussions and findings of the van Eysinga committee were concerned with problems of aggressive war as opposed to collective self-defense. The committee felt that aggressive war was outlawed since the Briand-Kellogg Pact of August 27, 1928, and certainly by the Charter of the United Nations, even though the Dutch constitution officially recognized war as a legal institution. Though it was thought unlikely that the Netherlands would par-

[20] Mimeographed statement of the Netherlands Delegation to the United Nations Press Office, June 23, 1955.

ticipate in anything but collective security action, the Dutch constitution contained no provision for such participation. The government, though favorable in principle to the adjustment of the omission, took the view that this question should be considered on the occasion of the more general revision of the constitution which is expected to take place within the next few years. It felt that this question falls rather within the framework of the constitutional provisions on military matters contained in the tenth chapter of the constitution.[21]

Guiding Principles of Dutch Foreign Policy

During the nineteenth and twentieth centuries, particular attention was given by the Dutch to their relationship with Great Britain, Belgium, and Germany. The conduct of relations with these powers, as with all powers, was guided by certain general principles which may be usefully reviewed at the beginning.

A small country is not interested in warfare; the main concern of such a nation is to remain at peace, not to be bothered by its neighbors, and to maintain a high standard of living. A trading nation such as Holland necessarily pursues the goals of open sea lanes and free trade and endeavors not to get involved in any policy that might interfere with such goals. A small nation must be more cautious than the big one; provocative statements may bring on the wrath of the great and thus endanger the little nation's existence. Certainly the Netherlands has done everything in order to avoid such provocations or anything that might lead to war, aggressive or defensive; for the country is not strong enough to risk the former nor to be exposed to the latter. Yet, though its policy had kept the country out of fighting in Europe for about 110 years, in 1940 the country was invaded without provocation and without any stated reasons.

RELATIONSHIP WITH GREAT BRITAIN. There has always been something special about the relationship of Great Britain and Holland. "England cannot tolerate a major power on the other

[21] For more detail see H. F. van Panhuys, "The Netherlands Constitution and International Law," in *American Journal of International Law*, October 1953, p. 543.

side of the North Sea. . . . It also is opposed to a weak power without resistance of its own power. Thus history shows the two countries, England and Holland, in an unbroken interrelationship. England was always for us when we were threatened, and against us when we were too powerful ourselves or when led by another power."[22]

The very creation of the new Netherlands following the Napoleonic wars, although the work of the great powers, was the special work of Great Britain. In fact, the independence of the Lowlands had been part of British foreign policy since the beginning of the modern nation-state in the sixteenth century. The continuing main reason for this stand had been that England, facing the European continent across a narrow channel, could not tolerate the existence of a hostile or potentially adverse great power opposite the Thames estuary; thus Great Britain was particularly interested in the neutralization of the Rhine-Scheldt-Meuse delta and in having Holland as a buffer state against potential enemies of the British on the continent—in former times the French, but after 1871 mainly the united and dynamic Germans. Another reason for the outspoken concern of Great Britain for Holland had been the common interest in colonial holdings, sea shipping, and trade. The Netherlands could count therefore on British good will in regard to the protection of overseas interests and on British support against danger in Europe. During the nineteenth century, the Dutch continued to look to the British for advice or help in foreign affairs.

There was much concern in England over the adventurous policy of Napoleon III and also over the annexationist pronouncements of Bismarck. There was also great anxiety as to the intentions of the Germans in regard to Dutch neutrality. During World War I there was no doubt that the British would have come to the help of the Dutch had the country been invaded by the Germans; in fact, there were offers of alliance in order to forestall such possibilities. Britain's main interest, however, was to have Dutch neu-

22 J. A. van Hamel, *Nederland Tusschen de Mogendheden* (Amsterdam, 1918) as quoted in B. Landheer, *The Netherlands in a Changing World* (New York, 1947), p. 123.

trality continued in order to keep the essential Dutch ports out of German hands.

The two nations have come very close to each other, since they have many interests in common. The Netherlands has learned by experience that the British are friends and will help them if there is need for aid. While in the field of economic relations there was some tension after the end of World War II, matters have considerably improved since 1954, particularly since the British government eliminated certain import restrictions so that Dutch exports to Great Britain have significantly increased.

RELATIONSHIP WITH GERMANY. Before the unification of Germany and its development into a great European power, little thought was given in the Netherlands to any danger that might come from Germany. In fact, a Dutch author felt that during the nineteenth century things were going rather well for Holland:

Holland's development in the nineteenth and twentieth century was stable and gradual until the supremacy of a new power began to threaten once more the balance of power in Europe. This time it was Germany who, having achieved unity in 1870, was determined to become the leading power and set about this task with energy and military might although with a considerable lack of judgment and without any moral justification. Thus, we see once more the same pattern in Holland's policy: a strong tie with England as the strongest maritime power and friendship with the second-strongest power on the continent: France.[23]

Although responsible persons in Netherlands scientific and military circles had expressed admiration for German achievements, and although the cultural influence of the Germans was steadily increasing, the Dutch had great misgivings as to the future. Before World War I broke out, Dutch leaders had become alarmed because of the strong language used by German leaders, and thus feared they might get involved in a general conflict in Europe. Landheer describes the feelings of the Dutch in those days as follows:

[23] Bart Landheer, *The Netherlands in a Changing World* (New York, 1947), p. 134f.

It was not due to any unusual statesmanship on the part of the Dutch that Holland did not become involved in World War I, but purely to accidental factors of a military nature which made the conquest of Holland irrelevant. A revised von Schlieffen plan envisaged a flank attack on France through Belgium, but not as the original plan through the southern part of Holland. If the Germans had won the war, they would undoubtedly have annexed Belgium, which would have made the position of Holland as untenable as that of Czechoslovakia after Munich. For this reason also, as well as to keep a neutral country open as a source of possible supplies, Germany did not invade the Netherlands.

On several occasions in World War I, the neutrality of Holland was severely threatened, and each time for the same reason, viz., that either Germany or England feared that Dutch territory was included in operational plans of the enemy.[24]

There was a feeling of relief in the Netherlands when Germany lost the war and concentrated on the problem of recovery from defeat. Yet within less than 25 years Germany invaded the Netherlands after having given solemn assurances that it would respect the integrity of the little country. Ribbentrop, on the morning of May 10, 1940, when the German attack on the Netherlands had already begun, told the Dutch minister that Germany was determined to safeguard Dutch neutrality "by military measures." Thus, Netherlands neutrality had been finally violated by one neighbor.[25] Queen Wilhelmina, with her daughter Juliana and her family, and members of the government were forced to flee the country and to go to London, where a government-in-exile took care of Dutch problems for the duration of the war.

Since the termination of the War the Netherlands government has always given expression to its feelings on future relations by emphasizing a need for an integrated Europe. They probably would prefer that Germany should remain disarmed. But they also have come to the conclusion that the postwar developments have changed matters so much that the West cannot do without German aid, particularly military aid.

NEIGHBOR IN THE SOUTH: BELGIUM. The Netherlands and

Belgium have always, since 1839, been concerned with the problem of close co-operation. After the great powers at the Congress of Vienna had created a union of the two countries into one state in 1815, there had been some hope that the new political entity could function. But for many reasons this union was not compatible with the general conditions of the period and broke up soon. The main reason for the union had been the British desire to see the Low Countries joined together to form a buffer state. The Belgians, however, discontented since they felt that they were not treated as well as the Netherlanders, revolted in 1830, when an insurrection took place in France. The great powers were approached by the Dutch king for help but they did not come to his aid. In fact, France, having no desire to see the barrier on her northern border continue for all the future, went so far as to threaten invasion should there be any military intervention by these powers. The British, though the development was a serious blow to their intentions, could not help in the situation, particularly since the Belgians had threatened that they might throw themselves into the arms of France if they were not given independence. The revolt of the Belgians finally brought on the recognition of the great powers meeting in London that the two nations should be separated, and by 1839 both countries were independent from each other.

This development returned the Netherlands to the status of a small nation again. Both nations assumed a position of neutrality, the Belgians forced to it and under the protection of the great powers, the Dutch voluntarily and abstaining from any active foreign policy. Yet there was no bitterness on either side, and before long there were attempts to obtain closer relations between the two countries, even proposals for military or economic alliances. Probably the Belgians were more in favor of such alliances than the Dutch, who feared that they might be regarded with suspicion by the powerful German neighbor. The proposals did not result in any official agreements between the two small nations.

Some problems interfered with the harmonious relationship of the two countries, such as the Flemish question and the problems arising from some of the waterways such as the Scheldt or the

Meuse. Also, after World War I, in which Belgium became involved, there was a chance of alienation because of the different experiences of the two nations during the war. Belgium had developed close relations with France, and the latter country, interested in the abolition of the neutral status of Belgium, seemed to be in favor of some alliance. The Belgians also expressed a desire to change the frontiers between Belgium and Holland. There was again the question of the waterways such as the connection between the Scheldt and the Rhine.

In the decade preceding World War II the nations again became close, though no military alliance was formed. In 1939 the monarchs of both countries offered their "good offices" to end the war. On several occasions in this time the solidarity of interests of the two countries was pronounced.[26]

The relationship between the two countries has been subject to great changes since the end of World War II. These are obvious in such a significant development as Benelux.[27] There had been attempts on both sides to discuss economic or at least customs union during the nineteenth century, but it was the great emergency caused by World War II that made the two countries, together with Luxembourg, come to such an arrangement.

If the First World War ended with annexationist demands of Belgium from the Netherlands, the Second one ended with an action not only of great economic but especially also of political significance. . . . Benelux has become something with a political meaning. . . .[28]

NEUTRALITY AND INDEPENDENCE UNTIL WORLD WAR II. The most significant manifestation of Dutch foreign policy has been the adherence to neutrality; the country was drawn into World War II against its own wishes. "The sanctuary of civilization," as the Netherlands was called by Georges Duhamel in Le Figaro of October 20, 1944, was completely innocent and "a little nation without arms, neutral in principle and without any

[26] For more detail see Vandenbosch, op. cit., pp. 141ff., and for the time between the wars, C. A. van der Klaauw, Politieke Betrekkingen Tussen Nederland en Belgie 1919-1939 (University of Leyden Press, 1953), passim.

[27] To be discussed in the next chapter.

[28] Smit, op. cit. in note 25 above, p. 468f.

temporal ambitions in the fights of nations." In all foreign relations, the Dutch until 1939 had steered away from political commitments that could have suggested any taking of sides and therefore might have invited hostile acts from other quarters. Even a treaty of political and military alliance suggested by the southern neighbor Belgium in 1907 had been rejected for that very reason by the Dutch, who then were interested only in economic relations.

The Dutch wanted to be left alone. When Belgium was granted independence in 1839, Britain insisted on the specific provision of perpetual neutralization of Belgium, to be guaranteed by the great powers. While the Belgians were thus forced to assume a position of neutrality, the Dutch developed a policy of utter passivity in world affairs. Any action of the Netherlands government which might have been considered as committing or compromising the country, or which might have been interpreted as taking some kind of stand, became subject to critical attacks by Parliament and public opinion. Three examples will show how careful legislature and public had become within a few decades.

In 1863 the Dutch Foreign Minister, together with his colleagues from the great powers, expressed disapproval of the Russian suppression of the Polish rebellion; this step led to severe criticism of the Minister by the States-General because he had departed from the honored policy of neutrality; in fact, a little later, when the Minister accepted an invitation to an international meeting on the Polish question, the whole budget of the Foreign Ministry was rejected by the States-General, an act that forced the Minister to resign.

A few years later, the Netherlands was in trouble because of the little Duchy of Luxembourg, then under control of the Dutch monarch. France, fearful of an expansion of Prussia after the Austro-Prussian War in 1866, had asked for the cession of Luxembourg from the Netherlands in exchange for some monetary indemnity. The Germans reacted strongly; in some parts of Germany there was even some sentiment for war in order to prevent French annexation of the duchy. Upon the suggestion of Great Britain a conference was called in 1867 to settle the matter of demilitarization and neutralization of Luxembourg. The newly elected States-General of Netherlands became nervous because the Dutch government had participated in this guarantee; such an action was considered by the legislators as dangerous for the future peace of their country. Therefore the Parliament rejected the budget for the Ministry of Foreign Affairs.

Perhaps the clearest example of the Dutch adherence to neutrality was presented during World War I. There was the repeated threat from Germany of impending hostilities, even though in general it was undoubtedly to the interest of the Allied Powers as well as of the Germans to spare the country from war. But the Dutch subjected themselves to limitations and economic losses in trade, and even introduced rationing in order to retain at all costs their sovereignty and unchanged boundaries. Neutrality did not have the meaning of appeasement and cowardice for the Dutch. Their decision to remain neutral did not mean that the nation was indifferent to the development of the war; the population in general was friendlier to the Allied Powers than to the Central Powers, especially Germany. A most generous treatment was given to the thousands of refugees from Belgium in 1914 who had escaped from the impact of war and German occupation.

The Dutch attitude of neutrality during the nineteenth century and up to World War I was somewhat different from that of Switzerland or of Belgium, since the neutrality of Holland was not guaranteed by the great powers as was the case with the two other nations. The Dutch did not seek such guarantee but preferred to be left alone, since they were apprehensive that such assurance might invite the meddling of the powers in Dutch affairs. They felt that real protection could be found only in their self-chosen and self-controlled stand for neutrality. They were not interested in territorial aggrandizement; in fact, when some parts of Germany were offered to the Netherlands after World War I, the offer was declined.

After World War I, since the neutrality of Belgium had meant very little to Germany in 1914, the Dutch felt a need to reassess their foreign policy:

A Dutch policy, although working along much the same lines as before, began to be called a "policy of independence." The new name implied a realization that the Netherlands might not be able to remain neutral in a war, but that she did not want to commit herself beforehand to any international grouping. She preferred to stand aloof as long as a deliberate choice did not become absolutely necessary. This policy of independence, although more realistic than the neutrality policy, could be selected according to Dutch preferences. It is hardly necessary to point out that this illusion was disposed of by what happened in the Second World War.[29]

It was consistent with this realistic change after World War I that Holland, while desirous to be free from political alliances or special military agreements, had joined the collective-security system of the League of Nations without any hesitation. While there were people in responsible positions who were fearful of entanglement and who considered membership in the League as a departure from Dutch traditional policy, the Foreign Minister, Dr. H. A. van Karnebeek, felt that membership was no contradiction but rather a shift in emphasis. The country had always been available for co-operation in the interest of peace; it had been opposed to entering political agreements and military alliances, and the affiliation with the League was neither.[30]

The Netherlands became one of the leading supporters of a policy of sanctions against the Italians during the Italo-Ethiopian War. It was the failure of this policy that made the Dutch come to the conclusion, together with other "neutral" powers, that the League was not strong enough to protect a weak state from reckless aggression. While the failure of collective security brought the Dutch back to their traditional policy of neutrality and independence, particularly after Hitler began his moves, they were nevertheless not willing to give in to any threats that came from Germany after the outbreak of World War II in 1939. Germany accused the neutral nations of being guilty of non-neutral actions by attending League meetings, calling the League an "Anglo-

---

[29] J. Barents, "New Trends in Dutch Foreign Policy," *Foreign Affairs* (January, 1947), vol. 25, no. 2, pp. 328ff.

[30] Amry J. Vandenbosch, "Netherlands Foreign Policy," *op. cit.* in note 11 above, p. 145.

French organ," but the Dutch did not weaken and refused to resign from membership.[31]

It was World War II and its terrible impact on little Holland that made the country decide to adopt a complete change in policy.

... The era of either a "neutrality policy" or a "policy of independence" is ended. The experience of the Dutch people with the German problem and the Indonesian question has brought home to them the truth that their foreign policy is dictated, not by themselves, and not even by the policies of the big Powers, but by the development of world forces.[32]

All are agreed by now that the old household word "neutrality" has lost its meaning for the modern Netherlands nation. The country has become a loyal and devoted partner in all organizations of the West, since it has realized that in a future major war or in any period filled with the threat of such a war, little Holland, owing to her geographical position in a shrinking and more and more interdependent world, would well-nigh automatically be drawn into such a conflict.

Bibliographical Notes are on page 612.

[31] *Ibid.*
[32] Barents, *op. cit.*, p. 333.

CHAPTER 17

THE FORMULATION AND RECENT CHARACTER OF NETHERLANDS FOREIGN POLICY

Political democracy cannot afford to put the executive branch of government in a position of complete control over any governmental activity. Some limitation must be imposed, be this through the United States system of separation of powers and checks and balances, or through parliamentary government and ministerial responsibility as in most European countries. The Netherlands, a typical country of the West and believing in the principles of political democracy, has rules by which executive and legislature are subjected to each other's check. Parliament, functioning as a balance against a powerful leader, has remained, at least in principle, *constitutionally* supreme, while the executive, in the modern political scene, has developed a position of *political* supremacy. In the Netherlands, as well as in other countries of the West that are using the parliamentary kind of government, the following analysis seems to fit the general condition: "The Ministry is omnipotent, but each day it is controlled by Parliament and public opinion."[1]

[1] B. Mirkine-Guetzevitch, *Les Nouvelles Tendances du Droit Constitutionnel* (Paris, 1931), p. 203.

The strength of the executive lies in its having initiative; in the conduct of foreign affairs the minister has the detailed knowledge of a situation, his representatives abroad are under his control, and he has the power of administration. But the strength of any political democracy is exhibited in the general safeguards against executive presumption, such as the ultimate check by a legislature, the impact of public opinion, and popular elections. Increases in the power of the cabinets in the Netherlands has been necessitated by emergencies and war; yet no student of the political conditions in the Netherlands could suggest that this development has led to arbitrary actions or to the usurpation of powers by the executive. In the field of foreign affairs the legislature maintains significant influence. Certainly, as a short historical survey will prove, the rights of the parliament in 1956 are much more impressive than they were in 1846.

Historical Developments

The participation of the executive and the legislature in the conduct of Netherlands foreign affairs has been subjected to many changes in the constitution of the country. Many amendments since the beginning of the last century have contributed to the growing influence of the States-General in this particular field.

The new Netherlands came into existence at the end of the Napoleonic wars. On November 30, 1813, William, Prince of Orange, landed in Scheveningen, after a period of exile in England. Holland had been liberated from France, into which it had been incorporated on July 9, 1810. On the day of his return he was proclaimed as William I, Sovereign Prince (Souverain Vorst). In March 1814, a constitution was put into effect, which gave to the Prince the authority to declare war and arrange for peace, to conclude treaties of any kind, to be in charge of diplomatic relations, and to hire and dismiss diplomatic personnel "at his pleasure." While a few leaders resented such unlimited powers, especially the power of declaring war, most people in the beginning showed a general willingness to accept these provisions—perhaps in reaction to the fact that, before the return of the monarch, the country as a republic had gained the international reputation of being "incredibly indolent" in its relations with other powers in Europe. Yet as early as 1815 the first limitations were introduced by the new constitution of that year that changed the title of Prince to that of King. Any treaty concluded in time of peace and dealing with the disposition over any part of the territory of the realm and its colonies could be ratified by the King only after approval by the legislature, the States-General.

The next significant changes were introduced through the constitution of 1848, under which, as in other European countries, some of the prerogatives and rights of the monarch were to be shared by the legislature. The new regulations demanded that all treaties containing additions to, or any change of legal rights, had to be first approved by the States-General. Also any disposition over the realm's territory, whether in times of peace or of war, had to undergo the same procedure. The subsequent constitutional developments during the second part of the nineteenth century and the beginning of the twentieth century made it more and more obvious that the powers of the executive in the field of foreign relations were to be subjected to increasing limitations. In 1887 other kinds of treaties were subjected to prior approval by the States-General: those that imposed any financial obligations on the realm. Finally, the constitutional changes of 1922 required all treaties to be approved by the legislature; also any declaration of war required legislative approval.[2] This latter right had been an unchallenged prerogative of the executive (the King) since 1814. But the 1922 constitutional amendment prescribed the "previous consent" of the States-General and only after the King had tried to settle any international conflict by peaceful means.

CONSTITUTIONAL CHANGES OF 1953. Further changes in the constitution on matters pertaining to the conduct of foreign affairs were made on June 22, 1953. Before then, all provisions on foreign relations were found in Articles 58-60, which left many gaps to be filled by constitutional practice. The revised constitution now con-

---

[2] For more detail see R. Kranenburg, *Het Nederlandsch Staatsrecht*, 7th edition (Haarlem, 1951), pp. 312-314.

tains much more detailed provisions in the following new Articles 58-67:[3]

Article 58: The King shall have the supreme direction of foreign relations. He shall promote the development of the international legal order.

Article 59: The King shall not declare the Kingdom to be at war with another Power except with the previous consent of the States-General. This consent shall not be required when as a result of an actual state of war consultation with the States-General has appeared to be impossible.

The States-General shall discuss and decide on these matters in united assembly.

The King shall not declare a war between the Kingdom and another Power to be terminated except with the previous consent of the States-General.

Article 60: Agreements with other Powers and with organizations based on international law shall be concluded by or by authority of the King. If required by such agreements they shall be ratified by the King. The agreements shall be submitted to the States-General as soon as possible; they shall not be ratified and they shall not enter into force until they have received the approval of the States-General.

The Courts shall not be competent to judge of the constitutionality of agreements.

Article 61: The consent shall be considered to have been given if within thirty days after the submission of the agreement no statement has been made by or on behalf of either of the Chambers of the States-General or by at least one-fifth of the constitutional number of members of either of the Chambers expressing the wish that the agreement shall be submitted to the decision of the States-General, or if both Chambers of the States-General state, before the termination of this period, that a decision is not desired.

The period referred to in the previous paragraph shall be suspended for the time of adjournment of the States-General.

In cases where the agreement is submitted to the decision of the States-General, the approval can only be given by an act.

Article 62: Except in the case referred to in Article 63, the approval shall not be required:

a. if the agreement is one with respect to which this has been laid down by law;

[3] The text of these amendments can be found in the Staatsblad of 1953 #261. The translation used in this volume has been taken from the article by H. F. van Panhuys, "The Netherlands Constitution and International Law," in *American Journal of International Law,* October 1953, pp. 538-540.

b. if the agreement is exclusively concerned with the execution of an approved arrangement; provided the States-General, when they gave their approval to the agreement, did not make a reservation in this respect;

c. if the agreement does not impose any considerable pecuniary obligation on the Kingdom and it has been concluded for a period not exceeding one year;

d. if in exceptional cases of an urgent nature the interest of the Kingdom requires that the agreement shall enter into force without delay.

An agreement of the kind referred to under d shall not be concluded except subject to the reservation that it shall be terminated if the States-General withhold their approval. The conclusion of the agreement shall be communicated to the States-General without delay. The agreement shall still be submitted for the approval of the States-General if within thirty days after the communication a statement has been made by or on behalf of either of the Chambers of the States-General or by at least one-fifth of the constitutional number of members of either of the Chambers expressing a wish to this effect. The provisions of the preceding paragraph shall not apply if this should be decidedly detrimental to the interests of the Kingdom. If such a case should arise, the agreement shall be submitted to the States-General as soon as possible and if they withhold their approval it shall be terminated as soon as shall be compatible with the provisions of the agreement.

Article 63: If the development of the international legal order requires this, the contents of an agreement may deviate from certain provisions of the Constitution. In such cases the approval of the agreement shall not be given by the States-General except by a two-thirds majority of the votes cast in each of the two Chambers.

Article 64: The provisions of the four preceding articles shall similarly apply to any accession to agreements.

As regards the denunciation of agreements Articles 60, 61 and 62 shall similarly apply, the second paragraph of Article 60 being taken to mean that the States-General shall be informed of the intention to denounce the agreement.

Article 65: Legal provisions in force within the Kingdom shall not apply if the application should be incompatible with agreements which have been published in accordance with Article 66 whether before or after the enactment of the provisions.

Article 66: Rules with regard to the publication of agreements shall be laid down in the law. Agreements shall be binding on anyone insofar as they will have been published.

Article 67: By or in virtue of an agreement certain powers with respect to legislation, administration and jurisdiction may be conferred on organizations based on international law.

With regard to decisions made by organizations based on international law Articles 65 and 66 shall similarly apply.

Van Panhuys evaluates the changes as follows:

In order to enable those who are not acquainted with Netherlands law to understand more easily the essence of the amendments, the purport of these amendments might be summarized as follows:

1. They adapt the constitutional provisions on the declaration of war to modern international law.

2. They put the treaty-making power of the Crown more strictly under the control of the "Staten-Generaal" (Articles 60, 62).

3. They provide for a more flexible procedure of parliamentary approval of international agreements (Article 61).

4. They render it possible to deviate from the Constitution if the development of the international legal order so requires (Article 63), and they accept the possibility of yielding authority to international organizations (Article 67).

5. They ensure the binding force of international law as prevailing over municipal law, and authorize the courts to test the national statutes as regards their conformity with international agreements and decisions of international organizations (Articles 60 [third paragraph], 65, 66, and 67 [second paragraph]).[4]

Constitutional Issues

While the Dutch Constitution clearly asserts the principle that all agreements with foreign powers and with international organizations must be given parliamentary approval, in practice it may be assumed that the government, in view of its initiative, the technical problems of diplomacy, and other considerations, can confront the legislature with a *fait accompli*.[5] The very important

[4] Ibid., p. 540f. The problem of the co-operation between the Executive and the States-General in the field of foreign relations had been discussed by the Cabinet, and in April 1950 a special commission had been instituted under the chairmanship of Jonkheer W. J. M. van Eysinga, retired professor at the University of Leyden and former Justice of the Permanent Court of International Justice. Members of this commission included parliamentarians, experts in the fields of international and constitutional law, and leading officials of the Ministry of Foreign Affairs. For more detail see *Jaarboek van het Ministerie van Buitenlandse Zaken 1950-1951*.

[5] Willem Frederik Wijthoff, *De Staatsinrichting van Nederland*, 7th edition (Haarlem, 1953), p. 270.

problem of the country's general interest and the related matters of security will impose restraint on the legislature and will force consideration of differences between the two branches into the sphere of confidential discussion rather than open and public debate.

In practice also, parliamentary committees furnish channels through which the ministry can inform members of the States-General on important diplomatic developments and negotiations, and also learn the views and get the suggestions of the legislators. These committees fit the principle of ministerial responsibility since they make it possible for the ministry to ascertain to some extent whether a planned agreement seems acceptable to the legislators.

TREATY VERSUS AGREEMENT. Until 1952 a constitutional distinction was made between "treaties" and other "agreements," but the 1953 changes in the constitution have eliminated the use of the word "treaty." The only term now used is the much wider description "agreements with other Powers and with organizations based on international law." According to the report of the van Eysinga committee, the word "agreement" is meant to include treaties, conventions, charters, statutes, acts, declarations, executive agreements, protocols, memoranda, and the like.[6]

BINDING FORCE OF AGREEMENT. Before the changes of 1953 discussions of constitutional issues were concerned with the problem as to whether international agreements were binding on Dutch citizens with or without a special law. Since 1952 there are no legal doubts, for Article 66 points out clearly that international agreements are binding on citizens. The government made clear in a memorandum of interpretation its rejection of the view that international agreements could be binding for the citizens only through the means of a special law. Indeed, in case of a conflict with domestic law, precedence is to be given to the later-created

---

[6] But according to some experts, it will probably not include such matters as the *agréation* of an ambassador, extradition, and other similar matters, nor any arrangements with other powers in the field of private international law. The government has been of the opinion that agreements which neither in form nor content contain elements of public law are not to be handled according to the procedure of Article 60. For more detail *ibid.*, p. 274.

international commitments. According to the new Article 65 these have force superior to "legal provisions in force within the Kingdom." "Legal provisions" include any provision that has been created by lawmakers in the national legislature or in provincial and municipal diets, in addition to governmental rules and orders. The constitution itself is not inferior to international agreements in view of the wording used in Article 63.[7]

CONSENT OF THE STATES-GENERAL. Dutch constitutional writers see three distinctive stages in the procedure of making and accepting international agreements: (a) the conclusion of the agreement by the monarch as the head of state; (b) the approval of the agreement by the States-General; (c) the ratification by the monarch.[8] While all agreements, according to Article 60, must be submitted as soon as possible to the States-General, exceptions are possible for agreements of a confidential nature; it is expected, however, that the agreement be placed before the Committee of Foreign Affairs. The ratification of an agreement by the King might under special circumstances not be necessary. But also in a situation of this nature approval by the States-General must be obtained, since the agreement cannot enter into force without its approval. Thus, it is evident that the King, with the exceptions provided by Article 62, cannot commit the country without the approval of the States-General.

While this approval is normally given by a law, the possibility of the silent approval is provided in Article 61; it was introduced into the constitution after the example of British practice, which developed because of the increased work load of Parliament. The government can, of course, ask for speedy handling by submitting a bill which will express the consent, as was the practice before the changes of 1953 in cases when consent was constitutionally demanded.

A special commission set up to advise the government on a further revision of the altered clauses on foreign relations in the constitution published its report in July, 1955. Headed by the constitutional expert, Professor R. Kranenburg, member of the Privy

[7] Ibid., p. 282.
[8] R. Kranenburg, op. cit., pp. 314ff.

Council, the commission concerned itself with the problem of the submission of agreements to the States-General and many other problems, such as the point of a belated approval of agreements which according to Article 62 thus far is not required "if in exceptional cases of an urgent nature the interest of the Kingdom requires that the agreement shall enter into force without delay."[9]

The Executive and the Conduct of Foreign Affairs

The supreme control of foreign relations is one of the most important tasks of the executive. The King, having "the supreme direction of foreign relations," represents the Netherlands before other countries. The most significant expressions of this representation are the maintenance of diplomatic relations, and the preparation, conclusion, and ratification of treaties and other agreements. While the King is charged with these tasks, the responsibility for the general and practical handling of these tasks before the States-General rests chiefly with the Minister of Foreign Affairs, but also with other appropriate ministers to whose province the special subjects mentioned in treaties are assigned.[10]

It should be mentioned that while the monarch officially enjoys the constitutional right to executive power, in practice the ministers execute the constitution and other laws, insofar as this execution depends on the Crown (Article 79, paragraph 3). While this provision and the general constitutional developments have contributed to lessening the influence of the King in executive matters, it should nevertheless be stated that the monarch retains at least some influence. The great prestige of the royal house and family gives it influence in domestic and foreign relations, and the voices of Queen Wilhelmina and Queen Juliana have been heeded with great respect.

But in general one should be reminded of the British situation where the exercise of the royal power by the bearer of the crown has gone over to the abstraction of the "Crown," which is actually the Council of Ministers. One or more ministers must countersign all royal decrees and orders, but the ministers must inform the monarch on all important matters of state.

[9] ANETA, July 15, 1955.
[10] Wijthoff, op. cit., pp. 269ff.

The Ministry, under the leadership of the Minister-President, concerns itself with many matters of foreign policy. The principle of collective responsibility is applied quite clearly; in fact, it may be said that, at least since the beginning of this century, the application of the principle in the field of foreign affairs is more typical than for internal policy and administration.[11] To begin with, the *Regulation of Order for the Council of Ministers* of November 10, 1945, provides for the joint deliberation and general decision between the Ministers for the purpose of assuring unity in government policy (Article 2). The specific language on foreign matters is that the Council deliberate and decide on

. . . treaties with foreign Powers, on momentous instructions to be given to the Ambassadors or Envoys, and on other important subjects in regard to foreign relations (Article 2, sec. e).

Some of the work can be handled by special permanent committees of the Ministry; yet even then, any minister who is not participating in such a committee may, if he so desires, attend the meetings of the committee (Articles 12 and 13).

The problem of ministerial responsibility gains in significance because of the fact that the ministers constitutionally cannot be members of the States-General. The 1938 revision of the constitution so provided in Article 99. Before this time there had been some doubt in the minds of some of the most outstanding Dutch experts and statesmen; J. R. Thorbecke, who has contributed so much to the modern constitutional system of the Netherlands, had given the best expression to the reasoning underlying this provision:

Certainly no office of the State is as little compatible as that of a Minister with that of a representative; for can the Minister as such, at the same time propose bills for the Government and judge them as a representative? Can he at the same time, demand, as a representative, any responsibility, and give it as a Minister?[12]

This thought is very much in opposition to the British constitutional custom; yet closeness between the ministers and the legis-

[11] Amry Vandenbosch and Samuel J. Eldersveld, *Government of the Netherlands* (University of Kentucky, 1947), p. 60.
[12] J. R. Thorbecke, *Aanteekening op de Grondwet*, 2nd edition (The Hague, 1906), p. 264f.

lators is assured since the ministers are constitutionally entitled
to have a seat and an advisory voice in both chambers.

The Minister of Foreign Affairs

The main work in the field of foreign relations is handled by the
Minister of Foreign Affairs and his staff. His is a most distinguished
assignment and he controls one of the oldest ministerial departments. It has been held by many leading and outstanding Netherlanders, and among them two ambassadors to the United States—
E. N. van Kleffens, who held the position from 1939 until 1946,
and Dr. J. H. van Roijen, who held it briefly from March to July,
1946.[13] It might be interesting to note that many of the Ministers were so-called nonpolitical or bureaucratic appointments,
since the Department was regarded as technical or purely administrative; typical departments of political character were always those
of Interior or Finance.[14]

While until lately one minister was in charge of the department, something unique has been done in the Netherlands. The
Ministry of Foreign Affairs is now divided between two persons;
in 1952 J. W. Beijen was made minister of Foreign Affairs, while
J. M. A. H. Luns was appointed Minister without Portfolio of the
Ministry of Foreign Affairs. Mr. Beijen was politically an Independent, while Mr. Luns represented the Roman Catholic People's
Party. It was explained by the Prime Minister, Dr. Willem Drees,
at the time of the appointment that the two Ministers would
exercise joint responsibility for foreign policy but that, for administrative convenience, they would divide their duties on a "functional" basis.[15] A government statement on the function of two
joint Foreign Ministers was given to the States-General at the end

[13] A list of all Ministers of Foreign Affairs since 1848 can be found in the
Gids van het Departement van Buitenlandse Zaken en de Buitenlandse Dienst.

[14] Vandenbosch-Eldersveld, *op. cit.,* p. 44.

[15] It was pointed out at the time by a part of the Dutch press, that the
allocation of the portfolio of Foreign Affairs had been demanded by the
Catholic People's Party, and was one of the principal reasons for the prolonged
Cabinet crisis; the appointment of two foreign ministers, one drawn from the
party and one an Independent, was, according to the press, a device to satisfy
rival party claims for the post. See *Keesings Contemporary Archives,* 1952,
p. 12435.

of August, 1952: Mr. Beijen would be concerned mainly with European affairs and problems of European integration; Mr. Luns was to deal with extra-European problems, including United Nations affairs. The same statement contained also the information that the appointment of the two Ministers was not due to party political considerations but had already been discussed by the previous cabinet, in view of the frequent absences of the Foreign Minister abroad for international conferences.[16]

Both Ministers are men of distinguished career. Mr. Beijen, lawyer and financial expert, was president of the Bank for International Settlements from 1937 to 1940, and after 1946 was a director of the International Monetary Fund in Washington. Mr. Luns, the younger of the two, studied law and political economy at Leyden, Amsterdam, and Berlin, and at the London School of Economics; he had held a number of posts in the foreign ministry and the diplomatic service. Prior to his appointment he had been a member of the Netherlands delegation at the United Nations.

Before a short description of the main aides to the Minister it might be opportune to review the history and organization of the Department of Foreign Affairs.

The Department of Foreign Affairs (Departement van Buitenlandse Zaken)

HISTORICAL BACKGROUND: 1815-1940. The liberation of the Netherlands from French domination toward the end of the Napoleonic era brought with it a provisional government under the guidance of Prince William as the Sovereign and Gijsbert Karel van Hogendorp, the key figure in the fight for liberation, as the new Secretary of State for Foreign Affairs. The daily work of the Department was under the supervision of the departmental secretary and was handled by about ten persons, of whom two were messengers.[17] When in 1815 the country became a monarchy,

---

[16] *Ibid.*, p. 12568. Upon appointment Mr. Luns became, in actual practice, also concerned with bilateral problems regardless whether such problems were concerned with European or with extra-European nations.

[17] Much of the following information is taken from *Organisatie en Reorganisatie van het Departement van Buitenlandse Zaken* (The Hague, 1950), pp. 21ff.

the Department began to grow, and it employed, by 1830, twenty-five persons.

The revolutionary impact of the changes of 1848 in Europe was also felt in the Netherlands, where a significant liberalization of the constitution was accepted, together with the institution of a much more powerful legislature and the establishment of ministerial responsibility. One of the first steps of the legislature was to introduce an economy program, so that by 1851 there were only seventeen officials working in the Department. It was a difficult, and sometimes hopeless, task for the organization to obtain any budgetary increase during the following decades.

During the second half of the nineteenth century, in 1876, the Department underwent a reorganization according to the modern principles of specialization. Until this time the Department had consisted of only one general office. Now two divisions were formed: the Cabinet of the Minister (under the leadership of a trained diplomat and in charge of political and secret affairs) and the Division of Consular and Commercial Affairs. The latter division became, after some time, the larger one because of the general need for increased consular representation abroad. Yet until the outbreak of World War I the general growth of the Department had been very slow; the number of officials in 1914 amounted to forty-five, under the permanent leadership of a Secretary-General whose office had been installed in 1902.

World War I and the period between the two World Wars created new and increasingly demanding tasks in the country's foreign relations and in the ministry concerned with their conduct. When the war broke out in 1914, it was immediately obvious that the staff was insufficient to deal with all the new problems that were facing the little country. Yet by the end of the war the Department had grown into a much larger and much more modern organization. Among many changes, a special division for diplomatic affairs was entrusted with political matters and the handling of the Foreign Service. After the League of Nations began with its work, a special Division for League of Nations Affairs was instituted. This general reorganization was undertaken by Foreign Minister Dr. H. A. van Karnebeek and it remained in force until the outbreak of World War II. The ministry reduced the number of employees during the depression years, however, and several people were entrusted with the handling of plural tasks and functions. Hence practically nobody could enter the service of the Department.

WORLD WAR II. The Department underwent its most critical experiences during World War II, when the German invasion forced Queen Wilhelmina and her ministers to flee to London in May 1940. But in the Netherlands itself, while the war was fought on Dutch soil, the actual leadership of the Department in the Hague was assumed by the Secretary-General of the Department, Jonkheer A. M. Snouck Hurgronje; another person left behind was the then Chief of the Bureau for Political Affairs, Dr. J. H. van Roijen, who in 1950 became the Netherlands ambassador to the United States. After May 15, 1940, when fighting in the country had ceased, no official was permitted by the Germans to enter the premises of the Department, which became the office of Seyss-Inquart, the German Reichs-Commissar for the Netherlands. Whatever work could be done by officials of the Department was handled in the offices of the Ministry for Colonies; even the small amount of work that could be handled was not done without many interruptions, since many officials were arrested, even if mostly for a short time; Dr. van Roijen, however, was arrested several times.[18] The work in the Netherlands became increasingly that of a contact organization, since the Department formed the link between other Dutch authorities and the Foreign Office of the Reichs Commissar.

In the meantime the work of the Dutch Foreign Office was performed by the government-in-exile. Yet from the standpoint of organization and administration it was, certainly in the beginning of its functioning, of a very makeshift character, since the events of May 1940 had made impossible any orderly evacuation and transfer of personnel, files, and offices. When the government began its work in London, the Minister of Foreign Affairs had

[18] In the beginning of 1945, Dr. van Roijen was asked by the Dutch government-in-exile to come to London, where he finally arrived after a highly adventurous trip by March 1945.

neither personnel nor archives. Only one diplomat of the Department, the Deputy Chief of Foreign Affairs, had come to London, as also had the Chief of the Code Section, who had saved some of the code materials from the Germans. Gradually more personnel managed to come to London from different diplomatic posts or by leaving clandestinely from the Netherlands and occupied Europe. While at first the Ministry settled down in the Embassy building in London, office materials and also clerical personnel were offered by some of the bigger Dutch commercial companies with a world-wide organization, such as Shell and Unilever. The Department grew in numerical strength through the arrival of personnel from the closed embassies to Italy and Japan, but many diplomatic posts had to be maintained. The legation, later embassy, in Washington even required additional personnel; in fact, the Washington embassy finally had more personnel than the Ministry at London. By October 1943 the Ministry had eleven officials assisted by service personnel amounting to thirty-one persons.

While the Department worked under the great handicap of being displaced and understaffed, it not only had tasks of the moment and of the war but also problems directed toward the future and the return to Dutch soil. Much thought was given to the reorganization of the Department and the future conduct of foreign affairs. Thus the work performed by a small staff had to include general dealings with the host country in all fields, the conduct of war in the West and the Far East, the practical problems of liberating the Netherlands, the ensuing steps of repatriation, the treatment of war criminals, the technical aspects of the reorganization of the Ministry, and the many questions of international law that arose particularly in connection with the coming United Nations.

AFTER 1945. Significant organizational changes took place after the return of the government-in-exile from London, but no complete overhauling of the Department. One of the outstanding innovations was the merger of the diplomatic corps, the consular corps, and the translators into one new body, the corps of "Officials of the Foreign Service," with personnel matters handled by a new combined Directorate of the Foreign Service.

Also subject to complete reorganization was the Division of

Juridical Affairs. Before the change this division had been entrusted with the treatment of the legal aspects of problems which, as to content, had been handled by the different specialized bureaus in the Department. Yet it had become obvious that legal questions were many times inseparable from the general problem and content of the question so that the final legal judgment depended on the detailed knowledge of the subject matter. There was a feeling that the legal department might be too theoretical and thus not too helpful to the rest of the Department. Hence it was planned to add permanently to the individual divisions jurists who could combine their legal experience with a thorough knowledge of the subject matter; however, in order to avoid too diversified or contradictory legal opinions emanating from different divisions, the office of a special legal adviser was to be instituted in order to check on the main points of legal opinions and decisions. In 1947 a second adviser was employed for the express purpose of giving exclusive attention to the legal aspects of the Indonesian problem.

Administrative tasks previously handled by the former Legal Division were turned over to a Directorate of Legal and Administrative Affairs.[19]

The Division for League of Nations affairs was not revived in its old form after the founding of the United Nations. Since it was recognized that the new international organization would be of greater political significance and influence than its predecessor, it seemed desirable to have a new Division for International Organization as part of the Political Bureau, but with a great amount of autonomy in its performance.

The Leadership in the Department of Foreign Affairs

Much of the daily and very special work with which a Minister of Foreign Affairs is confronted cannot be handled by him in

[19] Valuable information on matters such as the formation of the Department, its general organization, on the list of the personnel in the Department and in the Foreign Service, short biographic information on these officers, and other pertinent information can be found in the *Gids van het Departement van Buitenlandse Zaken en de Buitenlandse Dienst* (Guide of the Department of Foreign Affairs and the Foreign Service) (The Hague). Its third edition appeared in 1954.

person. Many of these tasks are therefore delegated to a staff of leading administrators who have been assigned specific tasks. Those of the Special Secretary of the Minister, the Secretary-General, and the Deputy and the Assistant Secretaries-General will be discussed. Other special administrators include the Financial-Economic Adviser, the Legal Adviser, and the Adviser for Traffic (concerning matters of air and river traffic).

THE SPECIAL SECRETARY OF THE MINISTER. The work load of the Foreign Minister requires a personal aide, in particular for the handling of work that had to be done by the Minister himself, including personal correspondence activities of such personal nature that they do not fall within the province of the Ministry itself. Thus the handling of correspondence and the preparation and arrangement of the many travels and appointments are the concern of the Special Secretary, as are the handling of matters and documents that have to be submitted to such groups as the Council of Ministers or the Council of Economic Affairs.

THE SECRETARY-GENERAL. In the Dutch administrative system the Secretary-General is considered the permanent head of the official hierarchy that assists the Minister in the execution of his decisions and orders. He also substitutes for the Minister in the handling of daily business when the Minister is absent. For this reason the Secretary-General has rarely participated in international conferences and delegations. This arrangement had been criticized before 1952, since it has been felt that the presence of the Secretary-General might be helpful especially in conferences concerning western and Atlantic co-operation. Plans for the future provide for increasing the number of top civil servants in the Ministry so that the Secretary can be used more frequently abroad.

Mention should be made at least of one outstanding person who had been in this office for more than a quarter of a century, Jonkheer A. M. Snouck Hurgronje; he held the office from July 1921 until January 1948 and died on March 26, 1951. He was one of the great civil servants of his country under whose control the great changes in the Department took place.

DEPUTY AND ASSISTANT SECRETARIES-GENERAL. The organization of the Ministry includes two positions of this kind. These offices are functional and do not carry official rank in the system of hierarchy. Dutch authorities compare these titles with such functional titles in the military field as Quartermaster-General or Adjutant-General.

There are two Assistant Secretaries-General in the Ministry, one of whom is concerned with the task of co-ordination rather than the direction of political affairs, mainly the co-ordination of the work of the Directorates of the Ministry, all of which are under the supervision of a special Director. It is the function of the Assistant Secretary-General, who is outside of the Directorates, to bring together the main points of the work of these different divisions; the handling of daily routine matters and specific questions remains within the Directorates. The Directors still have direct contact with the Minister and the Secretary-General.

It was not intended to make any of these Assistants substitutes for the Secretary-General in the latter's absence. Yet the fact that these two positions have been instituted suggests that the two Assistants together could handle most of the work in an emergency.

The Foreign Service

Until the end of World War II, the Netherlands Foreign Service consisted of separate services and was divided into the diplomatic, consular, and administrative branches, and translators. But the official separation was not always followed since in quite a few instances members of the diplomatic corps and of the professional consular service were detached to the other service; such matters as the education or promotion of the official remained, however, the concern of his specific service.

Nevertheless, in most instances, the separation was quite strict and applied even to admission to the services; special commissions were instituted to handle examinations and all questions concerning the new candidates for the consular or diplomatic professions. The diplomatic service was under the supervision of the Division for Diplomatic Affairs, while honorary and career consuls were supervised by a special office within the Division for Consular and Commercial Affairs. The translators, who were not numerous, were regulated by the Division for Diplomatic Affairs. The administrative personnel, depending on whether they worked for a diplomatic mission or for a consular office, were supervised by the division that was also responsible for the officers at the given post.

This split organization led to many unnecessary complications, particularly since there were only a few people in the two professional corps. Before 1940 there were about fifty officials in the diplomatic service, and about the same number in the consular corps, sometimes no more than a dozen in the translators group and in the group of the higher ranking administrative officials.

While in London, the government-in-exile faced the problem of a serious personnel shortage so that in this time the need for co-ordination in recruitment, pay, pensions, and other matters became acute. Initial arrangements were made for such consolidation of the different branches of the Foreign Service. As a result of this preparatory work the problem was solved as early as 1945, when the *Regulations for the Foreign Service (Reglement van het Buitenlandse Dienst)* were accepted.[20]

Pursuant to this change a new division was installed, the Directorate for the Foreign Service, in which all matters concerning the Foreign Service were concentrated; the new division was to deal not only with personnel questions but also with organizational and administrative problems. The tasks of the new division were manifold since, as a consequence of the war, the number of Foreign Service officers had been considerably increased; other problems that faced the administrators were such matters as the opening of new foreign posts and collaboration with other ministerial departments.

As in most modern countries, admission to the Netherlands Foreign Service is dependent on the passing of several examinations, which are open to any qualified Dutch citizen. The outstanding purpose of these examinations is to find out about the particular qualifications and interests of the candidates. The entrance examination is followed by specific examinations which are given to persons who have been admitted to the Foreign Service

[20] A more recent issue of these *Regulations* came out in 1951.

and have spent some time in it. The newcomer to the foreign service will be used at first as a probationary officer of the service and be employed as an Attaché or as an Aspirant-Vice Consul for a period of three years while working in the Department or at a foreign post. If he then has performed in a satisfactory fashion, he will be admitted to the so-called secretarial examination for which he may prepare himself during a special study period of five months. These examinations are given by a commission of five members, of whom four are completely independent of the Department of Foreign Affairs and the Foreign Service. The Chief of the Directorate for the Foreign Service is a member ex officio.

The Directorate for the Foreign Service is entrusted with all matters pertaining to the appointment, promotion, dismissal, transfers of all personnel of the Foreign Service, whether career officers, honorary consuls, or administrative or clerical personnel. In the year 1949 the office was therefore concerned with all questions pertaining to 231 officers of the foreign service, 63 administrative officials, and 550 persons of clerical and minor administrative capacity. This work included the supervision of 48 diplomatic and 28 professional (thus not honorary) consular posts. The Directorate is also concerned with all financial matters in regard to the Service, in particular with salaries, travel expenses, per diem expenditures, special pay for settlement in foreign posts, and like matters.

The Dutch diplomatic service has thus been completely recast. While before World War II Dutch diplomatic missions abroad have been described mainly as "centers of social intercourse," the changed world situation and the need for a more active participation of the Netherlands have created a new kind of Foreign Service with very capable, well-trained, and alert personnel contributing very much to the good name of their country.[21]

21 From time to time the Minister issues a list in the Dutch language mentioning the countries and cities where members of the Netherlands Foreign Service are stationed and giving their names, titles, districts and further particulars. This bears the title *Volledig overzicht der Vertegenwoordigingen van Nederland in het Buitenland* (Complete Review of Netherlands Missions Abroad). The Foreign Service Regulations can be found in the *Diplomatiek Reglement*, which gives information on ranks of the service. Similar informa-

The Legislature

The constitutional position of the legislature indicates the extent by which this body can be involved in the handling of foreign affairs. Nevertheless, as in other countries of the West, the executive dominates, since it exercises initiative and conducts the daily administrative handling of such problems. Yet the position of the Dutch Parliament is not weak. The legislators can exercise their influence through inquiry, through control of the budget, and in general through alert observation.

The parliament of the Netherlands (States-General—*Staten-Generaal*) is composed of two houses. The Lower House, the *Second Chamber* as it is called, is elected by direct popular vote and through a system of proportional representation. The Upper House, or *First Chamber*, is elected indirectly by the *Provinciale Staten* (provincial representative councils). The popularly elected Second Chamber has the right of initiative, but uses this right very rarely. Both chambers have the right of investigation, but the Upper House seldom makes use of this privilege. Both Chambers have the right of interpellation.

POWERS OF THE LEGISLATURE. The power of the legislature under the parliamentary system lies in the obligation of the prime minister to render account and to be generally responsible for the policies and actions of his administration. The States-General of the Netherlands have constitutional rights which assure them a permanent control of the work of the Cabinet. The avenues through which the States-General check governmental actions include: (a) interpellation, (b) question, (c) motion, (d) enquête, and (e) the budget. Their positive functions have been discussed, especially participation in the acceptance of agreements with foreign powers.

A much favored technique is the *written question*, but the

---

tion in regard to the consular service can be found in the *Consulair Reglement*.

It should also be mentioned that in addition to the regular Foreign Service, representation of the country abroad for very specific purposes is sometimes handled by special delegates or commissions with specific instructions and orders for negotiation.

Chambers in recent years have made more frequent use of the *motion*, especially in connection with the discussion of the budget when specific questions have arisen. The formal *enquête*, the inquiry, has also been used, notably after the termination of World War II, when a special committee concerned with the conduct of affairs by the government-in-exile dealt also to a considerable extent with the government's handling of foreign relations.

The States-General have become very active in regard to work in the field of foreign affairs. The matter of approval of agreements with foreign powers is responsible for this activity and contributes to the power the States-General exercise. The volume of treaties has been considerably increased since the end of World War II; between 1945 and January 1, 1950, the Netherlands became a party to more than 300 treaties and agreements.

CONTROL OF THE BUDGET. One of the most effective powers of the Dutch legislature (as in most democratic countries) is its control over the budget proposed by the executive. The States-General have, in several instances, made it impossible to fill an ambassadorial position by cutting out the salary of the ambassador. The salary of the Dutch ambassador to the Vatican, for example, was eliminated in 1869 from the budget of that year.

Reference has been made already to the rejection of the budget for the Department of Foreign Affairs by the newly elected Second Chamber in 1867. The Second Chamber had become uneasy because the Dutch government had participated in the guarantee of the neutrality of Luxembourg in the Treaty of London in 1867; this action had been considered dangerous for the future peace of the Netherlands. The cabinet regarded this attitude as a censure and asked the King to accept its resignation. The King refused and, a few days later, dissolved the Second Chamber. The ensuing elections did not bring any significant change in the distribution of parties in the Chamber. The new States-General approved a motion that "no interest of the land demanded the most recent dissolution of the Chamber"; the Cabinet refused to yield, and, consequently, during a vote on the budget for the Department of Foreign Affairs in April 1868, the Chamber again refused to approve it. The resignation of the Cabinet was accepted this time by the monarch. This episode established the parliamentary principle in the Netherlands.

Another significant example occurred in 1925, when the problem of a Netherlands embassy at the Vatican arose between the Roman Catholics and the Protestant Christian Historical Union in Parliament. Such an embassy had not existed since 1870, except temporarily during World War I. In the debate on the budget of the Department of Foreign Affairs, an amendment was proposed and carried that the embassy be closed (the Kersten Amendment). The Catholic members of the Cabinet immediately offered their resignation. A few days later the whole Cabinet resigned.

While these clashes indicate the strength of the Second Chamber, it should be pointed out that such feuds between the government and the parliament were more typical of the period up to World War I than of modern times. In the field of foreign relations the understanding between the government and the legislature has become better and by now can be described as being rather intimate and good. Such differences as the one in 1867 were exceptions, however significant ones, rather than the rule.

THE COMMITTEE ON FOREIGN AFFAIRS. While the legislature has always shown concern for foreign relations, its general attitude in regard to the conduct of these relations was greatly changed during World War I, when the importance of foreign policy was recognized. The questions both of the country's neutrality and of a future international organization gave the legislators a feeling for the many possibilities of the field. As early as 1915 a Socialist member of the Second Chamber, Dr. J. van Leeuwen, submitted a motion that, considering the general interest in foreign relations and the need for a good relationship between the executive and the legislature, the rules for the Second Chamber should be changed and in fact include the installation of a permanent Committee on Foreign Affairs. The motion was carried.[22]

---

[22] It should be noted that the Cabinet was not too enthusiastic about the general development, but neither were about one-fourth of the members of the Chamber who voted against the motion.

The members of the Committee for Foreign Affairs are chosen at the beginning of each session by the President of the Chamber, if the legislature does not decide differently. The task of the Committee is to promote the regular exchange of ideas on matters of foreign affairs between the government and the Second Chamber. It asks the government for information that it considers desirable and discusses with the executive all matters that he should hear about. The Committee is bound to secrecy in circumstances when the interest of the country is involved. But in all matters in regard to which it is not forced to secrecy by the Government, the Committee communicates them to the Chamber if the government itself has not immediately done so. The Committee is composed of seven members; the President and the Clerk of the Chamber are ex *officio* Chairman and Secretary of the body. The provision for the general function can be found in Article 151 of the *Regulations of Order for the Second Chamber.*

THE FIRST CHAMBER. The First Chamber has considerably less power than the Second, since it does not possess the powers of legislative initiative, nor, in theory at least, the powers of amendment; it has had the power of *enquête* since 1887 but has not used it. Although without direct influence on the formation of ministries, it has contributed to the fall of individual ministers. By rejecting a treaty with Belgium in 1927, it caused by its adverse vote the fall of the then Minister of Foreign Affairs, Jonkheer van Karnebeek.

The First Chamber also has a special permanent Committee for Foreign Affairs. In 1950 the Chamber changed its rules and provided for committees to be set up for the purpose of obtaining information.

Current Problems

Ruin in Europe and the loss of the greatest part of the colonial empire made Dutch affairs appear well-nigh hopeless for a relatively short period at the end of World War II. Since then the Netherlands has taken a clear orientation in the direction of Europe, where it sees the greatest need for an outspoken stand; as far as the future of the country is concerned, the most important questions in the direction of this future must be solved in Europe and in behalf of Europe.

With the end of the policy of neutrality since World War II, particularly since this policy was not paid any regard or respect, Holland has become one of the most pronounced supporters of western co-operation. The country has assumed to the fullest extent the responsibility to be expected from a nation of its kind. Queen Juliana in a speech before a Joint Session of the United States Congress in Washington on April 3, 1952, defined the country's devotion to this task as follows: "To accept freedom means to carry responsibility. Wherever this is recognized as a right and a duty for everybody, we call it democracy. It is the only form of fair government." It is this attitude of responsibility that should convince the observer of the reliability and the seriousness of purpose with which government and the people of the Netherlands have approached their new obligations.

The great specific problems now before the Dutch concern their collaboration with the West and their adjustment to the loss of their former holdings in the Indonesian Archipelago.

WESTERN COLLABORATION AND EUROPEAN INTEGRATION. As to the union of the West, it is important to know that the Netherlands has entered all alliances, agreements, and organizations for which arrangements have been made. And in addition, many concrete suggestions and detailed proposals as to the integration and unity of Europe have come from the Netherlands. All these departures have had the support of the overwhelming majority of the Dutch people. Polls taken by the Netherlands Institute for Public Opinion show that the population favors a united Europe under a European government with a democratic representation and under a European constitution. More than two-thirds of the population favor the economic union with the Belgians and Luxembourgers expressed in the Benelux arrangement between the three countries.

Alliances have been made with France, Great Britain, Belgium, and Luxembourg in the Treaty of Brussels (March 17, 1948), or with the nations that joined in the North Atlantic Treaty Organization (NATO) on April 4, 1949. The Netherlands Parliament was the first one to commit the country to the European Defense Community, and after the planned EDC did not come into existence, there was no doubt as to the country's joining the Western European Union (WEU). In the case of the European Defense Community, the Netherlands had initial objections such as losing its voice in the tightly constituted community in which there were to be three large partners: France, Germany, and Italy. There was concern as to whether Dutch participation in EDC might lead a changed relationship with Great Britain, which would not join the community. Still it was felt that, while the organization was far from perfect, it would have been also the best way to insure adequate defense of the European continent. In accepting WEU, the Netherlands had serious misgivings about the arms pool of the organization, which was to be instituted to co-ordinate the manufacturing and distribution of munitions. Yet when it came to the vote, the Dutch adhered.[23]

The Dutch also joined the European Coal and Steel Community, the first organization to start integration. They have stressed the need for a European Tariff Union as the first step toward a free common market of all goods within Europe by sending notes to all participants in the Schuman Plan (February 14, 1953). On December 17, 1953, the Minister for Foreign Affairs, J. W. Beijen, made a statement on European integration to the Second Chamber, in which he considered such a united Europe as the only possible solution to the German problem and as a defense against threats from the Soviet Union. Political integration must depend on economic integration:

. . . a supranational political community cannot exist and does not contribute to the unification of Europe if the powers transferred do not also include the promotion of economic integration. The Netherlands Government does not feel justified in taking part in a political community which does not possess such powers. Such a community is considered not only contrary to Netherlands interests but also to European interests: it could not contribute to the ultimate aim of the unification of Europe. . . . The Netherlands Government is prepared to

23 For detail see mimeographed sheet of the Netherlands Information Service, Western Division of January 6, 1955.

transfer powers for promoting economic integration to a political community, because it is convinced that without such a transfer economic integration could not be realized.[24]

Another Dutch hope has been expressed by the so-called Mansholt Plan for European agricultural integration, which was announced as early as 1950 and was considered as a contribution toward improving the standard of living of the people. This plan also needed a supranational organization to put it into effect. In this as in other situations the Government of the Netherlands has made it clear that military defense agreements do not suffice; economic co-operation has been considered imperative. The dangers threatening Europe's survival are not military only. Great hope has been put in the Council of Europe, of which the Netherlands has become a most devoted supporter, as it has of all organizations promising peace. This attitude has made a Netherlands a faithful and loyal partner in the United Nations.

Other organizations joined by the Netherlands are the Organization for European Economic Cooperation (OEEC) since its beginning in 1948 and the European Payments Union (EPU) which came into effect on July 1, 1950. The country thus participates in all international organizations that pertain to European recovery and integration.

BENELUX. Perhaps one experiment deserves more attention than others described, since it involves the Netherlands in particular: the arrangement between Belgium, the Netherlands, and Luxembourg.

On September 5, 1944, the governments-in-exile of the three countries signed a customs agreement in recognition of the fact that close economic co-operation between them was necessary for economic recovery and development in the postwar period. It was an extension of the Belgo-Luxembourg Customs Union which had been set up in 1922. A common customs tariff was adopted as of January 1, 1948. This meant abolition of duties but there were still restrictions in the form of import licenses and permits, excise duties, and the like. While the experiment is expected to become a complete economic union, quite a few things will have to be

[24] *News Digest from Holland,* January 25, 1954.

accomplished, such as the overcoming of differences in currencies, price levels, and wages. Much has been said about Benelux, that it is actually a failure or that it just did not live up to expectations. An objective and detached comment from a Swiss source of recent date might give some answers in regard to the many questions that have arisen about the organization. The *Swiss Review of World Affairs* in its February 1956 issue suggested that in the Netherlands in particular has always existed a considerable eagerness for the creation of such a union, while Belgium and Luxembourg feel that the economic integration has really progressed far enough and need not be further "consolidated" by an economic union.

It would be a mistake to assume that the development of Benelux has completely stagnated in the past year. On the political level the three countries gained a larger importance in international relations. An agreement has recently been signed for the establishment of a consultative interparliamentary Benelux Council, and cultural cooperation has made some progress. Finally the three countries arrived at an agreement on the conditions for an equalization of agricultural policy.

The problem of Benelux is the different approach of the three countries to economic life and principles, since the Netherlands has various measures for planned economy and the Belgians believe in minimal interference by governments. Nevertheless the Dutch feel that the issue of planned versus free economy is of no importance for the future of Benelux. The *Christian Science Monitor* in its issue of January 28, 1956, asking for patience and understanding, said that:

. . . Benelux has been steadily building, step by step. Customs and quota adjustments, special taxes put on goods crossing the frontier so they would not upset the other's internal market during the provisional period of gaining common internal levels, the money thus realized going into a special fund to help the situation develop—these have been typical of the many unspectacular but solid steps.

The article points out that in 1955 the organization was presented a single list by OEEC in connection with the raising of the compulsory level of liberalization of trade:

With the presentation of a single list OEEC granted official recognition of Benelux as a single entity, making it one of the foremost commercial powers in foreign trade in the world today. Benelux has succeeded in the toughest of all unifications, over-all economic union.

THE PROBLEM OF INDONESIA. Much has been said and written on this highly controversial issue so that it seems well-nigh impossible to find a neutral stand. From the viewpoint of the Dutch there is reason for disappointment that the Netherlands-Indonesian Conference at Geneva ended in failure on February 11, 1956. The Dutch felt strongly so, since at the Conference it had been agreed that the Netherlands-Indonesian Union should be dissolved and that the financial and economic agreements incorporated in the Union should be replaced by a new treaty. No arrangement had been obtained either for the handling of disputes or in regard to the problem of New Guinea. It was felt on the Dutch side that the Indonesians should have respected the agreements that had been made when the Netherlands-Indonesian Union was negotiated, particularly since they do not oppose Indonesian freedom. Yet the developments of August 1956 give the Dutch much reason for misgiving, since Indonesia's denunciation of her debts to the Netherlands is a breach of what had been considered voluntarily accepted in the round-table agreements of 1949. The Dutch are particularly outspoken in regard to New Guinea, since they feel that no historical or constitutional tie has ever existed beween Netherlands New Guinea and the territories now known as the Republic of Indonesia. The main concern for the Dutch appears to be the question of self-determination for the population which is one of the most primitive societies of modern times and which, according to the Dutch viewpoint, would have no chance for any development under the leadership of the ethnically different Malayan Indonesians. Dutch opinion considers the question as a matter of national conscience, since the Papuans of New Guinea, if given up by the Dutch, would be no masters of their own fate. The Dutch also maintain that there is no movement for affiliation with Indonesia among the indigenous population; finally that security in the Pacific, as guaranteed in the ANZUS and SEATO pacts, is closely related with the maintenance of the *status quo* of New

Guinea. Whatever the feelings of a world might be on this issue, one should at least understand the difficulty of a nation pressed to give up what has been a part of it throughout centuries. It should be also understood that the Dutch will carry on with new assignments. Some suggestion for that can be found in the comment of the Liberal Dutch newspaper *Het Algemeen Handelsblad* of Amsterdam of May, 1956, on the occasion of President Sukarno's visit to the United States:

> We now have other tasks in the world. After the separation between us and Indonesia had been completed, we were placed back in our original position, that of a seafaring trading people with no predominant military or maritime importance, [dependent] for its livelihood on sailing the seven seas and trading on all continents.

The differences with Indonesia have contributed to Dutch resentment of official United States behavior in the question. On March 22, 1956, the leader of the Catholic Party in the Second Chamber put questions to the Foreign Minister in connection with the visit of Secretary of State Dulles to the Republic of Indonesia and some of the statements made by him. Foreign Minister Luns answered the questions as follows:

> According to information available to the Government, . . . the U. S. Secretary of State during his recent stay in Jakarta did indeed give as his opinion that there is a strong resemblance with respect to the development of the United States and Indonesia from colony to independent state.

After Mr. Luns had referred to statements made by Mr. Dulles about being impressed with the "admirable patriotism" and "wisdom" of the Indonesian leaders and to his refusal to comment on the unilateral abrogation of the Netherlands-Indonesian Union, he gave expression to the Dutch government's disappointment and shock over the secretary's attitude:

> Foster Dulles, through these public statements, has created the impression that the U. S. Government approves the actions of the Indonesian Government against the Netherlands and the abrogation of formally concluded and ratified agreements. . . .
> These developments have led the Netherlands Government to ex-

press its extreme disappointment with the statements . . . The Netherlands Government believes that it may expect understanding and sympathy from the United States with regard to essential Netherlands interests, both in and outside Europe, under the existing allied relationship in which the Netherlands is continuously rendering loyal co-operation to the United States.

Epilogue

The Netherlands, a little country, eager to comply with the prescriptions of the law, too weak to be a menace to any nation, might well be considered as an example of peaceful living. The great gifts of the country to mankind, her concern for justice throughout the ages, and her fight for an integrated Europe as imperative for better living and world peace, should be regarded as a good suggestion for the conduct of foreign relations with an emphasis on consideration rather than on outspoken selfishness or self-centeredness. Such a lesson can be transmitted only by the small country, since its size and the experience taught from history, in old and in modern times, have forced it to gain in wisdom and understanding. We have witnessed the great changes in the guiding principles of the Netherlands that have moved the country from neutrality to a courageous and honest fight for western unity and strength. There is no doubt that the little nation will stick to its word, whatever may come.

BIBLIOGRAPHICAL NOTES

While quite a bit of material on the foregoing discussion can be found in Dutch publications, there is great difficulty in obtaining material in English concerned with the problem of Dutch foreign policy. Indeed, only one author in the United States has written chapters on the topic, Professor Amry Vandenbosch of the University of Kentucky. One of these can be found under the heading "Netherlands Foreign Policy" in B. Landheer, ed., *The Netherlands* (University of California Press, 1943). Another chapter dealing with the problem can be found in Amry Vandenbosch and Samuel J. Eldersveld, *Government of the Netherlands* (University

of Kentucky, 1947). Professor Vandenbosch has been also concerned with a very specific phase in a monograph, *The Neutrality
of the Netherlands during the World War* (Grand Rapids, 1927).
Reference to the general issues can be found in some of the publications of B. Landheer, such as *The Netherlands in a Changing
World* (New York, 1947).

There are some books that give some good information on the
general make-up of the little nation and thus appear valuable for
obtaining general information on power potential, population, attitudes, etc. Professor A. J. Barnouw's *The Making of Modern
Holland, A Short History* (New York, Norton, 1944) could be
mentioned as an example in this category. Many books appeared
during World War II and the period thereafter, as did pamphlets,
magazines, and booklets, most of which can be obtained from the
Netherlands Information Service in New York, or from its offices
in Holland, Michigan, or San Francisco. Many special questions
can be answered by these offices, all of whom gave splendid assistance to the author. Some of these publications are *Netherlands
News Bulletin*, published daily by the Netherlands News Agency
ANP at The Hague, or the booklet "The Netherlands 1952—
Political and Economic Life" (The Hague, 1953).

Specific topics on which information can be found in English
are, for example, United States economic aid and its impact on the
country. A very thorough report was issued by the Ministry of
Foreign Affairs, through the Director General for the Economic
and Military Aid Program of the Ministry: *Road to Recovery*
(The Hague, 1954). This is a very fine study and gives a good bit
of information on the struggle of the country at the end of World
War II and on the amazing amount of success that the country
had achieved during the few years since the end of the hostilities.
Some of the problems of the postwar period have been discussed
in J. Barents' article, "New Trends in Dutch Foreign Policy," in
Foreign Affairs (January 1947), vol. 25, No. 2, pp. 328 ff. The
issue of the most recent constitutional changes can be found in an
article by H. F. Van Panhuys, "The Netherlands Constitution
and International Law," in *American Journal of International Law*,
October 1953.

The Union of Soviet Socialist Republics

DAVID T. CATTELL

Department of Political Science
University of California, Los Angeles

The Union of Soviet Socialist Republics

CHAPTER **18**

BACKGROUNDS OF THE FOREIGN
POLICY OF THE USSR

Until the nineteenth century the Russian Goliath stood on the fringe of western Europe as the big, backward giant, who could be ignored in the general by-play and intrigues of European international relations. Only on occasion was the Colossus aroused to send its armies of peasant masses against the lords of the West, as when one of the more ambitious rulers of Europe tried to carve an empire for himself in the steppes of Russia. The massive army and the vast distances of Russia in the end always proved too much for the invader from the West. As a result Europeans acquired a respect for the might, if not the skill and culture, of the tsars and their cohorts. But by the nineteenth century the giant no longer seemed so awesome. Great navies and new technology had turned the countries of Western Europe into large empires with great land areas and large populations. Modern weapons made one Western-equipped soldier equal to tens of Russian soldiers. With vast spaces still to be bridged and without useable ports directly on the high seas, Russia was unable to keep pace with the development of the imperialist powers of the West.

The determination of Russian leaders, continued technical development, and the growing importance of air power have gradually redressed the balance and made Russia more fearsome than ever. The pinpointed naval bases of Great Britain have become strategically almost valueless under atomic attack, while great distances, dispersal of towns and industries, a large population, and a program of industrialization have strengthened the defenses of the USSR. Furthermore, with the increased potentialities of strategic air power, the landlocked position of Russia is no longer a hindrance to its expansion.

Natural Resources and Industrial Production

Geography

The total area of the USSR is more than 8½ million square miles, more than twice that of the United States. The country is almost entirely one vast plain, containing the largest single lowland area in the world. The plain is broken only by the relatively low Ural Mountains stretching north to the Arctic Circle and south almost to the Caspian Sea. Only in eastern Siberia and along the southern border in central Asia are there important mountain barriers, some of the highest in the world. The single central plain, however, is the dominating feature and influence of Russian topography.

To make Russia a great industrial power, space had to be conquered. Until the twentieth century the primary means of transportation were the rivers, which in the European part of Russia are well placed, connecting the central part of European Russia with the Baltic, Arctic, Caspian, and Black Seas. The Asiatic part of Russia is much less favored. Except for the Amur, the main rivers of Siberia flow north into arctic wastes; none connect Asiatic Russia with European Russia. In addition, the rivers are frozen and not navigable during several months of the year. Before the twentieth century, therefore, the resources of European Russia alone could be exploited and only that portion of the country could be tied together. Siberia remained remote—a place to send the castoffs from society. Even in European Russia, resource utilization was limited by the remoteness of some areas from navigable rivers, and by the short season of navigation, and by the shallowness of some of the rivers. It was with the introduction of railroads in Russia at the end of the nineteenth century that the country could be transformed into a modern industrial power. The railroads could and did overcome the long distances separating natural resources from each other and from the centers of population. In spite of the tremendous advancement of the Russian transportation system, the problem of adequately covering the enormous area of the country with a network of railroads and roads is still a crucial one and poor transportation is an important strategic weakness in the Soviet defense system.

Natural Resources

It is not surprising that in the highly mechanized age of today the two predominant powers, the United States and the Soviet Union, have the largest shares of the world's resources. For example, the Soviet Union has at least 20 per cent of the world's coal reserves, 1⅔ trillion tons, in numerous deposits throughout the country. The USSR's iron-ore reserves are abundant, more than 50 per cent of the total world's reserve. The Russian ores are of both high and low grades. The Soviet Union also claims more than half the world's oil potential, concentrated mostly in the area around the Caspian Sea both to the southwest and north; this claim is probably exaggerated. The Soviet Union in the past has actually suffered from the lack of oil, but the reason appears to have been more inefficient exploitation rather than lack of potential. Soviet hydroelectric resources are about three and one-half times those of the United States. Exploitation of this energy has been slow, however, because of its remoteness and the high capital investment necessary to build dams. The timber reserves are also more than enough for both domestic needs and export to western Europe, being one-fifth of the world's total. In addition the USSR has available most of the other mineral resources required by a highly industrial community: manganese (one-third of the world's reserves), lead, nickel, zinc, chromium, bauxite, copper, sulfur, tin, asbestos and many others.

Precise information as to the potential reserves of natural resources and their quality, however, is unavailable. It is believed that some of the ores are of quite poor quality, for example the bauxite and copper ores. But only in such cases as rubber, tungsten, and molybdenum, known to have been imported in quantity by the Soviet Union, is there any reason to suspect a deficiency of domestic sources.

The Soviet reserves of uranium, which have assumed primary importance in the last ten years, are also unknown. The intensive efforts which the Soviet Union made after World War II to obtain uranium from East Germany and Czechoslovakia suggested deficiency. The subsequent decline in the mining of uranium in this area may indicate either that the best ore has been removed or that the Soviets in their surveys have found adequate ores of their own.

The reasons why there is no accurate information on Soviet resources are several. Prior to the late 1930's no complete survey had been made of Soviet resources and since then detailed statistics on reserves have been classified as state secrets. Only broad categorical statements concerning Soviet potentials are made in the official and unofficial publications. Furthermore, even in the most ideal circumstances it is not easy to estimate mineral reserves accurately. Mineral estimates in the United States, for example, are constantly being revised in the light of new findings.

It is possible to conclude, in spite of a lack of specific information, that the Soviet Union has a rich abundance of the most important minerals—enough to be one of the leading industrial countries for some time to come, almost self-sufficient, and capable of sustaining a high standard of living for its people. More accurate information, especially concerning uranium deposits, however, is essential for making a precise equation of the Soviet's power position. Without it we must introduce a significant margin of error for any of our calculations.

Industrial Output

A margin of error must be allowed not only in estimating mineral reserves but also in calculating present exploitation. Precise figures on current production are classified in the USSR as state secrets. Industrial output is reported only in the form of general categories, in percentages of some base or in rubles.[1] These figures are

---

[1] More recently the Soviet Union has been willing to publish more exact production figures, but still in very general terms. In June, 1956, for the first time since 1939 a statistical yearbook for the USSR was published, but many of the important details were omitted.

meaningful only if the base and the cost assigned to each process and item are known. In addition there are the problems of evaluating quality, false reports by plant managers, statistical inflation, and the omission of unfavorable production figures. In spite of this cat-and-mouse game played by the Soviet Union in respect to economic statistics, western economists have been able to deduce certain broad trends and developments in the Soviet industrial picture.

The successful defense and counteroffensive against Hitler by Soviet forces in World War II proved that Soviet claims on production, no matter how extravagant they may seem, cannot be dismissed as propaganda. This lesson was again brought home by the successful detonation of both atomic and hydrogen bombs several years before Western economists and scientists had expected. Such nuclear weapons can be produced at the present time only by a highly developed industrial society.

The industrialization of Russia did not begin with the Soviet regime. By 1914, under the tsars, tremendous strides had already been made. The rate of increase of industrial production from 1885-1913 was more than 5 per cent per year—a little more than the rate in the United States for the same period. The annual production of coal, for example, increased from about 557,000 metric tons in 1870 to 29,100,000 in 1913. In the same period iron and steel production increased from about 237,000 metric tons to 4,000,000.

The following figures show the relative development of Russian industry under the Communists during recent years:

	Coal[1]	Oil[1]	Electricity[2]	Steel[1]	Cotton Cloth[3]	Shoes[4]
1913	29.1	9.2	1.9	4.0	2,227	—
1940	166.0	31.0	48.3	18.3	3,815	205.0
1953	318.0	52.6	133.0	38.0	5,300	242.0
1955	390.1	70.7	170.1	45.3	5,911	297.4
1960 (goal)	593.0	135.0	320.0	68.3	7,270	455.0

[1] Millions of metric tons.
[2] Billions of kilowatt-hours.
[3] Millions of meters.
[4] Millions of pairs.

These statistics indicate a large development of the means of production in the Soviet Union since the days of the tsars. This gain has been achieved by a continuous high rate of investment in the basic industries (20 per cent or more of the economy's total resources). Present goals indicate that the Soviet Union does not plan to relax its pace of development but intends to go right on pushing for the maximum output, that is, an annual rate of growth for the total economy of 6.5 to 7 per cent[2] as compared to only 2.5 to 3 per cent in the United States. The figures, however, say nothing about the cost of such achievements: the long extra hours of labor by the mass of Soviet citizens, the heavy taxes and forced deliveries, the terror, and the low level of consumer production and housing. One of the problems in estimating the future development of basic industries is to know how much longer and to what extent the Soviet people will tolerate these sacrifices. The answer is a primary concern not only of western analysts but also of the Soviet leaders, who have continued to seek the limit of endurance and the best methods to exploit the effort of the bureaucrats and the masses. Although the Soviet economy has the means to produce an abundance of consumer goods, the Soviet leaders have not yet been willing to let the people share in the fruits of industrial growth. The emphasis since the 1930's has been on the creation of basic industries and military potential. The Hungarian revolt in the fall of 1956 and the stirrings in the other satellites and even within the Soviet Union may, however, force the leaders to change production emphasis to consumer's goods at least temporarily in order to appease the cravings of the masses for better living conditions.

Military Production

One frequent mistake made by western observers in analyzing Soviet production figures for potential military power is to compare directly such items as the Soviet steel output of 46 million metric tons with the United States production of more than 100 million metric tons. Such a simple comparison is misleading. It is

---

[2] It is impossible to determine absolutely the rate of growth for the economy in the Soviet Union, but the consensus of western economists is about 5 to 8 per cent.

necessary first to adjust the figures to the amount of steel directly available for armament production. In the United States the civilian economy depends heavily on steel for its operation. Consequently, even in time of war a large portion of steel production in the United States must go for civilian purposes, reducing the amount available for armaments. In contrast, the Soviet civilian economy has always lagged far behind in its development and thus requires a minimum of steel for its continued functioning. A much larger portion of Soviet steel output, perhaps 90 per cent in contrast to about 50 per cent in the United States, is therefore available for war production.[3]

In view of a possible atomic war in which the initial blows may be decisive, long-range potentials for munitions output are less important than immediate military production. In current arms production the Soviet picture is more favorable than that of the United States because the entire Soviet economy has remained virtually on a war basis. Although only fragmentary information on this subject is available, the evidence indicates that current military production represents about 15 per cent of the total resources expended and that this production is equal to that in the United States if not greater. For example, it is estimated that the Soviet Union is producing in quantity not only supersonic and all-weather planes but also medium- and long-range bombers comparable to those being produced in the United States.

Agricultural Potential and Production

Natural Endowment

The Soviet leaders, in building Russia into the bastion of socialism, have not only made use of modern industrial techniques but

---

[3] The capacity of Soviet military production is indicated by World War II figures published by the Soviet Union. During the last three years of the war, for example, Soviet industry achieved an annual production of about 30,000 tanks, self-propelled guns, and armored cars; 40,000 planes; nearly 120,000 artillery pieces; almost 450,000 light and heavy machine guns; more than 3,000,000 rifles and about 2,000,000 submachine guns. (From *Bolshaya Sovetskaya Entsiklopediya, Soyuz Sovetskikh Sotsialisticheskikh Respublik*, cols. 827-28, cited in Harry Schwartz, *Russia's Soviet Economy*, 2nd ed., Prentice-Hall, 1954, p. 277).

have also sought to take the fullest advantage of the agricultural potential of the country. The need for efficient agriculture has been paramount because of the rapidly growing population and the demands of industry for more workers. The best means of increasing the industrial labor supply has been the release of peasants from the farm as the result of modern mechanized methods of agriculture.

In spite of occupying more than one-seventh of the earth and having a wide range of climate and soil, the Soviet Union is not well endowed with favorable agricultural conditions. A good portion of the country lies in the same latitudes as Canada and is subject to the extremes of continental climate: very cold winters and short but relatively hot summers. Consequently, the northern half of the Soviet Union has too short a growing season for most crops. However, it is not all waste. The portion which is south of the frozen tundra and includes about one-third of the country does contain excellent forests. In the southern half, where the season is long enough for many crops, the rainfall and soils are often deficient. In the Moscow area and the Ukraine the mean annual rainfall is twenty inches or more, enough to support ordinary grain crops; but the annual rainfall rapidly decreases further to the east so that at the mouth of the Volga River on the Caspian Sea it is only six inches. The extreme variation of even this rainfall from year to year makes crop production a problem. Furthermore, the acid *podsol* soil, which is relatively poor for agricultural purposes, is found over most of the Asiatic territories and the central part of European Russia. Thus only the relatively small area of the Ukraine, with its famous black earth of the steppes and good climatic conditions, is ideal for agricultural production. In fact, most of Russian farming can be found in the agricultural triangle marked by Leningrad, the southern end of Lake Baikal, and Odessa on the Black Sea—and even much of this is marginal land.

Soviet Techniques to Increase Output

By various means the Soviet Government has sought to make the best use of the land and to expand the amount of arable land.

These techniques include collectivization, mechanization, extensive use of fertilizer, land drainage, irrigation, new types of crops, intensive cultivation, putting virgin lands under crops, and building shelter forests. Irrigation has greatly increased the amount of cultivated land in central Asia, in the northern Caucasus region, and along the Volga. The Soviet Union in 1956 had about eleven million acres of irrigated land and is planning much further expansion in the near future. In the years just before Stalin's death, there was a rush of new ideas and projects, such as a 700-mile irrigation canal, several hydroelectric dams, and the unique fifteen-year plan to plant 15,000,000 acres of trees in eight giant belts running north and south in the eastern Ukraine and Volga regions. This last was calculated to retard the hot drying winds from Asia, which burn up crops and take the moisture from the ground. Some of these remedies appear to have been proved impractical and were probably discarded, as they are no longer mentioned in the press.

The most recent attempt to increase production has been a drive to add new acreage by plowing up empty grass lands. Beginning in the fall of 1953, the Soviet leaders asked for an increase of about 33,000,000 acres of cultivated land in 1955 and a total of 70,000,000 acres by 1956. There is some doubt as to whether this plan for immediate production is any more feasible than those of the early 1950's, because the area being plowed up is marginal land which, in a period of drought, is likely to turn into a huge dust bowl and be lost even for grazing. The crop failure in these regions in 1955 confirms these misgivings.

Agricultural Production

The appearance of these new and sometimes startling plans to increase agricultural output is a clue that agricultural production has not had the marked success of industrial production. Figures published by the Soviet Union on agricultural production, however, have always attempted to show a rapid increase in output. It was only after Stalin's death that the new leaders made public the true state of agriculture. From the figures given by Nikita Khrushchev in the fall of 1953 and from the estimates of western economists, it is evident that agriculture is a major problem. The essential element of the problem was made clear by Khrushchev when he said that from 1940 through 1952 over-all agricultural production rose by only 10 per cent; in the same years, the population rose by a little more than the same amount. Since the Russians were not well fed in 1940, they were not well fed in 1952—and their situation had not greatly improved in 1956. An even more startling revelation by Khrushchev was that the number of livestock in 1916 was 58 million head but in 1953 only 57 million. This 1953 figure represents a reduction of 3,500,000 below the livestock count before World War II and 8,900,000 below the 1928 figure. On the other hand, grain production increased from 1928 to 1950, but not markedly even according to official Soviet statistics.

Although Soviet agricultural production does not compare favorably with Soviet industrial output and although it is a problem which will tend to be aggravated even more as the population increases, it is dangerous to overemphasize its importance and label it a serious liability to Soviet strength. The diet of the average Russian is monotonous and starchy, but it is adequate. Furthermore, by careful stockpiling and restraint, the Soviet Union can avoid famines due to crop failures. The periods of acute food shortage in the past can be largely explained by political and social crises rather than by lack of agricultural potentiality. The period of World War II, when some of the best lands of Russia were fields of battle or under German occupation, is adequate proof that with careful stockpiling the Soviet Union can overcome short periods of crisis. Although the western Allies sent almost 2½ million tons of food to the Soviet Union during the war, especially animal products and processed foods, Russia itself supplied the bulk of the grain from current production and stockpiles. The prewar production and consumption of grain in the years just before the war had been around 80 million tons per year. What the Allies supplied was therefore but a small percentage of the food consumed by the Soviets during the war. Without doubt the Soviet Union in recent years has replenished her stockpiles of food, and has enough to cover successfully several years of crises which might cause a severe cut in grain production. But as long as the Soviet leaders continue to drive for autarchy, agriculture will be a pressing problem, although not completely unsolvable. Increased irrigation, greater intensification of crops, and improved grains and techniques undoubtedly offer the Soviet Union wide margins for crop expansion. Two important reasons for the low level of output compared with many other countries (less than 500 kilograms of grain per acre compared to 600 per acre in the United States) have been the resentment against collectivization and the lack of material incentives for the farmer. Farm workers are unable to exchange the results of their labor for an appreciable amount of consumer goods because of the extremely low prices paid for the agricultural products demanded by the state. The importance of incentives and private ownership is indicated by the amount produced by individual collective farmers on the small private plots allowed for their own use.[4] The land so used comprises 5 per cent of the arable land in Russia but accounts for about 20 per cent of over-all production. This produce is free from the heavy demands of state collections at very low prices and can be consumed by the farmer or sold on the free market as he chooses. The present regime has begun to recognize the importance of incentives to increase the yield and has reduced the amount of quotas to the government and raised the price paid for these quotas. For example, the price on quota cattle was raised from about 4 per cent to 27 per cent of the free-market prices. The main difficulty in increasing the farmer's share is that it decreases the amount of investment capital available for the government. Furthermore, it does not satisfy the persistent demand for individual farms.

Military Forces

Recruitment

The strength of the military forces of a country is the sum total of several factors that include industrial potential for munitions, the size and composition of the population, the military equipment currently on hand, and the training and morale of the troops. Traditionally the primary military advantages of Russia have been its stamina and the large population from which to recruit mass

---

[4] Another evidence of the desire for private ownership was the mass defections, particularly among the farmers, in World War II.

armies. The endurance of the Russian soldier, facing the enemy inadequately fed and equipped in both World Wars, has been proved. The Russian population has also been very prolific. The size and growth of the population is seen from the two general censuses taken in Soviet Russia in 1926 and 1939, which showed an increase from 147 million to 170 million people. By its territorial acquisitions in 1939 and 1940 the USSR increased its population by another 22 million, bringing the total in 1940 to about 192 million. Then, in spite of war-attributable losses of almost 40 million, the population by 1955 was reported to have surpassed the 1940 mark, reaching 200 million and increasing at a rate of more than 3 million a year. Although there are some indications that the rate of growth may be declining slightly, an appreciable increase in population can still be predicted.

Another important military asset of the Soviet population is that it is relatively young. A large number of youths are of military age or approaching it and only a small number of old people needs to be supported by the economy.

The Soviet Union also has made extensive use of its women in agriculture and industry, and during the war large numbers served in the armed forces.

Training and Morale

Hitler's attack on the Soviet Union on June 2, 1941, caught the military apparatus of the Soviet Union inadequately prepared and Russian troops were at first incapable of putting up much resistance. The morale of the troops was low and there were mass defections to the Germans because of the confusion and latent dissatisfaction with the Soviet regime.[5] Out of the chaos of the early months, the Soviet leaders, nevertheless, were able gradually to reorganize and forge a tightly knit, hard-hitting army. They were aided in part by the enemy's reign of terror in the occupied areas.

Military indoctrination begins at a very early age through the Communist Party youth groups, which inculcate discipline and

[5] Nikita Khrushchev in a secret speech before the 20th Party Congress in February, 1956, blamed the chaos on the refusal of Stalin to take heed of warnings that Hitler was about to attack, and Stalin's complete lack of knowledge of military matters.

teach the rudiments of military science, including the use of various weapons. On reaching military age, from one to two million conscripts are chosen each year to serve for periods varying from two to five years. The remaining are organized into the second-line reserve. Those in the services not only complete a rigorous military program but are subject to intensive political indoctrination. The Komsomol, the auxiliary of the Communist Party for older youths, assumes the special tasks of politically educating the young recruit in the military service, while the Communist Party itself provides tight political control over the officer ranks and the professional soldiers. To prevent contrary indoctrination, the Party seeks to isolate the soldier from all possible alien or subversive influences. Thus, the troops doing occupation duty in Germany and eastern Europe are indoctrinated with special care and their contact with the local people is kept to a minimum. The purpose of this hegemony by the organs of the Party has been both to prevent the army from becoming an independent source of power within the Soviet state and to insure the loyalty of the soldiers to the regime and to the Soviet Union.

An accurate evaluation of the combat potential of the Soviet troops is difficult. There is no question that in respect to military training and technical competence the Soviet troops are well qualified. On the other hand the morale and fighting spirit of the Russian soldiers cannot be measured. Only certain assumptions can be made. It is unlikely that the mass defections and panic of 1941 will be repeated in a future conflict. If history can tell us anything about the Russian military character, we must assume that in defense of his homeland the Russian conscript will fight tenaciously, but that in wars of aggression the lack of interest of the average Russian in building an empire or crusading for Communism would make him an apathetic soldier. Reports of the reluctance and even defection of some of the Russian troops during the Soviet repression of the Hungarian revolt confirm this hypothesis.

Equipment

Particularly important in estimating Soviet military strength is the fact that for the first time in over a century or more the Russian soldier is well equipped with modern weapons capable of sustaining him in a major war. The new class of Soviet scientists who emerged under the Stalin regime and during the initial Five-Year Plans has produced weapons of superior quality. By World War II Soviet tanks and artillery were among the finest in the world and Soviet industries were producing them in mass. In the postwar period, with the help of scientists brought from defeated Germany, the Russians have had a chance to improve their technical competence in other fields, such as guided missiles, aircraft, and atomic weapons. Consequently, there is every reason to believe that the former superiority of the United States in atomic weapons and aircraft has in recent years been cut down by Soviet advances. Recent Soviet air shows have displayed a number of long-range jet bombers which are believed to be almost equal in performance to those being produced in the United States. Even in the naval field, in which Russia traditionally has never excelled, the Soviets have been carrying out a large expansion program. They are trying particularly to build up their submarine force and smaller surface vessels.

The one outstanding feature about military equipment developed and produced in the USSR since 1950 has been the emphasis on the offensive ability of the armed forces—atomic weapons, guided missiles, and long-range aircraft. Even the expansion of the submarine fleet can be interpreted in this light. Submarines today can serve not only to cut supply lines but can also be used as a means to deliver the atomic bomb or as platforms for guided missiles. The question is whether the development of an offensive force means in the near future a new outbreak of Soviet aggression or whether the Soviet Union is following the United States and building for a strategy of mass retaliation on the premise that the best defense in an atomic war is an immediate counterattack.

The Satellites

To complete the analysis of Soviet military strength a brief mention should be made of the satellites. Their industrial capacity, particularly that of Czechoslovakia, East Germany, and Poland, adds significantly to the industrial potential of the Soviet Union. For example, in 1953 the satellites produced about 13.5 million tons of steel. So too the million or more troops being trained in the satellites can add considerable strength to the mass army of the Soviet Union, making its power even more impressive.

The actual effectiveness of satellite troops, however, is in some doubt. The riots of June 1953, when the East German workers attempted to revolt against their Communist leaders, and the almost complete defection of the Hungarian armed forces to the side of the rebels during the Hungarian revolt in October and November 1956, point clearly to the unreliability of satellite troops in times of crisis. In both cases Soviet troops had to be called in after the native troops not only refused to fire on the workers but joined them in their cause. Such orders to fire on fellow countrymen are extreme tests of a soldier's discipline; yet the very existence of these riots and revolt, together with the traditional enmity of the satellite peoples of eastern Europe toward their Russian conquerors and Communism with its rule of deprivation and terror, indicates that they are dubious allies.

The Soviet leaders have recognized the problem of disaffection in the satellite armed forces and have dealt with it in several ways, among them: (1) They have been careful to give the satellite armies technically inferior weapons. (2) They have furnished Soviet technicians and officers to train satellite troops and insure loyalty. A conspicuous example was the appointment of Soviet Marshal Konstantin Rokossovsky as commander in chief of the Polish army. The enmity of the Poles toward Russia has long been a recorded historical fact. Thus the Soviet leaders sought to be absolutely sure of their control over the Polish troops. In the other satellites the Soviet military "advisors" are present but in less prominent posts. (3) Most of the satellite countries still have Soviet troops in occupation, providing a double check on the loyalty of the local forces. (4) A multilateral defense treaty was signed in Warsaw in December 1954, and was followed by the agreement to form a defense organization and a united command (similar to NATO) for troops in the Soviet sphere of eastern Europe. One of the purposes of this new organization was to complete the integration of the military forces in the Soviet sphere. By the end of 1956 it was doubtful whether these precautions were enough. Marshal Rokossovsky and many other Soviet officers had been dismissed in Poland, the Hungarian people and army were in open revolt, and there were signs of ferment in varying degrees in all the satellites of eastern Europe. The likely consequence of these events will be the partial disarmament of the satellite armies and the writing off of these forces as an asset to the Soviet military strength.

An Evaluation

It is impossible to draw up an accurate balance of Soviet armed strength, and the large number of unknown factors has permitted western analysts to give play to their private feelings of pessimism or wishful thinking about the Soviet Union. Estimating military potential is always, even under the most favorable circumstances, a dangerous and doubtful game, as the various estimates by the analysts just before World War II clearly testify. A careful and balanced study of the evidence in respect to Soviet Russia, however, neither indicates doom nor justifies extreme optimism for the West. There is little doubt that the Soviet Union is a formidable military threat to the West. It is even quite possible that in the balance the Soviet Union has a slight superiority over the NATO powers. But the superiority, if it exists, is insufficient to reasonably assure the Soviet leaders of success in the great uncertainties of a war. Consequently, if they are reasonable men, it is unlikely they are calculating to launch a major war. The danger is too great that they might lose the war or that their leadership might be undermined by the internal strain.

National Character and Soviet Foreign Policy

National character is a nebulous term which cannot be easily defined and is often loosely used by analysts. To make this term meaningful in respect to the Soviet Union the characteristics which we attribute to the Russian people or leaders must be only those which can be clearly defined and proved by empirical data and historical continuity.

Soviet Stratification

One way to determine the character of a society is to examine the social stratification to be found within it. R. M. MacIver in his book, *The Web of Government*, defines and determines social stratification in terms of power, property, and status.[6] The importance of these elements is bound to differ from community to community.

Social status can be defined as the relative position occupied by a man or group in society regardless of personal achievements or qualifications. Status is closely associated to class, which denotes a well-defined system of status that is perpetuated from generation to generation. In the Soviet Union, status relationships have been changing and have not yet become so clearly defined or so lasting as to create real class distinctions, although the tendency is strong in this direction. Party membership has been the major exception in the changing social structure of the USSR; the holding of a Party card has always given a person preferred status. Intellectuals, engineers, plant managers, industrial workers, labor organizers, teachers, and to a lesser extent peasants and artists at various times since the Revolution have possessed different status depending on their usefulness to the current Party line.

In the Soviet Union, where all important property is controlled by the state, economic wealth has played a less important role than in countries with extensive private ownership. Thus it is useful in the case of Soviet society to confine determination of social stratification to the power and influence which persons or groups hold in the Soviet Union. Using this criterion it is possible to determine several important levels of social stratification in Russia today:[7]

[6] Robert M. MacIver, *The Web of Government* (Macmillan, 1947), Chapters 5, 6.

[7] For a more detailed and somewhat different breakdown of Soviet society see the article of Alex Inkeles, "Social Stratification and Mobility in the Soviet Union," reprinted in Reinhard Bendix and Seymour Martin (eds.), *Class, Status and Power, a Reader in Social Stratification* (The Free Press, 1953), pp. 609-622.

1. The ruling elite, composed of top Party, government, economic, and military officials. (The number in this group is very small, from fifty to three hundred. A precise count is impossible because little is known of the inner workings of the government and Party and how policies are determined.)

2. The intelligentsia and local leaders, consisting of the middle-ranking functionaries of the Party and government, such as the provincial Party secretaries, chief engineers, plant managers, top ranks in the armed forces, leading scientists, technical specialists, and the better-known artists.

3. The petty bureaucracy, which includes the lower Party and government functionaries, junior military officers, Stakhanovites or shock workers, collective-farm directors, and rank-and-file Party members.

4. The rank-and-file industrial workers.

5. The peasantry.

From this general division into strata it is evident that Party membership assures an individual of a preferred status in one of the upper three groups but that other criteria determine which of the three is his particular stratum.

Classification of Soviet strata by income would generally give a pyramid similar to that above. However, there would be some exceptions, such as top artists who often receive incomes that would put them in the highest bracket instead of the second. Many skilled workers in crucial industries and many well-to-do collective farmers would be in a higher stratum on an income basis.

Income differences are becoming increasingly important in determining an individual's social position in the Soviet Union. During the 1930's all pretense of equality of incomes was abandoned and incentive wages and bonuses of various types were instituted which created income differences not dissimilar to those in the United States. Thus the upper strata have multiroom apartments, cars, maids, and *dachas* or country homes in which to pass the hot summer months, while lower-income groups are barely able to make ends meet with the combined salaries of husband and wife in a one-room apartment. Wide differences in standards of living are not the only results of the disparity in incomes. Large incomes also provide the means of passing important advantages on to children. It is possible to will personal wealth—which may be considerable in the case of top leaders, artists, and technicians— to children with only a small loss through the inheritance tax. Until recently a high income also made it possible to pay the tuition for the less brilliant child who was unable to qualify for a government stipend. The restoration of a free-tuition system made this distinction less important, although the lower-income groups still tend to push their children out to work as soon as possible because the family needs the money and the wealthy can still give their children higher education regardless of ability.

From the evidence available it would appear that the Soviet social stratification is tending toward becoming a fixed system with the rank-order of the various groups remaining stable in respect to power as well as to property and to status. In addition the mobility between the various groups has been greatly reduced, so that birth plays an increasingly important part in securing positions. The tendency is in the direction of a pure class system, though whether it has been achieved is still a matter of controversy among observers. In their efforts to legitimize their power into justified authority the Soviet leaders have given impetus to this process and have introduced a large amount of rigidity into the rank-order of society. From the point of view of Soviet national power this marked distinction between ruling groups and ruled would appear to be a weakness. First, the difference between the professed aims of socialism as a society of abundance for all and the reality of Soviet society has developed a tendency towards cynicism, particularly among the lower groups. Second, the national unity of the Russian people has been damaged by the development of diverse interests among the various social groups. This situation is further aggravated by the presence of many nationality groups. During World War II, the loyalty of several of these nationality groups was not maintained. Although the Soviet Union has always sought to submerge these national differences as much as possible, the problem still remains.

Status and Foreign-Policy Decisions

Social stratification in Russia has traditionally corresponded to a division of functions among the various groups, in the pattern of a feudalistic society. Under the tsars, matters of government and particularly foreign policy, for example, were the exclusive domain of the tsar and his ministers. The Russian people have never taken part in any way or been interested in the conduct of foreign relations. Even if foreign relations led to war they were not concerned unless warfare involved the protection of their homes. Although the Communist leaders have professed democracy and the participation of the workers in the operation of all phases of government, in fact the tsarist tradition has been continued. Soviet foreign policy has never been considered a topic for general discussion by Soviet citizens. Detailed statements on Soviet foreign policy are made only infrequently by top members of the hierarchy. Other references to foreign affairs are confined to attacks on "the warmongering of the imperialist powers" and to "the dangers of capitalist encirclement," both in order to justify continued maximum efforts in the development of the Soviet economy. Consequently, public opinion plays almost no role in the making of foreign policy in the Soviet Union, nor is there any evidence that the masses in any way want or try to influence the leaders in this respect. Whatever influences the lower strata have on foreign policy are largely indirect and negative.

The conclusion must be that the national character of the bulk of the population, beyond its continued acceptance of the feudal-like division of functions, does not play an immediate role among the determining factors which influence Soviet foreign policy. The important characteristics, therefore, are those of the ruling elite.

The Ruling Elite

In spite of the very limited knowledge about the men in the ruling elite, some factors of their makeup can be deduced. One of the most controversial motivating influences on the top leaders is Communist ideology. There is no doubt that Marxism, for the present rulers of the Soviet Union, plays a far less important role in respect to decision making than it did for the original Bolsheviks who took over the Kremlin in 1917. Today the key elements of decisions are practical politics and opportunism. The continuous struggle for power with practically no ground rules, since Lenin's death in 1924, precludes any other possibility. Casual remarks made to westerners by Nikita Khrushchev and others on the theme of "living it up" indicate the present policy-makers in the Soviet Union are not men dedicated to the ideal of Communism. Even so, indoctrination in Communist theory has proceeded at all levels and has pervaded every function of society for a period of almost forty years. Every decision, every speech, every article, every book, and every decree is clothed and justified in Marxist-Leninist terms. Thus, it is not unreasonable to assume that Marxist methods of analysis and simplification have at least unconsciously affected policy; that in effect the Soviet leaders do closely associate capitalism with depressions, wage slavery, colonial exploitation, and imperialist wars. This rigidity of thinking in the terms of the Marxian dialectic is reinforced by the general isolation of the elite from the people and the world. The next chapter will deal in more detail with how this elite formulates and executes foreign policy.

Historical Factors: Tsarist and Soviet

A Common Political System

When the Bolsheviks came to power in Russia on November 7, 1917, they proclaimed they had broken with the feudal and bourgeois past, and that Russia and the world were entering a new era. But on taking up the reins of power to establish their new state, the dictatorship of the proletariat, they found the past was not dead. The habits and traditions of the tsars persisted, binding the old and new together irrevocably.[8]

It has already been noted that one of the most important conditioning factors of Russia's historical development has been its geographical position. Its continental, almost landlocked position, in the age of sea power cut it off from the rest of the world. The

[8] See George Backer, The Deadly Parallel: Stalin and Ivan the Terrible (Random House, 1950).

vastness of its flat topography at the same time intensified its isolation and exposed it to frequent invasions from both the East and
West. The civilizations of the Levant, the Far East, and the West
had combined to influence it toward a cultural and political development different from any one of the three. The political consequence of the Russian geographical situation has been the development and stability of the autocratic form of government. The
constant danger of invasions and three centuries of tutelage under
the oriental and despotic rule of the Tartar invaders from Mongolia
forced on the Russians, in self-defense, a political system of autocracy. As a result the concepts of the rule of law, the separation of
church and state, and the diffusion of authority under feudalism
were early abandoned in Russia because of the need for getting
rid of invaders. The system thus established has continued down
to the present. Accompanying absolute autocracy has been the
tough strength of the Russian people. Centuries of despotic rule,
alien and domestic, the need for sacrifices to rid Russia of the
Tartar yoke, the continuous heavy cost of protecting the Russian
steppes from invaders, the seclusion of the Russian people from
each other and the outside world, and the rigors of the climate
have created a hardy people capable of long periods of sacrifice
and privation with only an occasional anarchistic revolt against
their overlords.

These historical characteristics remain paramount in the Soviet
political structure. They are evidenced by the tight dictatorship
of Stalin and his successors, the drive for industrial output during
the first Five-Year Plans, and the tenacious defense efforts of the
Russian people in World War II. In respect to foreign policy the
absence of any popular participation and the desire to expand
the Russian empire are also historical characteristics inherited
from the tsars. Nor does the continuity of the two regimes end
here. Many of the current areas of interest and many current conflicts with the West find their origins under the tsars.

Parallels in Foreign Policy

Traditionally the foreign policy of Russia has been one of gradual expansion. From a small principality around Moscow under

tutelage to the Golden Horde during the middle ages, the princes of Moscovy have sought persistently to increase their realm. With only a few exceptions they were able from century to century to achieve their aim. One of the reasons for this expansion was to secure space, the primary strategic basis for Russian defense. But where the defense motive ended and pure ambition began was no more discernible in the tsars than in the Soviet leaders. The Soviet Union's expansion into central Europe after World War II was rationalized as necessary to establish a security zone against renewed German aggression. The interest of the tsars in part of the same area was one of the factors which led to World War I.

Just as Tsar Nicholas demanded the Turkish Straits as his reward for supporting the Entente Powers in World War I and as his share in a victory over the Central Powers, so Stalin asked for control of the same straits after World War II. Both rationalized their demands on the basis of the need to defend southern Russia from a naval invasion.

Russia has been interested in Turkey not only because of the Straits but also because of the strategic mountain heights which control the passes from the Caucasus area into the Anatolian plain of Turkey. Turkey, "the sick man of Europe," however, repeatedly resisted Russian pressure by allying itself with the western powers, particularly with the British. A similar situation existed after World War II, with the United States assuming the role formerly played by Great Britain.

The imperialist ambition of the tsars was also whetted by the continued decline of Persia (Iran). The tsars started to build a branch railroad into northern Persia, sent military instructors, extended loans guaranteed by customs and taxes, and granted special privileges to Persian merchants trading in Russia. Again the restraining influence was England, which also had interests in the area. When England was involved in the Boer War in 1899, the tsar's ministers even talked about annexing Persia right down to the Persian Gulf; but they could not be sure, in spite of the Boer War, that England would not take up the challenge. Russian interest and conflict with the West in Persia was repeated after World War II, when Soviet troops attempted to stay in Northern

Iran permanently and were forced out by the combined pressure of the western powers.

China also attracted the attention of the more imperialistically minded of the tsar's court. In the 1890's, Russia participated in the general land grabbing by the European powers at the expense of China, securing for herself the right to build and in effect to control the Chinese Eastern railroad across Manchuria. This meant a route four hundred miles shorter between Lake Baikal and Vladivostok, Russia's important warm-water port on the Pacific coast. A few years later Russia secured a naval base at Port Arthur in southern Manchuria and control over the railroad connecting it with the Chinese Eastern railroad. These acquisitions in effect put Russia in a position to exploit almost single-handedly the resources of Manchuria. It was only the Russian defeat in the Russo-Japanese War of 1905 that ended Russian paramountcy in this area. The Soviet recovery of the Chinese Eastern railroad and the naval base at Port Arthur, as a result of the Yalta agreement in 1945, matched tsarist exploits.

The imperialist school in the tsar's court was also responsible for expansion into Korea, but in this case Russian military power was not sufficient to support penetration. Consequently, when Russia pressed its expansion in opposition to Japanese interests in Korea, it blundered into war in 1905 and was defeated relatively easily by Japan, which was at this time only a second- or third-rate power backed by Great Britain. This defeat closed Korea to Russian interests for the time being but the dream was not forgotten. The Soviets revived Russia's imperialist interest in this area in 1945.

This brief review of the areas of tsarist expansion and resulting sources of friction with the western powers indicates that Russian imperialism, East-West rivalry, and mutual suspicion are not new phenomena. The diplomats sent by the West to Russia, yesterday as today, have approached this sprawling giant with the same apprehensiveness, with the same hostility, and with the same policy of containment, hoping to check its so-called "defensive" expansions.[9]

[9] See Marquis de Custine (translated by Phyllis Penn Kohler), *Journey for Our Time* (Pellegrini and Cudahy, 1951).

Dissimilar Factors

Although the direction of expansion and the interests of the two regimes are strikingly similar, it would be too hasty to conclude that Soviet foreign policy is merely the continuation of tsarist dreams. It is true that many of the elements which have influenced the two regimes have been constants or similarities, such as geographical position, a system of autocracy, and the lack of political consciousness among the masses. On the other hand, there are several factors of difference. The western diplomats were, for example, in closer affinity to the old rulers whose education and cultural background was similar to their own. This western cultural influence on the upper classes and the growing trade relations between Russia and the West were helping to break down the barriers of suspicion. The Entente of England, France, and Russia before World War I was an expression of this tendency. The Soviet rulers, however, were not touched by this earlier exchange and since they have come to power, they have rejected and have been rejected by the West. The reciprocal fears of both the East and West have kept cultural and trade relations at a minimum under the Soviet regime. More important, however, is that since 1917 many new components have entered into Soviet foreign policy. The Soviet Union has become a great industrial and military power second only to the United States. It proved its military strength in World War II and modern technology continues to alter and strengthen all of its military potentialities. In addition, a world-wide subversive movement in the form of international Communism is at the disposal of Soviet policy makers. Finally and most important, Communist ideology has provided a new way to perceive world politics and Soviet objectives.

Communist Ideology and International Relations

Lenin's Theory of Imperialism

Lenin, a follower of the revolutionary tradition of Marx, sought in his theory of imperialism to bring Marx up to date and fit his thinking to the Russian scene. The basis of Lenin's theory of imperialism was largely Rudolf Hilferding's *Das Finanzkapital* and J. A. Hobson's *Imperialism, a Study*. It was Hilferding's thesis that industrial capitalism was replaced by financial capitalism. The joint stock company came to replace the owner-manager, and control over industry passed into the hands of the great banks. Thus the process of consolidation of ownership continued with the concentration of industry into the hands of a few banks. The results of this amalgamation of capital into the banks is that business enterprises under capitalism became more and more impersonal, with their sole objective the making of money profits regardless of any other consideration. Furthermore, the banks through their increase in power and concentration were able to buy and control the bourgeois governments for their own benefit. Patriotism and the military might of the nation became the instruments of the great financiers in Wall Street and in the City of London.

Lenin carried Hilferding's thesis further, reasoning that the trend toward financial monopoly did not end at a country's border. Having exploited the home markets extensively, the capitalists necessarily sought new and more profitable markets. Having amalgamated political and economic power in their hands, the capitalists used the state to carry out imperialist economic objectives, and an era of imperialism began. The struggle for foreign markets turned into monopoly competition between countries. After the world was divided among the capitalist states the struggle became more intense as the monopolist blocs coveted each other's territories. Inevitably the capitalist states began to fight each other. No peaceful division of the spoils was or is possible. To secure their imperialist conquests and conduct wars the capitalists needed the support of the workers in their home countries both as fighters and producers. Such support could be secured only by creating a labor aristocracy paid from the monopolistic surpluses gained from foreign exploitation. This "bribing" of the workers in the capitalist countries with imperialist profits weakened the consciousness of the workers and tended to destroy the basis of the socialist revolution in the advanced industrial countries of the world. Lenin summarized his theory as follows:

Imperialism is capitalism in that stage of development in which the dominance of monopolies and finance capital has established itself; in which the export of capital has acquired pronounced importance; in which the division of all territories of the globe among the great capitalist powers has been completed.[10]

From this analysis of the development of capitalism Lenin drew conclusions concerning the socialist revolution which had not occurred to Marx. Imperialism could account for the improvement of the conditions of the workers in the advanced industrial countries; they had been bought off by the bourgeoisie out of the profits of colonial exploitation. Consequently, because a part of the laboring classes had thus been duped by the creation of a labor aristocracy, it was not possible to count on the mass of workers acting in their own interest to overthrow capitalism. If the workers were to act in their own interest, it was necessary to develop active class consciousness among them in order to counteract the influence of the bourgeoisie, that is, of the imperialist ruling class. And the best agent for developing the class consciousness was a revolutionary elite, to be created for leadership in the revolutionary effort.

It was Lenin's view that imperialism could not continue. For imperialism, he insisted, contained within itself mutually antagonistic inevitabilities ("internal contradictions") which would lead to struggles for the spoils in imperialist wars and to the inescapable collapse of capitalism. Lenin was able to point to World War I and his successors to World War II as the first two world wars of imperialism. Each created havoc, the second more than the first, and each undermined the strength of capitalism. Thus Lenin, like Marx, believed the destruction of capitalism to be ordained; but he did not hold the successful revolt of the working masses to be predestined without a class-conscious proletariat led by a revolutionary elite. Without the leadership of this revolutionary elite, civilization could retrogress into some dark age instead of moving toward the dictatorship of the proletariat and socialism. Lenin rejected, therefore, the idea of a mass, spontaneous action. The

[10] V. I. Lenin, *Imperialism, the Highest Stage of Capitalism* (International Publishers, 1939), p. 89.

bewitching of the proletariat by the bourgeoisie had made an automatic mass revolution impossible. A successful revolution depended primarily on a well-disciplined and centralized revolutionary party—a Communist party.

The appearance of imperialism as the highest and the last stage of capitalism also broadened the base of the struggle against the bourgeoisie, according to Lenin. The proletariat of the imperialist countries became allied with the "toiling masses of the backward countries" and a revolution was no longer exclusively for the advanced industrialist countries. This meant that the battle for socialism could not be confined to a single country but had to be world-wide. By this alliance of the proletariat with the toiling masses of the colonial countries the socialist revolution acquired two separate immediate goals. In the capitalist countries it was the creation of the dictatorship of the proletariat, while in the backward countries it was initially the struggle for national self-determination within the framework of bourgeois democracy.

Lenin further concluded that with the re-enforcement of capitalism by imperialism, the revolution would not come in the most advanced country, but rather "at the weakest link"; in the country where the capitalist-imperialist position was least secure. The profits which the monopolists derived from exploiting the backward countries permitted them to seduce the workers at home and thereby strengthened the capitalist position in the advanced countries. Consequently, it was unlikely that the socialist revolution could begin in the highly developed industrial countries where the capitalist class was strongest. It rather would begin in a more backward country where the capitalist development was just emerging and where the capitalists had not yet consolidated their hold on the proletariat. Such a country was Russia. Lenin saw the victory of the Bolsheviks in 1917 as the beginning of the world revolution and the introduction of a new world socialist society.

Although Lenin's successors have elaborated on his doctrines, Lenin's theory of imperialism in particular is still very much the vital essence of the Communist creed. It serves as the basis of both Soviet action and propaganda.

The New Soviet Regime and International Relations

Lenin's theses, applied to international relations, meant that with the victory of the world revolution the bourgeois practice of international relations would come to an end along with the breakdown of state boundaries. The new form of political power replacing the outmoded bourgeois states was to be a single world state under the dictatorship of the proletariat. The dictatorship itself in time would wither away, leaving only an economy of abundance and the administrative apparatus without any coercive instruments.

The Bolsheviks after coming to power did not, however, overlook the need in the short run to have dealings with capitalist states until the world revolution should triumph. But since the laws and customs of international relations were a bourgeois concept, the new Soviet government did not feel itself bound by these rules. It felt free to accept or reject at any time the traditional patterns of international relations. Thus the Soviet Union was quite willing to enter into treaties with capitalist powers but considered them temporary and not binding on itself, since international relations were due to end shortly and since the whole code was a bourgeois concept. This attitude of suspicion toward international relations has persisted in less extreme form to the present time, and the Soviet Union continues to qualify its acceptance of the principles of international law.

The Soviet Union considered its formal diplomatic relations with the capitalist states as not only the means to carry on official business and trade between states but also the tool for the export of revolution. Consequently, Soviet embassies abroad became the centers of underground revolutionary movements seeking to overthrow the various governments in favor of the Communist dictatorship of the proletariat. The Soviet embassy in Berlin during the revolution in Germany in 1918-1919 was particularly active in helping the more revolutionary Marxists in their attempt to overthrow the kaiser and the relatively moderate Social Democratic provisional government. To use embassies and trading corporations for the purpose of espionage and as a means of helping the underground Communist movement became a traditional feature of Soviet foreign policy. This aspect of Soviet conduct has been the subject of frequent disputes between the Soviet Union and other countries.

Parallel to the diplomatic institutions, on a nongovernmental level but directly supporting the foreign policy of the Soviet Union, were the Communist Party of the USSR and other revolutionary parties abroad, which from the beginning maintained close relationships. Their alliance was formalized in 1919 by the creation of the Communist or Third International (Comintern) as the instrument of world revolution and world socialism. In pursuing these objectives the Soviet Communists used the Comintern not only in attempts to ignite revolutions in the rest of the world but also as a means to protect the Russian revolution from interference by the victorious Entente powers of the West. When the Russian section assumed absolute dominance over the Comintern in 1920 it became even more a defensive tool of Soviet foreign policy rather than a revolutionary instrument.

From the beginning the Soviet propaganda appeal was anti-imperialist. To reinforce its appeal the Soviet government exposed what it considered to be the charlatanry of the bourgeoisie by publishing all the secret treaties which the tsar had concluded with the Entente powers and which had divided up the spoils of war in contemplation of victory. At the time of publishing these, the Soviet government declared its intention never to collect on these treaties and furthermore gave up Russia's special rights in the middle and Far East. The Soviet government proclaimed an end of the tsarist policy of imperialism in Turkey, Iran, and China in favor of the doctrine of sovereign equality. This gesture, motivated by the weakness of the Soviet regime and its inability to enforce these servitudes while fighting for its own existence in a civil war, fitted the Communist doctrine of anti-imperialism. In the same way, being unable to prevent it, the Soviet government accepted the independence of the Baltic countries, of Poland, and of Finland. The opportunism of this early policy is revealed by the events since 1939, when Stalin took advantage of the situation to reassert the USSR's hegemony over its neighbors.

The 1920's

The world-wide revolutionary fever which developed at the end of World War I receded within a year. By 1924, a new era of prosperity had opened up for Europe, making the possibility of revolution extremely remote. In this thriving environment the Soviet government found itself the only surviving revolutionary regime; it was not the leader of a new world order in the age of socialism but was looked down upon as the villain among nations. The Soviet Union was in great degree ostracized from international relations. Under these circumstances, Soviet foreign policy and methods were bound to change. As early as 1920 and 1921 the Soviet Union tried to normalize its associations with the capitalist countries by concluding treaties of nonaggression and friendship. Although it did not forgo the Comintern and subversive activities as means for its protection, the declining tide of revolution made these instruments unreliable for maintaining the security of the Soviet Union against intervention by the capitalist powers. Professed willingness to abide by the traditional rules of international relations offered greater assurance. In addition, the difficult and costly years of civil war from 1918 to 1921, when various anti-Bolshevik armies attempted to destroy the Soviet regime, had left the country depleted and exhausted. Only a few of the revolutionaries were still interested in leading a crusade of world revolution against capitalism. This change became apparent with the victory of Stalin, who came to power through defeating the international revolutionary Trotsky, with the slogan, "Socialism in one country."

Peaceful Coexistence

Putting the doctrine of world revolution second to nationalism was directly contrary to the generally accepted theory of international Communism, and in order to justify this radical change a new doctrine, "the rule of ebb and flow," was developed by Stalin. This rule became the new basis for Soviet foreign policy and for the strategy of the world Communist movement. In devising this new concept, Stalin was aided by the pragmatic approach which Lenin had always taken toward Communist theory and had used from the beginning in respect to Soviet foreign policy. As his starting point Stalin used the Leninist admonishment that it is necessary to be flexible in revolutionary strategy and tactics and to co-ordinate the "subjective" conditions or preparation with the "objective" conditions creating a revolutionary situation. Stalin pointed out that the "objective" conditions, largely outside of the control of the Communists, differ from time to time. Consequently, it is foolish to talk and plan for an immediate world revolution during a period when capitalism is consolidating and entering a period of relative prosperity. At such times the problem is the danger of counter-revolution and the destruction of the socialist gains already attained. In the 1920's and 1930's this meant the danger of renewed intervention in the USSR by the western powers to overthrow the Soviet regime. Planning immediate revolution during this period would only aggravate the situation and play on the fears of the capitalists. The proper strategy, therefore, would be to continue to prepare quietly for revolution, to make no attempts to start revolutionary outbreaks, but instead to discuss peaceful coexistence on the governmental level. Such a period can be considered one of revolutionary ebb.

The Bastion of Socialism

A corollary to this stratagem of temporary peaceful coexistence with capitalists is the necessity of using this period to consolidate and strengthen the USSR as the base for future socialist conquests and world revolution. Lenin had stressed that the victory of socialism would not come by itself and needed leadership; the leadership, according to Stalin, was best supplied by the Communist International supported by the military strength of the Soviet Union. It was impossible to think seriously about spreading Communism until the Soviet Union had become a great power. Even during the period of the depression in the 1930's, when capitalism was relatively weak from widespread mass unemployment and discontent, Stalin would not permit foreign Communists to attempt the seizure of power. The Soviet Union was too weak; it was in the throes of a new social and industrial revolution and could not help. There was danger that it might itself be a victim of counterrevolutionary activities if the revolutionary coups should fail. When Hitler came to power in Germany in 1933 and preached an anti-Communist crusade as a basic principle of his foreign policy, Stalin pressed even more urgently for peaceful coexistence with the democratic states. He initiated, through the Comintern in 1935, a popular-front program looking to the co-operation of all anti-fascists against Nazism and fascism. Also he tried to strengthen international collective security by joining the League of Nations, which Lenin had originally called a league of imperialist states bent on the destruction of Communism.

Thus Stalin saw the slump of 1929-1939 as not more than a period of ripening revolutionary crisis within the capitalist system. In his view it had not yet produced the proper "subjective" or "objective" conditions necessary to reverse the period of ebb into one of aggressive world revolution. The primary emphasis was to save the Soviet Union from the Nazi menace.

Stalin felt that the outcome of World War II made possible a new vigorous period of flow for the socialist revolution. World War II, the so-called great patriotic war in defense of the socialist fatherland, was in 1946 partially reinterpreted by the Communists as an imperialist war developing out of the internal contradictions in the capitalist system which result in the capitalist states fighting among themselves over the colonial spoils and weakening their economic and political systems. From about the middle of World War II until at least the time of Stalin's death, the Communists considered the "objective" conditions propitious for the spreading of Communism; but because the Soviet Union was involved itself in the war and was badly devastated, the "subjective" conditions were not immediately suitable for extensive Communist aggression.

SELECTED BIBLIOGRAPHY[11]

Those students wishing to delve deeper into affairs Soviet will find that in the post World War II period there has been a

[11] Prepared by Nancy G. Cattell.

veritable flood of new works on the Soviet Union, many of them important, scholarly and extremely necessary to a further understanding of this complex area. Only works in English have been cited below (except for a few books on International Law), since Russian-language works are not always available and the language itself is a barrier for most students. Needless to say, many worthy books have not been included since it would be impossible to list them all. An attempt has been made to enumerate here only generally accepted studies where a number exist covering the same or similar topics. In order to let the Soviets speak for themselves, books by Russian Communists are listed and it is hoped students will use these too, as without them one loses the real "flavor" of the subject.

Many current subjects are covered from time to time in various periodicals. Most of these articles are limited to narrowly specific subjects and constantly being augmented, so it appeared of more value to confine references to full-length studies.

Since the following bibliography is by no means complete, it is suggested some of the works below be consulted by those wishing to make more penetrating studies: American Friends' Service Committee, Committee on Russian-American Relations, *Suggestions for Reading and Study in Connection with the United States and the Soviet Union: Some Quaker Proposals for Peace* (Philadelphia, 1949); Alexander Dallin, *The German Occupation of the USSR in World War II: a Bibliography* (Washington, 1955); Division of Library and Reference Service, Department of State, *Soviet Bibliography* (A Fortnightly) [ceased publication in June 1953] (Washington); Philip Grierson, *Books on Soviet Russia, 1917-1942* (London, 1943); William Mandel, *Soviet Source Materials on USSR Relations with East Asia, 1945-1950* (New York, 1950); Nikolai N. Martianov, *Books Available in English by Russians and on Russia Published in the United States* (6th ed., New York, 1950); Harry Schwartz, *The Soviet Economy: a Selected Bibliography of Materials in English* (Syracuse, 1949); Jirina Sztachova, *Mid-Europe; a Selective Bibliography* (New York, 1953); United States National Archives, *Descriptive Guide to USSR-Related Records, 1918-1945, among the Collections of the*

National Archives (Washington, 1952); United States Library of Congress, *Monthly List of Russian Accessions* (Washington); United States Library of Congress, General Reference and Bibliography Division, *Guide to Soviet Bibliographies: a Selected List of References*, compiled by John T. Dorosh (Washington, 1950); United States Library of Congress, Reference Department, *Serial Publications of the Soviet Union, 1939-1951: a Preliminary Checklist* (Washington, 1951); United States Library of Congress, *Russia: a Check List Preliminary to a Basic Bibliography of Materials in the Russian Language* (Washington, 1945).

PRIMARY SOURCES AND GOVERNMENT PUBLICATIONS

Soviet theory and comments on political events are both available in the works of Lenin and Stalin and there are convenient collections in English. The contents of the numerous editions of Lenin's and Stalin's works in many languages varied with certain political changes, particularly after 1936, so caution and diligence must be exercised if the complete picture of any situation is to be ascertained. For V. I. Lenin a generally adequate collection is presented in *Selected Works* (London, 1936-1938), 12 vols. For J. V. Stalin, *Collected Works* (Moscow, 1953-1954), 8 vols. In addition Stalin's speeches and writings signaling such important changes as liquidation of the kulaks, liquidation of opposition to his regime and his comments on the new Soviet constitution, as well as his analyses of political situations abroad are contained in the single volume, *Leninism: Selected Writings* (New York, 1942).

For the war and post-war period Andrew Rothstein has a collection of translations under the title *Soviet Foreign Policy During the Patriotic War: Documents and Materials* (London, n.d.), 2 vols., and V. M. Molotov covers the immediate period following this in *Problems of Foreign Policy: Speeches and Statements, April 1945-November 1948* (Moscow, 1949).

Articles on current topics and some documents, such as constitutions and their changes in Soviet satellite countries and reports of international organizations, may be found in the Soviet journals *New Times* (Moscow), *International Affairs*

(Moscow), and the Cominform publication *For a lasting peace, for a people's democracy!* (Bucharest) [ceased publication in 1956].

The United States official view of Soviet Affairs is contained in the Department of State volumes *Foreign Relations of the United States; Russia 1918* (3 vols.), *Russia 1919, The Soviet Union 1933-1939* (Washington, 1931-1932, 1937, 1952).

Another United States government publication containing much primary material on theory and Soviet methods of operation is 84th Congress, 2nd Session, House Report No. 2241, *The Communist Conspiracy: Strategy and Tactics of World Communism, Part I—Communism Outside the United States,* Sections A-E (Washington, 1956).

A very useful chronological and subject guide to documents, newspaper articles and speeches is Jane Degras' *Calendar of Soviet Documents on Foreign Policy, 1917-1941* (London, 1948). Many of these materials are translated in her later works *Soviet Documents on Foreign Policy,* vols. I-III (London, 1951-1953).

The early period of the Communist International is quite thoroughly covered in Jane Degras' *The Communist International: Documents, 1919-1943,* vol. I (London, 1956). Other volumes for the later period are in progress.

Soviet treaties are conveniently gathered together and translated in Leonard Shapiro's *Soviet Treaty Series,* vol. I, 1917-1928; vol. II, 1929-1939 (Washington, 1950, 1955).

For translations from Russian newspapers aimed at researchers and analysts an indispensable publication issued weekly since 1949 is the *Current Digest of the Soviet Press* (New York).

NATURAL RESOURCES AND INDUSTRIAL PRODUCTION

On geography: S. S. Balzak et al., *Economic Geography of the USSR* (New York, 1949); L. S. Berg, *Natural Regions of the USSR* (New York, 1950); Theodore Shabad, *Geography of the USSR* (New York, 1951).

On Natural Resources: Heinrich Hassmann, *Oil in the Soviet Union* (Princeton, 1953); Dimitri Shimkin, *Minerals: a Key to Soviet Power* (Cambridge, 1952).

On Population: George B. Cressey, *How Strong Is Russia?*

(Syracuse, 1954); Basilius Martscheka, *Soviet Population Trends, 1926-1939* (New York, 1953).

On Industry: Abram Bergson (ed.), *Soviet Economic Growth: Conditions and Perspectives* (New York, 1951); Abram Bergson and Hans Heymann, Jr., *Soviet National Income and Product, 1940-1948* (New York, 1954); Nicholas De Witt, *Soviet Professional Manpower, Its Education, Training and Supply* (Washington, 1955); W. Galenson, *Labor Productivity in Soviet and American Industry* (New York, 1955); Donald R. Hodgman, *Soviet Industrial Production, 1928-1951* (Cambridge, 1954); Harry Schwartz, *Russia's Soviet Economy* (2nd ed., New York, 1954); Solomon M. Schwarz, *Labor in the Soviet Union* (New York, 1951).

Agriculture

Fedor Belov, *The History of a Soviet Collective Farm* (New York, 1955); Naum Jasny, *The Socialized Agriculture of the USSR: Plans and Performance* (Stanford, 1949); and the chapters on agriculture in Harry Schwartz, *Russia's Soviet Economy* (2nd ed., New York, 1954).

Military Forces

Harold J. Berman and Miroslav Kerner, *Soviet Military Law and and Administration* (Cambridge, 1955); Col. Louis B. Ely, *The Red Army Today* (Harrisburg, 1953); Raymond L. Garthoff, *Soviet Military Doctrine* (Glencoe, Illinois, 1954); B. H. Liddell Hart, ed., *The Red Army* (New York, 1956); Asher Lee, *The Soviet Airforce* (London, 1952).

National Character and Soviet Foreign Policy

On this complex subject it is difficult to select three or four books only. The following are listed from among many possibilities as they cover a wide range of views both as to subject matter and conclusions. All are provocative studies although their theories are often criticized and by no means universally accepted. Raymond A. Bauer, *Nine Soviet Portraits* (New York, 1955); Raymond Bauer, Alex Inkeles, Clyde Kluckhohn, *How the Soviet System Works* (Cambridge, 1956); Zbigniew K. Brzezinski, *The Per-*

manent *Purge* (Cambridge, 1956); Geoffrey Gorer and John
Rickman, *The People of Great Russia: a Psychological Study*
(New York, 1950); A. Inkeles, *Social Change in Soviet Russia*
(Maxwell Air Force Base, Alabama, 1952); Hans Kohn, ed.,
The Mind of Modern Russia (New Brunswick, 1955); Nathan
Leites, *A Study of Bolshevism* (Glencoe, Illinois, 1953); Mar-
garet Mead, *Soviet Attitudes Toward Authority* (New York,
1951); Barrington Moore, Jr., *Soviet Politics, the Dilemma of
Power, The Role of Ideas in Social Change* (Cambridge, 1950);
Barrington Moore, Jr., *Terror and Progress USSR: Some Sources
of Change and Stability in the Soviet Dictatorship* (Cambridge,
1955); Gerhart Niemeyer with assistance of John S. Reshetar, Jr.,
An Inquiry into Soviet Rationality (New York, 1956); John S.
Reshetar, Jr., *Problems of Analyzing and Predicting Soviet Be-
havior* (Garden City, 1955); W. W. Rostow in collaboration with
Alfred Levin, *The Dynamics of Soviet Society* (New York, 1954);
Ernest J. Simmons, ed., *Continuity and Change in Russian and
Soviet Thought* (Cambridge, 1955); Ernest J. Simmons, ed.,
Through the Glass of Soviet Literature: Views of Russian Society
(New York, 1953); Dinko Tomasic, *The Impact of Russian Cul-
ture on Soviet Communism* (Glencoe, Illinois, 1953).

HISTORICAL FACTORS: TSARIST AND SOVIET

Histories of Russia: Sir John Maynard, *Russia in Flux* (New
York, 1948); Anatole G. Mazour, *Russia Past and Present* (New
York, 1951); Sir Bernard Pares, *A History of Russia* (5th ed.,
New York, 1947); Hugh Seton-Watson, *The Decline of Imperial
Russia, 1855-1914* (London, 1952); George von Rauch, *A History
of Bolshevik Russia* (New York, 1954); E. H. Carr, *A History of
Soviet Russia* (New York, 1950-1954), 4 vols.

Foreign Policy: Three standard works covering the period from
the inception of the Soviet Union up to 1941 and Soviet foreign
policy are James Bunyan, ed., *Intervention, Civil War and Communism in Russia, 1918* (Stanford, 1936); Louis Fischer, *The
Soviets in World Affairs; a History of the Relations between the
Soviet Union and the Rest of the World, 1917-1929* (Princeton,

1951); Max Beloff, *The Foreign Policy of the Soviet Union, 1929-1941* (New York, 1947, 1949), 2 vols.

Books dealing with broader aspects of foreign policy, Soviet viewpoints or special topics of this area are W. P. and Z. Coates, *World Affairs and the USSR* (London, 1939); Committee on Un-American Activities, U.S. House of Representatives, *Soviet Total War*, 2 vols. (Washington, D.C., 1956); *Falsifiers of History (Historical Survey)* (Moscow, 1951); George F. Kennan, *Soviet-American Relations, 1917-1920*, vol. I, *Russia Leaves the War* (Princeton, 1956); Robert J. Kerner, *The Urge to the Sea* (Berkeley, 1942); M. M. Litvinov, *Against Aggression* (London, 1939); M. Ross, *A History of Soviet Foreign Policy* (New York, 1940); Frederick L. Schuman, *Soviet Politics at Home and Abroad* (New York, 1946).

COMMUNIST IDEOLOGY AND INTERNATIONAL RELATIONS

Soviet Works: A Commission of the Central Committee of the CPSU(B), eds., *History of the Communist Party of the Soviet Union (Bolsheviks), Short Course* (New York, 1939); V. I. Lenin, *Imperialism, the Highest Stage of Capitalism* (New York, 1939); V. I. Lenin et al., *Soviet Legal Philosophy* (Cambridge, 1951); V. I. Lenin, *State and Revolution* (New York, 1932); Joseph Stalin, *Leninism: Selected Writings* (New York, 1942); Joseph Stalin, *Foundations of Leninism* (New York, 1939); Andrei Y. Vyshinsky, *Law of the Soviet State* (New York, 1949).

Critiques of Communist Theory: 84th Congress, 2nd Session, House Report No. 2241, *The Communist Conspiracy: Strategy and Tactics of World Communism*, Part I—*Communism Outside the United States*, Section A: *Marxist Classics* (Washington, 1956); R. N. Carew Hunt, *Marxism, Past and Present* (London, 1954); R. N. Carew Hunt, *The Theory and Practice of Communism* (New York, 1951); Hans Kelsen, *The Political Theory of Bolshevism, a Critical Analysis* (Berkeley, 1948); John Petrov Plamenatz, *German Marxism and Russian Communism* (New York, 1945); Rudolf Schlesinger, *The Spirit of Post-War Russia: Soviet Ideology 1917-1946* (London, 1947).

CHAPTER 19

FORMULATION OF FOREIGN POLICY IN THE USSR

It is an established practice of the chancelleries of the world to hide as much as possible of their policy-making processes, in order to maintain a façade of unity and in order to conceal their sources of information, their techniques, and their final decisions before their actual execution. This is the practice even in democratic countries. But in the latter states the instruments for formulating foreign policy are usually defined by law and are well known. In the free give-and-take of debate over foreign policy and in the subsequent memoirs of the participants much of the actual process of decision-making is exhibited for scholars to study.

In the Soviet Union the efforts to conceal the techniques and results of policy formulation go much farther. Here even the instruments for making policy are hidden behind a deceiving democratic façade. The Presidium of the Party is known to be the central focus for decisions, but, except for its personnel, little else is known about this body. There is no free public debate over foreign policies, and when the "line" has been set a strict adherence to it is maintained by all discussants. Furthermore, none of the Soviet leaders since Stalin's domination of the Soviet apparatus has written any memoirs that provide an insight into the inner workings of the government and Party.[1] Consequently the story of

[1] The alleged memoirs of Maxim Litvinov, Commissar of Foreign Affairs during the 1930's, have been dismissed by most scholars as a fake.

policy formulation in the USSR must be pieced together from scraps of evidence and must be presented as a hypothesis rather than as a documented body of information.

The Structure

The Supreme Soviet

To the outside world the Soviet Union attempts to present a hierarchy of foreign policy-making institutions that parallels, in most respects, that of a democratic country. The Communists, of course, pride themselves that their institutions are basically different because they are "truly democratic" and are not designed, as are those in capitalist countries, to conceal from the masses the fact that the real rulers are the capitalists. In its theoretically sovereign capacity it is the Supreme Soviet, the two-house representative assembly, which has the right to make the ultimate decisions on foreign policy at any stage or in any form it wishes. In fact, the Supreme Soviet, which usually meets only once or twice a year for two weeks, hears a report on foreign policy by the minister of foreign affairs. There follows no more than a perfunctory debate in praise of the report, then its unanimous adoption. Although each chamber of the Supreme Soviet has a permanent committee on foreign affairs, which "considers" the minister's report and urges its approval, it is obvious that in practice the Supreme Soviet was never intended to control foreign relations; the foreign-policy report merely furnishes an occasion for the leaders to announce a new propaganda line or re-emphasize an old one. The Supreme Soviet has, however, been employed extensively by the post-Stalin leaders to publicize foreign policy. In 1955 the Supreme Soviet was convened twice for this purpose— in the summer to hear reports after the Four-Power Conference of heads of state at Geneva, and in the late fall after the trip of Party Secretary Nikita Khrushchev and Premier Nikolai Bulganin to Burma, India, and Pakistan.

The Presidium of the Supreme Soviet

According to the Stalin constitution of 1936, the Presidium of the Supreme Soviet carries on the work of its parent body (the

Supreme Soviet) when the latter is not in session. In respect to foreign policy, the constitution says that the Presidium

k. Institutes military titles, diplomatic ranks, and other special titles; . . .
m. In the intervals between sessions of the Supreme Soviet of the USSR proclaims a state of war in the event of military attack on the USSR, or when necessary to fulfill international treaty obligations concerning mutual defense against aggression;
n. Orders general or partial mobilization;
o. Ratifies and denounces international treaties of the USSR;
p. Appoints and recalls plenipotentiary representatives of the USSR to foreign states;
q. Receives the letters of credence and recall of diplomatic representatives accredited to it by foreign states.

The Presidium does in fact formally perform these duties; and for diplomatic functions it acts, usually in the person of its chairman, as the head of the state, receiving ambassadors, and issuing credentials for Soviet diplomatic representatives. In such matters as ratifying or denouncing treaties it is reported to act in conjunction with the two committees on foreign affairs of the Supreme Soviet. But it would appear that, like the Supreme Soviet, it does nothing on its own initiative.

The Council of Ministers

In foreign affairs the role of the Council of Ministers is theoretically to define alternative policies before they are debated and ratified by higher bodies, to make the less important decisions, and to initiate the execution of the policies. Because the operation of the Council of Ministers is obscure, a detailed account of its actual role is difficult. Certain observations, however, can be made. It is clear that the Council of Ministers does not prepare policies for ratification by the Supreme Soviet or its Presidium except for propaganda purposes. Whether or when it prepares them for deliberation by some other body is less clear. Furthermore, it is doubtful that the Council of Ministers meets as a whole and deliberates, since it is composed of more than fifty members of different political status. The deliberating process is provided for by two inner bodies: a steering committee of fourteen composed of the premier, first deputy premiers, and deputy premiers, and a still smaller executive committee (sometimes referred to as the Presidium of the Council of Ministers) composed of the premier and first deputy premiers. The composition of these committees, and particularly of the Presidium, makes it reasonable to assume that they play a very significant role in policy-making. Bulganin, Molotov, Kaganovich, Mikoyan, Malenkov, Saburov, and Pervukhin are among the present members of both committees. These men are also in the Presidium of the Party and are acknowledged leaders of the Soviet Union. The absence, however, of certain party leaders in these committees, most notably of Khrushchev, makes it questionable whether the basic policies on foreign affairs are determined here. As will be discussed in the next few pages, the Communist Party has always considered itself the leading initiator of all governmental schemes and plans, including foreign policy. Furthermore, Khrushchev, since his ascent to the position of the first secretary of the party, has obviously played an intimate role in the making and execution of foreign-policy decisions, often crowding out Bulganin, premier and acting head of the state.

In sum, it appears that the Council of Ministers, and more particularly its steering and executive committees, perform a preparatory and evaluation role very much like those of the National Security Council and Cabinet in the United States. And, like the latter institutions, the Council of Ministers is not the only organ in the USSR preparing material on which foreign-policy decisions are based.

The Party Presidium

The body in which focuses decision-making of every nature in the USSR is not a governmental organ but is rather the Presidium of the Central Committee of the Communist Party. It is the true sovereign of the Soviet Union, answerable to no one; and, as such, it wields and shares with no other body a concentration of powers to make and enforce decisions. Although it is a Party body made up exclusively of top Communists, its composition is also representative of the government, of the army, indirectly of the trade unions, and formerly of the secret police, because most of its members hold dual functions in the Party and in the government. In this way it brings all the political, economic, and coercive forces under the supreme control of the Party. The Communists have never denied that it is primarily the Party's task to issue the leading directives to the government; for the Party is the vanguard of the socialist masses and of their agent, the Soviet government. The role of the Party in respect to foreign matters was established at the beginning. Lenin considered the "fusion of Soviets and Party" in respect to international relations absolutely essential. As a result the agenda of the Politbureau, now the Presidium, has always been filled with problems of foreign policy. Furthermore, international politics has always received important consideration at the Party Congresses and at meetings of the Central Committee. For example, at the Nineteenth and Twentieth Party Congresses in 1952 and 1956 respectively, the main reports of the Central Committee, delivered by Malenkov and Khrushchev, considered in detail the international situation. There is no evidence that the Soviet leaders at any time have considered altering this basic direction of foreign policy by Party organs. Theoretically the Party's directives to the government are issued by the Central Committee, which is the highest representative organ of the Party (except for the Party Congresses which meet infrequently). Actually, the Central Committee articulates the orders of the real leaders who are in its Presidium. Recently it has been rumored, however, that the Central Committee is returning to the position of arbitrator which it held when Lenin dominated the Party.

The information and reports on foreign policy, upon which the Party Presidium acts, come from several sources. The inner committees of the Council of Ministers have already been mentioned as bodies for preliminary planning. It is not improbable that the foreign minister (in 1956 Dimitri Shepilov) also submits directly to the Presidium problems formulated by the staff in the Ministry of Foreign Affairs. Indeed, Foreign Minister Shepilov was made an alternate member of the Presidium. Still other channels are the

Foreign Branch of the Central Committee of the Party, the secret police, the army, the Cominform (until it was "disbanded" in 1956), and the Ministry of Foreign Trade (through its minister, Anastas Mikoyan, who is also a member of the Party Presidium). All these organs deal in one way or another with foreign affairs, as will be discussed later.

It has been assumed that, in order to handle the numerous and varied problems brought before it, the Presidium allows its sub-committee or expert in a given field frequently to dispose of a matter directly without reference to the full Presidium. At one time Molotov was considered the expert in foreign affairs for political matters, while in economic matters Mikoyan was the specialist.

How much free discussion takes place when the Presidium itself considers a question cannot be known. Khrushchev has reported that Stalin terrorized the members of the Presidium, much as he did the whole country, and consequently that the members were afraid to speak freely. Indeed, from Khrushchev's statement it would appear that the Presidium rarely met as a body. Stalin handled it in subgroups of three, four, and five and always kept for himself the final and definitive word. Although the reporting of Khrushchev may be exaggerated and defensive, it is abundantly clear from Stalin's actions at Teheran, Yalta, and Potsdam, and from his dealings with foreign diplomats in respect to foreign policy, that he made the final decision and could change the decision without reference to anyone else. No other person dealing in foreign affairs, not even Molotov and Mikoyan, could make such snap judgments. Western diplomats learned that, except for Stalin, there never existed a plenipotentiary representative from the Soviet Union. In negotiations it was unwise to push the Soviet representative for a decision until he had time to refer the matter back to Moscow. The situation after Stalin's death was less clear. The new regime claimed to be a collective leadership, and there were indications that in the beginning no one was strong enough to make foreign-policy decisions alone. Khrushchev's spontaneous remarks and declarations were perhaps an indication that he felt sure enough of his power to make quick decisions on foreign policy without the sanction of colleagues. This casualness, however, may have been more apparent than real.

Thus it is possible to say with some finality that the ultimate decision-making in respect to foreign policy resides in the Presidium of the Party, the real focus of power in Russia. The governmental organizations contribute to this decision-making role to the extent that their officers are also members of the Presidium— as are Premier Bulganin and Foreign Minister Shepilov—and to the extent that they supply needed information upon which the decisions are based.

Contact with the Outside World

The success of any process of policy formulation depends not only on an efficient top machinery with power to act, but equally upon the sources of information and the means of execution. Both Stalin, who kept himself a recluse from the world outside the USSR, and his successor group of Soviet chiefs, who for the most part are new participants in the field of international relations, had and have a particular need for adequate and reliable sources of information on world politics.

The Ministry of Foreign Affairs

The Soviet leaders have several channels for securing information from outside the Soviet bloc. The Ministry of Foreign Affairs serves in this capacity much in the same manner as comparable ministries in the West. The Ministry, however, has never acknowledged its similarity to the foreign offices of the West and in two matters on the surface has differed from the western pattern. Seeing itself as a dictatorship of the proletariat moving toward equality and socialism, the Soviet Union refused initially to adhere to the protocols of the Congress of Vienna of 1815 in respect to the status of embassies and diplomatic ranks—even though these protocols were followed by most of the other states of the world. The refusal of the Soviet Union to give its diplomats a designated status turned to its disadvantage because its rankless representatives were always put at the bottom of any list of protocol. The disadvantage forced the USSR to adopt titles and in 1943 to establish a full set of ranks (with uniforms for its diplomats), bringing its embassies into line with those of the West. In 1944 the Soviet Union inaugurated another innovation by turning the Ministry of Foreign Affairs into a union-republican ministry, which meant in theory that each of the separate republics of the USSR could have its own foreign minister and its representatives abroad, and could sign separate treaties with other countries.[2] This modification, however, was largely a political maneuver to increase Soviet representation in international conferences and bodies. The Russians had always claimed the British were overrepresented by the presence of separate delegations from the Dominions, and accordingly they sought to match the British Commonwealth by this new artifice. A compromise was ultimately worked out for the United Nations by which only the Ukrainian and Byelorussian republics were allowed separate delegations. In spite of the great fanfare heralding this constitutional change, which allegedly gave further expression to the sovereignty of the separate Soviet Republics, it was only a front. The Ukraine and Byelorussia do have separate delegations in the United Nations and representatives in some of the satellites. Their foreign ministries, however, have only small offices in Kiev and Minsk and their diplomats clearly take their orders from the main office in Moscow. This direction from the center is not even denied by the Soviet authorities. The other republics do not appear to have even these token ministries.

The Foreign Ministry in Moscow is subdivided into geographical, functional, and administrative sections. Like the United States Department of State, the Ministry has subdivisions dealing with Western Europe, Scandinavia, Central Europe, Middle East, Far East; legal, economic, consular and political matters; and personnel, finance, training and security problems. In addition the Ministry of Foreign Affairs operates the Moscow State Institute of Inter-

[2] A similar situation existed in Germany from 1871 to 1918, when separate entities of the German empire, like Bavaria, had diplomatic representation abroad.

national Relations, with a permanent faculty, as a training school for future Soviet diplomats.

Since the beginning of the 1930's the Soviet Union has had embassies in the leading capitals of the world. Also on a reciprocal basis, Soviet consuls are found in some of the leading cities abroad. But since the Soviet Union has few citizens outside the country, the main job of the Soviet consuls is political and economic reporting. In the Soviet embassies themselves, the collection of data is done through the usual military, political, and cultural sections with their attachés—all under the official direction of the ambassador.

The Ministry of Foreign Trade

Economic contacts with the outside world are in the province of the Ministry of Foreign Trade. It negotiates trade agreements with foreign nations, prepares the foreign-trade plans, arranges for credits, supervises all Soviet export and import agencies abroad, and directs the trading corporations within the Soviet Union. The Soviet government has sought as a matter of law to have its trade delegations in foreign countries accepted as an integral part of the Soviet embassies with diplomatic status. The purpose of the trade delegation is to act as the agent for the export-import corporations in the Soviet Union, to make market surveys, and to keep close watch on the economic conditions of the country. Neither the trade delegation nor the Ministry of Foreign Trade itself signs the contracts or carries on the actual trade. These activities are conducted by a group of specialized Soviet import-export corporations with their own economic accountability in the Soviet Union, and these are subject to suit in a court of law.

Some countries, especially the United States, have consistently refused to recognize the diplomatic status of the Soviet trade delegations. As a result, the Soviet Union has been forced to conduct its trade in the United States through the Amtorg Trading Corporation, owned by the Bank for Foreign Trade in Moscow but incorporated under the laws of New York State and subject to the usual liabilities of a commercial enterprise. In respect to the collection of economic information, Amtorg performs the same function as a trade delegation.

The Armed Forces

The military forces also have certain limited contact abroad. Soviet military attachés are found in the Soviet embassies throughout the world. Recently, military technicians from the Soviet bloc have moved into Afghanistan and Egypt and may in time move into other areas of the Middle East and South East Asia. Before World War II they were active in Spain during the Spanish Civil War and to a lesser extent in China during the war against Japan. In Germany and Austria, for a long time after the war, it was the Soviet military which conducted the day-to-day relations with the West. Traditionally, however, the Soviet military plays a distinctly subordinate role in collecting foreign information, making policy, and executing decisions. It is much more significant in co-ordinating the policies within the Soviet bloc, particularly through the Warsaw Pact of 1954. Since Stalin's death, the role of the army in Soviet leadership may be growing. One can assess Marshal Zhukov's presence at the 1955 summit conference in Geneva as signifying army influence or as an attempt to make advantage out of Zhukov's friendly personal relations with President Eisenhower.

TASS

The Soviet government's news agency TASS is largely responsible for disseminating special news items from the Soviet Union, for collecting news stories for Soviet publications, and for extensive reporting of comments from the foreign press. Undoubtedly TASS reports from abroad influence Soviet policy-makers in somewhat the same way that the New York Times and similar papers influence the policy personnel of the State Department in the United States. TASS communiqués, for example, are frequently quoted by Soviet negotiators. From the evidence of defectors from the Soviet Union, the TASS agencies abroad are also used as a "cover" for part of the Soviet espionage system with a large number of the employees serving a dual role.

The Secret Police

One of the most important organs in the government for collecting information—even though its activities are conducted *sub rosa*—is the secret police, formerly headed by Beria and after his downfall transferred to the administrative control of the State Security Committee. Working closely with the Communist parties in the various countries as well as with the official Soviet delegations abroad, the old Ministry of State Security set up an elaborate intelligence and espionage system, capable at times of penetrating deep into the innermost circles of the governments of the West. The importance of this branch of the government in foreign policy is seen from the fact that in the past the chief agent of the secret police operating through the Soviet embassy in a given country was often the real head of the embassy, giving orders even to the ambassador. For example, in Spain during the Civil War, the secret-police representative Orlov is alleged to have given all the orders. He dominated and controlled not only the Soviet embassy and the Soviet military personnel sent to Spain but also the Communist Party of Spain and all foreign Communists, including the International Brigade. He even took into his own hands the execution of measures against the enemies of Stalin in Spain.[3] Although this was an extreme case, the reports of defectors acquainted with Soviet foreign relations confirm the predominant role of the secret police in the past. Its position at the present time is not quite so clear. The purge of Beria and his subordinates beginning in July 1953 and the stripping from the secret police of many of its functions and single head would appear to put the Committee of State Security in a distinctly subordinate position in respect to foreign as well as domestic policy. Nevertheless its intelligence and espionage organizations undoubtedly continue to work and to collect valuable information.

International Communism

Outside and above the government, the Party organization is

[3] David T. Cattell, *Communism and the Spanish Civil War*, University of California Press, Berkeley and Los Angeles, 1955, pp. 74-75, 116-119, 133-135.

also in the foreign field. The Party maintains its own channels to the outside world through its agents and through legal and underground Communist parties in most countries of the world. The character of Communist parties as basic tools of Soviet foreign policy was established early. Lenin's pattern for organizing parties in Russia and elsewhere was to create an elite and tightly disciplined corps of revolutionaries. Absolute obedience was expected of members to orders from above, especially to directives issued by the Central Executive Committee of the Communist International (Comintern), which from the beginning was under the control of the Russian Communist Party. The Soviet leaders never have relaxed their authority over foreign Communists. Even though the Comintern was "disbanded" officially in 1943 in order to accommodate the sensibilities of the allies in World War II, it is now clear that the organization was in fact not dissolved but continued to operate and was restored to public life as the Cominform in September 1947. The Cominform was in turn publicly "dissolved" in June 1956; but in the long run this move, like its 1943 analog, probably will not change the fundamentally close-knit organization of international Communism, however much some of the national parties press for more independence.

One of the many services performed by members of foreign Communist parties on behalf of the Soviet Union is the collection of intelligence information. The leaders of these parties make occasional visits to Moscow not only to receive new orders but also to report on their activities and on conditions at home.

Information Bias

In spite of this elaborate system of reporting there are several factors which prevent the Soviet leaders from receiving accurate information. The traditional isolation of the Russian people has been reinforced by the Soviet dictatorship so that there is a minimum of contact with the outside world. While the post-Stalin Soviet leadership has been much more liberal concerning exchanges with the West, contacts have continued to be limited and controlled. Few Soviet citizens outside a small special group are allowed to travel abroad, and only a limited number of people have access to newspapers and books published abroad. At all levels of Soviet society, consequently, there is a general lack of knowledge and understanding of the real facts of the outside world.

Information received by the Soviet government is reported and interpreted through the prism of Communist ideology. The viewpoint of Marxian dialectics and of the inevitable contradictory forces in capitalism which are bringing about its decay is the only "truth" which is admitted. When Eugene Varga, a foremost Soviet economist, ventured to predict a new growth and consolidation of capitalism following World War II, he lost favor and was demoted. Thus, a report which is displeasing to the leaders because it does not conform to their own notions has serious consequences for the Soviet analyst. This condition further tends to distort information, because the Soviet agent over and above his Communist bias is likely to report back to his leaders only those things which he thinks the leaders want to hear. From the conversations of westerners with Soviet leaders and negotiators and from a reading of the Soviet press, it is clear that, in order to find a view which satisfies the current Soviet line, Soviet analysts are often forced to overlook predominant facts in favor of obscure items found in local foreign newspapers. An outbreak of violence, race discrimination, depression in a local area, or a small disagreement between the western allies is given national and international importance even to the point of predicting mass violence. This doctrinaire prepossession is particularly strong in respect to political matters. The influence is less prevalent in intelligence reports on military, scientific, and economic matters; in these, Soviet information excels. For example, during the period of lend-lease in World War II, Soviet negotiators revealed their comprehensive knowledge of the United States economy and often knew better than the War Production Board where in the United States some scarce item could be secured. Soviet success in securing atomic secrets is another case in point.

Such double distortion—the underlying bias of the political information on which foreign policy is formulated in the Soviet Union, plus the natural Communist bias of the policy formulators themselves—has created serious shortcomings in the Soviet scheme to spread Communist hegemony. These will be set forth in the discussion of Soviet relations with the West in the next chapter. The post-Stalin leaders in Russia are conscious of this deficiency. While they have not given up their ideological bias, they are willing to recognize and accept facts even though they may not fit into a preconceived Marxian dialectical pattern. Khrushchev has repeatedly cautioned against rejecting western advances and deprecating the strength of the West. Furthermore, Khrushchev and Bulganin are traveling abroad to observe for themselves. But while they take advantage of western methods and face the realities of western strength, the leaders persist in maintaining a rigorous competition with the West and a belief in the over-all superiority of the Soviet system. Because of long-developed habits, continued Marxian predilection, difficulties in administering the new line so as not to be accused of being pro-Western, and fear of a subsequent return to rigid isolationism, it is not likely that the new leaders are going to find an easy remedy to the problem of biased and distorted information transmitted by their agents abroad.

Execution of Policy

Diplomacy

The widespread and intricate system for the collection of information and for the analysis of international affairs, described above, is also available for the execution of foreign policy. Soviet diplomatic representatives in the United Nations and the capitals of the world respond instantly to changes in Soviet foreign policy. When it is peaceful coexistence they smile, mix, and talk freely with other diplomats. Their statements are phrased in polite terms and, if the policy dictates, they may give especially lavish attention to certain diplomats. In periods of hostility Soviet diplomats scowl and harangue in vitriolic terms. Taking the cue from their Soviet colleagues, the diplomats from the satellite countries fall into line and echo their Communist "big brothers."[3a]

[3a] Poland, having achieved a state of semi-independence from the Soviet Union in the fall of 1956, for the first time intentionally refused to follow the dictates of Moscow on voting in the United Nations. On November 5, 1956, while the USSR and its other satellites voted against the resolution in the General Assembly calling upon Hungary to admit United Nations observers, Poland abstained.

Trade treaties are negotiated usually with political purposes in mind. The Ministry of Foreign Trade, in response to the policy demands of the Soviet leaders for autarchy, generally restricts East-West trade to a minimum, but at the same time it makes attractive, well publicized offers to countries in the Middle East and elsewhere for propaganda purposes. At the meetings of the economic commissions of the United Nations, the Soviet trade delegations paint an attractive picture of possible Soviet trade to market-hungry western exporters, if only the strategic trade embargo against the Soviet bloc were relaxed. Within the Soviet bloc the Ministry of Foreign Trade integrates and brings under control the economies of the satellites.

Propaganda

The propaganda line is disseminated with the same dispatch and thoroughness. TASS handles the official and special news dispatches from the Soviet Union. The government censor handles the material sent out of the Soviet Union by foreign correspondents, permitting reports on the affable or hostile attitude of the Soviet leaders at cocktail parties according to whether such information is convenient to Soviet relations with the West. The World Peace Committee in Prague holds conferences and congresses and issues propaganda in order to convince world public opinion that the USSR is the leader for peace. Until 1956 there was the Cominform in Bucharest with its organ, *For a Lasting Peace, For a People's Democracy*, which guided the propaganda line to be supported by the foreign sections of the Communist movement. The Communist parties of the world, as well-disciplined cadres, have seldom deviated for long from a strict adherence to this line.

Foreign Communists

The Communist parties throughout the world are not only in the forefront as instruments for propaganda on behalf of Soviet foreign policy, but their domestic actions and reactions also follow closely the Soviet needs. Thus when Stalin still wanted to maintain at least the fiction of the grand alliance immediately after World War II, the Communist parties of France and Italy co-

operated with their bourgeois governments in bringing about a
rapid and democratic recovery from the devastation of war. But
when Stalin no longer felt the need of pretense and wanted to
destroy the Marshall Plan and NATO, the Italian and French
Communists tried to sabotage the plan and the defense efforts of
the West by strikes, espionage, obstruction, and derisive tactics
in parliaments. When domestic resources are lacking to carry on
the activities of the foreign Communist groups the Soviet Union
liberally helps in the financing. In the case of Italy the Communists have been benefited by sharing in the profits of Soviet
trade with that country. In most cases, however, money is trans-
ported through the diplomatic pouch of the Soviet embassy, protected from the snooping of customs and police agents.

The native Communist following abroad also serves as a source
of recruitment for the world-wide spy network of the secret police.

The absolute obedience, long associated with the Communist
movement, has been challenged recently by some of the foreign
Communist leaders. Several factors have encouraged them to pursue this course: the dissolution of the Cominform, the almost
complete repudiation of Stalin, the success of Tito in being accepted back into the fold in spite of following his own path to
socialism, Polish defiance of Soviet domination, and the rebellion
in Hungary. The brutal repression of the Hungarian workers by
Soviet troops and the denunciation of Stalin have been particular
sources of embarrassment to foreign Communists, who must now
eat their former words in public and rationalize their former position as sycophants and hirelings of the late tyrant and justify the
counter-revolutionary role of the Kremlin in the Hungarian revolt.
The result has been a flood of protests and moves for greater independence on the part of many sections of international Communism. It is doubtful, however, that the Soviet leaders will permit
this new assertiveness to progress far, since these parties have been
tools too useful to be allowed autonomy.

Espionage

The role of the secret police in executing policy varies from
espionage to direct interference in the politics of a foreign country.
In England and in the United States their job has been mainly to

get into high places informants and spies who can influence policy in these countries or at least can report on high-level plans. In Spain during the Spanish Civil War they directly dictated policy to the Loyalist government. In the same manner they controlled the countries liberated by Soviet troops during World War II. From the revelations since the war it appears the Communists were often successful in recruiting or planting their personnel in high places: for example, Alger Hiss in the United States Department of State, Dr. Klaus Fuchs, Guy Burgess, and Donald MacLean in Great Britain.

Thus, the Soviet leaders have at their disposal a widespread apparatus, larger and more responsive than is available to democratic states. To keep this network as efficient, responsible, and reliable organization requires special and constant attention to two problems: tight channels of control and constant preparation.

Training

The problem of preparation is mainly one of training personnel and maintaining an active underground movement in every country of the world. Lenin and Stalin persistently stressed the need of a carefully organized underground even in the countries where a Communist party could act legally. Although this preparation failed in Germany where, after the rise of Hitler, both the legal and illegal Communist party were eliminated in a matter of weeks, it was successful in France where the French Communists were able to organize a strong resistance after the collapse of France in 1940.

Training foreign-service personnel varies with the tasks they perform. All begin at a very early age with an intensive ideological indoctrination, and this never ceases. Largely on the basis of ability, personnel are then chosen for advanced training in the conduct of Soviet foreign policy. Candidate students in the diplomatic and consular service attend the Moscow State Institute for International Relations. The training period in the Institute is five years. Citizens of both sexes from 17 to 25 years of age who have completed a secondary education and have passed competitive examinations are accepted. The Institute is reported to graduate about 200 students per year.

All students in secondary schools and beyond learn a foreign language, and language study is intensified for those going into international work. Although Soviet delegates usually, as a matter of honor, refuse to speak anything but Russian in conferences, it is quite clear they have at least an excellent reading knowledge of foreign languages.

While training is concentrated on Soviet citizens going into foreign-service jobs, a great effort is also made to train foreigners to support Soviet policies. One of the more recent developments has been to offer generous scholarships and other attractions to students, particularly students from the less developed countries, as encouragement to attend universities in the Soviet bloc.

The long-standing program of intensive indoctrination for foreign Communists through the Comintern (later Cominform) proved useful in the spread of Communist influence. Although the results of the training program were not striking in the 1920's and 1930's, the careful groundwork of twenty-five years began to bear fruit in western Europe and Asia after 1945. A large number of Communist leaders in the satellites and outside have spent some time in the USSR working and studying for their roles. Earl Browder, one-time leader of the Communist Party of the United States; Georgi Dimitrov, late head of the Bulgarian Communist Party; Maurice Thorez, chief of the French Communists; and Palmiro Togliatti, leader of the Italian Communist Party—all were in the Soviet Union for training at one period of their careers and worked at the headquarters of the Comintern. The Sun Yat-sen University in Moscow, closely associated with the Comintern and Cominform, has graduated many of the leading Asian Communists, among them M. N. Roy, founder of the Indian Communist Party, and Ho Chi Minh, Communist leader of north Viet Nam.

Control

The matter of control and maintaining conformity is always of vital concern to a dictatorship; professed faith in the ideology alone is never felt to be sufficient security for the regime. The Soviet system is a labyrinth of controls both internal and external, all created by the Soviet leaders to assure the loyalty and enthusiastic support of their followers and to maintain the supremacy of the Communist Party. Thus, while the secret police play a dominant role in the security functions, the Central Committee of the Party holds tight control over the personnel assignments in all Party and government organs. Even the personnel of the espionage and security system are carefully screened and approved directly by the Foreign Branch of the Central Committee of the Party. An added insurance of loyalty has been the practice of holding the family criminally responsible for the acts of its members in the foreign services. Only the most trusted diplomats are allowed to take their families outside of Russia.

The problems of insuring the loyalty of foreign Communists are much more difficult. The same system of secret-police checks and confidential reports by colleagues is used, but in the case of foreign Communists the strong disciplinary instruments are lacking. It was Stalin's attempt to create a spy system in Yugoslavia to counterbalance and discipline Tito's organization that brought to a head the Yugoslav conflict with the Comminform. Tito refused to accept docilely the undermining of his position. Thus, too much pressure on citizens of foreign countries is ineffective because they can resign and repudiate the Communist movement with little fear of retaliation from the secret police or their own governments. Communists of special prominence, however, may be lured unsuspectingly to the Soviet Union so that more drastic punishment can be applied. On rare occasions assassination may be resorted to, but this is usually reserved for Soviet escapees of high rank. Excommunication is the most frequent and most drastic measure. As a precaution against deviation the Soviet leaders have preferred Moscow-trained Communists to native leaders whenever they have been in a position to dictate the choice. The reason is to be found also in the Tito dispute. Tito, although he had received training in Moscow, had grown away from its influence and had developed his own roots in Yugoslavia. Thus his obedience training had lapsed and he was no longer so docile to the dictation of Moscow.

A *Vast and Disciplined Network*

In summary, the Soviet leaders can normally count on a vast organization to respond quickly and decisively in fulfillment of their policies. The mechanism is so geared that it can completely shift its direction in the minimum of time. Thus the rapid shifts in foreign policy just before World War II (from Hitler as number one enemy to number one friend and back again) and since Stalin's death (the oscillation between the Geneva spirit of friendship and anti-imperialist tirades against the United States) were accomplished in remarkably short order. Although the system now and again is jolted by a defector escaping to the West and revealing a certain number of secrets, the surprising fact is that escapees are such a small fraction of the total foreign service personnel (much less than one per cent). This continued loyalty is maintained in spite of sudden changes in policy, changes in leadership, frequent purges by and of the secret police, strictness of discipline and constant insecurity. Even more startling is the way the Communist parties outside the Soviet bloc until recently remained solidly behind all directives issued from the Kremlin. This includes the sizable Communist parties of France and Italy, who still can count on the support of a quarter of the voting population.

The Soviet Union has created an organization that is not only disciplined and responsive but is also technically highly capable. For the periods of closer relations with the western democracies the Soviet system produced the very likable and charming Ivan Maisky, ten years ambassador to Great Britain, and Maxim Litvinov, an apparent Wilsonian idealist, supporting collective security and remaining at the same time a loyal Soviet citizen. For hard bargaining and polemics it produced Molotov and Vyshinsky. Among its foreign supporters the Soviet regime has also been remarkably successful in securing astute leaders in spite of the vicissitudes of the movement. The high level of capability in the politbureaus and cadre systems of the Italian and French Communist parties, for example, has been acknowledged even by their foes. But technical efficiency does not overcome the inherent difficulties of bias due to ideology and to the desire for conformity.

The Motives of Soviet Foreign Policy

The aims which the Soviet leaders and people hope to achieve in international politics are the ingredients to be considered finally in Soviet policy formulation. These fundamental motives are closely associated with the structure, the sources of information, and the instruments for the execution of foreign relations, because they determine the course and strategy of policy formulation.

World Revolution

It has been widely accepted that the primary motive of Soviet foreign policy is to achieve a Communist world revolution. This oversimplified explanation pleases both the Communists and the bitterly anti-Communists. The Communists interpret the alleged Soviet desire to spread Communism as the fulfillment of destiny, the beginning of working-class justice and equality for the masses, and the heralding of a new society of plenty. The anti-Communists interpret it as the gradual enslavement of the world to the despots of Communism. Both approaches overlook the role of personal ambitions and opportunism among the Soviet leaders and people in making foreign policy. They also ignore traditional factors and the possibility that policy may be based on ignorance and default rather than on the all-knowing master plan of world revolution.

The Tradition of Expansion

Rather than attempt to derive motives directly from Communist dogma, it is more fruitful to start empirically with what is known and observable about past Russian foreign policy and from this deduce possible motivations. The one persistent element of great importance which has been observed as an integral part of the foreign policies both of the tsars and of the Soviet regime has been the urge to expand. Except for very brief periods in her history, Russia has maneuvered and used every tactic and strategy available to it in order to add to its land mass. Even when Russia was relatively weak the move to expand continued, and traditionally a large amount of energy has been expended by Russians of all classes in this effort. The mere knowledge that such a drive to expand has existed does not define precisely the motives of Soviet foreign policy but it does eliminate certain alternatives. It means the makers of Soviet foreign policy are not interested, except tactically, in the principles of the United Nations (for example, "the equal rights of . . . nations large and small") and are basically opposed to national self-determination. They want the future of the world to be under their hegemony, or failing that ideal, under the control of the three or four great powers. They demanded after World War II, for example, that the peace treaties be dictated by the great powers without consulting the small allied powers. From the beginning they supported and insisted on that part of the United Nations Charter which puts primary responsibility for peace in the hands of the big powers. Thus, the presence of the urge to expand makes it possible to exclude some motivations from Soviet foreign policy (for example, striving for universal justice and for a democratic world community).

The next step is to deduce the exact operating motives from this policy of expansion. To arrive at them, it is necessary to evaluate the conditioning factors such as ideology and the domestic balance of forces. In short, it is necessary to investigate why this urge has existed and what form it takes.

Security

A partial explanation of the expansion tendency lies in the need for security against the unremitting danger of invasion. Within thirty years, Russia had its land twice laid waste and came very close to being completely overrun by German forces. Thus it is only natural that the more land it holds between itself and Germany, including German territory if possible, the more secure it feels.

Modern military techniques since World War II have served to strengthen this age-old Russian defense axiom. With the development of long-range aircraft and atomic weapons the importance of space has been recognized by all powers. Both East and West have tried to push back and contain the air bases of the other side and to move their own bases as far forward as possible toward the power centers of the other side.

Ambition and Nationalism

Another element in the urge to expand has been the personal ambition of the leaders—their aspiration to head a first-class power. To this can also be added the desire of the Great Russian people to be a great nation. A manifestation of this ambition for superiority under the tsars was the dominance of the Great Russian nationality and the policy of Russification of the other nationalities in the empire. There was a partial resurgence of these policies under Stalin during and immediately after World War II. Although the Great Russian masses have not themselves initiated policies of expansion, they have taken great national pride in the success of these policies. Thus, they have never supported any independence movements among the other nationalities and have co-operated in putting down national revolts. Even the anti-Bolshevik emigrés of Great Russian origin refused to co-operate with the minority peoples or to consider independence for them.

Communist Ideology

Communist ideology has given Soviet leaders a doctrine and a rationale for expansion far more flexible and dynamic than that available to the tsars or other imperialists of the nineteenth century. Marx had proclaimed the inevitable collapse of capitalism. Lenin echoed him but asserted that a resultant victory of socialism was not necessarily assured. Two roads would be open: descent into a new period of the dark ages or ascent to new heights, to socialism, under the dynamic leadership of the proletariat. Because the bourgeoisie had managed to bribe and beguile the workers, the second alternative was possible only under the leadership of a revolutionary elite. Consequently the Soviet Union, as the bastion of socialism and the home of the elite, was expanding not for selfish gains but rather to include new lands in the glories of socialism and to save the world from the dark ages. In adding new nations to its sphere the Soviet Union would be saving them from enslavement to the imperialist powers and from exploitation by their own bourgeoisie, who in their increasing decadence were turning to the fanatic and terroristic policies of fascism.

This rationale for imperialism is certainly no less plausible than the doctrines of "manifest destiny" and "the white man's burden" used by western expansionists in the nineteenth century. Communist ideology benefits the Soviet leaders because it is not a mere rationale to appease the conscience but is also, to their followers, a religion behind which is the strength of faith. Communist expansion can therefore be made a crusade for which great sacrifices are willingly made by the devout. But Communism, with mainly a materialistic goal, does not hold up as a pseudo-religion and is on the wane as such. Each year the number of Party fanatics who are willing to make sacrifices is declining, whereas the majority have become opportunists. On the evidence of recent emigrés from the Soviet Union it would appear that this process is well advanced. Even in Communist China, where the sweeping reforms of the victorious Communists in 1949 brought a surge of idealism, disillusionment set in.

A Communist Crusade

Although it might have been and may still be possible for Communist fanatics to generate a crusade of aggression against capitalism, Lenin and Stalin never supported such a cause. Instead, they turned the energy of these zealots toward internal reconstruction and industrialization. Trotsky's primary interest, on the other hand, was world revolution, and had he won the victory over Stalin he might have pursued an active crusade against the capitalist states. Lenin had been concerned above all with saving the Russian revolution and had felt himself fortunate that he could. Stalin's leadership went further and added oriental fatalism to Lenin's pragmatism. Stalin's theory of ebb and flow did not abandon the idea of world revolution, but it gave up any time-table for its achievement. Stalin stressed that good revolutionary strategy and tactics were not compatible with a monomaniacal drive against bourgeois capitalists. He went even further in his practice and stressed that sometimes it was necessary to ally with the capitalists against a greater enemy, such as Hitler.

Stalin was not only willing to postpone the crusade. He did not even consider it necessary to have a final showdown between the capitalist and Communist powers. His primary purpose in building Soviet industry was not preparation for a death struggle with capitalism. In the short range he wanted to make the USSR so strong that the capitalist powers would not attempt to overthrow his regime. In the long range he was interested in the strengthening process as a means to take advantage of the growing plight of the capitalist powers. Stalin felt, in the Marxist tradition, that capitalism contained the seeds of its own destruction. In his last theoretical dictum published in October 1952, he wrote that the next war would not be between the capitalist and Communist states but between the imperialist states. He predicted that the falling out of the NATO powers was leading to another destructive imperialist war. The legions of the Soviet Union would then be ready to take over in the resulting chaos.

Thus, it is clear that, although Lenin and Stalin used the danger of imperialist encirclement for internal purposes, they never allowed themselves to be committed to an all-out crusade against capitalism. Since the post-Stalin leaders have given little evidence of being Communist zealots and since their hold internally is still not certain, they are more likely to continue in the Stalin tradition than to revive the Trotsky doctrine of "permanent revolution." In their official dogma they have gone even further than Stalin in denouncing the inevitability of war between the camps of socialism and capitalism and in supporting the possibility of peaceful transition to socialism.

Internal Instabilities

Another factor which has played a role in the urge to expand has been unstable internal conditions. Tsar Nicholas, who ruled Russia from 1894 to 1917, made particularly noteworthy efforts to strengthen his internal control by a successful foreign policy. He felt that if he were successful in his expansion policies he would have enough prestige to overcome the disintegrating forces at home. One of the reasons he did not back down in the crisis with Austria that led to World War I was his hope that in the war the Russian people would reunite against the enemy. Statesmen at this time had thought it would be a short war. A quick victory, therefore, over a weak Austria would allow the tsar to penetrate into the Balkans and to solidify his position at home. During the initial stages of the war the Russian people did, in fact, rally behind the government. But the length of the war, the breakdown of the economy, and transportation difficulties broke the cord of loyalty.

Like their tsarist predecessors, Communist leaders have never felt they had a completely united country behind them. In contrast to the relatively few defections in the official foreign apparatus, the number of defections by soldiers and peasants during World War II and the tens of thousands of Soviet war prisoners and Nazi slave laborers who refused to return when the war was ended show that disunity is also a problem for the Communists. In order to consolidate their control, the Soviet leaders have used international politics. The threat of capitalist encirclement has been dramatized so that increased security measures and the activities of the secret police might be justified. The great purge of the 1930's was alleged to be the routing-out of imperialist and fascist spies who threatened to destroy the regime. After World War II, Soviet propaganda again called attention to the threat of the warmongering imperialists in an effort to promote quick reconstruction and further industrialization.

Nevertheless there is no evidence that the Soviet leaders have deliberately launched an active policy of imperialism in order to cover up internal dissensions as did Tsar Nicholas. Communist control over the people has been more firm and stable than that of the tsarist autocracy. Nor has the Communist dictatorship been predicated on a successful policy of expansion as was Hitler's regime. The whole life blood of Nazism was aggression; that is, undermining the Versailles Treaty, economic penetration and domination of central Europe, and finally enforcing German hegemony over all Europe.

The future is less certain. The hold of the present Soviet leaders is not yet so firm as that of Stalin and if the struggle for power should continue, their hold will undoubtedly become less firm. In this event it is not inconceivable that a new leader, having momentarily destroyed or weakened his opponents and being very unsure of his power, might initiate an aggressive foreign policy to rally the people against the capitalist infidel and internal schismatics.

Restraining Influences

The main deterrent against an aggressive war or any foreign policy likely to lead to one is the total destruction that will accompany a major war in the atomic age. Conquest and victory may have little meaning in the next war, unless the conqueror's military power can successfully administer a knock-out blow. Furthermore, there is every reason to believe that the people of the USSR want peace and would fight willingly only in the defense of their homelands. Finally, the Soviet Union feels restricted by world opinion. For its own security it has wanted to avoid taking a stand which would cause the rest of the world to unite against it, particularly during those periods when it is internally weak. The Soviet leaders thus bowed to world pressure on certain occasions in 1945-1946 when the country was in the initial stages of reconstruction. Indeed, Communist expansion is greatly facilitated by a friendly world opinion. The Soviet Union has therefore tried to play its hand cautiously and has spent millions of dollars in an effort to win world support.

SELECTED BIBLIOGRAPHY[4]

The Structure

Merle Fainsod, *How Russia Is Ruled* (Cambridge, 1954); George B. de Huszar and associates, *Soviet Power and Policy* (New York, 1955); W. W. Kulski, *The Soviet Regime, Communism in Practice* (Syracuse, 1954); Julian Towster, *Political Power in the USSR, 1917-1947* (New York, 1948); Karl W. Deutsch and John S. Reshetar, Jr., *Political Weakness of Dictatorship* (New York, 1954); John N. Hazard, *Law and Social Change in the USSR* (London, 1953); Harold J. Berman, *Justice in Russia* (Cambridge, 1950).

[4] Prepared by Nancy G. Cattell. Also see the introductory remarks preceding the Selected Bibliography for Chapter 18, pages 651-653.

CONTACT WITH THE OUTSIDE WORLD

Since there is no opportunity for scholars to study directly the Soviet internal policies toward contact with the outside world it is necessary to approach this by indirect methods. One of the sources of information is the innumerable works by those who have defected. Among the more interesting and informative of these is Alexander Barmine, *One Who Survived* (New York, 1945); Michael Bialoguski, *The Case of Colonel Petrov* (New York, 1955); V. A. Kravchenko, *I Chose Freedom* (New York, 1946); W. G. Krivitsky, *In Stalin's Secret Service* (New York, 1939).

For *Information Bias* see Frederick C. Barghoorn, *The Soviet Image of the United States; a Study in Distortion* (New York, 1950).

For the *Ministry of Foreign Affairs* see George Bilainkin, *Maisky: Ten Years Ambassador* (London, 1944); and Arthur Upham Pope, *Maxim Litvinov* (New York, 1943).

On *International Communism:* Franz Borkenau, *The Communist International* (London, 1938); Franz Borkenau, *European Communism* (New York, 1953); Georgi Dimitrov, *The United Front* (London, 1938); Mario Ernaudi et al., *Communism in Western Europe* (Ithaca, 1951).

EXECUTION OF THE POLICY

On *Espionage:* David J. Dallin, *Soviet Espionage* (New Haven, 1955); and Francis Edward Noel-Baker, *The Spy Web, a Study of Communist Espionage* (London, 1954).

On *Propaganda, Control, and Organization:* Alex Inkeles, *Public Opinion in Soviet Russia: A Study in Mass Persuasion* (Cambridge, 1950); Herbert S. Dinerstein and Leon Gouré, I—*Communism and the Russian Peasant,* II—*Moscow in Crisis* (Glencoe, Illinois, 1955); Philip Selznick, *The Organizational Weapon: a Study of Bolshevik Strategy and Tactics* (New York, 1952).

On *Foreign Communists:* 84th Congress, 2nd Session, House Report No. 2243, *The Communist Conspiracy: Strategy and Tactics of World Communism,* Part I—*Communism Outside the United States,* Section D—*Communist Activities Around the*

684 THE SOVIET UNION

World and Section E—*The Comintern and the CPUSA* (Washington, 1956); 80th Congress, 2nd Session, House Document No. 619, *The Strategy and Tactics of World Communism* (Washington, 1948).

THE MOTIVES OF SOVIET FOREIGN POLICY

On Imperialism: Waldemar Gurian, ed., *Soviet Imperialism: Its Origins and Tactics* (Notre Dame, 1953); C. Grove Haines, ed., *The Threat of Soviet Imperialism* (Baltimore, 1954).

On World Revolution: Stefan T. Possony, *A Century of Conflict: Communist Techniques of World Revolution* (Chicago, 1953); Hugh Seton-Watson, *The Pattern of Communist Revolution* (London, 1953).

On Nationalism: Frederick E. Barghoorn, *Soviet Russian Nationalism* (New York, 1956); Walter Kolarz, *Russia and Her Colonies* (London, 1952).

On International Organization and Law: J. Y. Calvez, *Droit international et souveraineté en URSS* (Paris, 1954); Hans Kelsen, *The Communist Theory of Law* (New York, 1955); Y. Lapenna, *Conceptions soviétiques du droit international* (Paris, 1954); André Vyshinskii, *The USSR and World Peace* (New York, 1949).

On Internal Instabilities and Restraining Influences: Edward Crankshaw, *Cracks in the Kremlin Wall* (New York, 1951); David J. Dallin, *The Changing World of Soviet Russia* (New Haven, 1956); George Fischer, *Soviet Opposition to Stalin, a Case Study in World War II* (Cambridge, 1952); Eugene Lyons, *Our Secret Allies* (New York, 1953).

See the sections on pages 654-655 on Communist Ideology and International Relations and Historical Factors: Tsarist and Soviet.

CHAPTER 20

RECENT AND CONTEMPORARY FOREIGN POLICY OF THE USSR

Objectives after World War II

The Soviet Union came out of the war both a victorious state and a devastated nation. The Russians estimated that the damage, over and above the millions of human casualties, amounted to $128 billion. Western observers in Russia at that time concluded that this figure was close to the true cost if not below it. As part of their defense, the retreating Soviet armies had carried out a scorched-earth policy. There had followed two years of German occupation and plunder and then a period when these areas had become battlefields and scenes of further destruction. By May 1945, the Russians had exhausted their strength and, in spite of their military might, needed time to recover. In contrast the United States, which had suffered comparatively little from the war, was just reaching the peak of its military power and production. The wasted condition of the Soviet Union dictated four basic foreign-policy objectives after World War II: (1) to lull the fears of the United States until the Soviet Union could again rebuild its economic and military strength, (2) in the absence of large amounts of economic aid from the United States without political strings, to collect from Germany and eastern Europe as much booty and reparations as possible for its own reconstruction; (3) to build up a security zone in eastern Europe, the Middle East and the Far East in order to prevent a future aggressor from invading the USSR; and (4) to neutralize the capitalist world through the United Nations and thereby prevent an anti-Communist coalition.

Deceiving the West

In respect to the first objective, the Soviet task was relatively easy. The United States never seriously considered taking advantage of its superior position to destroy Communism in Russia. The West was still in the aura of the Grand Alliance and based the future and the peace of the world on the continuation of this unity as represented by the Charter of the United Nations and other new international organizations. The United States and the West wanted Soviet friendship and were willing to make certain concessions for it, which meant that instead of the United States calling the cards, as it might have done, the Soviet Union often found itself in this favorable position. This did not mean that the democracies had adopted a policy of appeasing Soviet aggression. The West was striving to work out reasonable compromises without coercing the Soviets into acceptance of the western position.

Far from taking advantage of its strength, the United States facilitated the development of relative Soviet strength by destroying much of its own military equipment and by immediately demobilizing its troops. Finding within a few years that it was the number one power on the continent of Europe, the Soviet Union was able to establish a satellite empire in Eastern Europe virtually unopposed. Thus in 1948 it dared a Communist coup in democratic Czechoslovakia, confident that the United States was helpless to prevent it.

Reparations

Collecting reparations was not as simple or successful as deceiving the West had been. In the first place the war had strained all of central and eastern Europe: most of the reserves of this area were gone and the machinery worn out. The devastation during the last months of the war brought the economies almost to a standstill. Eastern Europeans were not able to supply and feed themselves, let alone pay large reparations. This poverty did not, however, prevent the Soviet rulers from demanding and extracting tribute wherever possible. The first step was to loot the countries of all readily removable objects that could not be hidden. This stripping was done by Russian soldiers who cleaned out the consumer and luxury goods, including bathtubs and light fixtures, and by Soviet government agents who moved in to dismantle factories. This same process was employed in Manchuria, which Soviet troops overran during the last days of war with Japan. The main difference in Manchuria was that looting was much more extensive because the Soviet Union did not expect to remain in occupation very long.

No doubt an important factor contributing to the looting was the sharp difference which the Soviet soldier found between the living standards he was used to and those enjoyed by the enemy. It was unthinkable, in the minds of the victorious Russians, to allow the conquered and hated Germans to live an easier and more comfortable existence than their own families at home. Communist propaganda had always stressed to the Soviet people the material advantages of living under a regime of socialism as compared to the impoverishment of the masses in the capitalist states. The shock of finding that the reverse was true was politically dangerous to the Soviet regime. It is probable, therefore, that in order to give vent to this frustration the Soviet soldiers' were permitted and encouraged to loot.

At Yalta in February 1945, the one subject Stalin wanted to discuss was reparations from Germany. He was especially interested in collecting reparations from the western zones of occupation not under his military control. The West was reluctant to discuss this problem but ultimately Stalin and Roosevelt made certain agreements in principle which were to be further defined by deputies. They established a tentative over-all figure of $20 billion as a basis for discussion, and the Soviet's right to at least half of all reparations from Germany was acknowledged. The fundamental differences in attitude of the East and West, however, prevented any precise agreement at that time or later. From their experiences after World War I the western powers were dubious about collecting large amounts of reparations from Germany and felt the total figure should be realistically set upon the basis of capacity. Furthermore, the United States felt that unless Germany first supplied its own minimum needs, the United States would in effect pay for reparations by being forced to continue its subsidization of the German economy. On the other hand, the Soviets, because of their reconstruction needs, would not and perhaps could not alter their demands for collecting the maximum reparations at any cost to Germany and the West.

Another attempt was made to bridge the gap at Potsdam in July 1945. This time a compromise was made, at least on the surface. The USSR, however, refused in practice to uphold its part of the agreement. At no time, therefore, did the East and West find common ground on the reparations question. The conviction of the Soviet leaders of their need for the absolute maximum was so strong that they were willing to sacrifice the good will which the Soviet Union had gained from the war.

The Amount of Tribute

It is impossible to estimate accurately the total amount of loot and reparations collected by the USSR, although fairly close appraisals have been made concerning removals of industrial equipment from Manchuria and eastern Germany. The amount of industrial machinery removed from Manchuria was valued at approximately $1 billion with a replacement value of $2 billion. The Soviet government denied this figure and placed the value of the property they removed as war booty at $97 million. In East Germany, by far the most important industrial area in eastern Europe, it was estimated that plant removals to the Soviet Union reduced over-all industrial capacity to 55 per cent of what it had been in 1936, and the capacity of heavy industry to 40 per cent of the 1936 figure. The value of these industries was estimated at about $1.5 billion calculated at 1936 prices. No attempts have been made to estimate the looting of personal goods, even in Manchuria where there was a temporary reoccupation by the Chinese Nationalists. The values above represent losses to the occupied countries but not gains to the Soviet Union, because the removals were handled so inefficiently that less than half the value was realized by the Russians.

Having exhausted most of the possibilities of looting, the Soviet Union turned its attention to means of securing long-term tribute. These new methods of exploitation included Soviet-owned corporations,[1] reparations from current production, slave labor, and terms of trade favorable to the Soviet Union.[2] A problem in respect to the collection of reparations was that the economies of the Soviet Union and eastern Europe were not complementary; they were competitive. Before the war neither party carried on more than 5 per cent of its trade with the other. Both areas, except for Saxony and Czechoslovakia, were agricultural-surplus areas and imported industrial goods. Except for Polish coal and Rumanian oil, eastern Europe is not richly endowed with natural resources. Industries of this area, including East Germany, depend heavily on imported raw materials. Consequently, the economies of eastern Europe, in order to recover and produce the reparations demanded by the Soviet Union, required the very materials and machinery the Soviet Union itself needed for reconstruction. A temporary solution was found in carrying on limited trade with the West.

Regardless of the obstacles, the Soviet Union successfully collected sizable amounts from the war-devastated areas it occupied. In addition to the $1 billion worth of looted equipment from Manchuria, the Soviet Union by 1950 received an estimated $4 to $6 billion from eastern Europe, of which almost $4 billion came from East Germany. Although the amount collected by the USSR

[1] Instead of moving factories to the Soviet Union, Soviet corporations were formed to take over German factories in place and make them an integral part of the Soviet economy even though in a foreign country. In this way the captors were able to save time and to use German labor and local resources when available. In 1947 there were about 200 of these Soviet corporations, which accounted for about 25 per cent of the total industrial production in East Germany. This same tactic was employed in the other satellites but to a much lesser extent, the usual form being a joint corporation with the satellite government. By 1949 this policy was reversed and the bulk of the Soviet corporations were turned over to the satellite governments.

[2] Adverse trade terms was one of the causes for the Tito-Stalin split in 1948. Yugoslavia complained not only of the bad terms but also of the failure of the Soviet Union to deliver goods on time. This was also a complaint of Poland and Hungary in their demands for more freedom in 1956.

was by no means comparable to the losses suffered, it did help its recovery.

Security Zone—Europe

Looting and collecting heavy reparations from eastern Europe was not a policy which won the Soviet Union many friends; rather it worked against the Soviet aim of building a security zone against Germany and the West. The complete success of such a defense system depended not only on the forced military and political integration of this area into the Soviet sphere but also on the winning over of the population to the Communist cause. Consequently, in 1947 when the need for reparations in the Soviet Union no longer was pressing, the Russians began reducing the reparation accounts of the former enemy states. They even initiated loans to some of the satellites, for example, a credit of $450 million to Poland in 1948 and another for an unspecified amount to Czechoslovakia in the same year.

Another obstacle to the creation of the Soviet sphere was the attitude of the western powers. At Potsdam, in answer to western demands for free elections and self-determination in eastern Europe, Stalin forthrightly declared that the Soviet Union was insisting on friendly states along its border regardless of how this "friendship" was secured. Any free election, he said, would be anti-Soviet, and the Communists would not allow it.[3] The United States and Great Britain, on the other hand, refused to accept the principle of spheres of influence except for military purposes of a temporary nature. They had, after all, just finished fighting a war against the Axis dictators who had also believed in dominating small nations. The democratic powers had fought to build the peace on freedom and self-determination. The Soviet leaders ignored these views of the West, considering them mere propaganda, and they misinterpreted or chose to interpret the temporary military division of Europe and Asia, devised for the purpose of war and occupation, as a division of political influence as well. They were allowing the democracies complete freedom in China

---

[3] Stalin's statement was verified in Hungary in 1947 when free elections gave the Communists only 17 per cent of the vote in spite of their advantages in campaigning.

and western Europe and had even ordered the large local Communist parties in Italy and France to co-operate in re-establishing democratic regimes. They expected in exchange the right to follow their own designs in eastern Europe, Turkey, and northern Iran. Thus they did not take the Yalta Agreement seriously and considered it a sop to democratic principles demanded by popular opinion. Yalta had explicitly supported the western principle of temporary tutelage by *all* the Big Three over liberated and conquered nations. This guardianship was to hold only until free elections could determine the nature of future governments, a pattern which was already being followed in respect to Italy. Within a month, the Soviets ignored the Yalta Agreement by unilaterally forcing King Michael of Rumania to appoint a new government friendly to the Soviet Union.

The West refused to accept the Soviet basis for the postwar settlement and tried every means short of force to prevent the creation of the Soviet sphere. The Soviet Union had to move slowly and cautiously in establishing outright satellite regimes in this area, but not until after Stalin's death in 1953 was there any indication it would be willing to relax its basic control as represented by the presence of its troops, secret-police agents, and Communist leaders. During the initial stage of occupation the Soviet Union permitted broad coalition governments and relatively free political activity for all antifascist parties, although administratively the Communist parties were favored. These periods of freedom differed from country to country, depending on the length of occupation and the strength of the democratic parties. It ended early for Bulgaria and Rumania (the beginning of 1945), in Hungary (February 1946), in Czechoslovakia (February 1948), but it may still be considered to exist in Finland. Poland, because of its traditional antagonism towards Russia and because it had developed a very successful and well-organized underground, was never allowed the same freedom for political activities. During the war the Soviet Union had tried its best to destroy the Polish underground. It was only the pressure from the United States and Great Britain which forced the USSR to permit some of the underground forces and leaders-in-exile to take part in the restored

Polish government, but the Communists made sure the power of these people was ineffective and short-lived.

By the middle of 1945 the U.S. Secretary of State, James F. Byrnes, felt the only way to stop the USSR from extending its control over eastern Europe was to conclude peace treaties with the former Nazi satellites as soon as possible. These, he felt, would stabilize these countries and stop Soviet interference in their politics. This policy was a stroke of luck for the Soviet authorities, who were finding themselves somewhat encumbered by the occupation regime which was, as stated explicitly in various agreements, under the sovereign control of the Allied Control Councils made up of the three powers. The Soviet Union had managed to bypass the Allied Control Councils on all important matters by generally ignoring these Councils and by restricting their freedom of movement, but this practice had created ill feelings. The USSR felt that its control would be made much easier by treaties that would turn the powers of the Allied Control Councils back to weak satellite governments and remove the West's legal right to object. The Soviet Union would, of course, still insist on the presence of its troops, because it needed to protect its supply lines to Austria and Germany, which were still under occupation. Consequently, the Soviet Union was quite agreeable to the plan for concluding immediately the peace treaties with the Nazi satellites. In the drafting, the Soviet negotiators, as usual, proved to be shrewd bargainers. They held out for the best deal possible: to limit to a minimum the West's future right to interfere in the area and to make the West think that they, the Russians, were making a big concession by signing the treaties. The Soviet negotiators managed to limit provisions for western influence to a few vague clauses which subsequently have proved ineffective. They were able also to end the participation of Britain and France on the international commissions for the Danube.

With the conclusion of the Nazi satellite treaties after a year and a half of strenuous bargaining, the peace treaties with Austria and Germany still remained to be settled. The Soviet Union was pleased to delay negotiating these treaties, when it became clear that its demands for reparations would not be met. This delay gave the USSR time to exploit its own zones, to establish a satellite regime in East Germany, and to redress the power balance in its favor so its demands at the peace conference could not be ignored. When the discussion of the German treaty finally began in December 1946, the Soviet Union had two objectives: (1) to share in the economic fruits of the western zones of Germany and (2) to prevent the resurgence of German aggression. However, until 1948 the weakness of the Soviet Union relative to the western powers forced it to play a defensive game—obstructing a peace treaty favorable to the West and blocking for as long as possible the unification of the three western zones. These tactics succeeded. In the case of Austria, which had a different system of occupation, the stakes were not so high. Here the Soviet Union was interested in exploiting economically its zone in Austria and in using it for bargaining purposes. Consequently, the Soviet Union was willing to negotiate a state treaty for Austria, but refused to sign it for many years.

Security Zone—the Near East

The Soviet Union did not have its way, however, on all issues or in all areas. The resistance of the non-Communist areas to Soviet influence increased steadily and forced the Soviet Union to moderate its demands and, on certain occasions, actually to retreat. At Potsdam, Stalin had opened the question of the Turkish Straits, having made it clear earlier that he wanted joint occupation of the Straits. He was put off by the United States and Great Britain, who suggested an international conference at some later date and an interim exchange of proposals on the future status to be communicated through Turkey. In August 1946, the USSR forwarded to Turkey its proposal for settling the Straits question. This included a proposal for their joint defense by the USSR and Turkey and for the creation of an international regime, exclusively composed of riparian states on the Black Sea, for their control. Turkey rejected the Soviet proposal absolutely. The Soviet Union also sought another approach through an intensified war of nerves against Turkey. This had already begun in March 1945, when the USSR denounced its treaty of friendship with Turkey. In addition

to the question of the Straits, the USSR put increasing pressure on
Turkey to change its government to a more friendly one and to
alter their common border in the Caucasus in favor of the Soviet
Union. Against these threats the Turks were forced to keep themselves in a state of partial mobilization, a heavy drain on their
backward economy. In 1947, however, the United States came to
their aid with the Truman Doctrine.

The Soviet Union was also embarrassed in the Middle East by
the persistence with which the West backed Iran's demand that
the USSR fulfill its 1942 commitment by withdrawing its troops
from Iran's northern provinces after the war. By bringing the
question before the United Nations, Iran made it a world problem, and as the first issue before the Security Council it became a
test case for this new world peace organization. The Soviet Union
was caught, both because it was not willing to wreck the United
Nations and arouse world public ire at this time, and because the
military balance of power was not yet in its favor. Consequently,
after several months of stubborn resistance, the USSR backed
down and withdrew its troops.

Security Zone—the Far East

The United States and the West also resisted the creation of a
Soviet sphere in the Far East. In the fall of 1945 the United States
backed China in insisting upon an immediate withdrawal of Soviet
troops from Manchuria. It is doubtful in this case, however,
whether the Soviet Union had really thought to keep its troops
permanently in occupation, or whether it hoped only to maintain
partial economic domination through control of the main railroads
and the naval base at Port Arthur. After many delays, the Soviet
troops, under continuous pressure from Nationalist China and the
United States, were withdrawn by April 1946 but not before the
Chinese Communists were given a head start in penetrating
the area. The Nationalists subsequently were able to clear the main
centers of Communists, but not the countryside.

Korea, like Germany, had been divided for the purposes of
surrender and military occupation; the Russians held the area north
of the thirty-eighth parallel, the United States the area south of

it. The vital strategic and economic importance of North Korea was in the Japanese-built power stations there and along the Yalu River, which supplied power for Manchurian industry. The USSR moved quickly to absorb its occupation area into the Communist sphere. It also tried to infiltrate the southern part, control of which was valuable to the Communists as a means of putting pressure on Japan, but this penetration met with strong resistance from the United States.

The Soviet Union, in accordance with its security policy, resisted all attempts to establish a single Korea, either as a United Nations trusteeship or as an independent nation under a government based on free elections. As was its custom, the Soviet Union never openly denied the principles of self-determination. Unless the united Korea could be tied to the Soviet sphere, the USSR was content in 1946 and 1947 with its control of the north, but it had no idea of retreating, at least not short of a threat of force by the United States. The United States, however, did not contemplate such a step because it was intent on building the future on peaceful negotiation and compromise.

Titoism

Except in Iran when the USSR was still weak, the West could do no better than contain Soviet expansion. It was not western policy but Stalin's own blunders that brought about one of his most serious setbacks: the defection of Tito in the spring of 1948. Stalin had underestimated Tito's strength as well as his independence. Tito had forged from his partisan guerrilla movement in World War II a personal following, primarily loyal to him. When Stalin attempted to undermine Tito and infiltrate the Yugoslav Communist Party and government, he found that neither Tito nor the Yugoslav Communists were the docile puppets he had believed. Tito chose to assert his independence rather than submit; and, with the help of the West, he won. This breach was a serious blow to Stalin's prestige and hegemony. He in turn tried to terrorize Tito and his countrymen in order to make them recant, but he failed primarily because Tito was able to bargain successfully for military and economic aid from the West. In the long run, however, the conflict was not without advantage to the Soviet Union. While the military loss of Yugoslavia was significant, it was not disastrous, and the dispute warned Stalin of other Titoist tendencies in eastern Europe and cautioned him against treating other indigenous Communist leaders, such as Mao Tse-tung, in such a capricious manner.

Soviet Relations with International Organizations

In keeping with its policy of maintaining a formal show of great-power unity, the Soviet Union did not reject entirely the host of new international organizations which were intended to introduce a new era into international affairs in the postwar period. The Soviet Union participated in the preliminary conference for the United Nations at Dumbarton Oaks from August 21 to September 28, 1944, and appeared to support the idea enthusiastically. The Soviet Union had also participated in the Bretton Woods Conference a month earlier for the creation of the International Monetary Fund and the International Bank for Reconstruction and Development. In this latter case, however, there is no reason to believe that the Soviet leaders, because of their Marxian economic thinking, ever seriously considered joining these organizations, except perhaps to secure large and unfettered credits from the West. More likely they participated only in the hope of influencing the structure of the organizations and for the sake of great-power harmony. It would appear that the Soviet Union, in contemplating a possible postwar world of coexistence between Communist and capitalist states, thought of co-operation only on a political and security level, but in all other areas wanted two systems. At Dumbarton Oaks, for example, the Soviet delegates wanted to have the United Nations deal exclusively with security matters and to create separate organizations for economic and social questions, although they did not insist on this point. After the war, the Soviet Union and its bloc refused to negotiate, join, or deal with any of the specialized agencies concerned with broad questions of social and economic welfare, even those closely associated with the United Nations and set up by the General Assembly. The Soviet Union did not become a member of such organizations as the Food and Agriculture Organization (FAO), the International Labor Organization (ILO), UNESCO, the International Civil Aviation Organization (ICAO), and the International Relief Organization (IRO). The main exception was the United Nations Relief and Rehabilitation Administration (UNRRA), which was a temporary organization to distribute relief during the last days of the war and in the immediate postwar period. The devastation and shortages in the Soviet Union qualified it to receive large amounts of relief, which explains its participation. Except for UNRRA and the United Nations, the Soviet Union confined its membership to technical international organizations with narrow goals, such as the International Postal Union and the Commission on Narcotic Drugs. In 1949 it even withdrew from the World Health Organization, allegedly because this was being used by the United States for political purposes.

Agencies dealing with social and economic problems, to which the Soviet Union automatically belonged as a member of the United Nations, were usually used by the Soviet representatives as means to spread propaganda and embarrass the western powers. The Soviet's record in the Trusteeship Council and in the Human Rights Commission clearly testifies to this fact. In the more technical and nonpolitical work of the commissions and subcommissions, however, its approach was ambivalent, at times being cooperative and at other times obstructionist.

By 1945 the Soviet enthusiasm even for an international security organization appeared on the wane. As its diplomats were busily occupied in eastern Europe, the Soviet Union decided not to send a top delegation to San Francisco for the final negotiations creating the United Nations. It was only Harry Hopkins' special mission to Moscow, just prior to the conference, which persuaded Stalin to send Molotov. The main reasons why the Soviet Union ultimately decided to join the organization were its own great-power status, the United Nations' potential power, and the possibility of the UN's becoming a hostile league of capitalist powers opposed to and sealing off the Communist sphere. Subsequently, the Soviet Union showed no interest in implementing the UN charter and, in fact, appeared intent on handicapping its operations. The USSR used the United Nations largely as a forum for accusing the western powers of colonialism in Greece, Indonesia, Indo-China, Korea, Africa, and elsewhere.

At Dumbarton Oaks the Soviet Union had discussed the development of an international air force for the purpose of maintaining security. But when attempts were made to implement Article 45 of the Charter, which provided for placing armed forces at the disposal of the Security Council, the Soviet Union helped to block agreement, although it still declared itself in principle as favoring an international armed force.

Disarmament

One of the first acts of the General Assembly was to approve, on January 26, 1946, a resolution establishing a United Nations Atomic Energy Commission with membership for all governments represented on the Security Council plus a permanent membership for Canada. Soon after the Commission began its work it was obvious that the USSR had four objectives, though these were never clearly expressed: (1) to outlaw immediately atomic warfare and to destroy all atomic bombs, which were possessed at that time only by the United States; (2) to prevent inspections of its own industrial and atomic installations by any international body; (3) to keep the proposed international atomic authority under the control of the Soviet veto in the Security Council; and (4) to prevent failure of agreement from being blamed on the Soviet Union. It refused to accept the decision of the Commission's majority, which proposed an independent authority with extensive powers of investigation and control and the gradual elimination of all atomic weapons. It was afraid the independent authority would come under capitalist control and discriminate against the Soviet bloc.

In the end the disarmament issue resolved itself into two questions: (1) whether the great powers were really serious in their desire to disarm, and (2) which should come first—disarmament or security. The Soviet Union favored disarmament as the first step, while the West insisted on security. Two years of work in the Atomic Energy Commission could not answer the first question or overcome the impasse on the second.

In order to offset its reputation for obstruction, the Soviet Union took the lead in advocating the creation of a commission for the reduction of traditional weapons. In its proposals to the Commission for Conventional Armaments, however, it persevered in backing the elimination of all atomic weapons along with reduction in other arms. The West again insisted that atomic disarmament depended on an adequate system of control. Furthermore, the West was reluctant to reduce conventional armaments until atomic control had been established. It was clear that the two problems were closely intertwined, and that deadlock over atomic control precluded any agreement on general disarmament.

Thus the Soviets successfully doomed any chance of achieving international security and peace by means of an international police force, great-power cooperation in the Security Council, or the reduction of national arms, either atomic or conventional.

The Marshall Plan

Another example of Soviet unwillingness to co-operate with the West was its attitude toward the offer of Marshall Plan aid. Although Soviet press comments were not favorable, the Soviet Union did not immediately reject the invitation extended in June, 1947, to all of Europe to discuss a reconstruction program on the basis of mutual planning and exchange. In fact Molotov, on June 27, arrived in Paris with an entourage of 89 people to discuss the problem with Britain and France. The conditions specified by Molotov for Soviet acceptance of the plan, however, made it clear that the USSR was in fact rejecting the plan. The Soviet Union wanted aid on a bilateral basis, with each country using its share as it wished. Furthermore, the Soviet Union wanted to discriminate against the former enemy states and give precedence to those countries which suffered most under German occupation. Since Secretary Marshall had made his offer on the basis of European self-help and co-operation, England and France were unwilling to accept the Soviet point of view; and the meeting broke up with western Europe determined to go ahead without the Soviet sphere.

It is probable that the USSR rejected the plan because it was not willing to divulge the necessary economic information and because its Marxian outlook made close economic relations with the non-Communist economies of the West impossible to contemplate. The USSR also may have hoped that its non-co-operation would sabotage the plan, thereby preventing the recovery of Western Europe, or that it could force the West to accept the Soviet conditions for individual programs. Finally, the USSR was obviously not anxious to expose its satellites to western economic penetration. But why did Molotov even bother to come to Paris with a corps of economic experts when he must have known the West would reject the basic ideas of his plan? Perhaps he realized this difference would be the final break between the East and West and he wanted to put the blame on the West. If so, he was unsuccessful.

Stalin's refusal to join this project was undoubtedly a major diplomatic error and demonstrates the rigidity of Soviet foreign policy at that time. As a result of its heavy war damages, eastern Europe would have been eligible for a large portion of the grants made under the Marshall Plan. Even if the Soviet Union was not interested in the funds and wanted only to sabotage the plan, there was no better place for a saboteur than the inside. Since the conclusive argument for the Marshall Plan was that it would build the defenses of western Europe against Communism, there is considerable doubt whether the United States Congress would have appropriated funds had the USSR been one of the major recipients. The Soviet rejection in this situation completed the East-West split and started the West towards recovery and mutual aid.

By 1948 the Soviet Union had accomplished its main objectives for the immediate postwar period except in respect to the Marshall Plan, Turkey, Iran, and Yugoslavia; but these setbacks did not greatly hinder its over-all accomplishments. Collecting heavy tribute in eastern Europe and Manchuria had helped the Soviet Union to overcome its war losses in a remarkably short time. The balance of military power, except for atomic weapons, had been reversed, and the Soviet Union was the most powerful force on the Eurasian continent. The Soviet Union was even making tremendous progress with atomic weapons and was about ready to explode its first atomic bomb. It had also been able to consolidate a security sphere in Eastern Europe. In the Far East it was assured of protection by a satellite in northern Korea and by the success of the Communist armies of China, although it may have had some misgivings about a large and aggressive Communist neighbor independent of Russian control. Finally, the USSR had succeeded in obstructing the work of the United Nations.

The period of consolidation and preparation of "subjective" conditions now came to an end, and the Soviet Union was ready to expand its sphere even further. Actually, the two periods of consolidation and renewed expansion were intertwined. Since 1945, for example, the Soviet Union had been demanding greater control in Germany and Japan. But 1948 marks an intensification of these efforts and the use of weapons other than propaganda and diplomatic pressure.

Period of Flow

Favorable "Objective" Factors

In addition to the USSR's own progress in reconstruction and the consolidation of its sphere, several "objective" factors appeared favorable to a more aggressive policy in 1948. The demobilization of the western powers was complete, and the ratio of forces showed a disparity of approximately 125 Soviet divisions to 16 western divisions in Europe, including two from the United States. Pacifism was particularly prevalent in western Europe—a reaction to the war—and the Soviet Union could count on the west European's desire to avoid war if possible. Furthermore, the countries of western Europe neither wanted rearmament nor were able to pay the cost of it. Their economies were in fact on the verge of bankruptcy, for after the first flush of reconstruction activity in 1945-1946 their economic position had deteriorated rapidly. Even though the United States, from V-E Day to the spring of 1947, provided Europe with $11 billion in the form of loans and grants, there remained a serious United States export surplus to western Europe which depleted the dollar and gold reserves of that area. In spite of an increase in population, agricultural production in 1947 was only 70 per cent of prewar; industrial production varied from less than 50 per cent of prewar in Germany and Austria to 100 per cent in England and 110 per cent in Norway. The formerly large overseas investments of western Europe were reduced or completely lost. If the Europeans had been unable to continue to buy food, machinery and raw materials on the dollar market, they would have had to cut drastically their industrial output and standard of living, already reduced by the war.

The continued division of Germany into four zones made that country a political vacuum and prevented its economic recovery. Since the German economy traditionally was closely tied to the economies of all western Europe and especially of the Low Countries, the delay in German recovery tended to postpone stability in the rest of Europe. In 1947 the future of Europe looked black and the time good for Communist activity.

In the Far East the situation also looked favorable to the Communists. The United States, having failed to settle the civil war in China and to strengthen the Nationalist regime, had abandoned the Chinese to their own future. By 1948 the Chinese Communist movement under Mao Tse-tung had proved the more vigorous and was winning the war over Chiang Kai-shek's Nationalist forces. A civil war was also in progress between Communist-led forces and the French in Indo-China. Communist guerrillas were active in the Philippines, the Malay States, and Burma. Although none of these Communist movements in the Far East were directly sponsored and supported by Moscow, they took their inspiration and many of their orders from the Soviet Union, and it stood to benefit by their success, although in the long run they posed a potential danger to Moscow's hegemony over Communism. Even where the Communists were not directly active, the situation was not stable. In both Korea and Japan the economies were weak and seriously off balance and dependent upon large subsidies from the United States. The Korean political situation was critical. The Indonesians were in revolt against the Dutch, and mediation efforts were running into serious difficulties. In the newly created republics of India and Pakistan, widespread religious riots caused thousands of fatalities and brought the two countries to the verge of war.

The Beginning of Western Unity

Contemplating the tremendous disparity of military power between the East and West and the political and economic instability of most of the non-Communist world, the USSR decided to discount the growing antagonism and alarm of the United States. The Soviet leaders, it would appear, felt that the United States was not really serious about defending all the western world and that the overwhelming power of the Soviet Union could, if necessary, bluff the United States' leaders into appeasement. They did, however, feel the need to act immediately, because the steps which the United States and the West were initiating would in time redress the balance. By the Truman Doctrine, announced in March 1947, the United States was replacing Britain as the protector of Greece and Turkey. The next important step was the launching of the Marshall Plan. About the same time the United States and Britain, reluctantly supported by France, declared, in the absence of a four-power agreement, their intention to create a West German government out of their three zones of occupation. Steps were also being taken to reconstitute the disbanded defenses of the West. On March 17, 1948, Britain, France, and the Benelux nations signed the Brussels Treaty of mutual defense. In view of these measures toward western unity, the Soviet leaders concluded that even though the Soviet Union's own reconstruction was not fully complete, the "objective" and "subjective" conditions for Communist expansion were the most favorable that would be available for some time. They launched a new drive to weaken western power and prestige.

The Character of the New Drive

Soviet aggression took many forms, from "peace campaigns"[4] to war. One step was the formation of the Communist Information Bureau or Cominform in September 1947. The prewar Communist International or Comintern had been officially disbanded during the war in deference to the Soviet alliance with the western democracies. Its partial reconstitution in the form of the Cominform was a sign the time was deemed ripe for an attack on capitalism.

[4] See below, page 707.

The Cominform became the center of a full scale propaganda attack on the West.

The Communist parties in the West were also ordered to take part in the cold war on behalf of the USSR. As early as 1946 the Communists of France had become restive following a policy of co-operation and participation in the governing coalition. Their obstructive activities became increasingly acute, to the point that they were forced out of the Cabinet in May 1947. In opposition, the Communists began openly to attack the democratic parties. As proof of their strength and growing aggressiveness, the French Communists took advantage of the discontent among the French workers to launch in November and December 1947 a strike that took a million and a half workers away from their jobs.

The Czech Coup

Beyond expressing open hostility, the Communists' first clearly aggressive move came in February 1948. This move, a coup in Czechoslovakia, was an outgrowth of their policy of consolidating eastern Europe. President Eduard Benes on February 25, 1948, yielded to the demand of the Communist Premier Klement Gottwald to accept the resignation of anti-Communist cabinet members and to approve a cabinet dictated by the Communist Party. The western powers could do nothing. As the Communists repeatedly stressed, this was an internal problem of Czechoslovakia, outside the jurisdiction of international law and politics by the West's own definition. Short of direct intervention, the democracies could only protest and ask the Security Council to investigate the coup. In the same month of February 1948, the USSR proposed a military pact with Finland, which was concluded on April 6. It looked as if another satellite was in the making, but internally the Finns, unlike the Czechs, were prepared to resist any Communist attempt to seize power.

The Berlin Blockade

As the next step in their campaign the Soviet Union undertook to challenge the western powers in Germany. Stalin probably hoped to accomplish four things in respect to Germany: (1) re-

move the western powers at least from Berlin, (2) retaliate against
the economic fusion of the United States and British zones of
occupation and the currency reform in the western zones, (3) prevent the economic consolidation of the three western zones and the
moves being taken to form a West German government, and (4)
undermine the United States' influence in Germany and western
Europe. The main target was Berlin, from which the Soviet Union
hoped to oust the western powers, or which it intended to use in
extracting bargaining concessions from the West. Berlin was particularly vulnerable to the Soviet attack because it was surrounded
by the territory of Communist East Germany.

In January 1948, the Soviet forces in Germany began a series of
minor annoyances in the form of regulating and inspecting Allied
and German transportation to and from West Berlin. These restrictions continued to multiply in the following months until
June 18, when all surface traffic into Berlin was halted in protest
against the introduction of a new currency into the western sectors
of Berlin by the western powers. The western powers immediately
took up the challenge and established an air lift. Although there
was some talk in the West of trying to force the way into Berlin
by sending an armed convoy, neither side wanted to provoke a
possible war in this tense situation. The Soviet forces permitted
the air lift and the West accepted temporarily the blockade on
land and water. The Soviet Union was no doubt surprised by the
positive reaction of the West in its refusal to be bullied. The crisis
did not appear fatal, however, because after some hesitation negotiations were initiated to settle the dispute. Although the talks
progressed satisfactorily and the western powers secured Stalin's
agreement in principle to their basic position, it proved impossible to work out the details. The Russians still hoped the hazards
of winter flying and the demand for large amounts of coal for
heating would defeat the air lift. All Europe was watching Berlin.
If the Soviet Union could have broken down confidence in the
United States, the resulting defeatism would have given the Soviet
Union and the large Communist parties in France and Italy the
means to exert tremendous pressure on the unstable governments
of these two countries. Considering the stakes and their chances

for success the Russians refused to settle the crisis even when it involved alienating world opinion and particularly the small powers in the United Nations, who were trying to find an equitable solution. They had not reckoned, however, with the technical skills at the disposal of the United States, nor with the West's determination to make the air lift successful.

The West gained immeasurably by this action. In Berlin, 86.3 per cent of those eligible cast their votes for the democratic parties in the elections during December 1948, in spite of the no-vote campaign conducted by the Communists (the Socialist Unity Party). The blockade, instead of delaying the formation of the (West) German Federal Republic as the Russians had hoped, moved the reluctant French to make common cause with the British and United States in launching it. Finally, and most important, the air lift gave western Europeans courage, and full evidence that the United States was determined to protect them. As a result the Soviet leaders were forced to accept the complete failure of their strategy in Berlin, and in May 1949 they agreed to lift the blockade in exchange for a new meeting of the foreign ministers. In the resulting Paris conference in May the USSR failed to obtain any concessions and failed to make any progress in convincing the European public that the West, not the USSR, was to blame for the failure to unify Germany.

Other Forms of Aggression

The Soviet offensive was also active on other fronts in Europe. In the fall of 1948, on the basis of genuine workers' grievances, the Communist Party of France repeated its activities of the previous year by starting a series of strikes, with the political intent of defeating the Marshall Plan. Work stoppage was widespread and armed clashes resulted. The strike did not last long, however. The French workers soon drifted back to work because they resented Communist use of their economic plight for political purposes. In Italy the Communist Party made a strong bid for power in the elections of 1948, but the efforts of the Church and the Christian Democrats, combined with early delivery of Marshall Plan aid and propaganda by the United States, prevented them from succeeding.

In a direct Communist attack on the Catholic Church, Josef Cardinal Mindszenty, primate of Hungary, was convicted in February 1949, of high treason, espionage, and black marketing. Then, on March 8, Bulgaria sentenced four leading Protestant clergymen to life imprisonment on similar charges. These two incidents were only part of a long series of attacks on the remaining influences of the western powers within the Soviet sphere. The USSR and satellite states closed western consular and information offices, expelled United States officials, placed travel restrictions on embassy personnel, arrested and tried United States citizens as spies, and fired on United States aircraft. The western powers protested and retaliated in kind, but the incidents continued.

Still another aspect of the Soviet expansion campaign was the peace offensive. The Soviet propaganda has always associated Communism with universal peace just as it has associated capitalism and imperialism with war. Beginning in August 1948, the Communists launched a world peace campaign through front organizations, which sponsored numerous congresses. In April of 1949 a permanent committee was established that later became known as the World Peace Council. This World Peace Movement was not without some success among non-Communist groups. The desire for peace and the fear of war were strong in western Europe, and many were duped by the peace appeal. As its close association with Soviet foreign policy became more obvious, however, the Movement's success in winning non-Communist adherents diminished. Nevertheless, the Communists kept up a strong campaign. In 1950, there was a World Peace Congress in Warsaw and a "Peace Partisan" meeting in Stockholm, and in 1952 Peace Congresses were held in Vienna and Peking.

Beyond their initial successes in achieving the coup in Czechoslovakia and consolidating the Soviet sphere, the cold-war offensive of the Communists in Europe was ineffective. It was met by the determination of the West to hold on, and it served as a catalyst for the rearmament, economic recovery, and increased unity of the western powers. Even though the USSR was vastly superior in conventional military power and could have overrun western Europe with relative ease, there is no evidence that the Soviet

Union at any time considered such a course in order to recover from its cold-war failures. The United States superiority in atomic weapons and the uncertainty of war appear to have precluded Stalin from adopting this alternative in Europe.

The Korean War

The Situation in the Far East, 1950

Although Stalin shied away from starting a third world war in Europe, he did not abandon entirely the instrument of war to gain his ends. In Asia, it would appear, he felt the opportunity presented itself to use armed force without the danger of world war. While the Soviet Union's situation in Europe was deteriorating by 1950, conditions in the Far East had become more favorable. The economic and political situation was still critical throughout the area. In December 1949, Chiang's Nationalist army was forced off the mainland of China with little chance of return. Thus, instead of having China oriented toward the United States as was contemplated in 1945, the USSR found itself with an important ally in a key position. With its population of more than 400 million people and large land mass, China was well suited to serve as a bastion for socialism in the Far East. The large number of Chinese nationals in every nation in the Far East was also a natural fifth column. An additional advantage was the proximity of the territory of China to Thailand, India, Indo-China, and Burma. In the latter two countries civil wars were in progress. Although Communist China came to power on its own and not as a Soviet satellite, it felt itself an ideological brother of the Soviet Union, and each country sought the other for mutual protection and support of like ambitions. It is rumored that Khrushchev, in a speech in Warsaw in 1956, reported that during 1948 and the beginning of 1949 Mao Tse-tung and Stalin were close to a break but that relations improved when Mao came to Moscow. In December 1949, a Chinese delegation, headed by Mao Tse-tung himself, went to Moscow to negotiate treaties of alliance and economic aid. These treaties were signed the following February 14. In addition to granting China a small credit of $300 million, the USSR renounced all its rights in Manchuria except for its commercial concessions in the port of Dairen. The transfer of bases and assets was to be completed by 1952 at the latest. The USSR further undertook to espouse the cause of the Chinese Communists in the United Nations. The situation in Asia by 1949 was therefore "objectively" suited for socialist aggression. The "subjective" conditions were being prepared. The Sino-Soviet pact was one step in this direction, but the main problem was to remove United States troops and interest from this area.

The Choice of Korea

Although it is possible that the Korean war was initiated by the North Koreans themselves without the knowledge of the Soviet leaders, this interpretation seems unlikely, considering the nature and discipline of the international Communist movement. Furthermore, the circumstances and timing would indicate the hand of the Kremlin. South Korea was a likely choice for initiating the expansion in Asia because of its geographical position and unstable political situation. Expansion elsewhere in the Far East was precluded, since the USSR lacked naval power and could not easily secure the immediate and direct participation of Communist China. At this time Mao Tse-tung was busy eliminating Nationalists, consolidating his internal control, and helping Ho Chi Minh in Indo-China. (It is possible only to guess whether Stalin anticipated that China would nevertheless enter a Korean war to protect its important industrial center in Manchuria.) Geographically, the addition of South Korea would have completed the Soviet security zone in the Far East and made possible pressure on Japan, still the most powerful industrial country in Asia. The internal situation in South Korea was extremely unstable. Democracy had not penetrated very deeply under the regime of Syngman Rhee, whose rule was not popular at home or abroad. The United States still supported the South Korean economy but was becoming reluctant to continue this subsidy indefinitely. In the long run South Korea was of little economic value to the West. On the other hand, North Korea had acquired a fair degree of economic and political stability under the Communists. Its superior military strength put it in an excellent position to overrun South Korea without help from Soviet troops. Furthermore, in the absence of a mutual-assistance treaty with Korea, the USSR had no obligations in case of a failure. And since the struggle was between the two zones of Korea, the Soviet Union could insist that North Korea's aggression was a civil war and that intervention by the West was a violation of the rules of international law. Finally, an attack in Korea seemed to involve the least risk of a big war in case the United States accepted the challenge, since neither side's interest in Korea was great enough to warrant a major struggle.

Preparation

During the latter half of 1948 the Soviet Union, in what later proved to be a feint, withdrew its troops from North Korea in order to let the Koreans "settle their own differences." As a result, the United States, anxious to lessen its financial burdens, decided that it could safely withdraw its troops. The South Koreans protested the departure of the United States troops because the North Korean army was reported to be far superior to theirs. In response to their plea the United States left behind a 500-man military training corps, and in January 1950 signed an agreement under the Mutual Defense Act to supply military equipment to the Koreans.

In withdrawing its troops from South Korea, the United States divested itself of sole responsibility for South Korea's security. On January 12, 1950, Secretary of State Dean Acheson declared the Republic of Korea must depend for its defense upon its own efforts backed "by the commitments of the entire civilized world under the Charter of the United Nations." Moreover the United States, in drawing its new defense lines, had reportedly put South Korea outside of its primary defense zone, as a position which it would be impossible to hold in case of war with the USSR. This latter fact or possibility may have been an important factor in convincing the Russians that the risk of war with the United States over Korea was not great and that its expansion in this area could be accomplished easily and possibly without United States interference.

Results of the War

On June 25, 1950, the forces of North Korea invaded South Korea. The United States, followed by the United Nations, did not hesitate to take up the challenge and Stalin's ambitions were again frustrated.[5] Even the direct participation of Communist China in the conflict did not shake the determination of the forces of the United Nations in the protection of South Korea. The war became stalemated. Thus by 1951 the Soviet Union's expansion in the Far East, as well as in Europe, was halted. Only the native Communist forces in the Malay States and Indo-China were still making progress and these movements were only indirectly inspired by Moscow.

In spite of Stalin's own admonishments concerning flexibility in foreign policy and tactical retreats when odds were unfavorable, the cold war continued after 1951 with no move to extract the Soviet Union from its fruitless and dangerous international position. Until Stalin's death in March 1953, East and West continued to face each other, poised for war. Even though the hostility of the Soviet Union had become the driving force of Western unity and rearmament, the Soviet attitude remained rigid. It may have been Stalin's senility that made him unwilling or unable to alter the direction of Soviet foreign relations. No one else in the top leadership was able to assume the responsibility, and only Stalin's death permitted a Soviet reappraisal of the cold-war policy and its results.

A Change of Strategy

For years newspaper reporters and commentators watched for Stalin's death and prophesied a struggle for power even if he were to name his successor. The stakes of absolute power are too high for those who lose out to acquiesce docilely. It was a fond wish of the West that Stalin's demise and a subsequent struggle for his mantle would spell the collapse of the regime. This hope had its unspoken counterpart in the USSR among the masses of

[5] See pages 134-137 for more detail on the war and diplomacy involved.

people who had borne the burden of Stalin's ambitions. For those in a position to take over the reins, however, the situation was one of apprehension rather than expectancy. Would the masses break out into revolt? Who would be strong enough to seize power and how long would the struggle last? Would the colleagues of Stalin be liquidated as Stalin had liquidated the old Bolshevik colleagues of Lenin?

The New Leadership

On March 5, 1953, the long-anticipated event occurred: Stalin died of a brain hemorrhage. There was obvious relief among the people. The contenders rushed in to fill the gap. In the first few weeks Malenkov, Stalin's first lieutenant in the Party, attempted to take over the reins alone but he was soon forced to share his power with the coalition of other lieutenants arrayed against him and to form a collective rule. Lavrentiy Beria, who had controlled the notorious secret police since the great purge of the 1930's, was momentarily rescued from the purge which Stalin had been hatching against him. Beria sought to make his comeback by appealing to the masses as a spokesman for justice and mercy, a role incongruous with his infamous past. By July 1953, however, he had been removed from all his posts in the government and Party and by December he had been executed. Two years later Malenkov was forced to resign as premier; but, unlike Beria, his demotion was not followed by his death. He remained in the Party Presidium and was elected by the Supreme Soviet to be Minister of Electrical Power and a Deputy Chairman of the Council of Ministers. This series of shifts apparently left only two outstanding personalities within the Soviet leadership who could conceivably take supreme command: Nikolai Bulganin and Nikita Khrushchev. Khrushchev was in the preferred position because of his role as First Secretary of the all-powerful Communist Party. Officially the new leadership, however, continued to adhere to the doctrine of collective rule, but the struggle was not over.

The precarious path of Soviet foreign policy in the cold war was ill-suited to a period of transition to a new regime. The consequences of Stalin's cold-war policies in the "period of flow" were too uncertain and raised the constant threat of a major war. Even more important was the doubtful support of the masses. As promoters and participants themselves in a revolutionary movement against capitalism, the new Soviet leaders were well aware of the discontent and possible revolutionary ferment released in the Soviet Union by Stalin's death. In such a situation they feared that a war with the West would mean revolt against their rule. This fear seemed justified by the outbreak of anti-Communist riots in East Berlin in May 1953 and by the prevalence of anti-Soviet strikes and minor disturbances in the other satellites.

Relaxation of Tension

The leaders immediately sought to alleviate the domestic danger by granting amnesty to many of the inmates of prison camps, ameliorating the most extreme forms of repression, reducing consumer prices, and making available stocks of long-sought consumer's goods. For international relations the new collective leadership resurrected the policy of "peaceful coexistence." The slogan had never completely died but it had lost its significance during the Korean War. After Stalin's death it was given new life and substance. To exhibit sincerity the Soviet leaders put pressure on their partner in aggression, China, to end the long wrangles over an armistice in Korea. In addition, they initiated a series of minor steps to relax tension. For example, they allowed Russian-born wives of United States citizens to leave the Soviet Union, permitted the election of Dag Hammarskjold as the new Secretary-General of the United Nations, invited Yugoslavia, Greece and Israel to renew normal diplomatic relations, dropped their demands for Turkish territory, and ceased to demand occupation costs from Austria. In addition, the vast propaganda mechanism at the Communists' disposal abandoned its war of nerves against the West.

It was not fear alone, however, which motivated this change in the Soviet attitude towards the West. The new Soviet leaders had to face the fact that the fruits of the cold war had been slight or even negative and had brought about the determination of the western powers to unite against them. As a result, Soviet policy-makers concluded that Communist foreign relations needed a reappraisal and a fresh approach. In the years following 1953 a new three-fold pattern of Soviet foreign policy gradually unfolded, reaching a climax at the Twentieth Congress of the Communist Party of the Soviet Union in February 1956, when the doctrines of Stalin were openly and decisively repudiated.

The Settling of Minor Disputes

As was mentioned above, the first new direction to become apparent was the settling of minor differences and the replacement of the most extreme cold-war pressures with invitations to friendship. The new leaders recognized that Stalin's peace campaign had fooled very few, since Soviet action had dramatized Soviet hostility toward the west. The new peace campaign was given substance and credibility by concrete acts.

The response of the West to this slight relaxation of tension was so favorable that the Soviet leaders apparently decided to make it a permanent part of Soviet policy. The doctrine of "peaceful coexistence" became the byword of Soviet policy. Communist propaganda continued in general to abstain from barrages of vitriolic attacks on the West. It stressed the claim that the peoples of Communist countries had no plans to destroy capitalism, and even asked for a renewal of the wartime friendship. To economic conferences and fairs the USSR sent affable delegations with huge exhibits, expressing a desire for trade. Soviet purchase of sizable quantities of consumer goods on the world market during 1953 and 1954 seemed to confirm this wish. In a still more concrete way, the Soviet Union proceeded to settle small differences that involved no real sacrifice on its part. As an example, after years of fanning the Trieste dispute between Yugoslavia and Italy, it willingly accepted and approved the Italian-Yugoslav agreement which divided the disputed area in 1954.

The year 1955 was particularly marked by reconciliations attempting to lull the democracies. In February the USSR declared its intention to end the state of war with Japan and to open peace negotiations. These were subsequently initiated in London on June 1. Then, dramatically in March, Austrian Chancellor Julius

Raab was invited to Moscow to settle the long-pending negotiations over the Austrian state treaty. Except for minor issues the treaty had been completed in 1949, but during the cold war the Soviet Union had refused to take the few remaining steps to its signature. By 1955 the Soviet Union had extensively exploited its zone; and, though it had failed to win the Austrian people or government over to Communism, it could withdraw without damaging its position strategically or economically, at least so long as Austria did not enter the western defense system. Assurance on this last point was accomplished by conditioning the treaty and the withdrawal of Soviet occupation troops on permanent Austrian neutrality and a guarantee that Austria would never allow foreign bases on its soil. In exchange the USSR agreed to relax some of its claims stipulated in the draft treaty. (1) It was willing to accept the $150 million compensation for German assets held by the Soviet Union in Austria in the form of goods rather than in freely convertible currency. (2) The USSR consented to surrender its claim, as recognized in the draft treaty, to 60 per cent of Austria's oil industry for 10 million tons of crude oil. (3) It promised to return to Austria, for compensation, title to the Danube Shipping Company, (4) the Soviet Union also agreed to return the Austrian prisoners whom it still held. On the basis of this Soviet-Austrian settlement the Big Four powers concluded and signed the Austrian State Treaty in May 1955.

A still more startling move on the part of the new Soviet leaders was their attempt to heal the breach with Tito. In a grand gesture of repentance Bulganin and Khrushchev, as the top government and Party leaders of the great socialist fatherland, made a trip of homage to the small renegade Communist state of Yugoslavia and begged forgiveness. Although they attempted to blame the original rift on the disgraced Beria, there was no concealing the lengths to which they would go in order to remedy Stalin's mistake. In asking Yugoslavia's return to the fold they did not demand that Tito or his party submit to the absolute discipline of Moscow or that Yugoslavia's socialism be altered to fit the Soviet pattern. The resignation of Tito's old foe, Molotov, as Minister of Foreign

Affairs and Tito's triumphant tour of Russia in June 1956 formally completed the rapprochement.

The Soviet Union also strove to relieve the tension around the German issue which had brought Europe to the verge of war in 1948. In January 1955, the Soviet Union ended its formal state of war with Germany. Then on June 8, the Soviets sent a note to West Germany inviting Chancellor Adenauer to visit Moscow. The Bonn Republic accepted. Talks were held in Moscow during September 1955, and resulted in the establishment of diplomatic relations and a verbal promise by the Soviet Government to return the remaining German war prisoners. Their partial return lent conviction to the view that the Soviet leaders were seriously determined to reduce tensions in this area.

When a United States Navy plane was shot down over the Bering Sea, on June 22, 1955, Soviet Foreign Minister Molotov, instead of following the usual practice of denying any responsibility, immediately sent apologies. He acknowledged that the Russian pilots might have erred in assuming the plane to be over the Soviet Union and promised to pay damages. A similar response occurred when an Israeli transport plane was shot down on July 27, 1955, on the Bulgarian border, killing 58 persons including British and United States nationals. The Bulgarian Government expressed its regrets and promised to investigate.

The high point in this new Soviet peace offensive was the Geneva meeting of heads of state of the four great powers in July 1955. In spite of certain disagreements, particularly among the foreign ministers who were meeting at the same time, the surface atmosphere of the conference was that of a meeting of old friends. Bulganin expressed the policy of the USSR: "If all participants in the conference display good will and sincerely seek to reach agreement, we shall undoubtedly be able to find common ground and chart feasible ways for an effective settlement of highly important questions on which the peace and well-being of the peoples depends." In keeping with this statement, the entire Soviet delegation sought to impress the world at this meeting that the USSR's protestations of good will were sincere and that it was confident of finding solutions. There is little doubt that many in the West were impressed by this new attitude and were tempted to forgive and forget. Following the conference the Soviet Union made strenuous efforts to preserve the "spirit of Geneva" and its role as espouser of a new era of friendship.

After the summit conference at Geneva, the Soviet Union seized several additional opportunities to press its "peace campaign." The exchange of visits of agricultural and housing experts with the United States created good will for the Russians, particularly among the traditionally isolationist elements in midwestern United States. In August the USSR announced the reduction of its armed forces by 640,000 men, and a few weeks later the satellites followed suit. On September 17, Bulganin declared that the USSR would give up the Porkkala Naval Base in Finland, which it had leased for fifty years under the 1947 Treaty of Paris. In the United Nations, during December 1955, the long deadlock on the admission of new members was broken with the co-operation of the Soviet Union. Sixteen new members were added, of which only four were Communist satellites.

The gestures of Soviet amity continued into 1956. Premier Bulganin in personal letters to Eisenhower proposed that the United States and Russia sign a twenty-year pact of friendship. In the spring Malenkov, followed by Bulganin and Khrushchev, made friendship tours to Great Britain, with indifferent success. At the Twentieth Party Congress in February 1956, the cold-war policies of Stalin were publicly castigated and the ideological sanction of the policy of friendship and peaceful competition with capitalism was given official expression.

Communist China also embraced the new policy. Although in no way bound by directives from Moscow, the Mao Tse-tung regime fell into line during 1955. Beginning the year with threats to take Formosa by force and apparently on the threshold of war with the United States, China unexpectedly called a temporary truce. At the Bandung Conference of Asiatic and African powers Chou En-lai made known his government's wish to open peaceful negotiations with the United States. In the subsequent negotiations the Communist Chinese government released thirteen United States prisoners of war condemned as spies and allowed a

few additional Americans still interned in China to leave by way
of Hong Kong. The Chinese Communists at the same time publicly endorsed the "spirit of Geneva" and praised the Soviet efforts
in this direction.

The Hard Core of Obstruction

Although the general response of the West to the gestures of
friendship and peace was extremely favorable, and although in
many quarters hope was expressed that peaceful coexistence was
possible, government leaders were more skeptical, especially since
major points of division still remained. Nevertheless, they were
encouraged to hope that perhaps they were seeing a sign of genuine
change or that the Soviet Union was talking from weakness, or
both. Since the West was entering a period of prosperity, was
united in its defense, and claimed to speak from a position of
strength, this seemed an opportunity to press the Soviet leaders
for a settlement of the major differences and test the genuineness
of their pacifism. Beginning in July 1953, England, France, and
the United States in a series of notes proposed to the USSR
a new meeting at the foreign ministers' level. The latter hesi-
tated, but finally—out of fear that further obstruction would undermine its international position—agreed to a meeting in Berlin in
January 1954.

The Berlin Conference of Foreign Ministers revealed other
aspects of the post-Stalin Soviet foreign policy. Primarily it demonstrated that, on the important problems involving great-power
status, the Soviet Union was unwilling to compromise or even
negotiate in a serious manner. On these issues the Kremlin evi-
dently felt that no equitable compromise was possible or feared
that any relaxation of Soviet control in the disputed areas would
go against the USSR. Perhaps it was significant that Molotov, the
work horse of Stalin's cold war, was still foreign minister and
headed the Soviet delegation. In any event the USSR was not
ready at the Berlin conference to settle either the German or the
Austrian question. Rather, it sought to delay the rearmament of
Germany, to reinforce its propaganda about peaceful settlement
of the cold war, and to support China in its expansion in

the Far East. Thus it continued the methods long associated with Stalin's era—the hard, shrewd bargaining and the refusal to compromise on vital issues; but, in a change from the blunt, older technique, the steadfastness of the Soviet position was now obscured by a series of tactical proposals from the Soviet delegation. These included a referendum asking the Germans to choose between a peace treaty and military association with the West, a plan to remove all occupation troops pending a peace treaty, and an all-European security system to replace the North Atlantic Treaty Organization. However, these tactics were only partly successful. They could not obscure the fact that the USSR was the power still obstructing solutions to major problems. Nevertheless, the maneuvers did raise doubts concerning the inflexibility and lack of initiative of the western positions as contrasted with fast-moving Soviet diplomacy. Moreover, the USSR succeeded in securing a meeting of the great powers with Communist China and other interested powers to consider problems in the Far East. This admission of Red China into the ranks of the great powers was regarded by the Soviet Union as a major triumph.

The Geneva Conference on the Far East which began in April 1954, disclosed the same basic hard line of the Soviet Union and her allies on big issues, this time on the questions of Korea and Indo-China. The Communists refused to make any concessions in Korea and they took advantage of their positions of strength in Indo-China to force a solution favorable to themselves with little regard for compromise or the interests of the people involved. The division of Indo-China along the seventeenth parallel was reminiscent of the still unsolved, unstable division of Germany and Korea under Stalin.

That the core of Soviet resistance did not change, even under the spirit of friendship launched by the heads of state at Geneva in the summer of 1955, was made clear by the subsequent conference of foreign ministers in November. Again Molotov led the Soviet delegation in rejecting any agreement on disarmament and the unification of Germany. He attempted to hide behind pleas for a general European security system, a decrease in the number of forces and bases on foreign territory, a reduction of general armaments, and a prohibition of atomic weapons. The conference did not succeed even in its minimum aims of arranging a greater exchange of ideas and information and an increase in normal trade between the East and West.

The disarmament question was another of the central disputes on which the Soviet Union remained fundamentally immovable, continuing the struggle of the cold war. It was well aware of the concern of the general public, especially in the small countries and among the victims of World War II, for the reduction of all arms as the main assurance against future annihilation. Even Stalin had always been willing to discuss the issues, although he refused to commit the Soviet Union to any concrete measures. After Stalin's death, the West took advantage of the change to try to break the deadlock on disarmament or at least to make clear to the world the responsibility of the Soviet Union. Beginning with President Eisenhower's dramatic proposal in December, 1953, for making atomic material available to the world for peaceful purposes, the western powers pressed the new Soviet leaders to end the obstruction of Stalin's policy on this question. It soon became clear that the Soviet Union still opposed a system of international control of disarmament. However, the Kremlin felt it necessary to take particular caution in rejecting western proposals. It is the artifice of the Soviet delegates never to reject a proposal immediately but to talk it to death and hide behind secret diplomacy, that is, until the Soviet Union can publish something favorable to its cause.

The main disagreement over disarmament continued to be the question of effective inspection to insure equal compliance by all nations. As did Stalin before them, the new directors of Soviet policy insisted on immediate banning of the use of atomic bombs in any future war as a prerequisite to disarmament. But because this argument and their delaying tactics had become tiresome, they dramatically offered in May 1955 concessions on this issue and on the problem of inspection, without granting the right of unfettered investigation of atomic and other facilities by an international team. At the Geneva meeting of heads of state in July, President Eisenhower again took the initiative and proposed, as a preliminary step toward disarmament and as a means for preventing surprise attacks, that the Soviet Union and the United States exchange complete blueprints of their military establishments and open both countries to unlimited aerial inspection. As before, the Soviets did not immediately reject the plan but first attacked it piecemeal, then denounced it at the disarmament talks in London in April 1956. Thus, in spite of diplomatic maneuvering and propaganda plays around the disarmament question, the situation remained deadlocked.[5a] Meanwhile the Soviet Union announced a reduction in armed forces on its own terms without international control. By the gesture of unilateral reductions in its military services, first of 640,000 persons, and then of another 1,200,000 persons on May 14, 1956, it hoped to end the rearmament efforts of the West.

Other examples of continuity between the old and new regimes on basic problems were the Soviet reactions to the rearmament of Germany, the Southeast Asia Treaty Organization, and the Bagdad Pact. The Soviet Union was elated with the defeat of the European Defense Community by the French National Assembly in August 1954, but it immediately became alarmed by the speed with which the western powers negotiated in October of the same year the London and Paris agreements which provided for the rearmament of Germany. In opposition, the Soviet Union at first tried to beguile the West through such delaying moves as proposing new talks on German unity among the four powers and extending invitations to an all-European conference, including the United States, to draw up the security arrangement previously proposed by Molotov at the Berlin conference. When these efforts failed, the Soviet Union resorted to threats. It claimed that the rearmament of West Germany would bar German unity indefinitely,[6] and warned that the USSR would denounce its mutual-

[5a] In April 1956, however, the Soviet Union did agree to the draft statute of the world-wide atoms-for-peace agency which was later approved by a conference of eighty-two nations in October 1956. The Soviet Union accepted this agency because of its popularity among the small nations and because the United States clearly intended to go along with the plan even without the Soviet Union.

[6] The true position of the USSR on German unification was probably expressed in the reported statement by Khrushchev to French Foreign Minister Pineau in May 1956: that the Soviet Government was not at all disposed to allow the reunification of Germany because of a possible renewed German threat.

assistance treaties with France and Britain if the Paris and London
agreements were ratified. Subsequently it carried out these threats.
Furthermore, in answer to West German rearmament and sovereignty, the East German Republic was given its sovereignty, including control over the East Sector of Berlin and the corridors to
West Berlin. Its sizable police force was recognized as an army and
further strengthened. An even more important counter measure
was the creation of a single military organization, similar to NATO,
for the Soviet Bloc. The Warsaw Pact creating this united command under Soviet Marshal Konev was signed in May 1955.

Neither did the Soviet Union stand idly by in the case of
SEATO and the Bagdad Pact. In notes to the participating powers
it denounced both pacts in strong terms. Although it was unable
to retaliate with alliances of its own, the USSR did what may
prove to be more effective in the long run: it made a determined
effort to win over to neutralism those states in the area not yet
committed to the pacts. This courting was begun in earnest by
Red China at the Bandung Conference in the spring of 1955 and
has since continued without interruption.

A New Type of Offensive

The Communist policy toward the Bandung Conference of
Asians and Africans was typical of another aspect of the new Soviet
foreign policy. In appraising Stalin's policies the new leaders of
Russia rejected, at least for the time being, the mode of expansion
used by Stalin for spreading Communist hegemony. The use of
terror and force had been singularly unsuccessful and had alienated
even neutralist opinion. Furthermore, the destructiveness of nuclear warfare and the danger of total destruction made the methods
of threat and coercion almost out of date. Beginning in January
1954, the Soviet leaders repeatedly warned the West that no one
can expect to win a nuclear war. The Geneva summit conference
appeared to have assured the Soviet policy-makers that the West
also realized the fatal character of a full-scale war. As a result,
Soviet stratagems in foreign policy have forgone at least temporarily in dealing with the West the use of force or the extensive use
of the cold war to accomplish their aims. This new Soviet line does

not mean, however, that the leaders have forgone their aims and hopes.

The startling success of Russian industrialization has given the Soviet Union a new means by which to extend its influence. The Soviet Union is now able to make available limited military and economic aid and technicians to neutralist countries. It has not yet matched the aid given by the United States and it must sacrifice some of its own industrial development and that of its satellites and allies to do it. However, it appears that on a limited scale the Soviet Union has decided the gain is worth the cost. And if the Soviet Union should decide to give up its struggle for autarchy and exchange industrial machinery for agricultural goods, the production of which in the USSR is expensive and in short supply, it would have an important instrument for influencing agricultural surplus areas. It would also have economic advantages for the Soviet Union.

Thus, the new leaders have realigned their assets and are concentrating on new methods of expanding and spreading Communist influence. Their new line is directed mainly toward the small powers and the undeveloped states. In the less developed countries the Communists preach anticolonialism, condemning France, Great Britain, and the United States alike. In western European countries the United States is singled out for attack. Although this is no new technique, it is being given special attention and substance by its direct support of anticolonialism in the Near and Far East and by overtly friendly acts and attitudes towards smaller powers. Thus when Khrushchev and Bulganin visited India and Burma in December 1955, their speeches centered abuse on Great Britain, trying to fire up old anticolonial issues among the Hindus, and supported India's demands for the Portuguese enclaves in India.

In western Europe the Soviet Union's propaganda has likewise been of a divisive nature. Initially the idea of a European security system as advanced by the USSR was to exclude the United States. In the various international conferences at Berlin and Geneva the Soviet delegation emphasized the contention that the presence of United States bases and troops in Europe kept alive world tension and fear of war. They promised that if western Europe would remove the Americans there would be peace in Europe and no need to continue the armaments race. They stressed to Germany that it would mean unity and to France that it would mean an end to German rearmament. Soviet propaganda has placed special emphasis on France as the weakest link of NATO and the country most susceptible to anti-United States feelings. The Soviet wooing of Yugoslavia was also intended to weaken Tito's close relationship with the West and to disrupt the 1953 Balkan Pact between Greece, Turkey, and Yugoslavia.

During the USSR's spree of buying consumer goods in 1954, the biggest plums were offered to the hard-pressed exporters of western Europe and the Soviet Union declared that there would be even more for them if the United States were not keeping them in bondage by the strategic-goods blockade against the Soviet bloc. The direct appeal of Premier Bulganin to President Eisenhower for a bilateral treaty of friendship with the United States, excluding its allies, was a subtle move to weaken western unity. The visit of Khrushchev and Bulganin to England, the extensive exchanges of other visits, and elaborate receptions for cultural and parliamentary delegations to the USSR from Western Europe were equally important divisive politics.

The primary emphasis of this new strategy of expansion has, however, been an attempt to increase the influence of the Soviet Union over policy-making and policy development in the small nations through the renewal of the popular front, diplomatic maneuvers, and economic and military aid. These devices work hand in hand with the Soviet plan to resolve the minor issues of the cold war. The Soviet offer to restore diplomatic relations with Germany and Japan was not only a means to reduce the tension in these areas but also a way by which the Soviet Union could extend its influence in the two countries and by-pass the United States, England, and France. The Soviet Union, as the only great power with diplomatic representatives in both Germanies, is now in a position to deal directly with them on the issue of unity. In Japan restoration of relations helps to revive the much needed trade between Japan and the Communist bloc and, through this instrument, gradually extend Communist influence.

Traditionally the Communist parties in the capitalist countries have shunned direct contact with other parties either of the right or left. But in the periods of 1935-1939, in the years of the grand alliance, and again since Stalin's death, Communists have adopted a policy of the united and popular front. In the 1930's the aim of the policy was to stop the spread of fascism but in the 1950's it is calculated to increase the role of the Communists in policy-making. During the campaign for the French elections in January 1956, the French Communist Party offered to co-operate and to ally with the Socialists and with the Radical Socialists of former Premier Mendès-France, and even asked to form a government with them. Their invitations have been repeatedly turned down. International Communism has not been abashed, and the Twentieth Congress of the Communist Party of the Soviet Union confirmed the tactic of the popular front.

Almost immediately after Stalin's death the Soviet Union and its satellites intensified their campaign in the Middle East. Communist officials publicly stated their desire for improving relations with Greece and Turkey as well as with the Arab states. In December 1953, they organized a Conference for the Defense of the Rights of the Peoples in the Near and Middle East. Contact was also attempted on the religious level.

It was in 1954 that the evidence of this new policy of developing friendship stood out in bold relief. The Soviet Union, which had previously shunned as imperialist shams the International Labor Organization, UNESCO, and the United Nations Technical Assistance Program, reversed itself and sought admittance in order to increase its influence among the laboring classes in backward areas. To the Technical Assistance Program it granted an initial sum of 4 million rubles and made known its intention of sending additional aid on a bilateral basis. This resulted in agreements with India to build a steel plant with a capacity of a million tons, to share experiences in industrial and atomic-energy matters, and to exchange experts in several fields. Through Czechoslovakia the Soviet Union performed an even more important service for

Egypt by supplying it with sizable quantities of armaments and military technicians which the western powers had refused for fear of igniting the Arab-Israeli conflict. In addition, the Soviet Union made specific offers of trade and economic aid to such countries as Burma, Afghanistan, Saudi Arabia, and Egypt. The amount of aid granted has been small compared to that from the United States, but each ruble is well publicized.

The effectiveness of this proffered aid is as much the consequence of the social and political contacts which have accompanied these offers as of the aid itself. The most dramatic action of this kind was the exchange of visits between Nehru, Bulganin, and Khrushchev during 1955. The greetings of both the Soviet Union and India to their visitors were overwhelming. In each country the government outdid itself in organizing for the visit and the masses of people responded enthusiastically with ovations of friendship. Both tours were triumphs for the Soviet Union in its effort to woo the neutralist nations.

The initial successes of Soviet penetration into the Middle East, due largely to the strong anti-Western attitudes of the Arabs, encouraged the Communists to become even more involved. During 1956 they increased their shipment of arms to Egypt and also began to supply Syria. It was estimated that within a year the nations of the Soviet sphere sent almost $500 million worth of military goods to Egypt and over $50 million to Syria. The rapid deterioration of British influence in Jordan, marked by the dismissal of the British commander of Jordan's Arab legion, opened up still further possibilities for Soviet infiltration. The Soviet Union also more and more openly sided with the Arabs against Israel and against France in North Africa, and increased its attack on the imperialism of the capitalist states. With the upset of the precarious balance achieved by the West in this area, the situation soon disintegrated into war. Algerians, encouraged by Egypt and by the success of Tunisia and Morocco in achieving self government, began a civil war against France; Egypt, with its newly acquired Soviet arms, sought to eliminate British influence permanently. In July 1956, President Nasser of Egypt nationalized the Suez Canal Company, largely a French and British holding. In the ensuing crisis the Soviet Union completely backed the Egyptian position against the British and French and encouraged President Nasser to resist any internationalization of the Suez Canal as proposed by the West. The collapse of the Suez negotiations and the Israeli attack on Egypt, supported by the armed intervention of France and England in the canal area in October, found the Soviet Union still giving President Nasser its full support. It even threatened to send or "permit" Russian "volunteers" to go to the aid of Egypt if the British, French and Israeli troops were not removed from Egyptian territory immediately. Soviet penetration into the Middle East now seemed well advanced. The only factor which saved the Western position in the area was that the United States also backed the Egyptians against the British and French invasion and was largely responsible for bringing about the evacuation of foreign troops from Egypt. Nevertheless the crises proved a success for Soviet diplomacy and would have been a major triumph if the USSR had not been embarrassed by events in Hungary at the same time.

The USSR and Its Satellites

The relationship of the Soviet Union toward its satellites in eastern Europe since Stalin's death has been a reflection of both Soviet domestic and foreign policies. Initially the satellite governments, as did the Soviet Union internally, reduced the tension and strain by which Stalin had ruled his empire. The reign of terror, which had haunted the satellite peoples since the war, was ended for the moment. The satellite leaders also tried to make more consumers' goods available. To do so, however, proved to be impossible, because tribute still had to be paid to the Soviet Union and the economies of the satellites were basically unsound. In the industrial sector there were many deficiencies and shortages, and the persistent opposition of the peasantry to collectivization kept the agricultural sector from fulfilling its part. Consequently drabness continued to burden life in eastern Europe.

In 1954-1955, with the general reappraisal of foreign policy, the Soviet leaders also systematized their relations with the satellites. The new pattern sought to rationalize the system of rule for the purpose of efficiency and to develop stronger bonds between the peoples of eastern Europe and the Soviet Union. In theory this program meant using positive encouragements in addition to indoctrination and in place of coercion. In practice it meant the reduction of pressure and bureaucratic weight in many minor matters, the end of general pressure towards collectivization, and, most important, the decentralization of decisions, thereby allowing the individual Communist parties to make many of their own plans. A strong reinforcement for this new policy was Tito. Tito had conditioned his reconciliation and continued good relations with Soviet Communism on the adoption of the doctrine that each Communist country must be permitted to find its own path to socialism. Thus the Soviet leaders were forced to repudiate the Stalin thesis that there was only his road to socialism and to allow that there could be different roads to the goal.

As in the case of foreign policy, however, basic positions towards the satellites remained firm. Thus it was never the intention of the Soviet leaders to permit real independence for the satellites. In fact, they increased coordination over general policies by moving toward a single economic plan for the whole Soviet sphere and by creating a single command for the armed forces under the Warsaw pact. Furthermore, they never willingly permitted any anti-Communist or anti-Russian manifestations in the satellites. They crushed immediately the East Berlin and associated riots in June 1953. They were ready to move against the Polish workers in Poznan when they struck in June 1956, in case the Polish troops were unable to handle the situation. Then in October 1956, when Wladislaw Gomulka led the nationalist wing of the Polish Communists in demanding less Soviet control and removal of certain Soviet agents in the Polish armed forces, Russian troops stood poised and ready in case the Poles went too far and demanded complete independence and immediate removal of Russian troops from Poland. When a similar movement in Hungary, shortly afterwards, got out of control of the local Communists and became an open rebellion, Soviet tanks moved in. In this case, however, the revolt spread rapidly, even involving Hungarian troops, and became a frenzy of revenge against the USSR and the Hungarian Communist quislings; the Russian forces had to retreat until they could move large reinforcements into Hungary.

The Hungarian rebellion made it clear the Soviet leaders had miscalculated concerning eastern Europe. They thought the ten years of intensive indoctrination under Stalin had laid the basis for a common socialist society within the Soviet sphere, particularly among the youth who were educated in the system. By the relaxation of terror and the gradual end of economic privation they had hoped the bond of Communism would be sealed. Instead, the youth provided the spark of the revolts and the policy of relaxation merely opened a Pandora's box of seething hatred against the Russian conquerors. By the end of 1956 it was doubtful that the new Soviet policy for eastern Europe would ever achieve success. Furthermore, Yugoslavia had again been estranged from the Soviet bloc and public opinion was alienated throughout the world, even in the Soviet Union according to reports.

From this review of Soviet actions in international affairs since Stalin's death, it is evident that a new pattern of Soviet foreign policy is emerging. It is not merely a change in tactics, which was first in evidence. Different methods and new directions of effort have been adopted. As in any military or power situation, the aim remains the same—victory over the opposition. This the new leaders do not deny—rather they repeat it at frequent intervals. But the strategy differs. The atomic stalemate and the obvious failure of the cold war turned Stalin's successors to both resurrected and new approaches. It is not surprising, therefore, that at the Twentieth Party Congress, just three years after Stalin's death, his ideology and methods were officially rejected and condemned while Leninism was reaffirmed. The new strategy in foreign policy has three parts, each complementing the other: (1) willingness to settle all minor differences in support of peaceful coexistence; (2) persistent obstruction on major problems for fear of losing a power position while at the same time hiding behind devious proposals; and (3) special concentration on the small nations to win them over to neutralism and eventually to Communism. It is still too soon to know the complete pattern or to estimate accurately the success of this new approach, although its future appears promising except within the Soviet sphere of eastern Europe.

SELECTED BIBLIOGRAPHY[7]

Works on the more recent events in the Soviet Union are listed below by area except for the following dealing specifically with analyses of developments since Stalin's death: Isaac Deutscher, *Russia: What Next?* (London, 1953); Barrington Moore, Jr., *Terror and Progress, USSR* (Cambridge, 1954); Philip E. Mosely, ed., "Russia Since Stalin: Old Trends and New Problems," *The Annals of the American Academy of Political and Social Science* (January 1956).

SOVIET RELATIONS WITH THE UNITED STATES

Thomas A. Bailey, *America Faces Russia* (Ithaca, 1950); R. P. Browder, *The Origins of Soviet-American Diplomacy* (Princeton, 1953); R. Dennett and J. E. Johnson, *Negotiating with the Russians* (New York, 1951); George F. Kennan, *American Diplomacy, 1900-1950, and the Challenge of Soviet Power* (Chicago, 1951); W. H. McNeill, *America, Britain and Russia: Their Cooperation and Conflict, 1941-1946* (London, 1953); Philip E. Mosely, ed., "The Soviet Union Since World War II," *The Annals of the American Academy of Political and Social Science* (May 1949); Henry L. Roberts, *Russia and America, Dangers and Prospects* (New York, 1956); Walter Bedell Smith, *My Three Years in Moscow* (Philadelphia, 1950); Joseph V. Stalin, *The Great Fatherland War* (New York, 1945); Edward Stettinius, Jr., *Roosevelt and the Russians, Yalta Conference* (Garden City, 1949).

SOVIET RELATIONS WITH GERMANY

Wladyslaw Anders, *Hitler's Defeat in Russia* (Chicago, 1953); Lucius D. Clay, *Decision in Germany* (London, 1950); Department of State, U. S., *Nazi-Soviet Relations, 1939-41, Documents from the Archives of the German Foreign Office* (Washington,

---

[7] Prepared by Nancy G. Cattell. Also see the introductory remarks preceding the Selected Bibliography for Chapter 18, pages 651-653.

1948); Gustav Hilger and Alfred G. Meyer, *The Incompatible Allies: A Mémoire-History of German-Soviet Relations, 1918-1941* (New York, 1953); J. P. Nettl, *The Eastern Zone and Soviet Policy in Germany, 1945-1950* (London, 1951); Angelo Rossi, *The Russo-German Alliance, August 1939-June 1941* (Boston, 1950); USSR, Ministry of Foreign Affairs, *The Soviet Union and the Berlin Question* (Moscow, 1948); USSR, Ministry of Foreign Affairs, *The Soviet Union and the Question of the Unity of Germany and of the German Peace Treaty* (Moscow, 1952); G. L. Weinberg, *Germany and the Soviet Union, 1939-1941* (Leiden, 1954).

SOVIET RELATIONS WITH CENTRAL EUROPE AND THE BALKANS

Hamilton Fish Armstrong, *Tito and Goliath* (New York, 1951); R. R. Betts, ed., *Central and Southeast Europe, 1945-1948* (London, 1950); Cyril A. Black, ed., *Challenge in Eastern Europe* (New Brunswick, 1954); V. Dedijer, *Tito* (New York, 1953); Edvard Kardelj, *On People's Democracy in Yugoslavia* (New York, 1949); Robert J. Kerner, ed., *Yugoslavia—United Nations Series XXI* (Berkeley, 1949); Stephen D. Kertesz, ed., *The Fate of East Central Europe* (Notre Dame, 1956); John A. Lukacs, *The Great Powers and Eastern Europe* (New York, 1953); The Mid-European Studies Center, Research Division of the Free Europe Committee, *East-Central Europe under the Communists* (New York, 1956), 7 vols.; Revers Opie et al., *The Search for Peace Settlements* (Washington, 1951); Hugh Seton-Watson, *The East European Revolution* (London, 1952); James T. Shotwell and Max M. Laserson, *Poland and Russia, 1919-1945* (New York, 1945); Gordon Shepard, *Russia's Danubian Empire* (London, 1954); *The Soviet-Yugoslav Dispute, Text of the Published Correspondence* (New York, 1948); Adam B. Ulam, *Titoism and the Cominform* (Cambridge, 1952); Robert Lee Wolff, *The Balkans in Our Time* (Cambridge, 1956).

SOVIET RELATIONS WITH THE MIDDLE EAST

Olaf Caroe, *Soviet Empire—the Turks of Central Asia* (New York, 1951); W. P. and Z. K. Coates, *Soviets in Central Asia* (New York, 1951); Department of State, U.S., *The Problem of* the Turkish Straits (Washington, 1947); George Lenczowski, Russia and the West in Iran, 1918-1948 (Ithaca, 1949).

SOVIET RELATIONS WITH THE FAR EAST

Max Beloff, Soviet Policy in the Far East, 1944-1951 (London, 1953); David J. Dallin, Soviet Russia and the Far East (New Haven, 1948); Malcolm D. Kennedy, Communism in Southeast Asia (New York, 1956); Ball W. Macmahon, Nationalism and Communism in East Asia (Melbourne, 1952); M. R. Masani, The Communist Party of India (New York, 1955); Harry Miller, The Communist Menace in Malaya (New York, 1955); Robert C. North, Moscow and Chinese Communists (Stanford, 1953); V. W. Purcell, Malaya: Communist or Free? (Stanford, 1954); W. W. Rostow in collaboration with Richard W. Hatch, Franck A. Kierman, Jr., and Alexander Eckstein, The Prospects for Communist China (New York, 1954); Virginia Thompson, The Left Wing in Southeast Asia (New York, 1950); O. O. Trullinger, Red Banners Over Asia (Oxford, 1950); USSR, Ministry of Foreign Affairs, The Soviet Union and the Korean Question (Documents) (London, 1950); Henry Wei, China and Soviet Russia (New York, 1956); Aitchen K. Wu, China and the Soviet Union (New York, 1950); Edward H. Zabriskie, American-Russian Rivalry in the Far East (Philadelphia, 1946).

Japan

JAMES T. WATKINS IV

Department of Political Science
Stanford University

and

KAZUO KAWAI

Department of Political Science
Ohio State University

Japan

CHAPTER 21

BACKGROUNDS OF JAPANESE FOREIGN POLICY

JAMES T. WATKINS IV

Japan's "unconditional surrender" in 1945 ended fourteen years of aggression that had begun in 1931 when the Kwantung Army leaders in defiant disregard of their government in Tokyo attacked and overran Manchuria. Defeat extinguished the designs of the Kwantung militarists and their dupes in Tokyo, but for their country much more was lost. The whole Japanese people, who by sacrifice and hard work under inspired leadership had in the space of a little more than two generations lifted themselves out of obscurity and isolation to make of Japan one of the Great Powers of the earth, now saw the fruits of all their efforts as well as their hope for security, prosperity and recognition gambled away by militarist folly and fanaticism. Defeat and enemy occupation are tragic for any people. For the Japanese, among whom there were not a few whose lives had spanned the whole period since feudalism, the tragedy was particularly bitter.

Their past is prologue as with any people. But in theirs is to be discerned a special dialectic giving it a pattern whose design suggests broadly the direction which Japanese policy will take in the future in so far as Tokyo is free to choose among alternatives. The alternatives are limited by the circumstances of geographic location, natural resources, industrial capacity, pressure of population, access to markets and raw materials abroad for their industrial plant, as well as by political experience and their national characteristics. But among these last are traits which pattern the history of the past century and provide the basis for optimism about Japan's future foreign policy.

Natural Resources

The basic "internal" resources upon which a state may draw in the conduct of its foreign relations are three: geography, population, and what may be called wealth for want of a better term.

The location and configuration of its territory; the number, character, and qualities of its people; the variety and riches and the use it can make of the raw materials within its boundaries—these constitute a state's internal elements of strength. Taken in combination with one another and with such "exterior" sources of strength as allies and access to markets and raw materials abroad, these internal resources provide the basis on which foreign policy rests for its long-range effectiveness.

But whatever their other scope, unless national resources include an extensive industrial establishment, the mechanized character of contemporary life in peace and war excludes a country from the ranks of the Great Powers—the oligarchs of the world community. Japan, fortunate in timing as in leadership, built one of the great industrial complexes in the world. By 1940, the Japanese economic and military strength had won the country a Great Power status. Like Italy, another defeated power, Japan has it no longer, and we may doubt whether she can ever regain it. Japan's rise to leadership in the world community had in it an important element of timing, and times have changed. That is to say, Japan's external resources no longer make up for the weaknesses in the foundations that supported Japanese economic and military strength of the past.

Geography

Japan in the 1950's, after a century of expansion, has been forcibly returned to substantially its original limits, a long crescent-shaped archipelago rising out of the continental shelf of the Eurasian land mass. This location off the eastern shores of Asia invites comparison with that of the British Isles off the coast of Europe. Japanese and foreign writers alike frequently propose the comparison. Both the Japanese and the British are island peoples. Both countries are dependent upon ocean traffic and foreign sources to keep their industries operating. Both have led their continental neighbors in building up industries. Both have created great naval and merchant-marine fleets. The straits of Tsushima and of Dover have played similar roles. So have the North Sea and the Sea of Japan. What the Lowlands have been to British security, Korea has been to Japan. But beyond these resemblances the analogy should not be stressed.

The Japanese archipelago consists of four large islands—Honshu, the main island; Hokkaido to the north, Shikoku and Kyushu to the south and southwest—and nearly a thousand small islands. Among the latter are Amami-Oshima and the other Ryukyu Islands between Kyushu and Okinawa, which have recently passed from United States to Japanese control. "Residual sovereignty" over the remainder of the Ryukyu chain, according to the official Washington position, remains with Japan despite United States occupation and use.

Altogether the peace settlement ending the war in the Pacific deprived Japan of one-third of its territory. Japan's geographic circumstances have come full circle in the period which began with the Treaty of Kanagawa in 1854 and ended with the Treaty of San Francisco in 1952. But the changes in Japanese strategic circumstances have taken a different course.

In the 1850's Japan found itself helpless in the face of western arms and warships, a nation of agriculture and handicrafts at the mercy of western technology. The amorphous continental mass of China lay on the Japanese flank, benignant and indifferent, wrapped up in pretensions to suzerainty and in foreign and domestic troubles of its own. In search of security Japan set out to acquire the new weapons, military and economic, which the West had developed. Once it could command these, there was hope that Japan might achieve predominance in Pacific Asiatic waters by capitalizing upon the weakness and sloth of China and the geographic remoteness of the western powers. In a world of aggressive states nothing less would spell security.

A century later, a different strategic situation prevails. Defeat in World War II brought to Japan for a brief period both total disarmament and foreign occupation. But since the outbreak of hostilities in Korea in 1950, rearmament has proceeded until in Japan's "Self Defense Forces" may now be seen the nucleus of a military arm. As of April 1955 these included about 150,000 ground troops, 19,000 naval personnel manning 101 small surface craft (the largest a 1700-ton destroyer), and 10,000 air personnel flying 250 planes. With a civilian force of about 14,000 added, the total rises to 193,000. Five years of further expansion are planned to bring these forces by 1960 to 180,000 ground troops, 125,000 tons of naval shipping supported by a naval arm of 180 patrol craft, and an air force with 1300 planes, of which 770 will be fighter craft. Moreover, though the "Self Defense Forces" have been equipped with United States arms, ships, and planes, the Japanese have begun the manufacture of all three.

But the "Self Defense Forces," even when outfitted by Japanese manufacture, fall far short of providing proper defenses for an island people of 90 millions. Japan's strategic position in 1956 and for the discernible future depends upon United States intervention, without which the outlook would be more ominous even than it was in the 1850's. Perhaps, as is hoped, it will not be necessary to maintain United States troops in Japan after the rearmament goals set for 1960 have been reached. But achieving these goals is not enough. Without protection in the sea and air around Japan, which can be provided only by United States forces, the islands cannot be secure. Meanwhile the weakest point in the fabric of national defense is the unwillingness of the majority of the Japanese to support rearmament.

Though the United States today lends Japan the shield it lacked in the 1850's, national security may be found to lie only in the direction of the United Nations and collective security. The two most threatening dangers appear to come from China and the Soviet Union. China, galvanized by a nationalism owed partly to

Japan, is no longer either benignant or indifferent. The USSR pursues the aims of tsarist Russia with the advantages supplied by modern technology. And both understand what the free world would lose if Japan's reservoir of highly skilled industrial workers were to be thrown into the scales on the side of Communism.

The land area of Japan totals 142,644 square miles, which is to be compared with California's substantially greater area of 158,693 square miles. The coastline of this island empire runs to 16,500 miles, more than thirteen times the length of California's 1200-mile coast and more than a fourth greater than the 12,500-mile coast of all the United States. Superimposed on a map of the eastern United States, Japan would stretch from northern Florida to eastern Maine; yet at its greatest width, in the island of Honshu, it does not exceed 180 miles. No place in the country is more than 90 miles from the sea.

The islands are blessed with abundant rainfall the year round and temperatures which allow a long growing season in most areas. But Japan does not have extensive areas suitable for cultivation. Three-fourths of the land surface is mountainous, with soil conditions that defy even the intensive methods of Japanese farming. There are no broad plains. The largest, which is that around Tokyo, is only some 5000 square miles in extent. Most of the rest of the flatland consists of sharply tilted patches built up at the heads of bays.

Intensive farming techniques based upon an unstinted investment of man-hours, fertilizers, terracing, wet-field cultivation, and reclamation give much of Japan the appearance of a well-kept garden of greens. But only 15 per cent of the land surface is cultivated, roughly 21,400 square miles. In almost any other country, much of what is now under cultivation would probably be left wild.

Population

Within its narrow, beautiful, but inhospitable confines, Japan crowds one of the world's great populations—89,269,278 persons according to the 1955 census. Although still greatly exceeded by China, India, the Soviet Union, and the United States, in that order, Japan ranks fifth in population among the nations of the world and is of the same order with Indonesia at 81 million and Pakistan at 76 million. Neither Britain nor France with, respectively, 50 million and 44 million, even come close. Japan's population density is 624 per square mile, a figure which soars to 4172 per square mile of cultivated area, the highest in the world.

As spectacular as the density of the population is its increase. The country was already densely settled in the Tokugawa era (1603-1867), when the population reached and remained stabilized around 30 million. Then, with the coming of industry and overseas commerce to support a larger population and of modern hygiene to reduce the death rate, the population tripled in the space of a century. The present figure includes 6 million added since the 1950 census, and 19 million since the end of the war in 1945; the latter figure, however, takes into account upwards of 6 million repatriated from the colonies and occupied areas.

The excess of births over deaths each year adds more than a million new mouths to the population. In one widely quoted estimate a Japanese is born every 13.4 seconds. Although there are signs that the rate of increase is beginning to fall with urbanization and further industrialization as it did in western Europe and North America, means will have to be found to support a population much greater than Japan now has. The Tokyo government foresees a hundred million before 1965. When will there be a leveling-off? The problem of support for the Japanese standard of living is appalling, the situation desperate.

Japan's population predicament is new only in degree. Until the 1920's, the new commerce and industry were expected to provide for the needs of the growing population. "Overpopulation" had not been thought of. Thereafter the predicament grew and remained acute, its remedy ever more baffling and elusive and its effects disastrous for domestic politics and foreign policy alike. We may doubt whether Japan, if left to its own devices, will be able to find a remedy in the future.

Emigration is no answer. It never was. The Japanese, despite government inducements, did not emigrate in any number. By the outbreak of World War II fewer than a million and a half were to be found away from the home islands. Immigration laws excluded them from the United States and from the Pacific states of the British Commonwealth. Adverse climatic conditions and lower standards of living deterred them from following the flag into their own colonies. Still less could they hope to compete economically in Asiatic lands where they did not enjoy government support. Today what emigration did take place has been largely undone by the return of Japanese to Japan after the war. There is no empire now and conditions abroad are even less inviting for emigration. According to a current report fewer than 14,000 emigrants, all but 5,000 with government aid, emigrated during the fifteen-month period ending March 1955, the great majority going to Latin America. A goal of 9,000 government-financed emigrants armed also with preliminary instruction in the language, customs, and conditions they will meet overseas, was set for the fiscal year ending March 1956. But what is that against the population increment of more than a million for the same period?

Wealth, Industry, and Trade

Since there is no promise of relief from agriculture or emigration, and since population control through changing social conditions and education is distant in the future, Japan must rely upon industry for economic salvation. The development of industry saved the Japanese during the second half of the nineteenth century from the colonial or semicolonial status which was the fate of other Asiatic peoples. The further development of industry must save them in the rest of this century from the inevitable consequences of overpopulation—grinding poverty and political upheaval—which have been the fate of the peoples of China and India. Japan needed and got outside help a hundred years ago; Japan needs it now.

Japan produces from a niggardliness of natural wealth. The land is poor in raw materials and in sources of energy. About two-thirds of it is in forests but, partly because Japan uses wood in more diverse and important ways than do most countries, it has an annual deficit in forest products.

Japan's coal reserves are the major power source for its industries, but while they are sufficient to make the country the chief coal-producer in the Far East, they have it trailing far behind the leading industrial states in the West. Moreover, the coal is low-grade.

Happily, Japan is well supplied with the "white coal" of water-power. The hundreds of hydroelectric plants which tap the water-power of the country's numerous and precipitous rivers make Japan the sixth-ranking consumer of electricity.

At the same time Japan is one of the world's poorest powers in oil from domestic sources. These are not adequate for present needs and will fall into ever shorter supply as Japanese dependence upon machinery grows. The discrepancy between supply and need is widening with the rehabilitation of the fishing fleet and with rearmament.

The picture is not much better for iron ore. The pig-iron produced from domestic sources amounts to only a few thousand tons from small deposits and supplies only a fraction of the country's consumption.

The only important minerals of which Japan has sufficient quantities, indeed, are lignite, sulphur, and zinc. Copper and manganese are available in significant amounts.

Such poverty in minerals means that Japan's heavy industry can operate only if heavy supplies are available from abroad. Not only must iron ore, coking coal, and oil be imported, but also bauxite, lead, phosphate rock, and tin. Nor is the situation better for fibers. For the cotton, wool, and silk textiles in which Japanese industry excels, only raw silk can be had from domestic sources. Sheep never were raised in Japan and the cotton which was once grown has long since given ground to food crops.

Japan's critical weakness, then, is the dependence of its industrial plant upon supplies from abroad. The country has had the workers and the power; it has lacked the raw materials. If the Japanese people are to sustain or advance their standard of living, raw materials must come from sources which are not under Japanese control.

Until Communist and United States policy combined to shut off the trade of continental China, Japan's location gave it easy access to sources both of food and industrial materials. So long as

Tokyo controlled the intervening seas, Japan's domestic deficiencies were in great measure supplied.

But access to raw materials without the means of purchasing them is as useless for nations as a candy counter is for small boys with empty pockets. Japan, dependent upon external sources of supply, is equally dependent upon external markets in which to sell. For only as a nation sells can it buy. To pay for food, for fertilizers, and for the raw materials to feed its machines, Japan must find overseas markets for the goods and services it produces.

Yet Japan's markets have been unstable ever since the beginning of its modern era, even while the industrializing of the country in adaptation to its inelastic cultivation areas has made for an ever-increasing need to buy and therefore to sell abroad. Control over the sea could secure little beyond physical access to markets, so when tariffs, boycotts, and other trade barriers began to interfere with the volume of Japan's foreign trade, an effort to control more than the sea was bound to be considered.

National Characteristics

Not least among Japan's resources are some of the distinctive characteristics of her people. All generalizing about the Japanese, as about any people, is subject to exceptions; but the culture of a people, transmitted by education beginning long before entrance into school, leaves its lasting mark. Certain Japanese traits will be recognized as sources of national strength and others as factors of weakness. With the qualities that are neutral in this regard we are not concerned.

National Cohesiveness

If there is one distinctive feature which marks the Japanese as different, albeit only in degree, from other peoples whether Asiatic or Western, it is their national cohesiveness. Not merely because of their numbers, concentration, and activity have the Japanese been likened to a beehive or an anthill. The analogy rests also upon such superficial qualities as the industry and energy of their members, their discipline and readiness for self-sacrifice in the common good, and the hierarchy of their social organization where each has his place. Though the analogy be exaggerated, the trait is important.

It is not merely that the Japanese are nationalistic, feeling themselves set apart from and perhaps superior to other peoples. Or that they take a deep pride in themselves and their culture. Or that they believe they have a national mission. Beyond these facts there is a national consciousness as well as an identification of himself with his country on the part of the ordinary individual which made something better than vainglorious nonsense such wartime slogans as "100,000,000 men as one." It is no accident that with all Japan's political turmoil during the past century, political refugees are practically nonexistent. The same national spirit accounts for Japan's lasting bitterness over the Russo-German-French intervention at the end of the Sino-Japanese War and over the United States' exclusion law of 1924, for the public's closing ranks in the face of foreign criticism of the Manchurian invasion in 1931, and for the widely felt almost personal shame over the sinking of the U.S.S. *Panay* in 1937. Such cohesiveness minimizes the upheavals caused by domestic strife and reforms, while it also makes for high morale and a maximum of effort in the face of external danger.

Other traits reinforce the cohesiveness of the Japanese. One is social conformity. Another is their acceptance of hierarchy as a universal principle applicable also to human affairs. A third is the high value they place on harmony in social relations. All three of these appear to have been evolved by the Japanese in answer to a felt interior need.

Social Conformity

Under their usually impassive exterior, their polite manner, and their famous smile, the Japanese cover a welter of emotion. The outward stoicism often hides a tortured, self-doubting, and insecure soul. High-strung, hot tempered, excitable and depressive, victimized by sentimentality and melancholy, they are subject to moods and impulses. It is not within our competence to account here for their psychological make-up; it is enough and it is necessary to point to the frustrations and explosions of the Japanese temperament and to the social controls without which the Japanese individual would have to go his own way, driven before every gust of feeling.

More than other peoples, therefore, the Japanese have been taught to deny their individual inclinations in the interest of conforming to acceptable patterns of social behavior from which little deviation is allowed. Ethics with them is a matter of status and circumstance, obligations being determined by the relationship of the particular persons concerned. Right conduct is attained through devotion to a rigid formalism unknown to the West. It is by a careful observance of rules that the individual will be spared loss of face and the disastrous embarrassment which accompanies it. For without face nothing and no one can succeed. Out of faithful conformity to rules comes the social behavior which means social success (to the Japanese there is no other success) and which contributes importantly to the cohesiveness of the nation. In the field of government, however, this kind of social behavior does not make for individualism, experimentation, or daring.

Hierarchy

The Japanese belief in hierarchy has a similar effect. It is not surprising to find that a people whose system of ethics has imperatives varying from individual to individual according to circumstance should elevate hierarchy into a universal principle. The Japanese do not regard men or any other of nature's creatures as "equal." The inequality of all things is with them a simple matter of observation and common sense. Social relations are expected to reflect inequality among men. The result is an ordering of society upon a strict system of hierarchy. To the Japanese this ordering is only "natural."

Hierarchy is an all-pervasive social principle in Japan; it goes beyond the armed forces, the political parties, the families of distinguished lineage, the business firms, and the religious orders, where hierarchy is found also in other countries. Japanese apply the principle to rank business firms, sports teams, classes within a school grade and the schools themselves, artists, relatives, village elders; indeed, everything has its foremost, behind which come the rest, each in his proper place. Age confers on the Japanese a special dignity unknown even among the Chinese and the Jews, who also treat the old with deference. The dominance of the male is found to a degree unique among advanced nations. But with each individual keeping to the place assigned him by circumstances and meticulously meeting the obligations which his place imposes, an orderly world is the result—an orderly world and a cohesive society. But the institution of hierarchy is not easily reconciled with democracy or with a family of nations which is made up of equals before the law.

As might be expected, the acceptance of hierarchy as part of the natural order leads the Japanese to put great stress upon the related virtues of loyalty to superiors, obedience to authority and, on the part of superiors, a paternalistic responsibility for those below. Loyalty to the overlord, the sovereign virtue of the ruling class in feudal Japan, has been transformed in modern times into loyalty to the Emperor on the part of all classes. At the same time there has developed an expectation of loyalty on the part of subordinates to their superiors in all walks of life.

Offsetting the unifying force of loyalty, however, are two besetting sins of the Japanese, jealousy and factionalism. Jealousy among colleagues often paralyzes their work and leads to personal defeat and to frustration of the common effort. Jealousy makes any successful figure the target of intrigue and opposition, be he the number-one student in class or the prime minister in Tokyo. Factionalism grows out of the loyalty of followers to their patrons and leaders. Like jealousy, factionalism operates to hamper the work of the body it afflicts, from a schoolboy club to the national parties and the Cabinet itself.

Obedience to authority, a conspicuous virtue of the Japanese, extends beyond loyalty to leaders and superiors. In varying degrees the father receives obedience from his family, the elder brothers from the younger, the teacher from his students (and even more the master from his disciples), the artisan from his apprentice, the business employer from his employees, the military officer from his men, the government official from the people, and above all the Emperor from his subjects. The modern Japanese are not so far removed from the feudalism their grandfathers knew as to forget the Confucian maxim, "Let the people depend upon the government; let the people not know the business of the government." This attitude militates against popular participation in the conduct of public affairs, and the dependence it encourages belongs to a social pattern extending far outside the political sphere.

The converse of the duty of obedience is the obligation of superiors towards inferiors. For with the Japanese, paternalism is as inseparable from hierarchy as is obedience. The duty of the individual extends not only up toward superiors, backward toward ancestors, and outward toward his peers (when by force of circumstances he has incurred obligations to peers); duty extends also downwards from the father to the children, from the officer to his men, from the rulers to the ruled. If superiors are to be looked up to and obeyed, subordinates are to be looked after and cherished. The individual exists for the whole community, all of its members contributing to the health of the whole, each as required by his station in life. Like the habit of compromise, which we shall examine, paternalism goes a long way toward easing the rigors of the Japanese system.

Finally, the cohesiveness of the Japanese nation grows in part out of the emphasis placed upon social harmony, a natural corollary of the preference for conformity and hierarchy. The Japanese ideal is a social system operating not so much like a machine of well-oiled and intermeshing parts as like an organism whose many organs each make an effortless, noiseless, and unnoticed contribution to the health of the whole. To the attainment of this ideal the individual Japanese expects and is expected to sacrifice his personal preferences—whether in family affairs, in business, in politics, or in other social contexts. The degree of sacrifice will vary with the circumstances of the particular case. The governing rule is that of compromise and the mechanism for the adjustment of interests is some form of group council, whether formal as in the family conference or informal as in the use of the time-honored "go-between." Operating to prevent or minimize rents in the social fabric, the value attached by the Japanese to harmony strengthens the social structure and exerts a powerful if uncertain influence upon politics.

Compromise

Related to their love of harmony and pervading human relations in Japan, government included, is the element of compromise. The Japanese compromise is not on the basis of an equal division or exchange, hence the political picture frequently remains obscure even when we think we have made allowance for compromise. We might be helped here by what one could call the "80 per cent rule," although the Japanese do not formulate the problem in those terms. But as a rough generalization the 80 per cent rule will help to account for the obscurity of Japanese politics. By this rule, the law is the law—but only for four-fifths of the time and to four-fifths of its ostensible limits. Your rights, legal and social, are yours —but don't push them the whole way; stop 20 per cent short. Power is exercised by those who have it but only to 80 per cent of the limit. Triumphs, in politics and elsewhere, are not more than four-fifths won; defeats not more than four-fifths disastrous. And the 80 per cent rule is only 80 per cent applicable. This is the element of compromise which everywhere blurs Oriental and especially Japanese relationships. Like paternalism, it greases the wheels of Japanese society, softening the impact upon the individual of law and social obligation, and easing the relationship of rulers and ruled. Like paternalism, obedience to authority, and social conformity, the habit of compromise helps explain the success with which the Japanese made the transition from feudalism to modern life and from all-out war to Occupation and then to peaceful independence.

Conciliar Decision-Making

In reaching compromises where there are conflicts of interests or differences of opinion respecting policy, the Japanese prefer to reach decisions in consultation among a group. From the club committee and the family council to such exalted organs of government as the former Supreme War Council and the present Cabinet, conciliar decision-making is the rule. Not only does council make compromise easier; more than that, it relieves the individual of personal responsibility for the decision. Should a policy determined upon in a group consideration go wrong, no one individual would be known and blamed as its author. To be sure, there is titular responsibility: and often a Japanese will publicly take responsibility for acts committed by others within his jurisdiction. But in reaching decisions, the Japanese clings to the group, where, the risks being shared, he feels safer. The ubiquity of the family council and of its analogues in business and in government reflects the Japanese propensity for committee decisions and concerted action. It is one of the many social consequences of the personal insecurity characteristic of Japanese psychology.

Self-Consciousness

Personal insecurity accounts for much in the Japanese social scene besides decision-making in groups to avoid individual responsibility. From self-doubt flows a painful self-consciousness. Lacking all his life what Europeans would consider elementary privacy, and kept in line from childhood by fear of social disapproval, the Japanese never quite relaxes. He is always acting to an audience, real or fancied. He is always alert for the cues which will prompt the next lines in the role he feels bound to play. Fearful of losing face, he plans everything ahead, striving to know where a given road will take him and to foresee all contingencies in order to fend off the undesirable. He is self-conscious both as an individual and as member of the Japanese people, which for him is a "chosen people." Whether at home or abroad, he stands in his own mind as a representative of the whole Japanese nation, playing to a world audience. That the audience may be paying him little attention does not occur to him; the act goes on as if in the glare of a spotlight, and success or failure are met as coming not to the individual in his loneliness but to the whole body of the people to which he belongs. Burdened with this responsibility, the Japanese can never let down his guard.

Self-Discipline and Emotionalism

The natural consequence of such self-consciousness is self-discipline. To overcome the stresses and strains of his emotions, to fulfill the demands imposed by his place in life, to avoid false moves that will invite disdain from what he thinks is an unsleeping audience, the Japanese cultivates self-discipline with a single-minded devotion approaching the heroic. Few western peoples can match his success. The Japanese recruit on half-rations, the religious devotee subjecting himself to outdoor ablutions of a January midnight, the Zen Buddhist student's austerities, or of the tea ceremony's exacting demands—these are only the more conspicuous examples. The peaceful crowds, the rarity of disorder, the even greater rarity of raucous public dispute so commonly found on the streets of other Asiatic lands, attest in part to the self-discipline of the Japanese.

But these same orderly and self-controlled people, so prudent and careful in the ordinary events of life, are susceptible under provocation to panic and to outbursts of violence. Times come when the volcanic emotionalism of the Japanese breaks through the crust of habit and discipline. Such contradiction is not without explanation. The Japanese tend to be intuitive, literal-minded, and unanalytic. They respond to fine phrases rather than to logical argument; they have convictions rather than conclusions. Unimaginative as well as unanalytic, they do not readily adjust to unexpected and unplanned developments. Not only do such people find themselves at a loss to improvise when plans go awry; they are also liable to sudden breaks under great strain. The high rate of suicide in peacetime and the *banzai* charges by last-ditch defenders in wartime, the hunting down of Korean immigrants by berserk mobs (who blamed them as arsonists) during the 1923 Tokyo earthquake and fire, illustrate what can happen because of this side of the Japanese psychological make-up.

Self-Centeredness

In another direction their lack of imagination and reasoned analysis prevents the Japanese from comprehending how non-Japanese think, what motivates them, and what is likely to be the foreign reaction to a given Japanese policy. The Japanese are by no means unique among nations in predicating foreign policy upon misconceptions regarding the psychology of their rivals, and they seem to share with the Germans a peculiar blindness as to foreign powers which repeatedly has spelled disaster. The barbarous rape of Nanking in 1937 and the air strike at Hawaii in 1941 are two instances where Japanese measures produced the very opposite of the reactions intended: the Chinese fought back with renewed determination and the Americans girded themselves for all-out war. But so dense is this blind spot of the Japanese that opposition is ascribed to base motives and wilful misrepresentation when other governments refuse to go along with them in such self-assumed roles as that of pacifier of China or king-maker in Manchuria.

Characteristics of Political Decision-Making

Besides taking into consideration such general national characteristics as have been discussed in the preceding pages, it is also helpful in thinking about government and foreign policy in Japan to keep in mind a number of illuminating peculiarities of the Japanese political scene itself.

Unstable Political Institutions

For one thing there is a special fluidity or mutability of political institutions in Japan. Though change is characteristic of all living institutions, in Japan since the Meiji Restoration of 1867 it has proceeded at a far greater rate and with greater violence to institutions than is compatible with orderly government. The institutions which replaced those of feudalism never attained the stability which is expected of governments that have not been defeated in war and are not prone to revolution. For this instability there appear to have been two general causes. On the one hand, none of the institutions, not even the Emperor cult, was deeply rooted in Japan's past. On the other, the institutions were in the aggregate a Japanized composite of various European contributions, a jerry-built structure European in appearance but Japanese in use and function. So long as its architects, the leaders who engineered the modernizing of Japan, remained united in their management of the structure, it had a certain sturdy quality. But from the time their unifying influence was lost through internal quarrels, there was a constant shifting of the political center of gravity, a con-

stant process of erosion and accretion of power among the organs
of the government and the political factions controlling them, a
constant change in the role each played. This instability is confusing to observers.

Incomplete Revolution

In a sense, Japan throughout the modern period may be regarded as in a state of latent or continuing revolution. The Meiji
Restoration was no true revolution. It could not be one so long as
the transfer of political power was not from one class to another
and so long as the change in form was not accompanied by a change
in spirit. The traditional ways continued. Japan did not come
abreast of the developments which had taken place in other parts
of the world during the centuries of its seclusion because its technological revolution was not matched by any social and political
revolution. The leaders of the Restoration attempted to graft upon
their traditional pagan society the outward forms of modern industrial society, and the attempt kept the upheaval brought about by
the events of the Restoration from ever wholly subsiding. This
continuing revolution is another thing to be borne in mind while
thinking about government in Japan.

Government Behind the Curtain

A third key to understanding is the principle of indirect government, variously called invisible government or government behind
the curtain. To this ancient political phenomenon in Japan, the
figurehead role of the English monarch and boss rule in the United
States present, in their different ways, analogies. In Japan at all
levels of government, however, one man might have the title and
another the power, the powers and duties nominally vested in one
official or organ of government being exercised in fact by others.
The political process in Japan will not be clear if the locus of power
is not perceived to be different from what the institutional façade
would suggest.

The Japanese National "Family"

Another peculiarity of Japanese government is the familial character of the nation in the eyes and sentiments of the people. Here

we must stop for a moment to note the distinctiveness of the Japanese family itself, for this by extension explains the distinctiveness of the Japanese state. Traditionally, the individual Japanese depends upon the family in all important decisions all his life. All members except infant children enter into the decisions of each member. The family is an organism of which the head may be the most important in one sense, but in which each part has its place and importance. No member suffers or prospers but that all suffer or prosper with him. Here, as elsewhere in Japanese social relations, no individual has the moral right to make any decision in any matter that impinges on the lives of those around him without their participation in the making of that decision. It is a group matter and a group decision.

In medieval Japan the unit of society was not the individual as in the United States nor the family as in China, but the community, the clan, which in its internal relations, so far as the ruling samurai or warrior class was concerned, was the family writ large. The individual was completely identified with his clan, to the exclusion of all more personal interests. With the Restoration the mores of the samurai class, which had long since begun to permeate the lower classes, were generalized throughout the population by universal education but with a new orientation. The feudal loyalty to the clan and to the overlord was transferred to the country and to the Emperor.

Since the country, thereafter, was the clan on a grander scale, just as the clan itself was a grander family, political relations in Japan were familial. The rulers, like elder brothers and clan leaders, were to be looked up to and obeyed. The people, like children and weaker members of the clan, were to be protected and guided. Government did not exist for the benefit of the governed. Rather, the individual existed for the community, with all parts of the community serving the common welfare, each person receiving what was his due and contributing what was required by his station in life. Paternalism, as we have noted, has ever since been characteristic of government in Japan. To the Japanese, too, since Japan is a great family and political affairs tend to be determined as family affairs are determined, policies were expected to be made by agreement among the leading members, not by a majority vote of the infant children.

Two peculiar features of the Japanese political scene remain for consideration: the influential roles of oligarchy and Emperor.

The Oligarchy

Among the changes produced by the reopening of Japan to foreign intercourse in the 1850's was the creation of a radically new form of government to replace the defunct shogunate. For the fourth time in the long history of the islands, the ancient Japanese practice of revolution from on top—with one section of the ruling class usurping the place and role of another—was followed by the establishment of a new structure of government. The events of the period between 1867 and 1890—from the collapse of the Tokugawa regime to the adoption of the Meiji Constitution—are known to history, at least to Japanese historians, not as a reformation, still less as a revolution, but, though euphemistically, as the Restoration. According to official doctrine, the Meiji Emperor was restored to the rule from which the usurping soldier had thrust his ancestors seven hundred years before. But in fact, the extremely able young samurai who engineered the overthrow of the shogunate and the establishment of the new government did no more than substitute one figurehead monarchy for another. The emperor had not ruled before 1867; he did not rule afterwards. The real change effected was a transfer of power, including the powers of the Throne, from one oligarchy to another, both of them part of the same section of the ruling class which had dominated society in Japan since the end of the sixteenth century—the soldier class. The Constitution of 1890 was designed to sustain the transfer.

The Constitution admirably fulfilled the intentions of its authors. All substantive power was ascribed to the Emperor in such language that the man, controlled in all official acts by the oligarchy in the role of advisers, could be confused with the institution, the Throne (Japan's analogue to the British Crown) and both of these with the state. Like its Prussian model, the Japanese Constitution wove into a single fabric the fiction of divine-right monarchy, the form of popular representation, and the fact of oligarchical control over both Emperor and government.

In their new system the oligarchs permitted outsiders only token participation in the governmental process through representation in an impotent House of Representatives. Their own position of control was amply protected. Direction of the apparatus of government was preserved by making the executive, the Cabinet, responsible only to the Emperor—which was equivalent to making it irresponsible—and by dividing the power of the state among the Cabinet, the Privy Council, the military and naval high command, and the officials of the Imperial Household. Actual control of policy was provided by the time-honored institution of government behind the curtain. That is, acting in the name of the Emperor, whom it controlled although popularly and officially he was equated with the state itself, the oligarchy insured that all strategic posts were filled by its members or by their protégés and gave the government unity of direction by concerting their policy behind the scenes and then carrying it out through the organs of the state.

Except for the oligarchy, the government thus constituted, with the Emperor at once its capstone and foundation, had in fact no final authority. For the Emperor qua Son of Heaven, acting only on the advice of his irresponsible ministers, was in relation to the government the Emperor qua state, and a state has no practical existence. The Meiji Constitution gave Japan a government of discrete parts cemented together by the oligarchy. So long as the cement held, the structure was reasonably stable; so long as the oligarchs were united, the Constitution worked.

What loosened the cement and weakened the structure, at times to the point of collapse, was the pervasive solvent of oriental loyalties: personal jealousy. The day came when the founding fathers of modern Japan, in sheer jealousy of one another, disagreed among themselves to the point of bringing their internecine struggles into public view. Thereafter, their failure to provide a unifying factor in place of their disunited selves made of each organ of government a bastion from which one entrenched faction might war upon factions entrenched in other organs. The Cabinet, the Privy Council, the high command, the Imperial Household, lent themselves in varying degrees to the struggle for power among the factions within the oligarchy and later among the groups which arose to take its place.

Only the veneer of constitutional terminology obscured for the public the underlying reality: the Hydra-headed monstrosity with its four constitutionally irresponsible organs of government, a multiple executive whose members warred among themselves as each "advised the Emperor" in the vaguely defined areas of their jurisdiction.

In the context of Japanese politics the structure was saved from total collapse by the native genius for compromise, on the one hand, and on the other by the emergence of an extraconstitutional body of elder statesmen, known individually and collectively as the Genro, in whom the Japanese tradition of indirect government found its most notable modern expression. These were some of the leading younger men among the early oligarchs who, as age caught up with them in their turn and the long years of association with the Meiji Emperor invested them with a special aura, came to have in the public view a national role not unlike that of the elders in a village or family. In this role, in some degree, they managed to supply to affairs of state the element of unity which the Constitution and they themselves as oligarchs had failed to supply.

The full weakness of the governmental structure was not felt until the end of World War I. By then the grip of the divided and warring oligarchy upon the reins of government had been relaxed through death of some members and the rise to power of the great industrial families, the bureaucracy, and the political parties. The Genro notwithstanding, no group appeared, however, to fill the position uniquely held by the oligarchs for two generations. Henceforth the contestants for power were the great factions into which the ruling class became divided: aristocrats, industrialists, party politicians, the navy—but above all the army and the bureaucrats.

The Emperor

A word needs to be added about the near miracles which have been worked by the government's invoking the power of the Emperor. This feature of the Japanese scene has no real counterpart anywhere else in the realm of modern government.

In a real but highly peculiar sense, to a Japanese nurtured in the *Tenno* mystique, the Emperor is a god in human form. But Shinto makes little distinction between the natural and the supernatural, between gods and men. This confusion of mortal and divine does not raise human beings to the plane of the gods so much as it brings divinity down to a human or at best heroic level. Moreover the world, seen and unseen, is populated with myriads of gods whose very abundance depresses their value.

The Son of Heaven, however, is no ordinary god. He is the last in a line of heaven-descended sovereigns into whose hands has been entrusted, originally by the Sun-Goddess herself, the governance of the "land of the gods." Caesar equally by divine descent and by divine right, the Emperor is both "visible deity" and high priest, the former representing upon earth the whole host of invisible deities, the latter representing the Japanese people before the heavenly hosts. At the same time he is the head of the vast Japanese family, the nation. To the Japanese faithful he incarnates divinity, ancestors, and the glory of Dai Nippon past, present, and future. Their attitude is thus a blend of religion, patriotism, and family affection, a very powerful force when adroitly invoked.

To the leaders of the Restoration, in their need for a symbol around which to unite the feudal loyalties of the many little clans, the Emperor cult came ready-made. High-pressure indoctrination— through school, army, patriotic societies, and the press—gave a patriotic bias to the ancestor-worship inculcated by Japan's brand of Confucianism; it redirected from the overlord to the Emperor the fierce loyalty inculcated by Japan's brand of feudalism; and it diffused these two class values of the samurai among the whole population.

One political consequence was that the Emperor became in the hands of his ministers a power of almost miraculous effectiveness. Time and again, dangerous opposition melted and storms of popular clamor ceased after an indication of the Imperial pleasure. The object of the Japanese faith was a completely helpless mortal like his subjects, a puppet in the hands of other mortals like themselves. But the majestic vision of the God-King-Patriarch hid from them the pathetic human figure.

Miracles, however, can be wrought only in an atmosphere of faith, and political miracles in Japan are no exception. There are limits beyond which the power of invoking the Emperor's pleasure failed to have effect (an instance, perhaps, of the 80 per cent rule). For the Japanese developed a mild corrective to the dangerous situation in which they were placed by the Emperor cult. They came to believe that the Emperor could not act contrary to what was right, that is, to what they thought was right. When he appeared to do so, it was out of "insincere advice" from his ministers. Such a conviction could and did lead to vigorous protest and often to outright violence. But when the spirit of the times was favorable, when what the Emperor did or seemed to do comported with what the Japanese were ready to accept—as in 1881 or 1945—the effects of the Imperial pleasure were instantaneous and unlimited.

Foreign Policy

As we have seen earlier in this chapter, Japan has an area less than California and a population more than half that of the United States, arable land insufficient to supply the food needs of its people, and an industrial plant—the most significant outside of Europe and North America—dependent upon foreign markets and foreign sources of raw materials. Having been defeated in World War II and then stripped of its arms, the country must look for its security to other powers at a time of world-wide international tension and "cold war." Yet Japan stretches along the great-circle shipping lanes from the New World, a screen of islands between the land mass of China and the Pacific Ocean. Its strategic situation, coupled with its industrial strength, makes the country a prized ally, the object of diplomatic attention and the subject of diplomatic maneuver. Japan is the keystone of the free world's defenses in the Pacific and stands squarely athwart the Sino-Russian bloc's road to the western hemisphere. Were Japan's allegiance to change, the balance of power would shift dangerously in favor of the Communist world. Japan would then constitute an island shield for the protection of the Asiatic continent against the West and a chain of anchored aircraft carriers threatening the sea lanes between the United States and Southeast Asia.

For a powerful nation, which Japan is not, this position would be difficult economically but enviable politically. For a defenseless nation it is deplorable on both counts. Security, a viable economy, and—because men and nations do not live by bread alone—recognition as a respected member of the world community are today the chief ends of Japan's foreign policy as they were before World War II. We shall be better able to judge whether there is hope that Japan will attain these ends and to anticipate the means through which they will be sought if we first look at the nation's record in the past century.

The Record

A century ago, in response to western pressures, the Japanese emerged from the self-imposed seclusion of more than twice that period of time, wiping from their eyes the cobwebs of insularity and finding themselves face to face with imminent disaster. The world that met their gaze in the mid-nineteenth century was strange and frightening. It grew more so as the 1860's came and went. The technological changes introduced by the Industrial Revolution and the accompanying improvements in commercial and financial structures, coupled with advances in large-scale organization of production, had transformed Europe and North America.

Japan found herself in a highly precarious situation. The island empire was a country with few resources, no modern armament, and little capital for investment in industry. Its chief asset was a disciplined, obedient, industrious population.

Encroaching from all directions were the predatory denizens of the fiercely competitive world of nineteenth-century imperialism. The European powers, which could be stood off by fiat in the simpler days of the seventeenth century, were now returning armed with weapons both military and industrial against which Japan had no adequate defenses. In the dozen years before Commodore Perry's black ships were sighted off Yedo (now Tokyo) Bay, China had twice been beaten by European arms, and China's Son of Heaven forced into flight from the Forbidden City in Peking as western troops neared the capital. This repeated humbling of China was seen by the Japanese against the background of European expansion throughout Asia and the Pacific.

On all sides, except due west where China lay, the horizons were threatening. Russia sprawled across Siberia, from the Urals to the Pacific north of Japan. The United States had reached the Pacific on the east. Britain and France were extending their dominions into regions to the southwest. Spain was ensconced in the Philippines. The tides of imperialism and conquest were washing steadily closer—out of India and the Indies and the south Pacific, out of Siberia and California. Events in Siam, Indo-China, the Maritime Provinces of Siberia, and Alaska marked their approach as significantly as did events in China.

Having abandoned its policy of seclusion and nonintercourse and having learned its inferiority in the modern sinews of power, Japan saw itself as vulnerable to attack as a hermit crab without its shell. There was clear warning that *bushido*—the ideology of her ruling warrior class—must find other than the traditional weapons of feudalism if security was to be regained for the country. Whatever may have been the intentions of the powers with respect to Japan, to the Japanese the implications of their advance were obvious: the face of imperialism was the face of jeopardy.

The threat could be met only by immediate and radical action. The first task of the makers of modern Japan was to unify the numerous feudal domains within the empire into a single state commanding the loyalty of all the people. The industrial sinews of modern power had to be acquired. Modern defenses must be built up. All must be done in the face of often violent opposition within Japan. All must be accomplished before disaster overtook the country in its defenseless condition, and the accomplishment must depend upon native wit, inspiration, and leadership, however much these might lean upon foreign models and instructors.

The genius of the Japanese was such that, having been forced by the technologically superior West to abandon their traditional policy of seclusion, they responded by adapting to their needs the very technology in which the West had shown itself to be superior. They learned the secrets of the power of the West so as to become able to cope with the West on the West's own terms and with the West's own techniques.

The question was whether the transformation could be effected before disaster struck. Could the Japanese move fast enough and with great enough force, learning from the West the secrets of its superiority in arms, industry, and finance in time to turn these against the imperialists?

The first essential was the establishment of an orderly government to guide the country's development with a minimum of internal dissension. The government created by the leaders of the Restoration was designed to act as a sort of combined brain trust and general staff able to devise long-term programs of development, to command compliance of the many sections of the public, to improvise in the face of necessity, and to change tactics whenever it seemed best to do so. Before and after the promulgation of the Meiji Constitution in 1889, the governmental system was such as to enable the ruling oligarchy to channel the whole force of the Japanese people into a concerted effort sufficient to bring about the required transformation of the country in time to prevent a fate similar to India's or to China's. The time-consuming and uncertain ways of democracy would have poorly served the pressing needs of Japan and the daring plans of the oligarchs. Democracy was a luxury beleaguered Japan could ill afford—even if the Japanese had been disposed to look for a model in the political systems of the United States (whose claim had been weakened by the Civil War), of Great Britain (whose Second Reform Bill doubling the franchise antedates the end of the Tokugawa era by only a few weeks), or of France (whose Second Empire ended in 1870 just a year before feudalism was abolished in Japan) rather than to those of Prussia and eastern Europe.

What the Japanese leaders were quick to learn from their western tutors were the sources of the latter's power: unity, industry, literacy, capitalism, and—above all—armaments. Its shocked awakening to the power of the West stirred Japan in self-defense to emulate the West. The Japanese adopted and adapted the West's legal systems and parliamentary forms along with the latest in communications, machinery, manufactures, and a thousand and one gadgets and gimmicks which happened to catch their eye or which they thought helped them measure up to western standards. But they soon learned that in the eyes of the modern world national greatness is measured only in military terms. No contributions of their arts, no excellence in the public service, no works of science, philosophy, or religion, but only military power proved on the field of battle would gain Japan the respect of the other powers where it counted, namely, in the inner circle of the world's oligarchs, the so-called Great Powers.

The pressure of the West upon Japan does not by itself account for the political changes which overwhelmed the feudal system of the shoguns and led to the creation of a unitary state under a constitutional monarchy. Domestic developments, some having roots extending far back into the Tokugawa era, also played their part. But to the external menace must be attributed the shape and direction of Japanese foreign policy once seclusion had been cast aside in favor of international intercourse with its manifold hazards.

The First Phase

In the three-quarters of a century between the start of the Meiji era (1867-1912) and the start of the Allied Occupation (1945-1952) the evolution of Japan's foreign policy may be said to have passed through three phases. There is a long period ending about the time of the peace settlement of 1919, which brought World War I to a close. This is followed by shorter second and third periods, each lasting not much more than a decade. The second ends abruptly with the launching of the Manchurian invasion in September 1931; the third, no less abruptly, with the fall of General Tojo as prime minister in July 1944.

During the first phase Japan was guided by the personal rule of the oligarchs, the men who had been associated with the Restoration and the revered Meiji emperor. The period fades out as the reins of government begin to slip from the aging fingers of the second generation of these oligarchs.

Except for a brief time at the start when questions of foreign policy were allowed to divide them, there was general agreement among the oligarchs as to the grand lines of foreign policy. United in opinion, armed with the power and prestige needed to carry the country with them, the oligarchs guided Japan through the jungle of international politics during the nineteenth and early twentieth centuries, using every means at the nation's command—and in those days of unbridled nationalism all means were legitimate if they were effective. At the end of the period Japan's leaders could look with pride upon the fruits of their labors. For in less than two generations Japan's international position had been raised from that of an insignificant people with little voice or weight in international counsels to that of a world power, one of the international oligarchy, the intimate circle of Great Powers. The nation had attained security and had exacted recognition, the two dominant purposes of its foreign policy in this first phase.

The lines followed by Japanese foreign policy during the first phase were four: the building up of an empire, the attainment of hegemony in eastern Asia and the western Pacific, the expansion of overseas trade, and admission, with full rights and privileges, to the world community as a leading member. In pursuing these objectives, Japan reflected, in part deliberately and in part unconsciously, the world in which she found herself.

The world of the late nineteenth century made much of national honor and sovereign irresponsibility on the part of state, justified imperialist ventures with high-sounding phrases such as the "white man's burden" and "la mission civilatrice," talked in terms of spheres of influence and Monroe Doctrines, employed investments for political purposes and diplomacy for investments. It was a world of scientific progress, philosophical ferment, political experimentation, and economic expansion. The Japanese entered into this world with zest.

For many years, however, the Japanese leaders were much too busy with fast-moving events in the modernization of their country at home to worry about expansion abroad. It was more by accident than as the result of policy that they inaugurated their acquisition of overseas territories. But before the adoption of the Constitution in 1889 they had absorbed the Ryukyu Islands, the Bonins, and the Kuriles.

The Ryukyus, stretching south from Kyushu to Formosa, became an issue with the disappearance in 1872 of the Japanese feudal domains, one of which, Satsuma, had claims (disputed with China) of suzerainty over the islands. In 1879 they were incorporated as an integral part of the Japanese homeland and divided between the prefectures of Kagoshima and Okinawa. About the Bonins, on the other hand, there never was much question despite sporadic and unauthorized claims by agents of other powers. Always considered a part of Japan, they were formally recognized as such in 1873 and in 1880 were placed under the municipal administration of the city of Tokyo. Controversy over the Kuriles, stretching northward from the Hokkaido to the Kamchatka Peninsula, was the inevitable result of Russia's expansion to the Pacific and Japan's return to the family of nations. The issue was settled by peaceful negotiation in 1874, when Russia abandoned her claims to Kurile territory and Japan did the same with respect to Saghalin.

Expansion began in earnest with controversies over Korea, first with China and then with Russia. With the former, the issue was whether Korea should continue as one of the vassal states which ringed China or whether it should enter into diplomatic and trade relations with other countries and especially with Japan. The quarrel was resolved by the defeat of China in the Sino-Japanese War (1894-1895), itself a test of how well Japan had learned its lessons in the art of western-style warfare. Japan as a result not only ended interference by her rival in Korean affairs but also acquired possession of Formosa and of the nearby islands called the Pescadores. To insure that there would be no future difficulties in Korea either from China or from Russia hovering to the north, Japan also secured the cession of the Liaotung Peninsula, which stretches out of Manchuria into the waters of the Yellow Sea. The cession further jeopardized the independence of Korea and promised to thwart Russia's hope of profiting by China's weakness to acquire a warm-water ocean outlet in the East.

To clip the wings of Japanese aspiration, Russia, Germany, and France—the famous *Dreibund*—intervened and successfully pres-

sured the bitterly disappointed Japanese into giving up the Liaotung Peninsula. This lesson the Japanese never forgot or forgave.
And nothing, except possibly the United States' exclusion law of
1924, had a comparable effect upon Japanese unity at home and the
Japanese policy of expansion abroad. The score was repaid to Russia
in 1904, to Germany in 1914, and to the French in 1940.

Russia came first. Once more the issue was Korea, in whose
affairs the Russians now replaced the Chinese as counterfoil to the
Japanese. But there were other pressing considerations. Russia,
continuing to penetrate Manchuria, had secured from the Chinese
a leasehold including the Liaotung Peninsula and refused to withdraw troops deployed in Manchuria. The European powers were
preparing to exploit what looked like the imminent break-up of
China. The Spanish-American war had brought the United States
into the Philippines. For the Japanese, time was running out.

Emboldened by the outcome of the Sino-Japanese war a decade
before and by the heady flattery implicit in the Anglo-Japanese
Alliance of 1902, the Japanese resorted to war against their Russian
adversary early in 1904. Japan won. The Portsmouth Treaty ending
the hostilities in 1905 left Japan with the southern half of Saghalin
island, the Russian leasehold of the Liaotung Peninsula together
with the Russian railway zone stretching as far north as Changchun
(= Hsinking), and a free hand in Korea. Eighteen months later
Korea became a Japanese protectorate and in 1910 it was formally
annexed. Japan proceeded apace with exploiting the economic opportunities presented by her treaty rights in Manchuria and her
occupation of Korea.

Then came World War I. Exposed to Japanese arms were the
German concessions on the Shantung Peninsula across the Yellow
Sea from Japan, and the German island possessions in the Pacific.
Japan, as Britain's ally, made short work of taking both, and the
Paris settlement in 1919 left them in Japanese hands—Germany's
Chinese holdings still as a concession and the Pacific islands as a
mandate under the League of Nations.

At the end of the first phase in the record of Japan's foreign
policy, thus, the empire extended through the Kuriles and Saghalin
on the north and northeast, the Ryukyus and Formosa on the

southeast, the Bonins and the mandates to the south and southeast, and Korea and the South Manchurian and Shantung concessions on the northwest. Japan had shown herself an apt pupil of
the imperialists. Indeed, she had beaten them at their own game,
for in this same period the force of Japanese arms and the effects
of World War I upon Japan's European rivals in China's affairs
made Japan the paramount power in the western Pacific. Hegemony, the second principle of Japanese foreign policy, had been as
much of a success as empire. One by one those who would have
balked the Japanese were met and removed from their path. China,
traditionally the Great Power of eastern Asia, had been humbled
in 1894 and her freedom of action prejudiced in Japanese favor by
diplomacy in 1915 (the Twenty-one Demands). Russia, the Siberian colossus, had been pushed back in 1905. Germany, the most
truculent challenger after Russia, was eliminated by World War I,
which also weakened the French and English. Even in the United
States, which had reverted to isolation, voices were raised in favor
of getting out of the Philippines.

Obviously Japan could not have built an empire and become the
principal power in eastern Asia unless its industry and trade had
made phenomenal strides during the same period. In both, Japan
quickly forged ahead of all its Oriental neighbors—despite the
paucity of its natural resources and the consequent necessity of
supplying a growing industrial plant with imported raw materials,
and despite the insatiable demands for foreign products imposed
by the westernization policy. Foreign trade kept pace with the
need, imports being paid for out of the profits from Japanese shipping and from the export of raw silk and processed goods and
foods. Nevertheless, a persistent excess of imports over exports in
the years before World War I boded ill for the future. But the war
reversed the tide, first with a flood of war orders from the belligerents and then with the opportunity to sell in markets previously
dominated by European products. By 1920, as compared with 1914,
Japan's horsepower had doubled, the number of her factory hands
had nearly doubled, the factories had tripled, and the value of
foreign trade had all but quadrupled.

Above all, success brought to Japan the prestige, the face, that the nation felt it must have—success in acquiring an empire, in attaining dominance in east Asian waters, and in expanding its industrial and commercial strength. Recognition came partly as a result of events themselves, above all of events on the battlefield, but it came also in answer to Japanese diplomatic efforts to secure the outward signs of respect. The first series of such efforts achieved its object in 1899, when the western powers abrogated the "unequal" treaties that had been imposed on Japan in the early years of intercourse. In 1900 Japan had the satisfaction of finding herself the only Asiatic power represented in the international expedition sent to the relief of the Peking legations besieged by the Boxers. In 1902, the Anglo-Japanese Alliance made Japan a partner with the greatest of the western powers; this alliance was revised in 1905 and 1911. The Japanese-American "Gentlemen's Agreement" of 1908 protected Japanese sensibilities in the matter of immigrant labor, while the Lansing-Ishii Agreement with the United States in 1917 acknowledged that Japan's position gave her special interests in China. The crowning gestures from abroad came at the Paris Peace Conference in 1919. Despite the adage that a "Great Power is a state that can lick a Great Power," Japan had remained in the world view a minor power during the decade and a half after the Russo-Japanese War. But at Paris, Japan was acknowledged to be a Great Power both by her place in the inner circles of the Conference and by her being named in the Covenant of the League of Nations for a permanent seat on that body's Council. Japan had arrived.

The Fork in the Road—the Second Phase

With the end of World War I and the first phase of Japanese foreign policy, the country's leaders had every reason to be satisfied. An adroit and often daring use of the West's techniques in war and diplomacy had achieved for Japan both security and a place among the world's Great Powers. In record time, the feudal domains of the shogun had been developed into a unified modern state, one of the world's leaders in industry and commerce. The decline in the influence of China, now only a congeries of local warlords, and of the European imperialists once so threatening in eastern waters, had left Japan the dominant power in eastern Asia. In naval arms Japan was counted one of the Big Three, exceeded only by the United States and Great Britain. At the Paris Peace Conference Japan had been one of the Big Five, and it had become one of the Big Four (with the United States out) in the League of Nations, the new world order planned to insure the defense of all countries. With such a record of success in foreign policy, Japan could face the future with confidence.

At about this time, however, the grip of the oligarchy upon the reins of government began to relax. The contestants for power now became the factions that divided the ruling class: the aristocrats, the industrialists, the party politicians, the navy, and—especially—the army and the bureaucrats. In the field of foreign policy also a sharp divergence of opinion developed. The industrialists, whose views were espoused by the bureaucrats, saw in international co-operation, peaceful diplomacy, and trade the wisest course for Japan to pursue in striving to maintain its dignity and security and to enhance its standard of living. But the militarists, a younger generation of army extremists, argued that regional autarky, won if necessary by further resort to war, was the only sure guarantee for Japan's future. For them the immense prizes gained by Japan when she had struck out for herself in 1894 and 1904 and 1914 conclusively demonstrated the superiority of the old ways.

Because of defects in the constitutional system, which we have noted, the conflict of policy could not be satisfactorily resolved. The military high command, within whose sole jurisdiction lay military questions deemed beyond the competence of civilians, was necessarily dominated by the army and the navy. The Imperial Household officials, deriving their obscure but important powers of interference thanks to their close association with the Emperor, were staunchly bureaucrat but had allies among the more moderate navy men. No group dominated the Privy Council, which had important powers of veto, but its conservatism inclined it toward the ambitions of the military. In the struggles between factions, the real prize was the Cabinet, the principal organ of the executive. Here the high commands had one final trump. The War and Navy Ministers, each of whom had to be a high-ranking officer, took office on sufferance of their respective general staffs. By the simple device of refusing to let an officer serve in the Cabinet, a general staff could cause the fall of a government, prevent the forming of a Cabinet, or even dictate the choice of Prime Minister.

In the last resort, therefore, government policy was at the mercy of the armed services. But three elements prevented the complete ascendancy of the military in the nation's councils, at least until General Hideki Tojo took office as Prime Minister in 1941. First was the tendency to compromise characteristic of Japanese conduct; second was the antimilitarist bias of the surviving Genro, Prince Saionji, who held the post alone from 1924 to 1940; third was the international atmosphere, the Zeitgeist, of the 1920's.

It was this Zeitgeist of the postwar world that more than anything else tipped the scales in favor of the industrialists and the bureaucrats rather than the militarists, and started Japan along the road of international co-operation and conciliation in foreign affairs rather than along that of war and aggression. The reasons are not hard to see. Japan, for all her triumphs, was still the pupil of the West. Throughout the century of her borrowings from Europe and America, she mirrored, though often with distortions, the developments abroad. Always there was an eager search for the secret of the West's superior strength vis-à-vis the non-European peoples.

The world of the 1920's was dominated by the democratic powers who had triumphed in World War I. It was an exhausted world committed to international co-operation and peaceful trade. In Japanese eyes, the outcome of the war and the collapse of the authoritarian regimes in Russia and in the Central Powers were proof of the superiority of the states with parliamentary regimes and party governments. Japan fell into line. Eager to be strong like the democratic powers, the Japanese were influenced by their example and their policies. It is not entirely a coincidence, therefore, that the first commoner was made Prime Minister in 1918, manhood suffrage was achieved in 1925, and the alternation of Cabinets based upon party control of the lower house of the Diet became the rule.

By the same token, it is not surprising that when antimilitarist policies, international co-operation, and reliance upon industry and

commerce for the answers to economic problems tended to characterize the former Allies, as these did during the 1920's, the
Japanese should be moved to adopt similar policies. Despite lapses,
during most of this second phase, which spans the 1920's, Japan's
foreign policy was co-operative and conciliatory. Few nations appear to have entered more wholeheartedly into the spirit and work
of the new League of Nations than did Japan. The Japanese made·
or were ready to make significant concessions in the Washington
Disarmament Conference of 1921-1922 and in the later conferences
at Geneva in 1927 and at London in 1930. At one point, in 1925,
Japan went so far as to reduce its standing army by four divisions
unilaterally. Although becoming alarmed about the problem of
exploding population after the first census in 1920, Japan's leaders
sought its solution by commercial rather than territorial expansion.
In the face of the growing turmoil next door in China, Japan was
notably patient and restrained.

The period thus was one in which the militarists did not get
much of a hearing in the "family council" of the Japanese nation
and could not take full advantage of their constitutional powers
vis-à-vis the Cabinet or the Throne. Indeed, as the decade drew to a
close, a popular clamor was raised in the Diet and in the press for
further reductions in the armed forces, to save money which might
be used in rural relief, and for constitutional reforms which, by
making the government both more unified in its decision-making
and more responsive to public opinion, would put greater limitation
upon the role of the military in the determination of national
policy.

The Third Phase

Japan's invasion of Manchuria in 1931 marks the end of the
second phase in Japan's foreign policy and the start of the third.
The industrialists and the bureaucrats still urged the policies followed before, but conditions at home and abroad played into the
hands of the militarists. Once more it was the posture of world
events that tipped the scales, this time in favor of the militarists,
and turned Japan from the road of international co-operation into
that of territorial expansion and armed aggression.

The Manchurian invasion which was launched on September 18, 1931, without the prior knowledge of the Japanese government, was planned in what amounts to a conspiracy among the Kwantung Army Headquarters in Manchuria and certain high army officers in Korea and Tokyo. They were moved less by consideration for conditions in China than by consideration for conditions at home. There the military party, out of public favor for more than a decade, was out of sympathy with the trends in Japanese affairs. Control of the army had long since passed into the hands of a younger group of officers drawn largely from the peasantry and educated in the narrow specialization peculiar to Japanese army institutions. Reflecting the discontents of rural Japan from which they came, contemptuous toward capitalism and party politics of which they had no understanding, these officers were imbued with patriotic and chauvinistic sentiments growing out of the official cult of Shinto, the national religion, and referred to as *Kōdō*—the Way of the Emperor.

Regarding themselves as the real custodians of Japanese traditions, they viewed with dismay the antimilitarist bias which the 1920's produced and the widespread demands in the press for reducing military expenditures. Naval forces had already been curtailed as a result of the naval disarmament conferences at Washington in 1921 and at London in 1930, and now a world disarmament conference was summoned to meet in Geneva under the auspices of the League of Nations in February 1932. The army did not propose to accept further reduction at the hands of misguided diplomats and civilian politicians. Foreign war was its maneuver against them.

The surprise attack upon the troops and installations of Marshal Chang Hsüeh-liang, in Mukden and along the South Manchurian Railway zone's perimeter, raised an outburst of criticism in the home press and among the military party's political opponents. But these objections soon subsided. Within a few weeks the country had rallied behind its armed forces, and the third period in Japan's foreign policy had begun.

It is not hard to account for the alacrity with which the Japanese public was brought to accept the army's leadership in place of the leadership it had followed until then. By 1931 the policies, both foreign and domestic, of the government seemed all but bankrupt. At home the government was struggling in vain with the economic depression which had rapidly deepened since 1929. Meanwhile the venal and corrupt party cliques in the Diet made a disgusting show of their self-seeking quarrels. Abroad the government's policy of conciliation and co-operation failed to maintain the proud position which Japan had reached at the end of World War I. The stigma of inferiority implied in the exclusion clause of the United States immigration law of 1924 still hurt seven years after, but the United States lawmakers gave no sign of understanding, much less of relenting. Japan's export trade (upon which rested the government's hope of meeting the population problem, about which the Japanese were now acutely conscious) suffered a catastrophic decline from 2,148 million yen in 1929 to 1,147 million yen in 1931, caused in great part by a world-wide rise in tariffs in which the United States led with its Smoot-Hawley Act of 1930. The silk industry, for which a third of Japan's farmers produced on a part-time basis, lost most of its market. It had sent 90 per cent of its exports to the United States alone. When the latter reduced its purchases more than two-thirds between 1929 and 1932, it was the Japanese farmer who bore the brunt. On the continent of Asia, at the same time, the growing power of the Nanking Government and the Kuomintang was threatening Japan's "special position" in Manchuria. Moreover, as the educated classes of Japanese looked abroad they could see that it was not only in Japan that parliamentary government appeared incapable of coping with the economic ills of the body politic. The same weaknesses were evident in the governments of all democracies.

There was consequently in Japan in the summer and fall of 1931 an atmosphere of desperation and a readiness to believe that the domestic and foreign policies of the previous decade were mistaken and their proponents false guides. Thus when the army, forcing the issue in Manchuria, proclaimed at home that salvation could be achieved by the sword, the public, having no answer of its own, was prepared to give the army a hearing. The logic of war itself did the rest.

War is the dominant theme of Japan's foreign policy throughout its third phase. From the outbreak of hostilities at Mukden in September 1931 to the surrender ceremonies on the deck of the *Missouri* in September 1945, despite intervals of armistice, Japan was for all practical purposes continuously at war. In the first stage of operations the army overran Manchuria and then consolidated its position; in the second, beginning in 1937, Japanese armies vainly tried to subjugate China; finally, in 1941, Japan threw down the gauntlet to the United States, Great Britain, and their allies.

The conquest of Manchuria was followed by the creation of "Manchukuo," as the new "state" was called, with a "government" headed by the former Manchu emperor who had been deposed by the Chinese Revolution in 1911. A transparent fraud, the Manchurian regime set up by the Japanese served as a façade behind which to exploit their conquest. But when the League of Nations Assembly declined in 1933 to ratify the seizure of Manchuria and all but a handful of states refused to recognize Manchukuo, Japan withdrew from the League into diplomatic isolation. Then, in April 1934, through the Foreign Office spokesman Eiji Amau, Tokyo proclaimed what amounted to a Japanese "Monroe Doctrine" warning the western powers not to interfere with Japan's schemes for a new order in Asia.

The economic experiment in Manchuria was even more disappointing than the political one. High hopes had been entertained for establishing, under the guidance of the Japanese army, a socialistic state free from the corrupting influences of capitalism and politics. But as the Japanese came to grips with administering their new preserve, neither the experience of the South Manchurian Railway officials nor the experimenting of certain industrialists willing to serve the army's purposes could make of Manchuria the bonanza which had been expected.

Unwilling to believe that their grandiose plans were inherently unworkable, the new empire-builders seized upon the continued Chinese underground resistance as the cause of their difficulties.

Eventually, as the only solution to the Manchurian problem, the Japanese in the summer of 1937 took advantage of what seems to have been an accidental collision between Chinese troops and some of their own troops on night maneuvers outside Peking to embark upon a campaign against China itself. But first, as a precautionary measure largely psychological in value, Tokyo eased the strain of her diplomatic .isolation by concluding with Nazi Germany an anti-Communist pact with a secret provision directed against the Soviet Union as the common menace.

Once more the Japanese met with initial successes followed by grave frustrations. The Chinese, exchanging space for time, drew the invading armies into an overextension of their lines during indecisive operations that continued year after year. At the same time Tokyo was kept on tenterhooks by sporadic outbreaks of hostilities between troops of Japan and the Soviet Union stationed along the Siberian border. Yet in treaty ports and other occupied areas the Japanese troops baited the western powers in a long succession of outrages against the property and persons of their nationals. The approach of war in Europe found the Japanese bogged down in China with no discernible way of extricating themselves so as to be ready to profit from Europe's troubles as they had done during World War I. Chiang Kai-shek would neither admit defeat nor come to terms, and the western powers, though unwilling to meet force with force, would not concede the justice of Japan's claims. The Japanese were convinced that only the support Chiang received from the western powers enabled the Chinese resistance to continue. Certainly that combination blocked Tokyo's grandiose scheme of a "Greater East Asia Co-prosperity Sphere" by which would be assured not mere hegemony but actual dominion over the coveted regions. Even after the outbreak of war in Europe, the high command temporized. But two years later, emboldened by the German successes on the western front in 1940 and on the Russian front the following year, Japan finally turned upon the United States and Britain in the hope of driving them and the remaining westerners once and for all out of eastern Asia. It was in seeking a solution to the

Chinese problem, therefore, that Japan launched the war in the Pacific.

It may also be said that during the decade between 1931 and 1941 the Kwantung Army, which conquered Manchuria, also conquered Japan itself before going on to the subjugation of China and South East Asia. Within Japan (from December 1931, when General Sadao Araki, one of the ideological leaders of the army's extremist wing, was made War Minister) there was an increasing militarization of the government. The alternation of cabinets based upon political parties ended in May 1932, after a series of terrorist acts on the part of ultranationalist fanatics had culminated in the assassination of Prime Minister Ki Inukai. The crisis led the Genro Prince Saionji to recommend a supraparty Cabinet with Admiral Viscount Makoto Saito, the greatly esteemed Governor-General of Korea, as Prime Minister. Two years later the assassination of Saito himself and other high officials by another group of ultranationalists had the contradictory effects of discrediting the army extremists while fastening a tighter military grip upon the Cabinet.

For the next four years, through a succession of supraparty Cabinets, the army called the tune despite the selection as prime minister of men who sought to brake the headlong descent of Japan into the bottomless pit of the China war. One of these was Prince Fumimaro Konoye, a figure of such exalted status that for him to become Prime Minister was an act almost of condescension. By 1940, when he accepted the post for a second time, the political situation had degenerated so far that although Konoye had been put forward as the last trump of the moderates the attendant compromise secured several Cabinet positions for the Kwantung clique, including that of War Minister for General Hideki Tojo, former Chief of Staff of the Kwantung Army. Later in the year, the Genro Prince Saionji died, removing one more block from the army's way. Then, when Konoye left the leadership of the Cabinet for the third and last time, Tojo succeeded him as Prime Minister and the Kwantung Army's triumph was complete.

Or as complete as triumphs usually go in Japan. For though

forced into compliance by the militarists, the industrialists (the Zaibatsu) and the bureaucracy, together with the moderates in the navy, remained in latent opposition. If they had little effect upon the course of Japan's foreign policy henceforth, their opposition was influential in keeping Japan from becoming the totalitarian state planned by the Kwantung clique. Then, when in 1945 the fall of Saipan signaled Japan's failure in the Pacific War, the irremediable loss of face for the war's principal authors unseated Tojo and the group he led. In the subsequent cabinets of General Kuniaki Koiso and Admiral Kantaro Suzuki, the moderates staged something of a come-back, if only long enough to negotiate the end of hostilities. Thereafter, until the Treaty of San Francisco brought to a close six years of Occupation and reform by making the Japanese once more masters in their own house, policy-making for Japan was in the hands of the victors.

Foreign Policy Today

In the light of the foregoing analysis of Japan's strength, its national characteristics, and its century of experience with foreign policy in the community of nations, what do we find today and what is to be expected of tomorrow?

There has been no change in the objectives of Japan's foreign policy. These remain as before. Security of the homeland from foreign aggression and recognition by the other members of the family of nations are sought by the Japanese today as they have been from the earliest days of the Restoration. The third objective, which dates from the 1920's, is a viable economy by which to support the islands' dense and growing population. The goals are the same but their attainment has become immeasurably more difficult.

As we have seen, Japan's security is threatened by the ambitions of the Communist colossi, the Soviet Union and Red China. To meet these threats to peace and safety, after being disarmed and demilitarized in the course of the Allied postwar Occupation, Japan in 1956 has only the insignificant "Self Defense" establishment at which we have looked earlier in this chapter. As we have also seen, Japan has been forcibly returned to the territorial limits it had at the start of the modern period. The war, moreover, has left it in a strategic situation increasingly similar to that of Britain, since both off-shore island peoples have been reduced to dependence upon the United States for their defense and prosperity and each continues in a pivotal position in the struggle between the Communist world and the free world.

Japan's fight for recognition or prestige has lost ground as a consequence of defeat in war and loss of control of its affairs during the six years of the Occupation by the forces under the command of General MacArthur. The loss is greater in the minds of the Japanese, with their feeling for face, than in the eyes of others. But paradoxical as it seems to us, the Japanese find a good deal of consolation in the prestige of having been defeated by the world's greatest power. How different a matter it would have been if they had been forced to pull out of China by nothing more than the drain on the nation's economy and military strength! The greater calamity spared them the greater indignity. But because of the calamity they have no hope today of regaining the privileged status of a Great Power. Here their disappointment is diminished because France and Italy have suffered much the same fate.

The hope of developing an economy adequate to support the Japanese population as it expands has been encouraged, in the short run, by the good prospects that as long as the "cold war" lasts there will be economic aid from the United States. In the long run, however, the problem has been aggravated by such sequels of the Pacific War as the communizing of China, economic nationalism in the emergent states of South East Asia, and higher costs of production which have weakened the country's competitive position vis-à-vis other powers.

Not only have the objectives of foreign policy become more difficult of attainment for Japan in the postwar era, but the lines of policy open to use have become fewer as well. Two traditional lines must be eliminated as no longer practicable. These are the two in which Japan was conspicuously successful before the 1920's, namely, the acquisition of an empire and the establishment of itself as the dominant power in the Pacific Asiatic region. Both belonged to an age of imperialism and to a society of states wherein war was a legitimate means of forwarding national interests. Both could be pursued without serious risk, owing to the weakness of China and other immediate neighbors and to the remoteness of rival seats of power. In the circumstances of today, however, both are ruled out of consideration. For one thing, we live in an age of fading empires. For another, the resurgent tide of Chinese power has at last come flooding back to fill completely the place once left by the ebbing power of the Manchu Dynasty. Then, too, the world has grown small enough to cancel out the advantages that used to come with the region's remoteness from Europe and America. In the anticolonialism first introduced by the Covenant of the League of Nations and now reinforced by the provisions of the United Nations Charter, an empire-seeking Japan would find a powerful deterrent. Finally, there seems to be no way by which Japan might amass the resources necessary for renewed policies of empire and hegemony.

Two lines remain: international co-operation and commercial expansion, both to be sought by peaceful diplomacy. Japan will regain the respect of the world community in the same way the country first gained it: by showing itself to be worthy of respect.

The furious pace with which the Japanese pursued modernization before World War I must be attributed in part to the desire to earn such respect on the part of the treaty powers as to induce the latter to free Japan from the bonds of extraterritoriality and the conventional tariff. In much the same spirit and determination, the Japanese embraced the reforms of the Occupation after World War II, including the constitution they were made to adopt. Since the Treaty of San Francisco rewarded this conduct by restoring Japan to full dignity in the family of nations, the Japanese have not flagged in their effort to regain the good opinion of others.

But the spirit of the times itself has encouraged international co-operation and peaceful commerce on the part of Japan. Notwithstanding the fall of France before the onrushing German armor in 1940, and notwithstanding the presence of the Soviet Union among the victors at the end of the war, the superiority of the western democracies was demonstrated in Japanese eyes for the second time in the twentieth century by the acid test of the battlefield. It is these same powers who have led the way, again for the second time, in a postwar struggle to establish an international order which would eliminate empire-building and other forms of aggression and would promote mutual effort for the general welfare. The opposition of the Soviets within the council chambers of the United Nations and the new imperialism by which they have operated outside of the United Nations have neither frightened nor misled the Japanese. The latter have correctly read such signs of firmness in the new order as the Truman Doctrine with its first application to Greece and Turkey in 1947, the Berlin air lift, NATO, and above all the collective police action against armed aggression in Korea. At the same time, on the economic side, Tokyo has found encouragement in the joint actions of the free nations. The European Recovery Program, Point Four or technical-assistance programs for underdeveloped areas, GATT and other reciprocal trade agreements, and the European Coal and Steel Community are a far cry from the damaging autarky policies after World War I. With this evidence that the free world under the leadership of the democratic countries is profiting from the lessons taught by the experience of Manchuria, the undermining of the League of Nations, and the depression, the Japanese have not waited for membership in the United Nations to begin acting in line with its underlying principles.

This conduct, moreover, is influenced today by Japan's experience in the 1920's and the contrasting experience in the years thereafter. No Japanese will deny that the policies which prevailed in the 1920's were disappointing in their results. These policies did not move the United States to change the exclusion law with its implied slur upon the Japanese people. They did not assure protection for Japan's interests from nationalist pressure in China. They did not maintain a level of foreign trade sufficient to support the increasing population in spite of world-wide depression, rising tariffs, and declining purchasing power abroad. But bleak as were the prospects by the end of the 1920's, Japan in 1931 remained one of the world's Great Powers, the only Asiatic state to have mastered the modern technology of the West, and the acknowledged leader in Pacific Asia. Perhaps the face of the future was perplexing but it was not the face of danger. Greater challenges had been met in the past and with fortitude and industry had been overcome.

Japan's leaders in government contrast this 1931 situation with that at the end of World War II. In 1945 the country was suffering the disastrous consequences of the aggression undertaken first in Manchuria, then in China proper, and finally throughout Pacific Asia, all in disregard of Japan's commitments under the League of Nations Covenant and in defiance of the rest of the world. In 1942, as Japan's far-flung lines buckled and began to break under the assault of her enemies the folly of the militarists in launching the country upon a career of aggression began to be understood at last. In the end, the failure had cost not merely lives and treasure expended for overseas campaigns but also, for the first time in Japan's history, vast destruction and suffering in the home islands themselves. Nearly a hundred and fifty cities had been burned out by bombing raids, with an estimated loss of two million buildings and between two and three million lives. For the first time, too, the country felt the heel of a foreign conqueror. Little wonder that the post-Occupation Japanese government, once again free of external interference in determining its foreign relations, should prefer the less glorious policies of the 1920's.

In the present foreign-policy phase, which began with the San Francisco Treaty, Japan's enduring objectives are being pursued through peaceful co-operation and expanding commerce with a program in which eight points are significant.

1. *Attachment to the United States.* This is the keystone in the arch. For Japan and the United States, the treaty of peace was indeed the treaty of reconciliation which John Foster Dulles, then President Truman's special agent in its negotiation, intended it to be. The leniency of the treaty's terms and the magnanimity of its spirit reflected the mutual admiration of conquered and conqueror, the conviction in Washington that punitive treaties of peace are self-defeating, and enlightened self-interest on the part of all the signatories. Japan and the United States are also joined in bilateral agreements for mutual assistance in their com-

mon defense. The assistance is by no means one-sided, for if Japan's defense depends upon United States arms, Japan is also essential for the defense of the free world. Because of the Japanese revulsion against war and the quixotic antiwar provision written into their constitution, the Japanese have not been happy at having to share the burden of their defense, but their responsible leaders have faced up to the need.

Supporting the Japan-United States alliance is the obvious fact that for Japan there is no practical alternative. Japan has irrevocably lost the opportunity it once had to throw the country's weight into the scales on the side of the emancipation of Asia through a genuine Pan Asiatic movement. No longer able to lead in such a movement, Japan is also too proud to follow India's leadership and too fearful of the consequences to turn to Red China. Anti-Communist by conviction, and by long tradition anti-Russian, Japan has nothing to look for in Moscow. Since the war, more-over, the Soviets with characteristic ineptness have continued to add to Japan's grievances.

2. *Peaceful Relations with the Soviet Union.* Alone among Japan's wartime enemies, the USSR refused either to accept the San Francisco Treaty or to negotiate a separate treaty of peace in order to put the relations of the two countries on a conventional basis. A technical state of war existed between the two until October 1956, when it was ended by a joint declaration signed in Moscow. The declaration also announced that there would be an exchange of diplomatic representations and that pending the nego-tiation of a trade treaty the most-favored-nation rule would govern their commercial relations. The negotiation of a future treaty of peace was intimated, but because eighteen months of discussion looking to such a treaty had foundered upon the question of title to the Kuriles, which the war had left in Soviet hands, there ap-peared to be no immediate likelihood that a treaty could be concluded. Until the declaration is replaced by a treaty, however, one of the principal points in the present foreign policy of Japan will be regularizing her relations with her powerful northern neighbor.

3. *Irredentism.* The two most painfully felt desires of the Jap-

anese are the return of those territories which they regard as having been unjustly seized at the end of the war and the repatriation of those nationals who remain in Soviet custody as prisoners of war. In both cases the injury done the Japanese is further resented as being irreconcilable with the principles of fair play and mutual concern which the new morality of the Charter of the United Nations was expected to put into postwar international relations.

The lost territories in question are not those great portions of the former empire like Formosa, southern Saghalin, Korea, or Manchuria. Unless in the daydreams of a few unreconstructed nationalists, these play no part. They were taken in war and their loss in war now is not resented. It is otherwise with the Kuriles, held by the USSR, and the Bonins and Ryukyus, held by the United States. Japan's unwillingness to surrender her claims to the Kuriles was what blocked the peace treaty with the Soviets even though the latter apparently were ready to give back Shikotan and the Habomai islets lying off Hokkaido. The Soviet concession may have been offered after the example of the United States, which earned Japanese gratitude in December 1953 by returning the northern Ryukyus lying between Okinawa and Kyushu. Both the Soviet Union and the United States decline for strategic reasons to release their island chains, but such reasons fail in Japanese eyes to offset either their own claims to the territories or the claims of the inhabitants. There is every indication that the Japanese will not soon be reconciled to the loss of the islands or to their continued occupation—even where, as in the case of the Ryukyus and the Bonins, "residual sovereignty" admittedly rests with Japan.

4. *Prisoners of War.* The second acutely resented condition is the Soviet failure to return all Japanese prisoners of war. At the end of hostilities in 1945, six million Japanese nationals were caught overseas. Almost all were brought home as part of the liquidation of the empire or in the demobilization of the armed forces. But an estimated 300,000 war prisoners and other nationals were believed by MacArthur's command and the Tokyo government to have remained in detention in the Soviet Union, Red China, or Northern Korea. A few were sent home after some years, but an

undisclosed number have never been accounted for. In the October 1956 declaration, the Kremlin officials committed themselves to repatriate those prisoners who survive and to "clear up" the fate of those who have disappeared. Such an accounting is not likely to mollify the Japanese or to lead them to view the Soviets in a happier light.

5. *Fishing Rights.* An issue only less important than the Kuriles and prisoners of war in Japan's foreign relations involving the Soviet Union is that of the deep-sea fisheries in waters controlled by the USSR. Fishing rights in the Sea of Okhotsk and in the coastal waters east of Kamchatka have had a long and controversial history. Moscow's occupation of the Kuriles since the war has aggravated the difficulty.

Much of the protein in the island diet is secured from the sea. Because some 10 per cent of the catch comes from the disputed fisheries, continued access to them is of vital importance to the Japanese. At present, in 1956, restricted fishing is permitted under a temporary agreement between the two countries. But the Soviets have refused to negotiate a long-term agreement before the conclusion of a peace settlement. They have used Japan's need to exploit the fisheries as a powerful argument for coming to terms. Except for the Soviet demands respecting title to the Kuriles, the Japanese would long since have yielded. Meanwhile the fisheries question is permitted by the Soviet Union to continue embittering diplomatic relations with its island neighbor.

6. *Improved Relations with China and South East Asia.* Even though the United States was able, not without great patience and diplomacy at the San Francisco conference and in the preliminary negotiations, to achieve a peace settlement for the Pacific, Japan has found it hard to follow up the treaty with bilateral agreements resuming cordial relations with the countries which suffered at its hands during the war. Only the government of Chiang Kai-shek, acting upon the assumption that normal relations were to be preferred, entered immediately into a conventional agreement. Elsewhere memories of Japanese arrogance and brutality were too strong. Burma, Indonesia, and the Philippines demanded heavy reparations. Korea would not accept help from Tokyo even during

the United Nations action against the Communist invaders. Australia has been especially unbending in its attitude. There has been no headway in the case of Red China, though here failure has been the fault less of the principals involved than of the United States. Left to themselves, the foreign offices of Peking and Tokyo would long ago have made overtures to one another. To do so is part of the Japanese policy of reconciliation with her former enemies.

7. *Stimulation of Exports.* The dependence of Japan upon foreign trade to support its ever-increasing population has inspired frantic diplomatic activity and salesmanship in the post-Occupation era. Yet the cool political relations between Japan and its neighbors aggravates what has always been a weakness in Japan's economy.

Japan developed its prewar trade thanks to its technological head start over the rest of Asia, whose less developed mainland has contributed raw materials for Japan's industry and provided markets for its finished goods. Since 1946, however, the higher costs of Japanese labor, together with the development of industry in neighbor nations, have cut down Japan's commercial advantage. To meet the new situation great effort has been expended in promoting trade. At the same time, like Britain in an earlier day, Japan has turned from a prewar emphasis upon consumer goods to a new emphasis upon materials of heavy industry—machinery, iron and steel manufactures, concrete, and chemicals—which now amounts to about a third of her exports. The recollection of the one-time disastrous dependence upon silk and the United States market, together with the decline of the former and boycotts in the latter, has led to a new diversification both of products and markets. The expanding economy of the North Atlantic countries also has encouraged Japanese exports, and these have made conspicuous gains in South America and South Asia.

The United States is still Japan's best customer; no other country takes as much as a twentieth part of total Japanese exports. A contributing factor in developing foreign markets has been the production of high-quality goods like cameras and precision instruments and the growing influence which Japan is exerting upon tastes in the United States.

Consistent with diplomatic support for foreign trade has been

Japan's eagerness for admission to the trade arrangements under the General Agreement on Tariffs and Trade (GATT), whose generalized relaxing of tariff barriers has had a salutary effect upon world trade ever since 1947. With the negotiation of reductions affecting Japanese goods and the promise of nondiscriminatory treatment by other members of GATT, Japan's accession to GATT will lead to further improvement in her trade situation. At the same time the inroads made by Germany and Italy and other new competitors, in Asiatic markets, the barring of Japanese trade with Red China, and the reappearance of private boycotts in the southern regions of the United States come as warning signals that progress is going to be slow despite Japan's best diplomatic efforts.

8. *Participation in International Organization.* Finally, for a variety of reasons, the Japanese attach great importance to taking part in the highly developed institutional life of postwar international relations. It has been a cause of deep chagrin that Soviet vetoes have blocked Japan's admission to the United Nations since application was first made in 1952. Accordingly, one of the principal hopes that Tokyo entertained in opening the negotiations which led to the October 1956 peace declaration was that Moscow would agree to withdraw its veto. Moscow did agree. The Japanese satisfaction at this minor concession by the Kremlin must be viewed in the light of Japan's activity in the work of the League of Nations during the 1920's, when the spirit of international cooperation was still high. Now that it is high again, the Japanese, characteristically, have reverted to their old enthusiasm. This explains also the alacrity with which Japan has accepted admission to such other international organizations as UNESCO, the World Health Organization, the Food and Agricultural Organization, and the International Bank for Reconstruction and Development. The same desire is satisfied in another direction by the Colombo Plan consultations, in which Japan has taken part since 1954.

There is something of the search for renewed recognition in the Japanese policy towards international organization. What it meant to the Japan of an earlier day to be invited to the Hague Peace Conference of 1899 and 1907, to become an ally of Great Britain in 1902, and after the First World War to find itself in the inner circle at the Paris Peace Conference is recalled to a degree by this generation's response to participation in contemporary international organization. The practical and material advantages are secondary in importance; the prestige of membership and the feeling of renewed belonging count more.

The foregoing eight points may seem to add up to something less than a vigorous foreign policy. Probably they do. But Japan is too recently out of the immobilizing cast in which it was held by the Allied Occupation to be very steady on its feet. As yet the country must cautiously feel its way.

Conclusion

The Treaty of San Francisco, with which the latest phase in Japanese foreign relations was inaugurated, came almost a century after the Treaty of Kanagawa, negotiated by Commodore Perry and the agents of the Yedo Government, brought Japan back into the community of nations. The intervening century was for Japan a drama of spectacular successes, tragic mistakes, and condign failure.

Only half a century sufficed for the quaint little people of western imagination to become the formidable power that humbled the Russian giant on the Mukden plains and in the straits of Tsushima. Only fifteen more years were to pass before the representatives could meet as peers with the representatives of the Great Powers, first at Paris Conference of 1919 and thereafter in the Council of the League of Nations and in the other conferences of the interwar period. What other people could boast so meteoric a rise? And what other Asiatic people held off the western imperialists and learned from them the secrets of capitalism and modern arms well enough to match them?

But the mistakes are as obvious as the successes. In emulation of the imperialist Great Powers, Japan followed the policy of exploiting the weakness rather than building up the strength of the other Asiatic powers. Japan sabotaged the interwar peace structure when it defied the League of Nations in the Manchurian dispute of the 1930's. The invasion of China in 1937 and the attack upon United States and British possessions in 1941 were further steps into the abyss. Good reasons were adduced to justify both, but the abyss remained. And at its bottom waited defeat and Occupation.

In the Treaty of San Francisco, Japan, chastened and penitent, was restored to good standing in the community of nations and invited to make a new beginning. The Japanese task would be harder this time, the obstacles to success more formidable, the ultimate goal more modest. None who knew the Japanese could reasonably doubt that they would go to work with characteristic industry, fortitude, and patience rebuilding with worn-out and battle-ruined tools the broken monuments to a century's progress.

A Selected Bibliography is on pages 828-833.

CHAPTER 22

THE FORMULATION AND RECENT CHARACTER OF JAPANESE FOREIGN POLICY

KAZUO KAWAI

Japan's surrender on August 15, 1945[1] marked the end of an era. The catastrophe had been brought on by a wrong policy decision in foreign relations. That decision, while stemming ultimately from basic background factors, had been facilitated by the defective system for the formulation and control of Japanese foreign policy. Whether this defect has been completely eliminated from the postwar Japanese government, which in some ways is so transformed but in others so unchanging, remains to be seen.

From the surrender in 1945 until the restoration of full independence in 1952,[2] Japan remained under Allied military Occupation. During this period, although the native government was at no time supplanted by a foreign military government, the Occupa-

[1] The formal signing of the "instrument of surrender" on September 2, 1945 passed relatively unnoticed among the Japanese; for them the Emperor's radio broadcast of August 15 (August 14, United States time) announcing his decision to surrender rang down the end of their old world and ushered in a new one.

[2] The peace treaty was signed on September 8, 1951 but did not become effective until April 28, 1952.

tion authorities—who were almost exclusively from the United States—supervised the actions of the Japanese government and in effect made all the important decisions.

The Japanese government was permitted to retain its Foreign Office, but was not permitted to maintain official representatives abroad. Foreign diplomatic representatives in Japan were accredited not to the Japanese government, but to the Supreme Commander for the Allied Powers (SCAP), who represented Japan in dealings with foreign nations. Between SCAP and the Japanese government there could ostensibly be no "negotiation" as between equals. In practice, however, working arrangements between SCAP and the Japanese government were handled through the Central Liaison Office, which was nominally an independent agency of the Japanese government but in effect an extension of the Foreign Office. Relations with SCAP comprised, in a sense, Japan's foreign relations during this period.

In the later stages of the Occupation period, contacts between SCAP and the Japanese government came to be handled directly between individual sections of SCAP headquarters and individual departments of the Japanese government. The Japanese government also gained the right to maintain "Overseas Agencies" abroad, manned by Foreign Service officers who performed quasi-consular and quasi-diplomatic functions. But the temporary and anomalous features of Japan's foreign relations did not disappear until it was restored to a normal independent status in 1952. A study of foreign-policy formulation and control in contemporary Japan must logically start from this point.

Formulation of Policy

Constitutional Bases of Foreign Relations

The constitutional bases for the conduct of foreign relations in the Japanese government after World War II differ radically from those of the prewar government.

Under the 1889 Meiji Constitution the Emperor, as the sovereign, was the fountainhead of all authority and foreign relations were conducted in his name.[3] His powers, however, were essentially nominal; he reigned but did not rule. He could take no official action without the countersignature of a responsible minister of state, which meant that the advice of his ministers was in practice mandatory.[4]

This concentration of such extensive theoretical powers in the person of the Emperor, with the practical requirement that he follow the advice of his ministers, had made for confusion. The executive branch of the prewar Japanese government was a multiple one in which the civilian component and the military component wielded virtually independent and co-ordinate powers. On civil matters the Emperor was bound to take the advice of the Cabinet, while on military matters he was bound to take the advice of the Supreme Command. Where the line of demarcation between civil and military matters was not clear, as was usually the case in matters of high policy, conflict of jurisdiction and conflict of advice were almost inevitable. Each set of advisers—being executive officers as well as advisers—would then go its own separate way, each with the mandatory acquiescence of the Emperor. Consequently, in time of greatest crisis, the Japanese government frequently tried to go in two different directions at once, until finally the military arbitrarily resolved the intolerable conflict in its own favor by resorting to the characteristic weapons it possessed. However natural and understandable were the historical circumstances that had created such a system, the results had been disastrous.

The Constitution of 1947 provides altogether different conditions with respect to the conduct of foreign relations. Drafted by the Occupation authorities and forced on the Japanese, who were

[3] Note the furor over Article I of the Pact of Paris of 1928 (Kellogg-Briand Pact), which bound the signatories "in the names of their respective peoples." Japan was able to ratify the pact only after attaching the reservation that this particular phrase, "viewed in the light of the provisions of the Imperial Constitution, is understood to be inapplicable in so far as Japan is concerned."

[4] This fact was recognized by the International Military Tribunal for the Far East, when it absolved the Emperor of any responsibility for the war while it held his advisers accountable for acts committed in his name. The Emperor's seemingly personal decision to surrender in 1945 was not an exception to the constitutional practice, for in this case he merely accepted the advice of the overwhelming majority of his advisers as against a small but obdurate minority.

given opportunity to make only minor modifications, some of its provisions and language strike the Japanese as quaint. But, in general, this Constitution commends itself as being so reasonable and so desirable that, while the Japanese may eventually amend it to some extent, its essential features appear secure enough for the foreseeable future.

This Constitution stipulates that the Emperor no longer possesses any power related to government but is a "symbol of the State and of the unity of the people, deriving his position from the will of the people in whom resides sovereign power." The "highest organ of state power" is the National Diet, comprised of the elected representatives of the people. As is characteristic of parliamentary governments, the executive branch is responsible to the legislature. The Diet thus designates the Prime Minister from among its own members. He in turn selects the other members of the Cabinet, at least half of whom must also be chosen from among members of the Diet. The multiple executive of the prewar Japanese government has been abolished; executive power is now vested solely in the Cabinet. As part of its executive functions, the Cabinet is specifically charged with the management of foreign relations.

The actions of the Cabinet must be acceptable to the Diet. The Diet has the power of the purse. Furthermore, whenever the lower house of the Diet expresses lack of confidence in the Cabinet, the Cabinet must promptly resign to make way for a new Cabinet more acceptable to the legislators; or else the lower house must be promptly dissolved so that the electorate may decide the issue in the general election which must immediately follow. In addition to this general ministerial responsibility, the Diet has a further check on the Cabinet's conduct of foreign relations in the requirement that treaties must obtain Diet approval.

The Constitution also provides for judicial review "of any law, order, regulation or official act"—an innovation for Japan—which may well bring the judiciary into the realm of foreign relations with authority to rule on the constitutionality of treaties or other official acts pertaining to foreign relations. An additional condition to the conduct of foreign relations exists in the constitutional provision renouncing war and prohibiting the maintenance of armed forces or "other war potential."

It now remains to examine in detail how these constitutional provisions are implemented in practice.

The Emperor

Although the Emperor has no powers related to government, he does have certain ritualistic functions related to the conduct of foreign relations. He attests to the appointment and dismissal of ministers of state, which naturally includes the Minister of Foreign Affairs. He attests to the powers and credentials of ambassadors and ministers. He receives foreign ambassadors and ministers. He formally promulgates treaties, once they have been signed and ratified by the competent authorities. In all of his official functions, however, he can act only on the advice and with the approval of the Cabinet, which is held responsible for his actions.

In view of the national mythology and historic prestige surrounding the Emperor, he obviously continues to be capable of exerting an influence far beyond his nominal powers. This influence is difficult to measure for, while in general the Japanese attitude toward the Throne is moving in the direction of the British attitude toward the Crown, the uniquely Japanese elements of semireligious veneration persist in many sectors of Japanese society. The influence of the present Emperor Hirohito, however, seems to be quite definitely in the direction of increasing rationality and modernization. He appears to be a shy and gentle person, much more at home with his hobby of marine biology than with affairs of state. He obviously finds his present role as a symbol of a demilitarized and democratic state much more congenial than posing in uniform astride a white steed as he formerly had to do. He fits the pattern of the proper constitutional monarch.

The Cabinet

As was already noted, the 1947 Constitution specifically entrusts to the Cabinet the management of foreign relations. In this task, the Cabinet no longer has to worry about challenge from the military, for nothing remains of the formerly complex executive but the Cabinet. With the constitutional ban on armed forces, the Supreme Command has naturally disappeared. The Constitution further provides, perhaps redundantly, that all members of the Cabinet must be civilians. Such modest "Self Defense" forces as Japan now manages to maintain through a flexible interpretation of the Constitution are clearly the creatures of the Cabinet. Even should the Constitution be amended eventually to permit the open establishment of armed forces, most Japanese are so nervous about the military dominance of recent memory that adequate safeguards will undoubtedly be maintained to keep the military subordinate to civilian control.

While accountable to the Diet and subject to various pressures, the Cabinet is the most important factor in the formulation and control of foreign policy. Not only is the Cabinet specifically entrusted with this task, but it is particularly capable of asserting its power. The executive in Japan has long overshadowed the legislative, not only because the 1889 Meiji Constitution conferred greater power and advantage upon the executive, but also because the legislators, being generally less experienced and less competent than the administrators, were unable to utilize fully even such powers as they might have constitutionally asserted. Under the 1947 Constitution, the legislature has come to enjoy legal dominance over the executive. And although, as compared with the past, the Diet is increasingly exercising its power, the traditional prestige of the executive is too much for the legislators to overcome entirely.

Not only the prestige but the disparity in actual abilities also persists. The Diet, preoccupied with the game of politics, often appears undignified and uninspiring. The Cabinet, though itself not unpartisan, looms more impressively as a select group of men whose responsibilities force them to consider broader national interests. Moreover, while postwar Japanese Cabinets include fewer men of bureaucratic background than prewar Cabinets generally, the Cabinet still commands the services of the civil-service bureaucracy. The technical competence of this bureaucracy helps the Cabinet to continue overshadowing the Diet despite the change in their constitutional relationship.

Furthermore, it is misleading to think of the Cabinet solely in juxtaposition to the Diet. In parliamentary governments, cabinets are in a sense executive committees of legislatures. Instead of a separation of powers, there is—to use the British expression—a fusion of powers. The Japanese Cabinet, composed mostly of members of the Diet and responsible to the Diet, possesses not only executive functions but also the legislative function of initiating and preparing the legislative program of the Diet. Most legislative bills are government bills originating in the Cabinet and formally sponsored by the Cabinet. The Cabinet's activities in steering these bills through the Diet naturally tend to develop a pattern of Cabinet leadership in the Diet. This leadership pattern is strengthened by the fact that Cabinet members are almost always important party leaders to start with. While the legislative leadership of the Cabinet has no direct relation to the Cabinet's executive functions in foreign relations, it is only natural for this habit of leadership in the legislative field to be carried over—perhaps unconsciously—into the executive field. It means that, unless forced to do otherwise, the Cabinet is disposed to formulate foreign policy on its own initiative without seeking the advice of Diet members, then to use its legislative techniques to marshal the post facto approval of the Diet.

Finally, it should be noted that in its conduct of foreign relations, as in all its activities, the Cabinet acts as a whole and bears collective responsibility. Although the Meiji Constitution had seemed to hold each minister individually responsible to the Emperor, in practice the doctrine of the Cabinet's collective responsibility had come to be quite securely established, although there was ambiguity as to where this collective responsibility was directed. The 1947 Constitution continues and formalizes this traditional collective responsibility and furthermore makes clear that it is now to the Diet that the Cabinet is responsible. Because foreign affairs comprise a specialized province often not familiar to many Cabinet ministers, any Minister of Foreign Affairs often finds his colleagues disposed to allow him a pretty free hand. In Japan, in the immediate prewar years, a small inner group within the Cabinet—consisting of the Prime Minister, the Minister of Finance, the Minister of War, the Minister of the Navy, and the Minister of Foreign Affairs—used to concern itself particularly with foreign affairs. But whatever its actual powers, such a group remained more or less an ad hoc committee; no inner cabinet as such ever attained recognition in Japan as a formal institution. Nominal responsibility for all decisions, therefore, remained with the Cabinet as a whole. It is too early (in 1956) to discern any clear trend in postwar Cabinets, but there is nothing in Japanese precedent to indicate any tendency toward change in the collective responsibility of the Cabinet.

The Prime Minister

Despite the corporate character of the Cabinet, the Prime Minister of Japan is not a simple primus inter pares like his British counterpart. He enjoys a legal authority not possessed by his colleagues. He alone is formally designated by a resolution of the Diet. He not only appoints the other members of the Cabinet, but he has the legal power to remove any member of the Cabinet as he chooses. He has the sole authority to consent to legal action being brought against other members of the Cabinet, who otherwise are immune from such action during their tenure in office. He countersigns all laws and all Cabinet orders signed by other members of the Cabinet.

While members of the Japanese Cabinet do not derive their powers from the Prime Minister in the way United States Cabinet members derive their powers from the President, the special powers of the Japanese Prime Minister might further his personal domination of the Cabinet. In fact, under former Prime Minister Shigeru Yoshida, who held office during what was for Japan the unprecedentedly long tenure of more than five years, something close to arbitrary personal rule did develop. During the important concluding years of the Occupation period and the initial years of restored independence, Yoshida in large part personally shaped Japan's foreign policy. But the situation was very unusual, not only with respect to Yoshida's personal qualities, but also with respect to the absolute majority in the Diet his Liberal Party was able to maintain through his control over his party machine. It is significant, however, that despite general recognition of his personal abilities and his unimpeachable motives, widespread resentment against his "one-man rule" resulted in the defection of his outraged associates and eventually in his downfall.

Men like Yoshida are hardly likely to appear frequently. It is no accident that none of the other postwar Prime Ministers has been a strong figure, notwithstanding the strong constitutional authority of the office. The existence until recently[5] of four major parties of roughly comparable strength has meant that the tenure of most Prime Ministers was apt to be precarious. Inasmuch as no party in such a multiparty system was likely to have an absolute majority in the Diet, the designation of a Prime Minister was almost always the result of a series of complicated deals by which the plurality party secured the temporary support or acquiescence of one or more of the rival parties. A Prime Minister chosen under such conditions, presiding over a coalition or a minority-party Cabinet existing only on the sufferance of other parties, was hardly in a position to make unchallenged use of his full legal powers.

The usual political weakness of Japanese Prime Ministers is further accentuated by the traditional pattern of Japanese society and of Japanese social dynamics, which tends to discourage the emergence of forceful characters. The Japanese social system tends to enforce dependence on the collective will. It affords little scope for the activities of rugged individualists and little opportunity for the exercise of personal power. Although Japanese society is not egalitarian but strongly hierarchical, the hierarchy is not monolithic. Though in idealized conception a pyramid, this society is actually more a web of overlapping and interlocking groups. Within a group a hierarchical boss-henchman relationship (*oyabun-kobun* system) may prevail, but the different groups interact among themselves as rival free agents in a more or less covert power struggle for positions of relative advantage. In efforts to enhance their competitive positions, groups seek to bind one another in

[5] In the late autumn of 1955 the Left-wing Socialists and the Right-wing Socialists reunited to form a single Socialist Party, while a few weeks later the conservative Liberals and Democrats merged to form the Liberal-Democrat Party. Despite the emergence of what appears to be a two-party system, internal dissension causes both of these parties to remain unstable.

complex alignments and tacit contractual obligations ramifying in all directions and into all levels. The man who succeeds in this kind of society is one who can subtly take advantage of the constantly shifting balance of power among these interacting groups to maneuver his own group to the top. The social process involved calls for a wily bargainer, rather than for a leader who issues commands.[6]

The Cabinet is the focal point where the interaction among the rival groups within the Japanese government comes to a head. The Prime Minister is likely to be the representative of the group that has temporarily maneuvered itself into position atop a precarious balance of power. He has probably selected his Cabinet members from among several groups with an eye to maintaining this balance. Rather than take imperious action which might upset it, he is much more likely to try to perpetuate it by continuing to bargain with various groups within the Cabinet and make concessions to them. He needs collective approval and group co-operation in order to survive, whatever may be his legal authority. He is therefore apt to be the kind of person whom the group will consider "safe," rather than an individual with forceful leadership qualities.

All the postwar Prime Ministers before Yoshida, and indeed most of the prewar ones, were of this common type or else were even less powerful figureheads "fronting" for manipulators. Ichiro Hatoyama, who succeeded Yoshida, was also a typical example. Such Prime Ministers are not likely to dominate the Cabinet's management of foreign relations. Hatoyama's attempts to carry out his election promise of "normalizing" Japan's relations with the Communist countries, for instance, were long nullified by his own strongly anti-Communist Minister of Foreign Affairs, Mamoru Shigemitsu. The election promise had been a gesture of conciliation toward the neutralist groups which Hatoyama had need to

---

[6] Even Tojo was not a personal dictator like Hitler or Mussolini, but was more a representative of an army clique (the *Toseiha*) which had maneuvered itself to the top. Therefore he and his group could be jockeyed out of power, as they were in 1944, by another clique (the Navy-Industrialist group) without causing much dislocation in the government. Japan during the war was authoritarian but hardly "totalitarian," for Japanese society with its interacting groups could never be wholly regimented or disciplined under a single leadership.

conciliate; but he then had to defer to Shigemitsu, who represented a rival faction in his own party which also had to be conciliated.

The Minister of Foreign Affairs

With a generally weak Prime Minister and with many Cabinet members unfamiliar with foreign affairs, the Minister of Foreign Affairs usually bears almost alone the actual burden of the Cabinet's responsibility for foreign relations. Foreign Ministers of Japan have in the past almost invariably been career diplomats or former diplomats turned politician,[7] and this precedent has so far not been abandoned nor is it likely to be abandoned soon. However, it is significant that, although all had diplomatic experience, every Foreign Minister of the postwar period except Katzuo Okazaki has come to his post more as the result of his role in domestic politics than in consequence of his role as a diplomatist. Even Okazaki, a Foreign Office functionary whom Prime Minister Yoshida elevated to the ministership, found it expedient to enter party politics following his appointment. This record may indicate a trend from the professional to the political Foreign Minister. Nevertheless the professional tradition still continues to give this office more the character of Foreign Office representation in the Cabinet than of a Cabinet supervision over the Foreign Office. The professional tradition has generally made for a notable level of technical competence in Japanese Foreign Ministers, but at the same time it has also often resulted in a specialized outlook causing alienation from popular political currents.[8]

Relative unfamiliarity with domestic politics may cause a Foreign Minister to lean heavily on his Parliamentary Vice Minister. Where the Minister himself is an experienced politician, as is usually the case with holders of most other portfolios, the position of Parliamentary Vice Minister serves as a sinecure with which to reward some deserving party faithful in the Diet. But where the Minister is not primarily a politician, as has until recently been

[7] On a few occasions in the immediate prewar period when the Army was strongly challenging the Foreign Office, the Foreign Affairs portfolio was given to a Navy man in the hope of warding off Army pressure.

[8] The experience of the United States Department of State might indicate, however, that a political department head is no sure talisman against popular suspicion.

usual with Foreign Ministers, the Parliamentary Vice Minister must be an influential member of the Diet who can cultivate favorable Diet reaction to the policies of the Minister.

The Foreign Office and the Bureaucracy

The *Gaimushō*, officially translated as the Ministry of Foreign Affairs but commonly called the Foreign Office, is the instrument for carrying out the foreign policy formulated by the Cabinet and particularly by the Foreign Minister. But it is much more than just an instrument. While the Foreign Offices of all countries influence the views of their governments, to an unusual degree the Japanese Foreign Office is itself likely to shape the policy it carries out. The special importance of the role of the Japanese Foreign Office is explained by the importance in the Japanese government of the bureaucracy in general, by the particular position of the Foreign Office within this bureaucracy, and by the unusually close identification of most Japanese Foreign Ministers with the Foreign Office because of their personal background.

The bureaucracy in Japan is an established institution whose historic prestige goes back to the seventh century, when the Japanese adopted the Chinese model of the civil service system. In the nineteenth century, when Japan undertook to modernize itself on the western model, the rapid transformation of the nation was made possible by direction from above, and the instrumentality for this controlled change was the bureaucracy. To a peculiar extent, therefore, modern Japan is the handiwork of the bureaucracy, a fact of which the bureaucrats are proudly aware. In such a paternalistic government, bureaucrats were numerous and ubiquitous. Also, as was previously noted, the Meiji Constitution had given the executive a pre-eminence over the legislative; and the bureaucracy, as the operational arm of the executive, enjoyed great power. Theoretically the bureaucrats could regard themselves as agents of the sovereign Emperor, superior to legislators who were mere representatives of the subject populace.

In the last analysis, however, the power and prestige of the bureaucracy rested on its actual abilities. To a much greater extent than in most countries, government service in Japan attracted the best brains of the nation. While the lowest category of civil-service jobs (the *hannin* class) was open to those with only secondary-school education, "The Bureaucracy" was generally considered to consist of the so-called "higher officers," so designated by their having passed the *kōtōkan* examination. Though the younger ones among them might still occupy lowly posts, these were the men who were eligible for eventual promotion to the highest positions in the government service. Their examination was highly competitive, requiring the most rigorous university training. About three-fourths of all who succeeded in passing were graduates of the Law School of Tokyo Imperial University. This university was specifically designed to produce government officials, it had by far the most distinguished faculty and the best facilities of any university in the nation, and its reputation attracted the most ambitious and most capable students from all over the country, selected through a mercilessly competitive entrance examination. Although professors of this institution generally served on the examining board, this fact probably had relatively little bearing on selection. By any objective standards, it would have been strange if the products of this competition mill were not successful. The bureaucracy thus comprised a recognized elite group, arrogant and headstrong in the consciousness of its own prowess.

Despite a heavy sprinkling of men of aristocratic birth and favored social origin, the bureaucracy was by no means a sheltered preserve for an effete privileged class. It was the road to power and position for the relatively unprivileged young man of ambition and ability. If he had the plenitude of brains and the modicum of means necessary to be admitted to Tokyo Imperial University, which was not an expensive school, his abilities alone generally determined how high he could go. A promising young official, even of undistinguished family background, usually had little difficulty in marrying a daughter of some well-placed parents who could give him wealth and social connections. While the bureaucrat's pay was comparatively modest even by Japanese standards, many official positions carried attractive perquisites and he was sure of a comfortable pension when he retired—at least in the days before post-

war inflation. If he chose to retire early, or if he reached an impasse in his official career, his government connections usually enabled him to find a good position in some private business company. The morale of the bureaucrats was therefore high; and their common educational preparation, their common career experiences, and their common pride in having achieved recognized status served to weld them, despite their diverse family backgrounds, into an exclusive, tightly knit, self-conscious, and self-assertive fraternity.

The bureaucracy was identified with no particular social or economic interests; it might ally itself from time to time with one political element or another, but its primary loyalty was always to itself. As a highly select group of professionals, it felt it knew best how to govern the nation; and its chief concern, while appearing to serve any political group that happened to be in power at the time, was to preserve its own monopolistic control over the mechanics of governmental power. With this control over the mechanics of government, the bureaucracy could even manipulate the formulation of the substance of policy, and it did so with bland assumption that its own interests coincided with the interests of the nation at large. It thus came to constitute an independent political force largely responsible only to itself, concerned primarily with preserving the *status quo* which assured it of such power.

The Japanese bureaucracy naturally had all the faults one might expect of such a group. Although personally the bureaucrats were generally highly intelligent individuals, in their official capacities they were often singularly unperceptive and devoid of common sense in matters that deviated from the established routine. Their intense but narrow legal training and their sense of their own importance inclined them to place great value on elaborate regulations and procedures which mere laymen could not hope to comprehend. Japanese bureaucracy was among the world's worst for red tape,[9] and while it was sometimes very efficient, it was more often maddeningly cumbersome. It presented a strong united front against all other groups, but it had internal jealousies. The "empire-building" by the various ministries and the resultant jurisdictional

[9] Even worse than the United States Army, which however gave the Japanese government some close competition during the Occupation.

disputes, common to all bureaucracies, were particularly evident in Japan. Advancement was nominally on the basis of merit, but seniority actually counted for a good deal. Hence there was more encouragement to put in time shuffling paper and "yessing" one's superiors than to take the risks of originality and initiative. With all these faults, the bureaucracy nevertheless constituted the most capable and effectively organized sector of the Japanese government.

Since World War II, many of these conditions have changed. The civil-service examinations have been modified in character to break the near monopoly of Tokyo Imperial University graduates and to facilitate the entrance of those with more heterogeneous preparation. Changes in job classifications and new practical examinations at various levels as prerequisites for promotion have been designed to overcome some of the traditional weakness for legalism and time serving. The growth of the power of the Diet threatens the privileged position of the bureaucracy. Lip service, at least, is being paid to the new concept of the public servant as opposed to the old concept of the agent of the Emperor. In the fluid and uncertain economic and social conditions of postwar Japan, the income from government employment—both financial and psychic—is not nearly as rewarding as it used to be. While the bureaucrat has always been unpopular with the general public, he now evokes more contempt and less fear than before.

Yet, despite these not inconsiderable changes, the bureaucracy remains the aspect of the Japanese government which has changed the least from prewar days. Many of the same individuals still remain in the government service. Much the same types of young men continue to enter the civil service for the same motives. Both the Occupation authorities and the postwar Japanese governments found the bureaucrats indispensable in keeping the machinery of government functioning. In fact, the complexities of postwar administration and reforms have helped to expand the powers of the bureaucrats. The bureaucracy still largely holds its traditional position of importance in the Japanese government.

The Foreign Office, as part of the bureaucracy, embodies all the characteristics described above, and a few special characteristics besides. It is by far the smallest of the ministries, its personnel numbering only about 1,500,—as compared with more than 260,000 in the Ministry of Postal Services or 85,000 in the Ministry of Finance—out of a total of approximately 1,500,000 in the national civic service as a whole. Its smallness does not mean that it constitutes the most elite group within the elite bureaucracy. The Japanese, with their strong sense of hierarchy, tend to rank everything in a clear order of precedence. In the past, the Finance Ministry has clearly ranked first in prestige among the ministries, because its budget-making authority gave its higher officers great, if indirect, power over all the other ministries. It was the goal for the most ambitious and brilliant aspirants to government office. The Home Office ranked second, because its control over the police and local administration afforded the most direct opportunities for the display of power. The Education Ministry unquestionably ranked the lowest and had to content itself with the grubbiest of those who passed the civil-service examinations.

The Foreign Office generally ranked somewhere near the middle of the scale. Sometimes it went as high as third place, next only to the Finance Ministry and the Home Office; but more often, pushed around and humiliated by its archenemy the Army, its stock fell far lower. Popular stereotypes of Foreign Office officials curiously resembled popular stereotypes of the State Department "cookie-pushers" in the United States. Foreign Office men were commonly suspected of being un-Japanese, of being affected dandies enamored of foreign ways and supercilious toward native virtues. But despite relatively low popular esteem, the Foreign Office, with its associations of high life among the foreigners, had a glamorous appeal to some individuals and managed to attract its share of men of good quality. These were selected through a foreign-service examination, which was a variation of the standard kōtōkan examination,[10] supplemented by personal interviews with a selection board of Foreign Office officials. Although originally there

[10] The Foreign Office and the Ministry of Justice were the only ministries that did not recruit their personnel from those who passed the general kōtōkan examinations but made use of special examinations. This practice was a recognition of the specialized character of the foreign service and the judiciary, rather than a recognition of any preferred status for these two ministries.

had been a legal distinction, in effect no practical differentiation in personnel was made between the Foreign Office and the Foreign Service or between the diplomatic service and the consular service; for they came to constitute virtually a single service within which individuals were freely transferred from one function to another.

The present prestige status of the Foreign Office is not clear. During the Occupation, Foreign Office personnel assigned to the Central Liaison Office enjoyed great importance, because they controlled the contacts with the all-important SCAP headquarters. But their glory was short-lived. Japan, though restored as an independent nation since 1952, is relatively so impotent a force in international affairs that the Foreign Office has had no opportunity to acquire any prestige. But because Japan in the future is bound to be so dependent on international conditions, the importance of the Foreign Office may eventually come to be more highly appreciated than in the past. Present plans for a considerable increase in its personnel indicate some growing recognition of its importance.

The Internal Organization of the Foreign Office

The Japanese have a penchant for neat, symmetrical organization, which in practice they proceed to circumvent by irregular, informal working arrangements. They also have a love for constantly tinkering with the nomenclature and details of the formal structure, rationalizing the changes on highly legalistic or technical grounds but actually acting out of considerations of political expediency. The Foreign Office reflects these characteristics, so that no description of its organization can remain up-to-date for long. The frequent changes, however, generally affect minor details so that the essential character of the Foreign Office organization has remained quite constant throughout Japan's modern history except for the recent wartime and Occupation periods.[11] The present or-

[11] Soon after the start of the war, the Foreign Office lost jurisdiction over relations with Asian nations to the Greater East Asia Ministry created at the instigation of the Army. When the Koiso-Yonai Cabinet replaced the Tojo Cabinet in 1944, the Foreign Office regained partial control through the concurrent appointment of the Foreign Minister as Greater East Asia Minister. At the end of the war, the Greater East Asia Ministry was abolished and its functions restored to the Foreign Office. During the Occupation, when a large

ganization[12] may therefore be considered typical in its essentials.

At the top is the Minister of Foreign Affairs, the characteristics of whose office have already been noted. Among his staff is the Parliamentary Vice Minister, a political appointee who, as previously mentioned, has nothing to do with the internal functioning of the Foreign Office but aids the Minister in his contacts with the Diet. There may also at times be a Parliamentary Counselor, likewise a political appointee, who supplements the Parliamentary Vice Minister. Sometimes certain senior diplomats may be temporarily designated as Ministry Advisers or Ministry Counselors to advise the Minister in policy matters. The designation may keep them nominally employed while awaiting some other assignment, or it may exclude them from more active positions.

Inasmuch as the Minister is largely absorbed with his Cabinet duties and with matters of general policy, the actual day-to-day operation of the Foreign Office is entrusted to the Administrative Vice Minister, generally called simply the Vice Minister. He is a personal appointee of the Minister and is generally replaced whenever the Minister changes. But he is invariably chosen from among the top half dozen or so permanent career officers of the Foreign Office—men of the rank of ambassador or sometimes of director of bureau. Like all good bureaucrats, the Vice Minister is supposed to be nonpartisan, but it is considered advisable to permit the Minister to select as his deputy a man who is congenial to him and who can be relied on to work for him. In certain ministries which used to elevate their highest-rated career officer automatically to the position of Vice Minister, nonprofessional Ministers sometimes found themselves virtually boycotted and kept in ignorance of the ministries' affairs by unco-operative professional Vice Ministers.

The structure of the Foreign Office follows closely the general pattern of organization which is pretty well standardized for almost all Japanese establishments—for large private corporations as well as for government agencies. Thus the ministry (shō) is

---

portion of its personnel was assigned to the Central Liaison Office, the Foreign Office retained not much more than a skeleton organization.

[12] As of January 1956.

divided into several bureaus (*kyoku*) and sometimes departments (*bu*), a department standing on the same level as a bureau in the organizational hierarchy but being generally somewhat more specialized and less important. Bureaus and departments are in turn divided into sections (*ka*) which may sometimes be further divided into subsections (*han*). The divisions of the Foreign Office are both functional and geographical. In 1956 they were as follows:

(1) The Minister's Secretariat, including a general planning council and separate sections dealing with administration, personnel, protocol, archives, and communications; (2) the Asian Affairs Bureau, divided into separate sections dealing with different countries and regions; (3) the European and American Affairs Bureau, with separate sections dealing with different countries or regions (including Africa!), and a special section dealing exclusively with matters pertaining to the military security arrangements with the United States; (4) the Economic Affairs Bureau, with some sections dealing with certain types of economic relations and other sections dealing with particular geographical areas; (5) the Treaties Bureau, including a section dealing with relations with the International Court of Justice; (6) the International Co-operation Bureau, dealing with relations with the United Nations and other international organizations; (7) the Public Information and Cultural Affairs Bureau; (8) the Emigration Bureau, which includes the Passport Section; and (9) Auxiliary Organs, among which the most important are the Foreign Service Personnel Committee and the Foreign Service Training Institute.

After the wartime bombing of its buildings, the Foreign Office occupied a succession of temporary quarters in Tokyo, first in a section of the Education Ministry Building, then for many years on the rented upper floors of an office building, and after 1956 in a portion of the Finance Ministry Building returned to the Japanese after use as a United States military billet. Authorization to start construction of a new Foreign Office Building on the original bombed-out site was voted by the Diet in 1956.

The Foreign Service

After the disruptions of the war and the Occupation, Japan's representation abroad had been restored through the establishment up to 1956 of 26 embassies, 29 legations, and one mission, as well as 18 consulates-general and 12 consulates. Japan had yet to enter into formal relations with any of the Communist nations, although an agreement with the Soviet Union to resume diplomatic relations had been reached. Japan had just been admitted to the United Nations at the end of 1956, but had previously had a permanent observer at the United Nations headquarters with the rank of ambassador.

Whereas before World War II the embassy in China was the largest and most important of Japan's diplomatic establishments abroad, since the Occupation the embassy in the United States ranks in first place, reflecting the special nature of contemporary Japanese-American relations. Assisting the ambassador in Washington are two ministers plenipotentiary, one of whom is not a regular member of the foreign service but a financial expert assigned from the Ministry of Finance. Below the ambassador and the ministers are four counselors, several secretaries (first, second, and third), and numerous attachés and clerks, numbering about 70 in all. (The United States Embassy in Tokyo has a staff of several hundred.) The embassy in London is the second largest of Japan's missions abroad, with a staff of about 50, followed by the embassy at Bonn. None of the others approaches these in size. The consulate-general at an important city like New York has a staff exceeding in size those of most legations and many embassies, and is headed by a man of standing comparable to a minister plenipotentiary or even to an ambassador.

All of these establishments are headed by professional diplomats. The staffs of these establishments, except for locally recruited clerical and menial help, are also composed almost exclusively of career officers. Unlike the United States, Japan has seldom used as ambassadors men who have not come up through the ranks of the diplomatic service. The few exceptions have almost all proved disappointing.

As was mentioned earlier, in the Japanese service there has never been any practical differentiation in personnel between the Foreign Office and the Foreign Service, or between the diplomatic and the consular branches of the Foreign Service. These are merely different functions within the same service, and an official normally alternates quite frequently between assignment in Tokyo and assignment abroad and between diplomatic duty and consular duty. Ambassadors are potential Ministers or Vice Ministers and vice versa; ministers plenipotentiary and consuls-general often exchange assignments with directors of bureau; first secretaries of embassy and consuls are interchangeable with heads of section. While individuals naturally tend to develop specialties to a certain extent, and some indeed become quite expert in some particular field, the official policy has been generally to transfer men at quite frequent intervals to a wide variety of assignments to broaden their experiences and their perspective. As a rule, every official in the Foreign Office at some time serves abroad and every representative abroad has at some time served in the Foreign Office.

This policy is incidentally abetted by the fairly widespread reshufflings that occur whenever a Cabinet change brings a new Foreign Minister into office. The reshufflings are apt to be quite frequent in view of the instability of most Japanese Cabinets. Because Foreign Office officials are permanent members of the civil service who cannot be removed or demoted without cause, there can be no clean sweep nor anything that looks too obviously like a spoils system. The reshufflings are therefore less conspicuous than the changes that take place at the higher levels of the State Department and among ambassadorial ranks with almost every change of administration in the United States. But, as was previously explained, the Foreign Minister does select his own Vice Minister, although the choice is limited to the senior career officers of the ministry. The Vice Minister in turn naturally likes to have in the key positions under him subordinates with whom he is sure he can get along. Hence, favorites of the Minister or Vice Minister soon find themselves quietly transferred to the more strategic and desirable posts accessible to those of their respective grades, while the less favored ones are shunted off to less desirable assignments. With each change of Minister, this process is repeated.

This game of musical chairs results from, and also contributes to, the existence within the ministry of several rival factions. No lone wolf can expect favors from anyone. To get ahead in the service, a junior needs the patronage of some superior; the superior on his part profits from the support of capable juniors. Each man, by the time he attains the stature of a possible contender for the Ministership or Vice Ministership, therefore finds himself at the head of a string of proteges who have hitched their wagons to his star and whom he pulls along whenever opportunity affords. Political views usually do not figure importantly; the attachments are mostly matters of informal personal connections and mutual advantage. An occasional individual may show a genius for hopping profitably from faction to faction. But most officials find it safest to play the game conservatively, remaining faithful to one faction, hanging on as long as possible when in power and intriguing to maneuver back into power when rival factions are having their turn. This type of intra-office factionalism and politicking is a feature common to practically all Japanese organizations, governmental or private; and, while traceable in part to the feudal boss-henchman (*oyabun-kobun*) or lord-vassal tradition, it has a very practical contemporary motivation in its bearing on one's immediate career.

Under such conditions, frequent changes and transfers of assignments are not only expected but often welcomed. When an official finds himself abroad at one post for as long as three or four years, he fears that he is being forgotten and becomes impatient for a tour of duty in Tokyo where he can strengthen his ties with the leader and other members of his faction. Yet he does not want to be tied down too long in Tokyo because he might become an office drudge and because prestige accrues from service abroad. Furthermore, in Tokyo he receives only the meager salary of the domestic variety of civil servant, whereas abroad he receives special allowances scaled to enable him to uphold the prestige of Japan in the social life of the foreign country. This pattern of peripatetic job assignments must significantly condition the attitudes of the Japanese official toward his work.

Another factor which affects the capabilities of the Japanese foreign service officer is the native environment from which he comes, which is very different from anything he encounters abroad. To be sure, by the time he enters the service he is a well-educated and sophisticated person; modern Japan is moreover sufficiently westernized and cosmopolitan in its external aspects so that nothing he sees abroad will be particularly new to him. But with respect to tradition, social customs, and personal relationships, a Japanese finds it difficult to shed completely his unique and insular background. While a Japanese diplomat is usually quite competent in the business side of his duties, he is apt to be clumsy in the social aspects of his activities. He can seldom sparkle at dinner-table conversation with a foreign dignitary's wife or engage in successful repartee with foreign correspondents. His social endeavors are likely to be correct but dull; his sense of public relations is generally poor, and he often puts his worst foot forward. The difficulties are not merely matters of language handicap, which is serious enough; they are even more matters of psychology. A Japanese may quickly attain an intellectual comprehension of foreign countries, but it takes him an exceedingly long time to acquire an intuitive rapport with foreign peoples.

In an effort to overcome these weaknesses, a newly appointed young officer is put through the Foreign Service Training Institute where, in addition to the more conventional diplomatic studies, he is systematically drilled in such exotic mysteries as mixing cocktails and matching the proper wines to the different foreign dishes. Then, as his first assignment abroad, he is sent to some embassy, nominally as an attaché, but is actually enrolled as a special student in some foreign university, where he is expected to concentrate not on academic studies but on social and other extracurricular activities. Only after a year or two of such seasoning is a Japanese considered ready for his first post as a vice consul or a third secretary.

The senior members of the postwar Japanese foreign service underwent this seasoning process before the war, but the enforced isolation of Japan during the war years and the Occupation period denied it to a large class of younger officers who are now of necessity being assigned to moderately important overseas posts without having had the benefit of a proper apprenticeship. Furthermore, the unsettling effects of the postwar social and economic conditions have bred in the younger generation of Japanese a rebellious mood and a cynical questioning of traditional authority which have inclined many of them to be attracted to Communism. Some of this attitude seems to have infected the junior grades of even the Foreign Office bureaucracy. As long as the present generation of properly trained senior officers is in control, the Japanese Foreign Office will remain a stronghold of the traditional type of diplomacy, but some of these senior officers look with misgivings on the unconventional character of their prospective successors.

Other Agencies Concerned with Foreign Relations

Several other units of the executive branch of the Japanese government have some interest in foreign affairs. The Ministry of Finance is concerned with reparations arrangements, foreign loans, foreign-exchange controls necessitated by Japan's usually unfavorable foreign trade balance, and similar financial matters involving foreign relations. The Ministry of International Trade and Industry is concerned with the promotion of foreign trade and with problems arising out of commercial activities overseas, matters of utmost importance to a nation so dependent upon foreign trade. The National Defense Agency, attached to the Office of the Prime Minister but under the immediate direction of one of the Ministers without Portfolio, is concerned with the close relations between Japan's embryonic defense forces and the United States military authorities necessitated by the Japanese-American security arrangements. The Procurement Board, an independent executive agency usually headed by an official not of Cabinet rank with Foreign Office experience, is responsible for supplying the services and facilities which the Japanese government must provide to the United States military forces in Japan under the terms of the mutual security arrangements. Its work may involve such awkward tasks as mediating in labor disputes between United States military organizations and their Japanese employees, or coping with the resistance of villagers who are being displaced to make room for United States military installations. Other governmental agencies may also be concerned from time to time with matters that involve foreign relations.

These various agencies may conduct their own preliminary planning and may even engage in informal direct contacts with foreign representatives; officials of these various agencies may be stationed abroad as attachés of embassies or legations. But all formal official negotiations are channeled through the Foreign Office. Policy matters are co-ordinated at the Cabinet level, while administrative co-ordination between the Foreign Office and the other interested agencies is achieved through consultations among the Vice Ministers or comparable officials.

Judicial Agencies Concerned with Foreign Relations

Through its new power of judicial review, the judiciary may eventually find occasion to intervene significantly in the field of foreign relations. Lack of a tradition of judicial review, however, will probably cause the Japanese courts to proceed very gingerly in this regard.

The Japanese courts are involved in the relatively minor but emotion-laden matter of Japanese jurisdiction over offenses committed by United States military personnel in Japan while off duty. Because of their historical experience with extraterritoriality, the Japanese are abnormally sensitive to crimes committed by foreigners; many Americans are unhappy about yielding criminal jurisdiction over United States service men to native authorities. Fortunately no serious issue has as yet arisen; but, because the 1947 Constitution safeguards the complete independence of the judiciary, the Foreign Office or the Cabinet could do little to contrive a diplomatically expedient settlement if the courts should choose to be adamant in a disputed case involving a foreigner.

Role of the Diet in Foreign Relations

Because the Cabinet is responsible to the Diet, which is the "highest organ of state power," the Diet possesses the authority to exercise ultimate control over the Cabinet's conduct of foreign relations. The Diet could, if it chose, assume a controlling role in the formulation of foreign policy. It would appear, however, that the Diet has as yet not gone noticeably beyond the functions of questioning and criticizing, which it used to exercise even in the prewar period.[13]

[13] Diet interpellations on foreign policy were often encouraged by the Cabinet before World War II, because Diet influence—slight though it used to be—could generally be counted on to favor the Cabinet in its perennial feud with the Supreme Command.

The reason for the Diet's seemingly modest role is to be found not only in the continuing pragmatic pre-eminence of the executive over the legislative, explained earlier, but also in the nature of the relations of the political parties to the Cabinet. Japanese political parties maintain a tight internal discipline so that no member of the Diet can deviate from the line adopted by his party executive or in his party caucus.[14] If he is a member of the Government party, he is committed to supporting the Cabinet policy; if he is a member of an Opposition party, he is committed to attacking the Cabinet policy. There is little room for flexibility of action on the part of individual Diet members which would permit the hammering out and shaping of foreign policy in the Diet.

The Diet merely furnishes the arena for the confrontation of the already settled positions of the opposing parties; the positions themselves have previously been determined within the councils of each of the parties. Inasmuch as the Cabinet comprises the leadership of the Government party or parties, it assumes the responsibility for policy formulation, while the Opposition is reduced to the merely negative function of criticizing. This practice is further accentuated by the fact that the conservative parties, which have been in power during most of the postwar period, generally see eye to eye with the professionals of the Foreign Office and are therefore quite willing to entrust the initiative in foreign-policy formulation to them.

Yet, behind the apparent rigidity of party positions and the initiative of the Foreign Office, individual members of the Diet can and occasionally do exercise greater influence over policy formulation than appears on the surface in the sessions of the Diet. The real hammering out of the substance of policy is carried on within the councils of the parties. Here is where the clash and adjustment of individual and factional views take place. The Government party not only has to resolve intraparty differences, but also—since it often lacks an absolute majority in the Diet—it needs to appeal for the support of some other party. This search for support involves direct bargaining between parties and often results in important

---

[14] This intolerance by the parties of individual deviations is one of the major reasons why Japanese politicians so frequently bolt from their parties to form splinter groups, or go over to a rival party.

modifications of the Cabinet's programs before they are proposed to the Diet as administration policy. Thus, while the individual Diet member may have little room for maneuver once the great foreign-policy issues are joined on the floor or in the committees of the Diet, he does have considerable opportunity to make his influence felt in the earlier exploratory stages of the process of policy formulation. He may act in the capacity of a party member rather than as a legislator, but he can at least indirectly influence foreign policy.

A marked change may come about if the Socialists should ever come to power. Inasmuch as most of the Foreign Office personnel would not be sympathetic toward the Socialist viewpoint, a Socialist Cabinet might rely heavily on Diet pressure for forcing the Foreign Office to toe the line. Initiative in the formulation of foreign policy might then pass from the professionals of the Foreign Office to the Socialist parliamentarians, and the Foreign Office would thus be reduced to its proper legal status as a mere instrument rather than an initiator of policy.

But that time has not yet come. Meanwhile, through backstage pressure and through interpellations, particularly in the Foreign Affairs Committee of the House of Representatives, members of the Diet keep a healthy check, if a largely negative one, on the Cabinet's conduct of foreign policy.

Political Parties and Interest Groups

From the foregoing analysis, it can be seen that, in so far as foreign policy is shaped at all outside of the Foreign Office and the Cabinet, it is shaped within the councils of the political parties rather than in the formal sessions of the Diet. Inasmuch as the bureaucrats of the Foreign Office are beyond direct reach while the Cabinet is sensitive to the inclinations of the political parties, popular influences on foreign policy can most effectively be brought to bear through pressure on the political parties. Hence, while unsophisticated interest groups may direct demonstrations at the Foreign Minister or address petitions to the Diet, knowledgeable pressure groups concentrate their attention upon the political parties. Lobbying as practiced in the United States hardly exists;

interest groups seek to gain more direct control over the party organization. Thus, business groups that contribute heavily to the campaign funds of the conservative parties can influence conservative politicians to espouse policies which the business community favors. Labor unions whose members furnish the bulk of the Socialist votes can influence the policies advocated by the Socialist party.

Incidentally, business and labor constitute the best organized and most powerful of the special-interest groups. The farmers are also well organized through agricultural co-operatives and other organizations, but they have relatively slight interest in foreign relations.

The business class, although tempted by possibilities of trade with Communist countries and sometimes irked by the attitude of Western nations, has a natural fear of Communism and believes that Japan has most to gain from close economic ties with the Free World. The conservative Liberal-Democratic party, which is largely dependent on business support, can therefore be counted on to favor intimate co-operation with the United States.

Organized labor, whose influence is dominant in the Socialist party, tends to favor a policy of neutralism. It fears that alliance with the United States will necessitate rearmament and that rearmament in turn will entail a financial burden which will necessitate the curtailment of the government's social-welfare activities in which labor is especially interested. It also suspects that the United States represents Big Business, which is unsympathetic to the interests of the laboring class, as evidenced in the favor allegedly shown to Japanese business as against Japanese labor by the Occupation authorities in their efforts to rebuild Japanese economy. The large group of intellectuals who support the Socialist party also suspect that the United States is more interested in using Japan as an instrument for combating international Communism than in nurturing democracy in Japan for the sake of the Japanese. Finally the Socialists, as the Opposition party, tend almost automatically to oppose any policy which the dominant Liberal-Democratic party espouses. If the Socialists should ever find themselves in a position of real responsibility, however, it is probable that practical necessity would cause them to follow a foreign policy not very different from that of the conservatives. At least the right-wing Socialists indicate that they understand this situation.

There are other groups that show a strong interest in certain aspects of foreign policy from time to time, but their interest is not sustained nor well organized. For instance, inhabitants of certain localities may demonstrate against the encroachment of United States military installations on their land. Peace groups may agitate against nuclear test explosions in the Pacific. Relatives of Japanese still detained in Communist countries may petition for their speedy repatriation. But, while such groups may at times generate tremendous pressures which political parties must heed or may seek to exploit, they do not have long-range influence over the parties in the way that business has over the Liberal-Democratic party or labor over the Socialist party.

These transitory pressure groups are aided by media of mass communication which are highly developed in this nation of practically universal literacy. Although the conservative point of view has its quota of able spokesmen, the majority of the intellectuals who write for the newspapers, magazines, and books are liberal or even radical. The two major newspapers of national circulation—the *Asahi* and the *Mainichi*, each with a circulation of more than three million daily—are somewhat to the left of center. The serious magazines, which have surprisingly large circulations, are almost all distinctly leftist. Hence pressure groups critical of the conservative government receive strong stimulation and support from the press. The general public is constantly influenced by reading matter which advocates a more leftist position than the majority of the people themselves hold. In the long run, the effect on the shaping of public opinion must be tremendous, but the immediate political effectiveness of the press is blunted by two factors. One is that the rural population, though well-organized, tends to be politically complacent and passive. The other is that the urban population, while susceptible to press stimulation and easily moved to temporary mass action, finds it difficult to carry on sustained political activity; for luncheon clubs, women's clubs, church groups, community forums, and other organizations that serve as channels for public action in the United States are less developed in Japan.

Organized business and organized labor alone have the machinery and the interest to exert constant systematic pressure on the political parties with respect to foreign policy.

The groups that support the extremist parties deserve little attention. The Japanese Communists are essentially identical with Communists the world over. Although noisy and troublesome, they are so few as to be a negligible political force at the moment. The neofascist and ultranationalist groups are so confused, disunited, and discredited as also to be insignificant political factors. Of course both of these extremes are potentially dangerous, but they could become powerful only if economic collapse were to drive the Japanese into a course of desperation.

Contemporary Policy

Basic Factors

On being restored to independence in 1952, Japan found itself in circumstances completely changed from those of the time when it had last participated in international affairs. Japan's overseas empire had vanished; its military establishment was gone; its economy was only partly recovered from the devastation of the war; its political, commercial, and cultural contacts with the rest of the world lay shattered. The old problems continued to plague the nation, but in a much accentuated degree—it had larger population, much smaller area, and less of natural resources than ever before. It had sunk from a first-class power to what the Japanese themselves, with not too much exaggeration, termed a third-class or fourth-class nation. Although a remarkably generous "peace of reconciliation" had restored Japan to full legal equality and freedom among the nations of the world, the peace treaty was tied to a security agreement with the United States which left United States military forces on Japanese soil. While theoretically free, as a matter of practical reality Japan was hardly capable of full independence of decision or of action.

Japan was further limited by being suddenly set loose, after the years of isolation during the war and the Occupation, in a strange new world to which it had to make radical readjustments. Great

Britain, France, and the Netherlands had withdrawn from Japan's part of the globe; the United States and the Soviet Union had become overtowering colossi; China under Communist rule was becoming a formidable power; a dozen new independent nations had come into existence in Asia, some of them friendly but others with hatred, suspicion, or jealousy of Japan. It would take some time before the Japanese could get the feel of this unfamiliar international environment and evolve a new foreign policy suitable to these revolutionized circumstances. Meanwhile Japanese foreign policy was bound to be one of impotence and drift.

But even at its lowest ebb, Japan retained some significant elements of power. It had strategic geographic location. Its industrial power, even after the ravages of defeat, still towered over that of the other countries of Asia. It possessed a completely literate population and an abundance of experienced scientists, technicians, and administrators which no other Asian country could hope to match for several generations. It had almost three generations of experience as a member of modern world society,[15] whereas most of the other countries of Asia were just emerging from colonial dependence. Although probably destined to be overshadowed by China and India in the long run, Japan for the foreseeable future seems certain to remain an outstanding power center of the Far East.

Already the Japanese have recovered from their demoralization of the immediate postsurrender years and are beginning to demonstrate anew their national cohesion, industriousness, and disciplined dynamism. Japan can no longer hope to play an important independent role in world politics, but might easily prove to be a decisive factor in a close balance of international alignments. As the Japanese people regain their bearings and realize their poten-

[15] "Approximately three generations are required for a folk-population to assimilate a machine-based way of living. The first generation copies, blunders, attempts to force muscle into unfamiliar patterns. The second generation accepts and uses new devices without much insight or assured skill and continues to copy. But the third generation, reared on mechanical toys and at home in mind and muscle amid machines, no longer need imitate. They assimilate, select, and invent devices adapted to their unique needs." (Douglas G. Haring, "Land and Men in Asia," *Far Eastern Survey,* vol. XXV, no. 1, January 1956.)

tialities, their government will undoubtedly evolve an increasingly positive and active foreign policy.

Such a foreign policy, whatever the political complexion of the government that happens to be in power at any particular time, must be directed toward three basic objectives, namely: physical security, economic viability, and prestige. These objectives are of course interdependent and inseparable, but the major issues of contemporary Japanese foreign policy may be arbitrarily grouped in relation to one or another of them for convenience in examination.

Issues Relating to National Security

In a world dominated by the confrontation of the United States and the Soviet Union, lesser nations like Japan must seek national security either through identifying themselves with one of the giants as opposed to the other, or through avoiding so great a dependence on one as to invite the enmity of the other. The first carries the risk of losing full freedom of action; the second carries the risk of being left with no protector at all.

The article in Japan's 1947 Constitution providing for perpetual demilitarization had been premised on the hope, which still prevailed at the time it was drafted, for a peaceful "One World." As the result of the subsequent polarization of the world into two antagonistic camps, Japan has created modest "Self Defense" forces under a flexible interpretation of the Constitution pending outright amendment. But even a rearmed Japan would be helpless if caught in the crossfire between the United States and the Soviet Union.

The Japanese government has therefore formally committed itself to the side of the United States through a mutual-security pact. Under the terms of this pact and its supplementary arrangements, the United States maintains armed forces in Japan to aid in the defense of that country, while the latter contributes facilities and services. These arrangements are to continue until such time as Japan's own defense forces become capable of assuming responsibility for the nation's security. Meanwhile the United States is pressing Japan for a more rapid and extensive build-up of its military capabilities than the Japanese are willing—or feel able—to undertake.

This situation gives rise in Japan to the related issues of whether or not this intimate relationship with the United States is desirable, whether or not the Constitution should be amended to remove legal restrictions on rearming, and how rapidly and extensively rearmament should be carried out. In the main, the conservative parties, which have been in power virtually throughout the postwar period,[16] favor continuation of close co-operation with the United States, amendment of the demilitarization provision of the Constitution, and rapid rearming, although not to the extent desired by the United States. The Socialists and many politically independent individuals incline toward neutralism, oppose amendment of the Constitution, and manifest opposition or extreme reluctance toward rearming, although most of them probably favor the continuation of some co-operation with the United States. None but the insignificant minority of confirmed Communists favor alignment with the Soviet Union, and even they find it politic to pretend to be in favor of mere neutralism.

The close association of Japan with the United States is not due solely to the persistence of United States power in Japan since the Occupation. A majority of the Japanese have reasons of their own for favoring this association. Fear and suspicion of Russia are strongly rooted in Japan's historical experience. As the most highly developed industrial and commercial nation in Asia, Japan has large and powerful business and industrial classes who have no desire to throw away their vested interest in capitalism in exchange for the Communist economic experiment. Most Japanese believe that their chronic economic difficulties can best be ameliorated through continued close co-operation with the United States and the free world.

The United States Occupation, moreover, has given to Japan a strong democratic orientation. Despite the superficial character of some aspects of the Occupation program and the resultant present

---

[16] The only exception was from May 23, 1947 to February 10, 1948 when Prime Minister Tetsu Katayama, a moderate Socialist, headed a coalition of the Socialist, Democratic, and People's Co-operative parties.

tendency toward backsliding on the part of the Japanese, it is unlikely that the profound changes wrought by the war and the defeat and the tremendous impact of the Occupation can ever be completely undone. Furthermore, the general trend of Japanese political and social development for the past hundred years has been toward gradually increasing westernization and democratization, halted only temporarily by the decade or two of reactionary militarism before and during World War II. The Occupation revived and strengthened this historic trend and created new vested interests—the beneficiaries of the land reform, organized labor, women, intellectuals, and others—which, however critical they may be of the United States, profited from the Occupation reforms and will fight to retain their new stake in a democratized Japan. The weight of all these factors will tend to hold Japan to the side of the western democracies.

At the same time, there are important factors that tend to weaken Japan's ties with the United States. A conspicuous point of disagreement concerns the extent of the military build-up which the United States is urging Japan to undertake. The Japanese contend that, even with substantial subventions from the United States, the burden of rearmament would so overtax Japan's still precarious economy as to depress the standard of living, causing social unrest which the Communists would be quick to exploit. Why guard against the external Communist threat if it will only lead to the growth of Communism from within? Some Japanese also fear that democracy in Japan is still so fragile that even a small military establishment might prove to be an entering wedge for the revival of militarism and authoritarianism. The threat of Communism seems to them to be less dangerous than the threat that democracy might be stifled in the effort to combat Communism. They are disturbed over the apparent inclination of some Americans to prefer militant anticommunism over true democracy in Japan.

But reluctance to rearm goes beyond rational considerations into realms where emotion plays a large part. Grateful as the Japanese were for the benevolent character of the United States Occupation, no foreign military occupation is a pleasant experience for the occupied. There is too much about the mutual-security relationship between Japan and the United States that reminds the Japanese of the recent Occupation. They question whether nations so disparate in power can really be equal partners; they suspect that the present alliance actually represents a continuation of the Occupation in disguise. Since they are comparatively powerless to influence United States policy positively, it is only by occasionally refusing to co-operate with the United States that the Japanese can reassure themselves that they really enjoy independence. Frustrated by their relative impotence, they unconsciously find relief in a hypercritical and supercilious attitude toward supposed American shortcomings.

Many Japanese suspect that the United States is so preoccupied with military measures against the Communist threat as to be neglecting possible political measures to lessen the danger of war. They fear that Japan is being used as a cat's-paw of this unwise United States policy and that Japan, transformed into a virtual United States military outpost, unduly risks being forced to absorb the first shock of a possible Communist assault. Some Japanese question the value of any military force for Japan at all, on the ground that any military force it could afford would be insufficient to assure successful defense while sufficient to provide an aggressor with a pretext for attack. They hold that the safest course for Japan would be to adhere to strict neutralism and strict pacifism so as to offer no provocation to anyone. They offer a rationalization to many more who, with traumatic memories of their terrifying wartime experience, recoil unreasoningly from all suggestion of rearming and are eager to believe that by their own will they can escape involvement in any future war.

For some Japanese, neutralism represents not only a flight from war but a more general form of isolationism. Confused and frustrated by the complexities of life in an interdependent international community, they would like to forget the rest of the world and retire within the reassuring confines of their familiar local concerns. They would like to ignore the United States; for to them it is the United States that represents entangling alliances, that is trying to get Japan committed in the cold war, and that is urging expensive rearmament with the unwelcome reminder that Japan has international responsibilities.

For other Japanese, neutralism represents not isolationism but a form of Pan-Asianism. They believe that Japan's future lies naturally with Asia rather than with the West. They, in common with many other Asians, regard the struggle between democracy and Communism as essentially a civil war between two Occidental ideologies in which Orientals have no direct concern. Their awareness of Communist imperialism and their memory of the colonialism of the western democratic countries are about equally vivid, and they take the attitude of a plague on both houses. They therefore feel that Japan should dissociate itself from the United States and identify itself with the Asian nations that are trying to avoid commitment to either side in the rivalry between the United States and the USSR. For still other Japanese, Pan-Asian neutralism is sublimated into an idealistic internationalism. They believe that Asians, as disinterested third parties, have a moral duty to try to moderate the intolerance of the western and the Communist antagonists and to serve as impartial mediators in the interests of the peace of the world.

While these attitudes may be dangerously unrealistic, their appeal to many Japanese is understandable. So far, hard-headed practical considerations have kept the Japanese government loyal to its commitments to the United States and the West. Increasing experience with the realities of postwar international politics should strengthen this official policy. But it involves many issues that must yet be argued out by the Japanese public.

Issues Involving Economic Viability

Pressed by a large and growing population on very limited land, Japan must normally import about 20 per cent of the food its people consume. This food import can be paid for only by the export of its products, but lacking adequate raw materials and natural resources Japan must import these as well. It can therefore survive only by importing cheap food and raw materials and exporting manufactures whose value has been enhanced by the labor of the Japanese people. This problem has become particularly acute

824 JAPAN

since the loss of Japan's overseas possessions and favorable trading
position has forced the country to resort to expensive sources of
imports and to more restricted and difficult market areas.

Although United States economic aid and military spending,
occasional bumper harvests, and native industriousness have provided a temporary disguise of outward prosperity, Japan's economy
remains basically unsound. In the postwar period Japan has not
been able to sell abroad enough to balance its essential imports. In
addition, it must earn enough to repay a good portion of the
United States aid which was in the form of loans, to pay reparations
to various Asian countries, to provide for the cost of rearmament,
and to provide for the social welfare and higher living standards
which the Japanese people are increasingly demanding.

The Japanese, by reason of their business background and their
close political ties with the United States, would prefer to earn
their livelihood by trading within the free world. Actually, the bulk
of Japan's foreign trade since the war has been with the United
States. But Japan has usually been buying about twice as much
from the United States as it has been able to sell to the United
States. Only recently has this imbalance been moderated somewhat, but one of the major issues of Japanese foreign policy is how
to overcome the tariffs, quotas, and public resistance in the United
States that obstruct the expansion of Japanese sales. Many other
western nations have raised more discriminatory barriers against
Japanese trade. These pose additional problems in Japanese foreign
policy.

Theoretically the best prospects for Japanese trade seem to lie in
South and Southeast Asia. Here is an undeveloped region which
can advantageously use Japanese goods and technical services. But
in practice, Japanese trade in this area is hampered by the residue
of wartime animosities, by European—particularly British—competition, by political instability in some countries, and by low purchasing power due to the generally underdeveloped state of this area's
economy. Japan hopes to overcome some of these handicaps by
very circumspect conduct and by making as conciliatory reparations settlements as its own economy can stand. With the active
support of the United States, Japan is also advocating the establish-

ment of an improved organization for regional economic co-operation and the employment by the United States of Japanese goods
and services in its program of economic aid to this region. But the
results may not appear soon enough to be of much help to Japan.

In this situation the Japanese are sorely tempted to trade with
Communist China, for China used to account for about one-third
of Japan's foreign trade. Prospects of violent United States dis-
pleasure, fear of being pulled into the Communist orbit, and the
likelihood that Japan will only be exploited cannot wholly end the
dreams of a profitable economic relationship with Red China as
long as the Japanese face the alternative of bankruptcy. The respect
and racial pride which most Asians have come to feel—though
often reluctantly—for the undoubted achievements and growing
power of Communist China tend to blind the Japanese to the
repulsive methods employed by the Communists. Even the conservative and anti-Communist administration of Prime Minister
Ichiro Hatoyama was constrained, therefore, to attempt negotiations with the Soviet Government in the hope that establishment
of formal relations would lead to profitable economic intercourse
with the entire Communist bloc. The popular pressure to enter
into close relations with Communist China will be even stronger
than the pressure to enter into relations with the Soviet Union.
How to adjust this pressure to the also obvious desirability of maintaining close ties with the United States constitutes a major problem of Japanese foreign policy.

Among the other less important foreign-policy problems relating
to Japan's economic situation are the friction with Korea, the
Soviet Union, and Communist China over access to fishing waters,
and the damage to Japanese deep-sea fisheries operations caused by
United States nuclear tests covering vast expanses of the Pacific.

Issues Involving Prestige

As a colored nation in a world still largely dominated by the
white nations, Japan is highly sensitive to the intangible factors of
prestige, recognition, and acceptance in the world community.
Even Japan's lawless international behavior before and during
World War II was, in a sense, but a perverse response to the

world's supposed unwillingness to accord the country its rightful due, and represented a hypersensitivity—albeit a misdirected one— to world opinion. Now Japan is eager to regain the reputation it forfeited through the war. With attainment of respectability again within reach, the Japanese are motivated toward a very proper international conduct as much by a sense of self-satisfaction as by the dictates of prudence.

So long as this mood prevails—and it is likely to prevail as long as Japan meets with no violent disillusionment—the Japanese are likely to play a co-operative and constructive role in all good international undertakings. Cultural and scientific exchanges, international gatherings of all kinds, self-restricting international agreements for the conservation of fish, seals, and whales, and all such good works meet with the enthusiastic support of the Japanese government and people. Their prewar dreams of power gone, they would now attain glory through peaceful modest deeds.

Delay in gaining membership in the United Nations was a bitter disappointment to the Japanese people, for they prize this membership more as a tangible symbol of their acceptance in the world community than for any practical benefits that might accrue. Meanwhile, they worked hard in UNESCO and the Economic Commission for Asia and the Far East and in other bodies to which they had been admitted.

Conclusions

Japan's postwar governmental organization certainly provides for a more effective mechanism for the formulation and control of foreign policy than its prewar counterpart. In contrast to the uncoordinated agencies that used to compete for the control of foreign policy, the Cabinet today possesses the sole responsibility for the conduct of foreign policy, the Cabinet is strictly accountable to the Diet, and the Diet is directly responsive to the general electorate. The pattern conforms to that found in the most advanced of the western democratic governments. In so far as any system can be devised to do so, it should produce a foreign policy that truly represents the will of the people.

But no political system can assure perfect results inasmuch as the human factor is concerned. It is still too early to tell just what the Japanese will be able to do with what they now have. Japanese national characteristics and social dynamics should throw some light, however, on what they are likely to do.

If the new mechanism for the formulation and control of foreign policy should fail to work, one reason for the failure might be the tradition of executive pre-eminence which predisposes the Cabinet toward seeking to minimize the influence of the Diet and the general public. Another reason might be the tendency of the Foreign Office bureaucracy, as an elite professional group, to be disdainful of popular controls. Still another reason might be the factionalism inherent in the Japanese social process, which causes rival groups to seek to outmaneuver each other for power and results in stultifying deals in the Cabinet, sterile personal politics in the Foreign Service, and irresponsible brawling in the Diet, all of which might well drive the discouraged public into fatalistic lethargy. Despite the safeguards embodied in the new mechanism, these traditional defects may prove to be too pervasive.

In the short period that the new system has been in operation, however, these traditional defects—while still all too evident—have not been evident to a fatal degree. If anything, the Japanese have been doing better in this regard, as indeed with almost all aspects of their new constitutional system, than their earlier record would have given reason to expect. Credit may be given to the essential merit of their new constitutional system, to the lessons learned from their past mistakes, and to the changes in the general social and political climate of Japan brought about by defeat in war and by its aftermath.

In the long run, however, it is not the forms of governmental organization nor the effects of historical events that determine success in any aspect of government, or specifically in the formulation and control of foreign policy. The basic nature of the society and nation is more important. In this regard, Japan suffers from its relatively recent feudal background with its authoritarian tradition, hierarchical social structure, particularistic human relationships, factionalism, and subordination of the individual to the group.

These are hardly compatible with democratic ideals or with modern democratic government.

On the other hand, the history of Japan has ever been characterized by dynamic changes. Despite persistence of many traditional features, Japanese life has been undergoing a fundamental revolution over the past one hundred years. The leaders of Japan may have originally intended that in adopting modern technology and widespread industrialization they would merely provide their country with material power while leaving its traditional social ideals and spiritual values intact. But in the nature of things, they could not. Modern technology and widespread industrialization, wherever introduced, inevitably bring in their train a transformation in the nonmaterial aspects of life. Rational modes of thinking, new forms of administrative organization and procedure, new types of social relationships, greater social mobility, respect for individual worth, different standards of values, and substitution of a universalistic ethic for the old particularistic ethic inevitably follow.

Although still lagging behind the older industrialized countries of the West, Japan has been undergoing this process for a century. Despite reactionary resistance and occasional setbacks, Japan more than any other nonwestern country has come to approximate the basic general conditions of life that prevail in the modern nations of the West. It may be that Japan is reaching the stage in its historical evolution where the political practices heretofore identified with the western nations fit Japanese national conditions more naturally than the traditional practices of the nation's receding past. If so, its new political system stands a good chance of success and growth.

SELECTED BIBLIOGRAPHY

I. GENERAL WORKS, AND PREWAR PERIOD

Inasmuch as there are almost no books that bear directly on the subject of foreign-policy formulation and control in Japan, pertinent information must be pieced together from a wide variety of works. An indispensable general orientation is provided by Edwin

O. Reischauer, *The United States and Japan* (Cambridge, Harvard University Press, 1950), which under a deceptively simple style presents a most astute and judicious appraisal of Japan's problems and its national characteristics. For further study, a useful starting point and guide is *A Selected List of Books and Articles on Japan in English, French, and German* (Cambridge, Harvard University Press, 1954), compiled by Hugh Borton, Serge Eliséeff, William W. Lockwood, and John C. Pelzel.

For the historical background, Sir George B. Sansom, *Japan: A Short Cultural History* (New York, Appleton-Century, rev. ed., 1944), is the acknowledged "classic" for the premodern period; the same author's *The Western World and Japan* (New York, Knopf, 1950) deals with similar brilliance with the western impact on Japan to about the end of the nineteenth century. Standard authorities on the modern period are Chitoshi Yanaga, *Japan Since Perry* (New York, McGraw-Hill, 1949), which is rich in factual detail; and Hugh Borton, *Japan's Modern Century* (New York, Ronald, 1955), which is valuable for its thoughtful interpretations although foreign policy is not as expertly handled as some of the other subjects. A more specialized basic work analyzing the forces underlying Japan's entrance into modern international society is E. Herbert Norman, *Japan's Emergence as a Modern State* (New York, Institute of Pacific Relations, 1940). A clear, concise summary of the whole of Japanese history is presented by Edwin O. Reischauer, *Japan Past and Present* (New York, Knopf, rev. ed., 1953).

Readable works dealing with the bases of Japan's national power are few and generally inadequate. The geographic bases are covered in Glenn T. Trewartha, *Japan: A Physical, Cultural, and Regional Geography* (Madison, University of Wisconsin Press, 1945). The economic aspects are interestingly surveyed in John E. Orchard, *Japan's Economic Position* (New York, Whittlesey, 1930), and penetratingly interpreted in William W. Lockwood, *The Economic Development of Japan, 1868-1938* (Princeton, Princeton University Press, 1954).

Sound, scientific studies of Japanese national traits are still in their infancy. Ruth Benedict, *The Chrysanthemum and the Sword*

(Boston, Houghton Mifflin, 1946), is the pioneering work which has opened up a highly suggestive new approach, although the book must be used with caution because of its sometimes fanciful overgeneralizations. Delmer M. Brown, *Nationalism in Japan* (Berkeley, University of California Press, 1955), carefully traces the development of nationalism as one of the dynamics of Japanese life.

For government and politics, the standard work on the prewar period is Harold S. Quigley, *Japanese Government and Politics* (New York, Century, 1932). A shorter but more interpretive work is Robert Karl Reischauer, *Japan, Government—Politics* (New York, Thomas Nelson, 1939). Of value are the articles on various aspects of the Japanese government by Kenneth W. Colegrove in *The American Political Science Review*, vols. XXV, nos. 3, 4 (1931); XXVI, 4, 5 (1932); XXVII, 6 (1933); XXVIII, 1 (1934); and XXX, 5 (1936); and particularly his article on "The Japanese Foreign Office" in *The American Journal of International Law*, vol. XXX, no. 4 (1936). The same author's *Militarism in Japan* (Boston, World Peace Foundation, 1936), is also useful. Tatsuji Takeuchi, *War and Diplomacy in the Japanese Empire* (New York, Doubleday, 1935), presents detailed case studies of the formulation and control of Japanese foreign policy. F. C. Jones, *Japan's New Order in East Asia* (London, Oxford University Press, 1954), is a masterly account of the unfolding of Japan's foreign policy during the climactic years of its imperialistic program. William Henry Chamberlin, *Japan Over Asia* (Boston, Little Brown, 2nd rev. ed., 1939), gives a journalistic but illuminating explanation of the forces competing for the control of Japanese foreign policy. Robert J. C. Butow, *Japan's Decision to Surrender* (Stanford, Stanford University Press, 1954), presents a dramatic illustration of the interaction of complex forces in the formulation of a policy decision in Japan.

II. POSTWAR PERIOD

Among the host of general works which have appeared on postwar Japan and the Occupation, the more notable are: Baron E. J. Lewe van Aduard, *Japan: From Surrender to Peace* (New York,

Praeger, 1954), which is probably the most balanced; Harry Emerson Wildes, *Typhoon in Tokyo* (New York, Macmillan, 1954), episodic and overdetailed but valuable for authentic atmosphere; Robert B. Textor, *Failure in Japan* (New York, John Day, 1951), highly unbalanced in its general conclusions but sharply perceptive in many of its details; W. MacMahon Ball, *Japan, Enemy or Ally?* (New York, John Day, 1949), an Australian criticism of American occupation policy; Edwin M. Martin, *The Allied Occupation of Japan* (Stanford, Stanford University Press, 1948), and its sequel, Robert A. Feary, *The Occupation of Japan, Second Phase: 1948-1950* (New York, Macmillan, 1950), which together present unexcitingly but accurately the official Washington point of view.

Scholarly works dealing with the postwar government and politics, with implications concerning foreign policy, are: Chitoshi Yanaga, *Japanese People and Politics* (New York, John Wiley, 1956); Nobutaka Ike, *Japanese Politics* (New York, Knopf, 1957); Harold S. Quigley and John E. Turner, *The New Japan, Government and Politics* (Minneapolis, University of Minnesota Press, 1956); Paul M. A. Linebarger, Djang Chu, and Ardath W. Burks, *Far Eastern Governments and Politics: China and Japan* (New York, Van Nostrand, 1954); and a somewhat outdated but still helpful short textbook treatment in Philip W. Buck and John W. Masland, *The Governments of Foreign Powers* (New York, Henry Holt, rev. ed., 1950). Of the many scholarly articles in this field, of most general use is the symposium "Postwar Politics in Japan," edited by Harold S. Quigley and composed of contributions by Kenneth E. Colton, John Saffell, Harry Emerson Wildes, and Justin Williams, which appears in *The American Political Science Review*, vol. XLII, nos. 5, 6 (October, December, 1948).

Among the great mass of source materials yielded up by the Occupation, the most pertinent to the subject of government and politics is SCAP, Government Section, *The Political Reorientation of Japan*, 2 vols. (Washington, Government Printing Office, 1950). In Major General Charles A. Willoughby, *MacArthur, 1941-1951* (New York, McGraw-Hill, 1954), and Brigadier General Courtney Whitney, *MacArthur: His Rendezvous with History* (New York, Knopf, 1955), two high Occupation officials who played significant roles in the reshaping of postwar Japan present their hardly objective but highly illuminating memoirs.

As to the bases of Japan's national power in the postwar period, Edward A. Ackerman, *Japan's Natural Resources* (Chicago, University of Chicago Press, 1953), is an extensive study whose ramifications are wider than indicated by its title. The economic aspects of national power are treated in Jerome B. Cohen, *The Japanese Economy in War and Reconstruction* (Minneapolis, University of Minnesota Press, 1949).

As for national characteristics, Jean Stoetzel, *Without the Chrysanthemum and the Sword* (New York, Columbia University Press, 1955), reports a research on the changing behavior pattern and character traits of postwar Japanese youth.

Study of the foreign policy of postwar Japan is so new that chief reliance will have to be on ephemeral periodical literature. The following books have some bearing on this subject: Edwin O. Reischauer, *Wanted: An Asian Policy* (New York, Knopf, 1955); Edwin O. Reischauer (editor), *Japan and America Today* (Stanford, Stanford University Press, 1953), containing contributions by Japanese and United States experts on problems of Japanese-American relations; Jerome B. Cohen, *Economic Problems of Free Japan* (Princeton, Center of International Studies, 1952).

Among recent periodical literature, the following might be particularly useful: Hitoshi Ashida, "Japan and Its Role in the World Today," *World Affairs Interpreter*, Spring 1954; Hugh Borton, "The Relation of Japan to the Continent," *Proceedings of the Academy of Political Science*, January 1955; Arthur G. Coons, "Neutralism: The Problem of Japan in East-West Relations," *World Affairs Interpreter*, Winter 1955; Toshikazu Kase, "Japan's New Role in East Asia," *Foreign Affairs*, October 1955; Kazuo Kawai, "The New Anti-Americanism in Japan," *Far Eastern Survey*, November 1953; Douglas H. Mendel, Jr., "Revisionist Opinion in Post-Treaty Japan," *The American Political Science Review*, September 1954; Joseph Z. Reday, "What of Japan?" *United States Naval Institute Proceedings*, July 1955; Walter S. Robertson, "United States Policy toward Japan," *U.S. Department of State Pamphlet*, Series S-No. 5, 1954; John D. Rockefeller III, "Japan

Tackles Her Problems," *Foreign Affairs*, July 1954; Tatsuji Takeu-chi, "Basic Issues in Japan's Foreign Policy," *Far Eastern Survey*, November 19, 1952; Mary Clabaugh Wright, "Japan and China," *Vassar Alumnae Magazine*, February 1955; Shigeru Yoshida, "Japan's Place in Asia," *Atlantic Monthly Supplement on Japan*, 1954; "On the Japanese Economy," Background Notes No. 3, Public Services Division, U.S. Department of State, November 1954.

To keep abreast of current developments, in addition to the usual news sources the following publications are helpful: *Journal of Asian Studies* (formerly the *Far Eastern Quarterly*); *Pacific Affairs* (a quarterly); *Far Eastern Survey* (formerly a biweekly, now a monthly); *Far East Digest* (a mimeographed monthly ab-stract of periodical literature); *Japan Report* (a mimeographed biweekly news bulletin issued by the Embassy of Japan, Washing-ton); *Japan Times* (formerly the *Nippon Times*, an English-lan-guage Tokyo daily).

CHAPTER 23

THE FUTURE OF THE CONDUCT
OF FOREIGN RELATIONS

QUINCY WRIGHT

Department of Political Science

University of Chicago

It has often been suggested that international relations are moving toward one world or none. The optimists rely on human reason. Aware of the general disaster which would result from atomic war and the human benefits to be gained by peaceful international co-operation to ameliorate conditions of poverty, ignorance, disease, and strife, the optimists anticipate that governments will emancipate themselves from concepts of national sovereignty, power rivalry, and ideological conflict, and organize the world to maintain order and justice, and promote human welfare and progress. "What we seek," wrote Woodrow Wilson, "is the reign of law based upon the consent of the governed and sustained by the organized opinion of mankind." World institutions, reflecting this opinion, say the optimists, will inevitably gain in strength and subordinate the independent decision-making of nations to the general good.

Some of the optimists would give the nation-states a secondary role, anticipating eventual organization of the world as a federation, in which central law-making and law-enforcing authorities operate upon individuals in defined spheres considered necessary to keep the peace, to enforce the law, and to promote justice. Others would give the nations a larger role, foreseeing a perfection of the United Nations to assure pacific settlement, collective security, disarmament, and international co-operation under a general regime of international law among sovereign states.

Pessimists, on the other hand, doubt whether human nature can be so educated as to eliminate the propensity of men to organize in groups for promoting selfish aims at the expense of other groups, using force and fraud, if suitable, to the ends sought. They emphasize the experience that political organizations have not been able to survive unless faced by an external political organization so obviously threatening their existence that they are obliged to cohere for common defense. Ambition and fear, the pessimists say, have together been the great political cement. Faced by the predominance of passion over reason in human motivation, and contemplating the proposition that an in-group maintains political solidarity only when facing a hostile out-group, they do not believe that the continuous danger of war can be avoided or that international relations can take a form other than that of power politics. Furthermore, they argue that the differences of climate, resources, culture, ideology, economy, and government in different parts of the world are so great and so founded on unchanging and unchangeable conditions that these differences will always persist and will always breed conflicting group interests transcending possibilities of peaceful accommodation. Accordingly, they say, the influence of international law, international organization, and international ethics will always be secondary to the influence of conflicting national interests. The society of nations will always, say the pessimists, be anemic and ineffective, while many of the nations will always be strong, dynamic, and aggressive. Consequently, international relations will always be characterized more by conflict than by co-operation. The demand for security will dominate in national policy-making and the satisfied and dissatisfied states will always threaten the peace by their different conceptions of what security requires. This situation, the pessimists say, can be expected, even though reason teaches that with such international anarchy war is probable and that war waged with hydrogen bombs would probably destroy civilization.

The idealists and realists struggle in the battle of words with perhaps insufficient consideration of the potency of ideas in influencing conduct, and of the tendency for close observation of actual situations to evolve ideas of change. Was Winston Churchill an idealist or a realist when he said "When the advance of destructive warfare enables everyone to kill everybody else, nobody will want to kill anyone at all"?[1]

It seems likely that, in the future as in the past, some tendencies will work together in influencing individual and national behavior toward the conquest of physical nature and, more gradually, toward the conquest of human nature: ideas of reform will grow from current observations and dissatisfactions; the way things have worked out in the past and the present will be observed, and generalizations will be made; traditional impulses, customs, policies, and human irritations and passions will also be influential. Toynbee in his *Study of History* finds that behind the rise and fall of states and of civilizations there has been continuous progress in science and technology on the one hand, and in more comprehensive values and higher religions on the other.

The progress of the world in technology during the twentieth century has been so phenomenal that human institutions, not surprisingly, have lagged behind in arrangements to control new forces which have become available. John Von Neumann, eminent atomic scientist, has pointed out that the effect of scientific progress has been to increase the capability of men to act at one point in time and space with effects devastating or beneficial over larger and larger areas.[2] In a world where individuals have such capability, no one can escape by flight or concealment. If a madman is at the controls, all may perish. The only security for anyone lies in assuring that those who have these vast capabilities shall use their power responsibly. Threats of retaliation which mean suicide if carried out

[1] House of Commons Debate, Nov. 3, 1953, *Parl. Deb.*, vol. 520, col. 30.
[2] John Von Neumann, *Fortune*, June, 1955, p. 106.

are less promising than the organization of control through law, but the one may lead to the other. If power of retaliation exists and if that power is understood by all, then the atomic stalemate—suggested by Churchill and apparently accepted by the leaders of the four great powers of the Summit Conference of August 1955—may have created a situation in which international organizations to prevent "nibbling aggressions," to reduce tensions, to develop international law, and to promote international co-operation may increase in effectiveness.

The history of the last century is one of continuous but unostentatious progress in international organization. During the period of the international unions from 1870 to 1899, the governments spent little over $100,000 a year on these agencies. In the Hague period from 1899 to the end of the first World War, their annual expenditures averaged ten times as much, nearly $1,000,000 a year. In the League of Nations period they averaged $10,000,000 a year, and in the United Nations period over $100,000,000 a year—a geometric progression. If these expenditures continue thus to be multiplied by ten each generation, they would reach a very large figure—a trillion dollars in another century, nearly twice the present annual income of the world. This rate of increase in the expenditures for international organization cannot continue, but the trend suggests that international organization is likely to grow. Furthermore, although during this same period national expenditures have increased, they have not increased as rapidly as have expenditures for international organization. We may, therefore, anticipate that in total government expenditure a larger proportion will be given to international organization. It is true that that proportion is still very small, only about one part in 2000; nevertheless it can be expected to grow, and if the rates of change over the past century continue in any degree, in another century a large proportion of governmental expenditures will be devoted to international organization.

If the trend toward progress in international organization continues, as technological progress and recent history suggest it will, the problem of gearing decision-making at the national level into that at the international level will increase in importance.

The desire of states for self-determination and efficiency in making foreign policy induces efforts toward more effective co-ordination of all agencies in the government toward accepted policies. These assume the practical form of securing consultation, before policy decisions are made, among all relevant executive agencies as well as the legislature, the parties, and public opinion. In spite of the desire of the executive authorities of states to emancipate themselves from such consultations and to act freely, the trend of national decision-making in foreign policy has been in the direction of co-ordinating the interests and action of all agencies to a common policy.

Such national co-ordination means that instructions to representatives in international organizations must be inflexible. Changes in a position which has resulted from such elaborate consultation cannot be made without treading on the toes of some interested national agency or violating commitments inherent in the process of consultation. The result is that national representatives in international organizations are so bound by instructions that they cannot moderate their positions as a result of discussion in the international body. Complete co-ordination at the national level destroys the possibility of any co-ordination at all at the international level.

On the other hand, flexibility in instructions, often the practice of governments of smaller states, means that the national representative in each international agency is free to change his position and to act in conformity with the course of discussion. If the representatives of all nations in the international body are thus free, co-ordination at the international level is possible. But the result may be national confusion. Representatives of a government in the International Labor Organization may be assuming a position inconsistent with that of the representative of the same government in the Food and Agriculture Organization. If there is no co-ordination nationally and the Labor Department instructs the ILO representative while the Agriculture Department instructs the FAO representative, inconsistent positions are almost certain, and the decision reached at the international level may reflect back on the respective national departments and lead to conflict and confusion in national policy. Such results were sometimes observed in connection with the League of Nations; it was said that under the enthusiasm of the atmosphere of Geneva, statesmen would approve resolutions which would have no chance of execution when subjected to the atmosphere of London, of Paris, or of Berlin.

This dilemma as to national and international co-ordination would be obviated in a World Federation in which both national organs and world organs derived their powers from the people in respect to well-demarcated functions. So long, however, as the world is organized internationally rather than federally, inconsistencies of co-ordination at the two levels appear to be inevitable. The solution can be found only in a spirit of tolerance and accommodation. Perfect co-ordination cannot be expected either in national governments or in international organs. Governments must be prepared to give their delegates some flexibility in order to accommodate their positions to the trend of discussion in the international agencies even at the expense of some inconsistencies in national policy. On the other hand, international agencies must realize that national co-ordination, demanded by the sentiment of national solidarity and self-determination, inevitably makes progress in international co-ordination slow.

Perhaps the problem can best be met by leaving the instruction of national delegations primarily to the functional department most interested in the subject matter, with supervision by the foreign office only to eliminate gross inconsistencies with its own foreign policy. Such a practice would permit co-operation and co-ordination at the international level in each functional field on its own merits. Foreign-office policy, dominated by considerations of security, is likely to insist that policies on matters of health, labor, agriculture, trade, and education be regarded from a political point of view to favor friends and weaken potential enemies; such policies tend to an organization of the world on the basis of power politics, making for bipolarization and war. Instances have been known where United States representatives in Specialized Agencies have been unable to support policies favorable to the distribution of information on the manufacture of antibiotics for purposes of health, or of technological information of agricultural value, because it might give strategic assistance to countries behind the Iron Curtain as well as to others.

On the other hand, the development of close co-operation on a universal basis in such fields as health, trade, labor, communications, education, technical assistance, and capital investment, making no distinction between political friends and enemies, tends to build the world community, ameliorating the absolutism of lines of political cleavage. During the nineteenth century, the growth of international trade and finance, conducted as it was largely by private enterprise, ameliorated the political cleavages of power politics and made the world relatively stable and peaceful and increasingly prosperous.[3] In the twentieth century, the development of international co-operation in many functional fields by the United Nations and the Specialized Agencies could serve a similar purpose. International co-operation in these fields might develop human interests without primary consideration to political oppositions, especially if an atomic stalemate should minimize the danger of actual hostilities across iron, bamboo, or other curtains.

With such a decentralization of foreign policy-making in functional and political fields within national governments, public opinion might be educated in a more rational manner. National nongovernmental opinion groups might interest themselves in each of the major functions and might associate with similar nongovernmental groups in other nations, forming international nongovernmental groups on many of the functional interests which concern human welfare. Through such groups a world public opinion in respect to certain functions might develop, thus ameliorating the tendency of opinion to be organized on the political lines of states or political blocs. It has been noted in United States history that the growth of political parties and of private associations on national lines, crossing the political boundaries of states and regions, ameliorated the conflicts inherent in the relations of the latter, and, although not sufficient to prevent the Civil War, made it possible to heal the wounds and eventually to build a national consciousness superior to such local and regional political interests.

[3] Quincy Wright, "Economic and Political Conditions of World Stability," *Jour. Econ. History*, vol. 13 (Fall, 1953), pp. 363ff.

Similarly, functional groups crossing national boundaries might develop a broader international consciousness.[4]

Complexity is the mother of peace, simplicity of war. The complex development of opinion and decision-making at the national and international level suggested in this chapter is difficult to grasp and may appear to involve inconsistencies and departures from logic. But in such complexity peace, order, justice, and progress can be achieved in a complex world.

Simplicity in a nationalistic world seems to demand complete co-ordination of national policies and the complete co-ordination of allies against enemies, but such simplicity tends toward a division of the world into two great groups, establishing a balance of power completely simple, completely intelligible, and completely unstable. As Clausewitz pointed out, it is the natural tendency for war to become total, and it is also the natural tendency for the world to become bipolarized. The two tendencies in the atomic age work toward a holocaust.

Working against that tendency toward simplification, distributing decision-making capabilities among many centers—intranational, national, regional, and universal—can bring into being an international order of such complexity that it can be at the same time stable and progressive. It cannot be said that the process of decision-making in international affairs will inevitably move in this direction, but it would seem to be the task of men of good will and of understanding to attempt so to move it.

---

[4] Frederick Jackson Turner, "American Sectionalism and World Organization," *Amer. Hist. Rev.*, Vol. 48 (April, 1942), pp. 545ff.

INDEX

843

Eisenhower, Milton, 147, 170
  cited, 187-188
Eldersveld, Samuel J., 591n, 592n
El Glaoui, 545
Elizabeth II, 301-302, 314, 369
El Salvador, 176, 185, 217-221
Emperor, of Japan, 756-758, 789-792
Empire Economic Conference,
  Ottawa (1932), 367
England, see United Kingdom and
  British foreign policy
Estrada, Genaro, 174
Estrada Doctrine, 173, 174-175
Europe:
  federation concept, 512-517,.
    606-610
  natural resources, 689
  Soviet security zone in, 690-693,
    723-725
  United States economic aid to,
    125-127
European Coal and Steel Com-
  munity, 140, 286, 514, 607
European Defense Community
  (EDC), 140, 287, 516-517,.
    543, 607, 721
European Payments Union (EPU),
  285, 608
European Recovery Program, 126-127
Evatt, H. V., 354, 365, 368, 382
Exclusion Acts, U.S., 58, 765, 772,
  779
Executive, the:
  in Ceylon, India, and Pakistan
    foreign policy, 464-469
  in France, 523, 527-531
  in Japan, 811-812
  in Latin America, 196-197
  in the Netherlands, 587n, 589,
    590-592
  in the United States, see United
    States Executive
Export-Import Bank, 119, 148, 152
External Affairs, Departments of, 366
  Australian, 351
  Canadian, 344
  in New Zealand, 363
  South African, 357, 358
  in the United Kingdom, 259-275

Eysinga, Jonkheer W. J. M. van,
  571, 587n

Falcon, 27
Farmers' Union, The, 43
Farouk, King, 292
Faure, Edgar, 520, 528, 533, 544,
  545
Federal Bureau of Investigation
  (FBI), 85
Federal System, United States,
  foreign-policy controls, 66-69
Federation of British Industries
  (FBI), 252
Ferry, Jules, 530
Fez, Treaty of (1912), 546
Figueres, José, 213
Filisola, Vicente, 218
Finland, 646, 691, 704, 717
Flandin, Pierre E., 535-536
Flourens, Pierre, 532
Food and Agriculture Organization
  (FAO), 697, 785
Foreign Affairs, Department of, the
  Netherlands, 592-599
Foreign Affairs Minister, France,
  531-533
  Japan, 798-799
Foreign Affairs Ministry, Soviet,
  662-664
Foreign Department, Brazil, 204-206
Foreign Office:
  Japan, 799-806
  United Kingdom, 264-269,
    272-277, 290-291
Foreign Operations Administration,
  U.S., 80
Foreign relations, 3-18
  Communist ideology and, 641-649
  factors influencing decision-making,
    6-8
  future of conduct of, 835-842
  goals, standards, and rules, 15-18
  personality in, 8-9
  procedures in conduct of, 9-15
  protocol in, 662-663
Foreign Secretary, British, 261-264
Foreign Service:
  Bolivia, 202

Isolationism, United States, 46-48,
142
Israel, 131, 145, 156, 159, 292-293,
726
Italy, 120, 127, 283, 714
Communist Party in, 670-671, 675
Ethiopian war, 330, 333-335, 580
Itamaraty, 205
Iturbide, Agustín de, 211, 217, 218

Jains, 421
Japan, 53, 150, 368, 695, 702, 709,
714
Australia and, 330-331
constitution of, 754-756, 790-792,
794
economy of, 741-743, 772
geography, 736-739
government organization in, 756-
758, 761-762, 792-814
industrial growth, 767-770
oligarchy in, 754-756
peace treaty, 137
political character of, 751-758
population of, 739-741, 743-751
rearming of, 820, 821
Soviet policy toward, 724
surrender of, 74
United States policy toward, 157-
158, 820-821
Japanese-American "Gentlemen's
Agreement" (1908), 767
Japanese foreign policy, 735-828
bibliography on, 828-833
bureaucracy and, 799-806
Cabinet in, 792-795
current and future aspects, 776-
787, 817-819
Diet in, 812-814
economic issue, 823-825
Emperor in, 789-792
executive in, 811-812
on exports, 784-785
on fishing rights, 783
historical record, 759-770
international-organization participation, 785-786
irredentism, 781-782
judicial agencies and, 812

military phase, 770-776
neutralism, 822-823
Occupation and, 788-789
organizational agencies, 798-811
political parties and, 814-817
prestige issues, 825-826
prime minister in, 795-798
on prisoners of war, 782-783
security issue, 819-823
Jebb, Richard, 316
Jefferson, Thomas, 55
Jennings, Sir Ivor, 440, 451, 463n,
466
Jessup, Philip, 130
Jinnah, Mohammed Ali, 418, 423,
424, 437-439, 442, 444n,
445, 456, 457, 462
João VI, King, 203
Joint Chiefs of Staff (JCS), U.S.,
87
Jordan, 156, 726
Juárez, Benito, 224
Juliana, Queen, 563, 575, 590, 606
Junagadh, 448-449
Junior Chamber of Commerce,
U.S., 43
Jusserand, Jules, 539

Kaganovich, L. M., 659
Kanagawa, Treaty of, 786
Karachi, 459
Karnebeek, H. A. van, 580, 594, 605
Kashmir, 131, 448-449, 483-485
Katayama, Tetsu, 820n
Kawai, Kazuo, 788-842
Kefauver, Estes, 75
Keith, A. B., 320n, 325n
Kellogg, Frank, 22
Kellogg-Briand Pact, 55, 790n
Kemal Pasha, 321
Kennan, George F., 31n
cited, 98, 123, 124, 149, 160
Khrushchev, Nikita, 149, 150, 154,
625, 631, 637, 659, 660, 661,
669, 708, 712, 715, 717, 723,
724, 726
King, Mackenzie, 305, 324, 326-329,
338, 345, 349, 377
Kisan Mazdur Praja Party, India, 471

Klaauw, C. A. van der, 577n
Kleffens, E. N. van, 592
Klingberg, Frank L., 114
Knappen, Marshall, 146n
Knight, W. S. M., 568n
Knowland, William F., 105-106
Kōdō, 771
Koiso, Kuniaki, 776
Konev, Marshal, 722
Konoye, Fumimaro, 775
Korbel, Josef, 483n
Korea, 640, 694-695, 702, 764, 765
Korean War, 34, 379, 515
　Soviet policy in, 708-710
　United States policy in, 134-148
Kossuth, Louis, 56
Kotelawala, Sir John, 464, 469, 473, 489
Kranenburg, R., 584n, 589
Kriesberg, Martin, cited, 40
Krishna Menon, V. K., 468-469, 486
Kunzru, H. N., 455n
Kuriles, the, 764, 781, 782
Kwantung Army, 735, 771, 775, 776

Labor, United States, 42
Labour Party, Australian, 310n, 317, 331, 337-338, 354-356, 382-383
Labour Party, British, 260, 293-295
Labour Party, New Zealand, 310n, 317, 335-337, 364-365
Lacoste, Robert, 547
Lall, Diwan Charman, 437
Landheer, Bart, 573n, 574-575
Langer, Prof., cited, 48, 79
Laniel, Joseph, 542
Lansing-Ishii Agreement (1917), 767
Laos, 138
Lasswell, Harold D., 8n
Latin America, 153, 169-234
　bibliographies of, 192-195, 232-234
　collective security issue, 177-180
　democracy urge in, 182-186
　economic co-operation in, 186-188
　foreign-relations controls, 196-200
　health in, 200-201
　international policy in, 169-195
　map of, 198-199

national sovereignty issue, 170-175
peaceful coexistence in, 175-177, 180-182
political asylum in, 185-186
racial equality in, 186
United States and, 127, 131-133, 144, 146-148, 188-190
see also separate countries
Laurier, Sir Wilfrid, 338
Laval, Pierre, 509
League of Nations, 59, 78, 181, 226, 280, 326, 475, 570, 580, 838-840
　Canada and, 327-328
　Japan and, 767-770, 773, 780, 785, 786
　New Zealand and, 335-336
League of Women Voters, 43
Lebanon, 117
Leeuwen, J. van, 604
Lend Lease Agreement, 74
Lenin, V. I., 667, 672, 678, 729
　theories of, 642-645, 648, 660, 679-680
Lesseps, Ferdinand de, 228
Liaotung Peninsula, 764-765
Liaquat Ali Khan, 437, 445, 457
Liberal-Country Party, Australia, 383
Liberal-Democratic Party, Japan, 815
Liberal Party, Australia, 354
Liberal Party, Canada, 317, 349-351
Libya, 131
Lippmann, Walter, 41
　cited, 7, 37, 60, 124
Litvinov, Maxim, 656n, 675
Litvinov Agreements, 74
Lloyd George, David, 320-321, 322
Locarno Treaties, 281, 283, 321, 322, 535
Locke, John, 9, 14
Loder, B. C. J., 570
Lodge, Henry Cabot, 101, 106, 148
Logan Act of 1799, 70
Loubet, Émile, 211, 528
Louis XI, 538
Louis XIV, 504, 538
Luce, Henry, 41
Lucknow Pact (1916), 435